COLLECTABLES
PRICE GUIDE **2009**

COLLECTABLES
PRICE GUIDE **2009**

Judith Miller
and Mark Hill

MILLER'S

Miller's Collectables Price Guide 2009

First published in Great Britain in 2008 by Miller's, a division of Mitchell Beazley,
imprints of Octopus Publishing Group Ltd, 2-4 Heron Quays, London E14 4JP.
Miller's is a registered trademark of Octopus Publishing Group Ltd..

An Hachette Livre UK Company.
www.octopusbooks.co.uk

While every care has been exercised in the compilation of this guide,
neither the authors nor publishers accept any liability for any financial or
other loss incurred by reliance placed on the information contained in
Miller's Collectables Price Guide 2009.

ISBN 978 1 84533 442 0

A CIP catalogue record for this book is available from the British Library.

Set in Frutiger

Colour reproduction by Fine Arts, Hong Kong
Printed and bound in China by C&C Offset Printing Co., Ltd

Authors Judith Miller & Mark Hill

Publishing Manager Julie Brooke
Editors Sara Sturgess & Daniel Goode
Editorial Assistants John Parton & Katy Armstrong

Photography Graham Rae, Jeremy Martin, Robin Saker

Design Tim & Ali Scrivens, TJ Graphics;
additional design by Jeremy Tilston, The Oak Studio
& Philip Gilderdale
Indexer Hilary Bird
Production Lucy Carter
Jacket Design Tim Foster & Juliette Norsworthy

Photographs of Judith Miller and Mark Hill by Graham Rae

CONTENTS

LIST OF CONSULTANTS

BOOKS

Roddy Newlands
Bloomsbury Auctions,
London

CERAMICS

Beth & Beverley Adams
Alfie's Antiques Market,
London

Dr Graham Cooley
Private Collector

Patrick & Petra Folkersma
outernational.info

Kevin Harris
undercurrents.biz

Michael Jeffrey
Woolley & Wallis, Salisbury

Steven Moore
BBC Antiques Roadshow

CHESS & GAMES

Luke Honey
Bonhams, London

FASHION & ACCESSORIES

Kerry Taylor
Kerry Taylor Auctions,
London

Sparkle Moore & Cad van Swankster
The Girl Can't Help It!,
London

GLASS

Dr Graham Cooley
Private Collector

William Farmer
Fieldings Auctioneers,
Stourbridge

Kevin Harris
undercurrents.biz

Marcus Newhall
sklounion.com

Alison Snelgrove
thestudioglassmerchant.co.uk

INUIT ART

Duncan McLean
Waddingtons, Toronto,
Canada

MARBLES

Robert Block
Private Collector

SPORTING

Graham Budd
Graham Budd Auctions,
London

TOYS & DOLLS

Colin Lewis
The Magic Toybox, Drayton

WATCHES

Mark Laino
Mark of Time, Philadelphia,
USA

We are also very grateful to our friends and experts who gave us so much help and support – James Bassam of T.W. Gaze & Sons; Nigel Benson of 20thcentury-glass.com; Conrad Biernacki and Brian Musselwhite of the Royal Ontario Museum in Toronto; Ian Broughton of Alfie's Antiques Market; Michelle Guzy; Jeanette Hayhurst; Gary Hendy; Chris Marks; Geoffrey Robinson of Alfie's Antiques Market; and Ron & Ann Wheeler of Artius Glass.

HOW TO USE THIS BOOK

Subcategory heading Indicates the sub-category of the main heading.

Caption The description of the item illustrated, including when relevant, the period, the maker or factory, medium, the year it was made, dimensions and condition. Many captions have **footnotes** which explain terminology or give identification or valuation information.

Essential reference and **expert eye** These are where we show identifying aspects of a factory or maker, point out rare colours or shapes, and explain why a particular piece is so desirable.

The price guide These price ranges give a ballpark figure for what you should pay for a similar item. The great joy of collectables is that there is not a recommended retail price. The price ranges in this book are based on actual prices, either what a dealer will take or the full auction price.

Page tab This appears on every page and identifies the main category heading as identified in the Contents List on pages 5-6.

Essential reference Gives key facts about the factory, maker or style, along with stylistic identification points, value tips and advice on fakes.

The object The collectables are shown in full colour. This is a vital aid to identification and valuation. With many objects, a slight colour variation can signify a large price differential.

Source code Every item has been specially photographed at an auction house, a dealer, an antiques market or a private collection. These are credited by code at the end of the caption, and can be checked against the Key to Illustrations on pages 486-488.

INTRODUCTION

A pair of 1950s Herbert Levine printed polka dot slingbacks. Worth £70-90

The world of collectables has never been so vibrant and international. When I produced the first edition of Miller's Collectables Price Guide 21 years ago, I could never have envisaged the speed at which the market would change and develop. Of course, much of this has been due to the internet which has given collectors from Chicago to London to Sydney unprecedented easy access to all manner of items in countries across the world. This has resulted in a general levelling of prices, regardless of whether the collector and object are in the same country, or thousands of miles apart.

But this doesn't mean prices have fallen, in fact many collectable areas have seen prices rise as the number of collectors and demand grow. It seems we still can't resist the lure of adding that elusive piece to our collections, the pull of nostalgic yearning for our childhoods, or the joy of finding something simply great that just 'speaks' to us in some way.

Like our desire to collect, another thing that hasn't changed is our need for accurate information. The internet may be an excellent place to buy or sell, but knowing what you're looking at, and how much it is really worth, is as important as ever. Just think of the lucky buyers who spotted a rare Worcester jug on eBay. Mis-described as being Italian, they bought it for £100 and shortly after sold it at auction for £50,000! Had the unfortunate seller known what he had, the story would have been very different.

That's where a copy of a Miller's price guide is essential. Useful as the internet is, information is not always accurate, and is often conflicting. Buying a copy of Miller's each year will enable you to build up an invaluable and reliable library that will help you make the most from buying, selling and collecting – be it at a car boot sale, auction, dealer's shop, or via eBay.

To celebrate the 21st edition of Miller's Collectables Price Guide, and my return this year to the company I co-founded, we've had a make-over. As you will see, the book is bigger than ever before, with larger images and more colour, enabling you to see even greater detail that might make all the difference. We've also increased the number of 'Expert Eye', 'Essential Reference' and footnote features to help you understand more, and pick up tricks of the trade.

Another exciting development is our new Miller's website, www.millersantiquesguide.com, which will be launched in October 2008. This has been developed over the past year and aims to provide a site for everyone who loves the world of antiques and collectables. It will appeal to both the committed expert and the inquiring novice. You can search our database of tens of thousands of antiques and collectables from around the world – each with fully authenticated captions and price ranges. We also include useful and easy to understand extra information, including top tips and special features to look for. In addition, you have access to fully illustrated features by myself, Mark Hill and our team of experts including many names from the Antiques Roadshow, both in the UK and the US. The best dealers and auctioneers can be tracked down through our dealer and auctioneer locator, which is linked to Google Maps. We'll keep you up-to-date with antiques news, and you'll also be able to view videos that will help you get more out of antiques as we walk you through all aspects of buying, selling, identifying and valuing. We may be involved in treasures of the past, but we also embrace the technology of the future.

This year's edition offers as much variety as ever, from advertising to ceramics, fashion, glass, toys and games, and even collectable hair! Popular markets that have remained strong, such as Clarice Cliff, are well represented with longer sections. Miller's also keeps up with the latest trends, bringing you hot, new collecting areas such as Meakin ceramics and postwar Czech glass. With pieces from auction houses, dealers and private collectors from across the world, Mark Hill and I have ensured that Miller's continues to reflect the market today – vibrant and international.

A 1950s-70s Czechoslovakian Borské Sklo 'Large Olives' pattern optical ball vase. Worth £80-120

A Clarice Cliff Bridgewater pattern Conical vase. Worth £1,800-2,200

Judith Miller.

A Coca-Cola printed and embossed tinplate thermometer sign, with gold-coloured bottle.

1936   *15.75in (40cm) high*

£140-160   SOTT

A Coca-Cola printed tinplate 'silhouette lady' thermometer sign.

1939   *16in (40.5cm) high*

£70-100   SOTT

EXPERT EYE – A DR PEPPER TIP TRAY

These rare items used to sell for around £450, but Dr Pepper collectables have fallen out of fashion slightly, which has affected prices.

Dr Pepper advertising memorabilia is harder to find than that for Coca-Cola. Early examples include a full stop after the 'Dr'.

A 1950s Coca-Cola enamelled tin bottle sign.

12.5in (31.5cm) high

£80-120   SOTT

Furthermore, as examples have become more widely and easily available via the internet, prices have been further affected.

The artwork of the pug puppies is appealing, adding to the desirability.

A very rare Dr Pepper printed tinplate tip tray, with pug dogs and scalloped rim.

2.5in (6.5cm) diam

£250-300   SOTT

A Coca-Cola printed celluloid sign.

c1950   *9.25in (23cm) high*

£70-100   SOTT

A Coca-Cola printed Masonite sign.

Masonite is a type of hardboard made from wooden chips that are blasted with steam to form fibres, it is then heated and compressed into boards. No glue or other material is used. It was developed in 1924 by William H. Mason of Laurel, Mississippi, with manufacturing beginning in 1929. It is also used for roofing, desktops and even canoes.

1952   *14.25in (36cm) high*

£70-100   SOTT

A Dr Pepper 'Hot or Cold' printed tinplate thermometer sign.

16.25in (41cm) high

£80-120   SOTT

ADVERTISING

ESSENTIAL REFERENCE

- Vintage advertising and packaging provides a fascinating and accessible record of social trends and aspirations over the past century, and more. Collectors tend to focus on one subject area, such as tobacco advertising, or on one type of object, such as tin signs. Some also focus on a particular brand, such as Kellogg's, or even a character. As such, these categories tend to attract the most collectors, and so the highest values.
- Most pieces found by collectors will date from the early 20thC or later, with 19thC examples generally being scarcer. Much of the market is driven by nostalgia or an interest in design and brands of the past. Advertising diversified rapidly during the early years of the 20thC and as the market expanded with more and more manufacturers. It became all-important to catch people's attention and make them buy a particular product over another.
- Tins and signs are two of the most important and sought-after areas. Both have typically eye-catching visuals, with bright colours and the use of logos and characters. Always examine surfaces closely for signs of damage, such as scratches or losses to the surface, and dents. The more

colours used in a printed design, and the better it is printed, the more valuable it is likely to be. Look for cross-market interest, such as railway or automobile related items, as this can increase value.
- Always look for items in good condition that represent the brand, subject area or period well. Items in the late 19thC and early 20thC Art Nouveau style will be sought-after. Similarly, those produced during the late 1920s and '30s that are in the popular Art Deco style will generally be desirable, as will those with typically 1950s artwork. The colours, style of lettering and often the logo used will help you to date a piece to a period.
- Also consider items that would have usually been thrown away. Although many may have been produced, fewer may have survived, making them scarce today. Much packaging falls under this category and was not made to last, making surviving examples in mint condition more desirable. The presence of the original contents does not necessarily add to value unless the package has intact seals or sealing labels, such as the tax seals on tobacco packets.

A 1950s German 'Veedol' advertising sign, transfer-printed and embossed tinplate, with some scratches.

17.25in (44cm) high

£80-120　　QU

A 1950s German 'Veedol' advertising sign, transfer-printed and embossed tinplate.

14.25in (36cm) high

£150-200　　QU

A 1960s German 'No. 4711 Kölnisch Wasser' cologne printed paper and wood life-size advertising standee.

A 1950s German 'Blaupunkt Autoradio' car radio advertising sign, transfer-printed tinplate.

18in (45.5cm) high

£180-220　　QU

A 1950s German 'Adox' camera film near life-size advertising standee, printed paper and wood, restored.

53in (135cm) high

£450-550　　QU

65.5in (166.5cm) high

£250-350　　QU

A Y-front 'Skants' advertising board, for Lyle & Scott.

14in (35.5cm) high

£20-30   MA

A 1950s Marconi 'Marconiphone' radio sign.

The hand is somewhat surrealist and also harks back to motifs used in more esoteric Shell advertising posters.

15.5in (39cm) high

£8-12   MA

A 1940s 'Drink Cliquot Club Beverages' printed tinplate thermometer sign.

13.5in (34.5cm) high

£40-60   SOTT

A Tetley Tea advertising sign, embossed metal on card, with folding arm to act as a counter-top standee, and hole to hang it up.

11.5in (29cm) high

£60-80   SOTT

A Peek, Frean's Teddy Bear Biscuits die-cut card advertising sign.

Advertising showing teddy bears is both hard to find and enormously appealing to teddy bear collectors. The craze began in 1902 when Theodore Roosevelt refused to shoot a bear on a hunting trip. The outstretched arms inviting a hug are a nice touch.

4.25in (11cm) high

£30-40   SOTT

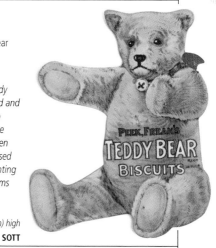

A 1950s German Palmolive Schwarzkopf Extra-Blond printed paper shampoo packet, with image of a woman's head.

6.25 in (26cm) high

£20-25   QU

A 1950s German Henkel Persil printed card 250g washing powder box, with original contents.

6in (15cm) high

£40-60   QU

A 1950s German Palmolive printed card box of wrapped soap bars.

5.25in (13cm) high

£20-25   QU

ADVERTISING

A 1950s American Cheramy 'Heaven Sent' cylindrical powder box, by Helena Rubenstein.

4.25in (10.5cm) diam

£35-45   QU

A 1950s American Cheramy 'April Showers' cylindrical powder box, by Helena Rubenstein.

4.25in (10.5cm) diam

£35-45   QU

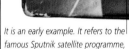

A 1950s German Burnus washing powder card box, showing a young housewife holding clean white sheets.

4.5in (12cm) high

£28-32   QU

A German Spleen soap powder card box, marked "Spleen Maurer + Wirz Stolberg", with original contents.

c1955   *4in (10cm) high*

£55-65   QU

EXPERT EYE – A RUSSIAN CIGARETTE BOX

Cigarette and tobacco advertising and packaging is one of the most collectable subjects.

The artwork, showing a satellite orbiting Earth amid the stars, is also highly appealing. Space Race memorabilia is desirable.

It is an early example. It refers to the famous Sputnik satellite programme, first launched in October 1957.

It is also Russian, making it scarce on the Western market. Most of these would have been thrown away after their contents had been enjoyed.

A late 1950s Russian 'Sputnik' colour-printed card cigarette box, marked "Sputnik" in Cyrillic.

4.5in (11.5cm) high

£60-80   QU

A 1950s German Knorr baby food card box, with image of baby eating from a spoon.

10.25in (26cm) high

£35-45   QU

A Julius Schmid of New York, NY, 'Ramses' transparent condom tin.

Early condom tins are now highly collectable, and some can be very rare. Sold discretely during a more prudish time when talk of sex was largely forbidden, they were often thrown away rather than being re-used around the home, like other tins.

1947   2.75in (7cm) wide

£25-35   **SOTT**

A 1950s Permatex Airplane Wash tin, with contents.

The artwork on this tin is particularly good, and typical of its period.

7.75in (19.5cm) high

£2-4   **AEM**

A 1920s-30s R.J. Reynolds Prince Albert Crimp Cut cigarette tobacco tin, with pull-off lid and transfer-printed design.

The Prince Albert this tobacco was named for is not the husband of Queen Victoria, but rather their eldest son, who became King Edward VII in 1901. The brand itself was mystifyingly still launched with his previous title after his Coronation, in 1902. The tobacco is still produced in the US today, but saw its heyday during the 1930s.

6.5in (16.5cm) high

£22-28   **AEM**

EXPERT EYE – A POCKET TOBACCO TIN

These slim, sometimes curving, tins were made to fit snugly inside the pocket of a gentleman's jacket without causing an unsightly bulge.

Bold colours and strong imagery are also highly sought-after. Look out for patriotic themes or those that cross collecting areas.

This is both a scarce tin and has an image of a fisherman that would appeal to collectors of fishing memorabilia.

Condition is important. This tin is in good condition, scratched and dented examples will not be worth as much.

A Canadian Imperial Tobacco Company 'Forest And Stream' pipe tobacco pocket tin, with scene of a fisherman.

4.5in (11.5cm) high

£100-150   **SOTT**

A 1950s Esüdro 'Vaseline' pocket-sized tin, transfer-printed tinplate, with friction-fit lid.

An Esso 'Sprite' 2-T litre oil can, with artwork of 'Happy' and his girlfriend on a scooter, with some scratches and denting.

Happy the oil drip and his un-named girlfriend promoted Esso's 'Happy Motoring' campaign.

3.5in (9cm) diam   9.25in (23.5cm) high

£35-45   **QU**   **£8-12**   **BH**

ADVERTISING

A Lipton Tea transfer-printed advertising mug.

3.75in (9.5cm) high

£2-3   AEM

A Pristalit salesmans sample of a miniature enamelled metal Dutch oven.

Pristalit were a maker of fine porcelain cookware.

5.5in (13.5cm) wide

£25-35   BH

A 1950s German 'Dr. E. Richter's Breakfast Herbal Tea' brass, aluminium and glass counter-top advertising display.

43in (110cm) high

£300-400   QU

A Kellogg's Frosties 'Tony The Tiger' advertising plush stuffed toy, made in China.

1997   *8in (20cm) high*

£2-3   AEM

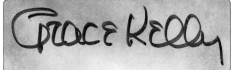

A Grace Kelly signed photograph.

Photographs are one of the most popular media for signatures – primarily as they make such a great display. Dedications to a person, unless that person is famous or connected to the star, usually reduce value.

10in (25.5cm) high

£350-450   **MAS**

A Luciano Pavarotti signed 'Verisimo Arias' album cover.

£350-450   **MAS**

United States Senate
WASHINGTON, D.C.

January 18, 1955

Dear Howard:

   I want to thank you for your very nice Christmas card. It was most kind of you to remember us and we appreciate your thoughtfulness more than we can say.

   I hope to be back to work in the not too distant future and look forward to seeing you some time soon.

   With every good wish for the New Year, I remain

             Sincerely your friend,

             John F. Kennedy

Mr. Howard T. Sniffin
116 Shaw Street
Braintree, Mass.

Sincerely your friend,

John F. Kennedy

A John F. Kennedy signed letter, on US Senate stationery.

The content of letters is also important to value. If the letter concerns important matters that the person is known for, or shows a personal or emotional side to a personality, values can rise.

1955

£650-750   **MAS**

A Screen Actors Guild document signed by Ronald Reagan.

1948

£280-320   **MAS**

A set of four Margaret Thatcher signed photographs.

£150-200   **MAS**

A Margaret Thatcher signed baseball.

A baseball is an unusual choice of object for Thatcher to sign - this factor and the apparent rarity can be appealing to certain collectors.

£200-300   **MAS**

ESSENTIAL REFERENCE

- Automobilia is a wide ranging subject area, and includes everything from car parts to items relating to automobile associations, car sales, repair and garaging. As the area is so wide, many choose to focus on a particular area, period or brand of car. In general, prestige marques such as Bentley and Rolls Royce attract the highest prices, although early or rare pieces for any brand can be desirable.
- Car mascots are one of the most popular areas, with the most desirable typically dating from the 1910s to '30s. There are a number of different types including manufacturer mascots, accessory mascots and advertising mascots. Dramatic, lively and well-modelled designs that represent speed or strength, or major marques, tend to be the most desirable. Reproductions do exist and beware of re-plated examples that have been over-polished, as this affects value.

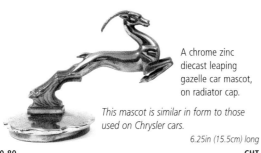

A chrome zinc diecast leaping gazelle car mascot, on radiator cap.

This mascot is similar in form to those used on Chrysler cars.

6.25in (15.5cm) long

£60-80   **CHT**

A 'First Past The Post' chrome-plated car mascot, on wooden plinth.

6in (15cm) high

£150-200   **CHT**

A Bruce Bairnsfather 'Old Bill' large car mascot, impressed copyright to base and "S" underneath scarf, on radiator cap.

5in (13cm) high

£250-300   **CHT**

A car mascot in the form of a fireman's helmet, with Staffordshire Fire Brigade crest, on plinth.

4.25in (11cm) high

£100-150   **CHT**

A Rolls Royce 'Kneeling Spirit of Ecstasy' car mascot, with underwing registration mark, on radiator cap, the base signed "C Sykes".

As used on Phantom III, Silver Dawn and Wraith models.

£180-220   **CHT**

A Bentley 'Flying B' chrome-plated car mascot, impressed "807924", on radiator cap.

Earlier examples from c1920 have the wings outstretched from the sides of the 'B'. Many were made by Joseph Fray of Birmingham.

c1936   *Mascot 4in (10cm) wide*

£280-320   **CHT**

A 1920s-30s Royal Automobile Club nickel-plated brass full member's badge, type 3A, no. D8079, with an enamelled Union Jack.

5.25in (13.5cm) wide

£100-150   **CHT**

A 'Monte Carlo XXIme Rallye Automobile' enamel badge, for grill mounting.

1951   *3.5in (9cm) wide*

£180-220   **CHT**

An Automobile Association 'Motor Cycle Specialist' double-sided enamel sign, black script on a yellow ground, some minor enamel losses and corrosion.

25in (64cm) high

£300-400   **CHT**

A nickel-plated 'boa constrictor' horn, with the remains of leather cloth sleeve and perished bulb.

74.75in (190cm) long

£200-300   **CHT**

A pair of Lucas Kings Own brass oil side lamps, no. NOF141, with flange side mounting bracket.

9in (23cm) high

£350-450   **CHT**

A Shell petrol pump glass globe, with chips to neck.

17.5in (44cm) high

£150-200   **CHT**

ESSENTIAL REFERENCE

- Notaphily, the collecting of paper money, has grown in popularity since the 1960s. As the area is so wide, many choose to focus on one area, such as particular country or time period. Some also focus on an element or theme in the design, such as wildlife, battles or famous people. As well as being decorative, the complex designs were aimed to foil counterfeiters.
- Look out for large denominations, as generally fewer of

these were produced. Variations including errors can also affect value. Early notes are not always valuable, so consult a reference book if you are planning on building a collection. Condition has an enormous effect on value, with notes in truly mint, un-circulated condition being highly sought-after. Store banknotes flat in specially produced wallets and handle them as little as possible.

An Algerian ten dinar note.

1964   *7.5in (19cm) long*

£10-15   **CN**

A Bahamian one pound note, featuring King George VI.

c1950s   *6in (15cm) long*

£70-100   **CN**

A Biafran five shilling note.

1967   *4.5in (11.5cm) long*

£4-5   **CN**

A Jordanian one dinar note, featuring King Hussein of Jordan.

c1960s   *7in (18cm) long*

£7-10   **CN**

A Maltese five pound note.

This was the highest denomination available at the time. Apart from British notes, five pound notes from any Commonwealth country at this time showing Queen Elizabeth II are generally desirable. For example, a Jamaican five pound note may be worth anything from £500 to £1,000. Condition, however, is vital, with values plummeting downward if the note is not in truly mint condition.

1968   *6in (15cm) long*

£70-100   **CN**

A Libyan one dinar note, featuring Colonel Gaddaffi.

1990   *6.5in (16.5cm) long*

£1-2   **CN**

A WWII Maltese emergency issue one shilling overprint on two shilling note.

4.5in (11.5cm) long

£40-50   **CN**

BANKNOTES

A Japanese occupation of Burma (Myanmar) ten rupee note, without water mark, with block letters.

Despite its apparent rarity, these notes are comparatively common.
1940   6.5in (16.5cm) long
50p-£1   CN

A Norwegian ten kroner note.
1939   5.25in (13.5cm) long
£7-10   CN

A very rare and early Thai one tical note.

The tical was the original name for Thailand's currency, and was used as its name in the English text on banknotes until 1925, even though the baht was established as the Thai name during the 19thC. In 1919, one British pound bought 12 baht.
1920   6.5in (16.5cm) long
£300-400   CN

A Reserve Bank of Rhodesia five pound note.

This note is valuable for the same reason as the Maltese five pound note on the previous page. Rhodesian and Maltese five pound notes are the most affordable of this type.
1964   6.5in (16.5cm) long
£100-150   CN

A Confederate States one dollar note, with green 'one'.

This is an early 1861 issue in excellent condition.
1862   6.5in (16.5cm) long
£200-250   CN

ESSENTIAL REFERENCE

- True first editions are those from the first print run (impression) of the first published hardback edition of a book. A first edition may then have subsequent impressions, which may be changed in some way, such as errors being corrected. Paperback first editions can also be collectable, but tend to be less valuable, and are not yet as widely collected.

- Numbers of true 'firsts' are limited – value rises as desirability increases. Very famous, iconic titles will always be prized, but a classic title published at the height of an author's career will often be worth less than an early or less-well received work, mainly as fewer copies of the 'first' will have printed.

- To check if you have a first edition – learn how to recognise the different styles of numbering. Look for a number '1' in the series of numbers on the inside copyright page. Some publishers state clearly that a book is a first edition, and some use a sequence of letters. Always check that the publishing date and copyright date match, and check the original publishing date and publisher in a reference book. In general,

book club editions tend to be ignored by collectors.

- The smaller the edition is, and the more renowned the title, the higher the price. Authors' signatures add value to a first edition, particularly if it is a limited or special edition. Dedications are less desirable, unless the recipient is famous in their own right, or connected to the author in some way.

- There are many consistently popular authors such as Ian Fleming, but fashion plays a large role in value. First editions can also rise in value if the story is adapted into a successful film or TV series. Jacket artwork can also make a difference to value.

- Always consider condition. Dust jackets should be clean, unfaded and undamaged – values can fall by over 50 per cent without them. However, damage can often be restored. Check the book is complete, and has not been damaged or defaced. Books in truly perfect condition will always fetch a premium, particularly if from a smaller print run.

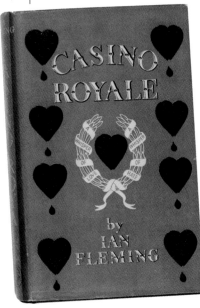

Ian Fleming, "Moonraker", first edition, published by Cape, with dust jacket, some scratches and spine slightly dulled, otherwise an unusually fine example.

Only 9,900 copies of the first edition were printed, making this example in excellent condition very rare.
1955

£3,200-3,800   BLO

Ian Fleming, "Casino Royale", first edition, first issue, published by Cape, overall a fine copy with dust jacket, some rubbing and wear to extremities.

Being a first issue of the first edition of Fleming's first Bond book, this example is a true first edition. Under 5,000 of these were printed, many going to libraries. As it is signed in the same year it was published with a charming dedication, it is all the more desirable.
1953

£6,500-7,500   BLO

Ian Fleming, "Dr. No", first edition, published by Cape, with dust jacket, some foxing and marks, and ink scribbles to front endpaper, otherwise a very good example.
1958

£450-550   BLO

Ian Fleming, "For Your Eyes Only", first edition, published by Cape, with dust jacket, slightly darkened to spine, otherwise a near fine copy.
1960

£320-380   BLO

BOOKS

Ian Fleming, "On Her Majesty's Secret Service", first edition, published by Cape, with dust jacket, bookplate inscribed by Ian Fleming to 'Eileen' [Cond].

Eileen M. Cond was a socialite and book collector who sent bookplates to a number of authors, requesting their signatures. Fleming corresponded with her and signed a number of his books for her.

1963

£1,500–2,000   **BLO**

Ian Fleming, "Thunderball", first edition, published by Cape, with dust jacket, minor rubbing to corners, light spotting to top edge, otherwise an unusually fine example.

1961

£700-800   **BLO**

Ian Fleming, "You Only Live Twice", first edition, with dust jacket, an unusually fine and bright example.

1964

£250-350   **BLO**

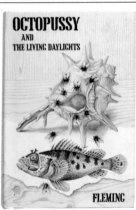

Ian Fleming, "Octopussy and The Living Daylights", first edition, published by Cape, with dust jacket, signed by Maryam D'Abo on title, a fine copy.

D'Abo played Bond Girl Kara Milovy in the 1987 film version of 'The Living Daylights'. Copies with no remains of price stickers and unclipped jackets, like this one, are preferable.

1966

£320-380   **BLO**

EXPERT EYE – FROM RUSSIA WITH LOVE

Fleming's fifth Bond novel is widely said to be his best book, as well as the best film. As such it attracts a large number of fans keen to own copies.

Although it bears a personal inscription seemingly unrelated to Fleming, it is still nicely signed by the author, which adds to its value.

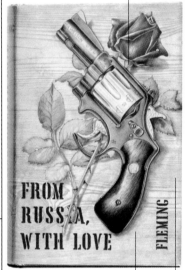

15,000 copies of the first edition were printed. Although the very first batch of printed pages were sent to a book club due to their poor quality, this effective second printing – marked Cape – is considered the true first edition.

The cover was the first to be designed by artist Richard Chopping, who worked closely with Fleming over the designs. His style has become a hallmark of Fleming's first editions.

Ian Fleming, "From Russia, With Love", first edition, near full-page signed inscription from the author on front free endpaper, original boards, dust jacket, price-clipped, otherwise a fine example.

Inscribed to Geoffrey van Dantzig.

1957

£6,500-7,500   **BLO**

Ian Fleming, "Thrilling Cities", first edition, published by Cape, with dust jacket, the bookplate signed and inscribed by Ian Fleming to 'Eileen' [Cond].

This is a collection of travel articles Fleming wrote for the Sunday Times following trips in 1959 and 1960. His travels appear to have influenced some of his future Bond novels and short stories.

1963

£1,000-1,500   **BLO**

J.G. Ballard, "The Drought", first edition, published by Jonathan Cape, with fellow author Angela Carter's bookplate on front paste-down, skillfully restored spine ends and corners, lightly rubbed.

This is an expanded version of "The Burning World", published in 1964.
1965

£200-300   BLO

J.G. Ballard, "The Crystal World", first edition, published by Jonathan Cape, with dust jacket, rubbed at extremities, otherwise very good.
1966

£100-150   BLO

J.G. Ballard, "The Atrocity Exhibition", first edition, published by Jonathan Cape, with dust jacket, a little darkening, otherwise very good.
1970

£80-120   BLO

J.G. Ballard, "Crash", first edition, published by Jonathan Cape, with dust jacket, small inked name to upper fore-corner of front paste-down, with slight rubbing and one tear.

"Crash" is a controversial novel dealing with the sexual fetishism of car-crashes. It was made into an equally controversial film by David Cronenberg in 1996, which was nominated for the Golden Palm at the Cannes Film Festival and won the Special Jury Prize.
1973

£350-450   BLO

J.G. Ballard, "High Rise", first edition, published by Jonathan Cape, with dust jacket, with minor creasing and a tear, but overall a very good copy.
1975

£100-150   BLO

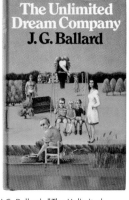

J.G. Ballard, "The Unlimited Dream Company", first edition, published by Jonathan Cape, with dust jacket, unclipped but without price sticker.
1979

£12-18   BLO

Peter Benchley, "Jaws", first edition, published by Bantam, New York, signed by the author, very slightly chipped at spine ends, otherwise a fine copy.

Both the cover artwork and the one-sheet movie poster for the Spielberg film version were drawn by Roger Kastel, who was also responsible for the 'Gone with the Wind' style poster for 'The Empire Strikes Back'.
1974

£250–350   BLO

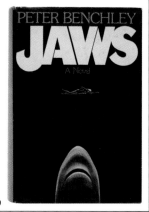

Raymond Benson, "The World is Not Enough", first edition, with dust jacket, signed by Goldie on front free endpaper, two cut signatures of the author loosely inserted.

Drum and bass legend Goldie, signed this copy both as Goldie and "The Bull", the character he played in the movie, with a bull monogram.
1999

£120–180   BLO

BOOKS

Raymond Chandler, "The Little Sister", first edition, published by Hamish Hamilton, with price-clipped dust jacket, worn at joints and fore-edges with slight loss to spine ends.

1949

£300–400   BLO

Tracy Chevalier, "Girl With a Pearl Earring", first edition, first issue, published by Harper Collins, with dust jacket and misspelling on lower panel, a fine copy.

1999

£150-200   BLO

Arthur C. Clarke, "2001, A Space Odyssey", first UK edition, published by Hutchinson, with dust jacket, with author's signature on loosely inserted card.

This was published by New American Library in the US, which can be worth up to £1,000 in similar fine condition.

1968

£500-600   BLO

Richard Chopping, "The Fly", first edition, published by Secker & Warburg, with dust jacket.

Best known as the cover artist for most of Fleming's James Bond titles, this was Chopping's first novel – naturally he designed the cover too. The story is unrelated to the 1986 film with Jeff Goldblum.
1965

£220-280   BLO

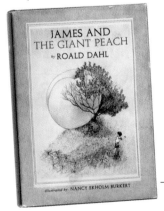

Roald Dahl, "James and the Giant Peach", first US edition, first issue, published by Alfred Knopf, with dust jacket, illustrations and plates by Nancy Ekholm Burkert, inked name on front paste-down.
1961

£700-900   BLO

Arthur Conan Doyle, "Uncle Bernac", first edition, published by Smith Elder, with 12 plates, and original cloth, slightly cocked and bumped, otherwise very good.
1897

£50-80   BLO

Arthur Conan Doyle, "The Green Flag", first US edition, published by McClure Phillips, with original pictorial cloth, spine very slightly sunned, otherwise a fine copy.
1900

£50-80   BLO

Lawrence Durrell, "Justine", first edition, published by Faber & Faber, signed and dated in 1985 by the author on title page, with price-clipped dust jacket, frayed at corners and spine ends.
1957

£500-600   BLO

EXPERT EYE – A JOHN GARDNER BOOK

John Gardner revived the James Bond series in 1981, finishing in 1996. Raymond Benson took over until recently, with Sebastian Faulks' writing 'Devil May Care' which was published in May 2008.

This was Gardner's ninth Bond story. This example is signed by the author on the title page. Unsigned it may still be worth around £400-500.

As well as being the first UK edition, it was also first of the Armchair Detective Library trade editions.

Gardner wrote the novel based on Richard Maibaum and Michael G. Wilson's screenplay for the 1989 film. Although accurate to the film's plot, many consider the book to be much better, though both have inconsistencies related to certain characters, such as Felix Leiter.

John Gardner, "Licence to Kill", first UK edition, published by the Armchair Detective Library, with dust jacket, signed by the author on the title page, slight darkening to page edges, an excellent copy.
1990

£650-750   BLO

John Gardner, "Seafire", first edition with dust jacket, published by Hodder & Stoughton, signed by the author on the title page, and signed by the jacket artist with stamp on front free endpaper.
1994

£150-200   BLO

John Gardner, "Goldeneye", first edition, third impression, published by Hodder & Stoughton, with dust jacket, signed by the author on the title page.
1995

£100-200   BLO

John Gardner, "COLD", first edition, published by Hodder & Stoughton, with dust jacket, signed by the author on the title page, slightly rubbed at extremities.
1996

£400-500   BLO

Nick Hornby, "Fever Pitch", first edition, published by Victor Gollancz, with price-clipped dust jacket, signed dedication by the author and inscribed on the title page.

This was the author's first novel. 1992

£200-300   BLO

Kazuo Ishiguro, "A Pale View of Hills", first edition, published by Faber, with dust jacket, very slight sunning to spine, overall a fine copy.

This was the author's first novel. 1982

£550-650   BLO

EXPERT EYE – THE VELVETEEN RABBIT

Margery Williams Bianco (1881-1944) lived between the US and UK. She wrote 30 children's books, although this is her best known and most loved around the world.

Williams was inspired by Walter de la Mare's poetry, which focused on the imagination, and particularly a child's imagination. In the story a soft toy rabbit is loved by a boy, leading to it coming to life as a real rabbit.

The illustrations were by William Nicholson (1872-1949), father of British abstract painter Ben Nicholson, and one of the most influential British illustrators and poster artists of the time.

Not only is this a first impression of the first edition, but it is in unusually good condition for a children's book, with bright images and only light signs of age.

Margery Williams, "The Velveteen Rabbit", first edition, first impression, published by Avon Books, with seven colour plates by William Nicholson including three double-page illustrations, some marks and spotting and with skillful repair to spine, edges and corners.
1922

£4,000–5,000   BLO

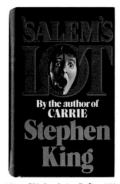

Stephen King, "'Salem's Lot", first UK edition, published by New English Library, with dust jacket, a fine copy.

1976

£350-450   BLO

Alistair MacLean, "H.M.S. Ulysses", first edition, published by Collins, with dust jacket, signed by the author on the title page, with pictorial endpapers.

This was the author's first novel. 1955

£450-550   BLO

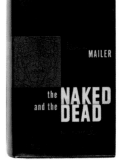

Norman Mailer, "The Naked and the Dead", first US edition, published by Rinehart, with dust jacket, publisher's device on the copyright page, sympathetic restoration to spine ends, corners and one edge.

1948

£200-300   BLO

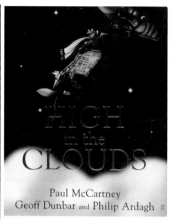

Paul McCartney, Geoff Dunbar and Philip Ardagh, "High in the Clouds", first edition, published by Faber, with dust jacket, signed with doodle by McCartney on half-title, and with colour illustrations throughout, in mint condition.

2005
£650-750   BLO

EXPERT EYE – A LARRY NIVEN BOOK

First published in 1970, Ringworld won both a Nebula award and a Locus award for Best Novel in the same year, and a Hugo award for Best Novel in 1971.

The first hardback version of this title is scarce, particularly in this excellent condition.

It is considered a classic work of science fiction and was followed by three sequels – the series is enormously popular with many fans.

Arthur Miller, "Death of a Salesman", first US edition, published by Viking Press, the dust jacket with unclipped $2.50 price and pictorial endpapers, skillfully restored at spine ends and corners.

1949
£650-750   BLO

The first edition of the paperback contains a number of mistakes, the most notable being that main protagonist Louis Wu travels the wrong way around the Ringworld, arriving in Munich from Greenwich, in an attempt to extend his birthday – later editions have him arriving in Beirut.

Larry Niven, "Ringworld", first UK and hardback edition, published by Gollancz, with dust jacket.
1972
£1,200-1,800   BLO

Patrick O'Brian, "Master & Commander", first edition, published by Collins, with price-clipped dust jacket, slightly frayed but otherwise very good.
1970
£500-600   BLO

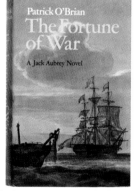

Patrick O'Brian, "The Fortune of War", first edition, published by Collins, with dust jacket, spine very slightly sunned.
1979
£170-200   BLO

Patrick O'Brian, "The Surgeon's Mate", first edition, with original boards and dust jacket, a fine copy, scarce.
1980
£750-850   BLO

BOOKS

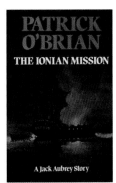

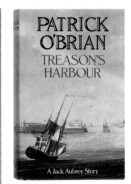

Patrick O'Brian, "The Ionian Mission", first edition, published by Collins, with dust jacket, spine slightly sunned.
1981
£250-350   BLO

Patrick O'Brian, "Treason's Harbour", first edition, published by Collins, with dust jacket, spine faded.
1983
£220-280   BLO

Danny Moynihan, "Boogie-Woogie", first edition, published by Duckworth Literary Entertainment, from an edition of 500 copies stamped and signed by Moynihan on the title page, jacket designed by Damien Hirst and signed by him on lower panel of jacket.
2000
£200–300   BLO

Philip Pullman, "His Dark Materials", three volumes of first editions, published by Scholastic, signed by the author on the title pages, comprising a first issue of "Northern Lights", the price-clipped jacket with Carnegie sticker on upper panel; "The Subtle Knife" and "The Amber Spyglass".

Prices for Pullman's first editions are beginning to rival those paid for J.K. Rowling's Harry Potter series, which previously eclipsed them. Even though it was released earlier, "Northern Lights" gained from the popularity of Rowling's books due to new interest in fantasy stories. The release of 'The Golden Compass', the film version of "Northern Lights", in 2007 drew further attention to the series, which may continue to rise as more films are made. Values are raised as each of these is signed, and the first bears its rare gold Carnegie Award sticker.
1995/1997/2000
£2,800-3,200   BLO

Pullman, Philip, "Northern Lights", first edition, first issue, published by Scholastic, with dust jacket, signed inscription from the author on the half-title page, with original boards.

The book was released under the title "The Golden Compass" in the US, referring to the fictional alethiometer, a device for detecting the truth, which features on the dust jacket and prominently throughout the book.
1995
£2,200-2,800   BLO

J.K. Rowling, "Harry Potter and the Deathly Hallows", first edition, published by Bloomsbury, signed with birthday greetings from the author on the title page, together with a letter of authentication from Rowling's personal assistant loosely inserted.
2007

£1,500-2,000   **BLO**

EXPERT EYE – A HARRY POTTER DELUXE SET

Each of these books is a rare original first edition that has been rebound in very high quality gilt-tooled morocco leather by London's notable 'Chelsea Bindery' – each book also has its own matching slipcase.

The front covers have an inset leather image based on the illustrations on the original covers - each also bears J.K. Rowling's impressed signature in gilt.

The colours have been carefully chosen to match those of the original covers, which may become damaged or dirty when they were being read originally.

Rebound books of this very high quality are scarce and sought-after by collectors and the army of Potter fans – it is also very rare to find a set of six Rowling first editions.

A set of six J.K. Rowling first 'deluxe' editions by the Chelsea Bindery, published by Bloomsbury, comprising "Harry Potter and the Philosopher's Stone"; "Harry Potter and the Chamber of Secrets"; "Harry Potter and the Prisoner of Azkaban" (first issue); "Harry Potter and the Goblet of Fire"; "Harry Potter and the Order of the Phoenix" and "Harry Potter and the Half-Blood Prince", the page edges stamped in silver with hologram stars.
1999-2005

£6,500-7,500   **BLO**

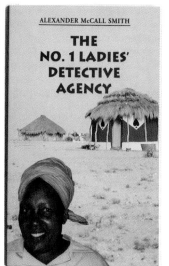

Robert Sabbag, "Snowblind", first edition, published by Rebel, from a limited edition of 1,000 with foreword by Howard Marx and packaging designed by Damien Hirst, signed by Sabbag, Hirst and Marx, complete with packaging including a rolled-up $100 bill, fake Amex credit card, original mirror covers, silver edges, slip-case with repeated $100-dollar bill design, in original publisher's box.

The cover artwork and accessories indicate the subject of the book – the cocaine trade. Always check the last three digits of the real $100 bill – these should match the edition number of the book.
1998

£1,200-1,800   **BLO**

Alexander McCall Smith, "The No. 1 Ladies' Detective Agency", first edition, published by Pantheon, Edinburgh, with dust jacket, signed by the author on the title page.

This is the scarce true first edition. At the time of writing, a BBC TV series of the books is being filmed, and will be shown in the US on HBO.
1998

£500-600   **BLO**

Paul Stewart & Chris Riddell, "Stormchaser", first edition, published by Doubleday, with price-clipped dust jacket, illustrations and map endpapers.
1999

£200–300   **BLO**

Hunter S. Thompson, "Hell's Angels", first US edition stating "first printing", with dust jacket and small ownership inscription on front free endpaper, published by Random House.
1967

£700-800   **BLO**

Hunter S. Thompson, "Fear and Loathing in Las Vegas", first US edition, published by Random House, with dust jacket and blind-stamp on preliminary, with illustrations by Ralph Steadman, slightly sunned at top edge.

This is Thompson's most famous novel. It was successfully filmed by Terry Gilliam in 1998, with Johnny Depp in the lead role, a character based on Thompson himself. This renewed popularity in Thompson, together with his death in 2005, has lead to an increase in prices.
1971

£700-800   **BLO**

Graham Swift, "Waterland", first edition, published by Heinemann, with dust jacket.

1983
£150-200   **BLO**

J.R.R.Tolkien, "The Lord of the Rings", published by George Allen & Unwin, comprising three first editions of "The Fellowship of the Ring", fifth impression; "The Two Towers", fourth impression; and "The Return of the King", second impression, each containing maps and with dust jackets, uniformly darkened.
1955-56

£500–700   **BLO**

William Trevor, "The Day We Got Drunk on Cake", first edition, published by Bodley Head, with dust jacket.

This is the author's first collection of short stories, and is sought-after.
1967

£500-600   **BLO**

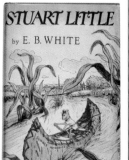

E.B. White, "Stuart Little", first edition, first issue, published by Harper & Brothers, New York & London, with dust jacket, illustrations by Garth Williams, with "10-5 & I-U" on copyright page.
1945

£250-350   **BLO**

Douglas E. Winter (editor), "Prime Evil", produced by Donald M. Grant and published by Bantam Press, from a limited edition of 250 copies signed by the contributors, containing colour plates and illustrations, and with original black rexine, black drop-back box.

Contributors include Stephen King, Clive Barker, Peter Straub, Ramsey Campbell and Whitley Strieber.
1988

£200–300   **BLO**

P.G. Wodehouse, "Summer Moonshine", first UK edition, published by Herbert Jenkins, with dust jacket, containing eight pages of advertisements, abrasions to spine, some skillful restoration to spine and edges.
1938

£400–600   **BLO**

John Wyndham, "The Day of the Triffids", first edition, published by Michael Joseph, with dust jacket, minor restoration to foot of spine.
1951

£850-950   **BLO**

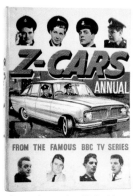

A 'Z-Cars' annual, published by World Distributors, Manchester.

1964   10.75in (27cm) high
£7-10   **MA**

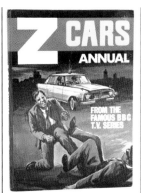

A 'Z Cars' annual, published by World Distributors, Manchester.

1966   10.75in (27cm) high
£7-10   **MA**

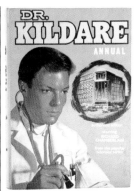

A 'Dr. Kildare' annual, published by Dell Publishing.

c1962   10.75in (27cm) high
£5-7   **MA**

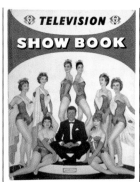

An 'ATV Television Show Book', published by Adprint, London.

1959   11in (27.5cm) high
£6-8   **MA**

A 'Radio Fun' annual, with UFO and alien cover.

The fun and quirky cover, with the UFO and alien representing the popularity of science fiction and outer space at this time, adds to the appeal of this annual.

1957   9.5in (24cm) high
£7-10   **MA**

A 'This Show Business' hardback book, published by the Daily Mirror, with Jayne Mansfield cover.

The presence of Jayne Mansfield raises the value of this book. Covers featuring popular stars who have a wide following will generally add to desirability - and often value - particularly if well photographed or showing their private life.

10in (25.5cm) high
£15-20   **MA**

A 'Radio Fun' annual, with Norman Wisdom cover.

1959   9.5in (24cm) high
£7-10   **MA**

A 1950s 'Stars Off The Record' annual, published by Eldon Press, with Johnnie Ray dust jacket and Frank Sinatra interview.

11in (28cm) high
£6-8   **MA**

BREWERIANA

'Opening Time is Guinness Time' advertising poster, no. GA/P2/2035, designed by John Gilroy and printed by Sanders Phillips.

1952   40.25in (102cm) high

£280-320   ON

'After Work Guinness' advertising poster, no. GA/4PU/2539, designed by Tom Eckersley and printed by Mills & Rockley.

1961   59.75in (152cm) high

£300-400   ON

A 1950s Guinness printed card beer mat.

4in (10cm) diam

£3-5   MA

A rare 1950s Carlton Ware 'Draught Guinness' penguin advertising figurine, with printed factory marks to base.

Carlton Ware's hard-to-find ceramic Guinness advertising figurines have been reproduced over the past decades. The beak colours on fakes or reproductions tend to be more clearly delineated than on originals, where they are more graduated.

3.75in (9.5cm) high

£500-800   BEV

One of a pair of Brewmaster advertising figures, by Carlton Ware, decorated in colours and gilt on inscribed black bases.

9.25in (23.5cm) high

£50-80 (pair)   SAS

A rare Beswick 'Double Diamond' beer advertising figurine, with printed marks to base.

8in (20.5cm) high

£250-300   BEV

ESSENTIAL REFERENCE

- The Blue Mountain Pottery was founded by Czech immigrant Josef Weider (1909-71) in Collingwood, Ontario, just after WWII. The name was taken from the neighbouring Blue Mountains, which are a haven for skiers. Founded to provide a steady income and work throughout the year, the pottery took on fellow Czechs Dennis (Zdenek) Tupy to develop the moulds and Mirek Hambálek, the glazes.
- Vases, ashtrays and bowls were sold to skiers and tourists. By 1955 production increased to cope with rising sales. Expansion continued into the 1960s, and Weider sold the successful company in 1968. After a further sale and financial problems, it was bought by Robert Blair in 1968. While the 1980s and early '90s proved strong for the company, it was forced to close in 2004 due to falling orders, the factory lease ending and competition from Far Eastern makers.
- The vast majority of pieces were made using the local red clay and a slip-moulding process. The most characteristic, popular and prolifically used glaze was a streaky, flowing green, said to be inspired by the mountains' spruce and pine trees. Blue and brown were also popular. Due to the two-step, brushed and dipped production process, the glaze on each piece is unique. The glaze formulae were complex and specially developed by the company.
- Other glazes are rarer. Among the most desirable today are Harvest Gold, Autumn Mist and Cobalt Blue, and rarer glazes include Slate and Mocha. Glaze is one of the most important considerations for value. A superbly varied green glaze on a good form may be worth as much as a poor example of the rarer Slate glaze. Look at the green vases shown below for an example. In general, the stronger and more tonally varied, the better.
- Look for early pieces from the 1950s or ranges produced for short time periods, as these tend to be more desirable and valuable. Some early pieces can be identified from the presence of three pin marks on the base, left by kiln stilts. Rarer or more sought-after ranges include a series of Noah's Ark animals, Apollo, the Native Artists' Collection, and Canadian Decorator.
- Unusual or rare forms are also sought-after. Long-necked swans, stylized fish that represent the period and clean-lined modern forms all find fans. Although shapes had their own numbers, many have been given names by collectors, such as the Angel Fish. As well as the glaze, consider how sharp and detailed the moulded forms are, as this counts too.
- As well as being successful within Canada, over 60 per cent of the company's production was exported abroad, 40 per cent of that to the US, with much of the remaining 20 per cent going to the UK and the rest of Europe. Prices have been growing rapidly over the past five years, but much is still affordable. As the pottery was so successful, more treasures may be waiting to be discovered.

A Blue Mountain Pottery asymmetric organic form 'Duckbill' vase, shape no. 55 designed by Dennis Tupy, with dripped green glaze.

12in (31cm) high

£15-25   TWF

A Blue Mountain Pottery 'Bowling Pin' jug vase or pitcher, shape no. 25a designed by Dennis Tupy, with mottled and dripped green glaze.

19in (48cm) high

£20-30   TWF

A Blue Mountain Pottery cylinder vase, with scooped rim, the base with moulded 'three tree' mark.

The glaze on this example is not as good or desirable as on the vases on the left.

11.5in (29cm) high

£15-20   TWF

A Blue Mountain Pottery vase, in the form of two stylized curving leaves, with green dripped glaze, the base with 'three tree' and "Canada" marks.

11.25in (28.5cm) high

£20-30   TWF

A 1950s Blue Mountain vase, shape no. 36 designed by Dennis Tupy, with long, flared neck, the early avocado green glaze with dripped light green and blue-tinged cream glaze.

5.75in (14.5cm) high

£10-20   TWF

CERAMICS

A Blue Mountain Pottery 'Spitoon' vase, shape no. 32A, with mottled, dripped green glaze.

This is one of the most commonly seen shapes in one of the most commonly seen colourways. It is the variety of green tones on this example that makes it this valuable.

5.25in (13cm) high

£15-20   **TWF**

A Blue Mountain Pottery cornucopia vase, with a good green dripped glaze, the base with moulded "BMP Canada" mark with curling "M".

This form is similar to, and may have been inspired by, the success of Royal Haeger's cornucopia vases.

10.75in (27.5cm) wide

£20-25   **TWF**

A Blue Mountain Pottery dolphin sculpture, with green dripped glaze.

16.5in (42cm) long

£15-20   **TWF**

EXPERT EYE – A BLUE MOUNTAIN FISH

This is one of the largest and most dramatic forms produced by Blue Mountain and was made from the early 1950s until c1986. Despite its success it was never copied by other makers.

It is usually found in this green glaze, which is well displayed by the large flat sides. Examples in Harvest Gold are rare, and it has not yet been found in any other colourway.

The production process was time-consuming as they were so large and fragile. Tupy is said to have joked that the glaze held the sides together.

Although prices have been rising in recent years, this is only for undamaged fish - always check carefully for signs of damage, particularly on the fin tips.

A Blue Mountain Pottery 'Angel Fish' vase, shape no. 58 designed by Dennis Tupy, with a graduated green dripped glaze, the base moulded "BMP Canada".

17.5in (44cm) high

£80-120   **TWF**

A Blue Mountain Pottery 'Swan' tall bird sculpture, shape no. 48 designed by Dennis Tupy, with green dripped glaze, the base with Blue Mountain Pottery paper label.

Birds with elongated necks were typical forms used by glassmakers on Murano during the same period. Examine the necks carefully as they were frequently broken and reglued.

18.25in (46cm) high

£20-30   **TWF**

A Blue Mountain Pottery Fish sculpture, with long, curving tail, in a dripped and mottled green glaze.

18.5in (47cm) high

£20-30   **TWF**

A Blue Mountain Pottery 'Ginger Jar', with the 'Celadon' glaze, the base moulded "750".

The form and glaze appear to be inspired by ancient Oriental ceramics. This shape was not popular at the time, making it harder to find today.

9in (22.5cm) high

£40-60   **TWF**

A pair of Blue Mountain Pottery 'Peacock' bookends, with green dripped glaze.

Peacock bookends are harder to find and more desirable than the more common horse head bookends.

8.5in (21.5cm) high

£35-45   **TWF**

A Blue Mountain Pottery camel figurine, with green dripped glaze.

8.75in (22cm) high

£25-35   **TWF**

A 1960s-70s Blue Mountain Pottery jug, with a dripped and mottled cobalt and light blue glaze, the base with moulded 'three tree mark'.

10.25in (26.5cm) high

£25-35   **TWF**

A 1950s Blue Mountain vase, shape no. 36 designed by Dennis Tupy, with long, flared neck, and Aurora Borealis glaze.

5.75in (14.5cm) high

£20-30   **TWF**

A Blue Mountain Pottery bottle vase, with shaped bulb, tall neck and flared rim, decorated with a streaked and dripped glaze, the base with moulded 'three tree' mark.

It is the highly appealing complex glaze, which contains different tones of light blue, green, cream and pink, that makes this vase so valuable.

6in (15cm) high

£70-100   **TWF**

A Blue Mountain Pottery dolphin sculpture, with dripped cobalt blue glaze.

7.75in (19.5cm) high

£18-22   **TWF**

CERAMICS

A Blue Mountain Pottery 'Spitoon' vase, shape no. 32A, with Harvest Gold glaze.

5.25in (13cm) high

£18-22   **TWF**

A Blue Mountain Pottery jug vase, shape no. 19 designed by Dennis Tupy, with handle and Harvest Gold glaze, the base with 'three tree' mark.

This glaze remains as popular with collectors today as it was with buyers during the 1970s.

13.75in (35cm) high

£25-35   **TWF**

EXPERT EYE – A BLUE MOUNTAIN VASE

The style of glaze and form are very similar to contemporary West German pottery that was being imported into Canada and sold inexpensively, competing for market share with Blue Mountain pottery.

The pitted surface and Apollo glaze name were inspired by the 1969 moon landing, and are unique to each piece as they were applied by hand.

Examples are hard to find as it was produced for only three years, from 1977 until 1980.

The thick and randomly bubbled glaze can be found on a number of different shapes including pitcher forms.

A Blue Mountain Pottery baluster shaped vase, shape no. 856, with the Apollo dripped and bubbled glaze, the base with circular factory mark and moulded "856".

13.5in (34cm) high

£80-120   **TWF**

A 1970s Blue Mountain Pottery wine carafe and two goblets, each with the Mocha glaze, the base with moulded "BMP" mark.

1965-84   Carafe 10.25in (26cm) high

£40-50   **TWF**

A 1970s Blue Mountain Pottery jug vase, with Mocha glaze, the base moulded "BMP Canada".

Produced from 1965 until 1984, Mocha was a popular glaze during this time, undoubtedly due to its (then) fashionable colour. It can be found on a large number of shapes, however, examples with the widest and most dramatic variety of tones, including the almost reflective dark brown shown here, are more desirable and valuable.

10.5in (27cm) high

£35-50   **TWF**

A late 1950-early 60s Blue Mountain Pottery tapering vase, with Plum glaze, the base impressed "B.M.P. Canada" mark.

10.5in (26.5cm) high

£40-60   **TWF**

ESSENTIAL REFERENCE – BLUE MOUNTAIN MARKS & LABELS

Over the years, Blue Mountain Pottery used different styles of marks and labels to identify their production. While this does not provide precise dating of a piece, it does allow you to date a piece to a period. The earliest marks during the 1950s were printed in ink. The most common moulded marks found show the words "BMP CANADA", and were used for the longest periods of time. The styles vary for two reasons. Firstly due to a change in the style of the 'M' in "BMP" and secondly, less easily detected, different moulds had slightly different styles along the same theme, as they were made by different people. If a piece had a small base without enough space for the full mark, only "BMP" would be used. The mountain-like 'three trees' mark was the work of graphic designer Chris Yaneff in 1967, and was used until 1976 on many pieces. However earlier moulds with "BMP CANADA" marks that were still useable were also used after this date. Paper labels may have been used at different times depending on factory stocks. Research work is currently being undertaken that will hopefully reveal more precise date periods for each mark.

A 1950s plain "MADE IN CANADA" mark

A mid-1960s "BMP CANADA" mark, with curling 'M'.

A 1980s-90s "BMP CANADA" mark.

A 1980s-90s "BMP CANADA" mark, with wider 'M'.

The 'Three tree' mark, designed by Chris Yaneff in 1967, used until 1976.

A late 1960s-mid-1970s 'vase and waves' mark and shape number.

A 1960s 'trillum' paper label, with Josef Weider's 'signature'.

A stylized tree paper label, used from 1968 onwards.

A late 1960s-mid 1970s 'vase and waves' paper label.

A Blue Mountain Pottery cylindrical vase, with scooped rim, and cobalt Granite glaze.

Produced from 1973-80, although it appears black, the background is actually a very dark blue.

11.5in (29cm) high

£35-50   **TWF**

A Blue Mountain Pottery wine goblet, with Slate glaze, unmarked.

Produced from 1965 until 1984, Slate can be hard to find today as it was not popular when it was originally produced, meaning comparatively few pieces were made.

5.5in (14cm) high

£8-12   **TWF**

A Blue Mountain Pottery vase, shape no. 33 designed by Dennis Tupy, with flared rim, with a greeny silver glaze dripped over black.

This was the first shape Tupy designed and was thrown on a wheel. The horizontal bands left by the potter as he formed the piece on the wheel show the influence of studio pottery, which emphasised handmade qualities.

7.25in (18.5cm) high

£40-60   **TWF**

CERAMICS

A Blue Mountain Pottery miniature duck figurine, covered with the Mustard glaze.

2.75in (7cm) high

£20-25   **TWF**

A Blue Mountain Pottery owl figurine, covered with a mottled and dripped brown glaze.

5.25in (13cm) high

£22-28   **TWF**

A Blue Mountain Pottery miniature cockerel figurine, covered with dripped and streaked light blue, yellow, brown and green glazes, unmarked.

This is an extremely unusual, colourful and scarce glaze combination. Blue Mountain produced a number of miniature animal figurines, some based on larger forms, as with the dolphin shown here. Their small sizes do not necessarily mean small values. Some animals are scarcer than others, and as usual the glaze is also of paramount importance. After 1980, animal figurines became a mainstay for the company, along with giftware. Swans were the most common animal shape produced.

3.5in (9cm) high

£35-50   **TWF**

A Blue Mountain Pottery miniature fox figurine, with the Harvest Gold glaze, unmarked.

3in (7.5cm) high

£18-22   **TWF**

A Blue Mountain Pottery miniature reclining seal figurine, with the 'Celadon' glaze.

4.5in (11.5cm) high

£30-35   **TWF**

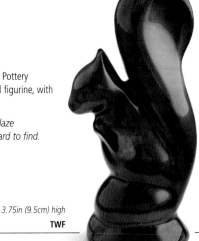

A Blue Mountain Pottery miniature squirrel figurine, with the Flame glaze.

This shape and glaze combination is hard to find.

3.75in (9.5cm) high

£20-25   **TWF**

A Blue Mountain Pottery miniature dolphin figurine, covered with a graduated cobalt blue glaze.

3.75in (9.5cm) long

£18-22   **TWF**

A Blue Mountain Pottery miniature tortoise figurine, covered with a mottled brown and green glaze, unmarked.

5.25in (13cm) long

£20-25   **TWF**

FIND OUT MORE...

'Blue Mountain Pottery', *by Conrad Biernacki, published in Antique & Collectibles Trader, Winter 2005.*

Blue Mountain Pottery Collectors' Club: *www.bmpcc.com*

'On The Table: 100 Years of Functional Ceramics in Canada', *by Sandra Alfoldy & Rachel Gotlieb, published by Gardiner Museum, 2007.*

ESSENTIAL REFERENCE

- The Briglin Pottery was founded in Baker Street, central London, in June 1948, and took its name from the combined forenames of its founders Brigitte Appleby and Eileen Lewenstein. In 1959, the company moved south to Mayfair, London, and Lewenstein left. The company became known for its simple and functional tablewares and decorative vases and bowls that were entirely hand-potted and hand-decorated.
- The Briglin style was inspired by Scandinavian Modernism, with themes taken from the natural world, such as leaves and country flowers, placed on very simple, clean-lined forms. The natural motifs were accentuated by earthy browns and beiges, as well as creams, green and light blues. Although stocked by fashionable department stores such as Heal's and Peter Jones, prices were largely affordable. Briglin was, in effect, mass-produced handmade studio pottery that could be used around the home.
- The pottery was enormously successful during the 1960s and '70s, but by the 1980s fashions had changed and their handmade, naturally inspired earthy pottery was no longer fashionable. With a drop in sales and rising competition from other makers, the pottery closed in 1990. Briglin languished in charity and junk shops for around 10-to-15 years, but prices have begun to rise recently. Vases and bowls tend to be more desirable than kitchenware and novelty forms such as money boxes, but always consider the level of decoration, the rarity of the pattern and the form when assessing value.

A Briglin tapering cylinder vase, with glossy cream glaze, and copper oxide, wax-resist and sgraffito decoration of a thistle, the base impressed "Briglin".

7.75in (19.5cm) high

£60-80   GC

A Briglin vase, with wax-resist and sgraffito sycamore leaf design, the base impressed "Briglin".

9.5in (24cm) high

£40-50   GC

A Briglin small vase or pen pot, with blue Japanese-style floral decoration on a glossy white ground.

4.25in (11cm) high

£20-30   GROB

A Briglin cylindrical vase, with a wax-resist closed thistle on one side and an open thistle on the other, painted with a glossy cream and green oxide glaze, the base stamped "Briglin".

7.5in (19cm) high

£35-45   GC

A Briglin cylinder vase, with hand-painted wax-resist bamboo decoration and brushed bands, and all-over glossy glaze, the base stamped "Briglin".

Here a wax-resist has been applied over the light beige glaze to mark out the leaves, before the final brown glaze was brushed on.

9.5in (24cm) high

£30-50   GC

CERAMICS

ESSENTIAL REFERENCE – BRIGLIN DECORATION

Briglin's decorators used three primary techniques to decorate their pottery, all executed by hand. The first, and most obvious was wax-resist, where wax would be applied to the areas where the glaze was not to appear, marking out a design. When the glaze was brushed on, it would not adhere to the wax, and when fired, the wax would burnt off, leaving the natural clay underneath. Sometimes this raw clay was coloured with darker matte tones by applying manganese oxide. The second is sgraffito, where a sharp point would be used to incise lines into the leather-hard dried clay prior to firing. Sometimes lines would be scratched through a wax layer, allowing glaze to be applied in fine lines. Thirdly, a piece could be painted with a design in glaze. A combination of these techniques could be used on the same piece, as here. This is also a very rare geometric pattern, and a very large size, hence its higher value.

A 1970s Briglin large cylinder vase, with sgraffito and green mottled cream gloss glazed circle design, the base stamped "Briglin".

10.75in (27cm) high

£150-200　　　　　　　　　　　　　GC

A Briglin 'Scroll' pattern tall mug, with swirling wax-resist decoration.

This was Briglin's longest running pattern, and is commonly found today.

5.25in (13.5cm) high

£15-20　　　　　　　　　GROB

A Briglin tall mug, with wax-resist decoration of leaves against a blue-green glossy glaze, the base impressed "Briglin".

4.5in (11.5cm) high

£20-30　　　　　　　GROB

A Briglin large tankard/mug, with wax-resist flower decoration.

This is another commonly found pattern, particularly on tableware.

4.75in (12cm) high

£20-25　　　　　　　GROB

A Briglin Japanese-style teapot, with wax-resist and manganese oxide flower decoration, and bent bamboo handle.

7.5in (19cm) high

£40-60　　　　　　　　　　　　　GROB

A Briglin small dog money bank, with sgraffito 'fur' and cream glaze, the base stamped "Briglin".

3.5in (9cm) long

£10-15　　　　　　　GC

A Briglin small bunny money bank, with sgraffito 'fur' and cream glaze, the base stamped "Briglin".

4.5in (11.5cm) high

£10-15　　　　　　　GC

FIND OUT MORE...

'Briglin Pottery 1948-1990', *by Anthea Arnold, published by Briglin Books, 2002.*

ESSENTIAL REFERENCE

- Wiltshaw & Robinson established the Carlton Works in Stoke-on-Trent, in 1890. Wares were produced under the trade name Carlton Ware from 1894, and it became the company's name from 1958. The company produced moulded, hand-decorated ceramics in a variety of styles.
- The Art Deco styled lustre range was introduced in the mid-1920s in answer to the success of Wedgwood's Fairyland Lustre range designed by Daisy Makeig-Jones. Patterns were inspired by Eastern themes, Egypt, the Art Deco movement, and nature. Birds and stylized leaves and flowers were popular motifs. Colours were typically bold and strong.
- The 1930s saw the introduction of cottageware, which comprised tableware shaped like country buildings, as well as moulded floral table wares. Produced into the 1950s, these remain more affordable than the earlier lustre wares, which were costly to produce and expensive at the time.
- The 1950s was one of the most productive times for the company. The 1930s lustre ranges were refreshed with the Royale range, which came in Rouge, Verte, Bleu and Noire (red, green, blue and black). As before, Chinese-inspired patterns were key, and designs included Chinese landscapes, plants, birds and spider webs.
- From the 1960s onwards, the company changed with the fashion of the day, producing shapes and patterns that would have been popular at the time. These include the space age inspired Orbit and the 1970s range of Walking Ware. In 1989, the company went bankrupt, although the name and some moulds were bought by Francis Joseph in 1997.

A Wiltshaw & Robinson Carlton Ware bowl, decorated with hand-painted roses and black stripes, the base with Wiltshaw & Robinson mark and painted "2080".

c1895   *9.5in (24cm) diam*

£75-85   **W&L**

A 1930s Carlton Ware hand-painted cottageware biscuit barrel, unmarked.

6in (15cm) wide

£80-120   **BAD**

A Carlton Ware cottageware jam pot.

3.5in (9cm) wide

£45-65   **BAD**

A Carlton Ware cottageware toast rack.

4in (10cm) wide

£80-120   **BAD**

A Carlton Ware 'John Peel' musical tankard, with moulded decoration.

4.75in (12cm) high

£70-100   **BAD**

A 1930s Carlton Ware
hand-painted Handcraft charger, pattern 3801, with stylized flowers.

12in (30.5cm) diam

£200-250   **BAD**

An Art Deco Carlton Ware 'Gum
Flower' pattern tapering vase, on
a mottled green ground, the base
painted "0/10080 3790 17".

6in (15.5cm) high

£150-200   **BEV**

A 1930s Carlton Ware 'Carnival' pattern matte Handcraft vase, the
base impressed "463" and painted "6/6246 3305".

*The last numbers, 3305, relate to the pattern number, which is also
known as 'Carnival'. The overall design bears some similarities to Truda
Carter's popular designs for Poole Pottery, produced during the same
period.*

4.25in (11cm) high

£250-350   **BEV**

EXPERT EYE – A CARLTON WARE VASE

*Vases are more popular and
desirable than jugs or shallow
dishes. The form is attractive
and shows the pattern off well.*

*There is also a hint of Oriental exoticism in
the pattern. This is a theme that runs
through many of Carlton Wares patterns
and also the Art Deco movement.*

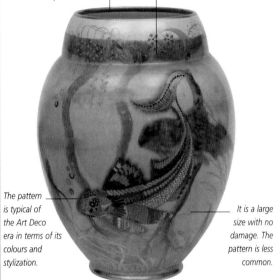

*The pattern
is typical of
the Art Deco
era in terms of its
colours and
stylization.*

*It is a large
size with no
damage. The
pattern is less
common.*

A 1930s Carlton Ware 'River Fish' pattern stepped ovoid vase, with
collar neck and gilt highlights, the base with printed marks.

9.5in (24cm) high

£1,500-2,000   **FLD**

A rare 1930s Carlton Ware
'River Fish' pattern conical
bowl, with gilt highlights,
the base with printed marks.

9in (23cm) diam

£700-800   **FLD**

A 1930s Carlton Ware 'Rainbow Fan' pattern inkwell, with cylindrical
integral well and stylized floral pattern, the base with printed marks.

8in (20.5cm) long

£700-800   **FLD**

A 1930s Carlton Ware 'Fan' pattern vase, with collar neck and gilt highlights, the base with printed marks.

9.5in (24cm) high

£1,300-1,800 **FLD**

A 1930s Carlton Ware 'Bell' pattern ginger jar, pattern no. 3788, decorated with a stylized floral and foliate pattern with gilt highlights over a red ground, the base with printed marks.

7.25in (18cm) high

£550-650 **FLD**

A 1930s Carlton Ware lustre 'Secretary Bird' pattern baluster vase, pattern no. 4018, hand-painted in vivid colours with a bird under stylized foliate and floral details, the base with printed factory and painted marks.

6in (15.5cm) high

£450-550 **DN**

A rare Carlton Ware Rouge Royale lustre 'Sketching Bird' pattern jug, pattern no. 3891, with hand-painted kingfisher and tree decoration, the base impressed "1676" and with Rouge Royal Carlton Ware mark.

This is both a rare and desirable pattern, and a rare shape.

7in (18cm) high

£450-550 **BEV**

A Carlton Ware Rouge Royale lustre 'Duck' pattern vase, pattern no. 4499, with hand-painted tree, ho-ho birds and plants, with ribbed base and gilt side handles.

4.25in (10.5cm) high

£80-120 **BEV**

A Carlton Ware Rouge Royale 'New Mikado' pattern ginger jar and cover, hand-painted in colours with a Chinoiserie scene, the base with printed factory and painted marks.

8.75in (22cm) high

£180-220 **L&T**

A Carlton Ware Verte Royal ginger jar and cover, hand-painted with a spider's web and a butterfly, the base impressed "125/3".

6in (15cm) high

£300-400 **BEV**

CERAMICS

ESSENTIAL REFERENCE

- Carn Pottery was founded by John Beusmans in 1971, in Nancledra, near St Ives and Penzance in Cornwall. Beusmans' parents had produced lamp shades for Troika Pottery, and he had studied throwing at the Redruth Art College. For each piece, Beusmans potted a master and then created a mould. This mould would be used with slip (liquid clay) to create the final range of pieces.
- Forms are linear and sculptural, ranging from simple cylindrical bottles to geometric fan vases. Patterns are abstract, yet inspired by the natural world around him. They include stylized leaves, sun rays and even pebbles on a beach. A number of moulds would be made from each master shape, each having a different pattern on the front and back. Colours are brushed on by hand with a mop, making each piece unique. Light green, blues, beiges and creams are typical.
- Most pieces are signed with a black printed mark, but some are signed by Beusmans, typically in pencil. Examine corners, bases and rims carefully as the ceramic tends to chip easily. As with Troika, interest in and values for Carn have risen in recent years, but seem to have reached a plateau. Fan vases, larger sizes and cats tend to be the more collectable forms. Look for those that combine two different shapes, one seen from the front and another from the back.

A Carn Pottery cylinder vase, with low relief moulded circular design of curving lines and brushed brown glaze, the base with factory black printed mark.

4.75in (12cm) high

£15-25　　　　　　UCT

A Carn Pottery hand-painted cylinder vase, with creamy green glazed circular motif, the base with factory black stamped mark.

5.25in (13cm) high

£15-25　　　　　　UCT

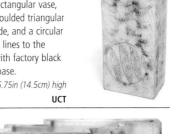

A Carn Pottery rectangular vase, with low relief moulded triangular pattern to one side, and a circular design of curving lines to the other, the base with factory black printed mark to base.

5.75in (14.5cm) high

£20-30　　　　　　UCT

A Carn Pottery rectangular vase, one corner cut with various angles, covered with a brushed light and dark green glaze, the base with factory black printed mark.

7in (18cm) high

£30-40　　　　　　UCT

A Carn Pottery asymmetric vase, with moulded low relief stylized flower design to one side and curving, beam-like pattern to the other, with cream and brushed green and blue glazes, the base with factory black printed mark.

£15-25　　　　　　UCT

A Carn Pottery fan vase, with low relief moulded curving design to one side and stylized flower design to the other, with cream and greeny blue glazes, the base with factory black printed mark.

6in (15cm) high

£20-30　　　　　　UCT

ESSENTIAL REFERENCE

- Chinese ceramics have hit the headlines over the past few years with millions of pounds being paid for rare, early and important examples. As well as existing collectors all over the world, buyers now include collectors from mainland China. A new class of wealthy businessmen lead a burgeoning, middle class now wishing to buy back their country's considerable heritage in ceramics.

- Away from these rarities, much late 19thC and 20thC export ware is comparatively affordable, with prices rarely rising above £1,000 for finer examples. Some pleasing and representative pieces can even be found for under £50. Pieces such as these are attracting the attentions of interior decorators and those looking for a unique or striking piece to add individualism, or a fashionable touch of the Orient, to a room.

- White ceramic pieces, hand-decorated in blue under the glaze, were exported to the West in their millions, and are perhaps the most commonly found type today. Forms include vases, bowls, dishes and larger chargers, and motifs are typically natural, including flowers, landscapes, trees, pagodas, figures, leafy vines and fish. The cargoes of shipwrecked vessels salvaged over the past decades typically comprised blue and white export wares, and examples from the 16thC can be had for as little as £50.

- Also popular are polychrome (multicoloured) wares, including famille rose (pink), famille jaune (yellow) and famille vert (green), all named after the dominant colour in the palette used. View museum collections and examples being sold at auction or in dealer's shops to enable you to spot finer quality pieces. The decoration should be well applied in sympathetic colours with a good level of detail. Marks can help with identification, so consult a specialist guide. However, it is worth bearing in mind that many early marks were applied to later pieces out of respect for, and in veneration of, ancestors.

A Chinese famille rose pear-shaped vase, probably 20thC, with flared rim, decorated with figures and an attendant beneath a pine tree, the base with Qianlong seal mark.

9in (23cm) high

£320-380   **DN**

One of a pair of large 19thC-20thC Chinese famille rose vases, of shouldered form, the flared rim enamelled with floral scrolls leading to a slender neck, the body finely painted in orange, red, green and blue to show a fishing hamlet.

22in (56cm) high

£300-500 (pair)   **FRE**

A large Chinese Republic period famille rose vase, of tapering ovoid form with a short slender neck, the body painted with a continuous landscape of green rock work, mountains and seascape, with small black inscription to shoulder.

15in (38cm) high

£220-280   **FRE**

A 20thC Chinese famille rose large vase, decorated with panels on a leaf scroll ground, some damage.

c1900   *22.5in (57cm) high*

£450-550   **WW**

A small 19thC Chinese famille rose vase, painted with two panels of birds on a turquoise ground decorated with birds, flowers and foliage.

6in (15cm) high

£150-200   **WW**

A 19thC Chinese famille rose moon flask, painted with a central cartouche depicting a battle scene, the reverse one with a phoenix perched on a branch, the neck restored.

8.75in (22.5cm) high

£150-200   **WW**

A large 19thC Chinese famille rose dish, painted with six figures at play.

14.5in (37cm) high

£100-150   **WW**

CERAMICS

A 20thC Chinese famille rose dish, decorated with nine peaches issuing from leafy branches, with six character Qianlong mark.

13.75in (35cm) high

£500-700 WW

A large Chinese ovoid vase and cover, decorated with prunus on a blue ground.

c1900 *12in (33cm) high*

£60-80 WW

A 20thC Chinese blue and white beaker vase, the centre painted with taotie masks between stiff leaves.

15in (38cm) high

£50-80 WW

A pair of 18thC Chinese export blue and white octagonal platters, one decorated with figures on a bridge and pagoda within a riverside landscape, the other with a fenced garden with exotic birds.

Largest 16.5in (42cm) wide

£500-600 L&T

A near pair of 19thC Chinese Canton famille rose vases, decorated with panels of figures and birds amid foliage.

10in (25.5cm) high

£180-220 WW

EXPERT EYE – A CHINESE BRUSH POT

Famille rose is named after the opaque pink colour used in the range of colours. It was first used in c1720 and could be shaded with opaque yellow and white.

The decoration intentionally does not cover the entire surface, allowing the fine quality, bright flawless white porcelain to be shown off.

Scenes showing people working are popular among collectors.

Particularly good examples have faces with individual expressions, unfortunately this example does not.

A 19thC Chinese famille rose brush pot, of deep circular form, well enamelled to show ladies in the pursuit of leisure, recessed base.

6.5in (16.5cm) high

£400-600 FRE

A early 20thC Chinese mille-fleurs large baluster vase, the base with a four character Qianlong mark, two small rim chips.

Used primarily in the 19thC, 'mille-fleurs' probably inspired the transfer-printed chintzware patterns produced by Royal Winton, Shelley and others from the 1920s to '50s.

18in (45.5cm) high

£250-350 WW

ESSENTIAL REFERENCE

- Clarice Cliff was born in Tunstall, Stoke-on-Trent in 1899. Hailing from the heart of the Staffordshire Potteries, she joined the local company of Linguard Webster & Co. as an apprentice enameller in 1912. In 1916, she moved to the larger firm of A.J. Wilkinson.
- Cliff showed great promise at A.J. Wilkinson and in 1925 the company's owner, Colley Shorter, gave Cliff her own studio in the recently acquired Newport Pottery. Cliff decorated the large number of defective blank wares with vivid colours in thickly applied, striking patterns, which hid any faults in the wares. Floral designs and angled, geometric patterns are typical. A new range was developed around Cliff's designs, which was given the name Bizarre, and launched in 1928. The range proved extremely popular and was produced until 1935.
- The Bizarre name does not belong to a particular pattern or shape, but was used as a general title, as was the name Fantasque, also first used in 1928, but phased out in 1934.

- To ensure that demand for her designs was met, Cliff trained a dedicated team of female decorators at the pottery and developed a series of new modern shapes and patterns. The dates included in captions refer to the period the pattern was produced for.
- Many patterns were produced in a range of colourways, some of which are now rarer than others. Orange is a common colour while blue and purple are often rarer and more valuable. Pieces in muted colours are less sought-after. Rare variations in colour or pattern will tend to attract collectors' interest.
- Earlier Art Deco shapes or patterns are popular with collectors, as are pieces which display a pattern well, such as chargers, plates and Lotus shape jugs and vases. Pieces displaying a combination of an Art Deco pattern applied to an Art Deco shape will generally attract the greatest interest. Condition is very important, any damage or wear will reduce the desirability on all but the rarest pieces.

A Clarice Cliff Bizarre 'Autumn Crocus' pattern grapefruit bowl, shape no. 476.

A Clarice Cliff Bizarre 'Autumn Crocus' pattern octagonal bowl.

1928-63	*9in (23cm) wide*	*1928-63*
£50-70	**GHOU**	**£120-180**

7in (18cm) wide

GHOU

A Clarice Cliff Bizarre 'Autumn Crocus' pattern Hiawatha circular tray.

3in (7.5cm) diam

£45-55　　　　**GHOU**

A Clarice Cliff Bizarre 'Autumn Crocus' pattern Ivor shape bowl.

5in (12.5cm) diam

£60-80　　　　**GHOU**

A Clarice Cliff Bizarre 'Autumn Crocus' pattern fern pot.

3in (7.5cm) high

£80-120　　　　**GHOU**

ESSENTIAL REFERENCE – CROCUS PATTERN

Crocus was the best selling of Cliff's many patterns. It sold in such large numbers during the late 1920s and early 1930s that a special decorating department was set up in the factory, with 15-20 'Bizarre Girls' devoted to painting it. However, sales declined in the late 1930s, and it was absorbed back into the general decorating department. Production was interrupted during WWII, but was restarted afterwards, continuing until 1963. It is known in a number of different colourways. This 'Autumn' version, with its earthy brown stripe, being the most common. Other colourways include 'Spring', with its pastel colours and green stripe produced from 1933-68, Purple and Blue, which were both produced in the early to mid-1930s. Popular forms, such as this sugar sifter, are usually the most valuable.

A Clarice Cliff Bizarre 'Autumn Crocus' pattern conical sugar sifter.

5.5in (14cm) high

£280-320   **GHOU**

A Clarice Cliff Bizarre 'Autumn Crocus' pattern candlestick, shape no. 310.

3in (7.5cm) high

£150-200   **GHOU**

A Clarice Cliff Bizarre 'Autumn Crocus' pattern vase, shape no. 280, the base with early painted green mark.

3in (7.5cm) high

£180-220   **GHOU**

A Clarice Cliff Bizarre 'Autumn Crocus' pattern cube candlestick, shape no. 658.

2.5in (6.5cm) high

£180-220   **GHOU**

A Clarice Cliff Bizarre 'Autumn Crocus' pattern beehive honey pot and cover, with early painted green mark.

3in (7.5cm) high

£150-200   **GHOU**

A Clarice Cliff 'Autumn Crocus' pattern beehive honey pot and cover.

4in (10cm) high

£150-200   **GHOU**

A Clarice Cliff Bizarre 'Autumn Crocus' pattern toast rack, shape no. 477.

This is a rare shape. Here, the handle is undamaged, which is also rare.

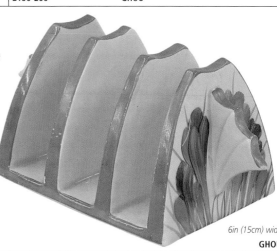

6in (15cm) wide

£250-350   **GHOU**

A Clarice Cliff Fantasque Bizarre 'Secrets' pattern vase, shape no. 264.

1933-37   8in (20.5cm) high

£320-380   **GHOU**

ESSENTIAL REFERENCE – SECRETS PATTERN

Secrets was Cliff's most popular landscape pattern, and was produced from 1933 to 1937. The rarest colourway was in brown, orange and purple, and is known as 'Orange Secrets'. A Blue colour variation was also produced. Towards the end of its production period, the design was simplified and used on tablewares.

A Clarice Cliff Fantasque Bizarre 'Secrets' pattern cauldron.

1933-37   3in (7.5cm) high

£200-300   **GHOU**

A Clarice Cliff Fantasque Bizarre 'Secrets' pattern cigarette/match holder, shape no. 463.

1933-37   2.75in (7cm) high

£500-600   **GHOU**

A Clarice Cliff Fantasque Bizarre 'Secrets' pattern Daffodil preserve pot and cover.

1933-37   5in (12.5cm) high

£200-300   **GHOU**

A Clarice Cliff Fantasque Bizarre 'Secrets' pattern stepped bowl, the base with printed factory marks, with minor chips to base rim.

1933-37   8in (20cm) diam

£200-300   **WW**

A Clarice Cliff Fantasque Bizarre 'Secrets' pattern beehive honey pot and cover.

Honey pots are desirable shapes, and this is an unusual colour variation, having seven colours.

1933-37   4in (10cm) high

£400-500   **GHOU**

A Clarice Cliff Bizarre 'Secrets' pattern octagonal side plate.

1933-37   5.75in (14.5cm) wide

£100-150   **GHOU**

A Clarice Cliff Fantasque Bizarre 'Secrets' pattern toast rack.

1933-37   5in (12.5cm) wide

£100-150   **GHOU**

A Clarice Cliff Bizarre 'Cafe Au Lait Autumn' stepped jardinière, with printed marks to base.

Café au Lait is the term used to described the mottled brown glaze effect. The technique was used on a number of patterns between 1931 and 1933, with a special 'Café au Lait' mark being used on bases.

1931-33   3.5in (9cm) high

£300-400   **WW**

A Clarice Cliff Fantasque Bizarre 'Blue Autumn' pattern vase, shape 360.

1930-34   8in (20.5cm) high

£500-600   **GHOU**

EXPERT EYE – A BRIDGEWATER CONICAL VASE

Bridgewater was only produced in 1934 in two colour variations – on the other, the tree has green foliage.

This was part of the Conical range, introduced in May 1929, which was inspired by a metal bowl produced by French company Desny.

Modern, geometric forms such as this, with its conical body supported on triangular feet, are very popular with collectors and typify the Art Deco style.

A much rarer lidded biscuit jar can also be found in this shape. The lid is a smaller version of the bottom half of the body.

A Clarice Cliff Bizarre 'Orange Bridgewater' pattern Conical vase, shape no. 400, painted in colours, with printed factory mark.

1934   6in (15cm) high

£1,800-2,200   **WW**

A Clarice Cliff Fantasque Bizarre 'Autumn' pattern conical cup and saucer.

1930-34

£250-300   **GHOU**

A Clarice Cliff Fantasque 'Berries' variant pattern ashtray, shape no. 503.

Berries is usually on a white, rather than black, background.

c1930   5in (12.5cm) diam

£80-120   **CW**

A Clarice Cliff Bizarre 'Branch and Squares' pattern plate.

1930   8in (20cm) diam

£170-200   **GHOU**

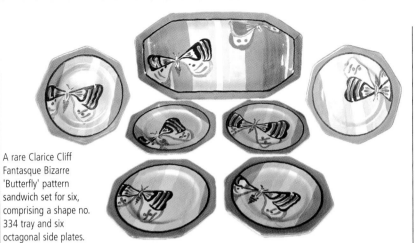

A Clarice Cliff Bizarre 'Orange Bridgewater' pattern clog, the sole with printed mark.

This is a rare and desirable shape.

1934   4in (10.5cm) long

£600-700   **WW**

A rare Clarice Cliff Fantasque Bizarre 'Butterfly' pattern sandwich set for six, comprising a shape no. 334 tray and six octagonal side plates.

This is a rare pattern dating from 1929, and was copied from a pattern produced by French painter, textile designer and bookbinder Edouard Benedictus. Sandwich sets with this many pieces are hard to find.

1929   Tray 12in (30.5cm) wide

£4,000-6,000   **GHOU**

A Clarice Cliff Fantasque 'Butterfly' pattern cylindrical preserve pot and cover.

1929   2.5in (6.25in) high

£320-380   **GHOU**

A Clarice Cliff Bizarre 'Canterbury Bells' pattern plate.

1932   9.75in (25cm) diam

£100-150   **GHOU**

LEFT: A Clarice Cliff Bizarre 'Red Carpet' pattern Conical jug.

1930   7in (18cm) high

£1,200-1,800   **GHOU**

RIGHT: A Clarice Cliff Bizarre 'Red Carpet' pattern wall plate.

Abstract designs such as this are very popular. 'Carpet' was copied by Cliff from a magazine photograph of a Da Silva Bruhn carpet, hence its name. However, it is perhaps not as impactful as those where colour covers the entire surface. The Conical range is desirable, as are chargers as they display the pattern very well.

1930   12in (30.5cm) diam

£1,200-1,800   **GHOU**

A Clarice Cliff Bizarre 'Coral Firs' pattern Conical sugar sifter, with grind mark to the foot rim.

1933-38   5.5in (14cm) high

£400-500   **GHOU**

A Clarice Cliff 'Elizabethan Lady' wall pocket, with original mirror-back mount.

7.25in (18.5cm) high

£80-120   **WW**

A Clarice Cliff Fantasque Bizarre 'Red Gardenia' pattern Coronet jug, with some fading.

1931　　　　*7in (18cm) high*

£140-200　　　　GHOU

A Clarice Cliff Bizarre 'Gay Day' pattern Athens shape teapot.

1930-34　　　*6.5in (16.5cm) high*

£50-80　　　　GHOU

EXPERT EYE – A LATONA SUGAR SIFTER

Sugar sifters are one of the most characteristic and popular of Clarice Cliff's shapes. This popularity means they are usually valuable.

Latona is the name given to a group of free-hand floral patterns produced from 1929 to 1930. This is closest to 'Latona Daisy'.

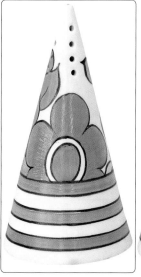

This is reputed to be the only known 'Latona' pattern sugar sifter ever to appear at auction.

The combination of the geometric lines and stylized flowers is typical of Cliff's more popular designs.

A rare Clarice Cliff Bizarre 'Latona' pattern Conical sugar sifter, painted with orange flowerheads and green foliage over three horizontal bands, small chip restoration to the base rim.

5.5in (14cm) high

£1,800-2,200　　　　GHOU

A Clarice Cliff 'Hollyhocks' pattern Conical sugar sifter, tip broken.

1936-37　　　*5.5in (14cm) high*

£120-180　　　　GHOU

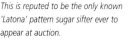

A Clarice Cliff Bizarre 'Latona' pattern coffee can and saucer, painted with orange flowerheads and green foliage.

1929-30

£60-80　　　　GHOU

A Clarice Cliff Fantasque Bizarre 'Limberlost' pattern Stamford tea for two set, comprising a teapot and cover, milk jug, sugar basin, two Conical cups and saucers and a side plate.

1932

£1,500-2,500　　　　GHOU

A Clarice Cliff Fantasque 'Melon' pattern Conical bowl candlestick, shape no. 384.

1930   *4.5in (11.5cm) diam*

£220-280   **GHOU**

A Clarice Cliff Bizarre 'Moonlight' pattern Conical sugar sifter.

A similar pattern but with stronger colours and orange, red and black bands, is known as 'Devon'.

1932   *5.5in (14cm) high*

£1,000-1,500   **GHOU**

EXPERT EYE – A STAMFORD TEA SET

The 'Mountain' pattern was produced only briefly from 1931 until 1932 and is very rare.

Any single piece would be a challenge to find, particularly the teapot, but to find a complete teaset in such excellent condition is very unusual.

The geometric, Art Deco Stamford shape with its shaped teapot and milk jug, and Conical cups with triangular handles, are popular.

Note the unpainted mountain top on the sugar bowl. This is typical of Cliff's hand-painted wares, where colours used on different elements could be changed by the Bizarre Girls, or accidentally be left unpainted.

A Clarice Cliff Bizarre range 'Mountain' pattern Stamford shape tea for two part service, comprising teapot, milk jug, sugar bowl, two teacups and saucer and a side plate, with date mark for 1932.

1932   *Teapot 4.75in (12cm) high*

£13,000-15,000   **WW**

A Clarice Cliff Bizarre 'Orange Patina Tree' pattern spherical vase, with spatter effect ground, the base with printed marks.

Patina has a lightly textured surface as it was splashed with liquid clay prior to being decorated. Difficult to paint over, a small number of patterns were produced including 'Tree' shown above, and the landscape 'Coastal' and 'Country'.

1932   *6in (15cm) high*

£500-600   **FLD**

A Clarice Cliff Bizarre 'Blue Patina Tree' pattern stepped cylindrical vase, with tapered neck, the base with printed marks.

1932   *7in (18cm) high*

£500-600   **FLD**

CERAMICS

A Clarice Cliff 'Rhodanthe' pattern ginger jar, with printed factory mark to base.

This pattern took over from Crocus in the popularity stakes, and was produced from 1934 until after WWII. It is known in other colours, which appear mainly in the flowers - green is known as 'Aurea', blue as 'Viscaria' and pink as 'Pink Pearls'.

7.75in (17cm) high

£200-300   **WW**

A Clarice Cliff 'Café au Lait Red Roofs' Mei Ping vase, painted in colours on a mottled yellow ground, printed mark, minor painted wear.

As the name of this vase shape suggests, it was inspired by Oriental ceramics.

1931   *9in (23cm) high*

£850-950   **WW**

A Clarice Cliff Fantasque 'Pebbles' pattern vase, shape no. 206.

This was one of the first 'Fantasque' range patterns, and was produced from 1929 to 1930. These simple vases show off the colourful, all over pattern extremely well.

1929-30   *6in (15cm) high*

£800-1,200   **GHOU**

A Clarice Cliff Bizarre 'Rudyard' pattern candlestick, shape no. 384.

1933-34   *4.5in (11.5cm) diam*

£250-350   **GHOU**

A Clarice Cliff 'Tiger Tree' pattern cauldron.

1937   *3in (7.5cm) high*

£350-450   **GHOU**

A Clarice Cliff Fantasque Bizarre 'Red Tulip' pattern globe vase, shape no. 370.

This is both a desirable and rare shape, and a scarce pattern, hence its high value.

1931   *6in (15cm) high*

£2,500-3,500   **GHOU**

A Clarice Cliff Fantasque 'Trees & House' pattern ashtray.

Although the house is missing, the pattern can be recognised from the style and colour of the tree and clouds.

1929   5in (12.5cm) diam

£100-150   **CW**

A Clarice Cliff Bizarre ashtray, shape no. 503.

The gate and trees, seen above, appear in a pattern from 1934 called 'Tulips'.

c1934   5in (12.5cm) diam

£150-250   **CW**

A Clarice Cliff Fantasque 'Umbrellas and Rain' pattern hexagonal vase, the base with printed marks.

1929   7.5in (19cm) high

£450-550   **FLD**

ESSENTIAL REFERENCE – FAKE LOTUS JUGS

Lotus jugs are one of the most popular and collectable shapes produced and are generally valuable. As a result, they are often faked, and early geometric patterns like this are the most common targets. The simplest way to identify a fake is to look at the inside edge of the handle. If a small hole is found towards the top, it is a modern reproduction or a fake. The interiors of reproductions and fakes also tend to be glazed 'too well'. Originals often have glaze runs or an uneven application of glaze. The colour tones of glazes also tend to be different. Always examine marks closely as many are not right, despite appearing so. Always compare marks to examples in a reference book. Lastly, look at the base and exterior for signs of wear over time, as these are often not present.

An authentic Clarice Cliff Bizarre 'Whisper' pattern Lotus jug.

1929   11.5in (29cm) high

£1,600-2,000   **GHOU**

A Clarice Cliff Fantasque 'Umbrellas and Rain' pattern angular vase with flared rim, the base with printed marks.

1929   7.75in (19.5cm) high

£500-600   **FLD**

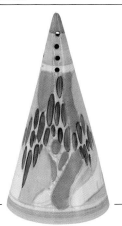

A Clarice Cliff Fantasque Bizarre 'Windbells' pattern conical sugar sifter.

1933   5.5in (14cm) high

£500-600   **GHOU**

CERAMICS

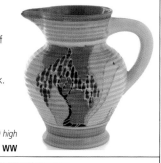

A Newport Pottery Clarice Cliff Fantasque Bizarre 'Windbells' pattern octagonal side plate.

1933   5.75in (14.5cm) wide

£280-320   **GHOU**

A Newport Pottery Clarice Cliff Fantasque Bizarre 'Windbells' pattern George shape jug, the base with printed factory mark.

1933   6.75in (17cm) high

£300-400   **WW**

A limited edition Wedgwood Clarice Cliff Age of Jazz 'Latona Red Roses' figure, printed and painted marks, boxed.

A series of company mergers and acquisitions led to Wedgwood owning the right to the Clarice Cliff name, brand and designs. During the 1990s, at the height of the market, the company released limited numbers of reproductions to allow collectors to own designs they may not be able to afford in vintage form. Produced until 2002, they are clearly marked on the base and should not be deemed 'fakes'. Always aim to buy examples that are complete with their boxes and paperwork, as these have already begun to rise in value.

8.25in (21cm) high

£80-120   **WW**

A limited edition Wedgwood Clarice Cliff Age of Jazz 'Twin Dancers', shape no. 434, from an edition of 1,000, with box and certificate.

5in (12.5cm) high

£100-150   **GHOU**

A limited edition Wedgwood Clarice Cliff Bizarre 'Farmhouse' pattern Mei Ping vase, from an edition of 250, boxed.

12in (30.5cm) high

£80-120   **GHOU**

A limited edition Wedgwood Clarice Cliff Bizarre 'May Avenue' pattern Isis vase, from a limited edition of 250, with box and certificate.

8in (20.5cm) high

£80-120   **GHOU**

A Wedgwood Clarice Cliff Bizarre 'Red Roofs' pattern vase, shape no. 461, with box and certificate.

7.5in (19cm) high

£40-60   **GHOU**

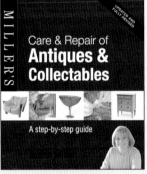
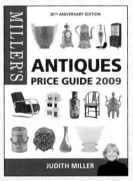

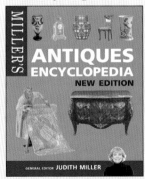

CERAMICS

A Royal Doulton cup and saucer, in dark red with gilt panels, marked "10" in gilt.

Saucer 4.25in (11cm) wide

£40-60   BAD

A Royal Doulton cup and saucer, marked "702 852".

Saucer 4.25in (11cm) wide

£35-45   BAD

A Royal Worcester cup and saucer, decorated with a pale blue band and hand-painted floral sprays, with gilt trim.

Saucer 5.5in (14cm) diam

£50-60   W&L

A 1980s Sarah Grosse cup and saucer, with printed and painted pattern of boxers, the base with printed marks.

c1986   Saucer 6.5in (16cm) diam

£7-10   MTS

A Royal Crown Derby trio set, with cobalt blue and transfer-printed gilt decoration, the base painted "8309S".

Plate 7.25in (18cm) diam

£55-65   W&L

A Royal Albert Crown China trio set, decorated with a transfer-printed and hand-painted with roses in dark blue and iron red, and with gilt highlights, the base painted "2946".

Plate 6in (15cm) diam

£18-22   W&L

A 1930s Old Royal China trio set, decorated in blue mottled 'malachite' effect and transfer-printed gilt trim.

Saucer 6.25in (16cm) wide

£20-25   W&L

A 1930s Melba bone china trio set, with hand-painted yellow flowers.

Note the angled handle, which is typically 1930s, as well as echoing popular, and now desirable, designs by Shelley.

6.25in (15.5cm) diam

£18-22   W&L

A pair of Denby Danesby ware 'Pastel Blue' stepped vases, modelled in low relief and painted with a stylized floral design, the bases with printed marks.

7.5in (19cm) high

£60-80   WW

A 1960s Denby Pottery 'Burlington' range vase, designed by Albert Colledge in 1959.

11in (28cm) high

£120-180   GGRT

A 1960s Denby Freestone range footed cylinder vase, designed by Glyn Colledge, with incised lines, with printed factory and signature marks to base.

12in (30.5cm) high

£80-120   GC

EXPERT EYE – A DENBY VASE

Just after the WWII, the production of colourful patterns was banned as materials were limited and could be better used elsewhere.

Jacobean Ware is very rare, and is characterised by its thickly hand-painted animal or figural designs in bright colours on a glossy black ground.

This piece was possibly made for export. If export sales could be proven, it was easier to obtain materials and licenses.

The short-lived range was designed by Albert Colledge – this example is also signed by him.

A rare Denby Pottery Jacobean Ware vase, designed and signed by Albert Colledge.

c1948   *6in (15cm) high*

£250-350   GGRT

A Denby flower pot, with factory marks and "WTL 1970" printed to base.

1970   *5.5in (14cm) high*

£25-35   GC

A 1980s Denby Savannah range footed plant pot, designed by Glyn Colledge in 1978, with hand-painted swirled pattern and fluted bands.

5.25in (13.5cm) high

£20-30   GC

A 1980s Denby Savannah range jug vase, designed by Glyn Colledge in 1978, with hand-painted swirled pattern and fluted bands.

7in (17.5cm) high

£20-30   GC

A Doulton Lambeth cylindrical biscuit barrel, decorated by Hannah Barlow with a central band of sgraffito ponies in a landscape, with a silver-plated rim, handle and cover, the base with impressed and incised marks.

Barlow is well-known for her designs incorporating horses and other animals.

6.75in (17cm) high

£800-1,200   **FLD**

A Doulton Lambeth large circular wall plaque, by Harry Simeon, decorated with an incised and glazed stylized interwoven floral pattern, the base with impressed and painted marks.

13.5in (34cm) diam

£250-300   **FLD**

EXPERT EYE – A DOULTON LAMBETH ISOBATH

The Isobath is a rare inkwell. It was made for Thomas De La Rue Ltd, who later made fountain pens, many under the 'Onoto' brand introduced in 1905.

The lid and hemisphere are often missing, which reduces the value by over 50 per cent. This example retains both.

They were made in a wide variety of forms with different styles of decoration, some with trays with crimped edges that act as pen rests.

The interior contains a swinging black hard rubber hemisphere, the weight of which forces ink into the side well, meaning a consistent level of ink is maintained.

A rare Doulton Lambeth 'Isobath' stoneware inkwell, designed by Thomas De La Rue Ltd, with lid, stylized floral and foliate decoration and impressed and inscribed factory and decorators' marks to base.

4.75in (12cm) high

£200-300   **L&T**

A Royal Doulton Slater's Patent baluster form vase, painted in colours with bands of flowers and foliage, impressed mark and "X2031 A.M." to base.

Slater's Patent involved the use of real lace impressed onto the body to act as a guide for the coloured pattern, which was hand-enamelled over the glaze.

17.25in (44cm) high

£100-150   **ROS**

A Royal Doulton flambé vase, designed by Charles Noke, modelled as a lotus flower and covered in a rich flambé glaze, printed marks and Noke facsimile signature.

7.5in (19cm) high

£300-400   **WW**

A Royal Doulton Brangwyn ware ovoid vase, designed by Frank Brangwyn, painted with stylized flowers and foliage on a graduated creamy ground, with green border to base, the base with printed marks and painted "D5081".

7.25in (18.5cm) high

£100-150   **WW**

A Royal Doulton Chang ovoid vase, decorated by F. Allen, minor flake to foot ring, marked "Royal Doulton Chang Noke F. Allen".

The Chang glaze was developed by Charles Noke and was used from 1925 to 1939. It is identified by the thickly dripped glaze that created random, abstract patterns. Examples, particularly of this size, are rare and sought-after.

9.25in (23.5cm) high

£1,000-1,500　　　　　　　　　　　　　　　　　**DRA**

A Royal Doulton Siliconware ewer.

c1905　　　　　　　　6in (15cm) high

£150-200　　　　　　　　　　　　**PGO**

A Royal Doulton 'Isaac Walton' pattern Seriesware water jug.

5.5in (14cm) high

£50-60　　　　　　　**PSA**

A Royal Doulton 'Coaching Days' Seriesware miniature tankard.

This is a scarce size for this pattern, which comprises over 20 different scenes. Coded as R or Y 433, it shows an innkeeper talking to the driver as a passenger boards.

3in (7.5cm) high

£40-60　　　　　　　**BAD**

A rare Royal Doulton 'Comical Bird', painted in bright colours and mounted on a creamy alabaster dish.

Figure 1.75in (4cm) high

£350-450　　　　　　　　　　　**WW**

ESSENTIAL REFERENCE

- German ceramics maker Goebel first produced Hummel figurines in 1935 using drawings of children by a nun, Sister Berta Hummel (1909-46), as inspiration. The first was 'Puppy Love' and was part of a range of 46 modelled by Arthur Moeller. Many of these original designs are still available today, although the range has grown to over 500 figurines, offering great scope to collectors.
- Three key points to consider are the date of the figurine, its size, and variations in modelling or colour. Earlier examples from the 1930s-40s are generally the most valuable. Familiarise yourself with the marks on the base as they changed over time and this is the easiest way to attribute a figurine to a period. Impressed 'Crown' marks are usually the earliest and were used from 1936 until 1950, but if printed together with the words 'Goebel' and 'Germany', the figurine will date from between 1991 and 2000.
- Hummel's most famous mark is the 'bee in a V' mark. Used from 1940 until c1980, the style changed over time. The larger the bee is, the earlier a piece will be. By 1958, the bee had shrunk in size, become very stylized and moved inside the 'V'. Dates shown here relate to the period the mark on the base was in use, combined with the dates that the model was produced.

- Impressed numbers relate to the mould number (often called the 'Hum number' by collectors) and the size. Numbers or Roman numerals after a '/' indicate the size. Roman numerals indicate a larger than standard size – the higher the number, the larger the piece. Arabic numbers indicate a smaller than standard size – the higher the number, the smaller the piece. Larger figurines can be worth many times more than standard sizes pieces.
- Also look out for variations in colour or moulded form, as these can affect value. Some forms were remodelled over time, and earlier examples are usually more desirable and valuable. All authentic Hummel figurines are properly marked. Beware of unmarked pieces and those of poorer quality as reproductions and fakes produced in the Far East are common.
- Always examine pieces closely before buying as the bisque used is fragile and easily chipped or cracked. Also be careful when moving them around on display shelves. Crazing of the glaze can also affect desirability. Many figurines are still being produced today, so consult a reference book to check production dates. Prices for figurines that are still available will usually be much lower than for those which are no longer produced.

A Goebel Hummel 'Hello' figurine, no. 124, the base impressed "124/0" and painted "G80" with 'three line mark'.

Designed by Arthur Moeller and introduced in 1939, alternative names have included 'The Boss'. Look out for variations wearing green trousers and a pink waistcoat with the brown coat, as these are the rarest and most valuable. The earliest models have grey trousers and coats.

1964-72   5.75in (14.5cm) high
£40-60   BH

A Goebel Hummel 'Valentine Joy' figurine, no. 399, the base impressed "399" and printed "Exclusive Limited Edition for Members of the Goebel Collectors Club Goebel W. Germany 1979".

Designed by Gerhard Skrobek in 1979, this figurine was released in 1980 and was the fourth special edition available only to Collectors' Club members.

1979   5.5in (14cm) high
£35-50   BH

A Goebel Hummel 'Merry Wanderer' figurine, no. 11, with stylized bee "W. Germany" mark.

1958-72   4.25in (11cm) high
£15-20   BH

A Goebel Hummel 'Little Tooter' figurine, no. 214H, the base with printed 'three line' mark.

1964-72   4in (10cm) high
£30-40   BH

A Goebel Hummel 'March Winds' figurine, no. 43, the base with printed stylized bee mark.

1958-72   5in (12.5cm) high
£30-40   BH

A Goebel Hummel 'Begging His Share' figurine, no. 9, with candle-holder hole in cake, the base with stylized bee mark.

A Goebel Hummel 'Good Hunting' figurine, no. 307, with brown rabbit, the base with 'two line' Goebel bee mark.

1972-79   5.25in (13.5cm) high

£50-80   **BH**

Designed by Arthur Moeller in 1935, this was originally intended to be a candle-holder – hence the hole in the cake. In 1964, the figurine was redesigned and the hole was removed, making this particular figurine easy to date. Very early examples have brightly coloured socks.

1958-64   5.5in (14cm) high

£40-60   **BH**

A Goebel Hummel 'Band Leader', no. 129, the base impressed "129", and with 'full bee' mark.

1940-59   6in (15cm) high

£35-50   **BH**

A Goebel Hummel 'Apple Tree Boy' figurine, no. 142, the base with 'three line' mark.

1964-72   4in (10cm) high

£25-35   **BH**

A Goebel Hummel 'Umbrella Boy' large figurine, no. 152, the base impressed "152/0A", with 'three line' mark.

Designed by Arthur Moeller in the early 1940s, this figurine has a companion piece, 'Umbrella Girl'. It has the same model number but was introduced a few years later, in the late 1940s.

1964-72   4.75in (12cm) high

£120-180   **BH**

EXPERT EYE – A HUMMEL FIGURINE

Designed in 1996 by Helmut Fischer, this figurine was released in the US in 1999 costing $185 (approx. £115). It has now been discontinued.

Her companion piece is 'Pretzel Boy', no. 2093, which is still available new.

A number of Special Event collectors' versions have been issued, including one with two US flags, but values are roughly the same.

Pieces produced in the inaugural year bear the 'First Issue 1999' stamp, as on this example.

A Goebel Hummel 'Girl with Doll' figurine, no. 239B, the base with printed "Goebel Germany" crown mark.

1991-99   3.5in (9cm) high

£10-15   **BH**

A Goebel Hummel 'Pretzel Girl' figurine, no. 2004, the base impressed "2004 16" and "1996", and printed "First Issue 1999" in blue.

1999   4in (11cm) high

£35-50   **BH**

CERAMICS

A Goebel Hummel 'Knitting Lesson' figurine, no. 256, the base with 'three line mark' and impressed "256 33 1963".

Although impressed "1963", which probably indicates the year of design and copyright, the figurine was introduced a year later in 1964.

1964-72   7.25in (18.5cm) high

£80-120   BH

A Goebel Hummel 'Little Thrifty' figurine, no. 118, the base impressed "118" and with "Goebel W. Germany" 'two line' bee mark.

This can also be found as a money bank. Examples made before 1963 have a thicker base than later examples.

1972-79   5in (13cm) high

£35-50   BH

A Goebel Hummel 'Auf Wiedersehen' figurine, no. 153, the base impressed "153/0" and with stylized bee mark.

1958-72   5.75in (14.5cm) high

£40-60   BH

A Goebel Hummel 'Wash Day' figurine, no. 321, the base impressed "321" and with 'three line mark'.

Look out for examples with 'longer' washing that looks like a pair of bloomers. These are much earlier in date and are much rarer and more valuable, often being worth over four times the value of this version.

1964-72   5.75in (14.5cm) high

£28-38   BH

A Goebel Hummel 'Blessed Event' figurine, no. 333, the base impressed "333", and with 'three line mark'.

Although this was designed in 1955, it was not released until 1964. However, a small quantity of trade samples were made in the late 1950s, bearing the 'full bee' mark. These are extremely rare and can be worth up to ten times the amount as this more common example.

5.25in (13.5cm) high

£70-100   BH

A Goebel Hummel 'Little Gardener' figurine, no. 74, the base with printed large stylized bee and "W. Germany" mark.

Examples from before the 1960s have an oval shaped base.

c1963-72   4.25in (11cm) high

£20-30   BH

A Goebel Hummel 'Happiness' figurine, no. 86, the base with 'three line' mark.

1964-72   4.75in (12cm) high

£15-25   BH

A Goebel Hummel 'Friends' figurine, no. 136, the base with printed 'three line' mark.

1964-72   5in (12.5cm) high

£12-18   BH

FIND OUT MORE...

'The No.1 Price Guide to M.I. Hummel Figurines, Plates & More', by Robert L. Miller, published by Reverie Publishing Company, 2006.

ESSENTIAL REFERENCE

- Italian ceramics of the 1950s to '70s have grown in popularity over the past few years, alongside West German ceramics of the same period. At this time, the influx of money and the renewed confidence of postwar Italy saw many potteries producing and exporting large numbers of brightly coloured, affordable ceramics.
- Shapes were typically simple and traditional with hand-painted patterns, which were sometimes highlighted with sgraffito, where a design is inscribed into the surface with a point. Patterns tended to be abstract, inspired by modern art of the day, and often based on natural or figural motifs. Most pieces were slip-moulded, meaning bodies could be turned out on a factory production line.
- Examples were sold in design shops, department stores and lower market discount shops. They were imported by numerous companies including Raymor in the US and Hutcheson & Son Ltd in the UK. The primary indicators to value are the style, colours and quality of the application of the design – abstract and modern patterns on unusual forms are highly desirable. The size is also important, and whimsical pieces can also be desirable.
- The most valuable pieces are by notable designers such as Guido Gambone (1909-69) and Marcello Fantoni (b.1915). Their work also influenced many other potteries stylistically. Another popular name is Bitossi, who produced a range known as 'Rimini Blu', designed by Aldo Londi in 1953. The range is typified by rows of impressed geometrical motifs, and can be found in red, yellow and a scarce speckled orange.
- Most pieces are marked simply on the base with a number and the word 'Italy'. Currently, very little is known about the factories or designers that produced these designs. The name of a town or resort is also often found on the base – this indicates that a piece may have been sold as a souvenir to tourists, although some towns, such as Deruta, had a long established reputation for their ceramics. Always examine pieces closely as the ceramic is generally fragile and easy to chip.

A 1950s-60s Italian Ronzan table centrepiece, modelled as a mermaid and child riding the back of a large fish, with circular dish below decorated in a turquoise glaze, with painted and printed marks.

15.75in (40cm) high

£1,500-2,000   **FLD**

An Italian Lenci figurine of a child playing with a ball, with transfer-printed floral pattern, and painted marks to base.

7in (18cm) wide

£350-450   **WW**

A 1950s Italian Lenci pottery jug, of angular form, covered in a green and brown glaze, with painted marks "11-7-57".

11.75in (30cm) high

£300-400   **WW**

A 1950s Italian Guido Gambone vase, of asymmetric form, decorated with white panels with green lines over a textured black oxide ground, the base with hand-painted signature.

13.25in (32.5cm) high

£1,500-2,000   **FLD**

A 1950s Italian Guido Gambone faience vase, painted with horses, signed "Gambone Italy" with donkey motif.

12in (30.5cm) high

£500-600   **SDR**

CERAMICS

A 1950s Italian ovoid vase, with flared rim, decorated with a pattern of turquoise, red and white leaping horses with sgraffito outlines on a black ground, restored rim.

11.5in (29cm) high

£100-150   QU

An Italian pottery vase, painted with a figure on horseback in the style of Marino Marini, in rough textured glazes, indistinct painted factory marks to base.

8.75in (22.5cm) high

£100-200   WW

EXPERT EYE – AN ITALIAN VASE

The flower form with its petal-like rim echoes the floral pattern.

It is made from a fragile white ceramic, but has remained undamaged. It is also a large size, smaller sizes have been found and can be worth around £30.

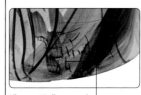

Like most Italian ceramics of the period, the abstract design was inspired by both modern art and nature. It is signed by the artist and dated "64".

The irregular form and the presence of ribs inside shows it was coil-built on a wheel by hand, rather than being slip-cast as many others are.

A 1960s Italian hand-built vase, the exterior painted with a multi-coloured abstract design, illegibly signed, and dated.
1964

15.5in (34.5cm) high

£200-300   BEV

A 1950s Italian vase, with a curving rim, decorated with a stylized lady's head in sgraffito and gloss glaze, unmarked.

8.75in (22cm) high

£30-40   GC

A 1950s-60s Italian blue textured jug, with hand-painted black lines and multicoloured ovals, the base painted "6320 Italy".

7in (17.25in) high

£20-30   GC

A 1950s-60s Italian vase, the crazed thick white glaze with hand-painted multicoloured stripes, and yellow interior, unmarked.

7.25in (18.5cm) high

£30-40   GC

A 1950s-60s Italian vase, with hand-painted swirling and geometric designs, the base painted "Italy".

The decoration strongly shows the influence of abstract paintings of the period.

6in (15cm) high

£40-60   GC

A 1950s-60s Italian hand-painted urn vase, with stripes and sea life motifs, the base painted "Italy London 3457/15".

6in (15cm) high

£20-30   MHC

EXPERT EYE – A BITOSSI BIRD

This charming and whimsical bird is part of a range of vases, bowls, lamp bases and animal figurines designed by Aldo Londi in 1953 for Bitossi of Montelupo, Italy.

This vintage form has not been re-introduced and is comparatively scarce, meaning the value has not fallen due to newer examples appearing on the market.

It is fully marked on the base and also bears a foil label for Illums Bolighus, the renowned Danish department store that specialises in modern design.

Many shapes have been in constant production since then, or have been re-introduced in response to the recent surge in popularity.

A 1960s Italian Bitossi 'Rimini Blu' range bird, designed by Aldo Londi, the base painted "800 Italy" and with impressed mark and oval silver foil sticker for Illums Bolighus.

6.5in (16.5cm) high

£70-100   MHC

A 1950s Italian vase, with hand-painted stylized leaf designs and hand-applied tube-lined white trails, the base painted "14799/136 Made in Italy".

11in (28cm) high

£30-40   MHC

An Italian Schiavoli, Venezia wall plaque, painted with a geometric Venetian landscape in colours, incised marks.

12in (30.5cm) high

£50-70   WW

A 1950s-60s Italian pottery elephant, with orange and white abstract design, the tummy painted "Italy 639".

7in (17.5cm) long

£50-80   GC

A 1960s Italian hand-painted cat money box, with a daisy motif, the base painted "SA 105 100P Italy" and with a 'Mr Norman Creation Italy' black and gold foil label.

7.25in (18.5cm) high

£7-10   AEM

ESSENTIAL REFERENCE

- While the market for Chinese ceramics has boomed in recent years, a weak domestic stock market and lack of wider interest has meant that the Japanese market has not enjoyed such popularity. Many pieces, therefore, are more affordable at present, particularly pieces dating from the late 19thC and first half of the 20thC. As with Chinese ceramics of these periods, many are collected for their decorative nature.

- Popular styles include the detailed Nabeshima, which is typically found in underglaze blue, but can also have red, green and yellow enamel highlights; the gilt and coloured Satsuma; and the vibrant and bold blue, red and white Imari. Look at examples in museums and compare pieces to learn how to spot the more finely painted examples. As well as a greater level of detail, faces may have individual expressions on better quality examples.

- As well as more traditional, historic styles, Japan exported vast numbers of hand-decorated Western style ceramics from the 1910s onwards. The major force was a company founded in 1904 by Ichizaemon Morimura, which became known as Noritake later in the century. Brightly painted roses and other flowers are typical, usually combined with lavish gilding. In general, the more gilding present, the earlier a piece will be.

- The first mass-produced designs were exported in 1910, and the company produced its first dinnerware for the US market in 1914. The US was its largest market, but pieces were also exported to Europe. Marks on the base can help with dating, and look for well-painted pieces with realistic and detailed imagery. Examine gilding for signs of wear as this reduces value, as does any damage.

- After the war, production continued, and pieces were marked 'Made in Occupied Japan' between 1947 and 1952. The production of novelty figurines and other small objects that grew during the 1930s also continued. As with tableware and decorative objects, the subject, motifs and how well they are executed is the main indicator to value.

An early 19thC Japanese Nabeshima footed dish, of blue floral underglaze, decorated with floral sprigs and a tightly painted 'comb' pattern to the well-potted foot.

8in (20.5cm) diam

£120-180   **FRE**

A Japanese Nabeshima footed dish, probably Edo period or later, with underglazed, blue floral motif to white ground, floral underglaze to underside and 'comb' design foot.

£100-150   **FRE**

A 19thC Japanese Nabeshima footed dish, with blue underglaze decoration and enamelled with yellow, iron-red and green to show a junk transporting auspicious items over a ground of red scrolling sea, well underglazed coin and ribbon to underside and 'comb' design foot, some wear to base, minor wear.

8.25in (21cm) diam

£180-220   **FRE**

A 19thC Japanese Nabeshima footed dish, slightly rounded over a short foot, painted with red and yellow seeded fruit and green and blue leaves, ribbon coins to underside, 'comb' design foot, some wear to base of foot.

7in (18cm) diam

£300-400   **FRE**

An 18thC/19thC Japanese Kakiemon octagonal bowl, with brown rim, interior of rim painted with blue, green and yellow enamel to show blossoms issuing from scrolling leaves, the central medallion as a floral spray flanked by eight floral garlands painted in reverse.

8.5in (21.5cm) diam

£400-500   **FRE**

A 19thC Japanese studio earthenware baluster vase, painted to show hagi (Japanese clover) and other autumn flowers and sprays, moon applied in light relief, signed and impressed "Itozan".

9in (23cm) high

£450-550   **FRE**

A 20thC Japanese porcelain bowl, decorated with two frogs and an octopus on a brown ground.

5in (12.5cm) high

£50-80   **DN**

A Japanese porcelain vase, decorated with two panels containing figures, the body decorated with a profusion of flowers and birds, restored rim.

c1880   *18.5in (47cm) high*

£200-300   **SWO**

A pair of Japanese celadon ground ovoid vases, Meiji period, each decorated with a bird standing beneath flowers and foliage, each with a six character mark.

14in (35.5cm) high

£150-250   **WW**

EXPERT EYE – A PAIR OF KAKIEMON VASES

The double gourd form is made from a single piece and requires great skill to pot – however, the example on the left leans slightly, a fault which probably occurred in the kiln.

Despite appearing to be a pair, there are differences in the sizes and proportions. This indicates they were not produced as a pair, which reduces the value.

The gourd form is considered auspicious, and is the Taoist symbol of longevity and good health. In Feng Shui it is a receptacle of good fortune.

They are decorated over the glaze in the Kakiemon palette, if they had stronger and richer colours, they would have been more valuable.

A matched pair of late 19thC/early 20thC Japanese Kakiemon vases, of double gourd form, with long slender necks, and moulded bodies decorated in iron red, blue and green to show mythical ho-o birds.

8in (20.5cm) high

£400-600   **FRE**

A Japanese blue and white rectangular vase and cover, each side painted with scenes of lakes before mountains, and with elaborate dragon and ring handles to the shoulders, the base with four character mark, some restoration and staining.

c1900   *7in (17.5cm) high*

£100-200   **WW**

A Japanese blue and white model of a well bucket, painted with sparrows in flight above breaking waves, with six character mark.

c1900   *7in (17.5cm) high*

£100-150   **WW**

A small Japanese blue and white teapot and cover, probably 19thC, painted with small huts in a rocky landscape.

5in (13cm) high

£25-35   **WW**

CERAMICS

ESSENTIAL REFERENCE – NORITAKE MARKS

The Morimura brothers' company, that became Noritake, has used a large number of different marks in its history. Three of the most common are shown here. The 'M' stands for the family name and the laurel wreath is derived from their family crest.

Marks with the 'M' in a wreath and 'Nippon' (the native name for Japan) were used from 1911–21. In 1921, the second McKinley Tariff Act declared that pieces imported into the US should have the country of origin marked in English. Hence, from that date, the wording 'Japan', and 'Made in Japan', replaced 'Nippon'.

During the 1920s, the word 'Noritake' also replaced 'Hand Painted' on some marks. In 1953, the 'M' was replaced with an 'N' for the company name. The commonly found maple leaf mark, introduced in 1891, follows the same rule as 'Nippon'.

Other marks include the 'komaru' symbol of a cross with a vertical line through it. The style of the cross and the presence of other motifs and wording can help to date a piece to a period. Beware of fake marks, which are becoming increasingly frequent – the quality of the mark is usually very high and it is always under the glaze.

A Japanese Nippon chocolate set, comprising chocolate pot and six cups and saucers, hand-painted with roses over black lines in bands, the base with printed blue "Hand Painted Elite Nippon" with 'B' in wreath motif mark.

Pot 8.25in (21cm) high

£100-150 (set)   **BH**

A Japanese Noritake coffee set, comprising teapot, four cups and saucers and matching tray, each with hand-painted and transfer-printed gilt stylized floral and scrolling design, the bases with printed "Made in Japan Handpainted No. 37532" mark, together with "M" in a laurel wreath motif.

Pot 6.75in (17cm) high

£100-150   **BH**

A Japanese Nippon melon or gourd form teaset, comprising teapot, creamer and sugar, ornately decorated with roses in medallions on a blue and white ground, with gilt highlights.

Teapot 8in (20.5cm) wide

£70-100   **BH**

A Japanese Noritake creamer and sugar bowl, hand-painted with pink magnolia blooms and autumnal leaves over a transfer-printed gilt band, with gilded feet and printed marks to bases.

Bowl 7.5in (19cm) wide

£50-70   **BH**

A Japanese Noritake China chocolate pot, painted in gilt with a stylized leaf design, the base with "Handpainted Japan" mark with an "M" in laurel wreath motif.

10in (25.5cm) high

£25-35 BH

A Japanese Nippon low pitcher, with shaped lip and scroll handle, hand-painted with pink and red roses, the base marked with printed leaf mark, also marked "Nippon Handpainted".

5.5in (14cm) high

£70-100 BH

A Japanese Nippon sugar shaker, hand-painted with a pink floral and foliate garland and with gilt highlights, the base with blue "M" mark in a laurel wreath.

5in (12.5cm) high

£40-50 BH

A Nippon three-piece condensed milk container, hand-painted with green bands and panels with gilt highlights and frames containing pink flowers, the base with "Japan Handpainted" mark with leaf motif.

6.25in (16cm) high

A Japanese Nippon coffee pot, with hand-painted pink roses on a blue and white ground, with gilt highlights, and scroll handle, unmarked.

10in (25.5cm) high

£100-150 BH

£100-150 BH

A Japanese Nippon covered bowl, with hand-painted red and gold borders and pink and red roses, unmarked.

10in (20.5cm) wide

£100-120 BH

A Japanese Nippon baluster vase, hand-painted with roses, other flowers and leaves on a graduated cream ground, the rim and foot with gilt bands, the base with printed green "M" in laurel wreath mark.

8.5in (21.5cm) high

£35-50 BH

A Japanese Nippon baluster vase, with hand-painted stems and traditional roses on graduated brown, green and yellow ground, the base with printed blue "Nippon Handpainted" leaf motif mark.

6.25in (16cm) high

£50-70 BH

CERAMICS

A Japanese purple and gold flower slightly waisted gourd type vase, with blue leaf and 'hand painted' script to right logo.

6.25in (16cm) high

£70-100   BH

A Japanese Imperial Nippon three handled vase, with hand-painted scene of native Americans under a palm tree at a riverside watching a boat, the base with printed circular light blue "Nippon Hand Painted" mark.

8.5in (21.5cm) high

£100-150   BH

A Japanese tapered cylindrical vase, with small neck and flared rim, painted with foliage and trees in a stylized lakeside setting, the base with indistinct printed red "Handpainted Japan" mark.

10.25in (26cm) high

£70-100   BH

EXPERT EYE – A NIPPON VASE

It is marked with a patent date identifying the earliest year it can be dated from – dated patent markings are more common in the 1930s-40s.

This is a pleasant and well-proportioned form, with restrained use of gilding.

Coralene is the term given to tiny glass beads that are sprinkled on to the surface. They are a very unusual feature and usually wore off over time.

The form of the vase and the floral motif recalls US art pottery by companies such as Rookwood – albeit in much more vibrant colours.

A Nippon vase, decorated with yellow and orange lilies on a shaded ground, with gilt and Coralene highlights, some wear to gilding, the base stamped "US Patent 917, Feb 9.1909".

8.75in (22cm) high

£550-650   DRA

A Japanese spherical tripod vase, with double handles modelled as branches, with hand-painted pink and white flowers on a blue and white ground with gilt highlights, the base with printed "Japan Handpainted" mark.

5.5in (14cm) high

£50-70   BH

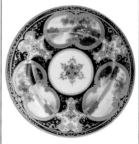

A Japanese Nippon plate, with three gilt-framed panels containing small hand-painted landscape vignettes, with printed marks to base.

7.75in (19.5cm) diam

£35-50   BH

A Japanese Nippon bowl, with a gilt scalloped edge, the hand-painted flowers with gilt highlights on a white ground, the base with printed "Japan Handpainted" mark with cherry flower motif.

8.75in (22cm) diam

£25-35   **BH**

A Japanese Nippon bowl, the scalloped edge decorated in blue with gilt highlights, the bowl with a hand-painted lakeside scene, the base with printed green "M" in laurel wreath mark.

10in (25.5cm) diam

£50-70   **BH**

A 1950s Paulux 'Made in Occupied Japan' bisque group of children playing in a garden.

5.5in (14cm) high

£28-32   **TOA**

A 'Made in Occupied Japan' figurine of a girl, from the 'Country Life' series, wearing a blue and pink dress and with a toy elephant by her side, with an "A" printed mark.

5.75in (14.5cm) high

£22-28   **TOA**

A 1950s Japanese hand-painted rooster matcholder or small vase, the base stamped "Japan" in red.

3.25in (8cm) high

£7-10   **BB**

A 1950s 'Made in Occupied Japan' putto blacksmith bisque figurine.

This appears to be an unusual theme, until you realise that the figure is Cupid is forging a wedding ring.

5in (12.5cm) high

£32-38   **TOA**

A 1950s-60s Japanese Lefton 'hands' porcelain pin or jewellery dish.

6in (15cm) long

£12-15   **AEM**

CERAMICS

ESSENTIAL REFERENCE

- J. & G. Meakin were founded in 1851, in Hanley, Staffordshire and produced tableware that sold both within the UK and was exported to other countries, particularly the US. Patterns were traditional, typically comprising of flowers and scrolling border patterns and were either transfer-printed or hand-painted, or both. During the 1930s and '40s, they produced a range of plain wares in pale colours, marketed under the 'Sol' brand.

- However, it is primarily the company's post-war designs that are of interest to collectors today. In 1953, the company was revolutionised by the introduction of the modern Studio range that grew to be their most important postwar range. Designed by Frank Potts, with patterns by Frank Trigger and Robert Williams, inspiration was taken from ranges seen on a sales trip to the US.

- The Studio range was redesigned in 1964, with the simple cylindrical shapes that have become characteristic of the

company being introduced. These were decorated in a variety of brightly coloured transfer-printed patterns that epitomised period tastes and styles. Designers included Tom Arnold and Alan Rogers, as well as the better-known Jessie Tait and Eve Midwinter. Midwinter and Meakin in 1968. Dates in captions indicate the year of design of the pattern, not the production run of the pattern or shape.

- The company was taken over by the Wedgwood group in 1970 and continued to be highly successful. Other shapes, such as Habitat, Trend and Studio Stone, were also introduced. The company was then taken over by Johnson Bros., who phased out certain ranges during the 1990s as tastes changed. The company closed in 2000.

- Although pieces are still available at comparatively reasonable prices, interest and values are rising due to the recent publication of a book, listed at the end of this section.

A J. & G. Meakin transfer-printed 'Arcadia' pattern meat dish, with scalloped edge and printed marks to base.

c1910   11.75in (30cm) long

£20-30   SMP

A 1920s J. & G. Meakin oval platter, transfer-printed with an Arabian scene, with printed marks to base.

16.25in (41cm) long

£40-50   SMP

Two late 1960s J. & G. Meakin Sheraton shape transfer-printed 'Welcome Home' pattern plates, with printed marks to base.

Scenes on this range were of the US countryside.

Larger 9.5in (24cm) high

£10-20 (each)   SMP

A J. & G. Meakin Grace/Lyric shape transfer-printed 'Dutch Scenes' pattern plate, with printed marks to base.

1961   7in (18cm) diam

£10-15   SMP

A J. & G. Meakin Grace/Lyric shape transfer-printed 'Sea Breezes' pattern plate, with printed marks to base.

The Grace and Lyric shapes were aimed at the Canadian market, and can be found in a variety of patterns.

1961   7in (18cm) diam

£10-15   SMP

A J. & G. Meakin Studio shape yellow teapot, blue milk jug, yellow sugar bowl and grey pitcher, from the Holiday range, with printed marks to base.

This early version of the Studio shape was designed in 1953. Inspired by a sales visit to the US, it is very similar in form and style to Russel Wright's notable American Modern range produced by Steubenville, particularly in these solid colours. It can also be found with over 30 different patterns.

Teapot 12.25in (31cm) long

Teapot & Pitcher: £30-40 (each) Others: £5-15 (each)   SMP

CERAMICS

A J. & G. Meakin Studio shape transfer-printed 'Golden Chain' pattern coffee-pot, platter and sugar bowl, with printed marks.
1965 Coffee-pot 10.25in (26cm) high
Coffee-pot: £8-12
Plate & Bowl £3-8 (each)   SMP

EXPERT EYE – J. & G. MEAKIN HABITAT SHAPE

The Habitat shape was designed in 1970 and is similar to Midwinter's MQ2 shape.

This shape was only produced with five different patterns, all of which were designed by Jessie Tait.

Midwinter and Meakin merged in 1968, meaning the same designers worked concurrently for both companies at this time.

The choice of a colourful stylized floral motif against a plain white background is typical of Meakin.

A 1970s J. & G. Meakin Habitat shape transfer-printed 'Fleur' pattern coffee-pot, plate, and teacup and saucer, with printed marks to bases.
Plate 10in (25.5cm) diam
Coffee-pot: £15-20 Others: £4-10 (each)   SMP

A J. & G. Meakin Sterling shape transfer-printed 'Orange Grove' pattern teapot, coffee-pot, sugar bowl, cup and saucer, and dinner plate, with printed marks to base.
1967   Coffee-pot 11in (28cm) high
Teapot & Coffee-pot: £15-20 (each) Others: £4-10 (each)   SMP

Left: A 1970s J. & G. Meakin Studio shape transfer-printed 'Mandalay Variant' pattern coffee-pot, with printed marks to base.
12.25in (31cm) high
£10-15   SMP

Middle & Right: A 1970s J. & G. Meakin Studio shape transfer-printed 'Mandalay' pattern tea cup and saucer, and coffee-pot, with printed marks to base.

The Mandalay pattern was designed in 1970 by Jessie Tait, who is best known for her work for Midwinter.
Coffee-pot 12.25in (31cm) high
Coffee-pot: £10-15 Teacup & Saucer £3-5 (each)   SMP

A J. & G. Meakin Studio shape transfer-printed 'Poppy' pattern teapot, coffee-pot, sugar bowl, mug, dish, and cup and saucer, designed by Eve Midwinter in 1973, with printed marks to base.

1974   Coffee-pot 12.25in (31cm) high
Teapot & Coffee-pot: £15-20 (each)
Others: £4-10 (each)   SMP

A J. & G. Meakin Studio Stone shape 'Aquarius' pattern coffee-pot and dinner plate, with printed marks to base.
1974   Plate 10.75in (27cm) diam
£6-12 (each)   SMP

FIND OUT MORE...

'J & G Meakin Pottery – History in the Making', by Chris Marks, published by SMP Ltd, ISBN 978-0-9557171-0-9 www.antiquexplorer.com

CERAMICS

ESSENTIAL REFERENCE

- William Moorcroft (1872-1945) began working as a designer at James Macintyre & Co. in 1897, being promoted to manager of Ornamental Ware in 1898. His first designs were the Florian and Aurelian ranges, which are typified by their complex Moorish-inspired symmetrical patterns of natural themes including leaves and flowers. Highly stylized, they are typical of the Art Nouveau style prevalent at the time.

- Moorcroft's hand-thrown shapes were decorated with a tube-lining process, where liquid clay was piped onto the surface, outlining the desired pattern. The 'cells' within the pattern were then filled with liquid glaze. Moorcroft left Macintyre in 1912 in order to found his own company with backing from important London retailer Liberty. By 1929, Moorcroft had been awarded the Royal Warrant.

- Colours are typically rich and deep, and patterns continued to be inspired by the natural world, although the Art Nouveau stylization was abandoned and new ranges were introduced. After William's death, his son Walter took over and continued many of his father's designs as well as introducing some of his own.

- The most desirable and valuable ranges tend to be early, from the 1900s to '20s, and include Florian, Claremont and any of the landscape patterns. Many of William's patterns were so popular, they were produced throughout the 20thC. However, more modern ranges produced by recent designers including Sally Tuffin and Rachel Bishop are also growing in value on the secondary market, particularly if they are from a limited edition or an unusual variation in terms of colour, form or pattern.

- Patterns produced for long periods tend to be the most affordable, particularly if the piece is small. The pattern, shape, size and type of marks on the base can help to date a piece. Always examine the entire body for signs of damage.

A James Macintyre & Co. large 'Dianthus' pattern Florian ware vase, designed by William Moorcroft, of slender high-shouldered form with a slightly everted rim, the base with printed marks and full green flash signature, with small restoration to rim.

12in (30.5cm) high

£700-800   **FLD**

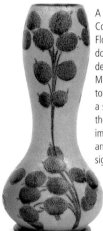

A James Macintyre & Co. 'Honesty' pattern Florian ware footed double gourd vase, designed by William Moorcroft, with two-tone blue glaze over a stippled ground, the base with impressed monogram and green painted signature.

11in (28cm) high

£1,200-1,500   **FLD**

A James Macintyre & Co. 'Blue Poppy' pattern Florian ware jardiniére, designed by William Moorcroft, with white ground and frilled rim, the base with printed and painted signatures.

6.75in (17cm) high

£1,200-1,800   **FLD**

A Moorcroft 'Anemone' pattern vase, designed by William Moorcroft, the base with impressed factory marks, signed "W.M." in green and dated "11-20-80".

1980 12.5in (31.5cm) high

£180-220   **BEL**

A Moorcroft 'Anemone' pattern vase.

c1940   *3.25in (8.5cm) high*

£220-280   **PGO**

A 1940s-50s Moorcroft 'Anemone' pattern vase, designed by Walter Moorcroft, with a green background, the base with impressed and painted marks.

5.5in (14cm) high

£200-300   PGO

A Moorcroft 'Revived Cornflower' or 'Brown Chrysanthemum' pattern circular footed fruit bowl, designed by William Moorcroft, with an ochre ground and applied loop handles, the base with green painted flash signature and dated "November 1913".

1913   *8.5in (21.5cm) wide*

£800-1,000   FLD

EXPERT EYE – A MOORCROFT VASE

Claremont is an early design that was produced and sold under the Liberty name – in fact, Liberty devised the name for the range, which Moorcroft then continued to use.

Early examples have dark green and blue mottled backgrounds similar to the Hazeldene design. They became darker and stronger during the 1920s, with bolder designs.

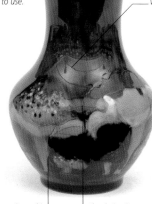

The pattern was registered in October 1903 and was produced for nearly 40 years.

The design is comparatively scarce, and highly desirable. This form is also appealing and the pattern is designed to fit the form.

A Moorcroft 'Claremont' pattern ovoid shouldered vase, designed by William Moorcroft, the base with impressed marks and full blue painted signature.

7in (17.5cm) high

£2,000-2,500   FLD

A Moorcroft 'Dahlia' pattern ovoid vase, designed by Walter Moorcroft in 1960, the base with impressed and painted marks.

This is reputed to be one of only 50 produced in this pattern, which was used experimentally.

8.5in (21.5cm) high

£600-700   FLD

A Moorcroft 'Finches Blue' pattern wall charger, designed by Sally Tuffin in 1988, the reverse with green WM monogram.

14in (35.5cm) diam

£280-320   WW

A 1960s-70s Moorcroft 'Hibiscus' pattern bowl, designed by Walter Moorcroft in 1949, the base with printed and painted marks.

3.75in (9.5cm) diam

£100-150   PGO

CERAMICS

A Moorcroft 'Moonlit Blue' pattern inkwell, designed by William Moorcroft, with integral cube-form well and pen rest to front, the base with impressed marks and painted signature.

Launched in 1922, 'Moonlit Blue' was the first of three landscape designs that also included 'Eventide' (1923) and 'Dawn' (1926). This is a scarce form.

9in (23.5cm) wide

£700-800   **FLD**

A Moorcroft 'Frilled Orchid' pattern baluster vase, designed by William Moorcroft, with a deep blue ground, the base with paper label.

3.75in (9.5cm) high

£150-200   **WW**

A 1920s Moorcroft 'Pansy' pattern bowl, designed by William Moorcroft, the base with printed and painted marks.

6in (15cm) diam

£300-400   **PGO**

EXPERT EYE – A MOORCROFT VASE

The Pansy pattern was introduced in 1911, a year after the popular 'Pomegranate' pattern.

Early backgrounds on 'Pansy' are lighter, comprising white, cream or celadon. After c1916, they became dark blue.

While the Florian wares that preceded them were patterned all over the body, 'Pansy' and 'Pomegranate' had single bands of decoration.

Pansy was available on tablewares and decorative wares and was produced until the late 1930s.

A James Macintyre & Co. 'Pansy' pattern baluster vase, designed by William Moorcroft, with a white glazed ground, the base with printed marks and painted signature.

3.75in (9.5cm) high

£1,200-1,800   **FLD**

A Moorcroft 'Pomegranate' pattern plate, designed by William Moorcroft, the base with impressed marks and signed in green.

8.25in (22cm) diam

£150-200   **L&T**

A limited edition Moorcroft 'Polar Bear' vase, designed by Sally Tuffin, from an edition of 250, with a tube-lined design on a light flambé ground, the base with impressed and painted marks, with firing crack to rim.

This design was produced for the Canadian market. The pink background is extremely unusual, as the standard colourway was white with a gently graduated pink outline accentuating the tube-lined designs. Suggesting warmth and comfort, pink is not a colour usually associated with the Arctic.

1988   *7in (17.5cm) high*

£550-650   **WW**

A Moorcroft 'Pomegranate' pattern flared cylindrical footed vase, designed by William Moorcroft, the base with impressed marks and green painted flash monogram.

The quality on this example is extremely high. A number of imitations produced in China have flooded the market recently. Often in large sizes, they are usually unmarked and the quality of decoration is very poor.

12.5in (31cm) high

£1,200-1,800   **FLD**

A Moorcroft 'Pomegranate' pattern vase, designed by William Moorcroft, the base with impressed and painted marks.

This is an unusual form.
c1928   4.5in (11.5cm) high
£300-400   **PGO**

A Moorcroft 'Pomegranate' pattern bowl, designed by William Moorcroft, the base with impressed and painted marks.

c1913-25   4.5in (11.5cm) high
£200-300   **PGO**

A Moorcroft 'Big Poppy' pattern double-handled pedestal bowl, designed by William Moorcroft, with a blue glazed ground, the base with impressed marks and painted monogram.

9in (23cm) wide
£750-850   **FLD**

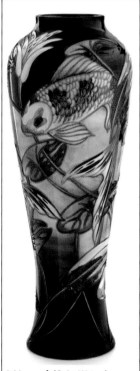

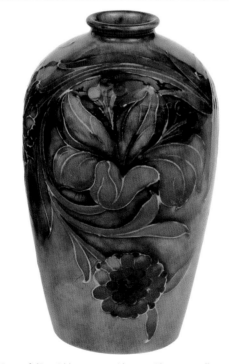

A 1920s-30s Moorcroft 'Big Poppy' bowl, designed by William Moorcroft, the base with impressed and painted marks.

6.75in (17cm) high
£400-500   **PGO**

A Moorcroft 'Quiet Waters' pattern vase, designed by Philip Gibson, the base with painted and impressed marks.
2002   14.25in (36cm) high
£450-550   **WW**

A Moorcroft 'Spanish' pattern ovoid vase, with narrow collar neck, the base with full green painted signature and date for 1914.

The richly coloured Spanish pattern was introduced in 1910 and was produced into the 1930s.
1914   5.25in (13cm) high
£1,600-2,200   **FLD**

A Moorcroft 'Violet' pattern vase, designed by Sally Tuffin, the base with impressed and painted marks.
1987   7in (18cm) high
£500-600   **WW**

ESSENTIAL REFERENCE – MOORCROFT MINIATURES

- Despite their diminutive size, there is nothing small about the prices of these scarce objects. Moorcroft's miniatures were most probably produced from the late 1910s to '20s as salesmen's samples, enabling travelling sales representatives to show prospective retailers the patterns available. Patterns are extremely well-applied and painted, and forms precise, despite their size. Some may also have been sold as novelties.

- The idea was revived in the 1970s, but the backstamps differ, so consult a reference work to ensure that you are buying a period piece. A further series of miniatures was offered later still, but the patterns are much later and include those by Emma Bossons and Sally Tuffin. All later examples can fetch anything from £70 to £200 depending on the date, pattern and location and type of seller. Later examples are often sold boxed in sets.

A 1970s Moorcroft 'Anemone' pattern miniature vase, designed by Walter Moorcroft, the base with printed marks.

2.5in (5.5cm) high

£120-180   WW

A 1970s Moorcroft 'Anemone' pattern miniature vase, designed by Walter Moorcroft, the base with printed marks.

2.5in (5.5cm) high

£120-180   WW

A James Macintyre & Co. 'Forget Me Nots' pattern miniature vase, designed by William Moorcroft, the base with printed marks and painted signature.

Exhibited at the 'William Moorcroft & Walter Moorcroft 1897-1973' exhibition at The Fine Art Society, London, in 1973, this vase also features in the accompanying catalogue.

3.25in (8cm) high

£1,500-2,000   WW

A rare Moorcroft 'Hazeldene' pattern miniature vase, designed by William Moorcroft, the base with painted signature, the rim restored.

Exhibited at the 'William Moorcroft & Walter Moorcroft 1897-1973' exhibition at The Fine Art Society, London, in 1973, this vase also features in the accompanying catalogue.

c1911   *3.25in (8cm) high*

£2,000-2,500   WW

A Moorcroft 'Pomegranate' pattern miniature vase, designed by William Moorcroft, the base painted "WM".

Exhibited at The Fine Art Society, London in 1973, and included in the catalogue.

2.5in (6cm) high

£1,200-1,800   WW

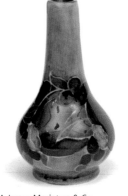

A James Macintyre & Co. 'Pomegranate' pattern miniature vase, designed by William Moorcroft, with green flash painted monogram.

2.5in (6cm) high

£750-850   FLD

A James Macintyre & Co. 'Tulip' pattern Florian ware miniature vase, designed by William Moorcroft, the base with painted signature and printed mark, with restored rim.

Exhibited at The Fine Art Society, London in 1973, and included in the catalogue.

c1902   *2.5in (6.5cm) high*

£1,000-1,500   WW

FIND OUT MORE...

'Moorcroft', by Paul Atterbury, published by Richard Dennis, 1996.

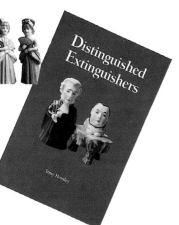

CERAMICS

ESSENTIAL REFERENCE

- In 1921, the Carter & Co. Pottery in Poole, England acquired a subsidiary that became known as Carter, Stabler & Adams Ltd. Known from early on as Poole Pottery, the company became well-known for its decorative wares. Early pieces were decorated with traditional floral and striped patterns, some with lustre glazes. All pieces were hand-thrown and hand-decorated, making each piece unique.

- During the mid-1920s a new range was introduced with stylized floral and foliate patterns. Designed by Truda Carter, and typical of the prevalent Art Deco style, the range dominated production into the 1950s. Look for examples with geometric patterns and animals as these tend to be rarer and more desirable.

- After WWII, the company continued to be at the forefront of ceramics design with their Contemporary and Freeform ranges. The modern, curving shapes were designed by Guy Sydenham, and the linear or stylized foliate patterns were designed by Alfred Read and decorator Ruth Pavely. In 1958, Robert Jefferson was employed as designer and the company entered another new phase, with the Poole Studio becoming increasingly important.

- The first results from the Studio were shown at an exhibition in London in 1961, these became the Delphis range, which typified production during the 1960s and '70s. In 1966, a Craft Section was founded, and led to the development of the Aegean, Ionian and Atlantis ranges. The bright oranges, reds and greens were typical of the period. Many new glazes were developed by Tony Morris in the early 1960s.

- Poole underwent a renaissance during the 1990s, with new designers such as Sally Tuffin, Janice Tchalenko and Anita Harris joining. In 1999, Tony Morris introduced the innovative Living Glaze range. Some pieces were offered as limited editions, and many are sought-after today, particularly those released in low numbers. After recent financial problems, the company still produces new designs.

A Carter's Poole Pottery baluster stoneware vase, with everted rim, and a blue-green lustre glaze, the base inscribed "Carter's Poole 1903".

1903   *5in (12.5cm) high*
£250-300   **WW**

A rare Carter's lustre wall charger, designed by James Radley Young, modelled in relief with a galleon at sea, covered in a ruby and blue lustre glaze, with impressed Carter's Poole factory mark to reverse.

c1910
£3,200-3,800   **WW**

A Poole Pottery 'Portuguese' stripe pattern vase, designed by James Radley Young, with hand-thrown red earthenware body.

1922-24   *4in (10cm) high*
£45-55   **C**

A Carter, Stabler & Adams 'The Bull' moulded stoneware figural group, designed by Harold and Phoebe Stabler, the base with impressed factory mark and dated 1914.

Designed in 1914 and produced at Poole from 1922-30, this figurine was exhibited at a number of influential exhibitions, including the 1925 Exposition des Arts Decoratifs in Paris, that later gave its name to the 'Art Deco' style.

1914   *13.5in (34cm) high*
£3,000-4,000   **WW**

A Poole Pottery 'DR' pattern vase, designed by Marian Heath, painted with Art Deco flowers and foliage on a mint green ground, impressed and painted marks.

8.25in (21cm) high

£120-180   **WW**

EXPERT EYE – A POOLE POTTERY WALL CHARGER

The design was produced from a 1940 drawing by artist Arthur Bradbury, who also produced designs for similar ship plates.

Approximately six examples are known, of which this is one.

The town of Poole became an important commercial and military destination for flying boats. The Empire flying boats ran scheduled flights from Poole from 1939 to 1948.

Another plate was presented to US President Roosevelt's envoy, Harry Hopkins, when he passed through Poole in 1941, after finalising the historic Lend-Lease Agreement.

A Poole Pottery 'Port of Poole Empire Airways' wall charger, designed by Arthur Bradbury and decorated by Margaret Holder, the back with printed mark.

1940   *14.5in (37cm) diam*

£3,500-4,000   **WW**

A 1930s Poole Pottery 'Persian Deer' pattern vase, shape no. 966, designed by Truda Adams and decorated by Ruth Pavely, the base impressed "966", with painted "SK" pattern code and with decorator's mark for Ruth Pavely.

This vase was owned by Roy Holland, Poole Pottery's works manager and then managing director of Poole Pottery from 1962 to 1975. Animals, particularly gazelles, are a desirable and scarce motif in 1930s Poole designs. It could have been worth around twice this value if it wasn't cracked.

10in (25cm) high

£250-350   **WW**

A Carter, Stabler & Adams Poole Pottery 'EC' pattern vase, designed by Truda Carter and painted by Anne Hatchard, in shades of mint, silver, brown and black, impressed and painted marks, minor hairlines to top rim.

16.5in (42cm) high

£800-1,000   **WW**

An early 1930s Carter, Stabler & Adams Poole Pottery 'EP' pattern large jug, shape 897, designed by Ruth Pavely, and decorated by Ann Hatchard.

The marks on the base are extremely useful. The inscribed number is the shape number, the painted letters the pattern number. The painted monogram was used by the decorator from the late 1920s onwards, and this impressed factory mark was used from 1925 to 1934.

11.5in (29cm) high

£1,000-1,500   **BEV**

A 1950s Poole Pottery 'Leipzig Girl' pattern plate, designed by Olive Bourne, the reverse with painted "HD" pattern code, printed factory marks and decorator's monogram, possibly for Gladys Hallett.

Although the design was produced in 1927 and exhibited at the Exhibition of Industrial Art in Leipzig, hence the pattern's name, this piece was made in the 1950s.

12in (30.5cm) diam

£180-220   **WW**

A Poole Pottery 'X/PT' pattern jardinière, shape no. 653, pattern designed by Ruth Pavely, from the Contemporary range, the base with printed and painted marks.

7.5in (19cm) high

£100-150   **WW**

A Poole Pottery 'YFC' pattern carafe vase, shape no. 690 designed by Claude Smale and Guy Sydenham, pattern designed by Alfred Read, from the Contemporary range, the base with printed and painted marks.

12.25in (31m) high

£240-280   **WW**

A late 1950s Poole Pottery vase, shape no. 704, designed by Alfred Read and Guy Sydenham, from the Contemporary range, covered in a chocolate brown glaze, the base impressed "704", and with blue Poole Pottery printed mark.

7.5in (19cm) high

£40-60   **GC**

EXPERT EYE – A POOLE POTTERY TRIAL PLATE

Ann Read was Alfred Read's daughter, and studied at the Chelsea School of Art before joining her father at Poole Pottery.

In 1956, she produced the stylized 'Bamboo' design that was used on tableware. It comprised of similar lines on a black background.

This is from a small range of limited edition or unique examples designed and produced by Read around 1955-56.

The design is highly modern, showing the influence of art of the period, particularly Cubism, but also the early 1950s obsession with science and crystalline structures.

A trial Poole Pottery 'Rock Crystal' pattern oval plate, designed by Ann Read, painted in shades of white, purple and brown on a Black Panther ground, the back with printed and painted marks. *c1956*

12.25in (31cm) wide

£240-280   **WW**

A trial Poole Pottery 'Philodendron' pattern oval plate, by Ann Read, painted in shades of white, black and brown on a black ground, the back with printed and painted marks.

Here, Read turns her attention to another 1950s fad – houseplants.

12.25in (31cm) wide

£240-280   **WW**

A Poole Studio charger, covered in a geometric design in textured coloured glazes, the reverse with printed "Studio" mark.

17in (43cm) diam

£500-600　　　**WW**

A Poole Studio charger, painted with a geometric abstract design in shades of green and blue, the reverse with printed blue Studio mark.

This pattern is very similar to designs by Robert Jefferson from c1962 to 1963.

13.5in (34.5cm) diam

£800-1,200　　　**WW**

EXPERT EYE – A POOLE STUDIO CHARGER

Tony Morris joined Poole in 1963 after studying at the Newport School of Art.

He worked closely with Robert Jefferson to produce new colourways using bought-in glazes. The blue palette is early, dating from before 1970.

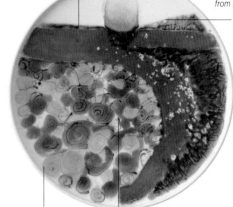

Abstract designs were typical, and also formed the basis of what was to become the immensely popular Delphis range.

This is a one-off, unique piece decorated by Morris himself and bears his monogram on the reverse. Look out for his desirable abstract face patterns.

A Poole Studio charger, designed and decorated by Tony Morris, painted in colours with an abstract landscape design, the base with painted "TM" mark.

14in (35.5cm) diam

£1,800-2,200　　　**WW**

A Poole Studio plate, painted with a stylized, geometric face, the reverse with printed and painted marks.

8in (20cm) diam

£650-750　　　**WW**

A Poole Studio plate, painted with a geometric face pattern in shades of green and brown, the reverse with printed Studio mark.

8in (20cm) diam

£380-420　　　**WW**

A Poole Pottery Studio small dish, with small mark to reverse.

5.25in (13.5cm) diam

£18-22　　　**GAZE**

CERAMICS

A Poole Pottery Delphis bowl, with printed and painted marks.

5in (13cm) diam

£60-80   WW

A Poole Pottery Delphis small dish, shape no. 86, the back stamped "86" and with decorator's mark.

5in (12.5cm) diam

£20-30   GAZE

A Poole Pottery Delphis tapering cylindrical footed vase, shape no. 85, covered with graduated and mottled yellow to brown to green glazes, with printed and painted marks, hairline crack to rim.

7in (18cm) high

£240-280   WW

A Poole Studio bowl, the interior with a mottled blue-green glaze, the base with printed blue Studio mark.

10.75in (27cm) diam

£100-150   WW

A Poole Studio vase, probably designed by Robert Jefferson, modelled in low relief with a grid design and glazed in green and brown, the base impressed with a triangle mark and with printed factory mark.

3.5in (9cm) high

£220-280   WW

A Poole Studio bowl, probably designed by Robert Jefferson, incised with a hatched design, with printed "Poole Studio" mark, and small glaze chip to top rim.

7.75in (19.5cm) diam

£200-300   WW

A Poole Studio vase, designed by Robert Jefferson and thrown by Guy Sydenham, carved with triangles in shades of blue on a creamy white ground, the base with printed mark.

Jefferson left Poole in 1966, but his influence remained strong during the following years.

15.75in (40cm) high

£750-850   WW

A Poole Pottery Delphis bowl, shape no. 85, carved with a geometric design and glazed in black, vivid red and orange, the reverse with printed and painted marks.

This bowl was owned by Roy Holland, managing director of Poole Pottery. It is decorated with colours typical of the Delphis range.

£500-600

13.75in (34.5cm) diam

WW

A Poole Pottery Delphis dish, boldly painted with a stylized design on a red ground, printed mark in black.

£120-180

LFA

A Poole Pottery Delphis charger, shape no. 54, decorated with an organic cell-like design in blues, greens, reds and oranges, with printed and painted marks to reverse.

16.25in (41cm) diam

£120-180

WW

A Poole Pottery Delphis plate, decorated with a geometric design, printed and painted marks.

10.5in (26.5cm) diam

£200-250

WW

A Poole Pottery Delphis charger, shape no. 54, painted with a geometric design in shades of yellow, orange, blue and green textured glazes, printed and painted marks.

16.25in (41cm) diam

£400-600

WW

A Poole Pottery Delphis charger, shape no. 54, decorated with a geometric design in shades of yellow, black and turquoise, printed and painted marks.

16.25in (41.5cm) diam

£400-600

WW

A Poole Pottery Delphis charger, shape no. 54, painted in colours with a geometric stained glass design, printed and painted marks.

16.5in (41.5cm) diam

£400-600

WW

CERAMICS

ESSENTIAL REFERENCE – ATLANTIS

The Atlantis range was the brainchild of talented potter Guy Sydenham (1916-2005). Sydenham joined Carter, Stabler & Adams in 1931 and worked his way up to become senior designer in 1966. He worked closely with both Alfred Read and Robert Jefferson, particularly in relation to the in-house Studio range, that grew to prominence under Jefferson and was relaunched in 1961. The range was designed between 1965 and 1966 and was produced into the 1970s. Each piece was carved, as well as glazed, by hand. Sydenham was responsible for much of the work although others also produced it. Pieces he produced are marked with his 'GS' seal, shown on the base of this vase. Pieces typically have a strong texture, with geometric patterns, and made as much use of the colour of the clay as any glaze applied. Each piece is unique, with the range being as close to studio pottery as possible.

A Poole Pottery Atlantis vase, by Guy Sydenham, with carved geometric columns in shades of white and blue on a brown ground, the base with impressed and incised marks.

5.5in (14cm) high

£180-220   WW

A Poole Pottery Atlantis stoneware vase, carved with vertical columns and geometric design, and glazed in a creamy gloss glaze, the base with painted and incised marks.

8.25in (21cm) high

£220-280   WW

A Poole Pottery Atlantis stoneware vase, the carved vertical columns with a chevron design, glazed in brown and creamy gloss glazes, the base with painted and incised marks.

5.75in (14.5cm) high

£180-220   WW

A Poole Pottery Atlantis stoneware vase, by Guy Sydenham, carved with abstract sliced columns, the base with impressed marks and "GS" and "BB" monograms, with hairline cracks to rim.

8.25in (21cm) high

£40-60   WW

A Poole Pottery Atlantis vase, by Guy Sydenham, of ovoid form with impressed design, covered in an oatmeal glaze.

4in (10cm) high

£150-200   WW

A Poole Pottery Atlantis vase, by Jennie Haigh, with incised and applied wavy band, the base with impressed factory mark and incised "JH" monogram.

4.75in (12cm) high

£180-220   WW

EXPERT EYE – A POOLE POTTERY LAMP BASE

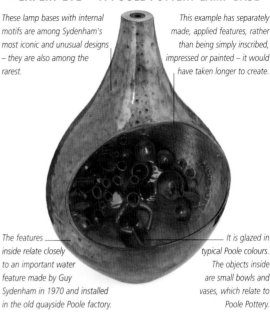

These lamp bases with internal motifs are among Sydenham's most iconic and unusual designs – they are also among the rarest.

This example has separately made, applied features, rather than being simply inscribed, impressed or painted – it would have taken longer to create.

The features inside relate closely to an important water feature made by Guy Sydenham in 1970 and installed in the old quayside Poole factory.

It is glazed in typical Poole colours. The objects inside are small bowls and vases, which relate to Poole Pottery.

A very rare Poole Pottery Atlantis 'Knight's Helmet' lamp base, by Guy Sydenham, of ovoid form internally modelled with a grimacing knight's face, the exterior modelled as chainmail, impressed "A12" and with artist cipher.

11.75in (30cm) high

£1,600-2,200   WW

A rare Poole Pottery Atlantis 'Mermaid' lamp base, by Guy Sydenham, of ovoid form internally modelled with a mermaid resting in a cave of 'Poole' vases, vivid orange glaze to the interior, the exterior mottled green, impressed "Poole England", with artists's cipher.

16.25in (41cm) high

£6,000-8,000   WW

A Poole Pottery Atlantis 'Pebble', shape A6, by Guy Sydenham, decorated with a spiralling pattern in slip, the base with impressed and incised marks.

4.75in (12cm) diam

£180-220   WW

A limited edition Poole Pottery 'Cathedral' wall plate, design no. 479 designed by Tony Morris, painted by C. Willis, from an edition of 1,000, with impressed, printed and painted marks.

The design was based on the 12thC stained glass window at the cathedral of Notre Dame, Chartres, France.

1973   *12.5in (32cm) diam*

£60-90   WW

A Poole Pottery 'peanut' vase, painted by Sue Pottinger, with stylized flowers in pastel colours on a banded cream and beige ground, the base with printed and painted marks.

14.25in (36cm) high

£120-180   WW

A Poole Studio Collection 'Bird' vase, designed by Sally Tuffin.

This vase was only made for approximately one year.

1996   *9in (20cm) high*

£150-180   KCS

CERAMICS

A Poole Pottery 'Old Harry Rocks' vase, by Karen Brown, from the Isle of Purbeck series, exclusive to Poole Collectors' Club members.

c1997   10.5in (26.5cm) high

£220-280   **KCS**

A Poole Pottery 'Viking' vase, by Karen Brown, exclusive to Poole Collectors' Club members.

8.5in (21.5cm) high

£150-200   **KCS**

A limited edition Poole Pottery 'Trewellard Red' charger, from an edition of 100, designed by Sir Terry Frost RA, with a hand-painted radiating design in red and black, the reverse with printed and painted marks, including a facsimile signature, together with box and certificate of authenticity.

This pattern was produced for the Royal Academy in 1996, with each plate being hand-decorated by Lindsay Stevens under Frost's supervision. A design with a black spiral on a cobalt blue ground was also produced, and is known as 'Arizona Blue'.

1996   16.5in (42cm) diam

£350-450   **WW**

Four limited edition Poole Pottery Collectors' Club 'CBC150' baluster vases, painted in shades of blue, the bases with printed and painted marks.

Each 4.25in (10.5cm) high

£60-80 (set)   **WW**

A limited edition Poole Pottery pair of grouse stoneware figural group, from an edition of 1,000, designed by Barbara Linley Adams.

£700-800   **C**

An early 1970s Poole Pottery stoneware mouse on corn figurine, designed by Barbara Linley Adams.

3.75in (9.5cm) high

£25-35   **KCS**

A Poole Pottery blue glazed tortoise figure.

1989-90   6in (15.5cm) wide

£65-75   **KCS**

A 1990s Poole Pottery gold glazed otter figure.

This unusual gold-coloured figure was probably used for advertising.

8in (20cm) wide

£80-100   **KCS**

ESSENTIAL REFERENCE

- Prattware is the generic name given to a particular type of underglaze transfer-printed ware. The patterns and manufacturers are related to pot lids of the same period. Although it is named after the prolific producer F. & R. Pratt, other companies, such as T.J. & J. Mayer, also produced it. Wares printed with colour transfers first appeared during the mid-19thC and reached the peak of production and popularity in the very late 19thC.
- Shapes vary from the functional to the highly decorative. Mugs, jugs and plates are among the more common shapes, as are jars that typically held meat paste. Shape is one of the main factors in value – a scarcer or more decorative shape, such as a vase or a rare eggcup, will be worth more than a dinner plate, which tended to be sold in multiples.
- The pattern is the other major factor to consider. Many were taken from pot lid designs. Look for strong colours and good quality images that have been printed well. Some subjects, such as Wellington's funeral, are rarer than others. Numbers given here relate to the pattern reference numbers in K.V. Mortimer's book listed at the end of this section.
- Also consider the surround, as the colour and the level of eye-appeal can add to desirability. White, red, dark green, burgundy and pink are the most common colours. Yellow, pale blue and black are rarer. Some have designs such as reclining ladies or arabesques, which are often more desirable when highlighted in gold.
- The level and style of the outer border decoration can also affect value. The most common border is Classical in style and known as the '1-2-3' pattern. A pattern with curving stylized wheat sheaves between small brooch-like turquoise spotted ovals is rarer. Pieces bearing advertising are generally rare. Always examine pieces for signs of wear or damage, looking closely at edges and the surfaces of dinner service plates.

A Prattware 'Haddon Hall' plate, no. 621, with classical reclining female border in deep crimson.

This is from a series of four historic houses, and was produced for many years. Early examples have borders like this example.

9.5in (24cm) diam

£220-280   SAS

A Prattware 'Tremadoc' plate, no. 620, with classical reclining female border in purple, lined in pink and gilt.

9.5in (24cm) diam

£60-80   SAS

A Prattware 'The Poultry Yard Trentham' plate, by Elliot & Son, no. 616, with gilded border, with title and with maker's mark.

Look out for the rare flask decorated with this pattern.

9.5in (24cm) diam

£180-220   SAS

A Prattware 'State House in Philadelphia 1776' dessert plate, no. 672, the maroon surround with a star and panel border and gold line decoration, the reverse with "R.J. Allen, Son & Co." retailer's mark.

This was produced in 1876 to celebrate the centenary of the Declaration of Independence in 1776.

9.5in (24cm) diam

£150-200   SAS

A Prattware 'The Hop Queen' plate, no. 676, with malachite border and gold line decoration.

This pattern can be found on large pot lids and circular comports.

9.5in (24cm) diam

£70-90   SAS

A Prattware 'The Irishman' side plate, no. 126, with an orange ground and '1-2-3' border with gold line decoration.

5.5in (14cm) diam

£50-80   SAS

CERAMICS

A Prattware 'The Truant' plate, no. 675, with maroon ground and '1-2-3' and scroll border with gold line decoration.

9.5in (24cm) diam

£80-120   SAS

A Prattware 'Pelargoniums & Moss Rose' plate, no. 459, the green border lined in yellow.

9.5in (24cm) diam

£40-60   SAS

A Prattware 'Shells' small side plate, no. 711, the pink border lined in green.

6.75in (17cm) diam

£100-150   SAS

A Prattware 'Orchids' plate, no. 454, with wavy outline, blue printed border, the reverse printed "No.94" in blue.

This is a dramatic and scarce combination with superb colouring reminiscent of 19thC botanical prints.

9.5in (24cm) diam

£300-350   SAS

A Prattware 'Uncle Tom and Eva' meat paste jar, no. 527, the neck with 'seaweed' ground.

A Prattware 'The Dragoon Charge, Balaklava' meat paste jar, no. 510, with minor hairline crack.

3.5in (8.75cm) high

£250-350   SAS

A Prattware 'Venice' meat paste jar, no. 517, by Mayer.

3.5in (8.75cm) high

£70-90   SAS

The companion piece to this shows an African slave being beaten and is known as 'Uncle Tom' (no. 526). A desirable set of three can be made by finding the version of this jar showing both scenes (no. 528). That double version has no seaweed decoration on the neck.

3.5in (8.75cm) high

£400-500   SAS

A Prattware 'The Fall of Sebastopol, 8th Sept. 1855' meat paste jar, no. 511, by Mayer.

3.5in (8.75cm) high

£350-450   SAS

MILLER'S COMPARES – TWO 'PASSING THE PIPE' JARS

The 'seaweed' pattern decorated neck on this example is not as fine.

As well as having a taller neck, it has a concave base. Some have internal collars.

This pattern was used on lids as well as jars and other wares.

The colours are stronger on this example.

A Prattware 'The Deer Stalker and Wild Deer' meat paste jar, no. 530, with 'Potted Meat' lid.

£220-280   **SAS**

A Prattware 'Passing the Pipe' meat paste jar, no. 525, the neck with mottled ground.

3.5in (9cm) high

£250-350   **SAS**

A Prattware 'Passing the Pipe' meat paste jar, no. 525, the neck with mottled ground.

4.5in (11.5cm) high

£450-550   **SAS**

A Prattware 'Exhibition Buildings 1851' Princess Christian sauce bottle or vase, no. 134, with a black mottled ground.

£200-300   **SAS**

A Prattware 'Convulvulus' jug, no. 458, with hinged pewter cover, gilt lining and minor hairline crack.

11in (28cm) high

£70-100   **SAS**

A Prattware tobacco jar, plunger and cover, with 'Cows in Stream near Ruins' and 'Halt near Ruins' scenes on a blue ground, with '1-2-3'-border and gold line decoration.

4.75in (12cm) high

£250-350   **SAS**

A Prattware cylindrical loving cup, decorated with 'Passing the Pipe' no. 525 and 'The Smokers', no. 524, on a malachite ground with gold line decoration.

4.25in (11cm) high

£200-300   **SAS**

FIND OUT MORE...

'Pot-Lids And Other Coloured Printed Staffordshire Wares', *by K.V. Mortimer, published by Antique Collectors' Club, 2003.*

CERAMICS

ESSENTIAL REFERENCE

- The Roseville Pottery Company began producing stoneware in 1890, in Roseville in the 'pottery state' of Ohio, USA. It initially produced utilitarian wares such as flowerpots, cuspidors (spittoons) and umbrella stands. As business grew, more factories were acquired and, by 1910, production was focused in the 'clay city' of Zanesville.
- Rozane, the company's first art pottery range, was designed by Ross C. Purdy in 1900 and mimicked Rookwood's successful Standard Glaze, as well as those Rookwood inspired like Weller's Louwelsa. Further successful hand-decorated art pottery ranges followed. However, by 1908, the demand for such expensive wares had declined and Roseville abandoned all but one hand-decorated range. The pottery adapted quickly, fitting a tunnel kiln to allow for less expensive mass-produced moulded wares.
- Frederick Rhead designed for the company from 1904 to 1908, introducing some of its most sought-after ranges, such as Della Robbia, and the squeeze-bag technique. Many later wares were designed by Frank Ferrell, who produced designs and shapes from 1917 to 1954, and

George Krause, who worked on glazes from 1915 to 1954.
- Moulded designs were typically based around flowers and natural motifs. The quality of the moulding counts considerably towards value – it should be clear and crisp. Similarly, the glazes should be well and correctly applied. Dull or unintentionally pale, sloppily applied glazes are less desirable. The colour of the glaze in a range can also affect value – blue is often more desirable than brown.
- Values also depend on the range itself. Common, later ranges from the 1940s, such as Bittersweet, tend to be less desirable. Although also easily found, the earlier Pinecone and Dahlrose are widely collected and desirable. Ranges that follow popular period styles, such as L'Art Nouveau and the Art Deco style Futura, are also consistently popular.
- Condition is also of paramount importance. Chips and cracks can devalue a piece by at least 50 per cent. Also beware of fakes and reproductions. Compare unusual glazes against colour photographs in a book and always carefully examine marks on the base.
- The plant closed in 1954.

A Roseville pink 'Apple Blossom' pattern vase, the base marked "Roseville USA 382-7".

7.25in (18.5cm) high

£60-90　　　　　BEL

A Roseville pink 'Apple Blossom' pattern ewer, the base marked "Roseville USA 316-8".

8.25in (21cm) high

£60-90　　　　　BEL

A Roseville pink 'Apple Blossom' pattern bowl, the bowl marked "Roseville USA 326-6".

8in (20cm) wide

£30-40　　　　　BEL

A Roseville pink 'Apple Blossom' pattern basket, the base marked "Roseville USA 309-8".

Examine handles carefully, as they are frequently broken. Apple Blossom was introduced in 1949 in blue, pink or green and is relatively common.

8.5in (20.5cm) high

£80-120　　　　　BEL

A Roseville green 'Apple Blossom' pattern jardinière, the base marked "Roseville USA 300-4".

4in (10cm) high

£50-70　　　　　BEL

A Roseville blue 'Apple Blossom' pattern jardinière and pedestal set, both marked, very minor nick to each piece.

£220-280　　　　　DRA

A Roseville 'Futura' pattern flared footed vase, with green stepped base and buttresses, unmarked, with three tight lines from rim, and a small nick to base.

12.25in (21cm) high

£500-700 DRA

A Roseville 'Futura' pattern cylinder vase, shape no. 381, with orange and green glazes, unmarked.

6.25in (16cm) high

£150-200 BEL

EXPERT EYE – A 'FUTURA' PATTERN VASE

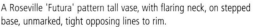

This is a rare shape, and is also large in size. However, it is cracked, which reduces the value.

The green leaf design near the rim recalls Roseville's traditional patterning, but here they are highly stylized in line with the Art Deco style.

The form is typical of the Art Deco period, with its clean lines based on geometric shapes.

The stepped base is another typical feature of the Art Deco style.

A Roseville 'Futura' bulbous vase, with stepped neck, covered in a turquoise glaze with charcoaling near base and paper label.

12.5in (32cm) high

£400-600 DRA

A Roseville 'Futura' vase, with stepped neck, decorated with a leaf-like design, unmarked, touch-ups to rim and base.

6in (16cm) high

£180-220 DRA

A Roseville pink 'Futura' pattern range four-sided vase, shape no. 399-7", with chevron design in green, unmarked.

Futura was introduced in 1928 and is usually labelled or marked with a red crayon only.

6in (16cm) high

£280-320 DRA

A Roseville 'Futura' pattern tall vase, with flaring neck, on stepped base, unmarked, tight opposing lines to rim.

12.25in (31cm) high

£600-900 DRA

A Roseville 'Futura' pattern jardinière, shape no. 616, with a tiny glaze flake and some glaze pops to the rim, unmarked.

9in (23cm) diam

£70-100 BEL

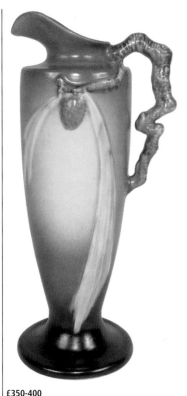

A Roseville blue 'Pine Cone' pattern ewer, shape no. 851, with branch handle and deep cobalt blue tones, two small glaze flakes to rim, the base marked "Roseville 851-15".

Designed by Frank Ferrell and rejected by other potteries, 'Pine Cone' was introduced by Roseville in 1935 and went on to become a best seller. It can be found in blue, brown or green, but blue tends to be the most desirable. Pink is extremely rare. Pieces with moulded, raised marks date from after 1939.

15.5in (39.5cm) high

£350-400   BEL

A Roseville blue 'Pine Cone' pattern double-handled vase, shape no. 747-10", the base marked "Roseville 747-10", with one restored handle.

10.5in (26.5cm) high

£80-120   BEL

A Roseville blue 'Pine Cone' pattern bowl, shape no. 278, with professionally restored rim and chip to twig.

The deep and varied blue tones are particularly appealing, as is the dramatically curving pattern on this form.

7in (18cm) diam

£70-100   BEL

A Roseville blue 'Pine Cone' pattern fan vase, shape no. 472, the base marked "Roseville USA 472-6".

This is a well-moulded example of an unusual and dramatic form.

6.5in (16.5cm) high

£150-200   BEL

A Roseville blue 'Pine Cone' pattern bowl, shape no. 322, the base marked "Roseville 322-12", with restored handle.

14in (35.5cm) wide

£50-70   BEL

A Roseville brown 'Pine Cone' pattern bowl, shape no. 279, the base marked "Roseville 279-9", in near mint condition with scratches to interior.

10.5in (26.5cm) long

£70-100   BEL

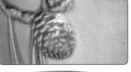

A Roseville brown 'Pine Cone' pattern vase, shape no. 704, with restored rim interior, the base marked "Roseville 704-7".

7.25in (18.5cm) high

£50-70   BEL

A Roseville brown 'Pine Cone' pattern cornucopia vase, shape no. 126, the base marked "Roseville USA 126-6".

6in (15cm) high

£60-90   BEL

ESSENTIAL REFERENCE

- Royal Copenhagen was founded in 1775 by Heinrich Frank Müller, under the royal patronage of Queen Julianne Marie of Denmark. Müller had devoted years of research into unlocking the secrets of hard paste porcelain, which was known only to a small number of European ceramics factories.
- Its first range, Blue Fluted, is still among its most popular today, but many collectors tend to focus on its 1920s to '30s, and post-WWII decorative porcelain and stoneware. Nils Thorsson was one its longest serving and most prolific designers, and other important names include Arnold Krog, Knud Kyhn, Axel Salto, and Johanne Gerber.
- Forms tend to be functional and Modernist, contrasting against the hand-painted patterns that were typically inspired by the natural environment. Colours, such as beiges, browns, and greens predominate, and patterns take the form of stylized leaves, sheaves and flowers. Abstract and surreal figural motifs were also used, often in less natural colours such as purple and blue.
- Marks on the bases can help you to find out more, including the range, the name of the designer and the decorator, whose monogram is hand-painted alongside the factory marks. Dates can often be identified by looking for a short line underneath a letter in the name 'Royal Copenhagen' and then consulting a reference table that allots a different year for each letter. Alumina marks often appear as the company acquired Royal Copenhagen in 1882.

A Royal Copenhagen Baca Fajance bottle vase, no. 704/3259, designed by Nils Thorsson, with blue on brown wax-resist design, and printed and painted marks to base.

9in (23cm) high

£70-90   **UCT**

A Royal Copenhagen Baca Fajance bottle base, no. 712/3259, designed by Nils Thorsson, with printed and painted marks to base.

9in (23cm) high

£70-90   **UCT**

A Royal Copenhagen Baca Fajance bottle vase, no. 711/3455, designed by Nils Thorsson, with printed and painted marks to base.

The monogram in the larger circular mark is that of Nils Thorsson (1898-1975), who worked at Royal Copenhagen from 1912 to 1975, becoming their chief designer in the 1950s. Collectors often call it the 'chop mark'.

7.75in (19.5cm) high

£50-80

A Royal Copenhagen Baca Fajance oval-section tall vase, no. 1780/3101, designed by Johanne Gerber, the base with printed and painted marks.

The mark on the base is very lightly scored through three times by a sharp knife, indicating this is a second. The more strikes through the mark, the more faults the piece contains. Despite being a second, the value is in the large size.

14.25in (36cm) high

£150-220   **UCT**

A Royal Copenhagen Baca Fajance chimney vase, no. 780/3121, designed by Johanne Gerber, with printed and painted marks to base.

This pattern, inspired by trees and Japanese art, is one of the more commonly found.

7.75in (19.5cm) high

£80-120 UCT

A Royal Copenhagen Baca Fajance 'funnel' vase, no. 714/3223, designed by Nils Thorsson, the base with printed and painted marks.

8in (20cm) high

£100-130 UCT

A Royal Copenhagen Baca Fajance ovoid vase, no. 719/3207, designed by Nils Thorsson, with printed and painted marks to base.

5.25in (13cm) high

£40-60 UCT

A Royal Copenhagen Baca Fajance dish, no. 790/2885, designed by Johanne Gerber, with hand-painted abstract design, the base with printed and painted marks.

10.75in (21cm) wide

£40-50 UCT

A Royal Copenhagen Baca Fajance dish, no. 962/3774, designed by Ellen Malmer, with hand-painted harvest design, the base with printed and painted marks.

8.5in (21.5cm) diam

£40-50 UCT

A Royal Copenhagen Baca Fajance lidded box, no. 704/3627, designed by Nils Thorsson, the base with Aluminia printed and painted marks.

3.25in (8cm) wide

£50-70 UCT

A 1950s Royal Copenhagen Fajance ovoid vase, no. 139/2878, designed by Inge Lise Sørensen and Marianne Johnson, the base with printed and painted marks and "4" decorator's monogram.

This vase is from what is commonly called the 'surreal' series, due to the range's unusual eye-like or abstract figural motifs.

7in (18cm) high

£110-130 UCT

A 1950s Royal Copenhagen Fajance oval-section vase, no. 182/3101, designed by Inge-Lise Koefoed, the base with gilt Aluminia printed mark, and other printed and painted marks.

14.5in (37cm) high

£200-230 UCT

A Royal Copenhagen Solbjerg range footed ball vase, no. 1605, designed by Nils Thorsson, with an alternating straight and wavy moulded pattern and light green glaze, the base with impressed and printed Aluminia marks.

8in (20.5cm) high

£180-220 **UCT**

A Royal Copenhagen Solbjerg range footed ball vase, no. 1680, designed by Nils Thorsson, with a moulded cross-hatched pattern and reddish brown glaze, the base with impressed and printed Aluminia marks.

4.75in (12cm) high

£100-130 **UCT**

EXPERT EYE – A ROYAL COPENHAGEN 'SOLBJERG' VASE

Colours are typically bold but restrained, or pale. The moulded motifs work well with the form, with neither dominating.

The decoration echoes the form.

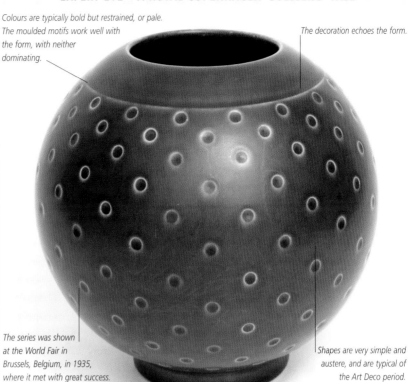

The series was shown at the World Fair in Brussels, Belgium, in 1935, where it met with great success.

Shapes are very simple and austere, and are typical of the Art Deco period.

A Royal Copenhagen Solbjerg range footed ball vase, no. 1605, designed by Nils Thorsson, with a moulded dot pattern and reddish brown glaze, the base with impressed and printed Aluminia marks.

5.5in (14cm) high

£100-130 **UCT**

A Royal Copenhagen Solbjerg or Scripto range bowl, no. 1692, designed by Nils Thorsson, with bands of moulded wavy lines, the base with printed Aluminia and painted marks.

3.5in (9cm) high

£110-130 **UCT**

A Royal Copenhagen Marselis small tapered vase, no. 2639, designed by Nils Thorsson, with moulded teardrop and dot design and reddish brown glaze, the base with Aluminia and Marselis printed marks.

4.25in (10.5cm) high

£90-120 **UCT**

A Royal Copenhagen Marselis small footed bowl, no. 2644, designed by Nils Thorsson, with moulded scale-like pattern and reddish brown glaze, the base with Aluminia and Marselis printed marks.

3.5in (9cm) high

£90-110 **UCT**

CERAMICS

A Royal Copenhagen Marselis green ovoid vase, no. 2628, designed by Nils Thorsson, with moulded fluted and linear pattern, the base with Aluminia and Marselis printed marks.

4.75in (12cm) high

£90-120 UCT

A Royal Copenhagen Columbine range baluster vase, no. 2768, designed by Nils Thorsson, with asymmetric blue and white glazed decoration, the base with printed and painted marks.

6.75in (17cm) high

£80-100 UCT

A Royal Copenhagen Columbine range double gourd vase, designed by Nils Thorsson, with asymmetric blue and white glazed decoration, the base with printed and painted marks.

The factory mark on this vase has been scratched through, indicating it is a second due to white marks in the black areas and the unbalanced shape. The single-piece double gourd form is challenging to pot. Nevertheless, this is a rare range, designed by Thorsson.

6.75in (17cm) high

£50-100 UCT

EXPERT EYE – A ROYAL COPENHAGEN VASE

Thorsson continued the theme of simple shapes moulded with patterns, and covered in a single colour glaze, with the Marselis range of the 1950s and '60s.

Forms tend to be more organic and rounded, and less austere – colours are also bolder, with thick glazes.

The tightly moulded designs are typically geometric and cover the entire body, rather than being spread over it, leaving plain areas, as with the Soldjerg range.

The beehive shaped mark on the base is that of the Aluminia company, who acquired Royal Copenhagen in 1882. The mark was used until 1969 when the Royal Copenhagen mark seen on the previous pages replaced it.

A Royal Copenhagen Marselis blue ovoid vase, no. 2631, designed by Nils Thorsson, with moulded square motifs, the base with printed Aluminia and Marselis marks.

7.75in (19.5cm) high

£140-160 UCT

A 1960s Royal Copenhagen stoneware vase, no. 21924, designed by Jörgen Morgensen, with high-relief stylized dog motif and a beige and brown graduated Sung glaze, the base with printed and painted marks and inscribed "jm".

These heavily moulded patterns of stylized animals are typical of Morgensen's designs at this time, and the Sung glaze is the most common on stoneware bodies.

6in (15cm) high

£120-150 UCT

A scarce Royal Copenhagen stoneware baboon figurine, designed by Knud Kyhn, the feet inscribed "KK" and with impressed marks.

4.5in (11.5cm) high

£120-140 **UCT**

A scarce Royal Copenhagen stoneware elephant figurine, designed by Knud Kyhn, the feet impressed "KK" and with impressed marks.

Like the baboon, the elephant is rarer – bears and other more cuddly and friendly animals are more common.

4in (10cm) high

£120-140 **UCT**

A Royal Copenhagen stoneware seated fawn figurine, no. 20183, designed by Knud Kyhn, the base moulded "KK" and with printed marks.

This style of glaze, with its brown and cream colours and green tones, is an early example. Later, the glaze became more chocolatey.

4in (10cm) long

£80-100 **UCT**

A Royal Copenhagen stoneware walking bear figurine, no. 20155, designed by Knud Kyhn, the feet impressed "KK" and with printed marks.

4in (10cm) long

£110-130 **UCT**

A Royal Copenhagen stoneware bear cub playing figurine, no. 21432, designed by Knud Kyhn, the base impressed "KK" and with printed marks.

This is typical of the later style of glaze colouring.

4in (10cm) long

£35-45 **UCT**

A Royal Copenhagen stoneware bear cub waving figurine, no. 21453, designed by Knud Kyhn, the base impressed "KK" and with printed marks.

4in (10cm) long

£35-45 **UCT**

A Royal Copenhagen stoneware seated monkey figurine, no. 20188, designed by Knud Kyhn, the base impressed "KK" and with printed marks.

4in (10cm) long

£40-50 **UCT**

A Royal Copenhagen 'Huguenot Girl' figurine, designed by Arno Malinowski in 1927, glazed in white brown and beige and with gilt highlights, the base with printed and impressed marks.

8.25in (21cm) high

£350-450 **WW**

CERAMICS

A Royal Worcester bottle vase, shape no. 2491, painted and signed by Harry Stinton, with Highland cattle, gilt rim, the base with printed crown and circle mark in puce, date code for 1915.

1915

£300-400   **NEA**

A Royal Worcester blush ground twin-handled vase, shape no. 2337, decorated by William Hale, with floral spray decoration, signed "W. Hale", factory printed and impressed marks, dated 1908.

1908   12.25in (31cm) high

£280-320   **SWO**

EXPERT EYE – A SCOTTIE WILSON PLATTER

Scottish born Scottie Wilson (1891-1972) turned to drawing late in life, at the age of 44, while running a second-hand shop in Toronto, Canada.

He is considered an 'outsider' artist, in other words an artist with no education or official training in art and who is not part of the 'art world'. The term is often applied to vagrants and the poor who survive by earning money from art.

After some success and his return to England in 1945, his art was admired and bought by famous artists including Pablo Picasso and Jean Dubuffet.

In in the 1960s, he was commissioned by Royal Worcester to produce a pattern for them to reproduce, which is shown below.

A Scottie Wilson hand-painted platter, decorated over the glaze in shades of yellow, rust and black with a panels of birds, flowers and fish within a stylized foliate frame, signed "Scottie" on the bottom right.

Despite claiming poverty throughout his life, and living very modestly, upon Wilson's death in 1972 bank accounts containing large sums of money were discovered – as was a suitcase full of money hidden under his bed.

15.5in (38.5cm) high

£300-400   **WW**

A Royal Worcester Art Nouveau twin-handled vase, with printed and impressed marks, restored.

16in (41cm) high

£120-180   **SWO**

A 1950s Royal Worcester transfer-printed 'Fiesta' pattern bone china plate.

8in (20cm) diam

£10-15   **BAD**

A Royal Worcester Crown Ware 'Tree of Life' pattern plate, designed by Scottie Wilson, with black transfer-printed decoration, the reverse with printed marks and facsimile signature.

8.25in (21cm) high

£80-120   **WW**

A Royal Worcester Crown Ware 'Tree of Life' pattern teapot, designed by Scottie Wilson, with black transfer-printed decoration, the reverse with printed marks and facsimile signature.

8.25in (21cm) high

£100-200   **WW**

A Rye Pottery mug, hand-painted with multicoloured pastel bands beneath a galleon at sea, and inscribed "Rye", the base with impressed mark, small hairline crack to rim.

5.25in (13.5cm) high

£80-120   WW

A Rye Pottery tankard, with yellow and blue bands and moulded ribs, impressed "Rye".

5in (13cm) high

£50-70   GAZE

A Rye Pottery tapering cylindrical vase, the beige glaze with crossing linear decoration, the base with "Made in Rye Pottery" blue ink stamp.

12in (30cm) high

£60-80   GAZE

A Rye Pottery Cockerel vase, by David Sharp, covered in a mottled blue and green glaze, the base painted "DT Sharp Rye", with hairline crack to top rim.

14in (35.5cm) high

£50-100   WW

A David Sharp Pottery vase, decorated by "TC", and signed to the base with monogram and date.

Pottery has been made in and around Rye since the Middle Ages. Just after WWII, the Cole brothers brought about a renaissance in ceramic design, introducing modern designs inspired by Stig Lindberg's work at Gustavsberg. They also trained a number of potters including George Gray, David Sharp and Dennis Townsend, who all left to found their own potteries. The David Sharp Pottery still exists, continuing the tradition of handmade and hand-decorated pottery, and is run by his family. This design was produced in 2004, and is signed and dated on the base.

2004   *6in (15cm) high*

£30-40   PC

A Rye Pottery shallow dish, hand-painted with a stylized fish, with impressed marks to the back.

The scales on the fish are decorated with Rye's typical modern and abstract patterns.

4.75in (12cm) diam

£30-50   GAZE

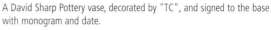

CERAMICS

ESSENTIAL REFERENCE

- Developments in Scandinavian ceramic design from the 1940s to '70s were influential and enduring, not only in Scandinavia, but across the rest of the world. Value mainly depends on the factory, the range and the designer. Also consider the form, size, glaze and production process. Learn how to recognise styles, key ranges and marks on the base. Currently few fakes are known but styles were often copied by other makers, often closely.
- Leading factories whose work is sought-after include Rorstrand (founded 1726), Gustavsberg (founded 1640), and Arabia (founded 1873). However, there are also a number of smaller factories that are growing in prominence as ranges by these main factories continue to rise in value. These include Stavangerflint (1949-79), Palshus (1949-72), and Upsala Ekeby (founded 1886).
- Designers to look out for include Stig Lindberg (1916-82), whose hand-decorated, brightly coloured faience works produced at Gustavsberg between the 1940s and '60s were particularly influential. Marks on the base help with identification and dating. Look out for a large 'G' with a hand motif, some also bear the wording 'Stig L'. The works of Wilhelm Kåge for Gustavsberg, Gunnar Nylund for Rorstrand, and Bjørn Wiinblad are also popular.
- Designs often combined stark modernism with a feel for traditional crafts and the natural environment. Colours range from bright and strong primary colours to more subtle, earthy tones, the former often used for tableware. Tableware also tends to be more affordable than decorative wares, but was often just as influential. Also consider studio ceramics, as interest and values are rising, and each piece is unique. These can be harder to spot, so always look on the base for marks that often include the country of manufacture.

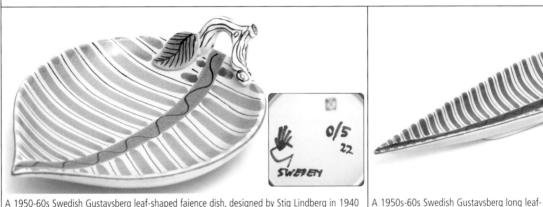

A 1950-60s Swedish Gustavsberg leaf-shaped faience dish, designed by Stig Lindberg in 1940 and painted by Franca Pugno, with applied branch and leaf handle and hand-painted pink stripes and black lines, the base with painted marks and decorator's monogram.
A similar example of this dish is shown in 'Scandinavian Ceramics & Glass in the Twentieth Century', by Jennifer Opie, published by the Victoria & Albert Museum.

7.5in (19cm) long

£150-200   UCT

A 1950s-60s Swedish Gustavsberg long leaf-shaped faience dish, painted by Franca Pugno, with hand-painted pink and blue stripes and black lines, the base with painted marks and decorator's monogram.

12.5in (31.5cm) long

£150-200   UCT

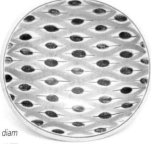

A 1950s-60s Swedish Gustavsberg faience dish, designed by Stig Lindberg and painted by Kurt Addin, with hand-painted yellow lattice design with brown dots, the base with painted marks and decorator's monogram.

5in (12.25cm) diam

£150-200   UCT

A Swedish Gustavsberg conical jug vase, designed by Stig Lindberg and painted by Sigrid Richter, with hand-painted blue stripes and orange lines, and applied handle, the base painted "G Sweden 159.AM.3" and with decorator's monogram.

8in (20cm) high

£180-220   UCT

A Swedish Gustavsberg melon-shaped vase, designed by Stig Lindberg, with pink stripes and scalloped rim.

c1940-50   8.5in (21.5cm) wide

£350-400   **GGRT**

EXPERT EYE – A GUSTAVSBERG REPTIL VASE

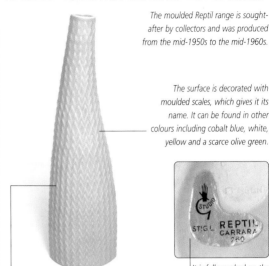

The moulded Reptil range is sought-after by collectors and was produced from the mid-1950s to the mid-1960s.

The surface is decorated with moulded scales, which gives it its name. It can be found in other colours including cobalt blue, white, yellow and a scarce olive green.

It is fully marked on the base with the Gustavsberg name and anchor mark. The label is a rare survivor.

This organic, asymmetric form is typical of the range and of Scandinavian Modernism of the time. Many shapes also have elongated necks on curving bodies.

A 1950s Swedish Gustavsberg light blue Reptil range vase, designed by Stig Lindberg, the base with impressed factory marks and foil label.

Some pieces in this range were designed by Berndt Friberg.

9in (23cm) high

£150-200   **UCT**

A Swedish Gustavsberg Domino range cylindrical vase, designed by Stig Lindberg, with brown glaze and spiralling ridges.

5.25in (13cm) high

£100-120   **UCT**

A Swedish Gustavsberg Domino range vase, designed by Stig Lindberg, with brown glaze and spiralling and chevron ridges.

5.25in (13cm) high

£120-140   **UCT**

A Swedish Gustavsberg little girl figurine, designed by Lisa Larson, with hand-painted clothes, the back with gilt foil label.

5in (12.5cm) high

£40-60   **UCT**

A Swedish Gustavsberg lion figurine, designed by Lisa Larson, with impressed and sgraffito details, the base impressed "LL".

This lion was also produced in larger sizes. Larson is better known for her popular 'Kennel' series of dog figurines.

2in (5cm) high

£40-60   **UCT**

CERAMICS

ESSENTIAL REFERENCE – THE ARGENTA RANGE

The Argenta range of mottled jade-green glazed decorative wares embellished with silver patterns was designed by Wilhelm Kåge (1889-1960), one of the company's most notable designers. It was introduced in 1930 at the 'Stockholdsutstallingen', Stockholm's major exhibition of art and industry. Expensive to produce and buy, it was always deemed a luxury line and was sold in high-end design and department stores. Motifs are typically inspired by the natural world and are strongly stylized. Figures were also used. Small dishes and bowls are the most common shapes seen, with larger sizes and vases being more valuable. Red is a very rare variation, with blue being even rarer.

A Swedish Gustavsberg Argenta range vase, designed by Wilhelm Kåge, with silver stylized floral and foliate design, the base numbered "9780".

5.25in (13cm) high

£140-160   ANT

A Swedish Gustavsberg Argenta range tapering vase, with silver decoration of a mermaid reserved on a mottled green ground, painted and printed marks "Gustavsberg/Argenta/ 978 II".

8.25in (21cm) high

£450-550   L&T

A Swedish Gustavsberg Argenta range small bowl, designed by Wilhelm Kåge, with turned linear design, and silver top rim and foot rim, the base with impressed and printed mark.

The impressed name "Kåge" and the style of the other marks indicate that this is an early piece.

2.5in (6.5cm) high

£40-50   UCT

A Swedish Gustavsberg Argenta range posy vase, no. 960, designed by Wilhelm Kåge, with scalloped rim and stylized flower motifs, the base with printed marks.

2.5in (6.5cm) high

£35-45   UCT

A Swedish Gustavsberg Argenta range pin tray, no. 924, designed by Wilhelm Kåge, with floral motif and scalloped design rim, the base with gilt printed mark.

3.5in (9cm) high

£35-45   UCT

A Swedish Gustavsberg Argenta range circular dish, no. 1003I, designed by Wilhelm Kåge, with floral motif, the base with gilt printed mark.

5.25in (13cm) high

£50-70   UCT

A rare Swedish Gustavsberg red Argenta range small footed bowl, no. 1094, designed by Wilhelm Kåge, with foliate motif and scalloped design rim, the base with gilt printed mark.

3.5in (9cm) high

£50-70   UCT

A Finnish Arabia ovoid vase, covered in a splashed orange and yellow lustre glaze, the base with printed mark.

10in (25.5cm) high

£60-80   WW

A Swedish Laholm footed bowl, with hand-painted and sgraffito designs to the exterior and interior, the base with impressed mark and incised "B.G."

3in (7.5cm) diam

£60-80   UCT

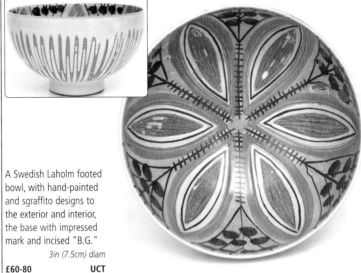

A Swedish Rorstrand candlestick, designed by Ingrid Pedersen, decorated with a dark and light blue glossy glaze, the base with impressed factory marks.

4.25in (11cm) high

£90-110   UCT

A 1950s Norwegian Stavangerflint bottle vase, with hand-painted bands of yellow and black stylized leaf motifs, the base with printed marks.

10.75in (27cm) high

£40-60   UCT

A Swedish Rorstrand Farina range jug vase, designed by Gunnar Nylund, with moulded abstract design, and asymmetrical neck and angled handle, the base impressed "7" and with blue printed factory marks.

The reflective glossy high glaze is a notable feature of this range.

12.25in (31cm) high

£80-120   UCT

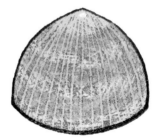

A Swedish Upsala Ekeby 'Fiorella' pattern dish, designed by Ingrid Atterburg, the base marked "2350".

This rare pattern was only in production from 1958 to 1960.

12.5in (31.5cm) long

£45-50   OUT

A Swedish Upsala Ekeby footed spherical vase, with tapered neck, decorated with bands of stylized leaf and linear patterns in grey and white, the base with incised marks, chip to foot.

3in 33cm) high

£100-150   WW

CERAMICS

ESSENTIAL REFERENCE – BJØRN WIINBLAD

Bjørn Wiinblad (1918-2006) was one of the most versatile Danish artists of the 20thC, working across poster, textile, ceramic, glass and metalware design. After studying at the Royal Academy of Arts in Copenhagen he started working in ceramics with Lars Syberg, before founding his own studio in 1952. Handmade limited production studio works were made throughout his career, however, his name is more commonly associated with Nymølle and Rosenthal. He began producing transfer-printed designs for Nymølle in 1946 and bought the company in 1976 – his designs were produced until the 1990s and were exported all over the world. Wiinblad worked with Rosenthal of Germany from 1956 until he bought Nymølle, producing similar transfer-printed patterns. His instantly recognisable and characteristic designs focus on fairy tale, myth and nature, with a unique style all of his own. Mass-produced pieces such as the seasonal plaques and these plates are commonly seen. His unique hand-decorated studio works are considerably rarer and more valuable. These plates were produced in four different sizes, of which this the largest. 11in (28cm) plates may be worth around half as much. Wiinblad's recent death has increased interest from collectors.

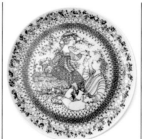

A Danish Nymølle 'Summer' transfer-printed large charger, designed by Bjørn Wiinblad, from The Seasons series.

14.25in (36cm) diam

£80-120   **GROB**

A Danish Nymølle 'Autumn' transfer-printed large charger, designed by Bjørn Wiinblad, from The Seasons series.

14.25in (36cm) diam

£80-120   **GROB**

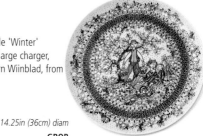

A Danish Nymølle 'Winter' transfer-printed large charger, designed by Bjørn Wiinblad, from The Seasons series.

14.25in (36cm) diam

£80-120   **GROB**

A Danish Nymølle 'Spring' transfer-printed large charger, designed by Bjørn Wiinblad, from The Seasons series.

14.25in (36cm) diam

£80-120   **GROB**

A Danish Nymølle transfer-printed planter, designed by Bjørn Wiinblad.

6in (15cm) diam

£70-100   **GROB**

A Danish Nymølle 'Masquerade' transfer-printed vase, designed by Bjørn Wiinblad, with printed mark to base.

6.5in (16.5cm) high

£60-80   **MHT**

A Bjørn Wiinblad figural triple candelabra, with modelled and painted face and painted stylized foliate and floral 'hair', the base with painted marks, with minor restoration.

8.75in (22cm) high

£170-200   **WW**

A Danish Palshus rounded square-section vase, designed by Per Linnemann-Schmidt, covered with a mottled cobalt blue glaze, the base with inscribed marks.

10.25in (26cm) high

£150-180   **UCT**

A Danish Palshus tapered cylindrical footed vase, no. 1182/1, designed by Per Linnemann-Schmidt, covered with a vibrant blue haresfur glaze, the base inscribed "Palshus Denmark PLS 1182/1".

The Palshus factory was founded by Annelise and Per Linnemann-Schmidt in 1949, and produced a range of pottery including chamotte wares, ceramics with glossy high-fired glazes, and pieces with scratched and roughly decorated surfaces. The highest prices and greatest interest tend to be for pieces covered with their beautiful matte haresfur glazes. Delicately graduated with fine lines and often in vibrant colours or earthy tones, they cover simple and well-balanced forms. The marks above are typical and include Linnemann-Schmidt's initials and the model numbers. The factory closed in 1972.

4.25in (11cm) high

£120-140   **UCT**

A Danish Palshus bulbous vase, no. 1155, designed by Per Linnemann-Schmidt, covered with a graduated brown haresfur glaze, the base inscribed "Palshus Denmark PLS 1155".

3.75in (9cm) high

£140-160   **UCT**

A Danish Palshus tapered rectangular vase, no. 401, designed by Per Linnemann-Schmidt, covered with a graduated brown haresfur glaze, the base impressed "Palshus Denmark" and inscribed "401".

3.25in (8cm) high

£130-150   **UCT**

A Danish Michael Anderson & Sons rectangular dish, with pattern designed by Marianne Stark, the base marked "5906 MS", with restored rim chip.

4.75in (12cm) wide

£22-28   **OUT**

A Danish Michael Anderson & Sons cobalt blue charger, the pattern designed by Marianne Stark, the base marked "4800-1 MS".

9.75in (24.5cm) wide

£40-60   **OUT**

CERAMICS

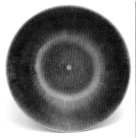

A Danish Eigil Hinrichsen studio pottery bowl, with green haresfur glaze, the base with painted mark.

10.75in (27.5cm) diam

£150-180   **UCT**

A Danish Ejvin Nielsen studio pottery tapering cylindrical vase, covered with a blue haresfur glaze, the base inscribed "Ejv. Nielsen".

At first glance, these are often mistaken for pieces designed by Per Linnemann-Schmidt for Palshus, until the marks on the base are seen.

8.25in (21cm) high

£80-100   **UCT**

A Danish Ejvin Nielsen studio pottery cylindrical vase, with low collar neck, covered with dripping and graduated brown tones and a beige haresfur glaze, the base inscribed "Ejv. Nielsen".

5.25in (13.5cm) high

£90-110   **UCT**

A Danish Nymølle stoneware vase, with long neck and everted dish rim, the edge unfinished, covered with a blue glaze.

The banded pattern indicates that this was decorated by applying the glaze with a brush as the vase turned on a wheel.

5.25in (13.5cm) high

£80-100   **UCT**

A Saxbo bowl, with moulded stylized leaf design and covered with a pale celadon glaze, the base numbered "123" and with impressed factory marks.

Many Scandinavian ceramics designers were influenced by ancient Oriental forms and glazes. This lotus-like form, with its gentle celadon glaze is typical. Other glazes focus on heavy browns akin to the tenmoku glaze. The base is marked 'Danmark', which was used between 1931 and 1949. 'Denmark' was used from 1950 until 1968.

3.25in (8cm) high

£130-150   **UCT**

A Søholm Pottery stoneware vase, with hand-painted abstract design, marked "Søholm Bornholm Denmark Stentoj Handmade" to base.

£70-80   **MHT**

ESSENTIAL REFERENCE

- The term 'studio pottery' is used to describe pottery made by the pottery owner, or by others under his or her guidance or supervision. As individual pieces are handmade or hand-decorated, or both, each piece is effectively unique. Much was intended to be functional, however decorative pieces were also made. Although there were some 19thC studio potters, the market largely focuses on pieces made during the second half of the 20thC, and primarily on the postwar period when the area boomed.
- Pottery by the most influential, and often earliest, studio potters tends to be the most sought-after and thus typically the most expensive. Key names include Bernard Leach (1887-1979), and his colleague Shoji Hamada (1894-1978), together with Lucie Rie (1902-95) and her one-time colleague Hans Coper (1920-81). Leach was particularly influential, and founded the St Ives pottery. He promoted functionality over decorative or artistic aspects. Both he and Hamada were strongly inspired by ancient Oriental examples – a theme that runs through many potters' work.
- Lucie Rie is primarily known for her post-WWII finely potted bottle and bowl forms. Although her work was intended to be functional, its architectural and often sculptural forms and wider range of less rustic, and sometimes brighter, glazes puts her work in a different league to that of Leach. Her assistant, and later colleague, Hans Coper's work is typified by its strongly sculptural forms, and the fact that many pieces were assembled after being thrown and were not intended to be functional. Both typically worked in a palette of brown, beiges, greys and creams.
- Bernard Leach was also a prolific teacher, and he and many of his contemporaries trained a new generation of studio potters, who then went on to teach a further generation. As the work of these important early pioneers is already valuable fetching many hundreds, if not thousands, of pounds, many collectors focus on the second and third generations, whose work is often more affordable. Some are also turning to the vibrant world of contemporary studio pottery.
- Always look on the base of a piece for an impressed or inscribed mark, as this can help you identify the potter. Look these up in a reference book, as some marks may not have been correctly identified by the owner. The work of some potters is yet to be 'discovered', so learn how to recognise the styles of certain potters, and find out a little of their background, such as with whom or where they studied and trained. Look for quality in terms of form and glaze, but also in terms of innovation. Always carefully examine a piece for damage such as chips or cracks as this will usually reduce the value dramatically.

A Hans Coper stoneware cup-form vase, comprising a tapered bowl over a cylindrical stand, with whitish glaze over a partially textured body, with an internal cylindrical candle-holder, the interior glazed manganese dark brown, with impressed "HC" seal.

This form shows both Coper's sculptural approach to studio pottery as well as his interest in ancient Cycladic pots or bronze vessels. The colours and texture are also typical of his work.

7in (18cm) high

£4,000-5,000   JN

A Lucie Rie mottled brown porcelain pedestal bowl, the flared rim with pink, blue and green bands, with impressed seal to base.

This bowl was purchased direct from Lucie Rie during the 1980s. A similar bowl is illustrated on p166 of 'The Potters Art, by Garth Clark, published by Phaidon.
c1979   7.5in (18.5cm) diam

£3,500-4,500   WW

A Lucie Rie porcelain bottle vase, with cylindrical body, waisted neck and flared rim, the bronze glaze with sgraffito lines to rim and shoulder, impressed mark to base.

The glaze gives the impression that this vase is made from bronze. The finely potted and balanced form dominates the simple, yet typical, decoration of incised lines.

9in (22.5cm) high

£5,500-6,500   WW

A Lucie Rie stoneware vase, with fluted sides and flared curved, spiral rim, covered overall with a heavily pitted white and grey glaze, with impressed "LR" seal.

8.5in (21.5cm) high

£3,500-4,500   JN

CERAMICS

ESSENTIAL REFERENCE – STUDIO POTTERY MARKS

An impressed seal mark for Lucie Rie.
Austrian-born Lucie Rie signed most of her work with her name or initials until 1939, when she introduced this combined 'LR' monogram. It was used increasingly from the late 1940s onwards, sometimes in association with Coper's inverted 'HC' seal mark from 1947 until 1958. The precise style of the monogram changed over the years, which can help date pieces more precisely.

An impressed seal mark for William Staite-Murray.
Staite Murray's (1881-1962) first marks comprised his inscribed or painted name over the word 'London'. Occasionally a number or date also appears, and his name may appear as an impressed 'W.S. Murray'. In 1924, he developed the impressed monogram mark seen here and used it until he stopped potting.

An impressed seal mark for Bernard Leach.
Leach used a number of marks during his career, most comprising his two initials. 'BHL' impressed monograms, that include his middle initial, are early and date from 1913 into the 1920s. The mark on the left, with two dots near the 'L' is the most commonly found. After 1940, Leach often also painted his initials in addition to the St Ives mark (see 'The Leach Family' section below), and his personal seal.

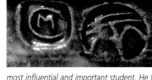

Impressed seal marks for Michael Cardew (left) and his Wenford Bridge Pottery (right).
Michael Cardew (1901-83) is often seen as Bernard Leach's most influential and important student. He founded the Winchcombe Pottery in 1926. In 1939, he left to establish Wenford Bridge Pottery, then moved to Africa, where he also founded a pottery in 1942. He returned to Wenford Bridge in 1949, and remained there until his death.

An impressed seal mark for the Lowerdown Pottery.
A number of marks were used by the Lowerdown Pottery and David Leach from 1956 onwards, including the one shown here. Variations include marks where a small 'D' replaces the small cross motif, marks with two small dots next to the 'LD' monogram, and marks combining the 'LD' closely in a circle.

Examine seal marks carefully, as minor variations can indicate different dates, or even a different potter. A number of fake, marked Lucie Rie iron glaze pieces have been identified by experts – these show less variation between the usual thicker, heavy bases and the thin rims Rie favoured, and have smoother glazes.

THE LEACH FAMILY

A St Ives Pottery stoneware ovoid vase, by Bernard Leach, decorated with simple brush stroke, impressed with "BL" and St Ives seal marks.

The impressed seal shown is the St Ives pottery mark, and is usually found along with a potter's personal seal mark.

4.75in (12cm) high

£320-380   **WW**

A Lowerdown Pottery teapot and cover, by David Leach, with painted decoration on an ash ground, the base with impressed seal marks.

Son of Bernard Leach, David Leach (1911-2005) founded Lowerdown Pottery in 1956 and worked there until his death in 2005.

9in (23cm) high

£300-400   **WW**

A Lowerdown Pottery studio pottery teapot, by David Leach, with 'sliced' body covered with a reduced copper red glaze, and with a bamboo handle and impressed "LD" seal to base.

5.5in (14cm) high

£250-350   **WW**

A David Leach tin-glazed earthenware bowl, the interior with a brown linear design on a blue ground, the base with impressed "LD" seal.

10.5in (26.5cm) diam

£250-350   **WW**

A David Leach tin-glazed waisted earthenware vase, painted with a stylized natural design in shades of beige and brown, the base with impressed "DL" seal.

7in (18cm) high

£250-350   **WW**

An early 1950s Ambleside Modernist footed studio bowl, with sgraffito decoration through the matte black glaze, the base inscribed "Ambleside".

This very rare form dates from early in founder George Cook's running of the Ambleside Pottery from 1948 to 1966. The irregular form and surface shows that it was hand-formed, rather than being moulded or cast, as later pieces were. The form and decoration are typical of early 1950s austerity and recall the work of Tibor Reich for Denby.

c1952   3.5in (9cm) high

£40-60   **PC**

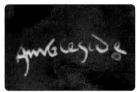

A Peter Beard stoneware studio vase, of ovoid form with inverted rim and inlaid mottled blue and terracotta chevron designs, with impressed seal to base.

8in (20cm) high

£450-550   **WW**

A Greendene Pottery vase or candle-holder, designed and made by Michael Buckland, with impressed marks to base.

The slightly recessed rim indicates that this vase could also be used as a candle-holder.

c1965   3.75in (9.5cm) high

£15-20   **MHC**

A Winchcombe Pottery ovoid vase, by Michael Cardew, decorated with brown bands, stripes and sheaves of wheat on an ochre ground, with impressed seal marks to base.

11.75in (30cm) high

£700-900   **WW**

EXPERT EYE – AN ALDERMASTON CANDLESTICK

The Aldermaston Pottery was founded by Alan Caiger-Smith in Berkshire, in 1955, and went on to be an important training ground for many 20thC studio potters.

The form and decoration recall Hispano-Moresque and late 19thC Medieval Revival designs, such as the work of William de Morgan.

Although Aldermaston is well known for its tin-glazed wares, Caiger-Smith also experimented, and was successful, with reduction-fired lustre glazes, as seen here.

The pottery closed in December 2006 when Caiger-Smith retired. Interest in his work has risen dramatically, particularly due to the recent sale of the pottery's collection.

An Aldermaston Pottery candlestick, by Alan Caiger-Smith, painted in ruby lustre, painted marks.

11.75in (30cm) high

£180-220   **WW**

An African Abuja Pottery stoneware 'Gwari' casserole dish and lid, by Michael Cardew, with pie-crust banding, with Abuja and "MC" seals to base.

c1957   11.5in (29cm) diam

£350-450   **WW**

CERAMICS

A large Wenford Bridge Pottery stoneware studio bowl, by Michael Cardew, decorated with stripes in shades of ash green and brown, with impressed seals for Michael Cardew and the Wenford Bridge Pottery.

A similar bowl, dated to 1967, can be seen on p165 of 'Studio Pottery' by Oliver Watson and published by Phaidon. The marks on this bowl can be seen on p112.

12.25in (31cm) high

£1,000-1,500   WW

A 1950s, unsigned studio pottery lamp-base, probably designed and made by Kenneth Clark, with Modernist sgraffito design through the brown glaze.

13.5in (34cm) high

£300-400   GC

A Fulham Pottery large charger, designed and decorated by Philip Sutton RA, the reverse with painted "JP" signature and dated 1987.

Philip Sutton is a member of the Royal Academy and produced some painted ceramic work for potteries, including the Fulham Pottery, for a few years from 1986. His free and expressive use of colour is one of his hallmarks.

1987   *21in (53cm) diam*

£200-300   WW

A St Ives Pottery stoneware studio vase, by Peter Bernard Hardy, covered in a thick, dark brown 'volcanic' glaze, the base with impressed "h" in a circle seal mark.

1970-73   *5.25in (13cm) high*

£70-90   WW

A Hilland Pottery bowl, with green and grey glaze, and sgraffito spiralling design, the base with printed windmill mark.

9.25in (24.5cm) diam

£40-60   GC

A Margaret Hine earthenware peacock, with incised and painted decoration and small chip to foot.

Margaret Hine (1927-87) worked with William Newland and Nicholas Vergette in Bayswater from 1949-54, marrying Newland in 1950. Together with Vergette, she produced a number of decorative sculptures of stylized bulls, goats, birds and other animals.

c1954   *9.5in (24cm) wide*

£300-400   WW

A Katharine Pleydell-Bouverie bowl, covered in a crackled ash glaze, incised marks, impressed seal mark.

Pleydell-Bouverie is particularly known for her ash glazes, and forms based on ancient Oriental examples.

10.5in (26.5cm) diam

£120-180   WW

A Katharine Pleydell-Bouverie stoneware flared bowl, with wrythen interior and carved bands on the exterior, milky-grey glaze, and impressed 'KPB' seal.

5in (12.5cm) diam

£180-220   **JN**

A Peter Simpson fungus-form porcelain vase, with matte blue/green glaze, the base with impressed artist's cipher and with paper exhibition labels.

As indicated by the labels, this piece was acquired from the Stephen Ferris Gallery, Nashville, probably around 1976.

c1976   *8.75in (22cm) high*

£150-200   **WW**

A William Staite Murray stoneware vase, of globular form with an everted neck and a veined thick blue glaze, the base with impressed seal and incised "1924 T.L.".

The influential William Staite-Murray shared Bernard Leach's and Charles Vyse's admiration of the forms and glazes of Oriental ceramics. He was particularly interested in high-temperature Chinese glazes, which were shown off on simple forms. The opposite of Leach, Murray saw himself as an artist, and created vases that were first and foremost intended to be decorative rather than functional. As such they were often exhibited alongside paintings and drawings by his avant-garde contemporaries. For the seal mark on the base of this piece, see p112.

1924   *4in (10cm) high*

£450-550   **WW**

EXPERT EYE – A STUDIO POTTERY VASE

These are known as cactus vases as the heads and bodies could be planted with cacti. They were popular at a time when houseplants, such as cacti, were novel and highly fashionable.

Along with Margaret Hine (see previous page) and William Newland, Vergette was part of a group Bernard Leach called the 'Picassiettes' as they were strongly, and openly, inspired by Picasso.

The whimsical, zoomorphic form of a dancing couple, as well as the sculptural stylization of their hand-built forms, is typical of his work.

This example has been broken and professionally restored – had it been in mint condition, it could have been worth twice as much.

A rare 1950s Nicolas Vergette studio pottery earthenware cactus vase, modelled as two dancing figures, incised and decorated in shades of aubergine.

17.75in (44.5cm) high

£550-650   **WW**

An Elizabeth Touroet studio pottery charger, with hand-painted abstract leaf design, the reverse inscribed "Elizabeth Touroet 1955".

1955   *14in (35.5cm) diam*

£80-120   **GC**

A Charles Vyse stoneware vase, painted with stylized floral and foliate sprays in a tenmoku glaze, the base incised "C Vyse Chelsea".

6.25in (16cm) high

£180-220   **WW**

CERAMICS

A Robin Welch flaring stoneware ovoid vase, with blistered graduated coloured glaze and impressed "Robin Welch" seal.

5.25in (13.5cm) high

£180-220   WW

A Robin Welch flaring stoneware pedestal bowl, with textured finish and glazed oatmeal rim, the base impressed "Robin Welch".

7.25in (18.5cm) high

£250-350   WW

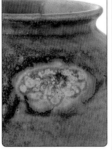

A Coldrum Pottery vase, by Reginald Wells, with a speckled green/blue glaze, the base impressed "Coldrum", with 'kiln kiss' to body and repaired rim.

Reginald Wells (1877-1951) studied at Camberwell College of Arts & Crafts before founding the Coldrum Pottery in Kent c1904. One of the first true studio potters in 20thC Britain, he moved to London c1909 and abandoned white slip-glazed red earthenwares in favour of potting large vases inspired by Oriental forms and glazes. In 1925, he moved to Sussex and developed his feel for Chinese styles with his blue and grey-white 'Soon' wares inspired by ancient Song wares. If the rim of this piece had not been damaged and if the glaze had not been disturbed by the kiln wall, the value could have been around £400.

9in (23cm) high

£150-250   WW

A Coldrum Pottery vase, by Reginald Wells, of shouldered form with a mottled blue and brown 'snakeskin' glaze, the base impressed "Coldrum".

8.25in (21cm) high

£180-220   WW

A Soon studio pottery vase, by Reginald Wells, covered in a thick, deep blue glaze, the base impressed "Soon".

4in (10cm) high

£100-200   WW

A Po Chap Yeap stoneware dish, of circular shape, painted with tenmoku and olive crayfish against a speckled grey-white ground, signed "Yeap".

Malaysian-born Po Chap Yeap (b.1927) took up pottery in Aarhus, Denmark in 1961, and became a research student in ceramics at the Royal College of Art in London in 1967. He is known for his throwing skills and for his bowls and dishes. His pieces are in collections across the world.

14in (35.5cm) diam

£450-550   JN

A 1970s Wenbury Pottery studio pottery vase, with hand-painted and moulded swirling design.

The form and swirling pattern was clearly inspired by the Whitefriars 'Guitar' vase, pattern no. 9675, designed by Geoffrey Baxter in 1967.

6.5in (16.5cm) high

£80-120   GC

FIND OUT MORE...

'Ten Thousand Years of Pottery', by Emmanuel Cooper, published by The British Museum Press, 2000.

'British Studio Potters' Marks', by Eric Yates-Owen & Robert Fournier, published by A&C Black, 2005.

ESSENTIAL REFERENCE

- The Troika Pottery was founded in 1963, at the Wells Pottery in Wheal Dream, St Ives, Cornwall. The founders were potter Benny Sirota, painter Lesley Illsley and architect Jan Thompson, who left in 1965. The first wares to be made were mostly functional or tablewares, including tiles, teapots and mugs. Glazes at this time tended to be smooth and glossy, often in white, and these can be challenging to find today.
- New shapes were introduced around 1965 and again in 1970 when the pottery moved to Newlyn in order to expand. The characteristic matte, textured glazes associated with the pottery were not in common use until c1974, although some examples were produced before this. Shapes were slip-moulded using liquid clay poured into moulds to ensure uniformity and ease of production.
- Marks on the base can help to date a piece and give you more information about who decorated it. Marks on pieces produced from 1963 to 1967 usually contain the word 'St Ives' together with a mark of a stylized trident in a square.

- After 1967 the trident mark was phased out. When the pottery moved to Newlyn in 1970, the 'St Ives' wording was dropped, although 'Newlyn' never appears.
- Painted monograms indicate the decorator responsible for the glazing. Refer to a guide, such as the ones listed at the end of this section, to identify these marks, although some have not yet been identified. The work of some decorators, for example those that became head designers, is more desirable than others – particularly on more common shapes. Dates shown here reflect the working dates of decorators combined with the production dates of a shape and any identifying marks.
- Consider the form, size, colours and style of decoration used. Practical rectangle vases are more common than items such as Anvil vases or Head Masks. Some hallmark shapes, such as Wheel vases, are consistently popular. Look for well-executed, complex geometric patterns – figural or pictorial images are rare. Always check carefully for damage, such as chips or cracks, as this reduces value considerably.

A Troika Pottery white square ashtray, the base with painted "Troika Cornwall" mark.

4.75in (12cm) wide

£180-220 **WW**

A Troika Pottery perfume flask, decorated by Anne Lewis, with glossy white glaze and stylized star and flowerhead design to each side, the base painted "Troika Cornwall England" and with 'AL' decorator's monogram.

1967-71 *6.75in (17cm) high*

£350-450 **WW**

A Troika Pottery white square dish, decorated by Ann Lewis, with glazed circular motif.

c1970 *4.5in (11.5cm) high*

£250-300 **JN**

A Troika Pottery white perfume flask, painted with a star and flowerhead design in blue, the base with painted marks.

6.75in (17cm) high

£250-300 **WW**

A Troika Pottery tall cylinder vase, decorated by Honor Curtis, with a circle design on a mottled turquoise ground, the base with factory mark and painter's monogram.

Head decorator from 1969 to 1974, Curtis decorated many cylindrical wares.

1966-74 *14.5in (37cm) high*

£200-250 **WW**

CERAMICS

A Troika Pottery Rectangle vase, modelled in low relief with geometric designs including figures, the base with painted marks.

8.75in (22.5cm) high

£120-180   **WW**

A 1970s Troika Pottery Rectangle vase, modelled in low relief with geometric patterns including figural designs, the base painted "Troika Cornwall" and with an unidentified decorator's mark.

8.75in (22cm) high

£150-200   **WW**

A Troika Pottery Rectangle vase, decorated by Alison Brigden, moulded in low relief with geometric motifs on a blue ground, the base painted "Troika" and with "AB" decorator's monogram.

1977-83   *9in (23cm) high*

£220-280   **WW**

A 1970s Troika Pottery vase, moulded with geometric motifs including a wheel and triangle, on a blue-green ground, the base painted "Troika Cornwall" and with "))" decorator's monogram for an unidentified decorator.

£180-220   **WW**

A Troika Pottery Cube vase, moulded in low relief with geometric designs and glazed in shades of beige, brown and green, the base with painted factory mark.

6in (15cm) high

£100-150   **WW**

A Troika Pottery rectangular vase, decorated by Alison Brigden, moulded in low relief with geometric shapes on a cobalt blue ground, the base painted "Troika" and with "AB" decorator's monogram.

1977-83   *7in (17.5cm) high*

£220-280   **WW**

A 1970s Troika Pottery large Cube vase, moulded with geometric patterns, the base painted "Troika Cornwall" and with an unidentified decorator's monogram.

5.75in (14.5cm) high

£250-300   **WW**

A Troika Pottery Chimney vase, decorated by Penny Black, modelled in low relief with geometric panels, in shades of blue and ochre with bronze shoulders, with painted marks and "PB" decorator's monogram.

7.75in (20cm) high

£300-400 WW

A Troika Pottery Double Base lamp base, modelled in low relief with geometric panels, in shades of ochre and blue, the base with painted marks.

Double Base lamp bases are hard to find and desirable. The pattern and bold colours on this example are highly appealing.

17in (43cm) high

£550-650 WW

EXPERT EYE – A TROIKA POTTERY ANVIL VASE

Introduced in 1965, Anvil vases are rare and highly desirable shapes.

Although the decorator is unknown, the pattern is excellent. If it been by a known decorator, it would have been worth more.

Anvil vases are typical of the geometric forms used by the pottery, but are more visually interesting than rectangular or square forms.

They are often damaged, but this one is in excellent condition.

A 1970s Troika Pottery Anvil vase, moulded with low relief geometric designs and decorated in shades of beige and blue, the base painted with "Troika", "WW" and another unknown decorator's monogram.

8.5in (21cm) high

£850-950 WW

A Troika Pottery Double Base lamp base, decorated by Alison Brigden, modelled in low relief, painted in shades of brown and green, with painted marks and "AB" decorator's monogram, restored middle section.

14.25in (36cm) high

£350-450 WW

A Troika Pottery Double Base vase, decorated by Anne Lewis, modelled in low relief and painted in shades of blue and ochre, with painted marks and "AL" decorator's monogram.

14in (35.5cm) high

£350-450 WW

A Troika Pottery Wheel vase, decorated by Sue Lowe, with different moulded geometric patterns to each side, the base painted with "Troika Cornwall" and "EW" decorator's monogram.

1976-77 *6.75in (16.5cm) high*

£250-350 WW

A 1970s Troika Pottery Wheel vase, moulded in low relief with geometric patterns on a textured and mottled beige ground, the base painted with "Troika Cornwall" and monogram for an unknown decorator, with restored rim.

6.5in (16.5cm) high

£100-200 WW

FIND OUT MORE...

'Troika Ceramics of Cornwall', *by George Perrott, published by Gemini Publications, 2003.*

www.cornishceramics.com, *includes a regularly updated list of decorators' monograms, and more.*

CERAMICS

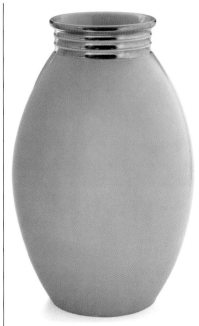

A rare Wedgwood earthenware vase, shape no.3985, designed by Keith Murray, with grey glazed body, the ribbed neck plated with silver foil, with printed factory mark and facsimile signature to base.

New Zealand-born architect Murray (1892-1981) produced Modernist designs for Wedgwood during the 1930s, which were produced until the late 1960s. Even though the simple form is typical, this glossy glaze is highly unusual, as is the colour. However, perhaps the most unusual feature is the silver neck, as all other designs were undecorated apart from the simple glaze and moulded pattern.

12.75in (32cm) high

£1,400-2,000   WW

A Wedgwood 'Dolphin' plate, designed by Laurence Whistler, with printed and painted design including a Classical dolphin, the reverse with printed marks.

11in (27.5cm) diam

£70-100   WW

A Wedgwood Fairyland Lustre 'Leapfrogging Elves' York Cup, designed by Daisy Makeig-Jones, printed and painted in colours and gilt on a black lustre ground, printed and painted marks.

4.75in (12cm) diam

£750-850   WW

A Wedgwood 'Garden' pattern teapot, designed by Eric Ravilious, with transfer-printed pattern in yellow and black, the base with printed factory marks.

4in (10cm) high

£120-180   WW

A Wedgwood quatre-lobed teapot, cover and stand, moulded with bamboo branches, impressed marks including date mark for 1870, some damages.

8in (20.5cm) high

£100-200   WW

EXPERT EYE – A WEDGWOOD FAIRYLAND LUSTRE BOWL

Makeig Jones (1881-1945) was heavily influenced by the illustrated fairy books she read as a child, as well as the work of illustrators such as Arthur Rackham and Edmund Dulac.

Showing elves leaping over toadstools, this was one of her more notable and popular patterns, and was designed in 1916.

Bowls are a popular form as they can be decorated inside and out, unlike vases. This interior is not decorated – this would have added considerably to the value.

Wedgwood's Fairyland Lustre inspired the later Carlton Ware lustre ranges, and has grown enormously in desirability and value in recent years.

A Wedgwood Fairyland Lustre 'Leapfrogging Elves' small Empire bowl, designed by Daisy Makeig Jones, decorated in colours on a black lustre ground, the base with printed factory marks.

5.25in (13cm) diam

£1,000-1,500   WW

ESSENTIAL REFERENCE

- Wemyss was produced at the Fife Pottery in Scotland, under the guidance of its owner Robert Methven Heron. He was assisted by his sister Hessie, works manager Robert McLaughlin and a young Austrian painter called Karel Nekola. Production boomed in popularity from the 1880s until the outbreak of WWI.
- It is typified by cheerful, brightly rendered hand-painted patterns of flowers, plants, fruit, birds and other animals. Shapes are usually simple to show the pattern off to its best advantage, and comprise bowls, vases, candlesticks, jugs and basin washing sets, and tablewares. They also produced a range of unusual pig and cat figurines – look out for small sleeping pigs as these can be worth over £10,000.

- Patterns were primarily designed by Nekola, who trained a small team to reproduce them, as well as decorating examples himself. Apart from Nekola, the most talented decorators were James Sharp and, from 1916, Edwin Sandland. Pieces decorated by them, particularly Nekola, will be worth a premium. Consider the shape as well as the pattern – even a small matchbox cover may be valued at a few hundred pounds due to its scarcity.
- In 1930, the rights were sold to the Bovey Tracey Pottery in Devon. Karel Nekola's son Joseph moved with them, where he continued to paint until his death in 1942. Eccentric, colourful and charming, Wemyss has remained popular for many years and looks set to continue.

A Wemyss 'Gordon' pattern small plate, decorated with irises, impressed mark "Wemyss Ware/R.H. & S."

c1900   5.5in (14cm) diam

£150-200   L&T

A Wemyss 'Gordon' pattern dessert plate, decorated with purple irises, with impressed mark "Wemyss/R.H. & S.", and printed "T. Goode & Co." retailer's marks, restored.

c1900   8in (20.5cm) diam

£180-220   L&T

A Wemyss side plate, decorated with red clover, impressed mark "Wemyss/R.H. & S."

c1900   8.25in (21cm) diam

£170-200   L&T

A Wemyss small plate, decorated with blackcurrants on a branch, with impressed "Wemyss Ware/R.H. & S." mark, and painted "T Goode & Co." retailer's mark.

c1900   5.5in (14cm) diam

£180-220   L&T

An early 20thC Wemyss side plate, decorated with strawberries, impressed "Wemyss" mark and painted "T. Goode & Co." retailer's mark, one small chip to rim.

7.5in (19cm) diam

£150-200   L&T

CERAMICS

An early 20thC Wemyss sponge dish and liner, decorated by James Sharp with pink, purple and brown chrysanthemums, impressed and painted "Wemyss" mark and painted "T. Goode & Co." retailers mark, restoration to one handle.

7.75in (20cm) diam

£340-450   **L&T**

An early 20thC Wemyss 'Lady Eva' vase, decorated by Edwin Sandland with daffodils, impressed and painted "Wemyss" marks.

8in (20.5cm) high

£400-500   **L&T**

An early 20thC Wemyss frilled vase, decorated by Edwin Sandland with dragonflies, impressed and painted "Wemyss" marks, restored.

5.75in (14.5cm) high

£350-450   **L&T**

A Wemyss small beaker vase, decorated with a black cock and hen, indistinct impressed "Wemyss Ware/R.H. & S." mark.

c1900   *4.25in (11cm) high*

£150-200   **L&T**

An early 20thC Wemyss 'Bon Jour' pattern cream jug, decorated with a brown cock, inscribed "BonJour", impressed and printed marks, glaze frits to spout, stained rim.

2.75in (7cm) high

£250-350   **L&T**

A Wemyss pig, painted in shades of black and pink on a white ground, impressed marks, re-glued ear and hairline crack.

Had this pig not been damaged, it may have been worth more than twice as much.

A Wemyss pink glazed pig, impressed marks.

6.25in (16cm) wide

£400-500   **WW**

6in (15cm) wide

£500-700   **WW**

ESSENTIAL REFERENCE

- West German ceramics produced from the 1950s to the '70s have become highly collectable recently after being considered unfashionable for many years.
- This period saw an explosion of innovation and design in West German pottery, which changed considerably during each decade. Companies such as Bay Keramik, Dümler & Breiden, Emons & Söhne and Ruscha underwent a revival, and were joined by new companies such as Scheurich and Otto Keramik.
- During the 1950s, forms could be curving and organic, or simple and geometric. Angled handles and rims were common. Patterns were typically painted in bright, primary colours. Jug vases with handles became common and were produced for the next few decades. During the 1950s, handles were often strongly angled, taking on ring forms from the 1960s onwards. Although these jugs can be used, they were intended primarily as decorative objects.
- The 1960s and '70s saw a complete change in style, with the order of structured patterns giving way to glazes that were trailed, dripped or daubed over the body of the piece.

The colour and texture of the glaze became of primary importance. Many of these were thick, bubbling 'lava' glazes in bright colours such as orange and red, and were sometimes arranged in bands or stripes.

- Makers can be identified by considering the shape, colour and type of glaze, and the style of the moulded, inscribed or impressed marks on the base. Some may also have labels, although these have often been removed. The area is still relatively new, and original information is hard to come by, as many companies have closed or destroyed their archives, there is still much research to be undertaken.
- Look for the wilder thick glazes and often unusual forms from the late 1960s and '70s known by collectors as 'Fat Lava', as these tend to be more desirable and valuable. Many were only produced in limited numbers at the time, with 'tamer' designs in browns, beiges and other single colours on simple forms being much more common. Size is important, with large vases designed to stand on the floor being highly sought-after and comparatively rare today.

A 1950s-60s West German Scheurich jug vase, with gloss multicoloured chevrons and vertical lines on a matte cream background, the base moulded "627-29 W.Germany".

11in (28cm) high

£30-40   **GC**

A 1950s West German jug vase, with moulded "Made in Germany" mark and with other indistinct marks to the base, with remains of red and black triangular sticker reading "Seit 1858".

14.5in (37cm) high

£10-15   **GAZE**

A 1950s West German Silberdistel 'Kairo' pattern jug vase, the base marked "336-20", and with original foil label.

This pattern was introduced in 1957.

8in (20cm) high

£18-22   **OUT**

A 1950s West German Matrau pottery jug, with integral handle and glazed in matte black and glossy white.

13.5in (34cm) high

£70-100   **QU**

A 1950s-60s West German Ruscha jug vase, no. 314, with a turquoise crackle glaze, the base moulded "314".

This shape was designed by Kurt Tschorner, Ruscha's innovative and influential designer, in 1954.

14.25in (36cm) high

£50-80   **QU**

CERAMICS

A 1950s West German Hessiches Majolika Fritz Dienes ball watering can, hand-painted with blue and yellow stripes, with brass spout and handle.

c1953   *17in (43cm) long*

£50-80   **QU**

A 1950s West German Ruscha hand-painted 'Milano' pattern pot, designed by Cilli Worsdorfer, the base marked "232/2.5".

1954-60   *5in (12.5cm) high*

£22-28   **OUT**

A 1950s German Karlsruhe Majolika Manufaktur wall plate, with hand decorated scene of waterbirds on a lake at night, the back with factory mark and label.

16.5in (42cm) diam

£100-150   **QU**

A 1950s West German ES-Keramik charger, probably designed by Willi Hack, with hand-painted and multicoloured abstract pattern, unmarked.

This large example is decorated with a typically 1950s design.

8.75in (22cm) diam

£50-80   **OUT**

EXPERT EYE – A WEST GERMAN BAY KERAMIK DISH

The design is typical of the 1950s with its flat planes of bright, primary colours outlined in black.

The pattern was introduced c1956 and is seen to best advantage on dishes such as this.

Patterns are unique on each piece. The abstract, almost cell-like, style is also typical of the period.

Patterns were often named after exotic and romantic destinations, often in Italy. This pattern is 'Florenze', others include 'Milano', 'Venedig' and 'Palma'.

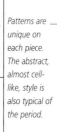

A 1950s Sgraffomodern blue and white glazed porcelain wall plate, with pattern of three stylized cranes and maker's mark to reverse.

12.25in (31cm) long

£80-120   **QU**

A 1950s West German Bay Keramik 'Florenze' pattern wall charger dish, the reverse moulded "West-German 447".

10.25in (26cm) diam

£70-100   **HLM**

A set of three West German ceramic vases, the bases moulded "West Germany", with indistinct numbers.

7.75in (19.5cm), 9.75in (25cm) and 11.75in (30cm) high

£30-40 **GAZE**

A West German Bay Keramik vase, with grey speckled finish and blue band with orange circular motifs, the base moulded '"West-Germany 660-20".

8in (20cm) high

£20-30 **GC**

A West German Scheurich vase, with red band printed with green squares, with matte textured white glazed upper and lower parts, the base moulded "203-32".

12.75in (32.5cm) high

£40-60 **GC**

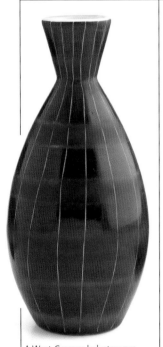

A West German baluster vase, with gun-metal matte grey and gloss red bands and white vertical scored lines, the base with hand-painted marks "KK 6196 Made in Germany Handpainted".

7.75in (19.5cm) high

£25-35 **GC**

A West German Bay Keramik vase, possibly designed by Bodo Mans, with glossy white and multicoloured linear and splodged design on a brick red ground, the base moulded "West Germany 1065-30".

12in (30.5cm) high

£40-50 **GC**

An Austrian Keramos waisted vase, with hand-decorated banded and dripped design, the base moulded "664-18 Austria".

The survival of the original label here is useful. It shows that this piece of Austrian pottery was produced by the German company Carstens. In 1953 they had signed a deal with the Goldscheider factory to produce a number of their products.

7.25in (18.5cm) high

£25-30 **GC**

CERAMICS

An early 1960s West German Scheurich vase, with light green pumice glaze and dripped streaks of brown and orange glaze, the base moulded "Foreign 244 22".

8.75in (22cm) high

£15-20   AEM

A West German waisted vase, with dripped silvery gun metal grey glazed bands over a thin black lined ground, the base impressed "3769/22".

9in (23cm) high

£40-60   GC

A West German Carstens tapering vase, with black cross-hatched pattern over a dark green ground, the base moulded "1227-21 W.Germany".

8in (20.5cm) high

£30-50   GC

A West German Ceramano 'Agina' pattern floor vase, with soldier and geometric pattern picked out with a creamy lava glaze, the base inscribed "106/3 'Agina' Ceramano W-Germany Handarbeit".

c1961   *18.5in (47cm) high*

£100-150   QU

A West German Ceramano 'Tourmalin' pattern large floor vase, shape no. 27, decorated with bands, incised marks.

Ceramano's wide range of designs have become highly sought-after recently. Each was hand decorated, so the designs vary from piece to piece. Ceramano pieces can be recognised by the marks which were inscribed by hand into the base. Typically these include the pattern name, the decorator's monogram, and the word 'Handarbeit' (handworked).

21.25in (54cm) high

£200-300   WW

A West German Bay Keramik 'Kongo' pattern ovoid vase, with incised lines and multicoloured gloss oval patterns, the base impressed "543/30 Germany".

c1960   *13.75in (35cm) high*

£200-300   GC

A very rare 1970s West German Carstens double gourd vase, with purple glaze and handle, unmarked.

6in (15cm) high

£22-28   OUT

A late 1960s West German Scheurich floor vase, with moulded and tube-lined multicoloured circles, the base moulded "529-38".

15in (38cm) high

£80-120   **OUT**

A Ruscha bottle vase, the matte textured dark grey glaze over-dripped with a white streaked blue 'lava' glaze, the base impressed "22/18".

These impressed numbers are an unusual form of marking for Ruscha, whose marks are typically moulded.

7in (18cm) high

£50-70   **MHC**

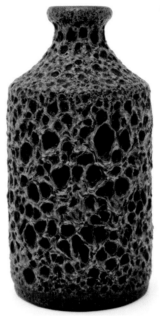

A late 1960s West German Ruscha vase, with banded form and dripped glossy brown and orange lava glazes, the base unmarked.

6.25in (16cm) high

£18-22   **OUT**

A West German Roth Keramik cylinder vase, with foamy white glaze over dark brown and glossy orange glazed band, with original gilt Roth label.

In a complete departure from 1950s styles, this almost looks like a machine component.

11in (28cm) high

£40-60   **GAZE**

A West German Roth Keramik square section jug, with inset handle and dripped and mottled brown, tan, blue and green glaze, unmarked.

This form was previously attributed to U-Keramik, but a US collector has now identified them as having been produced by Roth Keramik.

11.75in (30cm) high

£50-80   **GC**

EXPERT EYE – A ROTH KERAMIK VASE

These vases can be found in a number of different colours - red is the most common, followed by purple, with blue and yellow being rarer, and white the rarest.

On all other colours, the lava glaze is black – it is only known in black and white on the purple colourway.

Its unusual shape and design are typical of the late 1960s, as are the bold colours, which match plastic furniture designs and progressive interior designs of the day.

Prices for these hard to find vases have leapt in recent years, primarily as they are so visually stunning and unusual, yet typical of the period.

A West German Roth Keramik shaped vase, moulded with concave purple glossy glazed ovals between white and black textured bubbled strands, the base moulded "W.Germany".

10.25in (26cm) high

£150-200   **GC**

CERAMICS

A 1970s West German Otto Keramik cylinder vase, the glossy red glaze with matte cratered textured black glaze bubbling through, unmarked, with felt base.

9.5in (24cm) high

£50-80   **GC**

A 1970s West German Otto Keramik small posy bowl, with a bright yellow glaze over a matte black 'lava' glaze, the base with applied blue felt.

As well as being typical of the best 'fat lava' designs, this small size is extremely rare, perhaps as it was of only limited use at the time.

2in (5cm) high

£30-50   **OUT**

A West German Scheurich jug, with bubbling yellow glaze over a grey-blue ground, the base moulded "474-16".

6.25in (16cm) high

£25-35   **GC**

A West German Scheurich floor bottle vase, with a trailed, zig-zag brown lava glaze pattern over a matte cream and glossy blue glaze, the base moulded "241-64 W.Germany".

25.5in (64cm) high

£150-250   **QU**

A West German ovoid vase with curving rim, the white body with a semi-matte grey lava glaze over a bright orange vitreous glaze, the base inscribed "S".

The maker of this piece is not known, although the inscribed 'S' may indicate Silberdistel, who produced glazes with similar textures. Its stunning visual appearance makes it highly desirable.

7.5in (19cm) high

£60-80   **BH**

EXPERT EYE – AN ES-KERAMIK VASE

ES-Keramik stand for Emons & Söhne, which was founded in 1921 and closed in 1974. The company began producing art ceramics in 1954, with many being exported to Canada and Australasia.

Thickly applied, bubbling lava glazes are typical of the company's production at this time, but this combination of colours is very hard to find.

The form is also very rare, an example with a much shorter neck and no handle is also known, but is slightly more common.

It retains its original gilt foil label, which identifies it, as the base is unmarked.

A West German ES-Keramic jug vase, with tall neck and handle and dripped matte red and blue-grey lava effect glaze over a blue-grey ground, unmarked, with shield-shaped foil label.

11.25in (28.5cm) high

£70-100   **GC**

FIND OUT MORE...

'Fat Lava: West German Ceramics of the 1960s & 70s', *by Mark Hill, ISBN: 978-0-95528-650-6, www.markhillpublishing.com.*
'From Spritzdecor to Fat Lava', *by Kevin Graham, self-published, kj_graham@gmx.de.*
'Keramik der 50er Jahre, by Dr Horst Makus', *ISBN: 9783897902206, published by Arnoldsche, 2007.*

An Arts & Crafts porcelain vase, attributed to Amphora, fashioned to appear clad in hammered and rivetted copper, with two pierced handles and large panels of embossed stylised trees, stamped "552 N", a couple of glaze flecks and one small chip to base.

20.5in (52cm) high

£400-500   **DRA**

An Ault Pottery Propeller vase, designed by Dr Christopher Dresser, covered in a running green glaze, unmarked.

5.5in (14cm) high

£200-300   **WW**

EXPERT EYE – AN ETTORE SOTTSASS TEAPOT

The form was inspired by the Art Deco Odeon style with its clean-lined, stepped and architectural form.

It was designed by notable Postmodern architect and designer Ettore Sottsass. Sottsass's work, and Postmodern design in general, is rapidly gaining in interest and value.

The two handles mirror Mickey Mouse's ears and the form is almost cartoon-like. Popular culture was a strong influence on the Postmodern style.

Beware of unmarked examples without the moulded wording to the base as these are copies produced during the 1980s.

An Ablebest teapot, designed by Ettore Sottsass in 1971 and made by P. Hinton and G. Stevens, with cobalt blue glaze, moulded wording to base.

Ablebest was based at 296 Upper St, London, N1.

1971   *9in 23cm) high*

£250-300   **WW**

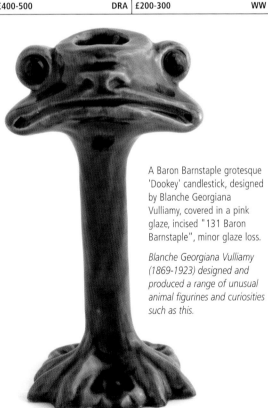

A Baron Barnstaple grotesque 'Dookey' candlestick, designed by Blanche Georgiana Vulliamy, covered in a pink glaze, incised "131 Baron Barnstaple", minor glaze loss.

Blanche Georgiana Vulliamy (1869-1923) designed and produced a range of unusual animal figurines and curiosities such as this.

5.75in (14.5cm) high

£220-280   **WW**

A 1950s-60s Beswick vase, shape no. 1343, shape designed by Albert Hallam in 1954.

This pattern may have been designed by James Hayward, who was decorating manager from 1932 to 1957, and then art director. He produced over 3,000 patterns and glazes.

10in (25cm) high

£80-100   **BEV**

A 1950s-60s Beswick tapered vase, shape no. 1370 designed by Albert Hallam.

12in (30.5cm) high

£200-250   **BEV**

CERAMICS

A 1950s-60s Beswick lipped globe bowl, shape no. 1352 designed by Albert Hallam in 1954.

1954-62   4.5in (11cm) high
£60-80   **BEV**

One of a pair of 1920s Bursley Ware short candlesticks, with hand-painted floral designs.

2.75in (7cm) high
£40-50 (pair)   **BAD**

An Italian Bitossi 'E-Vaso' double vase, designed by Paolo Palma and Carlo Vannicola in 1990, the central urn-shaped vase sliding out of the main vase.

This was available in many different colours and vase shapes, with a more curving form being designed in 1996.

9.75in (24.5cm) high
£120-180   **GM**

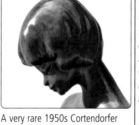

A very rare 1950s Cortendorfer Keramik room fountain, the seated figure of a young girl with a graduated mottled turquoise-black glaze, the figurine marked "315".

32.75in (83cm) high
£350-450   **QU**

EXPERT EYE – A BURSLEY WARE CHARGER

Charlotte Rhead (1885-1947) was the daughter of notable ceramics designer Frederick Rhead. She joined her father at Bursley in 1922 and worked there until 1927. She returned in 1947 after working for a number of other companies.

Not only is it a charger, a form that shows the pattern off well, but it is also extremely large and would have been expensive in its day, making it rare today.

Most of her designs were produced using the tube-lining technique, where liquid clay is piped onto the surface to outline the design. The areas created by the clay are then filled in by hand with a coloured glaze.

A Crown Ducal vase, pattern no. 5802, designed by Charlotte Rhead, decorated with tube-lined oranges and leaves picked out in gilt on a biscuit ground.

c1938   6.25in (16cm) high
£80-100   **JN**

A Della Robbia twin-handled amphora shaped vase, by Hannah Jones, covered in a dripped glaze, the base with incised marks and painted green monogram.

10.25in (26cm) high
£250-350   **WW**

A 1920s Bursley Ware 'Chinoiserie' pattern wall plaque, designed by Charlotte and Frederick Rhead, decorated with a central floral medallion within a floral painted border with panels, the reverse with printed marks.

18.25in (46.5cm) diam
£900-1,000   **FLD**

A limited edition Dennis China Works 'Polar Bear' pattern vase, designed by Sally Tuffin, from an edition of 29, the base with impressed and painted marks.

A version with a black, rather than blue sky was produced in an edition of only 14 examples. The pattern was retired in 2004.

8in (20.5cm) high

£100-200   WW

A 1930s Editions Etling pastille burner, designed by A. Godard, modelled as a Chinese scholar seated before a table, printed marks, small chip to tea cup.

6.75in (17cm) high

£180-220   WW

An Art Deco T.F.& S. Ltd 'Rainbow Phoenix' pattern hand-painted vase, the base impressed "6070/1".

T.F. & S. Ltd stands for Thomas Forester & Sons, whose factory in Longton, Staffordshire ran from 1883 to 1959.

8.75in (22cm) high

£100-150   BEV

A Fulham Pottery 'Priscilla' figurine, model no. GF2, designed by Eric Griffiths, glazed with a creamy glaze, the base with printed marks.

Priscilla was designed in 1956 and is from a set of six figurines, which were also available in unglazed natural stoneware or a 'Bronzeglow glaze'.

1956-60   *14.25in (36cm) high*

£100-150   GROB

A Goldscheider red clay wall mask, modelled as a young woman with white hair holding her hand to her face, the reverse with maker's marks.

12.25in (31cm) high

£80-120   QU

A 1930s Goldscheider 'Tragedy' wall mask, the reverse with printed and painted marks.

14.5in (37cm) high

£600-900   FLD

A pair of Gouda 'Juliana' pattern Ivora vases, with tapered tall necks and decorated with stylised floral motifs and scrolls, with hand-painted marks to bases.

12in (30.5cm) high

£300-400   FLD

CERAMICS

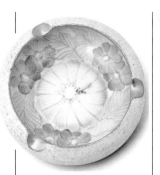

A Gray's Pottery ashtray, hand-painted with floral decoration and gilt trim.

4.5in (12cm) wide

£40-50   **BAD**

A Dutch Pieter Groeneveldt hand-built small cube vase, with mottled and lightly textured bronze brown glaze over a deep brown matte underglaze, on four feet, unsigned.

5.75in (14.5cm) high

£20-30   **PC**

EXPERT EYE – A GOLDSCHEIDER 'BUTTERFLY GIRL' FIGURINE

Goldscheider's Art Deco figurines are highly sought-after for their size, quality, grace and elegance. Examine all areas closely for damage.

It was designed by Josef Lorenzl (1892-1950), one of Goldscheider's most notable designers, along with Stefan Dakon, who also designed many elegant bronze figures.

Produced by Goldscheider primarily from 1922 to 1935, these figurines represent the fashions of the period, such as the flowing cape and bobbed hair shown here.

The complex form is made up of a number of moulded pieces which were assembled using liquid clay, known as slip, and then carefully 'finished'. Later figurines, such as those produced by Myott in England from the 1940s, are not as finely finished.

A Goldscheider 'Butterfly Girl' figurine, designed by Josef Lorenzl, with moulded signature to the stepped base and printed and painted marks.

18.75in (47.5cm) high

£2,200-2,800   **FLD**

A Dutch Pieter Groeneveldt hand-built small cube vase, with a lightly textured mottled blue glaze over a brown underglaze, on four feet, unsigned.

Pieter Groeneveldt (1889-1982) studied as a painter and draughtsman at the Academy of Arts in Amsterdam. He then turned to pottery, opening his first pottery near The Hague in 1923. Much of his production, which varied between unique studio works and serial studio works, was sold through his nearby flower shop Schéhérazade. His experimental glazes were inspired by Oriental glazes and typically covered simple, modern forms such as this.

5in (12.5cm) high

£30-50   **PC**

A Dutch Pieter Groeneveldt cylinder vase, with a deep purple grainy glaze, the base impressed "11 10".

4.75in (12cm) high

£18-22   **OUT**

A 1930s Belgian Roger Guerin small squat vase, with mottled brown, blue, red and green glazes, the base with impressed "R. Guerin" signature, and hand inscribed "007".

2in (5cm) high

£100-150   **TOJ**

A 1930s Hollinshead & Kirkham transfer-printed Chintzware triangular pin tray, with gilt rim, marked "H&K".

Hollinshead & Kirkham of Tunstall were active in the Potteries, Staffordshire, from c1876 to 1956.

5.25in (13cm) wide

£15-25 BAD

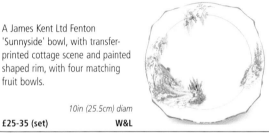

A Hornsea Pottery 'White Bud' pattern jardinière, no. 361, from the Home Decor range designed by John Clappison, covered in a matte white glaze, the base with printed mark and chip.

1960-62 8in (20.5cm) high

£60-80 WW

A Hancock & Sons Morris Ware tapering cylindrical vase, by George Cartlidge, decorated with stylised tulips in red and green over an ochre ground, the base with printed and painted marks.

8in (20cm) high

£300-500 FLD

A Hancock & Sons Morris Ware bottle, pattern no. C72-1, by George Cartlidge, decorated with a stylised flower motif in purple, green and ochre, the base with printed and painted marks.

12in (30.5cm) high

£400-500 WW

A James Kent Ltd Fenton 'Sunnyside' bowl, with transfer-printed cottage scene and painted shaped rim, with four matching fruit bowls.

10in (25.5cm) diam

£25-35 (set) W&L

A limited edition Kevin Francis 'Clarice Cliff' toby jug, designed by Douglas Tootle, from an edition of 350, the base with printed marks.

1990 9in (23cm) high

£250-300 WW

A late 1960s Langley cache pot, designed by Glynn Colledge, with hand-painted stylised floral and foliate pattern, the base with printed windmill mark and painted "P".

Staffordshire-based Lovatt & Lovatt, who produced Langley Pottery, was acquired by Denby in 1959. This explains how Colledge (1922-2000) came to design for Langley. The pattern and palette are loosely based on his 'Glynbourne' range for Denby, designed between 1960 and 1961 and produced into the 1970s.

4in (10cm) high

£20-30 MHC

A 1930s Art Deco Lemanceau cat figurine, designed by Charles Lemanceau, with graduated brown and beige glazes, with signature mark to the body.

11.75in (29.5cm) high

£180-220 WW

CERAMICS

An Art Deco John Maddock & Sons Ltd Royal Ivory 'Sunset Ware' hexagonal vase, with hand-painted decoration including cypress trees and gilt handles.

8.25in (21cm) high

£100-150   **BEV**

A Mak'Merry part-dinner service, comprising vegetable dishes and covers, plates, bowls, jugs, a collection of pots and covers, and salt and pepper shakers, each decorated with fruit and blossoms on a yellow ground, with painted marks.

The hand-decorated Mak'Merry pottery was produced during the 1920s by members of the Scottish Women's Rural Institute, founded in 1917 by notable suffragette and women's rights campaigner Catherine Blair.

£1,000-1,500   **L&T**

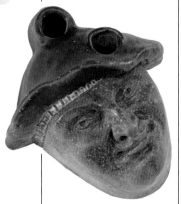

A Martin Brothers stoneware figural pencil holder, in the form of a Scotsman wearing a tam o'shanter, marked "Martin London".

3.5in (9cm) high

£450-650   **DRA**

A Maw & Co. large footed vase, by Charles Henry Temple, with flared neck, decorated with a band of stylised floral motifs within banded borders in tonal green and blue lustre over an oatmeal ground, with painted signature to base.

14.5in (37cm) high

£600-700   **FLD**

A 1950s-60s Midwinter Stylecraft plate, decorated with a black and white geometric pattern.

It is likely that this was decorated by a student, or was a sample piece made at Midwinter. The white areas were masked off before the black glaze was applied.

9.5in (24cm) wide

£80-100   **WW**

A Mettlach Art Nouveau charger, by R. Thevenin, with a maiden at a pond, marked "Mettlach VB Gegh…Nachbildung Geschutzt 2542, R. Thevenin".

The long-haired maiden and the natural surroundings are typical of Thevenin's designs, and the strong Art Nouveau style is highly sought-after.

15.75in (40cm) diam

£2,000-2,500   **DRA**

CERAMICS

A Midwinter hand-painted porcelain 'Larry The Lamb' figurine, the base stamped "Plichta H.H. & G Ltd Reg'd No 791377".

1934　　　　*8.75in (22cm) high*

£12-18　　　　**GAZE**

A Midwinter hand-painted and printed 'Capri' pattern television cup and saucer set, designed by Jessie Tate in 1955.

Saucer 8.75in (22cm) wide

£50-70　　　　**VC**

A Mintons polar bear figurine, covered in a uranium orange glaze, unmarked.

5.75in (14.5cm) high

£100-150　　　　**WW**

A Mintons Secessionist range jardinière, designed by John Wadsworth, with tube-lined decoration of panels and columns with flowers and leaves in shades of red and green, the base with printed marks.

8in (20.5cm) high

£150-200　　　　**WW**

EXPERT EYE – A PAIR OF MIDWINTER VASES

These were part of a range of studio wares designed by Jessie Tait and influenced by her return to the potter's wheel at the Burslem College of Art.

The monochrome patterns were mainly tube-lined by hand, and included the striped 'Tonga' and a pattern of short vertical lines known as 'Stubble'.

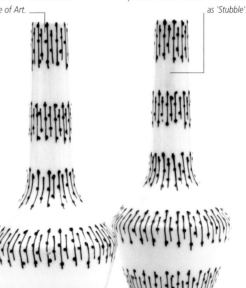

The range was introduced in 1956 and produced until 1960. It was important enough to be illustrated in 'Pottery & Glass' trade magazine in 1958.

They are not commonly found, particularly in pairs. Had one not been damaged they may have been worth 25 per cent more.

A 1950s Midwinter pair of 'Bands & Dots' pattern F201 shape vases, with black tube-lined design over a white glossy ground, the bases with printed marks, one with hairline crack to rim.

7in (17.5cm) high

£220-280　　　　**FLD**

A Mintons jam jar and cover, with hand-painted pansy designs and butterfly knop, the base painted "E435U .J".

The Minton mark was changed to "Mintons" from c1873, which can help with dating certain pieces. The style of this piece places it in the 1920s or '30s.

4in (10cm) high

£80-120　　　　**BEV**

A Pierrefonds large stoneware vase, covered in a blue crystalline glaze, with impressed and painted marks.

21.5in (54cm) high

£250-300　　　　　　　　WW

A Pilkington's Royal Lancastrian ovoid vase, by William S. Mycock, painted with a fish amid stylised ripples in shades of blue on a silvery ground, the base with impressed marks and date code for 1933.

1933　　　　　　　*5.5in (14cm) high*

£300-350　　　　　　　　WW

A Portmeirion Potteries Cylinder shape 'Greek Key' pattern coffee pot.

1968-late 1970s　　*13in (33cm) high*

£25-35　　　　　　　　FFM

A Portmeirion Potteries screen-printed 'Talisman' pattern storage jar, introduced in 1962.

6.25in (16cm) high

£10-15　　　　　　　　FFM

A set of three Portmeirion Potteries screen-printed 'Talisman' pattern storage jars with lids, introduced 1962.

4.75in (12cm) high

£35-45 (set)　　　　　　FFM

A German Rosenthal porcelain candle holder, with four curving legs and gilt trim.

c1952　　　　*5in (12.5cm) high*

£70-90　　　　　　　　QU

An Alfred Powell wash set, comprising a ewer, basin, soap dish and toothbrush holder, each painted with bands of foliage, painted marks.

£600-800　　　　　　　　L&T

A 1950s German Rosenthal porcelain trapezoidal dish, the interior glazed in black, the base with underglaze green factory mark.

9in (23cm) wide

£80-120　　　　　　　　QU

CERAMICS

A 1970s Rosenthal Studio Line porcelain vase, with transfer-printed black and gilt pattern, the base with underglaze green factory mark, decorator's monogram, and numbered "1584".

16.25in (41cm) high

£120-180 QU

A Royal Norfolk Petra range vase, shape no. 112, designed by Colin Melbourne, with facsimile signature to base and impressed marks.

6in (15.5cm) high

£40-60 GC

A Royal Stanley 'Pomegranate' pattern ginger jar and cover, decorated with a tube-lined pattern of fruits and leaves, the base with printed marks.

This was produced in imitation of Moorcroft's successful pattern.

8.25in (21cm) high

£300-400 WW

A Royal Dux classical figure group, model no. 1498, modelled as young love, painted in colours, the base with impressed marks and applied pink triangle mark, minor chips.

27.5in (70cm) high

£500-600 WW

A 1930s Grimwades Royal Winton yellow teapot, with a floral handle and knop, patent number "301262".

£70-100 BAD

A 1930s Royal Winton Beehive hand-painted milk jug.

5in (13cm) long

£30-40 BAD

An Art Deco Royal Winton sugar sifter, decorated with ducks in flight, with chrome-plated top.

6.25in (16cm) high

£80-120 BAD

A Royal Winton Chintz 'Fireglow' pattern Ascot shape sugar bowl.

4.75in (12cm) wide

£30-50 BEV

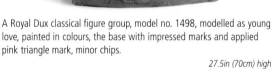

A Ruskin Pottery handled vase, decorated with a dripped, mottled green, cream and blue crystalline glaze, with impressed marks.

1933   8.25in (21cm) high

£200-300   WW

A Sadler novelty racing car teapot, covered with a green glaze, the base with impressed marks.

Look out for the rare cream version with transfer-printed designs by Mabel Lucie Attwell, as this can be worth over £500.

8.75in (22.5cm) long

£50-70   WW

A German Schmider black-glazed wall hanging hand, designed by Anneliese Beckh.

1957   8.25in (21cm) long

£80-120   QU

ESSENTIAL REFERENCE – SHELLEY HARMONY WARE

A Shelley conical Harmony Dripware 'volcano' vase, with impressed and printed marks to the base.

The Harmony Dripware range, with its characteristic dripped glazes, was released in 1932 and was produced into the 1940s. The designs were produced by Shelley's designer Eric Slater, who came up with the idea by accident. After mixing too much turpentine with a glaze, he found that when he applied the glaze to a vase, it ran down the sides forming drips. Slater developed the idea, combining two or more colours and eventually produced an entire range applied to simple, modern and clean-lined bodies that show the effects off to their best advantage. Some effects were accentuated by spinning the vase at speed. The pattern on each vase is unique due to the way it was produced. The range of shapes, sizes and colours is vast. Look out for teapots and coffee pots as these are rare.

5.25in (13cm) high

£80-120   BAD

A Shelley Harmony Dripware footed conical vase, the base with printed and impressed marks.

6.5in (16.5cm) high

£70-100   BAD

A Shelley Banded ware Regent shape plate.

1933-34   10in (25cm) wide

£15-25   BAD

A Shorter & Sons 'Fish' service, comprising two large platters, sauce boat and tray, and six plates, all moulded as scaly fish and painted in butterscotch with green highlights, the bases with printed marks.

Platter 13.75in (35.5cm) wide

£60-80   WW

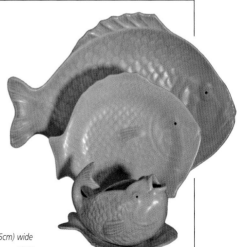

CERAMICS

A Staffordshire Potteries transfer-printed mug, made to commemorate the Apollo 11 moon landing, showing astronauts and the lunar module.

c1969   *3.6in (9cm) high*

£10-15   **MTS**

A SylvaC textured brickwork cylindrical vase, mould no. 3811.

8.5in (21cm) high

£12-18   **BAD**

A Watcombe Pottery jug, designed by Dr Christopher Dresser, covered in a running green glaze, unmarked.

8in (20.5cm) high

£180-220   **WW**

A 20thC ovoid presentation vase, painted with an Arabian horse 'Al-shawafah' in landscape frieze and with flowering plant to reverse,

18in (46cm) high

£400-500   **BRI**

EXPERT EYE – A WATCOMBE POTTERY JUG BY CHRISTOPHER DRESSER

Christopher Dresser (1834-1904) is widely acknowledged as Britain's first industrial designer. He also wrote about design and his work contributed to the development of the Arts & Crafts and late 19thC Anglo-Japanese movements.

His designs are highly sought-after and often display a quirky modernity.

The mark on the base was used to denote registered designs, the numbers and letters contained in this mark show that the design for this jug was registered on 3rd June 1872.

This jug can also be found glazed, as shown above, and also without the hallmarked silver mount, in which case the values can be reduced by up to 30 per cent.

A late 19thC Continental earthenware jug, moulded as a seated mallard duck.

15.75in (40cm) high

£80-120   **BIG**

A Watcombe Pottery terracotta jug, designed by Dr Christopher Dresser, the base with impressed factory mark and printed registered design diamond mark, the silver cover and mount with hallmarks for London 1872, minor chips.

9.25in (23.5cm) high

£250-300   **WW**

A late 19thC continental porcelain 'Out by Jingo!!' fairing, of dental interest, titled in gilt to base, rubbing to the gilt.

Fairings were mass-produced figurines made from the late 19thC to the early 20thC. Often featuring gruesome, salacious or amusing subject matter, they were given away or sold at fairs and fairgrounds. Many were damaged or thrown away over time, making some rare today. Although this is unmarked and most probably by another maker, many detailed fairings such as this were made by German company Conte & Boehme, who often used a mark of a shield with an arm holding a dagger.

5in (13cm) wide

£300-400   **WW**

A late 19thC continental porcelain 'A Long Pull and a Strong Pull' fairing, of dental interest, titled to base, hairline cracks and a small chip.

5in (13cm) wide

£250-300   **WW**

An English penguin figure, with hand-painted decoration, unmarked.

6.25in (16cm) high

£15-20   **BAD**

A hand-painted ceramic dog ashtray, probably Japanese.

3.25in (8cm) high

£40-50   **BH**

A Continental wall plate, decorated in the style of Gio Ponti, with a hand-painted design of a piper, the reverse with indistinct marks.

7.25in (18.5cm) diam

£60-100   **WW**

A German moulded blackbird ashtray, probably 1930s, with finely moulded details, unmarked.

This is very similar to pieces by Schaefer & Vader.

6.75in (17cm) high

£100-150   **BEV**

A 1970s Hungarian Zsolnay, Pecs glazed and cut large drum vase, stamped with the factory mark and inscribed "15 20".

This is a scarce and unusual design for Zsolnay, who are better known for their boldly iridescent glazes. The form, pattern and glaze recall West German ceramics of the time. It is also a large, monumental Modernist piece.

17in (43cm) high

£300-400   **GC**

ESSENTIAL REFERENCE

- Trained modeller, Andrew Clark, started the Sugarlump Studio in 1995 and, inspired by his love of children's TV, created a range of figures and scenes based on numerous TV shows, including The Clangers, The Magic Roundabout, The Herbs and Sooty. The studio closed in September 2002.
- As each piece was hand-painted by a small team, production numbers are limited, even for standard pieces. The rarest piece is the Magic Roundabout 'Potting Shed', identified by its green roof, as only 90 examples were produced between April 1995 and August 1996.

- Other pieces likely to be desirable are those produced in small limited editions, or those retired early. Examples should retain their original packaging and paperwork to be worth the values given here.
- Given the short life of the studio, the limited production numbers, and the continuing popularity of the subject matter, it is likely that Sugarlump figurines will remain sought-after.
- See the company's website, which is still maintained, for a full list of figurines produced: www.sugarlumpstudio.com.

A Sugarlump Studio 'Gabriel' figurine, from the Bagpuss collection, mint and boxed.

2000-02   *3in (7.5cm) high*
£25-30   **MTB**

A Sugarlump Studio 'The Mouse Organ' figurine, from the Bagpuss collection, mint and boxed.

1999-2002   *4.5in (12cm) high*
£25-35   **MTB**

A Sugarlump Studio 'Bagpuss' figurine, from the Bagpuss collection, mint and boxed.
1999-2002   *3in (7.5cm) high*
£30-40   **MTB**

A Sugarlump Studio 'Professor Yaffle' figurine, from the Bagpuss collection, mint and boxed.

1999-2002   *3in (7.5cm) high*
£25-30   **MTB**

A Sugarlump Studio 'Major Clanger' figurine, from the Clangers collection, mint and boxed.

1996-2002   *3.3in (8.5cm) high*
£20-25   **MTB**

A Sugarlump Studio 'Tiny Clanger' figurine, from The Clangers collection, mint and boxed.

1996-2202   *3in (8cm) high*
£20-25   **MTB**

A Sugarlump Studio 'Uncle Clanger' figurine, from The Clangers collection, mint and boxed.

1997-2002   *3in (8cm) high*
£20-25   **MTB**

A set of Sugarlump Studio 'Chive' figurines, nos. 1, 2, 3 and 4, from The Herbs collection, mint and boxed.

1999-2002   *2in (5cm) high*

£20-25 (each)   **MTB**

A Sugarlump Studio 'Sage The Owl' figurine, from The Herbs collection, mint and boxed.

A Sugarlump Studio 'Parsley The Lion' figurine, from The Herbs collection, mint and boxed.

1999-2002   *3in (7.5cm) high*

£25-30   **MTB**

1999-2002

2.5in (6cm) high

£20-30   **MTB**

A Sugarlump Studio 'Sir Basil' figurine, from The Herbs collection, mint and boxed.

A Sugarlump Studio 'Tarragon The Dragon', from The Herbs collection, mint and boxed.

A Sugarlump Studio 'Basil' figurine, from The Magic Roundabout collection, mint and boxed.

A limited edition Sugarlump Studio 'Buxton The Blue Cat' figurine, from an edition of 2,000, from The Magic Roundabout collection, mint and boxed.

1999-2002	*3in (8cm) high*	*2000-02*	*3in (7cm) high*	*1998-2002*	*2.5in (6.5cm) high*	*1999*	*3in (8cm) high*
£20-30	**MTB**	**£20-30**	**MTB**	**£25-30**	**MTB**	**£30-40**	**MTB**

A Sugarlump Studio 'Mr MacHenry' figurine, from The Magic Roundabout collection, mint and boxed.

1995-2002   3.5in (9cm) high

£30-40   **MTB**

A Sugarlump Studio 'Mr Rusty' figurine, from The Magic Roundabout collection, mint and boxed.

1995-2002   4in (10.5cm) high

£20-30   **MTB**

A Sugarlump Studio 'Paul' figurine, from The Magic Roundabout collection, mint and boxed.

1998-2002   3.5in (9cm) high

£22-28   **MTB**

A Sugarlump Studio 'Rosalie' figurine, from The Magic Roundabout collection, mint and boxed.

1997-2002   3in (7.5cm) high

£20-25   **MTB**

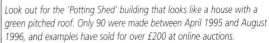

A Sugarlump Studio 'Ermintrude's Potting Shed', from The Magic Roundabout collection, mint and boxed.

Look out for the 'Potting Shed' building that looks like a house with a green pitched roof. Only 90 were made between April 1995 and August 1996, and examples have sold for over £200 at online auctions.

3in (7.5cm) high

£20-25   **MTB**

A Sugarlump Studio 'Roundabout', from The Magic Roundabout collection, mint and boxed.

Available for a long time period, this is a large and heavy piece. Its value today is usually close to its original retail price of £95.

1996-2002   10in (25cm) high

£80-100   **MTB**

A limited edition Sugarlump Studio 'Scene 2 featuring Ermintrude & Zebedee' mini-scene, from an edition of 499, signed by Andrew Clark, mint and boxed.

2001   4.75in (12cm) long

£35-45   **MTB**

ESSENTIAL REFERENCE

- Robert Harrop was a freelance modeller working in ceramic resin before setting up his own company in Shropshire, with his wife Margaret, in 1986.
- Their first range was the 'Doggie People', which became so popular the company was able to move to larger premises. It is still in production today. Further collections were soon added, primarily based on vintage children's TV shows, including The Clangers, The Magic Roundabout, Camberwick Green and Bagpuss, as well as comics The Beano and Dandy.
- A collectors' club was established in 1994 and some special models are released to club members only. Standard models are retired regularly and some designs are updated during the lifetime of the model.

- In general, prices for retired models have often remained at the level of the original selling price on the secondary market, which is unusual for such figurines. This is largely due to their collectability, quality and that collectors are still trying to complete collections or ranges, thus supporting the prices.
- Prices for some of the more popular figurines and ranges are also rising as new collectors come to the market, or as people collect popular characters such as Dennis the Menace or Gnasher.
- Look for early examples, those that were produced for only a short period, or special editions. Models should retain their original paperwork and packaging.

A Robert Harrop 'Andy Capp' figurine, no. AC01, from the Andy Capp collection, mint and boxed.

2006   *4.5in (11.5cm) high*

£20-25   **MTB**

A Robert Harrop 'Flo' figurine, no. AC02, from the Andy Capp collection, mint and boxed.

2006   *4.75in (12cm) high*

£20-25   **MTB**

A Robert Harrop 'Big Eggo' figurine, no. BD30, from The Beano & Dandy Collection, in mint condition with original packaging tube.

This card cylinder is an early form of packaging. At the time of writing, all models from the BD collection have been retired.

1999   *6.75in (17cm) high*

£40-45   **MTB**

A limited edition Robert Harrop 'Bagpuss Oh Hear What I Sing' figurine, no. BGLE1, from an edition of 1,500 and part of the Bagpuss collection, mint and boxed.

2005   *5in (13cm) high*

£20-25   **MTB**

A Robert Harrop 'Ship in a Bottle' figurine, no. BG07, from the Bagpuss collection, mint and boxed.

2005   *4.5in (11cm) high*

£18-22   **MTB**

A limited edition Robert Harrop 'Border Collie Graduate' figurine, no. CC131, from the Doggie People Collection, from an edition of 5,000, mint and boxed.

Bulldogs are particularly popular figurines from this collection. CC numbers before 20 tend to be worth around £30-40, depending on condition and presence of the box.

6in (15cm) high

£20-25   **MTB**

CHARACTER COLLECTABLES

A Robert Harrop 'Mr Platt Clockmaker' figurine, no. CG44, from the Camberwick Green collection, mint and boxed, retired in 2005.
2001-05   *4in (10cm) high*
£12-15   **MTB**

A Robert Harrop 'Windy Miller Hard At Work' figurine, no. CG61, from the Camberwick Green collection, mint and boxed.
2003   *4in (10cm) high*
£12-15   **MTB**

A Robert Harrop 'Tiny Clanger' figurine, no. CL04, from the Clangers Collection, mint and boxed, retired in 2007.
2005-07   *3.5in (9cm) high*
£15-18   **MTB**

A Robert Harrop 'Dougal' figurine, no. MR01, from the Magic Roundabout collection, mint and boxed, retired in 2007.
2006-07   *3in (7.5cm) high*
£20-25   **MTB**

A Robert Harrop 'Dylan' figurine, no. MR06, from the Magic Roundabout collection, mint and boxed.
2006   *5.75in (14.5cm) high*
£20-25   **MTB**

A Robert Harrop 'Bean - Fantastic Mr Fox' figurine, no. RD23, from the Roald Dahl collection, mint and boxed.

A Robert Harrop 'Fatty' figurine, no. DO03, from the Beano Dodgems Collection, mint and boxed.
2001   *6in (15cm) high*
£28-32   **MTB**

7in (18cm) high
£20-25   **MTB**

A Robert Harrop 'Parker' figurine, no. TBF06, from the Thunderbirds collection, mint and boxed.
2004   *6.75in (17cm) high*
£20-25   **MTB**

ESSENTIAL REFERENCE

- The market for character collectables is driven by nostalgia. Collectors often look for characters associated with childhood fun and games, or famously associated with the past. Pieces featuring characters from comic books, TV programs and films, or those associated with particular brands, are enthusiastically collected.
- More famous characters generally have larger collecting bases and tend to fetch the largest sums. However, do not ignore minor characters, these can be rarer and collectors will often need to complete a set. The rarest pieces can be those produced before a character became famous.
- Limited editions are of great interest to collectors as they become valuable if demand exceeds supply. Try to ensure limited editions are from genuinely small production runs. The quality of a piece is also important, detailed moulding

and decoration can add to desirability, as can an accurate depiction of a character. Always keep limited edition pieces in mint condition, with boxes and paperwork.
- As many items were intended for promotional use, they were not necessarily made to last. This ensures that the few pieces left in truly mint condition demand great attention. Officially licensed products will typically be more accurate and more sought-after.
- The nostalgic nature of this market ensures that it ebbs and flows as generations mature and begin to demand characters from their own childhoods. This means that collectors should always be on the hunt for the next potentially collectable character. Recent additions to the character collectables market have included Buzz Lightyear and Wallace and Grommet.

A Barbie hand-painted ceramic head mug, by Enesco, based on the 1959 Evening Splendour doll.

1997   5.75in (14.5cm) high

£10-15   BH

ESSENTIAL REFERENCE – CARE BEARS

The Care Bear characters were created in 1981 by the American Greetings company for use on greetings cards. This was followed by a range of plush toys by Kenner in 1983 and a number of animated TV series and films during the 1980s. The line was relaunched in 2007 and is still in production today. It is estimated that over 40 million Care Bears were sold during the 1980s, so standard bears in good, but used, condition are not difficult to find. Collectors often concentrate on prototypes, limited editions or samples, or may choose to collect by decade.

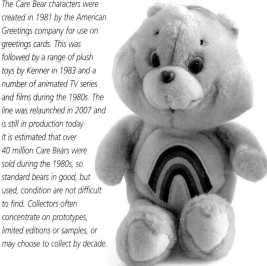

A Care Bear 'Cheer Bear' large pink soft toy, by Kenner, with fabric tag, in good condition.

1983   18in (45.5cm) high

£4-5   AEM

A Beverly Hills 90210 watch, by Fada Industries, the photographic dial showing Brandon and Ian, with original card box, in mint condition.

Box 3.5in (9cm) high

£4-6   BH

A Care Bear 'Wish Bear' soft toy, by Vivid Imaginations, in near mint condition with slightly water damaged original card shop tag.

These were released under the 'Those Characters From Cleveland' brand to celebrate the 20th anniversary of the first Care Bear.

2003   10.25in (26cm) high

£2-3   AEM

An American Bugs Bunny alarm clock, by Ingraham USA, marked "Bugs Bunny © Warner Bros. Cartoons, Inc." and "Time-Telling Dial © Richie Prem. Corp."

4.75in (12cm) high

£100-150   PWE

An Alvin the Chipmunk novelty telephone, licensed by Bagdasarian Productions and made in Hong Kong.

1984   15in (38cm) high

£12-18   AEM

EXPERT EYE – A CHRISTOPHER ROBIN NURSERY BOWL AND COVER

The Ashtead Pottery was in production from 1923 to 1935, a mere 12 years. Given the factory's short life, Ashtead pieces are scarce, and are sought-after when they come to the market.

Although the pottery was praised at the time for its fresh designs, particularly its Art Deco pieces, the factory closed in part due to the death of its founder Sir Lawrence Weaver.

A Christopher Robin nursery set was presented to the future Queen Elizabeth II in 1928.

The combination of a sought-after pottery and beloved childhood characters makes this a valuable piece. Pieces were easily damaged by children, making items in excellent condition rare.

An Ashtead Pottery Christopher Robin nursery set bowl and cover, printed in colours with characters from Winnie the Pooh, based on the designs of E.H. Sheppard, printed marks.

6in (15cm) diam

£400-500   **WW**

A Pizza Hut The Flintstones Kids 'Wilma' glass.

1986   *6in (15cm) high*

£2-3   **AEM**

A 1950s Noddy painted wooden eggcup, by Fairy Lite Products and licensed by Noddy Subsidiary Rights Co. Ltd, mint and boxed.

During the 1960s, these were made in plastic and are less desirable. They have a value of around £5-7 in this condition.

4in (10cm) high

£12-14   **MTB**

A Howdy Doody printed cotton handkerchief.

8in (20cm) wide

£28-38   **SOTT**

A Howdy Doody colour transfer-printed tin cookie jar, by Kagran Corp.

A pair of Dutch Laurel & Hardy moulded plastic money banks, modelled as policemen, with scales to each side showing the level of savings.

A Howdy Doody painted celluloid pin.

1.5in (4cm) long

£5-7   **TSIS**

8.5in (21.5cm) high

£50-80   **BH**

1968   *10.5in (26.5cm) high*

£15-20   **MTB**

A 1970s Magic Roundabout squirting 'Dougal', by Bendy Toy, mint and sealed in original packaging.

Loose without its packaging, this toy is worth around £10. Always examine Bendy Toys carefully, as the foam plastic is prone to 'dissolve' into a powder.

£32-38   MTB

A late 1960s Welsh The Magic Roundabout 'Ermintrude' hand-made shell sculpture, licensed by Serge Danot, with conch shell body.

4.25in (10.5cm) high

£10-12   MTB

A late 1960s Welsh The Magic Roundabout 'Florence' hand-made shell sculpture, licensed by Serge Danot, with sea anemone shell head.

Given the delicacy of these shells, it is surprising that Florence has survived intact for over 40 years.

7.25in (18.5cm) high

£20-25   MTB

EXPERT EYE – A SIGMA 'MISS PIGGY' MUG

Sigma Ceramics made a number of good quality Muppet Show collectables, many of which are highly sought-after.

As Miss Piggy and Kermit are the most popular Muppets, they are easier to find than characters such as Dr. Teeth and Animal, with Gonzo being the rarest.

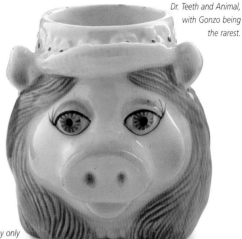

As the company only made Muppet merchandise from 1978 until the early 1980s, they are hard to find today. The attention to detail, note Miss Piggy's eyes for example, also make them desirable to collectors.

As well as 14 ceramic pieces, the company also produced papier-mâché Christmas ornaments,

A Muppet Show 'Miss Piggy' hand-painted mug, by Sigma Ceramics.

1979-81   *4.25in (10.5cm) high*

£8-12   AEM

A McDonalds 'Mayor McCheese' Collector Series transfer-printed glass.

1975   *5.75in (14.5cm) high*

£1-2   AEM

A Muppet Show Christmas satin glass ornament, dated 1983, featuring Kermit and Miss Piggy, in mint condition with box.

Out of the box, this delicate and colourful bauble can still be worth around £15.

1983   *Box 4.75in (12cm) high*

£20-30   MTB

A pair of Muppet Show child's slippers, by Cleverleys of England, unworn, with original box.

Box 8in (20cm) long

£12-18   MTB

A Shoe People 'PC Boot' money bank, by Action Games & Toys, mint and carded.

Although comparatively popular at the time, the Shoe People cartoon ran for one season only. Merchandise is hard to find today, but values are often low as there are so few collectors.

1986   9.25in (23cm) high

£18-20   **MTB**

A Planet of The Apes 'Galen' money bank, by PlayPal Plastics Inc. and licensed by 20th Century Fox.

The character of Galen was played by Roddy McDowall in the 1974 Planet of the Apes TV series. He previously played 'Cornelius' in two films and 'Caesar' in two further prequels. PlayPal also made a 'Dr. Zauis' money bank that is worth a similar amount.

1974   10.25in (26cm) high

£8-12   **BH**

A Popeye Speed Boat, by Harmony C&D Ind. Ltd, Hong Kong, licensed by King Features Syndicate Inc.

£22-28   **MEM**

A 1980s Rainbow Brite 'Starlite' plush horse stuffed toy, with fabric tag, in good condition.

1983   12.5in (32cm) high

£4-6   **AEM**

A Marx Toys Rupert the Bear plastic friction-driven tricycle toy, licensed by Beaverbrook Newspapers, mint and boxed.

1973   Box 4.25in (11cm) high

£30-40   **MTB**

A Superman game, by Hasbro Games, nearly complete, missing one flying card.

1978   Box 19.75in (50cm) wide

£10-12   **BH**

A 'Superman Time Capsule!' promotional comic, for Kellogg's Sugar Smacks, with artwork by Win Mortimer and Curt Swan.

There were two other titles given away with this promotion: "Duel in Space" and "The Super Show of Metropolis". All three titles are sought-after. This title was reprinted in 'Superman' issue 250, released in April 1972.

1955   7in (17cm) long

£50-70   **TSIS**

A 1940s-50s Superman large plaster shop display figure, unmarked.

The missing 'S' logo from his chest, shows it is an unauthorised figure.

15.25in (38.5cm) high

£150-250   **BH**

A Tarzan badge, with artwork by Ross Manning licensed by Edgar Rice Burroughs Enterprises.

1975   3.25in (8.5cm) diam

£4-6   **BH**

A limited edition Beswick 'Dr Mopp' figurine, no. TR5, from the Trumpton Series, from an edition of 2,500, mint and boxed with matching numbered certificate.

2001   *5.75in (14.5cm) high*

£40-50   **MTB**

A limited edition Beswick 'Windy Miller' figurine, from the Trumpton Series, from an edition of 2,500, mint and boxed with matching numbered certificate.

Beware of examples that come without their matching numbered certificates and without a limited edition number inscribed into the ceramic on the base. These are seconds and are generally worth under 50 per cent of this value.

2001   *5.75in (14.5cm) high*

£40-50   **MTB**

A Wizard of Oz 'Mayor' hand-painted figurine bell, by Presents, mint with original box.

1989   *6in (15cm) high*

£15-25   **MTB**

An Annie Oakley plastic mug, with photographic insert of Gail Davis playing the character in the 1954-57 TV series.

This plastic mug came from Gail Davis' personal estate, as she used to sign them for fans.

4in (10cm) high

£6-9   **BH**

A Davy Crockett mug, by Norton Ceramics, with impressed factory marks to base.

4in (10cm) high

£12-18   **BH**

A Hopalong Cassidy Med-O-Pure Cottage Cheese printed tinplate tip tray.

4.75in (12cm) diam

£12-18   **BH**

A 1950s Hopalong Cassidy paper-over-card pencil case, by Hasbro.

9in (23cm) long

£20-30   **BH**

A Lone Ranger hair brush, with worn transfer on the wooden handle.

1939   *4.25in (11cm) high*

£3-5   **BH**

A very rare 1950s Lone Ranger carnival hand-painted chalkware figure, marked with impressed name to the base.

These cheaply made figures were given away as prizes at carnivals and fairs. Due to their fragile nature, intact examples are scarce. Collectable in their own right, the subject matter makes this even more desirable.

10.25in (26cm) high

£50-70   **BH**

COMMEMORATIVES

A Royal Doulton Lord Nelson commemorative stoneware jug, glazed in blue with moulded portrait of Nelson flanked by moulded maritime scenes.

1905　　　　　　　*8in (20cm) high*

£80-120　　　　　　　　**SAS**

A Royal Doulton Lord Nelson commemorative small stoneware jug, with blue glaze, moulded portrait, wording and cartouche of his victory.

1905　　　　　　*3in (7.5cm) high*

£80-120　　　　　　　　**SAS**

A 19thC Staffordshire pottery 'Nelson' character jug, hand-painted in typical colours, with blue coat.

11.75in (30cm) high

£50-70　　　　　　　　**SAS**

A Wilkinson Ltd Sir John French 'French pour les Francais' character jug, designed by Sir Francis Carruthers Gould, issued by Soane & Smith Ltd during WWI, decorated in underglaze colours, enamelled and gilded, with printed marks.

10.25in (25.5cm) high

£250-350　　　　　　　　**SAS**

A Wilkinson Ltd Admiral Jellicoe 'Hell Fire Jack' character jug, designed by Sir Francis Carruthers Gould, issued by Soane & Smith Ltd during WWI, decorated in underglaze colours, enamelled and gilded, with printed marks and facsimile signature of Carruthers Gould.

10.5in (26cm) high

£200-300　　　　　　　　**SAS**

A Wilkinson Ltd of Royal Staffordshire Pottery Lord Kitchener 'Bitter for the Kaiser' character jug, designed by Sir Francis Carruthers Gould, issued by Soane & Smith Ltd during WWI, decorated in underglaze colours, enamelled and gilded, with printed marks and facsimile signature of Carruthers Gould.

For more information about Wilkinson's range of toby jugs designed by Sir Francis Carruthers Gould, please see p.385.

c1917　　　　　*10.25in (26cm) high*

£450-550　　　　　　　　**ROW**

A Kevin Francis 'Winston Churchill' character jug.

9in (23cm) high

£60-80　　　　　　　　**SAS**

A Continental porcelain 'Tommy Atkins' caricature figurine.

Tommy Atkins is the full term used to describe a common British soldier in WWI. 'Tommy' is the more commonly used, shortened form.

7in (18cm) high

£40-60　　　　　　　　**SAS**

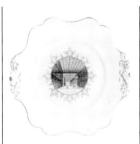

A Great Exhibition commemorative porcelain plate, printed with a 'View of the Interior of the Building for the Exhibition of the works of Industry of all Nations', chip to rim back, printed mark 'Green London' and registration mark.

1851   *10in (25.5cm) diam*

£12-18   **HAMG**

A 1901 Glasgow Exhibition commemorative plate, by the Nautilus Porcelain Company, with moulded rim.

A sepia version of this pattern can also be found, but is less valuable.

     10in (25.5cm) diam

£90-100   **RCC**

An Ashtead Pottery British Empire Exhibition commemorative lidded jar, the lid painted with the lion motif, the base with printed factory mark.

1924   *5in (12.5cm) diam*

£60-80   **WW**

A Wembley China binocular-shaped crested fairing, commemorating the 'British Empire Exhibition'.

This larger piece is based on miniature crested ceramics, such as those made by Goss and Carlton.

1924   *3in (7.5cm) wide*

£30-35   **RCC**

A Liptons brass tea caddy, commemorating the British Empire Exhibition of 1924, with impressed logo.

1924   *5.25in (13cm) high*

£10-15   **PC**

A Wedgwood 1951 Festival of Britain commemorative mug, chipped.

This rare mug was designed by Norman Makinson for Wedgwood, and is of higher quality than much Festival memorabilia.

1951

£250-350   **SAS**

COMMEMORATIVES

A Wallis Gimson commemorative pottery plate, for the 1887 H.M. Stanley Expedition, printed in black, with chipped rim.

9.5in (24cm) diam

£40-50   SAS

A Wallis Gimson octagonal plate, commemorating the Emin Pasha Relief Expedition, printed in colours and in mint condition.

Aiming to relieve the besieged Emin Pasha, this was the last major European expedition into Africa, and was led by Henry Morton Stanley.
c1887   9.5in (24cm) diam

£200-300   H&G

A pottery stand commemorating the 1875 Arctic Expedition, printed in pale blue with the expedition motif, the reverse inscribed 'Alert' above a fouled anchor, chipped and repaired.

7.25in (18cm) diam

£120-180   SAS

An early 20thC Norwegian commemorative parcel gilt spoon, for Roald Amundsen's successful expedition to the South Pole, 14-17th December 1911, no maker's mark.

c1912   6.5in (16.5cm) long

£250-350   WW

A rare Sarreguemine Nicholas II, Tsar of Russia commemorative plate, for his visit to France to sign a treaty between the two countries.

A companion piece was also made with a portrait of the Tsarina. They are more commonly found with the surrounding decoration in brown, which are usually worth under £100.
1896   8.5in (21.5cm) diam

£220-280   RCC

A rare T. & R. Boote commemorative jug, for Sir Robert Peel, the moulded ground with applied relief of Peel, the base transfer-printed with a design of a lady grieving beside a plaque.

Sir Robert Peel (1788-1850) is best remembered as laying the foundations for the police force in the UK. He was also instrumental in the repeal of the Corn Laws and oversaw the formation of the modern Conservative party from the Tory party.

6.75in (17cm) high

£300-400   SAS

A limited edition Chown commemorative teapot, for the state funeral of Ronald Reagan, with photographic image of Prince Charles and Margaret Thatcher attending the funeral, commissioned by Paul Wyton & Joe Spiteri, from an edition of five.
2004   7in (18cm) wide

£45-55   RCC

A Paragon commemorative bone china tazza, for the opening of the St Lawrence Seaway, with blue and gilt transfer-printed decoration.

The St Lawrence Seaway is a system of canals that permits ocean-going vessels to travel from the Atlantic Ocean to the Great Lakes, as far as Lake Superior.
1959   6in (15cm) diam

£30-50   TCF

A Metlox teddy bear cookie jar, with impressed marks to base and some damage to lip.

Without damage to the inside lid, this could be worth around £30-40.

11.75in (29.5cm) high

£8-12   **AEM**

A very rare Regal China Co. 'Goldilocks' cookie jar.

Regal's Goldilocks usually features on the top ten list of most wanted cookie jars. However, examples have been reproduced by Brush McCoy and are marked as such. Modern reproductions are also available over the internet. Reproductions are typically smaller, and may have different over-glaze colours. Look on the base for authentic Regal marks including '405' and 'Pat-Pending'.

12.5in (31.5cm) high

£200-250   **AEM**

A McCoy 'honey bear' cookie jar.

8.25in (21cm) high

£25-40   **AEM**

An American Bisque pig cookie jar, with hairline crack to neck and some chips to the internal rim.

Had he not been damaged, he could have been worth over twice as much.

12.25in (31cm) high

£25-40   **AEM**

A Treasure Craft 'graduate' owl cookie jar.

11in (28cm) high

£8-12   **AEM**

A Treasure Craft Victorian house cookie jar, with damage to the inside rim and a few chips.

11.5in (29cm) high

£10-15   **AEM**

A Metlox apple cookie jar, the base impressed "Made in U.S.A."

7.5in (19cm) high

£18-22   **AEM**

ESSENTIAL REFERENCE

- Vibrantly coloured Bakelite and plastic jewellery exploded onto the fashion scene during the 1920s. Great leaps in the development of plastics saw a wider variety of colours being introduced. They could also be economically moulded, or cast, and then carved with patterns by hand or machine.
- The Great Depression caused by the Wall Street Crash of 1929 meant less money was available to spend on luxuries. While jewel-encrusted, platinum cocktail jewellery remained popular with the very wealthy, Bakelite and plastic jewellery provided an affordable yet fashionable alternative for others. The bright colours, novelty shapes and themes also added cheer at difficult times.
- Generally, it is the better carved, brighter coloured, chunkier pieces that obtain the best prices today. Cherry red, bright green and orange are the most desirable colours. The creamy butterscotch, also known as 'creamed corn', is also desirable. Duller colours such as black or brown are less so. Novelty or quirky shapes such as human faces or animals are also popular. Later plastics from the 1950s are often of poorer quality, but are still collectable.
- Also consider the work that went in to making a piece. Assembled items, made up of different parts, or chunky pieces deeply cut by hand will be worth more than a thin piece cut by machine or with moulded patterns. Geometric patterns, typical of the Art Deco style, are also sought-after. Always examine a piece closely for signs of damage such as holes, cracks or chips, which are very difficult to repair.

A red stained cream plastic bangle, carved with rose and leaf motifs.

2.75in (7cm) diam

£45-55   P&I

A salmon pink stained cream plastic bangle, carved with rose, daisy and leaf motifs.

2.75in (7cm) diam

£25-35   P&I

A pale green, pink and butterscotch stained plastic bangle, well carved with flower and leaf motifs.

This is nicely carved and the complementary colours have been applied to mark out the individual flowers.

3in (8cm) diam

£45-55   P&I

A cream plastic, wide bangle, carved and pierced with rose, daisy and leaf motifs.

2.75in (7cm) diam

£30-50   P&I

A pale blue stained cream plastic bangle, well carved with flower and leaf motifs, and lightly stained in pink.

3in (8cm) diam

£30-50   P&I

A 1950s clear Lucite bangle, containing dried flowers and grasses.

3.25in (8cm) diam

£35-45   AEM

A 1930s hand-carved faux-tortoiseshell bakelite bangle.

As well as being cut on the round, the bangle is also cut and shaped to the sides, adding an extra level of detail and interest.

3.25in (8cm) diam

£50-80   BB

A 1930s carved butterscotch bakelite dress clip, the metal clip marked "Made in USA".

1.75in (4.5cm) high

£30-40   P&I

A cast and carved green and yellow mottled phenolic leaf brooch, inlaid with metal bead 'veins'.

3.25in (8.5cm) high

£60-90   P&I

A 1940s carved and painted lucite cicada brooch.

2in (5cm) long

£50-80   BB

A 1930s carved brown bakelite elephant brooch.

2.25in (5.5cm) long

£40-60   BB

A 1930s carved and painted Lucite horse brooch.

3.25in (8cm) long

£45-50   AEM

A 1930s black bakelite lifebuoy brooch, with original woven two-colour gimp 'rope'.

Naval and maritime themes were popular during the 1930s.

1.75in (4.5cm) diam

£100-150   BB

A 1930s chrome-plated metal sailboat brooch, with inset green bakelite sail.

1.5in (3.5cm) high

£22-28 P&I

A 1930s green plastic beaded necklace.

23.75in (60cm) long

£40-60 P&I

EXPERT EYE – A CARVED LUCITE SET

Lucite was a popular material for jewellery and handbags from the 1930s-50s. It can also be found in many different transparent colours, which are desirable.

As here, thick blocks of Lucite often contained designs, which were typically floral. Other, scarcer forms are known and these can add value.

A three-dimensional form was carved and hollowed out from the back.

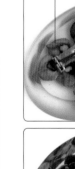

The space was then injected with coloured paste to give the design form and colour. The more detailed the design, the more valuable the piece will be.

A 1950s Charmeuse Lucite brooch and earrings set, reverse-carved and filled, with original flock-covered card box.

It is rare to find a complete set like this, particularly with its original box.

Brooch 2.25in (5.5cm) wide

£12-18 AEM

A 1930s chrome and coral red bakelite necklace, with bead drop.

17.75in (45cm) long

£50-70 P&I

A 1930s green bakelite cube necklace, with metal chain and nine cubes.

17.5in (44.5cm) long

£70-100 P&I

A salmon pink beaded necklace, assembled with plain and carved floral beads.

31.5in (80cm) long

£50-70 P&I

A 1930s carved yellow and green marbled bakelite ring.

1.25in (3cm) high

£22-28 BB

ESSENTIAL REFERENCE

- Costume jewellery in all its variety provides a look for every taste and every occasion. Due to its dramatically rising popularity over the past few years, values have risen considerably. While many pieces still remain affordable, the best and most iconic pieces have begun to obtain prices close to those paid for precious jewellery. These classic pieces are by renowned makers such as Trifari, Stanley Hagler, Elsa Schiaparelli, Miriam Haskell and Joseff of Hollywood. Names are usually marked on the back.

- The second most important consideration is style and eye-appeal. While this can help to identify the maker, it is also an important consideration on its own. As many people buy to wear, a great design with a strong 'sparkle factor' may command a higher value. Always look on the back as some pieces may be marked 'Sterling' indicating that the piece is made from solid silver. This material was commonly used during the 1930s and '40s.

- Missing stones will reduce value and, although many can be replaced, it can be hard to find ones that match exactly in size or colour. Some beads or faux pearls, such as those used by Miriam Haskell, are even harder to replace as they were supplied exclusively at the time and are not made to the same quality today.

- Also examine the way the stones are set as this indicates quality too. The best are held in place with small metal prongs, and this should be done by hand. Many have three-dimensional effects, and may be hand-wired onto a frame – these tend to to be worth more. The quality, colour and size of the stones is also important – look out for chunky 'baroque' faux pearls and vibrant Murano glass beads.

A Canadian Bond Boyd silver-plated flower brooch, with faceted amethyst rhinestones.

£40-60   TCF

A Canadian Bond Boyd silver-plated leaf brooch, with applied scrolling filigree decoration over metal mesh.

£25-35   TCF

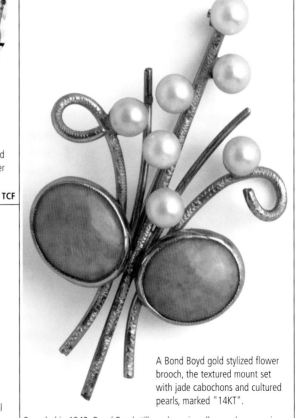

A Bond Boyd gold stylized flower brooch, the textured mount set with jade cabochons and cultured pearls, marked "14KT".

A Canadian Bond Boyd silver flower and leaves brooch, set with light blue rhinestones.

£80-100   TCF

A Canadian Bond Boyd vermeil brooch, set with faceted, colourless and light blue rhinestones, marked "Sterling".

£80-100   TCF

Founded in 1940, Bond Boyd still produces jewellery and accessories today, although much of it is for the corporate market or showing Canada's maple leaf symbol.

£150-250   TCF

COSTUME JEWELLERY

A Canadian Bond Boyd vermeil flower brooch, with textured petals and curling stem, marked "Sterling".

£40-60   **TCF**

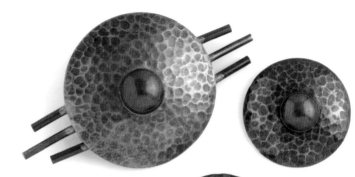

A Canadian Bond Boyd silver earrings and brooch set, with tarnished and hammered effect, and copper centres and rods.

Brooch 2in (5cm) diam

£150-250   **TCF**

A BSK gold-plated metal cat's head brooch.

1.5in (4cm) wide

£2-4   **AEM**

A 1960s Capri starfish-shaped textured gold-plated brooch, set with a faceted plastic 'stone'.

3.25in (8cm) widest

£6-9   **AEM**

A pair of Coro pink faux pearl cluster earrings, on original card.

Card 2.75in (7cm) wide

£2-3   **AEM**

A Coro silver-plated flower brooch.

3.75in (9.5cm) wide

£5-7   **AEM**

A Dodds rhodium or silver-plated maple leaf brooch, set with amber rhinestones.

2.75in (7cm) high

£5-7   **AEM**

A pair of 1960s Givenchy blue glass and silver metal oval 'Yin and Yang' style earrings.

1in (2.5cm) high

£12-18   **BB**

A Grosse gold-coloured metal stylized flower brooch, with inset turquoise nugget, the back stamped "Grosse 1961".

1961   *2.5in (6cm) diam*

£25-35   **BB**

A Har gold-plated branch shaped brooch, set with blossoms of turquoise and faceted ruby red rhinestones.

2.5in (6.5cm) high

£25-35   **AEM**

A pair of Miriam Haskell gold-coloured metal stylized flower clip earrings, set with faux pearls, the back stamped "Miriam Haskell".

1.25in (3cm) diam

£25-35   **BB**

A 1970s Miriam Haskell gold-plated necklace and earring set, with moulded Egyptian pharaoh and hieroglyph design.

This is likely to have been inspired by the 'Treasures of Tutankhamun' travelling exhibition, which ran from 1972 until 1979.

Pendant 1.5in (3.5cm) high

£100-150   **BB**

A Miriam Haskell gold-coloured metal quill-shaped brooch.

2.75in (7cm) high

£22-28   **BB**

A pair of Hobé gold-coloured metal drop earrings, set with green jade-like cabochons.

2.75in (7cm) high

£25-35   **BB**

A Kramer gold-plated leaf shaped brooch, prong set with multicoloured, faceted rhinestones and aurora borealis, and cast aurora borealis iridescent glass leaves, the mount marked "Kramer" and "Austria".

This is an interesting shape and is notable for the Austrian aurora borealis stones that are usually a sign of quality.

2.5in (6cm) wide

£40-60   **AEM**

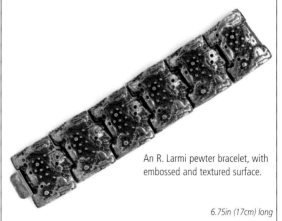

An R. Larmi pewter bracelet, with embossed and textured surface.

6.75in (17cm) long

£150-200   **TCF**

COSTUME JEWELLERY

A Canadian Rafael gold-plated pendant and necklace, with hammered effect, the inset red glass cabochon with black inclusions, the back marked "Rafael Canada".

Serbian-born Rafael moved to Canada in 1970 and began making jewellery shortly after. His avant-garde designs produced during the 1970s and early '80s are known for their moving parts, use of different metals and Murano glass.

£100-150   TCF

A Rafael copper pendant and necklace, the hammered surface set with deep red glass cabochons, the back marked "Rafael Canada".

5in (12.5cm) wide

£80-120   TCF

EXPERT EYE – A SCHIAPARELLI BROOCH

Elsa Schiaparelli (1890-1973) was a famous fashion designer whose costume jewellery, made from the 1920s to the 1960s, is highly collectable today.

The elements are wired by hand onto a supporting frame, showing the skill that went into making Schiaparelli's jewellery.

Themes from nature, such as flowers and leaves, are typical in her work – here the brooch resembles a peacock's tail.

The unusual long, oval faceted stones are prong-set, which is another sign of quality.

A 1950s Schiaparelli green rhinestone and faux mother-of-pearl 'peacock fan' brooch, the hand-wired back stamped "Schiaparelli".

2in (5cm) diam

£100-120   AEM

A Rafael brass brooch, with multicoloured inset glass cabochons around a faux pearl and cross motif, the back marked "Rafael Canada".

2in (5cm) wide

£35-50   TCF

A Rafael brass ring, with inset oval red glass, the back marked "Rafael Canada".

£40-60   TCF

A Schiaparelli gold-coloured metal brooch, the conical filigree mount set with a deep brown glass cabochon with gold foil inclusions, the back stamped "Schiaparelli".

1.75in (4.5cm) diam

£20-30   GCA

A Nettie Rosenstein vermeil Oriental piper brooch, with enamel highlights and inset rhinestone details, stamped "Sterling".

Vermeil is the term used to describe gold-plated solid silver.

2.75in (7cm) high

£100-150   BB

EXPERT EYE – A SHERMAN SET

Sherman is Canada's best known costume jewellery maker and was active from 1947 to '81.

This set is known as a demi-parure. If it included a brooch as well it would be a full parure and the set would rise in value by at least 25 per cent.

The fine quality pointed oval-shaped rhinestones, known as 'navette-' or 'marquise-cut', are typical of their designs.

Nearly all the stones are prong-set in flower or leaf shapes.

A Sherman demi-parure, comprising a necklace, bracelet and pair of earrings, set with light and dark blue spherical glass cabochons.

Earrings 1.5in (4cm) high

£350-500   TCF

A Sherman stylized floral brooch and matching earrings, with prong-set red and colourless faceted rhinestones.

Brooch 2.5in (6.5cm) wide

£250-350   TCF

A Sherman flower brooch and matching earrings, with prong-set red and colourless rhinestones.

Colour combinations are comparatively uncommon in Sherman designs – most are just one colour.

£60-90   TCF

A pair of Sherman 'chandelier' drop earring, set with faceted rhinestones.

3in (7.5cm) long

£350-450   TCF

A pair of Sherman drop earrings, with prong-set rose pink faceted rhinestones.

2in (5cm) long

£150-250   TCF

COSTUME JEWELLERY

A Sherman brooch, with prong-set iridescent faceted rhinestones.

£80-120   **TCF**

A Sherman stylized foliate brooch, with prong-set iridescent light blue rhinestones.

£180-220   **TCF**

EXPERT EYE – A TRIFARI BROOCH

Although the three-dimensional domed form and the curving effect to the outer ring are appealing, this is not the most lively of shapes.

It contains iridescent and multicoloured aurora borealis stones, which is a desirable feature.

The fact that the stones are prong-set is a sign of quality.

Green is a 'love/hate' colour in jewellery – while it will appeal enormously to some, others may pass it by.

A 1950s-60s Trifari round brooch, with prong-set green faceted rhinestones and aurora borealis stones, the back marked with crown above "Trifari".

2.25in (5.5cm) diam

£30-40   **AEM**

A Sherman bracelet, set with alternating small and large circular and oval iridescent rhinestones.

As well as a great sparkle factor, the use of different sized and shaped rhinestones adds interest.

7.75in (17cm) long

£150-200   **TCF**

An Adele Simpson three-dimensional triple flower brooch, set with blue faceted rhinestones.

2in (5cm) high

£10-15   **GCA**

A 1960s Giles Vidal Modernist necklace, with geometric textured design, the large squares containing gold-plated metal balls.

26in (66cm) long

£100-150   **TCF**

A 1960s Giles Vidal Modernist silver-plated pewter brooch, with textured surface and gold-plated balls.

The organic, moon-like surface is typical of Vidal's work, which is often juxtaposed against shiny smooth surfaces in silver or gold.

2in (5cm) diam

£70-100 **TCF**

A Warner cat's head brooch, pin-set with faceted red rhinestones.

1.25in (3cm) high

£15-25 **GCA**

A Warner swirling flower brooch, set with multicoloured aurora borealis rhinestones.

1.75in (4.5cm) diam

£15-25 **BB**

A Weiss circular brooch, set with faceted and baguette-cut light and dark blue rhinestones.

1.5in (4cm) diam

£22-28 **BB**

A Weiss gold-plated wreath brooch, set with amber rhinestones and aurora borealis stones.

1.75in (4.5cm) diam

£15-25 **AEM**

A Weiss strawberry fruit brooch, the black painted metal set with rhinestones.

1.5in (3.5cm) high

£10-12 **AEM**

A Weiss leaf-shaped brooch and matching earrings, prong-set with light blue and turquoise rhinestones.

Brooch 2.75in (7cm) wide

£35-50 **AEM**

A Weiss gold-plated and enamelled metal 'tremblant' flower and butterfly brooch, the butterfly set with multicoloured rhinestones.

'Tremblant' is the term used to describe jewellery, typically brooches, that appears to tremble as the wearer moves. To obtain this effect, parts are mounted on small, tight springs. The hand-applied enamelling on this piece is also a desirable feature that adds to the value.

2.75in (7cm) high

£30-45 **AEM**

COSTUME JEWELLERY

ESSENTIAL REFERENCE – CHRISTMAS TREE BROOCH

Although festive jewellery has been worn seasonally since the late 19thC, the fashion boomed in the US during the Christmas of 1950. Mothers whose sons where fighting in the Korean war had Christmas tree-shaped pins as reminders of their absent sons – some even sent their sons pins as gifts.

The trend continues today with costume jewellery makers releasing new designs, and reviving older ones, each year. Colours are typically festive, being predominately in green and red, as well as blue and yellow. Look out for named examples – those by Stanley Hagler can be worth in excess of £200. Hagler's pins are also complex pieces encrusted with beads and rhinestones – such detailed pieces are time consuming to make and the level of detail are other factors that affect value.

This dramatic example by Weiss is highly popular. It was produced in three sizes, of which this is the largest and most valuable.

A 1950s Weiss Christmas Tree brooch, set with green, red, yellow, pink and clear crystal rhinestones, marked "Weiss".

2.75in (7cm) high

£100-120   **GCA**

A J.J. Christmas tree brooch, set with multicoloured glass 'stones'.

2.25in (5.5cm) high

£4-6   **AEM**

A J.J. Christmas tree brooch, the gold-plated mount moulded as a fir tree and set with multicoloured glass 'stones'.

2.25in (6cm) high

£7-10   **AEM**

A Gerry's Christmas tree brooch, with red and green enamelled 'decorations'.

2.25in (5.5cm) high

£3-5   **AEM**

An unmarked prong-set faceted rhinestone Christmas tree brooch.

1.5in (3.5cm) high

£3-5   **AEM**

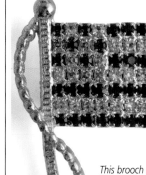

A gold-plated patriotic flag brooch, possibly by Raflatan, with prong-set red, clear and blue rhinestones.

This brooch has more stones, is large in size and has a simulated curling rope, hence the comparatively high value.

1.75in (4.5cm) high

£6-8   **AEM**

A Reja sterling silver United States Navy anchor-shaped brooch, set with rhinestones.

1.25in (3cm) high

£25-40   **BB**

A pair of Renoir embossed copper earrings, in the form of stylized sheaves of corn.

1.25in (3cm) high

£12-18 BB

A pair of Renoir embossed copper teardrop-shaped earrings.

1.5in (3.5cm) high

£10-12 BB

EXPERT EYE – A REBAJES BROOCH

In 1934 Spanish jeweller and sculptor Francisco Rebajes (1906-90) opened his first shop in New York City, which he ran until he returned to Spain in 1967.

His designs are Modern in style, and were usually inspired by foreign culture or ethnic designs. Here he has been inspired by a Chinese dragon's head.

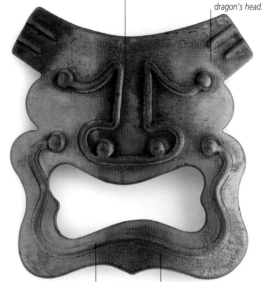

All his designs are made from die-cut and embossed copper. They have a distinctive soft patina that should not be polished.

Other makers also imitated his successful designs. All Rebajes pieces are marked on the back with his name.

A Rebajes Chinese dragon's head copper brooch, stamped "Rebajes" on the reverse.

1.75in (4.5cm) high

£22-28 BB

A pair of Bergere copper crescent-shaped earrings.

0.75in (2cm) high

£10-12 BB

A pair of Renoir copper earrings, set with opaque white glass cabochons.

1.25in (3cm) high

£10-15 BB

A pair of Rebajes earrings, with three lobes and a ring.

1.25in (3cm) high

£10-15 BB

A pair of Rebajes copper curving feather-shaped earrings, with screw-back fittings.

1.25in (3.5cm) wide

£10-12 BB

COSTUME JEWELLERY

A Nye embossed copper brooch, with ears of wheat.

Nye pieces are usually found in silver, making this copper example scarce.

1.5in (4cm) diam

£10-15   BB

A Renoir embossed copper leaf brooch.

3.25in (8.5cm) high

£22-28   BB

An unmarked 1960s copper bracelet, with ball and curving wing design.

2.75in (7cm) wide

£12-18   BB

A Nye embossed sterling silver pansy flower brooch, the back stamped "Sterling" and with three leaf clover mark.

Nye was founded by Stuart Nye in Asheville, North Carolina in 1933. Silver is typically used, although copper was added during WWII due to metal shortages, and brass from late 1979 due to the high cost of silver at that time. The company is still active today.

2in (5cm) wide

£12-18   BB

A Nye embossed sterling silver pansy flower brooch, marked "Sterling" and with three leaf clover mark.

1.5in (4cm) wide

£8-12   AEM

A Nye flower brooch, the back stamped "Sterling" and with a three leaf clover mark.

1.5in (3.5cm) diam

£8-10   BB

A Nye sterling silver rectangular brooch, with chased and engraved sheaves of wheat design.

2in (5cm) wide

£18-22   GCA

A Cini sterling silver 'Taurus' brooch and earrings set, the back stamped "Sterling".

Cini produced a set for each of the 12 signs of the Zodiac.

Brooch 2in (5cm) wide

£35-50   BB

An unmarked sterling silver leaf-shaped pin, probably by Nye.

2.5in (6cm) high

£12-18   BB

A Beau sterling silver curving leaf brooch, the back stamped "Sterling".

3.5in (9cm) long

£3-5   AEM

A Danish Anton Michelsen sterling silver lily of the valley brooch, with 'tremblant' flowers, the back stamped "Sterling" and with a crown and "AM" mark.

2.75in (7cm) high

£30-45   GCA

A Lang sterling silver lobster brooch and earring set, the back marked "Sterling".

2.5in (6.5cm) high

£20-30   BB

A Petersen sterling silver brooch, with embossed Art Nouveau style flowers and leaves.

Carl Poul Petersen (1895-1977) was apprenticed to famed Danish silversmith Georg Jensen. Many of his designs bear strong similarities to, or take their inspiration from, Jensen's style. Petersen emigrated to Canada in 1929 and opened his shop shortly after. It remained in business until 1975, showcasing his high quality jewellery and domestic silverware designs.

£220-280   TCF

EXPERT EYE – A CORO BROOCH

The back is stamped with a Viking longboat motif, as well as the Coro name and "Sterling", indicating it is from the Norseland range.

The range was made in the 1940s and includes a number of brooches with stylized flower and leaf designs.

The style is heavily influenced by the desirable and valuable designs by Danish silversmith and jeweller Georg Jensen.

It is well designed – perspective is shown by the way the branches curl in front of, and behind, the bird.

A 1940s Coro 'Norseland' sterling heart-shaped bird brooch.

2in (5cm) high

£90-110   BB

A 1960s Schluer sterling silver geometric brooch, with textured surfaces and inset cultured pearls.

Assembled from a number of pieces, this brooch is similar to Modernist wooden and metal sculptures produced at the same time.

£700-1,000   TCF

COSTUME JEWELLERY

An unmarked strawberry fruit brooch, set with faux pearl and coloured rhinestone studs.

1.75in (4.5cm) high

£10-12   BB

An unmarked strawberry fruit brooch, set with red rhinestones.

Note the good quality moulding of the strawberry's leaves.

1.75in (4.5cm) high

£5-8   AEM

An unmarked leaf-shaped brooch, set with faceted blue crystal rhinestones.

2.75in (7cm) high

£20-30   BB

A green faceted rhinestone leaf brooch, with gold-plated leaf mount.

2.75in (7cm) high

£12-18   AEM

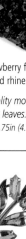

An unmarked gold-tone foliate sprig brooch, with curling leaves and prong-set multicoloured stones.

2.25in (6cm) high

£20-30   BB

A pair of unmarked purple faceted rhinestone earrings.

1.5in (4cm) high

£5-8   AEM

An unmarked red and clear faceted rhinestone floral spray brooch.

2.75in (5.5cm) high

£12-18   AEM

An unmarked Austrian faceted brown crystal articulated leaf and grape brooch.

Articulated pins such as this are popular as the light is reflected off the facets when the brooch moves, giving a sparkling effect.

2.75in (7cm) high

£22-28   BB

An unmarked heart brooch, prong-set with faceted black rhinestones.

The colour and sentimentality of the form brings to mind Victorian jewellery.

2.25in (5.5cm) high

£10-12   BB

EXPERT EYE – A CROWN BROOCH

Crown brooches were popular from the 1930s to '50s, coinciding with the release of a series of highly popular romantic-historical movies that fired public imagination about European aristocracy and royalty.

It is stamped 'Sterling' indicating that it is made from solid silver that has been gold-plated.

Trifari were the best-known maker, with their marked examples designed by the legendary Alfred Philippe being worth up to £300.

Consider the colours and the complexity of the design and setting – this is a comparatively simple and sober example.

A 1940s vermeil sterling silver crown brooch, with faceted yellow and ruby red glass stones, the back stamped "Sterling".

1.5in (3.5cm) high

£30-45   BB

A 1960s Czechoslovakian gold-plated brooch, set with blue rhinestones in different tones.

2.75in (7cm) wide

£30-40   BB

An unmarked scarecrow bar pendant, set with clear and multicoloured rhinestones.

Although this looks like a scarecrow, his hat may make him a 'rhinestone cowboy'.

3in (7.5cm) high

£25-35   AEM

A 1920s-30s unmarked 'Fu Manchu' fur clip.

Note the expressive face and curling beard, which raises this above the norm.

3in (7.5cm) high

£25-35   BB

COSTUME JEWELLERY

An unmarked large bee-shaped brooch.

This is very similar to the famous bee pins made by Joseff of Hollywood, although the gold-coloured metal is different.

2.5in (6cm) high

£15-20   BB

A 1950s unmarked gold-plated 'top hat and cane' brooch, set with red rhinestones.

2.5in (6cm) high

£4-6   BB

An unmarked gold-plated brooch, in the form of a pair of spectacles, set with blue rhinestones around the top rim.

As well as being decorative, the arms of this brooch could be used to hang your own spectacles from.

1.25in (3cm) high

£7-10   BB

A pair of 1960s gold-plated bamboo style earrings, with amber bakelite teardrops.

1.75in (4.5cm) high

£10-15   BB

An unmarked cocktail jewellery style expandable bracelet, set with pale blue rhinestones.

Although examples with colourless stones are easier to find, this attractive pale blue is scarcer.

2.5in (6.5cm) diam (unexpanded)

£20-30   BB

EXPERT EYE – A HUMMINGBIRD BROOCH

Although this is in the style of Trifari, Trifari pieces are always marked on the back. Considering the style, it is probably by Monet.

The wings are enamelled in alternate colours, showing some consideration to detail has been made.

The head is not set with rhinestones as it first appears, instead the textured surface has a bright silvered finish.

The eye is missing its inset rhinestone. Although this can be replaced, there will be an added cost.

An unmarked hummingbird-in-flight gilt metal brooch, with enamelled wings.

1.5in (4cm) high

£7-10   MHC

A 1930s unmarked paste cocktail jewellery style articulated bracelet.

Jewellery such as this was made during the 1930s in imitation of the platinum and diamond-set cocktail jewellery worn by the wealthy.

7.5in (19cm) long

£50-80   BB

FIND OUT MORE...

'Miller's Costume Jewellery: How to Compare & Value', by Steven Miners, Miller's Publications, 2006.

ESSENTIAL REFERENCE

- The Disney animation studios were founded in 1923 by Walter Elias Disney (1901-66) and his brother Roy (b.1930). Their most famous character, Mickey Mouse, was developed in 1928. Shortly after, merchandise was also produced, and it is this pre-war memorabilia that tends to be most sought-after and valuable today.

- Look for marks, as these can help with dating. Before 1939, the wording 'Walt Disney Enterprises' or, more rarely, 'Walter E. Disney' was used. From 1939 to 1984, the mark changed to 'Walt Disney Productions', with later marks including '© Disney' and '© Disney Enterprises'. Licensed items bearing one of these marks is generally more sought-after than unlicensed items, unless very early or rare.

- The style of a character, or the characters themselves, can also help with dating. For example, Mickey Mouse lost his toothy grin in the early 1930s and became more rounded and less rodent-like over time. Mickey and some characters have broader appeal than others, but do not ignore characters that are less well-known as they may be rarer.

- In 1961, Marx released its Disneykins ranges, which were produced until the company closed in 1973. These were tiny injection moulded, hand-painted figures that were sometimes included in detailed scenes. They were affordable and fun – in the US, in 1961, the small figurines retailed at 15 cents each, while larger TV Scenes retailed at 29 cents each. With over 160 figurines to find, there are a number of ranges, with 101 Dalmations being the largest with over 47 figurines.

- Condition is important to value as most memorabilia was played with or worn, and has become damaged. Disneykins should retain their colourful and appealing boxes, which should also be in good condition, to be worth higher values. Earlier examples produced in 'British Hong Kong' tend to have better quality moulding and painting.

A 1960s Louis Marx Disneykin 'Pinocchio' TV Scenes set, marked "Walt Disney Productions", mint and boxed.

3in (7.5cm) high

£20-25   MTB

A 1960s Louis Marx Disneykin 'Bambi' TV Scenes set, marked "Walt Disney Productions", mint and boxed.

3in (7.5cm) high

£20-25   MTB

A 1960s Louis Marx Disneykins 'Dewey' hand-painted miniature figurine, made in Hong Kong, mint and boxed.

Box 1.5in (4cm) high

£3-6   MTB

A 1960s Marx Disneykins 'Thumper' hand-painted miniature figurine, made in Hong Kong, mint and boxed.

Box 1.5in (4cm) high

£3-6   MTB

A 1960s Marx Disneykins 'Polly' hand-painted miniature figurine and bowl, from '101 Dalmations' made in Hong Kong, mint and boxed.

This figurine is one of the rarer and more sought-after from the series. It must be complete and in mint condition to be worth this amount.

Box 1.5in (4cm) high

£8-12   MTB

DISNEYANA

A 1960s Louis Marx Disneykin 'Soldier' hand-painted miniature figurine, from the Babes in Toyland series, made in Hong Kong, mint and boxed.

This series was released in 1962.

4.25in (10.5cm) high

£10-15   **MTB**

A 1960s Louis Marx Disneykin play set, including Mickey Mouse, Minnie Mouse and Pluto, made in Hong Kong, marked "Walt Disney Productions".

6.5in (16.5cm) wide

£40-60   **MTB**

A 1970s-80s Play Pal Plastic Inc. Mickey Mouse plastic money bank, impressed "Walt Disney Productions".

11.25in (28.5cm) high

£5-7   **AEM**

A Hoan Ltd Mickey Mouse cookie jar, impressed "©The Walt Disney Co."

10.75in (27cm) high

£20-30   **AEM**

A 1940s Ideal Novelty Co. Pinocchio painted composition and wood figurine, with flex-jointed arms and legs.

This Pinocchio is lacking his name, which is usually transfer-printed in white across his chest.

7.5in (19cm) high

£30-50   **AAC**

A 1970s-80s Play Pal Plastic Inc. Pinocchio plastic money bank, impressed "Walt Disney Productions".

11.25in (28.5cm) high

£7-10   **AEM**

A Snow White hand-painted carnival chalkware figure, with recently touched-up face.

These painted plaster figurines were usually sold or given away at fairs as prizes. Condition is usually very poor.

c1938   *14.5in (37cm) high*

£22-32   **BH**

A 1960s Louis Marx Mary Poppins clockwork plastic 'Whirling Toy', marked "Walt Disney Productions", mint with original printed card box.

Wind her up and she jiggles and jumps around.

10.75in (27.5cm) high

£40-60   **MTB**

A Mattel Pushmi-Pullyu double-headed llama soft toy.

This was produced in conjunction with the 1967 film 'Dr Dolittle' starring Rex Harrison as the Doctor. In the book it appeared as an antelope, but was portrayed as a llama in the film.

c1968   6.25in (16cm) high

£40-50   **MTB**

A Kohner plastic Pluto 'Peppy Puppet', marked "Walt Disney Productions", mint and carded.

1970   11in (28cm) high

£12-18   **MTB**

A unopened pack of 1950s Walt Disney Productions printed card 'Disneyland Party Decorations', including Bambi and Thumper.

13.5in (34.5cm) high

£3-5   **BH**

A 1930s-40s colour transfer-printed tinplate 'Mickey's Sand Pail', marked "Reg'd Design Shape No. 858445 Happy Nac Square Sand Pail 760 Made in England" and "By Permission of Walt Disney Mickey Mouse Ltd".

It is very hard to find UK licensed Walt Disney memorabilia with these marks. Sand pails are usually worn and damaged through outdoor play – this example is in excellent condition.

5.25in (13.5cm) high

£120-180   **BH**

EXPERT EYE – A PAIR OF SALT & PEPPER SHAKERS

Retailer Faye Bennison acquired the Poxon China Company of Vernon, California in 1931, renaming it Vernon Kilns.

He won a contract to produce characters from Walt Disney's 'Fantasia', 'Dumbo' and 'The Reluctant Dragon' films in 1940, which lasted until late 1941.

Having been made between 1940 and 1941, Vernon Kilns' examples are very rare. The ostrich ballerina figurines can be worth as much as £1,000 each.

Now being deemed a classic, Fantasia was not a commercial success when released, and sales of related memorabilia at the time were comparatively low.

A very rare pair of Vernon Kilns dancing mushroom salt and pepper shakers, from Walt Disney's 'Fantasia', impressed "Disney Copyright 1941".

The American Pottery Company continued producing some of Vernon Kiln's items, but these are not marked and are less sought-after.

1941   3.5in (9cm) high

£150-200   **BB**

A 1950s Walt Disney Productions transfer-printed metal bubblegum dispenser, with maker's mark to base.

23.5in (59.5cm) high

£250-350   **QU**

FIND OUT MORE...

www.disneykins.com
www.disney.com

ESSENTIAL REFERENCE

- The earliest dolls were generally home-made, carved from wood or sewn from scraps of fabric. The bisque-head doll industry grew in France and Germany from the 1860s onwards, and saw its golden age from the 1900s until the 1930s, when other materials such as composition (which had been traditionally been used for dolls' bodies rather than their heads), began to take over.
- The incised marks on the back of a bisque doll's head can help identify its maker, as can facial characteristics. Look for dolls by well-known makers such as Jumeau, Heubach and Armand Marseille. Collectors value clean, undamaged heads with expressive faces. Replaced bodies devalue a doll, while original clothes add considerably to value.

- Bisque and composition were used for dolls' heads from the 1900s to the 1950s when they were superseded by the more economical, and versatile, plastic.
- In recent years, hard and soft plastic dolls have seen a rise in interest and value, as those who loved them as children become collectors. Look for major names such as Madam Alexander, Terri Lee, Vogue, Ideal and Pedigree. Condition is one of the most important considerations for value. Hairstyles should also be original with restyled, and particularly cut, hair reducing value considerably. Look for detailed, original clothing and original boxes. Character dolls can also be sought-after, whether based on celebrities or story book characters.

A German Kammer & Reinhardt/Simon & Halbig bisque child doll, with weighted blue eyes, open mouth, pierced ears, brunette wig and pate, wood and composition jointed body, wearing woollen one piece long-johns and vest, socks, leatherette shoes, green velvet pantaloons and matching jacket and cap, the head impressed "Simon & Halbig k * R 39".

Simon & Halbig made heads for Kammer & Reinhardt, who purchased the company in 1920.

16in (40cm) high

£250-350   VEC

A German J.D. Kestner Jr. bisque doll, with weighted brown eyes, open mouth, blonde mohair wig, five-piece composition body, painted dark blue ribbed stockings and tan and brown shoes, cotton and woollen undergarments, white muslin dress, crochet bonnet, the head impressed "192".

1900   *9in (23cm) high*

£150-200   VEC

A German Armand Marseille for Edmund Edelman Melitta bisque doll, with open mouth with missing teeth, original brown mohair wig and pate, five-piece curved limb composition body, impressed "Melitta 11", blue weighted eyes detached but present, right thumb missing, toes detached.

c1910   *20in (51cm) high*

£35-55   VEC

A German Hermann Steiner bisque doll, with weighted brown eyes, open mouth with chipped teeth, blonde wig and pate, wood and composition ball-jointed body, cotton and woollen undergarments, silk, cotton and lace dress and lace bonnet, the head impressed "H St 9".

c1910   *17.5in (45cm) high*

£100-150   VEC

A German Walther and Söhn character bisque doll, with weighted brown eyes, open mouth, original blond wig and pate, five-piece composition body, dressed in original golden thread woven dress and matching head-band, impressed "200-14/0 W&S 14/0".

This character doll may have been used as a Christmas fairy judging by its clothing.

c1922   *9.25in (24cm) high*

£80-120   VEC

A 1930s American Effanbee Patsyette composition doll, with painted brown side-glancing eyes, painted closed mouth, moulded brown hair, five-piece body, impressed "Effanbee Patsyette Doll", slight crazing overall, reclothed.

9in (23cm) high

£50-80   VEC

A 1920s-30s moulded and painted felt and fabric 'Empress of Australia' souvenir sailor doll.

10in (25.5cm) high

£20-30   PC

A 1930s Chad Valley felt boy doll, with painted eyes, mohair hair, wearing socks, leather shoes, cotton shirt, brown spotty tie, green velvet shorts and felt jacket, with red embroidered label to left foot "Hygienic Toys Made in England by Chad Valley Co. Ltd", minor moth damage and fading.

16in (41cm) high

£100-150   VEC

EXPERT EYE – A STEINER CLOCKWORK BISQUE DOLL

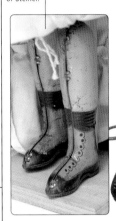

The tinplate boots are characteristic of Steiner.

Her face finely moulded with a charming expression, and she is beautifully dressed in well-made clothes, adding to her appeal.

Mechanical walking dolls are rare. The body of this doll has been opened to repair the mechanism, which reduces the value marginally.

The head is incised 'FS & Co' indicating it was made by German maker Franz Schmidt (founded 1890). This style of marking was used on their later dolls.

A Steiner clockwork walking doll, with Franz Schmidt bisque head, original period clothes and tinplate boots

12.75in (32cm) high

£3,000-4,000   MTB

A 1950s Betsy McCall cloth doll, together with her McCall's pattern and instructions.

17in (43cm) high

£35-50   BH

An Annalee 'Kid with Kite' poseable fabric doll, with fabric and card tags, the base stamped "2335".

1992   7in (18cm) high

£6-9   AEM

A Coleco Cabbage Patch Kid, with vinyl face and wool hair, dressed in a sailor suit.

Cabbage Patch Kids were devised by Xavier Roberts in 1978 and were made from cloth. They were initially sold at craft shows and later via the Babyland General Hospital in Cleveland, Georgia. Toy maker Colec mass-produced them with vinyl faces from 1982 until they went bankrupt in 1989. Since then, they have been made by a number of companies including Mattel, Hasbro and, most recently, Play Along.

1982-89   17.25in (44cm) high

£3-5   AEM

DOLLS

A Chad Valley Strawberry Shortcake vinyl doll, complete with comb, and mint and boxed.

1980   7.75in (19.5cm) high
£15-20   **MTB**

An Ideal Shirley Temple vinyl doll, with original sailor suit, shoes, bow and hat, and original red coat and hat, in mint condition.

1957   12in (30.5cm) high
£70-100   **SOTT**

EXPERT EYE – A PEDIGREE MARY POPPINS

Notable UK doll company Pedigree was commissioned by the film's New Zealand distributors to produce a Mary Poppins doll to promote the film.

The clothing is very close to that worn by the character in the film, including a working dress and apron.

Pedigree used a Sindy doll with chestnut hair that was in production at the time, dressing her in Mary Poppins' clothing.

Examples are rare. Those in mint condition, complete with their boxes, are rarer still.

A Pedigree Walt Disney's 'Mary Poppins' vinyl character doll, complete with original clothes, hat and bag, and in card box.

c1965   12in (30.5cm) high
£550-650   **MTB**

A rare 1963 Alexander-kins Queen Elizabeth II doll, no. 499, in mint, complete condition, with printed card box.

Do not confuse this earlier example with the later edition from 1992, that wears a crown and is dressed differently.

1963   7.75in (19.5cm) high
£400-600   **BH**

A 1950s Madame Alexander Maggie hard plastic walker doll, her black skirt printed with pink roses, with shoes and laces, and label on blouse.

14.25in (36cm) high
£120-180   **BH**

A 1950s English Rosebud hard plastic doll, with original suit, duster coat and ponytail.

13.75in (35cm) high
£35-45   **MA**

A Tiny Terri Lee hard plastic doll, with original clothes, socks and shoes, with curly hairstyle and fabric tag.

10.25in (26cm) high

£80-120   **BH**

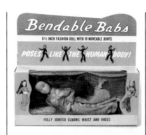

A 1960s Uneeda 'Bendable Babs' poseable fashion doll, from the Dollikin range, made in "The British Crown Colony of Hong Kong", mint in original box.

7.5in (19cm) wide

£25-35   **MTB**

A 1960s Uneeda Dollikin poseable fashion doll, with 14 different poseable body joints, mint and boxed.

11.25in (28.5cm) high

£60-80   **MTB**

A Vogue Lil' Imp soft vinyl walker doll, complete with original clothing and shoes, in excellent condition.

1959-60   *11in (28cm) high*

£60-90   **BH**

A 1950s Vogue Dolls Ginny hard plastic walker doll, with painted lashes and straight legs, mint and boxed with original leaflet.

7.5in (19cm) high

£220-320   **BH**

A Vogue Dolls Inc. 'Ginny' doll, with wrist tag and remnant of original label, in mint condition with box and instruction leaflet.

The high value of this doll and the one shown above far right can be attributed to the fact they are in complete, boxed and mint condition.

1953   *7.5in (19cm) high*

£220-320   **BH**

A Vogue Dolls Inc. 'Ginny' outfit, with dress and hat, in mint condition with original card and cellophane window box.

6.25in (16cm) wide

£30-40   **BH**

ESSENTIAL REFERENCE

- Just like salt and pepper shakers, eggcups have become a collecting field of their own. Over the past 300 years, many companies and makers have produced eggcups in different materials, with a great many being found in ceramic. Small in size, and usually affordable, they are easy to describe, ship and display. This makes them popular with shop-based dealers as well as internet-based sellers.
- There are a number of features to consider. Firstly, look for a maker's mark. Notable makers such as Spode or Wedgwood will add desirability. Secondly, look at the quality of the piece in terms of the moulding and the pattern. If it is hand-painted, look for good details and careful application of paint. Although small, transfer-printed designs should be carefully applied.
- Novelty forms are also popular, particularly if they relate to popular characters, cars or aeroplanes. Most novelty eggcups found will date from the 1920s and 1960s and were often made in Japan. Examples with designs by popular children's book illustrators such as Mabel Lucie Attwell will usually be worth more. Always look carefully for signs of damage as these were made to be used and typically saw great use.

A Washington 'Old Willow' pattern transfer-printed eggcup.

1.75in (4.5cm) high

£12-18   BEV

A Copeland Spode 'Italian' pattern transfer-printed eggcup.

Spode is collected in its own right, and 'Italian' is one of the more common patterns.

1.75in (4.5cm) high

£20-25   BEV

An English urn-shaped 'Imari' eggcup, with hand-painted and transfer-printed detailing and gilt highlights, the base painted "No 824 X".

2.5in (6cm) high

£35-45   BEV

A Japanese lustre painted combination whistle and train eggcup, the base stamped "Foreign" in red.

4.75in (12cm) long

£25-35   BEV

A Japanese combined whistle and 'man in a car' eggcup, the base stamped in red "Foreign".

This is valuable and desirable for a number of reasons. Combination eggcups and whistles such as this are scarce, particularly in good condition. The car shape is also highly desirable, and the level of moulded detail is very good.

4.5in (11cm) long

£80-120   BEV

A Japanese lustre painted train eggcup, unmarked.

2.5in (6.5cm) high

£20-25   BEV

A Japanese lustre painted Noah's ark eggcup, unmarked.

2.5in (6.5cm) high

£20-30   BEV

A 1920s-30s Japanese hand-painted chick clown eggcup, the base printed in red "Foreign".

Although the country's name is not printed, the lightweight white ceramic and the style of moulding and painting identifies this as Japanese. By the 1950s, marks such as "Japan" and "Made in Japan" were used.

2.75in (7cm) high

£35-45   BEV

A Japanese spray lustre seated teddy bear eggcup.

2.5in (6cm) high

£28-32   BEV

A 1930s eggcup in the form of a crouching rabbit, with spray-painted glaze, the base impressed "L".

2.75in (7cm) high

£25-35   BEV

An Australian hand-painted Sooty eggcup, the base printed "Keble St PTY Co. Ltd Reg. by Sooty Concessions Ltd No.743610".

2.5in (6cm) high

£30-40   BEV

A Japanese lion's head eggcup, with hand-painted mane.

2in (5cm) high

£18-22   BEV

MILLER'S COMPARES – EGGCUPS

This was made by notable German ceramics manufacturer Goebel, adding to its desirability.

As well as a mould or shape number, the base bears impressed marks of a crown and a 'WG' monogram (for founder Wilhelm Goebel), dating it to the 1920s to 1940s.

A 1930s German Goebel hand-painted smiling boy eggcup, impressed with the Crown mark and "E76".

2.5in (6cm) high

£40-50   BEV

The quality of this example is comparatively poor. Although lively, the character is not as expressive, the moulded details are not as good and the hand-painting is paler and poorer.

Although also German, and probably of the same period, this example is by an unknown manufacturer.

A 1930s German hand-painted smiling boy eggcup, the base impressed "5254".

3in (7cm) high

£25-35   BEV

A W.R. Midwinter Ltd 'Peggy Gibbons' transfer-printed eggcup.

Peggy Gibbons was Midwinter's most successful nurseryware range and was produced into the 1960s.

2.5in (5.5cm) high

£55-65   BEV

An American Marilyn Monroe erotic calendar, with posed photograph titled 'The Lure of Lace' and 'Posed by Marilyn Monroe. In the nude. With lace overprint'.
1954   *16.75in (42.5cm) high*
£550-650   **QU**

A 1950s American erotic promotional card calendar, printed for 'Tire Craft of N.Y.', with tear-off calender to base.
1956   *19.75in (50cm) high*
£100-150   **QU**

An American New Hotels Supply erotic promotional card calendar, printed by 'Jack's Stationery – The Store of Friendly Service', with complete tear-off calender to base.

Calenders such as these could be printed with any business name and given away as promotions.
1950   *20.5in (52cm) high*
£100-150   **QU**

A 1950s American erotic promotional card calendar, printed for 'New York Hotel Supply', with tear-off calender to base.

1956   *19.75in (50cm) high*
£100-150   **QU**

An American Esquire erotic calendar, with printed 'Robert Patterson' signature.
1952   *11in (28cm) high*
£100-150   **QU**

A pack of '52 American Beauties' playing cards, designed by Gil Elvgren, together with original card box and four coupons.

3.5in (9cm) high
£30-50   **SOTT**

A 1950s American erotic key ring, the leather cover opening up to reveal a concertina of black and white erotic photographs.
1.25in (3cm) high
£70-100   **QU**

A 1950s English Combex vinyl 'pin-up' plastic hot water bottle, wearing a turquoise bikini.

21.25in (54cm) high
£30-40   **MA**

ESSENTIAL REFERENCE

- Although there are still many who collect primarily to record optical developments and changing styles, today's market for vintage eyewear is dominated by those who buy to wear, and include prolific collectors such as Elton John. A decade ago, the focus was on 19thC and earlier examples, but today this has shifted to examples from the 20thC that are visibly more wearable, colourful and fun.
- The key factors governing value are: the style or look, the condition, the name of the maker or designer, and the materials used. Examples that sum up a particular period or style tend to be most popular, with those from the 1950s and '60s currently being seen as the most stylish. These include the 'cat's eye' styles of the 1950s and the over-sized rounded forms of the 1960s.
- Those in wilder styles, or in crazy colours or shapes, tend to be the most valuable. Sought-after today to give a truly individual look, they can be hard to find as their extreme styling made them either unpopular or too expensive at the time. More standard frames that sum up the period can make affordable and useable retro alternatives to today's frames.

- Consider the materials used and the work that went into making a pair. Hand-crafted elements such as enamelling, painting or complex laminating or cutting will generally add value. Look for a famous designer's name or monogram, as this will usually add value, particularly if the name is combined with great period styling. Some designers' monograms changed over time, which will help with dating.
- Always examine a set of frames closely before buying. Look for burn marks, and particularly for cracks or splits, as these cannot be repaired suitably, especially if the frames are intended to be worn. Some plastic can warp over time and bend out of shape. Providing this is not too serious, it can usually be corrected by a professional.
- The value is not usually affected if lenses are scratched, cracked or even missing entirely. Most buyers will prefer to choose whether frames are used as glasses or sunglasses, and may want to fit prescription lenses. However, if lenses were unusual, such as having a graduated tint in a matching or contrasting colour, the original examples will add value. Keep hold of them even if they are replaced with prescription examples.

A pair of 1950s American dark blue 'cat's eye' frames, with inset star-shaped screws, marked "Swan U.S.A. 51/2".

4.75in (12cm) wide

£15-25   BB

A pair of 1950s French grey pearlescent 'cat's eye' frames, inset with rhinestones and flashes, marked "France".

5in (13cm) wide

£20-25   BB

A pair of 1950s French gold pearlised, blue and red laminated plastic 'cats eye' frames, marked "Made in France".

5in (13cm) wide

£70-90   VE

A pair of 1950s French black frames, with inset metal lines and stars, marked "Frame France".

5in (12.5cm) wide

£20-25   BB

A pair of 1950s Christian Dior laminated pearlescent grey and clear plastic 'cat's eye' frames, set with rhinestones in gilt metal at the corners, and with a bow-shaped bridge, marked "Frame Austria".

5in (13cm) wide

£120-180   VE

A pair of laminated pearlised grey and black plastic 'snake' textured frames, with extended side wings over the hinges.

5.25in (13.5cm) wide

£70-90   VE

EYEWEAR

A pair of 1960s French floral fabric laminated plastic 'cat's eye' frames, marked "560" and "France".

Here, floral printed fabric has been sandwiched between two layers of clear plastic. Look out for examples marked 'Emilio Pucci' or 'Emilio', as Pucci's designs can be worth up to £200.

5.25in (13.5cm) wide

£150-180   **VE**

A pair of Raybert moulded plastic faux bamboo sunglasses, marked "Made in France".

Raybert is a very collectable name among the cognescenti.

5in (13cm) wide

£70-100   **VE**

A pair of 1950s laminated pink and clear 'cat's eyes' frames, inset with small star-shaped screws and 'starbust' designs.

5in (12.5cm) wide

£20-25   **BB**

A pair of 1950s Swank lady's white pearlised plastic 'cats wrap' frames, with applied gilt metal leaves and rhinestones, marked "Swank Frame France".

Swank are better known for their wide range of men's accessories that they distribute and manufacture across the US, including cufflinks and tie pins. Many of their pieces from the 1950s to '70s are highly collectable.

5in (13cm) wide

£150-180   **VE**

A pair of 1950s French pearlised pink champagne plastic frames, decorated with rhinestone, marked "Frame France".

5.5in (14cm) wide

£120-180   **VE**

A pair of early 1960s yellow and orange laminated plastic 'cats eye' Cabana sunglasses, stamped "TGS 723".

5.5in (14cm) wide

£80-120   **VE**

A pair of 1950s clear, blue and white striped 'cats eyes' frames, with hand cut zig-zag arms, stamped in gilt "Cabana TS-1139".

A pair of 1950s French blue and white striped over clear laminated plastic frames, with wrap sides, marked "France".

5.25in (13.5cm) wide

£120-180   **VE**

Here, alternating thin strips of opaque white plastic and clear plastic have been laminated together and cut vertically, and then laminated onto a sky-blue back. The angular cutting of the arms is highly unusual and draws attention to the angles of the frame.

5.5in (14cm) wide

£150-180   **VE**

A pair of 1960s French handmade gold-coloured and black laminated carved plastic sunglasses, with flower petal type decoration, the original lenses with "Fait Main Verres Filtrant" label.

The label indicates that the petal-like shapes were cut into the side of the frames by hand.

5.5in (14cm) wide

£150-180   **VE**

A pair of 1960s French orange and white laminated plastic frames, with hand-cut 'cookie cutter' edges, marked "Hand Made in France", with 'Fait Main' sticker.

6in (15.5cm) wide

£120-180   **VE**

A pair of 1960s black and white laminated plastic frames, unmarked.

5.5in (14cm) wide

£120-180   **VE**

A pair of laminated purple and white plastic 'Op Art' chequerboard frames.

5.25in (13.5cm) wide

£150-180   **VE**

A pair of 1960s convex 'bug eye' laminated white and black plastic frames, marked "Frame France".

The streaked wood effect is created by laminating thin strips or panels of black and white plastic together in different combinations and layers and then cutting it vertically to reveal the 'sandwich' of layers.

5.75in (14.5cm) wide

£150-180   **VE**

A pair of 1960s French translucent 'Jackie O' brown 'bug eye' sunglasses, the original lenses with sticker reading "Filtrant Vergo France", unmarked.

6in (15cm) wide

£120-180   **VE**

A pair of 1960s thick copper and black laminated plastic 'bug eye' frames, unmarked.

5.25in (13.5cm) wide

£120-180   **VE**

A pair of 1960s French laminated black and grey leopard skin effect on black plastic Lucite 'Eskimo' frames.

6.25in (16cm) wide

£25-40   **BB**

EYEWEAR

A pair of 1960s French transparent sky-blue plastic sunglasses, inset with metal dots and rhinestones, marked "Made in France".

5.25in (13.5cm) wide

£120-180   VE

A pair of 1960s French scalloped bone sunglasses, with original lenses, marked "Made in France".

5in (13cm) wide

£120-180   VE

A pair of 1960s French 'Op Art' black plastic hexagonal oversize sunglasses, with blue circular insets, marked "Made in France".

These bring to mind the boldly coloured 1960s geometric artworks of Victor Vasarely.

6in (15cm) wide

£150-180   VE

A pair of 1960s Op Art style white and black laminated sunglasses, stamped "Sun Sentry U.S.A."

Op Art is the name applied to an abstract style of painting comprising geometric monochrome or repeated colours, and making use of optical effects to blur the boundaries between the picture plane and illusion. Its champion was the British painter Bridget Riley, and its effects were seen in the fashions of Andre Courreges and Pierre Cardin.

5.5in (14cm) wide

£150-180   VE

EXPERT EYE – A PAIR OF DIOR SUNGLASSES

Christian Dior is a prestigious name. The frames are fully signed and retain their original case.

The large perfectly round frames and thick arms are typical of the most fashionable 1960s styles.

The brightly coloured stylized floral design has been hand-painted onto the moulded front, and is typical of the 1960s.

Dior also produced scarcer enamelled gold metal frames with similar decoration, inset rhinestones and glass jewels during the late 1960s. They can be worth up to £750.

A pair of 1960s French Christian Dior multicoloured handmade plastic sunglasses, the arms with impressed 'CD' monograms, together with original grey faux leather case with Dior logo.

6in (15.5cm) wide

£400-500   VE

A pair of 1960s 'Patriotic' cream plastic square sunglasses, cut with a square of lines and then block-printed with red or blue squares.

5.5in (14cm) wide

£120-180   VE

A pair of late 1960s Pierre Cardin light grey transparent plastic frames, in the shape of a pair of open lips, marked "Frame France".

5.75in (14.5cm) wide

£120-180   VE

A pair of 1960s French pink-striated transparent plastic large sunglasses, stamped "Made in France".

6.25in (16cm) wide

£120-180   **VE**

A pair of 1970s Italian Delotto laminated terracotta, white and faux tortoiseshell plastic sunglasses, with wavy arms and original graduated lenses, one arm marked marked "Made in Italy, Oris 112 Brown".

6in (15.5cm) wide

£120-180   **VE**

ESSENTIAL REFERENCE – GIVENCHY

A pair of 1960s Givenchy pink oversized curving 'bug eye' frames, with original graduated violet lenses and wavy arms, marked "Givenchy L Unico-Frame France".

The haute couture house of Givenchy was founded in 1952 in Paris by Hubert Givenchy (b.1927). He worked with a number of influential haute couture fashion designers including Jacques Fath, Lucien Lelong and Esla Schiaparelli. After his retirement in 1995, he was succeeded by John Galliano, who was followed by Alexander McQueen and then Julien MacDonald. Famous patrons include Audrey Hepburn (notably for her films such as 'Sabrina') and the Kennedy family, some of whom wore Givenchy to John F. Kennedy's funeral. Part of the LVMH conglomerate, Givenchy continues to produce luxurious and elegant eyewear that reflects today's fashions.

5in (13cm) wide

£150-180   **VE**

A pair of 1970s over-sized brown and amber graduated plastic frames, with cut-out bridge, unmarked but with Paco Rabanne inset metal decal.

5.75in (14.5cm) wide

£120-180   **VE**

A pair of 1970s German Christian Dior yellow-to-amber graduated plastic Optyl frames, with triangular pierced arms, marked "Made in Germany".

£120-180   **VE**

A pair of 1960s-70s transparent graduated green, pink and clear plastic frames.

5.5in (14cm) wide

£15-20   **BB**

A pair of 1970s American colourless and violet graduated plastic frames, with drop arms, inset 'WB' decal, and stamped "Satin Doll, American".

The 'drop' style of the arms is a typical feature of the 1970 styles.

6in (15cm) wide

£18-22   **BB**

EYEWEAR

A pair of 1970s blue aluminium oversized frames, with curving arms.

5.75in (14.5cm) wide

£30-40   **BB**

A pair of Ted Lapidus red plastic 'bamboo' sunglasses, with tubular wrapped gold sections.

Ted Lapidus founded his haute couture fashion house in 1957 and presented his first collection in 1963. In the mid-1980s, he was succeeded by his son Oliver.

6in (15cm) wide

£120-180   **VE**

A pair of 1960s-70s hexagonal framed tortoiseshell plastic sunglasses, unmarked, with brown lenses.

6.25in (16cm) wide

£120-180   **VE**

A pair of 1960s large transparent yellow frames, with wide arms and bat wing-like frames and black 'cat's eye' shape lenses.

5.75in (14.5cm) wide

£150-180   **VE**

EXPERT EYE – A PAIR OF PIERRE CARDIN FRAMES

The oversized dimensions of theses frames is typical of the 1960s, and the style followed through into the 1970s.

They were handmade, and the screen-like shape shape shows the Sixties obsession with television.

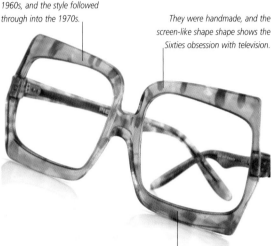

They were designed by Pierre Cardin (b.1922), who was a revolutionary designer during the 1960s and '70s.

Led by celebrity innovators, over-sized, shaped sunglasses such as these have seen a resurgence of popularity over the past few years.

A pair of large 1960s Pierre Cardin shaped square brown tortoiseshell plastic frames, marked "Cardin Handmade in France Vonni".

6in (15cm) wide

£150-180   **VE**

A pair of 1980s Helena Rubinstein 'Modele Depose' white plastic and silver lattice sunglasses, with original graduated violet lenses and 'HR' gilt decal.

Polish-born Helena (Chaja) Rubinstein (c1870-1965) founded her eponymous company in 1902, in Australia, moving to London and then the US, expanding it as she went. Her name is best-known in relation to make-up and skin care products.

5.5in (14cm) wide

£150-180   **VE**

A pair of 1980s Japanese aviator-style aluminium frames, stamped "Lugano WB Frame Japan".

The aviator style was popularised by the 1986 film 'Top Gun' about the life and love of 'Maverick', played by Tom Cruise.

5.25in (13.5cm) wide

£18-22   **BB**

A pair of 1970s Prince Michel de Bourbon laminated light and dark blue plastic sunglasses with graduated lenses, stamped with a gilt shield motif and marked "12300 C 30".

The faux horn effect is created by selectively carving back the darker top layer, revealing the lighter colour beneath.

5.75in (14.5cm) wide

£80-120   **VE**

A pair of French Emilio Pucci handmade faux tortoiseshell plastic frames, with gilt metal hinges and black lacquer panels, marked "Florence Made in France Fait Main EP274".

5.75in (14.5cm) wide

£120-180   **VE**

A pair of 1980s Italian Zagato 'New Dimension' black, red and white plastic sunglasses, marked "Hand made Italy" and with original swing tag.

6in (15cm) wide

£150-180   **VE**

A pair of 1970s French Balenciaga laminated red and clear plastic sunglasses, the corners overlaid with black cut with lines, together with the original tag marked "CR39" and "Handmade France".

Cristobal Balenciaga (1895-1972) opened his first boutique in 1914, and grew to be one of the most influential fashion designers of the mid-20thC. Described by Christian Dior as 'the master of all of us', he is particularly remembered for his tunic, chemise and Empire-style dresses of the late 1950s. His name continues today as part of the Gucci group.

6in (15cm) wide

£150-180   **VE**

A pair of 1980s Playboy yellow, white and black laminated Optyl plastic sunglasses, with original graduated lenses, gold Playboy bunny motif, marked "Made in Austria Optyl Playboy".

Optyl is a cast-moulded, thermo-setting plastic. It is used by Christian Dior, Dunhill and Paloma Picasso, among other, for their eyewear. Vintage licensed Playboy items are becoming increasingly collectable.

5.75in (14.5cm) wide

£120-180   **VE**

A pair of 1970s Occhi malachite green mottled laminated plastic over metal frames, with an applied metal stripe over one eye, the arms marked "Made in W.Germany".

£70-90   **VE**

A pair of 1970s Christian Dior ivory-coloured plastic curving sunglasses, with printed pattern, applied gilt shaped decal with 'CD' logo, and wide arms marked "Christian Dior", "Made in Germany" and "2346".

As with most frames, the addition of a designer's name, such as Dior's, from a classic period, such as the 1960s, indicates good quality and adds value.

5.75in (14.5cm) wide

£150-180   **VE**

A pair of American white plastic sunglasses, screen-printed with black and blue flag and circle motif, and with original sky blue lenses, marked "Cabana TS-1934".

The cat's eye shape is more typical of the 1950s, although the decoration indicates these are later.

5in (13cm) wide

£80-120   **VE**

EYEWEAR

A pair of aluminium frames, with matte 'glitter' effect to the top rim and protruding hinges, stamped "ALUM 46".

5.5in (14cm) wide

£25-40   **BB**

A pair of Bausch & Lomb 'Baluminum' gold-filled aluminium rimless frames, with inset rhinestones, the arms marked "Ballgrip 12KT GF.".

5in (13cm) wide

£180-220   **VE**

ESSENTIAL REFERENCE – VICTOR GROS

A pair of 1980s French 'Michele Lamy pour Victor Gros' Elisabeth black plastic asymmetric frames, with pearlised blue and gold plastic over one eye and arm.

Victor Gros was founded in 1872 by Edouard Gros to produce hair ornaments. They began producing glasses in 1930 when the company was being run by his son Victor Gros. Perhaps their most famous design was the oversized frame produced in 1968 for Jacqueline Kennedy Onassis, which became a hallmark of her look, and 20thC eyewear design. The design was exclusive to Onassis, who was a friend of the Gros family, until the 1980s but is now part of their Traction production range. Michele Lamy is a notable fashion consultant who once designed for Gros. Married to fashion designer Rick Owens, she is also is a backer behind fashion's avant garde ascending star Gareth Pugh.

6in (15.5cm) wide

£70-100   **VE**

A pair of 1960s purple and white woven fabric laminated in clear plastic frames, with 'VO' monogram.

5.75in (14.5cm) wide

£20-25   **BB**

A pair of 1960s French large tartan fabric and laminated plastic sunglasses, with graduated grey lenses, marked "Hand Made in France".

6in (15cm) wide

£120-180   **VE**

A pair of 1970s Ted Lapidus sunglasses, with original graduated UV lenses and wood-effect textured top rim, stamped "Paris Made in France" and "TL 63 02".

5.5in (14cm) wide

£120-180   **VE**

A pair of 1980s Nina Ricci 'Haute Couture' malachite green, white and clear cut and laminated plastic sunglasses, with applied gilt 'Nr' motif, stamped "Nina Ricci Paris", "Handmade" and "CR39" lenses, retaining original card.

The Nina Ricci fashion house was founded by Maria Ricci (1883-1970) in 1932. By the 1950s, she had retired from her active role in the company leaving it to her son Robert and, from 1954, the Belgian designer Jules-Francois Crahay.

5.5in (14cm) wide

£150-180   **VE**

A pair of 1980s French Alain Mikli grey pearlescent and black plastic laminated sunglasses, with original purple lenses, marked "Hand Made in France, C A.M. 88 706 366".

Alain Mikli (b.1955) founded his first eyewear design studio in 1978. Within a few years his innovative designs had attracted the attention of legendary collector Elton John.

5.75in (14.5cm) wide

£150-180   **VE**

A pair of curved rectangular tortoiseshell plastic gentleman's frames, marked "USA 5 3/4".

Striking low and wide rectangular forms such as these have seen a resurgence in popularity for men over the past few years.

5in (12.5cm) wide

£18-22   BB

A pair of American Optical laminated light blue over clear plastic small hexagonal frames.

5in (12.5cm) wide

£15-20   BB

A pair of transparent, pearlescent grey plastic gentleman's frames, with two inset metal star shaped screws, marked "Frame France".

5in (13cm) wide

£15-20   BB

A pair of 1970s American black plastic gentleman's frames, marked "U/Z 512 U.S.A."

Large, visually 'heavier' frames such as these have become fashionable for men over the past few years, particularly with the 'geek chic' trend.

5in (13cm) wide

£15-20   BB

A pair of 1970s deep blue plastic frames.

5.25in (13.5cm) wide

£15-18   BB

A pair of French Swank faceted black plastic gentleman's frames, marked "Frame France".

5.75in (14.5cm) wide

£15-18   BB

A pair of 1940s French handmade tortoiseshell plastic gentleman's sunglasses, the original blue lenses with rectangular "Fait Main Verres Filtrant" sticker and 'hockey stick' arms.

5.5in (14cm) wide

£70-100   VE

Four pairs of similar 1970s new-old stock frames.

The term 'new-old-stock' refers to vintage stock found in shops that was never sold or used. Old opticians are increasingly being used as exciting sources for vintage eyewear.

5.75in (14.5cm) wide

£20-25 (each)   BB

A pair of 1930s-40s light tortoiseshell plastic gentleman's frames, with half hexagonal top rims and 8mm thick arms.

This simple, curved style is known as 'hockey stick' and is desirable.

5.25in (13.5cm) wide

£70-100   VE

EYEWEAR

A pair of 1960s Swank tortoiseshell plastic folding frames, with folding metal parts, stamped "Frame British Hong Kong Swank".

These frames are hinged in a number of places enabling them to be folded down so they could be safely carried in a pocket.

5.5in (14cm) wide

£25-35   BB

A pair of American Dr Peepers black and white 'harlequin' asymmetric frames, marked "S68901".

6in (15.5cm) wide

£20-30   BB

A pair of Hamilton Bogue transfer-printed frames, the multicoloured diamond pattern set with diamanté, yellow lenses and hand-painted 'flag pole' arms.

5.5in (14cm) wide

£150-180   VE

A pair of 1990s pearlised grey laminated on black plastic novelty pig-shaped sunglasses, marked "Made in France CE".

6in (15cm) wide

£70-100   VE

A pair of late 20thC French laminated grey and amber plastic novelty 'gun' sunglasses, set with rhinestones, printed "Made in France".

6in (15cm) wide

£70-100   VE

EXPERT EYE – A PAIR OF NOVELTY SUNGLASSES

The 1960s saw many different decorative treatments applied to frames that did not necessarily focus on practicality, including squares, slits and even grids.

Many of these were inspired by the 'Space Race' and fashion designers' perceptions how we may live and what we may wear in the future.

This style is known as 'Eskimo' as the Inuit (Eskimo) people of Canada made the first sunglasses, which were made with discs cut with slits.

Minimalist styles comprising plain surfaces, curves and use of black, white and silver are also typical features.

A pair of 1960s black plastic 'Eskimo' frames, marked "Christan Frame Italy".

5.75in (14.5cm) wide

£150-180   VE

A unique pair of 1980s customised cocktail-themed sunglasses, on unmarked black plastic frames, one arm painted "J. Chase".

6.25in (16cm) wide

£150-180   VE

FIND OUT MORE...

'Specs Appeal' – Extravagant 1950s & 1960s Eyewear', by Leslie Pina and Donald-Brian Johnson, published by Schiffer Books, 2002.

'Eyeglass Retrospective – Where Fashion & Science Meet', by Nancy Schiffer, published by Schiffer Books, 2000.

ESSENTIAL REFERENCE

- Vintage fashion has moved into the mainstream over the past decade, a trend led by top models and celebrities such as Kate Moss and Sarah Jessica Parker. No longer just the preserve of costume or couture collectors, many buy vintage pieces to add an individual or classic look to an outfit. Although prices have risen, there is still plenty available to suit different budgets. Examples can be found at specialist auctions and costume dealers, and sometimes in charity shops.
- Designs by influential names such as Cristobal Balenciaga, Coco Chanel and Christian Dior will tend to be worth the most, particularly couture items made in limited quantities to exacting specifications. Pieces from notable collections will usually be the most sought-after, particularly if the collection is considered a classic of the designer's work or launched a new movement or style. The recent death of Yves Saint Laurent (1936-2008) may cause a surge of interest in his already iconic designs. Also consider lesser designers whose work is typical of a period.
- The 1950s and '60s, and the Disco era of the 1970s, have been collectable for a number of years and the High Street spawned many pieces copied or inspired by the work of leading designers, as it continues to do today. These are typically more affordable, but look out for the names of top retailers in prestigious locations, as these are often more desirable. Always consider the style of the label as many designers also produced diffusion ranges, which were considerably less expensive at the time and produced in greater numbers.
- Pieces from the 1980s are now rising strongly in value, particularly the work of innovative designers at the time, such as Gianni Versace and Thierry Mugler. A particularly notable example is the influential, and ever inventive, Vivienne Westwood, who became iconic for the Punk style of the 1970s, and went on to produce many important and sought-after collections during the 1980s and '90s.
- When buying, always consider the shape, construction, material, pattern and colour. Finer quality pieces will be well-cut, using high grade materials and stitching. Avoid pieces that are stained or torn – unless this is intentional. Look at fashion books and learn how to recognise the key looks of a decade. Away from the work of leading designers, the more desirable pieces of any decade sum up the age perfectly and have eye appeal.

A 1980s Koos Van der Akker patchwork wool and mink coat, of felted mohair, with printed and woven cottons and flannels and mahogany mink, lined in plaid flannel with slightly off-centre buttons, raglan sleeves, labelled "Koos Couture, Koos Van Der Akker New York".

46in (117cm) long

£500-700   **FRE**

A 1970s Loris Azzaro black jersey two-piece dress, with shirred waist, plunging neckline, rhinestone edging, and matching full length over-vest with rhinestone-encrusted shoulders and tie at neck, labelled "Loris Azzaro Paris/Made in France".

Size 4-6

£150-200   **FRE**

A mid-1960s Pierre Balmain pale green gazar ballgown, with crystal jewelled embroidered panel, labelled and numbered "136 76 2", with matching jewelled stole.

Gazar is a loosely woven silk with a crisp finish.

Bust 36in (91.5cm)

£900-1,200   **KT**

A mid-1960s Pierre Balmain pale green silk and jewelled evening gown, with raised white vinyl domes on silvered discs with aureoles of white beads and pastes, the bodice and hem borders with chunky hexagonal Perspex medallion bands, labelled and numbered "140,034".

Bust 34in (86cm)

£500-600   **KT**

An early 1980s Azzedine Alaïa perforated suede safari suit, the pale yellow lining revealed through the perforated roundels in the leather, labelled.

Size 40

£750-850   **KT**

FASHION

A late 1960s Geoffrey Beene jewel-tone metallic brocade A-line tunic evening dress, with Nehru collar, covered buttons, on-seam pockets, cuffs split and belled, labelled "Geoffrey Beene".

Size 10

£150-200   FRE

An early 1970s Biba cotton maxi dress, printed with large red and white ladybirds on a navy ground with an oversized pointed collar, red heart-shaped buttons on a fitted bodice with applied triangular breast pockets.

£120-180   FRE

A 1970s Bill Blass red chiffon evening gown, with attached scarf details, an under-column of rayon jersey and overlay and sleeves of sheer chiffon, labelled "Bill Blass".

Size 10

£80-120   FRE

A 1990s Bill Blass sequinned and feathered cocktail dress, covered in small black, grey and white sequins in a looping pattern, the skirt with 'salt and pepper' coloured ostrich feathers, labelled "Bill Blass" and "Martha".

Size 4

£550-650   FRE

A Bob Bugnand embroidered tulle evening gown, of pale blue tulle, embellished with bands of smoke grey sequins, gold embroidery and bugle beads and pale blue pastes, labelled "Bob Bugnand, Paris".

c1955-60   Bust 36in (91cm)

£500-600   KT

EXPERT EYE – A BALENCIAGA DAY DRESS

Cristobal Balenciaga (1895-1972) was one of the most influential couturiers of his day, working for the house he founded until 1968. This piece was produced in 1965.

It is made from brocatelle, a comparatively heavy, woven patterned fabric typically of silk and linen, similar to brocade. The use of heavy fabrics was typical of Balenciaga's designs at the time.

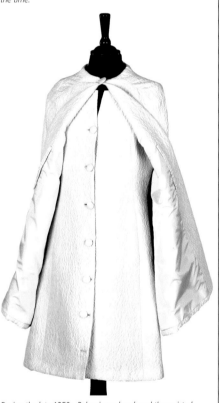

During the late 1950s, Balenciaga abandoned the waisted hourglass form of the New Look, designing more linear tunic, chemise and sack dresses. Jacket capes were another common part of his designs.

His day wear was highly influential, and was worn by celebrities and personalities of the day, including Jackie Kennedy, the Duchess of Windsor and Diana Vreeland.

A Balenciaga ivory brocatelle day dress and cape, the simple sleeveless shift dress fastened by buttons down the front, invisible pockets inset into the front side seams, simple cape with single button to fasten, both pieces labelled and numbered "100656".

c1965   Bust 32in (81cm)

£1,300-1,800   KT

A black moss crêpe wool evening gown, attributed to Pierre Cardin, the high neck with stand collar, V-shaped yoke to bodice echoing the pointed hem edged in streamers of fabric, black silk lining, unlabelled.

1970   *Bust 34in (86cm)*

£300-400   **KT**

A black moss crêpe mini dress, attributed to Pierre Cardin, with car-wash hem, and with gym-slip type bodice from which the bands fall and loop back into the Chinese lantern style skirt, unlabelled.

c1969-70   *Bust 34in (86cm)*

£500-600   **KT**

A contemporary Roberto Cavalli bias-cut silk gown, with spaghetti-straps and a naturalistically depicted snake and fruit motif, unlined, with a train and back zip closure, labelled "Roberto Cavalli".

Size small

£180-220   **FRE**

A 1990s bright coral-pink Chanel skirt suit, medium weight bouclé wool, with straight pencil skirt, double-breasted nipped-waist jacket with gold and velvet buttons, black velvet trim, labelled "Chanel Boutique".

Size 36-38

£400-500   **FRE**

A 1970s Chanel black silk chiffon metallic jacquard shirtwaist dinner dress, with bronze, gold and silver shaded dots, gold buttons, attached tie at the neckline, and calf-length gored-pleat skirt, labelled "Chanel Boutique".

£220-280   **FRE**

A Chanel white, pink and black tweed suit, with tousled edging to the short, boxy jacket, and matching skirt, labelled.

2005   Bust 38in (97cm)

£550-650   **KT**

An mid-1970s Ossie Clark/Celia Birtwell for Radley 'Floating Daisies' printed cream moss crêpe dress, with black and green printed bodice, and button front, labelled, with original shop tag.

Size 38

£400-500   **KT**

An Ossie Clark/Celia Birtwell printed muslin halterneck summer dress, with pale peach and black lily print overall, and wrap-around skirt, printed Ossie label.

c1970   *Size 14*

£320-380   **KT**

FASHION

ESSENTIAL REFERENCE – OSSIE CLARK

A late 1960s Ossie Clark/Celia Birtwell 'Floating Daisies' printed chiffon dress, the cream chiffon ground printed overall in black and green, with Alice Pollock printed label.

Bust 36in (91cm)

£500-600 KT

An Ossie Clark/Celia Birtwell printed chiffon dress, printed with a green lattice and purple flowers on a primrose chiffon ground, with button front with handkerchief flounces to cuffs and hem, printed Ossie label.

This dress was inspired by fashions of the 1920s.

c1969 *Size 12*

£500-600 KT

An early 1970s André Courrèges cotton summer dress, the bodice of white honeycomb mesh edged in appliquéd embroidered cotton rope-twist banding, with matching belt, labelled and numbered "102216".

Bust 32in (81cm)

£350-450 KT

Ossie Clark (1942-96) was one of the most influential and popular designers of the 1960s, and was dubbed the 'King of King's Road'. A year after he graduated from the Royal College of Art in 1965, he produced a range for Quorum, owned by Alice Pollock. Within a year, the company had run into financial trouble due to Pollock and Clark's excessive lifestyles, and the company was acquired by Radley. In 1968, his diffusion range 'Ossie Clark for Radley' was released. He is known for his use of flowing chiffon and moss crepe to give a flamboyant, romantic and floaty feel to his dresses, which is backed up by the use of printed patterns of stylized natural motifs. These were designed by textile designer Celia Birtwell (b.1941), who first met Ossie in 1959 and became his wife in 1969. They worked together until just after their divorce in 1974, with Clark continuing to design, albeit on a lesser scale, until the 1980s when the Punk era dawned.

An Ossie Clark/Celia Birtwell black chiffon wrap-over dress, printed with cream and pink star-like florets in differing sizes, and with contrasting flounces to the neckline, printed Ossie label.

c1970 *Size 12*

£550-650 KT

A late 1960s/early 1970s André Courrèges couture purple velvet trouser suit, comprising shaped, futuristic styled waistcoat with zip front, edged in purple vinyl, matching flared trousers, lined in white satin, labelled and numbered "122910".

Bust 36in (92cm)

£700-800 KT

A Marc Bohan for Christian Dior black and gold cocktail dress, with corseted inner bodice attached to the skirt, sleeveless brocade over-bodice, the fabric brocaded with tulips against a black ground in shades of gold, belt with large black jet-like stones, labelled and numbered "7521".

This dress was part of the Autumn/Winter 1962 collection. Bohan (b.1926) was the primary designer at Dior from 1958 to 1989, with his 1966 'Peter Pan' collection being particularly notable.

Bust 35in (89cm)

£600-700 KT

A mid-1960s Ekto for Harrods Op-art coat, with press-stud fastenings, oval patch pockets, leather tabbed detail to the chest, together with a matching head-dress with peak to the front and turban-like ties to the back, (not shown), labelled.

Chest 36in (91cm)

£250-350   **KT**

A 1970s Gaby Espagne midnight blue rhinestone-encrusted gown, completely covered in beads and multicoloured rhinestones, with embroidered label.

Size 4-6

£150-250   **FRE**

A mid-1950s Jacques Fath watermelon chiffon cocktail gown, with horizontal pleats to the breast in contrast to the narrow vertical pleats of the skirt, labelled.

Jacques Fath (1912-54) is considered one of the most influential couturiers of the immediate postwar period, along with Christian Dior and Pierre Balmain. Releasing his first collection in 1937, he is known for his wide fluttering skirts and his 1950 'Lily' collection with skirts shaped like flowers.

Bust 34in (86cm)

£800-1,200   **KT**

A probably 1990s/early 2000s Givenchy couture black bugle beaded cocktail dress, the column of black beads intersected with a flesh-toned organza and tulle band across the bodice, forming a T across the shoulders, labelled and numbered.

Size 38

£500-600   **KT**

A 1980s Hachi silver satin one-shouldered evening gown, the long sleeve and undulating neckline edged in shimmering silver bugle beads, gently blousing bodice over columnar skirt, labelled.

Bust 36in (91cm)

£500-600   **KT**

A late 1970s Halston red silk chiffon one-shouldered Grecian gown, the bodice in two sheer layers of silk fastening with a hook at one shoulder, with an elastic waist and long wrap-around skirt forming a flounce at one hip, with a long narrow scarf, labelled "Halston" and "B. Altman & Company", some damage to skirt towards hem.

Size 6-8

£400-500   **FRE**

COAT: A 1960s-70s Guy Laroche sheer black silk coat, in very sheer textured raw silk with open front, collarless, hand-finished on all edges, labelled "Guy Laroche Paris" with "4594" handwritten verso.

£150-200   **FRE**

DRESS: A 1960s-70s Guy Laroche white crepe jersey strapless column gown, elegant simple strapless sheath with built-in tulle corseting, double-zipper at the left side, full length, labelled "Guy Laroche Paris" and "2667" handwritten verso.

Size 6-8

£60-80   **FRE**

A 1970s Guy Laroche periwinkle satin silk and feathered pyjama ensemble, buttoned-down blouse with wide feather trimmed collar, with dyed feather vest with hidden hook-and-eye closures, labelled "Guy Laroche Paris, Made in France" with "8590" written on tape label, verso.

£150-200   FRE

A 1960s-70s Guy Laroche black and white paisley and floral-beaded column gown, with black silk satin empire-waisted bodice, attached back-fastening elbow-length bolero over-bodice, interior corseting at waist, labelled "Guy Laroche/Paris".

Size 4-6

£180-220   FRE

A Jean-Louis couture red ostrich feather coat, exuberant fire-engine red with long sleeves and a train, no closures, lined in red satin, labelled "Jean-Louis" and "Lacledes, Memphis".

£1,000-1,500   FRE

A 1980s Issey Miyake violet cotton dress, long sleeves, inset V-shaped bib buttoning at the shoulders, mirrored by inverted V-shaped insets at front and back, labelled "Issey Miyake".

Size medium

£70-100   FRE

A Claude Montana shocking-pink suede and leather bodice and skirt, in homage to Schiaparelli, the suede asymmetric top press-stud fastened down one side with single shoulder strap, the body-hugging skirt with flounced hem and back split, labelled.

c1980   *Bust 35in (89cm)*

£550-650   KT

EXPERT EYE – A MUGLER JUMPSUIT

Mugler's work has an individual style, yet one firmly grounded in the 1980s. He was known for almost harsh, angular designs, often with wide padded shoulders and cinched waists.

The heavy unpatterned grey is typical of his choice of colours and matches the theme perfectly.

Here he looked back to jumpsuits worn by Communist workers during the 1920s and '30s, but the design also hints at a world of the future and robots, two other themes that run through his work.

Seen as too extreme at the time, as well as very expensive, these jumpsuits are rare today.

An early 1980s Thierry Mugler Communist-style jump suit, of loosely cut grey gabardine, with red stand collar and square press-stud fasteners, with sun-ray stitched yoke, diagonal fastening, deep patch pockets and broad belt, labelled.

Size 38

£3,200-3,800   KT

A 1960s Norman Norell taupe wool ensemble, A-line sleeveless dress with princess seams, wide leather belt, vertical welt pockets and silver fox trim with matching cropped three-button jacket, labelled "Norman Norell/New York" and "Marsal".

Size 6-8

£250-350   FRE

A 1960s Mollie Parnis gold-beaded cocktail dress, sleeveless round collared sheath lined in silk, back zip, heavily encrusted with glass beads and rhinestones and with beaded fringe at the hem and with a narrow matching belt, labelled "Mollie Parnis New York".

Size 4

£120-180   FRE

A 1970s Jean Patou pink metallic brocade tunic and pants, asymmetrical button-down closure with high neck and long sleeves, hip pockets, matching straight-leg slacks, labelled "Jean Patou Week End, Paris" and "Couture Boutique, Bergdorf Goodman" etc.

£80-120   FRE

A 1970s-80s Oscar de la Renta feather and sequin gown, silk chiffon bodice with sequin decoration and black cock feather ruff collar and cuffs, satin bow at waist and floor-length sequin-decorated velvet skirt, labelled "Oscar de la Renta" and "Marsal".

Size 4-6

£220-280   FRE

An Oscar de la Renta tweed cocktail dress, sleeveless black and white bouclé tweed cocktail-length sheath dress with bead, ostrich feather and rhinestone accents and with wool-fringed and tulle hem, labelled "Oscar de la Renta".

Size 6

£250-350   FRE

A 1970s Nina Ricci black silk tuxedo yoke bubble dress, jacquard tiny heart patterned silk with long sleeves and high neck, micro-pleated silk chiffon ruffled yoke and shirtsleeve cuffs, falling to below the knee in a gathered ruffle, labelled "Nina Ricci Boutique, Paris, Made in France".

Size 6

£200-300   FRE

A 1980s Yves Saint Laurent silk grosgrain twill party dress, geometric stars and symbols in bright primary and jewel-tone colours on black, deep scoop neckline and puffed-shoulder three-quarter length sleeves, pleated from the natural waist and falling to the calf, labelled "Yves Saint Laurent/Rive Gauche".

Size 40

£60-80   FRE

A 1980s-90s Yves Saint Laurent black cocktail dress, long sleeved with a pleated pouffed-out skirt in black silk-blend taffeta, with large faceted black glass buttons from the waist down, V-neck neckline with gored pleat forming a faux interior layer, hidden hooks to close at bust, labelled "Yves Saint Laurent/Rive Gauche".

Size 38

£180-220   FRE

FASHION

A Vivienne Westwood 'Nostalgia of Mud' collection skirt, with Mudman print, of navy fleece fabric with textural grey 'mud' print, white stockinette waistband and side panels, World's End label.

1982-3   Bust 26in (66cm)

£500-600   **KT**

A Vivienne Westwood track-suit ensemble, probably 'Punkature' collection, top printed with combination Keith Haring and Buffalo Gal motifs, white side panels to bodice, buttoned fly and hems of the track-pants, World's Ends label.

1983   Chest 60in (152cm)

£700-800   **KT**

EXPERT EYE – VIVIENNE WESTWOOD ENSEMBLE

The 'Nostalgia of Mud' collection was Westwood's third, and came after the sex-and-bondage inspired Punk fashions of the 1970s.

It examined both African, Indian and other cultures that were beginning to become a more visible part of multicultural British life.

The name was also used for a shop opened in London in 1982, which sold similarly styled clothes. It closed in 1984, a year after Westwood split from collaborator Malcolm McLaren.

Torn, dishevelled and distressed fabric in muddy browns and beiges were typical, and her preference for unusual fabrics and cuts is clear.

A Vivienne Westwood 'Nostalgia of Mud' collection ensemble, comprising cable knit sweater dress, the blue-grey flecked knitted skirt cut higher at the front, together with a pair of brown leather shoes with triple straps, with World's End label.

1982-83   Chest 42in (102cm)

£1,200-1,800   **KT**

A Vivienne Westwood Punkature collection printed 'big collar shirt', striped bib-front inset into a gold toile-de-Jouy style print on a mottled pink and brown ground, extra wide neck; together with a pair of slate grey cotton trousers, worn high on the chest with leather braces inset with metal springs, deep button flies, World's End label.

1983   34in (86cm)

£850-950   **KT**

A Vivienne Westwood Keith Haring designed 'Smiley Face' top, from the 'Witches' collection, woven in shades of light and dark grey, World's End label.

1983-84   Chest 39in (96cm)

£700-800   **KT**

A Vivienne Westwood 'Time Machine' collection black leather 'Armour' jacket, the waistcoat section with press-stud fastening detachable sleeves with open inner arms, segmented shoulder panels, red label.

1988-89   Bust 40in (102cm)

£700-800   **KT**

FIND OUT MORE...

'Miller's Collecting Fashion & Accessories',
by Carol Harris, published by Miller's, 2000.

An early 20thC black beaver fur top hat, with a wool band, in fitted calfskin leather case labelled "Boyd's St. Louis", with handle, brass lock and key.

£65-75　　　　　　　　FRE

A black silk top hat, with band, in a leather box with fitted interior and handle, impressed "Paris Exposition Universelle 1900". *c1900*

£35-45　　　　　　　　WDL

A late 1920s woven straw cloche hat, with green velvet band and silk poppy flowers.

As this would only fit a small head, it may have been made for a child.

7in (18cm) high

£25-40　　　　　　　　LH

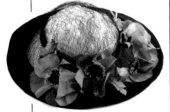

A 1930s wool felt and woven horse hair hat, with silk poppies.

14.25in (36cm) wide

£40-60　　　　　　　　LH

A 1950s-60s Lilly Daché pink cocktail hat, bright bubble-gum pink dupioni silk with banded and wide double-bow detail.

£50-100　　　　　　　　FRE

FASHION

ESSENTIAL REFERENCE

- Traditionally worn over the head as protection, the scarf as headwear gained further prominence during WWII when women wore them to keep their hair away from their work. During the 1950s, period colours and fashions drew designs away from more traditional and sober styles and patterns. Colours became brighter and motifs became light-hearted.

- The headscarf became an iconic form of headwear during the 1950s. Typical printed motifs included fashionable ladies, often walking their dogs, good luck symbols, polka dots and foreign places. As foreign travel also increased, souvenir scarves were produced. Notable names, such as Hermés or Pucci, will also add value, particularly if the patterns are typical of the company.

- Look for bright colours and motifs that are typical of the period. Silk is usually valued higher than cotton or other materials, as it would have cost more originally, but it is generally the theme and eye-appeal that contributes most towards desirability. Examine edges carefully and look out for tiny holes. Although it is best to ask a specialist to clean vintage examples, cotton and man-made fibre scarves can be carefully washed at home.

A 1950s yellow printed cotton good luck themed scarf, with black cat motifs and 'good luck' in numerous European languages.

24.75in (63cm) wide

£20-30   **GCHI**

A 1950s-60s printed sky blue silk 'Superstition' scarf, with diamonds containing lucky activities.

19in (48cm) wide

£20-25   **GCHI**

A 1950s printed red lucky charm scarf, with four-leaf clover, key, dog and horseshoe motifs.

19in (48cm) wide

£20-30   **GCHI**

A 1950s-60s printed fabric St Ives tourist souvenir scarf, with vignettes of scenes of St Ives.

16.25in (42cm) wide

£30-40   **GCHI**

A 1950s French RD Paris hand-painted silk scarf, with four scenes of stylized figures driving, taking a walk or undertaking other activities, and with frayed edges.

22.5in (57cm) wide

£20-30   **GCHI**

A 1950s American printed nylon 'Vermont – The Green Mountain State' tourist souvenir scarf.

29.5in (75cm) wide

£25-35   **GCHI**

A 1950s green and white printed silk harlequin scarf.

16.5in (42cm) wide

£18-22   GCHI

A 1950s printed silk dog walking themed scarf.

16.25in (42cm) wide

£25-35   GCHI

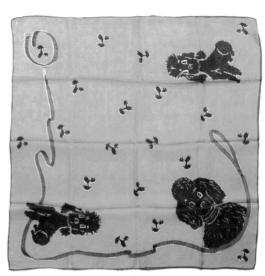

A 1950s turquoise printed silk scarf, decorated with poodles, retailed by Littlewoods.

Poodles and Scottie dogs are the most typical dogs shown during the 1950s – both evoke period style and fashion.

30.75in (78cm) wide

£25-35   GCHI

A 1950s Italian printed nylon 'perfume bottle' scarf.

27.25in (69cm) wide

£30-40   GCHI

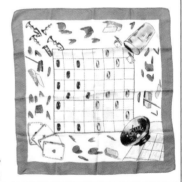

A 1950s printed silk gambling themed scarf, with draughts, roulette, cards and chess motifs.

Gambling is another theme typical of the 1950s – but one more commonly associated with men than women.

18in (46cm) wide

£20-25   GCHI

A 1950s printed cowboy and horse riding themed scarf, with central horseshoe motif.

Cowboys and cowgirls were clean-cut, popular All-American heroes and heroines during the 1950s. The trend was led by characters such as Hopalong Cassidy and Roy Rogers. The horseshoes also double as a good luck symbol.

21.25in (54cm) wide

£45-55   GCHI

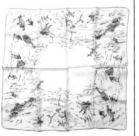

A 1950s printed winter sports themed scarf.

18.5in (47cm) wide

£20-25   GCHI

A 1940s printed fabric 'big band' pattern scarf.

31.5in (80cm) wide

£45-55   GCHI

FASHION

ESSENTIAL REFERENCE

- Even though men's clothes after WWII remained largely the same as those before the war, being somewhat sober and traditional, signs of brighter and more cheerful fashions began to appear. Much of these came from the US, where the teenager was becoming a force to be reckoned with, synthetic fibres were growing in popularity, and there was more freedom to experiment.
- One piece of clothing that changed dramatically was the tie. Designs became bolder, louder and more indicative of men's tastes at the time, moving away from traditional stripes and repeated motifs. Hawaii, gambling, drinking and naked or scantily clad pin-up girls, which gained

popularity with servicemen during the war, were key influences. Ties became wider to accommodate increasingly bold designs.
- Many were made on the West Coast of the US, and as well as being printed, a surprising number were hand-painted. Today, these have become immensely desirable once again as part of the trend for retro and vintage styles. Erotic or nude ties tend to be the most popular, but look out for any that show well-executed painted designs in a style typical of the period. Look carefully for holes, or minor tears. Ties should be taken to a specialist cleaner rather than washing them yourself.

An original 1940s painted silk 'showgirl' tie, with double showgirl decoration, recently assembled.

3.75in (9.5cm) wide

£120-180   **GCHI**

A 1940s 'South Pacific' hand-painted pin-up tie.

4.25in (11cm) wide

£120-180   **GCHI**

A 1940s-50s hand-painted nude pin-up tie, with 'Handpainted in California by Leon' label.

3.75in (9.5cm) wide

£100-150   **GCHI**

A 1940s hand-painted pin-up tie, showing a nude posing with her arms above her head.

4in (10cm) wide

£150-200   **GCHI**

A 1940s tropical themed pin-up tie, showing a nude on a beach.

4.5in (11.5cm) wide

£70-100   **GCHI**

A 1950s Cunningham Shields Topeka 'Blind Date' brown 'peekaboo' tie, with hidden printed glamour girl decoration.

Peekaboo ties reached the height of their popularity during the 1940s and '50s. Sober designs on the front hid a secret on the tie's lining. Originals are sought-after today, and the saucier the girl, the higher the price. The 'peekaboo' fad was re-introduced c2002, when designer Paul Smith printed nudes inside ties and in shirt cuffs. Even British Prime Minister Tony Blair was seen wearing one of his 'peekaboo' shirts.

3.25in (8cm) wide

£80-120   **GCHI**

The pointy headed fat dwarf is a Billiken, an ancient Egyptian or Alaskan character associated with good luck and fun.

It was popularized from 1908 by US illustrator Florence Pretz after she received a patent for her drawn designs, and was the subject of a craze lasting until c1912.

As well as being printed and painted, his eyes and belly button are highlighted with small rhinestones.

The Billiken was also used by the Royal Order of Jesters, founded as part of the Freemasons in 1911. Membership is by invitation and unanimous vote only, and is limited to 13 new members annually.

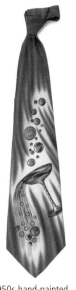

A 1950s hand-painted blue 'champagne' tie, with 'Made in California' label.

4.25in (10.5cm) wide

£70-100   **GCHI**

A 1950s French hand-painted silk 'Folies Bergere' tie.

3.75in (9.5cm) wide

£60-80   **GCHI**

A 1950s 'Desertones Marathon Cravat' hand-painted tie, made in San Francisco.

3.25in (8.5cm) wide

£100-150   **GCHI**

A 1950s Pilgrim hand-painted nylon tie, with a Mexican street scene.

4.5in (11.5cm) wide

£50-80   **GCHI**

A Pilgrim hand-painted marlin tie, with two fish and bands of brushstroke effects.

4in (10cm) wide

£50-80   **GCHI**

A 1950s Cutter Cravat Original 'Crooner' tie, showing a singer being applauded.

4in (10cm) wide

£70-100   **GCHI**

A 1960s burgundy 'Royal Order of Jesters' tie, with painted Billiken and applied jewels.

3in (7.5cm) wide

£60-90   **GCHI**

FASHION

A 1940s pair of red leather shoes, in mint condition and unworn.

These are typical of the period with their solid, blocky form and sensible, practical heels.

£80-120   GCHI

A 1940s pair of Palizzio of New York black suede sling-backs, with red and black beads in the form of a poodle, and black sequin detail.

8in (20cm) long

£180-220   GCHI

A 1950s pair of Mackey Starr of New York handmade 'Countess' last sling-backs, with diamanté studded Lucite high heels and applied gilt metal 'buckles' inset with multi-coloured rhinestones.

£120-180   GCHI

A 1950s pair of Dezario shoes, with multicoloured assembled Lucite semi-circular heels, the black straps with holes and applied Lucite cabouchons.

8in (20cm) long

£25-35   NOR

A 1950s pair of wooden heeled mules, with woven straw uppers and clear Lucite heels containing raffia flowers, with very light wear.

6.5in (16.5cm) long

£200-250   GCHI

A 1950s pair of Italian carved and painted wood and woven raffia mules, with multicoloured raffia trim and applied flowers, in mint and unworn condition.

The straps are lined with leather to prevent the raffia chafing the skin.

9in (23cm) long

£200-250 **GCHI**

A 1950s pair of Schiaparelli black patent leather shoes, with original ribbon, in excellent condition.

£220-280 **GCHI**

A 1950s pair of Gainsborough beige leather shoes, the silver leather and pink snakeskin toe decoration with three-leaf motif and applied metal circular decoration with inset rhinestones and turquoise enamel.

£100-150 **GCHI**

EXPERT EYE – A PAIR OF SHOES WITH INTERCHANGEABLE HEELS

Polish shoemaker Israel Miller began making shoes in 1892 for actresses in Broadway's theatrical productions. They were so beautiful and well-made that he was soon asked to make shoes for them personally.

In 1911, he opened a store on Broadway & 46th St in New York. In 1929, he adorned the building with sculptural wording by Alexander Sterling Calder concerning shoes, which can still be seen today.

The interchangeable heel system is rare and complex, and adds value, particularly as the three different heel styles are still together, and in mint condition.

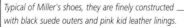

Typical of Miller's shoes, they are finely constructed with black suede outers and pink kid leather linings.

A 1950s pair of I. Miller 'Beautiful' Perugia style black suede shoes, from the Paris collection, lined with pink kid leather, with three interchangeable heels, one set with diamanté, one set with beading and one set plain.

Interestingly, during the 1950s, Miller hired Andy Warhol to illustrate the company's advertising in an attempt to revamp the ailing brand.

9.5in (24cm) long

£200-300 **GCHI**

A 1950s pair of wedges, with iridescent sequins sewn with turquoise miniature beads, and applied floral motifs made up of miniature turquoise beads and with faux pearl centres.

£70-100 **GCHI**

A 1960s pair of stiletto sandals, with gold leather and clear plastic straps, gold leather lining and multicoloured woven, striped decoration, in mint condition and unworn.

£80-120   **GCHI**

A 1950s pair of Dream Step Originals cream leather high-heeled shoes, the toes decorated with a hand-painted gold stylized foliate pattern highlighted with flowers and edged with metal studs with inset rhinestones.

The colour and curving, yet pointed shape of these shoes make them extremely elegant.

£100-150   **GCHI**

A 1960s pair of pumps, with multicoloured printed floral design overlaid with applied iridescent hexagonal glitter, together with matching handbag, in mint condition, the shoes hardly worn.

£120-180   **GCHI**

A 1950s pair of cream leather sling-backs, decorated with gilt-edged hand-painted floral design, in unworn ,mint condition.

£100-150   **GCHI**

A 1950s-60s pair of Italian Mazerio hand-lasted stilettos, with woven gold thread and silver glitter, together with matching clutch bag, in mint condition.

£50-70   **NOR**

A 1950s pair of Herbert Levine beige suede stilettos, with suede and 'jewelled' rhinestone tassels.

Size 6-61/2

£100-150   GCHI

A 1970s pair of Vivaldi high heels, with silver reflective plastic heels and black suede straps inset with rhinestone triangles.

8in (20cm) long

£50-70   NOR

EXPERT EYE – A PAIR OF HERBERT LEVINE SHOES

Herbert Levine shoes were designed by Herbert's wife, Beth Levine (1914-2006), who trained under Israel Miller and became his head designer.

Her shoes were worn by many celebrities and First Ladies, and she also invented the revolutionary Spring-O-Lator for mules.

She is best known for reintroducing boots to haute couture. Examples were famously worn by Nancy Sinatra when she sang 'These Boots Are Made For Walkin''"

She is also known for her sculptural heels, fine quality construction, maverick designs and colourful patterns – her shoes have become hot collectors' items.

A 1950s pair of Herbert Levine blue and white printed polka dot slingbacks.

£70-90   GCHI

A pair of 1970s-80s Cover Girl 'Go Bananas' pink suede shoes, with cut holes in the plastic heels.

These holes would have added a spring to a girl's step, making them more comfortable to wear.

8.75in (22cm) long

£20-30   NOR

A 1970s pair of Italian Carber platform shoes, with wooden soles and printed green and white flower fabric straps, with original box.

8.5in (21.5cm) long

£50-70   NOR

A pair of 1980s Napoleon of London gold glitter-on-leather high-heels, with block heels.

These sparkling disco-tastic shoes would have looked great on the dancefloor.

8.25in (21cm) long

£70-90   GCHI

A 1970s pair of yellow leather sandals, in very good condition.

£100-150 GCHI

A 1950s pair of Lady Studio patent yellow leather effect plastic open-toed high heels, with lace detailing.

8.75in (22cm) high

£15-25 NOR

A 1980s pair of The American Girl black, brown and white woven basketweave fabric high heels.

10.25 (26cm) long

£15-25 NOR

A 1950s pair of black fabric stilettos, with woven multicoloured rectangles, in mint condition.

£40-60 GCHI

ESSENTIAL REFERENCE – CHARLES JOURDAN

A 1980s pair of Charles Jourdan vivid purple suede shoes, with deep purple leather bows.

Charles Jourdan (1883-1976) is best known for his women's shoes, which he began producing in 1919. The 1950s saw expansion after great success, with a shop in Paris and sales to the UK. Along with Herbert and Beth Levine, they became notable for their use of unusual materials combined with fine construction and 'tailored' shapes and details. During the 1960s and '70s, their avant-garde advertising drew many to the brand, to which handbags were added in 1975. Although Charles died in 1976, the business continued to prosper under his sons into the 1980s. However, sales began to decline in the late 1980s, particularly after bad publicity in connection with Imelda Marcos, who owned many Jourdan shoes. In 2002, the company filed for bankruptcy despite the attempts of Patrick Cox as designer, but continues today under new ownership.

£100-150 GCHI

A 1950s pair of American Buster Brown black velvet children's 'Mary Jane' shoes, with transfer motif to the gilt interior.

6.75in (17cm) long

£25-35 GCHI

ESSENTIAL REFERENCE

- The 1950s saw an explosion in design following the restrictions of WWII. As well as serious new design movements, a sense of fun, colour and frivolity pervaded designs. Themes included glamour, scantily clad girls, polka dots and playing card motifs, as well as geometric or abstract patterns that followed on from the Art Deco movement of the 1930s. Forms and patterns were frequently curving and asymmetric, and were often inspired by futuristic molecular or atomic motifs.

- New materials, many developed during the war, also took hold – plastics in particular. Plastic could be moulded easily and economically into a range of forms, and could be brightly coloured, matching the hopeful outlook of the decade. The material really took hold during the 1960s, when it was used to make furniture and other items. Many were moulded into the space-age forms popular at the time. Formica offered similarly modern, affordable and easy to maintain pieces.

- The 1950s and '60s also saw the emergence of a 'throw away' culture, with many items being produced and sold inexpensively in fashionable styles. As styles changed, items were discarded and new ones bought. Young couples moved into new homes and decorated them in a colourful and modern way that rejected the styles of their parents. The teenager also emerged as a new and important part of society.

- The highest prices are reserved for those items by influential and important designers. However, representative pieces can be found at affordable prices. Always consider the style, pattern and colour, as well as the condition. Many pieces were not made for long-term use and were worn and damaged over the years. A piece that is colourful, appealing and typical of the period in mint condition is likely to be a good investment.

A 1950s bent wire musical note-themed glass side table, with magazine rack below.

26in (66cm) high

£25-35   MA

A 1950s Freemans Catalogue 'Home Sweet Home' bent wire 'musical' coat rack, with treble cleff and note motifs.

In 1957, this rack cost 21 shillings and 6 pence.

27.75in (70cm) wide

£70-100   MA

A scarce 1950s laminated wood cactus or jewellery stand, with three platforms.

Both the colours and the shape of the platforms are typically 1950s. The cactus was a relatively new favourite in the 1950s.

8in (20cm) high

£50-70   MA

A 1950s German flower table, with printed glass surfaces, wooden legs and metal detailing.

Ivy could be grown up the curving trellis. The pattern, colours and overall form are typical of the 1950s, which saw a boom in the popularity of houseplants with new, young home owners.

33.25in (84cm) high

£80-120   QU

A set of six 1950s Lyndalware place mats, made from laminated and printed wood, and plastic, in original box.

5.5in (14cm) wide

£35-45   MA

A 1950s German Goebel napkin holder, the glazed ceramic torso, arms and head on a wooden base with original printed folded napkins forming her skirt.

Goebel is a high quality German ceramics manufacturer, who also produced Hummel figurines.

A 1950s German tea cosy, the synthetic material with woven and printed geometric design.

12in (30.5cm) wide

£35-45   QU

A 1950s German tea cosy, the synthetic material with stylized foliate design and metal handle.

12in (30.5cm) wide

£35-45   QU

9in (22.5cm) high

£60-80   QU

A 1950s-60s fabric doll-shaped hat stand, unmarked.

15.75in (40cm) high

£15-20   AEM

An Alexander Backer Co. double-headed 'Janus' vase, the base with with "ABCO Hand-painted Made in the USA Alexander Backer Co. NY" brown foil oval label.

7.25in (18cm) high

£60-90   ANT

A pair of 1950s 'Plantation' pattern printed cotton curtains, designed by Lucienne Day, with printed wording to selvedge.

Lucienne Day became a renowned textile designer in the 1950s and '60s after she released her 'Calyx' design at the 1951 Festival of Britain. 'Plantation' was released in 1958. Values today depend on the size and shape of the curtain – many new homes in the 1950s had short, but wide, windows.

91.75in (233cm) long

£300-400 (pair)   WW

A pair of Heal's 'Chicane' pattern printed cotton curtains, designed by Philip Turney, with printed wording to selvedge.

81in (206cm) high

£40-60 (pair)   WW

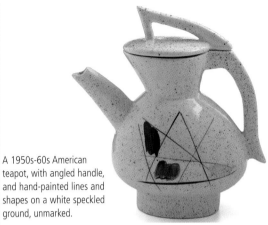

A 1950s-60s American teapot, with angled handle, and hand-painted lines and shapes on a white speckled ground, unmarked.

Despite the fact that the designer and maker of this teapot are unknown, the fantastic shape makes it a must-have for any Fifties fan.

9in (22.5cm) high

£15-25   TWF

A 1950s-60s American dish, hand-painted with lines and shapes on a white speckled ground, unmarked.

2.5in (6.5cm) high

£5-7   TWF

A 1950s hand-painted asymmetric vase, the base impressed "1042".

9in (23cm) high

£10-15   GAZE

A 1950s cruet set, with hand-painted zebra-like pattern and gilt rims.

The zebra pattern was popular during the 1950s, with Beswick and Midwinter producing their own market-leading examples. The organic, bud-like forms are also typical of the decade's style.

3.5in (9cm) high

£50-70   BEV

A set of six 1950s German ceramic ashtrays, of elliptical form with hand-painted designs of stylized animals including deer, birds, fish and a rabbit.

Each 6in (15cm) widest

£150-200   QU

A 1950s Belgian Henri Bequet Quaregnon organic form dish, decorated with green, yellow, pink and black stripes, and gilt detailing and rim, with two gilded balls, the base with decorator's signature and model number "485".

20in (50.5cm) widest

£70-100   QU

A set of 12 Fornasetti 'Grand Maestri' plates, decorated with black transfer-printed portraits of composers in the style of 19thC etchings, with gilt borders showing musical instruments, some wear to gilding.

10in (25.5cm) diam

£100-200   WW

A set of six 1950s colour lithographed can-can dancer tumblers, unused, with gilt trim and original card box.

Each 4.25in (11cm) high

£50-70   MA

A set of six 1950s small transfer-printed can-can dancer shot glasses, with gilt rims and original card box.

Each 2.75in (7cm) high

£30-50   MA

A set of six early 1950s colour lithographed tumblers, with gilt trim, in wire-framed carrying tray.

4.5in (11.5cm) high

£50-70   MA

A set of eight 1950s American textured and pressed glass beakers, in bent wire carrying frame.

12.5in (31cm) long

£60-90   QU

A set of six 1950s German shot beakers, in carrying frame, each lacquered in a different colour and with matte gold-coloured interiors.

7in (17.5cm) long

£20-30   QU

A mid-1950s American Swiss Harmony Inc. musical cocktail set, in metal, laminated wood and glass, with two decanters, a shaker and four shot beakers.

18in (45.5cm) wide

£40-60   BH

A 1960s Evers moulded plastic pineapple ice bucket, with glass liner.

This has become an iconic piece of retro kitsch. Although once easily found, they are becoming scarcer as more people add a bit of fun to their homes. This example still retains its glass liner, which is early in date and rare, as most were broken. Later liners were made from plastic.

11in (28cm) high

£25-35   MA

An early 1960s transfer-printed tinplate and plastic child's coffee set.

Coffee pot 5.75in (14.5cm) high

£18-22   BB

A 1950s Vogue large picture disc, no. R730, showing young couples jiving.

10in (25cm) diam

£35-45   **BH**

A pair of 1950s celluloid 'Kissing Dolls', made in Hong Kong, sold by Woolworths, mint and boxed.

These youthful and lusty bobble-heads have magnets inside the heads behind the mouths. When placed close together, the heads lean forward and lock to 'kiss'.

3.5in (9cm) high

£15-20   **MTB**

EXPERT EYE – A 1950s OLIVETTI TYPEWRITER

This typewriter was designed in 1969 by important and influential designer Ettore Sottsass (1913-2007), together with Olivetti design consultant Perry King.

It revolutionised typewriter design – the red plastic was typical of the period; fun, and also lightweight, meaning it could be easily carried.

Considered a design classic, it was also available in pink and grey. An example is in the Museum of Modern Art in New York.

Advertising for the typewriter featured people happily typing away outside cafés or on beaches. Many see both the typewriter and the advertising itself as a precursor to Apple's iMac.

An Olivetti Valentine typewriter, designed by Ettore Sottsass in 1969, red plastic fitted case, with moulded factory marks.

16.25in (35cm) high

£120-180   **WW**

A 'Sun Kissed' lemon nodder, wearing a red and white striped bikini, with some chips.

6.25in (15.5cm) high

£8-12   **BH**

Two Peter Max covered vessels; one made of ceramic and shaped as a man wearing hat, signed "Max" in the print; the other as an ice bucket, the metal exterior stencilled with a man's face, with purple plastic sunglasses handle, dented.

8.25in (21cm) high

£350-450   **SDR**

A Peter Max 'Hello' blow-up plastic cushion, decorated with a Pop Art smile to each side, signed in the design.

15.75in (40cm) wide

£30-40   **WW**

GLASS

ESSENTIAL REFERENCE

- Carnival glass is the name given to press moulded glass sprayed with chemicals to give it an iridescent surface effect. It was first made during the 1900s, and reached the height of its popularity during the 1920s and 1930s. Mass-produced on mechanised factory production lines, it was bright, vividly colourful and inexpensive.
- The effect was inspired by Tiffany's expensive iridescent Favrile glass, and as a result it was often known as 'Poor Man's Tiffany'. It came to be called Carnival glass during the 1960s, probably because it was used for prizes at fairs. US factories dominated production until the late 1920s, when countries such as Scandinavia, Germany, Australia and the UK began to take the lead.
- Major US factories included Northwood (1902-25), Fenton Art Glass (est. 1904), the Imperial Glass Co. (1901-84) and Dugan (1904-13), which became known as the Diamond Glass Co. after 1913. Most Carnival glass is unmarked and factories are identified from the moulded pattern. Northwood occasionally marked its glass with an 'N' in a circle.

- A number of criteria are used to value Carnival glass including pattern, the base colour of the glass, shape and level of iridescence. To see the base colour, shine a strong light through the piece. The orange 'marigold' is the most common colour, with sky blue and red being much rarer.
- Examine patterns carefully as they can differ minutely, and factories frequently copied each other's designs. Patterns that were popular when produced are likely to have been made in large numbers, making them more common and therefore less valuable today. Ruffled bowls are the most common shape, with plates being much rarer.
- Sometimes the combination of a particular pattern, shape or colour, even if each is individually common, can make a piece rare and desirable. Always examine edges for damage such as chips, which will appear shiny rather than silky matte. Carnival glass has been reproduced since the 1960s, particularly in the Far East, and Northwood's original designs are being used once again now the name has been revived.

A Northwood 'Good Luck' pattern marigold Carnival glass ruffled bowl.

Note the strong iridescence on this piece, which has subtle and varied colour tones. Look out for sparser leaf patterns and possibly stipples, which make this common pattern more desirable.

8.75in (22.5cm) diam

£80-120   BH

A Dugan 'Raindrops' pattern opalescent peach Carnival glass ruffled bowl.

'Raindrops' is a scarce and sought-after pattern. Look out for the rare purple colour, as this pattern is usually found in peach opalescent, as here.

8.25in (21.5cm) diam

£50-80   BH

A Dugan 'Six Petals' pattern peach opalescent Carnival glass ruffled bowl.

8in (20.5cm) diam

£20-30   SAE

A Fenton 'Pine Cone' pattern green Carnival glass sweet dish.

Fenton originally called their Carnival glass 'Iridill'.

6in (15cm) diam

£100-150   BH

A Fenton 'Pine Cone' pattern blue Carnival glass sweet dish.

6in (15cm) diam

£70-100   BH

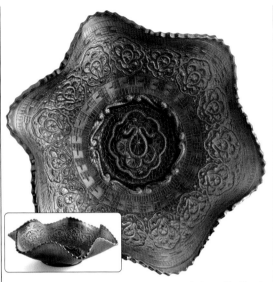

A Fenton 'Persian Medallion' pattern blue Carnival glass ruffled bowl.

This bowl has excellent iridescence all over, and extremely crisp moulding. The pattern is heavily inspired by Oriental motifs.

10.5in (26cm) diam

£100-150   SAE

A Fenton 'Horses' Heads' pattern marigold Carnival glass bowl.

6.75in (17cm) diam

£35-45   SAE

EXPERT EYE – PEACOCK & URN PATTERN

Seven variations of this classic and popular pattern were produced by Fenton, and from 1915 onwards by Northwood and Millersburg.

To distinguish them, pay close attention to the shape of the urn as well as the precise pattern of the leaves. Millersburg's version also has a bee near the peacock's beak.

With Fenton's version, the compote has a plain exterior while the bowl and plate are moulded with the 'Bearded Berry' pattern.

This example has superb iridescence, making it more desirable.

A Fenton 'Peacock & Urn' pattern amethyst Carnival glass ruffled bowl, with 'Bearded Berry' pattern moulded exterior.

9.25in (23cm) diam

£100-150   SAE

A Fenton 'Butterfly & Berry' pattern marigold Carnival glass ball-and-claw footed bowl.

Footed forms are typical of this prolifically produced range. White is a very rare colour.

1911-26   9.25in (23.5cm) diam

£50-80   BH

A Northwood 'Three Fruits' pattern marigold Carnival glass footed bon-bon dish.

This pattern is very similar to Northwood's 'Fruits & Flowers' pattern but without small flowers.

4in (10cm) high

£35-45   BH

A Dugan 'Wreathed Cherry' pattern amethyst Carnival glass banana bowl.

12.5in (30.5cm) long

£40-60   SAE

An Imperial 'Heavy Grape' pattern olive Carnival glass bowl.

6.75in (17cm) diam

£15-20   SAE

GLASS

A Fenton 'Pinecone' pattern blue Carnival glass large bowl.

This pattern was produced in two sizes of bowl and one plate. Teal is the rarest colour.

7.5in (18.5cm) diam

£15-25   SAE

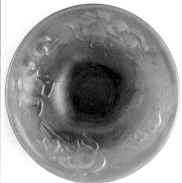

A Fenton 'Kittens' pattern marigold Carnival glass saucer.

Kittens, a charming pattern intended for children, is both rare and sought-after, perhaps as so many were broken at meal times. This may explain the comparatively high value for such a small piece.

4.5in (11.5cm) diam

£40-50   SAE

MILLER'S COMPARES – SINGING BIRD PATTERN

Even though these mugs are by the same maker, are the same size and have the same pattern, they are an excellent example of how values can vary based on different colours and levels of iridescence.

Although blue is hard to find, look out for 'smoke', which is the rarest colour.

Marigold is a much more common colour than blue, and the level of iridescence on the blue example is much stronger and considerably more desirable. Nevertheless, both are comparatively highly valued.

This is due to the fact that 'Singing Birds' is a popular pattern amongst collectors and is available in a wide range of shapes, making it an ideal pattern to focus on.

TOP: A Northwood 'Singing Birds' pattern blue Carnival glass mug.

3.75in (9.5cm) high

£80-120   BH

BOTTOM: A Northwood 'Singing Birds' pattern marigold Carnival glass mug.

3.75in (9.5cm) high

£40-60   BH

A Millersburg 'Mayan' pattern green Carnival glass ice cream bowl.

This example has very low levels of iridescence, and is in the most common colour for this pattern. The rarest colour is, surprisingly, marigold - only one example has been found to date.

8.5in (21.5cm) diam

£25-35   SAE

A Northwood 'Peacock at the Fountain' pattern blue Carnival glass tumbler.

Dugan produced some of the water sets found in this prolific pattern.

4in (10cm) high

£15-20   SAE

An English Sowerby 'Lea' pattern marigold Carnival glass creamer.

Along with the Thistle & Thorn pattern creamer to the right, this pattern is usually found in creamer, open sugar and bowl forms.

3.75in (9.5cm) high

£15-20   BH

An English Sowerby 'Thistle & Thorn' pattern marigold Carnival glass creamer.

4.25in (10.5cm) high

£10-15   SAE

A Fenton pink Carnival or Stretch glass candlestick, no. 232, with an internal stress fracture.

Although visually quite similar to Carnival glass, stretch glass is further worked after the metallic salts have been applied. This involves blowing or 'expanding' the piece, causing the iridescent surface to stretch and become cracked, resulting in a mottled, onion skin-like effect.

1915-c1925   8.75in (22cm) high

£30-50   SAE

A Northwood 'Fine Cut & Roses' pattern amethyst Carnival glass three-footed rose bowl.

4in (10cm) high

£25-35   BH

A Dugan 'Wreath of Rose' pattern marigold Carnival glass rose bowl.

Only available in rose bowls, spitoons, whimsies and ruffled bowl forms, this was an inexpensive, mass-produced pattern. Amber is a considerably rarer colour than marigold.

3.5in (9cm) high

£10-15   SAE

A Fenton 'Kittens' pattern marigold Carnival glass small ruffled vase.

2.5in (6.5cm) high

£30-50   SAE

A Northwood 'Bushel Basket' pattern lavender Carnival glass handled bowl.

Lavender is lighter than the standard blue, and is a scarce colour. The iridescence on this piece is particularly heavy.

4.75in (12cm) high

£80-120   BH

A Northwood 'Grape & Cable' pattern amethyst Carnival glass butter dish and cover.

Northwood's Grape & Cable range is as popular as it is expansive, being found on a vast variety of

objects in different colours. The pattern can vary from piece to piece, but do not confuse it with the similar pattern made by Fenton that has large single leaves and a different, more linear and larger grape configuration.

6in (15cm) high

£80-120   BH

A Northwood 'Grape & Cable' pattern purple Carnival glass powder jar.

3.75in (8.5cm) high

£60-90   SAE

A Fenton 'Orange Tree' pattern marigold Carnival glass hatpin stand.

Hatpin stands in any pattern are comparatively scarce and desirable. Orange Tree is also a desirable pattern as it was made in so many shapes, giving excellent scope to a collector.

6.5in (16.5cm) high

£140-160   SAE

An Imperial 'Ripple' pattern amethyst Carnival glass vase.

12in (30.5cm) high

£35-45   SAE

GLASS

ESSENTIAL REFERENCE

- The past few years have seen a rise in interest for postwar Czech glass design. As the country was behind the Iron Curtain until 1989, the major revolution in design has been largely ignored in favour of glass from countries, such as Italy and Scandinavia, despite the fact that exports were just as wide and prolific. As glass collectors and researchers have uncovered more information, prices have begun to rise and pieces have become harder to find.

- Complexity and rarity are currently the main indicators to value. The designer is also very important, but as the market is so new, many designers' names are not yet widely known. Hot-worked or enamelled pieces, as well as unique cut and engraved examples, tend to make the highest sums. These often inspired ranges that were produced on a larger scale in factories, and are more affordable.

- Many of these are hot-worked or pressed glass designs,

with the most desirable being those that are in the modern, avant-garde style that was developed by designers from the late 1950s to the early 1970s. Leading designers whose work is sought-after include Adolf Matura, Frantisek Vízner, Milan Metelák, Jan Gabrhel and Frantisek Zemek, as well as influential names producing more unique works such as Stanislav Libensky, Pavel Hlava, René Roubícek and Jirí Harcuba.

- As much glass is unmarked, particularly away from unique art masterpieces at the higher end of the market, it is best to consult a reference book so you can learn how to recognise designs. Many are currently mistaken for the work of factories on Murano or in Scandinavia. A considerable amount of research is yet to be undertaken, and the area looks set to grow in importance and relevance over the next few years.

A Czechoslovakian Harrachov Glassworks Evening Blue colourless cased vase, designed by Milan Metelák in 1968.

7in (17.5cm) high

£80-120   **GC**

A Czechoslovakian Harrachov Glassworks Evening Blue colourless cased vase, designed by Milan Metelák in 1968, with pulled rim.

9.75in (24.5cm) high

£120-180   **GC**

A Czechoslovakian Harrachov Glassworks Green colourless cased vase, designed by Milan Metelák in 1968.

9.25in (23.5cm) high

£120-180   **GC**

A Czechoslovakian Harrachov Glassworks Topaz colourless cased vase, designed by Milan Metelák in 1968, with internal bubbles.

9.75in (24.5cm) high

£150-200   **GC**

A Czechoslovakian Harrachov Glassworks Evening Blue colourless cased vase, designed by Milan Metelák in 1968, with internal bubbles.

This range of vases, both with and without bubbles, were previously thought of as having been made by Schott Zweisel due to the similarity of the blue. Recent research has uncovered that they are Czech, not German. Evening Blue was the most successful colour, and rare variations can be found with mica chips inside the bubbles.

9.75in (24.5cm) high

£200-250   **GC**

A late 1960s Czechoslovakian Skrdlovice hot-worked green cased amber vase, designed by Emanuel or Jan Beránek in 1964, with pulled lobes and 'Bohemia Glass' foil label.

This colourway is typical of the period.

9.75in (24.5cm) high

£80-100   **GC**

A 1970s Czechoslovakian Chlum u Trebone Glassworks mould-blown bottle vase, designed by Jan Gabrhel after 1969, with textured surface.

7.75in (19.5cm) high

£150-250   **MHT**

A 1990s Czechoslovakian Exbor cased vase, designed by Jirí Suhajek c1974, with applied blue trailing and blue or sandy forms, on a mottled beige and opaque white ground.

9in (23cm) high

£800-1,000   **GC**

A 1960s-70s Czechoslovakian Skrdlovice Glassworks light blue heart-shaped vase, designed by Vladimír Jelínek in 1965, with random pink and burgundy inclusions and a central well.

5.25in (14cm) high

£300-400   **QU**

A Czechoslovakian Moser vase, designed by Jirí Suhajek in 1974, the colourless ovoid form with green casing to sides and central applied abstract flower and stalk motif.

8.25in (20.5cm) high

£450-550   **QU**

A Czechoslovakian Borské Sklo 'Large Olives' pattern green mould-blown optic ball vase, with machine-cut rim.

8.75in (22cm) high

£80-120   **GC**

A 1960s Czechoslovakian Borské Sklo lustre painted mould-blown optic ball vase, designed by Max Kannegiesser in 1963, from the Nemo range.

4.25in (10.5cm) high

£15-20   **MHC**

A 1950s Czechoslovakian Borské Sklo gilded and painted grey mould-blown glass decanter, with stopper.

The amoebic painted forms are typical of the period, but are harder to find than more common, usually gilt, linear motifs. The angular form, reminiscent of a piston or machine part contrasts strongly with the organic pattern.

13.75in (35cm) high

£30-40   **MHC**

A Czechoslovakian Borské Sklo mould-blown smoked grey tapering vase, with thin white and gilt bands.

These can be found with clear and purple base glass, purple being the most desirable and valuable.

12in (30.5cm) high

£20-30   **GC**

GLASS

A Czechoslovakian Rosice Glassworks large light blue pressed glass 'lens' vase, shape no. 966, designed by Rudolf Schrötter and produced from 1955.

Although introduced in 1955, production of this vase continued into the 1970s in a variety of colours. A smaller example was also made, and the shape is one of the most commonly found today.

7.75in (19.5cm) high

£40-60   **MHC**

A Czechoslovakian Rosice Glassworks amethyst pressed glass vase, no. 482, designed by Jirí Brabec and produced from 1969.

4.75in (12cm) high

£25-35   **GC**

A Czechoslovakian Rudolfová Glassworks blue pressed glass vase, no. 13152, designed by Vladislav Urban and produced from 1963.

8in (20.5cm) high

£30-50   **MHC**

EXPERT EYE – A SKLO UNION VASE

The numerous factories that made the pressed glass vases on this page were amalgamated into the 'Sklo Union' group in 1965. It is by this name that these pieces are known by collectors.

This design was also produced in other colours including amber, green and colourless – purple is the hardest to find.

A number of shapes were produced including a lower vase, a jardinière and an ashtray, which is the most common shape found.

The clean-lined form and moulded hobnail textured pattern is typical of designs produced at this time. Jurnikl is also a noted designer.

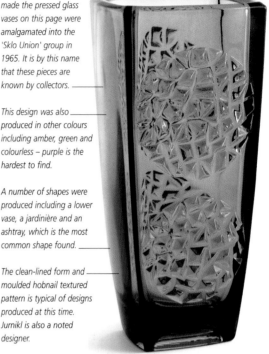

A Rudolfova Glassworks large purple pressed glass 'hobnail' vase, shape no. 13227, designed by Rudolf Jurnikl and produced from 1964.

9in (23cm) high

£60-90   **MHC**

A Czechoslovakian Hermanova Glassworks light green pressed glass vase, shape no. 20048, designed by Vladislav Urban and produced from 1962.

A very similar and more common shape, with fewer rounded undulations, was designed by Frantisek Vizner at the same time and is usually worth £100-150.

8in (20cm) high

£120-180   **MHC**

A Czechoslovakian Hermanova Glassworks colourless pressed glass vase, no. 20082, designed by Frantisek Vízner and produced from 1965.

This is one of the most commonly found designs. It was successful at the time.

9.75in (25cm) high

£20-30   **MHC**

A Czechoslovakian cut and engraved glass vase, with scene of a nude posed in a landscape within an oval frame, the base inscribed "Sklo Kodels 1944".

1944   6.75in (17cm) high

£100-150   **WW**

A pair of Czechoslovakian Borské Sklo lime green and opaque white cased cut glass attenuated bottles, designed by Jaroslav Lebeda, enamelled and gilded with geometric and other motifs.

These rare bottles are from a range first exhibited in the Czech Pavilion at the 1958 World Exposition in Brussels. They were made in a number of shapes and can also be found in red or blue. They represent the way designers modernised traditional Bohemian styles and techniques during the period.

12.75in (32cm) high

£400-500   **TCF**

A Czechoslovakian Novy Bor amethyst cased colourless cut vase, probably designed by Karel Wünsch from 1962, from the Dual range.

10in (26cm) high

£60-80   **L&T**

EXPERT EYE – A CZECH CUT GLASS VASE

Josef Svarc's signature indicates that this piece was either cut by him, or cut by someone under his supervision. The cutting is of exceptional quality.

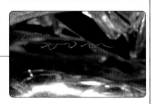

Svarc (b.1928) was one of the key designers responsible for re-introducing natural themes and motifs into postwar Czech cut glass designs.

This pattern was successful and produced in different shapes in large numbers, and can also be found with a coloured flashed (thinly cased) outer layer, which is cut through.

The back is also cut with stylized thorns in star formations, which emphasise the spiky nature of the thistles and gives a sense of perspective.

A late 1960s Czechoslovakian Svetlá & Sázavou Glassworks cut and engraved 'Thistle' vase, designed by Josef Svarc in 1962, deeply cut with a pattern of thistles to the front and stylized thorns in star formations to the back, the based lightly signed "Svarc".

10.25in (26cm) high

£100-150   **TCF**

FIND OUT MORE...

'Hi Sklo Lo Sklo: Post War Czech Glass From Masterpiece to Mass-Produced', *by Mark Hill, published by www.markhillpublishing.com, 2008.*
'Sklo Union: Art Before Industry', *by Marcus Newhall, published by Cortex Design and www.sklounion.com, 2008.*

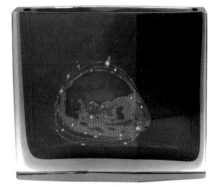

A Czechoslovakian Exbor cased and facet cut vase, designed by Pavel Hlava from 1964, with spiralling oxide inclusions.

5.5in (14.5cm) high

£100-150   **VZ**

GLASS

ESSENTIAL REFERENCE

- Depression glass is the term given by collectors to mechanically pressed glass, mass-produced from the 1920s onwards. It gained its name from its popularity during the Great Depression. Brightly coloured, durable, and inexpensive and made in a huge variety of patterns and colours, it brought cheer to those on hard times. As well as being retailed, it was also given away as a premium in petrol stations, cereal boxes or cinemas.

- Some of the patterns introduced during this period, such as Whitehall, were still being made as functional tableware into the 1960s. Although many companies produced Depression glass, the majority found today was made by six of the larger companies including Anchor Hocking, Jeanette, Indiana, and Hazel Atlas.

- Green is one of the most common colours found, along with pink. Scarcer colours include cobalt blue, red and black. A colourless variety, known as Crystal was also very popular, particularly from the mid-1930s onwards. Many of the patterns found in Crystal imitated the more expensive cut lead crystal, offering buyers the look of luxury.

- Most collectors collect by pattern, and then perhaps by colour. Natural themes predominate, often with complex patterns of stylized floral and foliate motifs. Each pattern has a name, often inspired by festive, historical, or natural themes. Pay close attention to the pattern, as some are very similar, but were produced by different companies, therefore having minor differences. 'Sandwich' is a good example.

- As well as colour and pattern, consider the form as certain shapes are scarcer than others. Plates tend to be one of the most common forms, primarily as people tended to own more than one. Scarcer forms include cruet sets and butter dishes, as a single example was all a household was likely to require. Always examine pieces closely, to check for chips and deep scratches which devalue a piece. Bubbles and ripples are, however, more acceptable to collectors.

- Reproductions are also known, particularly in rare shapes. Handle as many originals as possible to become familiar with their feel and appearance. In general, reproductions are paler in colour and the moulded detailing may be less sharp. Consult a reference book to check the shape was made at the time.

A Jeanette Glass Company 'Adam' pattern pink Depression glass creamer.

1932-34   *3.5in (9cm) high*

£8-12   **SAE**

A Jeanette Glass Company 'Adam' pattern pink Depression glass cup and saucer.

1932-34   *Saucer 6in (15cm) wide*

£12-18   **SAE**

An Imperial Glass Company 'Beaded Block' pattern pink Depression glass sugar.

Pink pieces embossed 'IG' are recent. Look for rare red examples – a bowl could be worth around £100.

1927-c1935   *4.5in (11.5cm) high*

£15-20   **SAE**

An Anchor Hocking 'Bubble' pattern Royal Ruby Depression glass cup and saucer.

This pattern was introduced in 1937 in Crystal, Sapphire Blue and Forest Green.

1963-65   *5.75in (14.5cm) diam*

£5-7   **SAE**

EXPERT EYE – AMERICAN WHITEHALL PATTERN

The popular hobnail style pattern was first introduced by Fostoria as 'American' in 1915 and was produced for decades by other companies under different names, including Colony Glass (Whitehall) and Jeanette Glass Company (Cube).

In the mid-1980s, Lancaster Colony Glass (as it was then known), who also owned Indiana Glass, purchased Fostoria and merged a number of Fostoria Lines into the 'Whitehall' range, renaming it 'American Whitehall'.

Despite being very similar, Whitehall and American Whitehall are different. 'American Whitehall' pitchers have shaped rims, while 'Whitehall' pitchers have flat rims, and Whitehall' beakers have wide, flaring rims that are not seen on 'American Whitehall' versions.

Colours are also important. 'American Whitehall' was produced in crystal, gold, amber, blue and peach.

A late 1980s Indiana Glass Company 'American Whitehall' pattern amber Depression glass pitcher.

8.25in (21cm) high

£20-25   **SAE**

An Imperial Glass Company 'Cape Cod' pattern Crystal Depression glass wafer-stemmed 8oz water goblet.

1932-84   *5.5in (13.5cm) high*

£3-4   **SAE**

An Imperial Glass Company 'Cape Cod' pattern Crystal Depression glass salad bowl.

Larger items, such as this bowl, are generally more expensive as they would have been when first purchased. Furthermore, although a family may have bought a number of plates, only one salad bowl may have been necessary.

1932-84   *11in (27.5cm) diam*

£30-50   **SAE**

An Imperial Glass Company 'Cape Cod' pattern Crystal Depression glass handled butter dish.

1932-84   *4.5in (11.5cm) diam*

£18-22   **SAE**

A 1930s Paden City Glass Company 'Crow's Foot' pattern red Depression glass soup bowl.

4.5in (11.5cm) diam

£8-12   **BH**

A Jeanette Glass Company 'Floral' pattern pink Depression glass creamer.

This pattern is also known as Poinsettia. Crystal, amber, red and yellow examples are harder to find as fewer were produced.

1931-35   *3.75in (9.5cm) high*

£5-7   **SAE**

A Hazel Atlas Glass Company 'Florentine' pattern pink Depression glass sherbet.

1932-35   *3in (7.5cm) high*

£5-7   **SAE**

A Paden City Company 'Glades' pattern silvered red Depression glass bowl.

Paden City operated from 1916-51 and, despite being grouped within Depression glass, produced hand- rather than machine-pressed glass. The company is known for its coloured glass, with red being commonly found. The company operated a decorating department which etched, silver-plated, painted and cut its wares.

4in (10cm) high

£25-40   **SAE**

A Fostoria Glass Company 'Jamestown' pattern light blue Depression glass iced tea glass.

1958-82   *6.25in (15.5cm) high*

£10-15   **SAE**

A Fostoria Glass Company 'Jamestown' pattern red Depression glass sherbet.

1958-82   *4.5in (11cm) high*

£7-10   **SAE**

GLASS

A Hazel Atlas Glass Company 'Moderntone' pattern cobalt blue Depression glass sherbet.
1934-42   3.25in (8cm) high
£3-5   SAE

A Hazel Atlas Glass Company 'Royal Lace' pattern pink Depression glass oval planter.
1934-41   12.5in (32cm) diam
£18-22   BH

A Hazel Atlas Glass Company 'Royal Lace' pattern green Depression glass dinner plate.
1934-41   9.75in (25cm) diam
£12-18   BH

An Anchor Hocking 'Sandwich' pattern Forest Green Depression glass 8oz tumbler.
1956-c1965   4in (10cm) high
£3-5   SAE

ESSENTIAL REFERENCE – SANDWICH GLASS

Sandwich glass refers both to the glass produced in the early 19thC by factories based around Sandwich, Massachusetts, such as the Boston & Sandwich Glass Company, and to a pressed glass pattern produced from the 1920s onwards. The most commonly found examples fall into the latter category. The pattern comprises a scrolling foliate motif on a background of stippled, slightly raised design, and was made by a number of factories. These include Anchor Hocking, Duncan & Miller, Indiana and Westmoreland. However, despite their similarities, each is slightly different. Duncan & Miller and Anchor Hocking are the most commonly found, with the former producing their version of the glass from 1924-55 and the latter from 1939-c1965. When building a collection, look closely at the designs of the scrolling form, the central pattern and particularly the flower to ensure you are adding the correct pieces to your collection. Duncan & Miller's flowers are more detailed, with lines through the centre of each raised relief petal, while Anchor Hocking's flowers have double outlines. Those by other makers tend to be less detailed.

An Anchor Hocking 'Sandwich' pattern Forest Green Depression glass custard and liner.

1956-c1965   Saucer 4.5in (11.5cm) diam
£3-4   SAE

A Duncan & Miller 'Sandwich' pattern Crystal Depression glass sugar, creamer and tray.

Note the difference to Anchor Hocking's version. Coloured examples by Duncan & Miller are harder to find than colourless Crystal.
1924-55   Tray 8in (20cm) wide
£12-18   SAE

A Federal Glass Company 'Sharon' pattern pink Depression glass sugar bowl.
1935-39   3.25in (8cm) high
£5-8   BH

FIND OUT MORE...

'Warman's Depression Glass', by Ellen T. Schroy, published by Warman's, 2003.
'Collectors' Encyclopedia of Depression Glass', by Gene & Cathy Florence, Collector Books, 2007.

ESSENTIAL REFERENCE

- Ronald Stennett-Willson (b.1915), began his career at London-based Scandinavian glass and ceramics importers Rydbeck & Norström in 1946. In 1951, he joined similar importer J. Wuidart & Co. Ltd where he became managing director. He also designed glass for them, which was made in Scandinavia by Björkshult and Johansfors, among others. During the 1960s, he was Reader in glass at the Royal College of Art in London, and ran his own modern design shop, Choses, and a glass import company, Wilmart.
- In 1967, he founded King's Lynn Glass in Norfolk, and was responsible for all their designs. Among his most notable is the 'Sheringham' candle-holder, with its characteristic discs. The number of discs vary from one to nine, and the more discs, the rarer and more valuable the piece. Surprisingly, each candle-holder is made from many separate gathers of glass – one with two discs is made from seven gathers formed and joined together by hand. Other notable designs include 'Brancaster' and 'Sandringham'.

- The modern Scandinavian inspired designs were popular and the successful company was sold to Wedgwood in 1969. They retained Stennett-Willson's services and continued to produce his designs, as well as introducing more. Vases with surface textures were popular, as were those with mottled or striated patterning cased in colourless glass. One-off vases and bowls in the Studio range were also made.
- Stennett-Willson also designed a range of animals. Look out for the rhinoceros and hippopotamus as these tend to be scarcer as fewer people bought them at the time, preferring more cuddly and jolly animals. The most common colours were topaz, sapphire and lilac, with pink and turquoise being the most common speckled colours. Sizes can vary widely, and depend on how much glass was used in the gather. In 1979, the Lilliput collection of miniatures was released. All first quality pieces were marked with the Wedgwood acid stamp.

A King's Lynn amber 'Sheringham' candle-holder, shape no. RSW13, with two discs, designed by Ronald Stennett-Willson in 1967.

5.25in (13cm) high

£25-30   **TGM**

A Wedgwood light blue 'Brancaster' small candle-holder, shape no. RSW15, designed by Ronald Stennett-Willson in 1967, the base with acid stamp.

This lighter blue is scarcer than the usual darker tone. Surprisingly, the stems on the Brancaster range are hollow.

5.25in (13.5cm) high

£20-25   **TGM**

A Wedgwood green 'Sheringham' candle-holder, shape no. RSW13, with two discs, designed by Ronald Stennett-Willson in 1967 for King's Lynn.

c1970   *5in (12.5cm) high*

£25-30   **GC**

A Wedgwood blue 'Sheringham' candle-holder, shape no. RSW13, with three discs, designed by Ronald Stennett-Willson in 1967 for King's Lynn.

c1970   *6in (15.5cm) high*

£35-40   **GC**

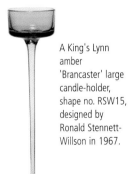

A King's Lynn amber 'Brancaster' large candle-holder, shape no. RSW15, designed by Ronald Stennett-Willson in 1967.

11.5in (29cm) high

£50-60   **TGM**

GLASS

A 1970s Wedgwood pink 'Sandringham' candle-holder, shape no. RSW22, designed by Ronald Stennett-Willson in 1967 for King's Lynn.

7.25in (18.5cm) high

£40-60   GC

A King's Lynn purple 'Sandringham' small candle-holder, shape no. RSW22, designed by Ronald Stennett-Willson in 1967.

5.25in (13cm) high

£20-30   TGM

A King's Lynn cased blue 'Top Hat' vase, shape no. RSW21, designed by Ronald Stennett-Willson in 1967 for King's Lynn.

8in (20.5cm) high

£70-100   GC

EXPERT EYE – A WEDGWOOD 'ARIEL' GLASS VASE

This vase is made using the Ariel technique, developed in 1937 at the Orrefors factory by Vicke Lindstrand, Gustav Bergqvist and Edvin Öhrstrom. Here, different coloured layers are sand-blasted away to create a pattern, before the piece is reheated, cased in colourless glass, blown and formed.

Some pieces took over five hours to make, meaning they were expensive and unprofitable – Stennett-Willson saw them as exhibition pieces and very few were made during the 1970s. This is an early example.

It is different from the similar graal technique as the finished product contains air bubbles under the colourless layer and the final design is typically much more fluid.

This and the other Ariel vase on the page were from the collection of Ronald Stennett-Willson and were first exhibited as part of the Graham Cooley Collection retrospective exhibition of Stennett-Willson's designs in 2004.

A unique Wedgwood Ariel vase, designed and made by Ronald Stennett-Willson, the ovoid body heavily cased with colourless glass over a tortoiseshell effect tonal brown interior, with grey fleck and stylized air bubble leaf forms, signed and dated 1970 to the base.

6.25in (15.5cm) high

£1,200-1,800   FLD

A unique Wedgwood Ariel vase, designed and made by Ronald Stennett-Willson, the ovoid body with cylindrical neck, heavily cased with colourless glass over a powder pink and white interior, with stylized chevron air bubble forms, signed and dated 1970 to the base.

1970   6.5in (16.5cm) high

£800-1,200   FLD

A King's Lynn or Wedgwood wine glass, designed by Ronald Stennett-Willson.

Intact examples are extremely hard to find, as the stem is so thin and delicate that most were broken.

c1967   7.5in (19cm) high

£40-60   GC

A Lemington Glass red 'Harlequin' tumbler, shape no. LSW17, designed by Ronald Stennett-Willson in 1959.

These were also available in green, blue, yellow, purple and grey at a time when domestic coloured tableware was uncommon. Their heavy bases and shape mean they are very hard to tip over. Red is a scarce colour.

1960-62

£7-10   PC

A Wedgwood mottled pink elephant with raised trunk, shape no. RSW405, designed by Ronald Stennett-Willson, the base with acid stamp.

Shape no. RSW409, an elephant with its trunk down, is worth around the same price.

3.25in (8cm) high

£30-35   TGM

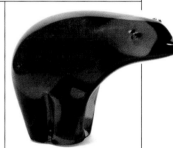

A 1980s Wedgwood mottled grey and colourless cased elephant with raised trunk, shape no. L5005, designed by Ronald Stennett-Willson, from the Lilliput series, the base with acid stamp.

3.5in (9cm) high

£40-45   TGM

A 1980s Wedgwood pink long-tailed bird, shape no. L5013, designed by Ronald Stennett-Willson (RSW73), from the Lilliput series, the base with acid stamp.

2.5in (6.5cm) high

£30-35   TGM

A Wedgwood graduated pink duck, shape no. RSW232, designed by Ronald Stennett-Willson, the base with acid stamp and the wing with gold foil label.

6.75in (17cm) high

£40-50   TGM

A Wedgwood colourless cased mottled grey squirrel, shape no. SG410, the base with acid stamp.

This is the most commonly found of Wedgwood's animals.

5.5in (14cm) high

£20-25   TGM

A Wedgwood Topaz polar bear, shape no. RSW267, designed by Ronald Stennett-Willson, the base with acid stamp.

3.5in (9cm) high

£30-35   TGM

A Wedgwood blue and green mottled and colourless cased Scottie dog, shape no. SG418, with acid stamp to base.

4.25in (11cm) high

£45-55   TGM

A Wedgwood mottled green frog, shape no. 404, the base with acid stamp.

3.5in (9cm) high

£38-42   TGM

GLASS

ESSENTIAL REFERENCE

- René Lalique (1860-1945) was born near Rheims, France, and began his career by designing and producing Art Nouveau jewellery. In the 1890s, he began experimenting with glass, both for jewellery and small vessels, using the lost wax technique. In 1905, he opened a shop in Paris, near perfumier François Coty.
- In 1907, Coty commissioned him to produce some perfume bottles and other small glass vessels, which were made at the Legras factory. In 1909, his success had grown, enabling him to buy his own glass factory. By the 1920s, his designs had expanded to include pressed and mould-blown vases, bowls and other shapes, and by the end of the decade he owned three factories.
- Lalique is loved for his speciality, which was opalescent

glass in the Art Nouveau, but particularly the Art Deco, style. Some pieces were stained with colour to highlight the moulded details. Coloured glass was also made, and can be scarce. Lalique glass is highly sought-after and is often valuable, but many smaller pieces are more affordable and just as representative of his pioneering style.
- Marks help with dating, and can be etched or inscribed. Before 1945, the initial 'R' was used, sometimes with the word 'France' and model number. The initial was not used after 1945. Many designs are still in production today. Use reference books and handle authentic pieces to learn how to spot Lalique – his designs were successful and widely imitated, and even faked, then and now.

EXPERT EYE – A LALIQUE CREAM POT

It does not bear Lalique's name although it was designed by him and produced by Legras & Cie before Lalique bought his own factory.

The floral design is typical of the Art Nouveau's emphasis on natural motifs, although the stylization and the fact it covers the whole lid hints at his later Art Deco work of the 1920s to '30s.

The depressions in the base and the moulded star cut through the knob enabled a cord to be tied around the pot, ensuring its precious contents were not spilt or spoilt.

At the time, cosmetics and perfume were sold in large volumes, with the customer bringing their own vessel to be filled, or buying a new one to be re-used.

A Lalique for Coty 'Clematite' cream pot, designed by René Lalique in 1911, the base moulded "Coty France".

2.75in (7cm) diam

£200-250   TGM

A Lalique for Houbigant 'Marguerites' face cream pot, designed by René Lalique in 1926, the body moulded with lines, the lid with stylized daisies, the base moulded "R.Lalique".

2.25in (5.5cm) high

£250-300   TGM

A Lalique for Coty 'La Jacée' powder or cream pot, designed by René Lalique in 1928, the base moulded "Coty France".

2.5in (6.5cm) high

£100-150   TGM

A Lalique 'Deux Zephyrs' opalescent ashtray, designed by René Lalique in 1913, with moulded scene of two puffing cherubs representing the winds amid swirling clouds, the base with acid-etched "R. Lalique France".

This is an early and relatively scarce design. Note the Art Nouveau style swirls and theme.

1913-47

3.25in (8cm) diam

£300-400   TGM

ESSENTIAL REFERENCE

- The influential Mdina Glass studio was founded by Michael Harris in 1968, at the Ta' Qali airfield on Malta. After graduating from the Stourbridge College of Art & Design, Harris completed a number of private commissions before becoming a tutor in, and then head of, the glass department at the Royal College of Art. In late 1966, he met Samuel Herman, who taught him the new studio glass techniques being developed in the US. Mdina Glass became one of the first commercial studio glass companies, producing unique, handmade art glass works.

- Colours are reminiscent of the Mediterranean, such as sea greens and blues, and sandy ochres and browns. Forms tend to be chunky, being rendered in thick glass, and comprise vases, bowls, dishes, paperweights and more abstract, sculptural forms. Production was aimed at the tourist market, but the factory's success was also due in part to increasing export sales to UK, US and German retailers. Most pieces are signed with the studio's name. Examples signed by Michael Harris with his name are rare and valuable.

- Harris left Mdina Glass in 1972 and founded Isle of Wight Studio Glass in the same year. His first ranges of the 1970s, such as Aurene, tended to be made with broad swirls of mottled colour in deep blues, ochres, browns and pink. The turning point came in 1978 with the introduction of the Azurene range, designed by Harris and RCA graduate William Walker. Using fragmented 22ct gold and silver leaf on coloured glass bodies, the range was, and continues to be, enormously successful and is exported around the world.

- Other popular ranges include Meadow Garden (1983-88), Kyoto (1982-88), and Golden Peacock (1982-2004). Look out for other, often experimental ranges produced for smaller periods of time, as these can be desirable. As with Mdina Glass, examples signed by Michael Harris with his name are rare and sought-after. Harris died in 1994, but his innovative flair, and the company he founded, are continued today by his son Timothy and widow Elizabeth. The market is continuing to expand, drawing new collectors and rising values.

A Mdina Glass 'Side Stripe' vase, with applied colourless glass base and side trails.

The colour and form indicate this is an early piece.

c1971   5.25in (13.5cm) high

£30-50   **GROB**

A Mdina Glass globe vase, with small button rim, the base inscribed "Mdina" in diamond point.

These vases were produced from the earliest days of the factory in 1968 into the 1990s, and beyond. Examples from before the mid-1970s have small rims such as this. Later examples are more flared and spun-out as shown on the other image on this page.

6.75in (17cm) high

£40-60   **TGM**

A late 1970s-80s Mdina Glass globe vase, with wide flared rim, the base inscribed "Mdina".
4.5in (11.5cm) high

£40-60   **TGM**

A mid-1970s-80s Mdina Glass 'Ming' bottle vase, with cylindrical neck and flared rim.
5.75in (14.5cm) high

£30-50   **GC**

A late 1970s-80s Mdina Glass 'Ming' stoppered bottle, with swirling, fragmented green pattern and blown stopper, the base inscribed "Mdina" and with shape number label to side.

This shape was also produced as a vase, shown on the left.

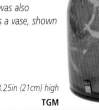

8.25in (21cm) high

£45-55   **TGM**

GLASS

A late 1970s-80s Mdina Glass 'Ming' stoppered bottle, with swirling, fragmented green pattern and solid stopper, the base inscribed "Mdina".

11.5in (29cm) high

£50-60   TGM

A Mdina Glass carafe, the applied prunt with impressed Maltese cross, the base with polished concave pontil mark and gilt retailer label.

Most of these carafes date from the mid-1970s onwards. However, this has two features that make it earlier. Firstly, it is more thinly blown than later examples and secondly, it has a polished concave pontil mark. This dates it to late 1969-70, shortly after the Boffo brothers, glassmakers from Whitefriars, had arrived, where this type of mark was common.

8.75in (22cm) high

£20-30   TGM

A Mdina Glass cylinder vase, with internal random bubbles and blue casing on the foot, the base with polished concave pontil mark.

c1970   6.5in (16.5cm) high

£30-50   TGM

A late 1970s-80s Mdina Glass 'Tiger' bottle, with brown, green and blue swirls cased in colourless glass, the base inscribed "Mdina".

13.5in (35cm) high

£50-70   TGM

A 1970s Mdina Glass 'Earthtones' tall bottle vase, in brown and yellow glass.

13in (33cm) high

£32-38   GAZE

A 1970s-80s Mdina Glass 'Earthtones' bottle vase, with flared rim.

5.75in (14.5cm) high

£30-40   GC

A late 1980s Mdina Glass 'Side Stripe' bottle vase, with ochre chevron pattern and applied colourless straps to each side and the base, inscribed "Mdina".

9in (22.5cm) high

£30-50   P&I

A mid-to late 1970s Mdina Glass Tiger 'Side Stripe' bottle, with coloured swirls, and clear supports.

8.25in (21cm) high

£60-70   **GROB**

A 1990s Mdina Glass 'Side Stripe' bottle, the cobalt blue body overlaid with gold leaf.

The use of fragmented gold leaf on the surface of the glass was pioneered by Michael Harris at the Isle of Wight Studio Glass in 1978.

8in (21cm) high

£20-30   **GC**

A very unusual mid-to late 1970s Mdina vase, with heavy blue casing, and cut and pulled rim.

5.5in (14cm) high

£100-150   **GROB**

EXPERT EYE – A MDINA 'CRIZZLE STONE'

Known as a 'Crizzle Stone', this form is related to Harris' celebrated 'Fish' vases – however, these pieces were spun when molten to give the evenly rounded sculptural form.

The mottled web-like pattern is created by dipping the hot glass into cold water momentarily, causing the surface to fracture. Metallic salts are used to mark out the shallow cracks.

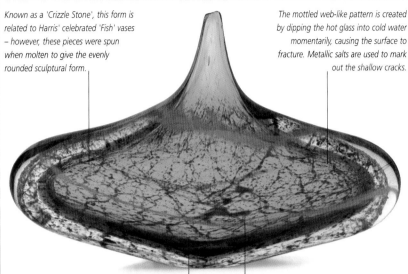

The production process is complex, involving a number of carefully applied layers, and the piece is heavy and large. Both factors are surprising for such an early date in the Studio glass movement.

Due to the immense skill required to make them, Crizzle Stones were only made by Michael Harris and are extremely rare – fewer than ten are known to collectors.

A Mdina Glass 'Crizzle Stone', designed and made by Michael Harris, with flat polished base and iridescent streak of silver chloride around the neck.

c1971   *7.25in (18cm) high*

£1,200-1,800   **WW**

A Mdina Glass display goblet, designed by Michael Harris, with trailed knop, the base inscribed "Mdina Glass 1977".

Squared-off bowls are indicative of production after Harris left Mdina Glass in 1972. Before this date, bowls tend to be rounded in form. Nevertheless, signed and dated examples tend to be popular with collectors, a similar unsigned example may be worth around £50-80.

1977   *7.5in (19cm) high*

£80-120   **GC**

A 1970s-80s Mdina Glass tapered cased vase, with applied blue and tortoiseshell trailing on a mottled sandy ground.

5.5in (14cm) high

£30-40   **GC**

GLASS

An Isle of Wight Studio Glass Seaward large attenuated bottle, designed and made by Michael Harris in 1973, the body overlaid with green and blue swirls of coloured enamel and silver chloride, the base signed "Michael Harris Isle of Wight".

Fragile attenuated bottles were generally made by Harris himself, particularly in the early years. They are hard to find, but this is even rarer as it is in Seaward, which was made for one year only and it is signed by Harris.

1973　　　　　　　　18in (45.5cm) high
£600-700　　　　　　　　　　**FLD**

An Isle of Wight Studio Glass Aurene bell vase, designed by Michael Harris, with spiralling iridescent streaks and impressed 'flame' pontil mark to base.

1974-c1980　　　　　8.25in (21cm) high
£200-300　　　　　　　　　　**VZ**

An Isle of Wight Studio Glass blue Golden Peacock globe vase.

1983-86　　　　　　　3.25in (8cm) high
£32-38　　　　　　　　　　**TGM**

An Isle of Wight Studio Glass Aurene globe vase, the base with impressed 'flame' pontil mark.

c1975-c1982　　　　　3.75in (9.5cm) high
£40-50　　　　　　　　　　**TGM**

An Isle of Wight Studio Glass Turquoise Azurene squat globe vase, the base with black triangular label.

This translucent colourway is among the rarest of the Azurene range. In production, most examples gained 'burnt' spots of the silver and gold foil (as here) which, combined with the fact that the colour was not popular, meant that the colour was discontinued a year after it was introduced.

1986-87　　　　　　　3.5in (9cm) high
£70-100　　　　　　　　　　**ART**

An Isle of Wight Studio Glass 'Poppy' vase, from the Meadow Garden range.

The crinkled rim is a hallmark of this range. Colours used in the Meadow Garden range can vary widely – this is closest to Poppy, although the green tinges hint at Clover.

1983-88　　　　　　　3.5in (9cm) high
£28-32　　　　　　　　　　**TGM**

An Isle of Wight Studio Glass 'Dog Rose' perfume bottle, from the Meadow Garden range, with correct colourless stopper.

1984-88　　　　　　　6.25in (15.5cm) high
£55-75　　　　　　　　　　**TGM**

A 1970s Isle of Wight Studio Glass paperweight, the base with impressed 'flame' logo.

This uses the same colour combinations and tones as Seaward, which may date it at around 1973-74, although similar colours were used throughout the 1970s, and indeed '80s.

2.25in (5cm) high

£18-22   **TGM**

A 1970s Isle of Wight Studio Glass large paperweight, with impressed 'flame' pontil mark and paper labels.

Large paperweights such as this are scarce, as they tended to crack when being 'annealed' and cooled due to internal stresses caused by the different rates of cooling.

4.25in (10.5cm) diam

£45-55   **TGM**

An Isle of Wight Studio Glass Azurene White egg paperweight, the base with black triangular sticker.

Azurene White is extremely rare as the production process was a largely unsuccessful and it was poor seller at the time. The rarest forms are vases and bowls.

1982-84   *2.5in (6cm) high*

£30-40   **TGM**

An Isle of Wight Studio Glass 'Goldberry' apple paperweight, from the heavily iridised Summer Fruits range.

1996-current   *3in (7.5cm) high*

£28-32   **TGM**

EXPERT EYE – AN ISLE OF WIGHT SEASCAPE VASE

Launched in 1985, Seascape was one of three linked ranges, along with the iridescent swirling 'Nightscape' and the rarer green-ish 'Landscape'.

The production process is complex involving applied canes, trails and shards of striped glass that are melted into the surface along with the studio's hallmark fragmented gold foil.

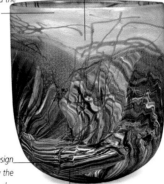

The abstract design was inspired by the storm-lashed rocky coastal area near the studio on the Isle of Wight, and was produced until recently.

This piece is unusually large and is signed by Michael Harris, which is a very rare feature. The limited edition style number and presence of 'England' indicates that it was made for export to US retailers like JC Penney, around 1987.

An Isle of Wight Studio Glass Seascape large bell-shaped bowl, designed by Michael Harris in 1985, the base signed "Michael Harris England" and numbered "54/500" on the base.

c1987   *8.75in (22cm) high*

£800-1,000   **FLD**

Two Isle of Wight Studio Glass Golden Peacock Royale large and small bird figurines, with original 'signature' card box.

This box bearing Harris' facsimile signature is hard to find. Despite the long production period, Golden Peacock Royale birds are scarcer than birds from other ranges, such as Meadow Garden, probably as they were more expensive.

1987-95   *Large: 2in (5cm) high Small 1.5in (3.5cm) high*

Large: £20-25 Small: £15-20   **TGM**

FIND OUT MORE...

'Michael Harris: Mdina Glass & Isle of Wight Studio Glass', by Mark Hill, published by www.markhillpublishing.com, 2006.

ESSENTIAL REFERENCE

- The founding of Mdina Glass by Michael Harris on Malta in 1968, which previously had no real history of glassmaking, led to other glass companies being set up both on Malta and its surrounding islands. All had connections with either Harris or Mdina Glass, and many of their ranges bear similarities to those by Harris. Phoenician Glass was founded by Leonard Mulligan, who had previously worked at Mdina, in the 1980s and continues today.

- Mtarfa Glass was founded in 1981 by Paul Said and is now known as Valletta Glass. Said and his brother Joseph both trained and worked at Mdina glass, with Joseph running Mdina from 1981 until today. Gozo Glass was founded by Michael and Elizabeth Harris in 1989 as a retirement project, with the initial ranges being designed by Michael and his son Timothy. After Michael's death in 1994, the company was sold and continues to produce glass today.

A Phoenician Glass perfume bottle, with blue, ochre and green mottled body and long colourless stopper and applicator, the base inscribed with factory marks and with "Artisans Centre Valletta Malta" gilt foil label.

4.5in (11.5cm) high

£18-22   TGM

A Phoenician Glass bowl, with trailed and iridescent decoration, the base signed "Phoenician Malta" and with black triangular label.

This design, which is similar to Nightscape by Isle of Wight Studio Glass, was also available in red, which is worth roughly the same.

2.5in (6cm) high

£10-15   TGM

A Phoenician Glass perfume bottle, with applied and melted textured surface and bands of fragmented gold and silver foil, with an iridescent effect, the base with inscribed factory marks.

4.5in (11cm) high

£32-38   TGM

A late 1990s Gozo Glass perfume bottle, from the Stone Collection, with opaque white interior and colourless coiled stopper.

The swirling technique was also used by Harris' Isle of Wight Studio Glass on their Gemstone range in 1993, and then their Golden Mosaic Range from 1995.

6.5in (16.5cm) high

£35-40   TGM

A Phoenician Glass pink perfume bottle, with mottled and striated body and opaque jade green applied foot and stopper, signed on the base.

4in (10cm) high

£18-22   TGM

A 1990s Gozo Glass pebble vase, designed by Timothy and Michael Harris in 1989, with white paper label.

Later examples include fragmented gold and silver foil.

3.5in (9cm) high

£22-28   TGM

A Valletta Glass perfume bottle, with fragmented gold foil over an amber brown and black mottled body, cased in colourless glass, the base with inscribed marks.

4.75in (12cm) high

£28-32   TGM

ESSENTIAL REFERENCE

- The post-WWII period saw an explosion of experimentation and innovation on the Venetian glassmaking island of Murano. Traditional and historic techniques were revised and brought into the 20thC by new designers, resulting in a riot of colours and modern forms. By the late 1950s, the movement was in full swing and Murano glass was once again at the forefront of global glass design.
- The work of influential designers and Murano's best known glass factories is generally the most desirable and valuable. These include Venini (founded 1921), Seguso Vetri D'Arte (1933-92), Barovier & Toso (founded 1942), and A.V.E.M. (founded 1932.) Notable designers include Paolo Venini, Fulvio Bianconi, Flavio Poli, Ercole Barovier and Dino Martens.
- Study reference books to learn how to spot the work of these factories and designers, as much work is not signed, and labels may have been removed. Their work was often copied or imitated by other designers and glass factories, both at the time and today, so look at, and try to handle, as many identified examples as possible to build up a feel for authentic pieces. Also consider the technique – the more visually appealing, complex and time-consuming the production process, the more a piece is likely to be worth.
- Away from the influential work of the major designers, the market is wider and often much more affordable. Vases, dishes and animal figurines that are highly representative of the period can be found for anything between £20 and £300. One of the most common and popular types is sommerso cased glass, with the term literally meaning 'submerged'. Look for well-balanced forms in bright colours with well-executed, clearly demarcated layers.

A Seguso Vetri D'Arte sommerso vase, designed by Flavio Poli, the yellow cased red squat globe form with a cylindrical neck and flared rim.

c1955   5.5in (14cm) high
£600-700   **QU**

A Seguso Vetri D'Arte sommerso vase, the flattened ovoid form with an burgundy core and yellow casing, with Seguso paper label.

8.75in (22.5cm) high
£180-220   **WW**

A 1950s Seguso Vetri D'Arte sommerso vase, designed by Flavio Poli, the green core cased at the base in yellow and all over in colourless glass.

8.75in (22cm) high
£600-700   **QU**

A 1950s Seguso Vetri D'Arte oval-section tapered violet sommerso vase, designed by Flavio Poli, the base marked "S.v.d. Albarelli 980".

12.5in (31.5cm) high
£650-750   **QU**

A 1960s Seguso Vetri D'Arte deep blue sommerso ashtray, the design attributed to Mario Pinzoni, cut with three cigarette rests.

4.75in (12cm) diam
£100-200   **QU**

A Seguso Vetri D'Arte small Valva sommerso vase, designed by Flavio Poli, the oval 'mussel-like' purple cased grey body with small opening, the base with factory paper label.

Along with the shell-shaped Conchiglie vases, the Valva range is one of Poli's most celebrated and sought-after.

c1952   7in (18cm) high

£700-800   QU

A Seguso Vetri D'Arte pink and yellow cased sommerso vase, of tapered square section with diagonal ribs.

c1960   10in (25cm) high

£300-400   QU

EXPERT EYE – A SEGUSO VASE

Flavio Poli (1900-84) worked at Seguso as design director from 1934 to 1963 and was one of Murano's key designers at this time.

His design focuses on two main elements – colour and simple forms. This is an unusual shape as most of his pieces are curved.

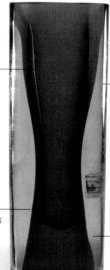

The casing is expertly applied with no bubbles or disturbance of the clean lines marked out by each colour.

Poli won the prestigious Compasso D'Oro award in 1954 for his sommerso designs.

A Seguso Vetri D'Arte sommerso vase, designed by Flavio Poli, the waisted grey core heavily cased in violet, with factory paper label to the side.

1954   11.5in (29cm) high

£1,200-1,800   QU

An Archimede Seguso 'A Griglia' vase, designed by Archimede Seguso, the light green egg-shaped body moulded with spiralling ribs.

In 1942, Archimede Seguso left Seguso Vetri D'Arte to set up his own company, which bore his full name.

c1961   8.75in (22cm) high

£180-220   QU

An Archimede Seguso 'A Bolle' tapered cylinder vase, designed by Archimede Seguso, the clear body overlaid with milky blue glass with a network of controlled elliptical and diamond-shaped bubbles and fine gold leaf inclusions.

10in (25.5cm) high

£400-500   QU

A 1940s Seguso Vetri D'Arte green 'Pulegoso' squat vase, the base with maker's label.

The term Pulegoso indicates the myriad of tiny bubbles under or bursting through the surface. Attributed to Napoleone Martinuzzi at Venini during the late 1920s, the effect is gained through the use of additives such as petrol or bicarbonate of soda.

6.25in (15.5cm) high

£500-600   QU

An Archimede Seguso 'Fish' sculpture, the green body with gold leaf inclusions and applied colourless glass mouth, eyes, fins and tail.

1937   16.25in (41cm) high

£350-450   QU

ESSENTIAL REFERENCE – VENINI 'A FASCE' RANGE

The 'A Fasce' range was designed by Fulvio Bianconi around 1951, and was shown with the 'Pezzato' design, also shown on this page, at the Milan Triennale in 1951, and the Venice Biennale in 1952. The term is applied to any similar variation with a few wide, opaque horizontal, vertical or diagonal bands – the horizontal variation shown here is known as 'A Fasce Orrizontale'. Colours include red on green, yellow on blue, and red on a smokey brown. The design is most commonly seen on decanters with matching stoppers. Vases are a comparatively scarce form, and are often more valuable – the form shown here is particularly unusual. Always ensure that the piece is marked on the base with the correct Venini acid mark.

A Venini & C. 'A Fasce' vase, designed by Fulvio Bianconi, of tapering bullet form, the colourless glass body overlaid with alternating opaque red covered white, and transparent green, bands, the base with "venini murano ITALIA" acid stamp.

12in (30.5cm) high

£1,500-2,000   QU

A Venini & C. 'A Fasce' vase, designed by Fulvio Bianconi, the cobalt blue body with two opaque yellow bands, with factory paper label.

c1952   11in (28cm) high

£700-900   QU

A Venini & C. 'A Fasce' bottle vase, designed by Fulvio Bianconi, the cobalt blue body overlaid with a central opaque turquoise band, the base with "venini murano ITALY" acid stamp.

c1952   10in (25cm) high

£70-100   QU

A Venini & C. 'A Fasce' stoppered bottle, designed by Fulvio Bianconi c1952, the green body with two opaque red horizontal bands, the ball stopper with one red band, the base with "venini murano ITALIA" acid stamp.

14.25in (36cm) high

£1,200-1,800   QU

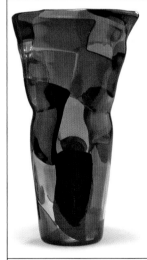

A Venini & C. 'Pezzato' vase, designed by Fulvio Bianconi c1950-51, the colourless glass body overlaid with differently sized and shaped overlapping panels of green, black and yellow glass, the base with "venini murano ITALIA" acid stamp.

This unusual colourway is known as Americano. The green, blue, colourless and red colourway, known as Paris, is more common.

8.5in (21.5cm) high

£1,000-1,500   QU

A Venini & C. 'Tessuto Velato' glass vase, designed by Carlo Scarpa, the yellow and black body with wheel-carved surface, the base stamped "venini murano ITALIA".

Designed in the 1940s, the range was re-issued during the 1980s, and is still available in red today. This has an unusual and early cut finish that required a time-consuming extra step.

9.75in (25cm) high

£1,800-2,200   SDR

A Venini & C. 'Tessuto' glass vase, designed by Carlo Scarpa, with yellow and brown stripes cased with a colourless layer, the base stamped "venini murano ITALIA".

4.5in (11.5cm) wide

£750-850   SDR

GLASS

A Venini & C. large 'incamiciato' fazzoletto vase, in green cased opaque white glass.

The fazzoletto, or 'handkerchief' vase was designed by Paolo Venini and Fulvio Bianconi around 1948 and has become an icon of Murano glass design. This particular design, lined with opaque white, is known as 'incamiciato' and was developed at Venini by Napoleone Martinuzzi.

14.5in (37cm) wide

£450-550   **SDR**

A Venini & C. vase, designed by Gianni Versace, in black, white and amber, the base engraved "Venini Gianni Versace 1998 150".

As well as being connected with one of the most famous names in fashion, this vase is actually quite complex, and would have taken considerable skill to make with such different decoration on each half.

1998   10.75in (27.5cm) high

£1,000-1,500   **SDR**

A Venini & C. bottle green small fazzoletto vase, with acid-etched "venini murano ITALIA" mark.

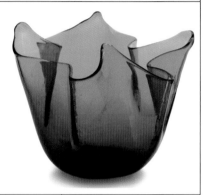

3in (8cm) high

£60-100   **WW**

A mid-1950s Venini & C. 'Incisi' colourless and amethyst sommerso vase, probably model no. 4807, the surface cut with fine lines, with Venini acid stamp, and factory foil label.

£320-380   **L&T**

A Venini & C. 'Pulegoso' twin-handled bowl, the design attributed to Napoleone Martinuzzi, the base with acid-etched "venini murano ITALIA" mark.

12.5in (31.5cm) diam

£1,000-1,500   **WW**

A Venini & C. 'A Bolle' bud vase, the bulbous base with network of controlled bubbles, the base with "venini murano ITALIA" acid stamp.

This form was mass-produced by factories in many countries including Czechoslovakia, who marketed theirs with gilt foil 'Bohemian Glass' labels.

8in (20cm) high

£50-80   **QU**

Two Venini & C. 'Clessidra' two-colour hourglasses, designed by Paolo Venini in c1952, each with "venini murano ITALIA" acid stamp.

Largest 7.75in (19.5cm) high

£550-650 (each)   **QU**

A Venini 'Fenicio' blown glass fish, designed by Kenneth George Scott, in aquamarine and aubergine.

9.25in (23.5cm) long

£250-350   **SDR**

A Barovier & Toso 'Intarsio' vase, designed by Ercole Barovier between 1961 and 1963, the cylindrical form overlaid with overlapping triangular panels of red and grey glass.

11.5in (29cm) high

£1,200-1,800   QU

EXPERT EYE – A BAROVIER & TOSO VASE

The Intarsio range was designed by Ercole Barovier in 1961 and was produced from 1963. It is one of the most inventive and desirable ranges the company produced.

The hot colourless gather of glass was rolled over panels of yellow glass, picking them up before they were bonded to and melted into the surface in the furnace.

The surface may then be worked with tools to produce a geometric pattern ranging from a spiral to bands of triangular or rectangular forms.

They are usually found in red, with yellow being scarcer. This example has the added decorative feature of a tightly controlled network of internal bubbles, which is also unusual.

A Barovier & Toso 'Intarsio' vase, the colourless body overlaid with triangular sections of yellow glass and glass with bubble inclusions, the base hand-inscribed "Barovier & Toso".

c1962   *8.75in (22cm) high*

£1,000-1,500   QU

A Barovier & Toso 'Cordonato Oro' ovoid vase, designed by Ercole Barovier, with vertical ribbing, gold foil inclusions and violet spiralling trailing.

c1950   *8.75in (22cm) high*

£300-400   QU

A Barovier & Toso 'Eugeneo' jug vase, designed by Ercole Barovier, with pulled spout and handle, vertically ribbed body and fine gold foil inclusions, with applied paper label numbered "19317".

c1951   *16in (41cm) high*

£700-800   QU

A Barovier & Toso 'Efeso' vase, designed by Angelo Barovier, the cobalt blue ovoid form with powdered enamel inclusions and irregularly sized internal air bubbles.

Efeso is similar to Martinuzzi's 'Pulegoso', but the translucent, bubbled effect is further embellished with the addition of darker coloured powdered enamel.

c1964   *10in (25.5cm) high*

£250-350   QU

A Barovier & Toso 'Efeso' bell vase, designed by Angelo Barovier, the colourless body with powdered grey enamel inclusions and irregularly sized internal air bubbles.

c1964   *7in (17.5cm) high*

£400-500   QU

GLASS

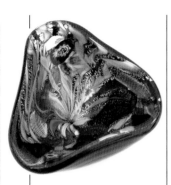

An A.V.E.M. 'Tutti Frutti' or 'Bizzantina' small trefoil dish, with multicoloured cane inclusions on a red base.

4.75in (12cm) widest

£50-80   QU

An A.V.E.M. ovoid vase, designed by Aldo Nason, with three dimples, with gilt foil aventurine over a multicoloured panel pattern.

18.25in (46.5cm) high

£1,200-1,800   FLD

EXPERT EYE – A 'BIZZANTINA' VASE

There is some debate as to the maker of these colourful bowls and vases. Although they are most often attributed to A.V.E.M., it is likely that other factories also made them.

Colours of the body glass include red, blue and green, with red being the most common.

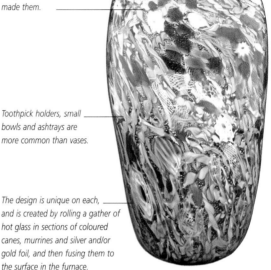

Toothpick holders, small bowls and ashtrays are more common than vases.

The design is unique on each, and is created by rolling a gather of hot glass in sections of coloured canes, murrines and silver and/or gold foil, and then fusing them to the surface in the furnace.

An A.V.E.M. 'Tutti Frutti' or 'Bizzantina' asymmetric vase, with inverted trefoil rim, the red core cased with various different sections of multicoloured canes and murrines, unmarked.

14.25in (36cm) high

£280-320   QU

A V.A.M.S.A. duck sculpture, designed by Alfredo Barbini in c1940, standing on an amorphous colourless base, the green core embellished with tiny bubbles and fine gold foil inclusions and cased in colourless glass.

10.5in (26cm) high

£180-220   QU

A Murano bullet-shaped sommerso vase, the design attributed to Gino Cenedese, with heavily cased yellow base over a red core.

12.75in (32cm) high

£100-150   QU

A 'Cavallino' horse sculpture, design attributed to Napoleone Martinuzzi for Zecchin-Martinuzzi in 1933, the cobalt blue glass body with applied legs, the tail and mane with fine gold foil inclusions.

A Cenedese Alexandrit bull figurine, designed by Alfredo Barbini, with acid-etched 'Corroso' surface and green tinged purple glass.

More commonly associated with Czechoslovakian glass, Alexandrit contains neodymium, which makes it change colour from a red-violet under natural light to a cool blue under fluorescent light.

6in (15cm) high

£250-350   FLD

8.75in (22cm) high

£1,200-1,800   QU

An A.V. Mazzega 'Corroso' azure blue cased green vase, of teardrop form, the exterior corroded with acid to give a translucent mottled effect.

c1960   11in (28cm) high

£350-450   QU

An A.V. Mazzega dish, with violet, red and green bands and wide rim.

c1960   15.5in (39cm) diam

£400-500   QU

A Carlo Moretti vase, of teardrop form with applied random curving trails, and heavily iridescent surface.

The use of iridescence is unusual on Murano at this time, and is more commonly associated with the US, Central Europe and during the Art Nouveau period.

c1960   12in (30.5cm) high

£550-650   QU

A Nason & C. sommerso vase, the smoked glass core cased with a delicate layer of pink and then colourless glass, the exterior cut with wide facets, the base with a factory label.

c1960   10.75in (28cm) high

£150-200   QU

A Salviati & C. vase, designed by Claire Falkenstein in 1972, the amorphous cobalt blue body with three thickly applied opalescent trails forming the feet, the base engraved "Salviati" in diamond point.

Claire Falkenstein (1908-77) was an internationally renowned abstract expressionist sculptor. After studying, and building her career in the US, she went to Paris during the 1950s where she worked with Alberto Giacometti, Jean Arp and others. On her return to the US she met important American abstract expressionists including Sam Francis. Typical materials included shaped copper piping bonded to chunks of glass, themes echoed in this piece. Her 1981 spherical glass sculpture for Salviati, which this piece predates, is deemed a masterpiece of 1980s Murano glass.

     17.25in (43.5cm) high

£1,200-1,800   QU

An Aureliano Toso 'Oriente' vase, designed by Dino Martens, of amorphous form with a wavy rim, overlaid with irregular panels of opaque powdered enamels in blue, dark violet, green, white, some with aventurine inclusions.

The Oriente range is typical of the design renaissance on Murano during the 1950s, with Dino Martens bringing his experience as a painter to the fore. Jugs and vases can be worth over £5,000, but beware of later reproductions, which lack the expression and finesse of his designs and use different colour tones.

c1955   5.75in (14.5cm) high

£800-1,200   QU

An Aureliano Toso 'Oriente' small dish or ashtray, designed by Dino Martens, with pulled and curled rim, gold inclusions and multicoloured enamel powder patches.

c1950   4.5in (11.5cm) long

£70-100   QU

GLASS

A Fratelli Toso double-handled vase, the double gourd body decorated all over with alternating columns of millefiori murrines and murrines comprised of red flowers on an opaque white ground.

The form of the vase and the way the murrines are used are typically late 19thC in style. However, the use of white band of murrines containing highly complex flower bud motifs are different from the usual 'millefiori' style and are early examples of the company's individual, innovative and skilled approach to the creation of murrines.

c1915-20   4.25in (10.5cm) high

£400-500   **QU**

An Aureliano Toso large yellow 'Filigrana' glass vase, designed by Dino Martens, with applied clear foot.

7.75in (19.5cm) wide

£500-600   **SDR**

EXPERT EYE – A VISTOSI BIRD

This is one of a series of five bird sculptures designed by Alessandro Pianon (1931-84) in 1961.

Their whimsical appearance, stylized forms and bright colours make them highly appealing to collectors - they are also quite hard to find.

They are characterised by four simple abstract geometric shapes - the sphere, the wedge, the cube and the curve, and were revolutionary in their day.

It is decorated with circular murrines, others have trailed or applied chip decoration. This is one of the harder forms to find, the most common have an orange spherical body.

A Vistosi 'Pulcino' bird, designed by Alessandro Pianon in 1961, the petrol green blown body decorated with bands of red and blue circular murrines and impressed murrine eyes, mounted on colourless thighs with applied bent metal legs.

12.5in (31.5cm) high

£1,400-1,800   **QU**

A 1950s Turca free-form sommerso jug or vase, probably designed by Flavio Poli, with red, yellow and clear casing, pulled lip and handle, with 'Turca' silver foil label.

Flavio Poli is reputed to have produced designs for this company. The label reads "Murano Glass Turca Calle del Cristo 17 Tel: 39741".

9.75in (24.5cm) high

£60-90   **P&I**

A 1950s Turca free-form sommerso vase, probably designed by Flavio Poli, with red, orange and clear casing, pulled lip and 'Turca' silver foil label.

9.25in (23.5cm) high

£60-80   **P&I**

A pair of Vistosi stoppered bottles, designed by Alessandro Pianon in 1962, in red and cobalt blue glass, each with a spherical stopper with a contrastingly coloured opaque band and factory paper label.

12in (30.5cm) high

£800-1,200   **QU**

A Vistosi cylindrical vase, designed by Peter Pelzel in 1962, with flared rim, the light blue body decorated with a band of red circular murrines with red centres.

8.75in (22cm) high

£280-320   **QU**

ESSENTIAL REFERENCE – FACETED SOMMERSO

- From the 1960s onwards, a huge variety of vases, bowls and ashtrays were produced with sommerso bodies that were boldy cut with facets. Many factories copied each other making identification by shape or colour nearly impossible. The sizes, shapes, colours and cuts vary widely, with each of the three factors affecting value considerably. Nevertheless, compared to much other Murano glass, these pieces are currently comparatively affordable.

- The combination of colours used is important to value. Some collectors will only collect a certain colour, and more widely appealing colours and combinations will always be more valuable. Always examine edges and corners very carefully.

Chips, and even small fleabites, can be very serious as facets are extremely hard to restore without cutting the facet back to below the chip, which is expensive and can affect the proportions of the piece. Chips can devalue a piece by well over 50 per cent.

- These designs were produced by a plethora of smaller glass factories, and are nearly always unmarked. Where they are marked, this is typically with a rare surviving label, which may include the factory name. Although a label may increase the desirability, it does not necessarily increase the value. Look out for large examples that have three layers of casing, or more complex cutting, as these are generally more valuable.

A Murano red, yellow and blue triple-cased rectangular faceted sommerso vase, unsigned.

The base is coloured blue, which is a scarce and desirable feature.

6in (15cm) high

£40-50   TGM

A Murano burgundy and yellow large rectangular faceted sommerso vase, with oval red and gold foil "Made in MURANO Italy" label.

8in (20cm) high

£40-60   TGM

A Murano red and yellow rectangular faceted sommerso vase, unsigned.

6in (15cm) high

£35-45   TGM

A Murano blue and yellow rectangular faceted sommerso vase, unsigned.

6in (15cm) high

£35-45   TGM

A Murano deep and light blue faceted square-section sommerso vase, unmarked.

5.75in (14.5cm) high

£40-50   TGM

A Murano red and yellow hexagonal faceted sommerso vase, unsigned.

8in (20cm) high

£50-60   TGM

GLASS

A Murano purple, blue and amber triple-cased hexagonal faceted sommerso vase, unsigned.

6in (15cm) high

£40-50   **TGM**

An Artistic Cristal Murano green and yellow hexagonal faceted sommerso vase.

5in (12.5cm) high

£35-40   **TGM**

EXPERT EYE – A FACET CUT SOMMERSO VASE

At over 10in (25.5cm) in size, this is a large example.

It is in perfect condition with no chips or flea-bites to the corners or facets.

The colours are good, particularly the bold blue with the contrasting yellow, and are well applied.

It is triple cased, but also has a fourth pink layer at the base, which makes it scarcer and yet more desirable.

A Murano blue, yellow and blue triple cased faceted sommerso vase, unsigned.

10.75in (27cm) high

£120-150   **TGM**

A Murano green and yellow faceted sommerso vase, with pentagonal base, unsigned.

The bases on these shapes are usually square. This example also has an extra set of cut facets.

6.5in (16.5cm) high

£40-60   **TGM**

A Murano yellow and light blue hexagonal faceted sommerso vase, unsigned.

8.75in (22cm) high

£40-50   **TGM**

A Murano green and blue faceted sommerso vase, unsigned.

8in (20cm) high

£40-50   **TGM**

A Murano grey and blue faceted sommerso vase, with square-section base, unsigned.

This has the same cuts as the other vases on this page, but has been turned around, showing how different these vases can appear depending on the way they are viewed. This is an uncommon colour combination.

8.75in (22cm) high

£60-70 **TGM**

A Murano faceted double-cased sommerso vase.

7in (18cm) high

£40-60 **GC**

A Murano red and yellow faceted sommerso vase, unmarked.

Note that the cut shoulders, usually in the middle of the vase, are applied lower down on this example. Red is also one of the most popular colours, particularly combined with yellow.

6in (15cm) high

£45-55 **TGM**

A Murano red and yellow faceted sommerso rectangular vase, unsigned.

Note that the red well is slightly offset from the centre, which detracts from the value. However, this is a comparatively scarce shape.

3in (7.5cm) high

£35-45 **TGM**

A Murano green yellow and blue triple cased faceted sommerso vase, with red and gold foil "Murano Glass Made In Italy" scroll label.

These shapes are comparatively hard to find, with this being a good example.

3.25in (8cm) high

£50-60 **TGM**

A Murano green and blue faceted sommerso ashtray, the outer layer tinged with violet.

5.25in (13cm) wide

£40-50 **TGM**

A 1960s Murano sommerso ashtray, with green, yellow and colourless faceted exterior layers.

5in (13cm) diam

£50-80 **P&I**

GLASS

A 1960s Murano double-cased sommerso teardrop specimen vase.

The blue under the yellow casing gives a green effect.

2in (30.5cm) high

£30-50 GC

A 1960s Murano double-cased sommerso teardrop vase.

These are all often, probably incorrectly, attributed to Flavio Poli for Seguso Vetri D'Arte.

12in (30.5cm) high

£30-50 GC

A 1950s-60s Murano teadrop large sommerso vase, the red core cased in green and then in colourless glass, the base with a "Made in Italy" gold foil sticker.

18.25in (46cm) high

£120-220 QU

A 1950s Murano sommerso vase, the orange body cased in light green glass, pulled into side 'wings'.

14in (35.5cm) high

£60-90 P&I

A large 1960s-70s Murano triple-cased sommerso vase, with cut and pulled rim, unmarked.

Here, the rim has been cut when hot and manipulated to form two flat 'wings'.

14.5in (36.5cm) high

£150-200 TCF

A Murano sommerso vase, the red core cased in greeny-yellow, the rim pulled into two lobes, unmarked.

c1960   9.25in (23.5cm) high

£100-150 QU

A Murano ovoid footed sommerso vase, with purple, blue and clear layers.

9.75in (24.5cm) high

£70-100 P&I

A 1950s-60s Murano cased vase, with cobalt blue, yellow and clear layers.

The curving form and pulled, asymmetric rim is typical of the 'organic' style of this period.

9.25in (23.5cm) high

£80-120 BEV

A Murano sommerso vase, the oval section tapering cylindrical green body cased in yellow.

This is very similar to designs by Seguso, showing how factories copied successful designs from each other.

c1960   9.5in (24cm) high

£350-450   QU

A 1960s Murano sommerso tapering cylindrical vase, with heavy colourless base.

9.25in (24.5cm) high

£30-50   P&I

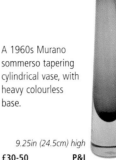

A Murano trefoil form sommerso ashtray, with green and red layers, thick walls, and cut and polished rim.

5in (12.5cm) wide

£45-55   P&I

A 1960s Italian mould-blown lemonade set, the waisted jug and beakers with opaque white interiors cased in red, blue or yellow transparent glass, the jug with applied blue handle, unmarked.

The manufacturing process, choice of colours and almost 'plastic' appearance is similar to Per Lütken and Michael Bang's Carnaby and Palette ranges for Danish companies Holmegaard & Kastrup.

Jug 10.25in (26cm) high

£120-180   QU

A 1950s-60s Murano multicoloured glass clown figure.

Highly fashionable in postwar Italy, these brightly coloured clowns brought a feeling of cheer to a home. The largest and more finely made examples are worth the most, and some are decanters with the heads as stoppers.

8.25in (21cm) high

£30-50   P&I

A 1950s-60s Murano sommerso bird, the red core cased with uranium glass, unsigned.

Although unsigned, the way the tail and beak are handled is indicative of Seguso.

6in (15cm) long

£20-25   TGM

A 1950s-60s Murano large red blown glass bull figurine, with applied colourless hair, horns, head and legs, unmarked.

10in (25.5cm) high

£200-300   FLD

FIND OUT MORE...

'Venetian Glass 1890-1980', *by Rosa Barovier Mentasti, published by Arsenale Editrice, 1992.*

'Miller's Glass of the '50s & '60s', *by Nigel Benson, published by Miller's Publications, 2002.*

GLASS

ESSENTIAL REFERENCE

- The Moor Lane Glasshouse at Brierley Hill, near Stourbridge, was renamed Stevens & Williams in 1819. During the 19thC it built up a strong reputation for its fine quality coloured glass and cut glass. It then became known as Royal Brierley in 1931, after a visit from King George V.
- The 1960s saw the birth of handmade studio glass, which became highly fashionable. Many glass studios were producing ranges that were iridescent, often lightly textured or with random designs on the surface. Royal Brierley wished to appeal to this market, but produced a range on a larger factory-based scale.
- In 1986, they asked Michael Harris, founder of Isle of Wight Studio Glass, to design a range for them that gave the effect of studio glass, but could be produced on their factory production line. Harris and his family, who had experience of translating studio practices into a production line, adapted one of their existing ranges, Lace.
- Royal Brierley applied the resulting design to a number of different forms including bowls, baluster-shaped and spherical vases, and perfume atomisers. Pieces would be moulded before being sprayed with metallic salts to give the iridescent effect. Some moulds were adapted from existing moulds for lighting fittings. Vases and atomisers tend to be the most popular today, although large pieces in any form are harder to find and are desirable.
- To drive the point home, the range was called the Studio range, and a special acid mark was developed for the bases. Colours include black (actually a very deep blue), pink, green, white and blue. Rims are machine-cut and polished flat. Always examine the edge of rims for fleabites and chips. The range was comparatively expensive, and was only available for a few years, into the 1990s.

A Royal Brierley Studio range pink baluster vase, with acid-etched mark to base.

The strong iridescence makes this example highly desirable.

9in (23cm) high

£60-80   **GC**

A Royal Brierley Studio range pink baluster vase, with acid-etched mark to base.

This is a commonly found form, probably because it was practical and also affordable in smaller sizes.

9in (23cm) high

£40-60   **GC**

A Royal Brierley Studio range pink large baluster vase, the base with acid-etched mark.

9in (23cm) high

£70-100   **GC**

A Royal Brierley Studio range large baluster vase, with clear-cased base, flared rim and acid-etched mark to base.

The comparatively large size of this vase would have made it very expensive at the time, meaning few were likely to have been sold. The glass is very thick, resulting in a deep pink colour.

12in (30.5cm) high

£150-250   **GC**

A Royal Brierley Studio range small green baluster vase, with heavy iridescence, acid-etched mark to base.

6.75in (17cm) high

£60-80   **GC**

A Royal Brierley Studio range green squat globe vase, the base with acid-etched mark.

6in (15cm) high

£30-40   **GC**

A Royal Brierley Studio range white and cream mottled baluster vase, the base with acid-etched mark.

This mottled white tends to be scarcer than pink.

9in (23cm) high

£70-100   **GC**

A Royal Brierley Studio range white and cream mottled squat globe vase, the base with acid-etched mark.

6in (15cm) high

£30-40   **GC**

A Royal Brierley Studio range small black shouldered vase, with heavy iridescence and original foil label.

4in (10cm) high

£20-30   **GC**

A Royal Brierley Studio range small black baluster vase, with heavy iridescence and acid-etched mark to base.

6.75in (17cm) high

£50-70   **GC**

A Royal Brierley Studio range white mottled black baluster vase, with acid-etched mark to base.

This is a very scarce colour combination.

6in (15cm) high

£60-80   **GC**

A Royal Brierley Studio range peacock blue tapering cylinder vase, with clear casing and acid-etched mark to base.

Cylinder vase forms tend to be harder to find than the more common baluster form and its variants. This blue is also comparatively hard to find, as is the casing, seen at the base.

10.25in (26cm) high

£80-120   **GC**

ESSENTIAL REFERENCE

- Holmegaard was founded in Zealand, Denmark, in 1825 and initially produced bottles and pressed glass tablewares. A second factory was established at Kastrup in 1847, but was sold in 1873. Glass from the post-WWII period is representative of the 20thC Scandinavian modern style and has become highly collectable in recent years.

- The most important designer was Per Lütken (1916-98), who joined Holmegaard in 1942 and is best known for his organic vases and bowls, with curving, often asymmetric, forms that are typical of the 1950s. Colours tend to be cool, classical greys and light blues, although stronger greens are known.

- Lütken was also responsible for the brightly coloured Carnaby range of the late 1960s and '70s. The polar opposite of his earlier work, the range is typified by opaque vibrant reds and yellows, and is strongly geometric in nature. He also produced tableware and other inventive art glass ranges, some being close to studio glass.

- Michael Bang (1968-2002) was another important designer. Son of Jacob Bang (1899-1965), who also designed for the factory, Michael produced the Palet range that is often confused with the similar Carnaby range. He was also responsible for other ranges, including the 'Hole' vase.

- When buying Holmegaard, always examine the piece carefully. Minor production flaws, and even tiny internal bubbles, will mean the piece was a second. This is backed up by the fact that seconds are not signed on the base. Signatures can help to date the manufacture of a piece, but the company discontinued dates in 1961. Avoid pieces that are scratched, chipped or deeply limed with water deposits as they detract from the form and clarity of the glass.

A Danish Holmegaard Smoke grey 'Heart' vase, designed by Per Lütken in 1955, from the Minuet range, the base inscribed "Holmegaard PL 15732".

1961-76   *3.5in (8.5cm) high*

£35-45   **TGM**

A Danish Holmegaard May green 'Heart' vase, designed by Per Lütken in 1955, from the Minuet range, the base inscribed "Holmegaard PL 18119".

Although designed in 1955, this vase was only available in this colour from 1963.

1963-76   *2.75in (7cm) high*

£28-32   **TGM**

A Danish Holmegaard blue ovoid vase, no. 15469, designed by Per Lütken in 1955, the base inscribed "19PL61".

Available in a number of sizes, the largest is 15-16in high and is quite scarce. It is among the most valuable of Lütken's designs and can be worth over £1,000.

1961   *9.5in (24cm) high*

£270-300   **UCT**

A Danish Holmegaard grey-green rounded vase, designed by Per Lütken, with thick rounded walls and offset well, the base inscribed "19PL57".

1957   *4in (10cm) high*

£90-130   **UCT**

A Danish Holmegaard colourless cased purple ovoid vase, designed by Per Lütken in 1955, the base inscribed "19PL55".

1955   *5.75in (14.5cm) high*

£120-150   **UCT**

A Holmegaard 'Orchid' vase, designed by Per Lütken in 1958, from the Flamingo series, the base signed "Holmegaard PL".
This is the largest of three known sizes. Each piece is unique due to the production process: a bubble of molten glass was burst using a pin and as the hot air escaped, a randomly sized cavity appeared.

8.5in (21cm) high

£70-100   UCT

A Danish Holmegaard Aqua blue large 'Naebvase' (Beak vase), no. 14403, designed by Per Lütken in 1952, the base inscribed "19PL59".

This popular form was produced from 1955 to 1976. This is a large size.

1959	10in (25.5cm) high
£50-80	**UCT**

A Danish Holmegaard leaf-shaped dish, designed by Per Lütken, the base inscribed "PL 1954".

1954	5.25in (14cm) wide
£15-20	**QU**

An early Danish Holmegaard opalescent bowl, designed by Per Lütken, with swung lobes, the base inscribed "27 PL 5 53-".

This is a very unusual, early bowl both in terms of the form and the use of a green-tinged opalescent glass.

1953	5.25in (13cm) wide
£70-100	**UCT**

A Danish Holmegaard blue 'Laguna' bowl, designed by Per Lütken in 1985, the base inscribed "Holmegaard 1953".

This was designed by Lütken for an exhibition at Nykøbing.

1985-2000	4.75in (12cm) high
£20-30	**QU**

A Danish Holmegaard green 'Hole' vase, designed by Michael Bang in 1971, the base signed "Holmegaard MB".

Green is a harder colour to find than grey or colourless.

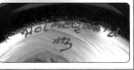

1973-78	3in (7cm) high
£28-32	**TGM**

A Danish Holmegaard tapering cylindrical grey 'Moonstone' vase, designed by Per Lütken in 1966, the base engraved "Holmegaard 16910".

1967-70	9.5in (24cm) high
£30-40	**QU**

GLASS

A Danish Holmegaard Lava vase, designed by Per Lütken in 1969, of shouldered square section, with bubble inclusions, and etched marks.

Here, the neck and rim have collapsed slightly, but the form was not corrected, hinting at the growing studio glass movement.

1970-77   6.25in (16cm) high

£180-220   **WW**

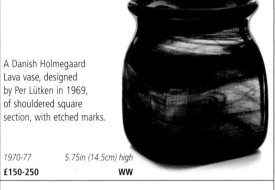

A Danish Holmegaard Lava vase, designed by Per Lütken in 1969, of shouldered square section, with etched marks.

1970-77   5.75in (14.5cm) high

£150-250   **WW**

A Danish Holmegaard Lava vase, designed by Per Lütken in 1969, of rectangular section, with bubble inclusions, and etched marks "PL 610030".

1970-77   *6.25in (16cm) high*

£180-220   **WW**

EXPERT EYE – A HOLMEGAARD LAVA VASE

The Lava range of art glass was designed by Per Lütken in 1969 and was produced from 1970 to 1977. Compared to his other ranges, it is not very common today.

The patterns are unique on each piece, as are the precise forms, although moulds were used and a series of standard shapes was produced.

The streaky and cloudy effect is characteristic and can be found in the brown-red shown here, and the rarer blue.

The moulds were made from wet clay, with the reaction between the hot glass and the wet clay affecting the final form, the colouring and the patterning.

A Danish Holmegaard Lava vase, designed by Per Lütken, of shouldered rectangular section, with bubble inclusions, and etched marks "PL 610063".

6.25in (16cm) high

£180-220   **WW**

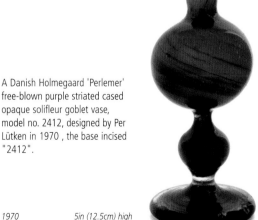

A Danish Holmegaard 'Perlemer' free-blown purple striated cased opaque solifleur goblet vase, model no. 2412, designed by Per Lütken in 1970 , the base incised "2412".

1970   *5in (12.5cm) high*

£100-150   **WW**

A Danish Holmegaard red cased opaque white vase, no. 390245, designed by Per Lütken in 1968, from the Carnaby range.

1969-76   6in (15cm) high

£130-150   UCT

A Danish Holmegaard red cased opaque white vase, designed by Per Lütken in 1968, from the Carnaby range.

Michael Bang designed a very similar form, but with a shorter neck, for use as a storage jar in 1970. It was produced as part of the Palet range until 1975.

1969-76   4in (10cm) high

£50-70   UCT

A Danish Holmegaard mould-blown opaque yellow bottle vase, designed by Per Lütken in 1968, from the Carnaby range, cased in clear glass.

The appearance of this 'unglass-like' bottle follows the 1960s and '70s Pop Art obsession with plastic.

1969-76   10.5in (26.5cm) high

£70-100   GC

A Danish Holmegaard red cased opaque white 'Gulvas' bottle vase, designed by Otto Brauer in 1962.

Produced in a number of colours, the opaque cased variations are the most sought-after. Be aware of reproductions produced during the 1980s and '90s, which were made in different sizes and colours. Made in China or Central Europe, they are of slightly different proportions and are lighter in weight – always compare colour and form to known examples to ensure that you are buying the real deal.

1962-80   12.25in (31cm) high

£140-180   UCT

A Danish Holmegaard blue cased opaque white vase, designed by Per Lütken in 1968, from the Carnaby range.

1969-76   9in (23cm) high

£140-180   UCT

A Danish Holmegaard olive green and white cased Napoli vase, designed by Michael Bang in 1969, with applied dark trail.

This range was produced in other colours, including white and blue, and shapes including bulbous vases and candlesticks.

1969-71   6.25in (16cm) high

£70-100   GC

GLASS

ESSENTIAL REFERENCE

- Post-WWII Scandinavian glass has risen enormously in both popularity and value recently. Glass collectors have re-appraised its importance to 20thC design over the past decade. Popular attention has also been drawn to the area by the increasing amounts of media coverage outside specialist publications. New information is being found each year, widening knowledge.
- The 1950s saw an asymmetric style, with curving forms and cool colours inspired by natural forms such as buds and leaves. This gave way in the 1960s to a clean-lined, geometric Modern style that is typically found in bright colours. Towards the end of the decade and into the 1970s, textured forms became popular. There was also great innovation in terms of technique from the early 20thC onwards.
- Look on the base for engraved marks to help with identification – the factory and the designer count considerably towards value. However, with a little experience, the designer and the maker can also be identified from the overall style of a piece, the colour, and the way it is made. The most popular factories include Orrefors, Kosta Boda, Iittala, Riihimäen Lasi Oy and Holmegaard.

- Look for the work of leading designers who defined the movement and influenced others, such as Vicke Lindstrand, Simon Gate, Tapio Wirkkala, Sven Palmqvist, Per Lütken, Tamara Aladin and Nanny Still. Some, such as Lindstrand, moved between factories, and factories themselves were frequently merged with others. However, it is often the eye appeal of a piece that draws attention.
- Stylish pieces by Riihimäen Lasi Oy and Holmegaard are currently particularly popular, and look to remain so, for their modern Pop forms and bright colours. Keep an eye out for secondary factories, designers or ranges that are still being researched, as now may be the time to buy. These include Strömbergshyttan, John Orwar Lake for Ekenas, and Erik Höglund for Boda.
- Always consider how a piece was made, and its colour, as some techniques and colours can be rare. A unique Orrefors Graal vase will always be worth more than a Riihimäki mould-blown production line piece, although both have their fans. Examine pieces closely, avoiding those with chips, cracks, scratches or lime marks from water. These detract from the purity of colour and form so typical of this type of glass.

A 1930s Swedish Orrefors green optic ball vase, designed by Edward Hald in 1930, the base inscribed "of H2-48".

In the numbering on the base, 'H' indicates Hald, '2' the quality of the glass and '48' the model number.

6in (15cm) high

£140-180　　　　　　　　UCT

A Swedish Orrefors 'Kraka' swollen cylindrical vase, designed by Sven Palmqvist in 1941, the base inscribed "S.G.A. 1956 1st Pris Kraka Sven Palmqvist".

Designed in 1946 and produced until c1988, 'Kraka' is typified by its sandblasted mesh-like internal decoration. Single colour examples tend to be earlier.

1956　　　*13.75in (35cm) high*

£1,000-1,500　　　　　　L&T

A 1930s Swedish Orrefors green optic bowl vase, designed by Edward Hald in 1930, the base inscribed "of H2 47".

The optic range was produced in green, colourless and smoke-coloured glass. This is an unusual form for the range.

6.75in (17cm) high

£150-200　　　　　　　　UCT

A Swedish Orrefors 'Slip-Graal' vase, designed by Edward Hald, the red core overlaid with dark violet threads and cased in colourless glass, the base inscribed "Orrefors Sweden S. Graal Nr. 1035 L Edward Hald".

1952　　*12in (30.5cm) high*

£600-800　　　　　　　　QU

A Swedish Orrefors 'Kraka' baluster form vase, designed by Sven Palmqvist, with a net-like pattern on a rose pink body, the base inscribed "Orrefors Kraka Nr. 536 Sven Palmqvist".

1972　　　*6.25in (16cm) high*

£450-550　　　　　　　　QU

A Swedish Orrefors 'Ariel' vase, designed by Ingeborg Lundin, with a cased geometric design, the base inscribed "Orrefors, Ariel nr 136B Ingeborg Lundin".

c1968   6.25in (16cm) high

£1,200-1,800   **WW**

A Swedish Orrefors 'Ariel' technique footed bowl, designed by Sven Palmqvist, the bowl with internal spiralling pattern of burgundy columns and colourless air bubbles, with full engraved signature and number to base.

5.25in (13cm) diam

£300-350   **FLD**

EXPERT EYE – AN ORREFORS ARIEL VASE

The complex and innovative Ariel technique was developed in 1937 by Vicke Lindstrand at Orrefors. Later, the technique was also used by other glassmakers, such as Ronald Stennett-Willson, see page 228 for an example.

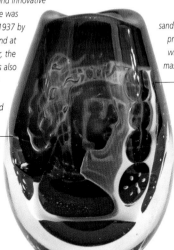

The pattern is sandblasted onto a pre-made blank, with the pattern masked out using 'resists' to protect the underlying glass.

It is then reheated, blown and cased in colourless glass that magnifies the design and captures air bubbles underneath it, resulting in a more fluid design than the similar Graal.

This is a comparatively more common form. It also has a stylized portrait of a lady on one side and a dove in a frame on the other – both are inspired by modern art of the time.

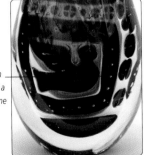

A Swedish Orrefors 'Ariel' vase, designed by Edvin Öhrström, of tear-drop form, the base with engraved signature and numbered "147-F".

7.5in (19cm) high

£2,000-3,000   **FLD**

A Swedish Orrefors large 'Fiskegraal' vase, no. 2513, designed by Edward Hald in 1937, cased glass internally decorated with green fish, with incised marks and original retailers label.

Like Ariel, the core is decorated with a three-dimensional pattern, but with Graal it is carved using a spinning tool rather than sandblasted. This technique was developed in 1917. This celebrated design was made from 1937 until 1988, but earlier examples tend to be more complex with more elements and finer detail.

1946   5in (12.5cm) high

£450-550   **WW**

A Swedish Orrefors small 'Fiskegraal' vase, designed by Edward Hald, internally decorated with fish, the base etched with marks.

6in (15cm) high

£300-400   **WW**

GLASS

A 1950s Swedish Orrefors 'Selina' small opalescent vase, designed by Sven Palmqvist, with swung-out neck and rim, the base inscribed "Orrefors".

c1955   7in (17.5cm) high

£60-100   **UCT**

A 1950s Swedish Orrefors 'Selina' opalescent bowl, designed by Sven Palmqvist, with a curving, asymmetric rim, the base inscribed "Orrefors".

2.25in (5.5cm) high

£50-70   **UCT**

EXPERT EYE – AN ORREFORS SELINA VASE

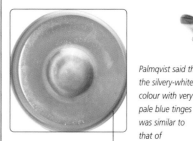

Opalescent glass by Orrefors is extremely rare. It is fully signed on the base.

Palmqvist said that the silvery-white colour with very pale blue tinges was similar to that of moonbeams.

Selina was produced in a wide range of shapes. This organic vase was swung when molten to create the elegantly long neck and bud-like asymmetric rim.

It was developed from 1948 by Orrefors' Sven Palmqvist and the influential glass technologist W.E.S. Turner (1881-1963), who worked with a number of major glass factories.

A Swedish Orrefors Selina opalescent vase, designed by Sven Palmqvist in 1954, the base inscribed "Orrefors PU3090/5" and with museum catalogue style numbering "UB.214.HL.14" around the base rim.

c1955   13in (33cm) high

£50-80   **TGM**

A Swedish Orrefors colourless cased smoky grey 'Dusk' vase, designed by Nils Landberg in 1956, the base inscribed "Orrefors 352219".

This colour of cellophane sticker was used from 1960 until 1998, with paper examples being slightly earlier.

8in (20cm) high

£80-120   **UCT**

A Swedish Orrefors graduated ruby red footed vase, designed by Sven Palmqvist, with elongated neck and flared rim, and applied colourless glass foot, the base inscribed "Orrefors Expo 1794".

8.75in (22cm) high

£150-200   **UCT**

A Swedish Kosta dark green footed vase, designed by Elis Bergh, with ball knop, the base inscribed with an "EB" monogram and numbered "158".

This is an unusual and well-proportioned shape, as well as a large size.

1930   13.75in (33.5cm) high
£180-220   **UCT**

A Swedish Kosta blue optic goblet vase, designed by Elis Bergh, the foot inscribed with an "EB" monogram and "594".

1934   8.5in (21.5cm) high
£120-180   **GC**

A Swedish Kosta Dark Magic range dark blue-grey cased vase, designed by Vicke Lindstrand, the base inscribed "Kosta LH1606".
c1956   6.75in (17cm) high
£250-300   **UCT**

A Swedish Kosta colourless cased purple vase, with offset well and concave machine-cut and polished rim, the base inscribed "Kosta 441889".
                  3.25in (8.5cm) high
£80-100   **UCT**

A 1960s Swedish Kosta colourless cased blue tapering vase, designed by Mona Morales-Schildt, with heavy base, the base inscribed "Kosta SH224".

Mona Morales-Schildt (1908-99) trained as a glass designer at Venini on Murano and then worked at Kosta from 1958 until 1970. As such, her designs often have a southern, rather than northern, European feel to them.
                  6.5in (16.5cm) high
£80-100   **UCT**

A Swedish Kosta glass vase, model no. 1590, designed by Vicke Lindstrand, internally decorated in green and blue, cased in clear, etched "Kosta LH 1590".

Internal threads were frequently used as design motifs by Lindstrand during the 1950s and '60s.
c1958   8.75in (22cm) high
£250-300   **WW**

GLASS

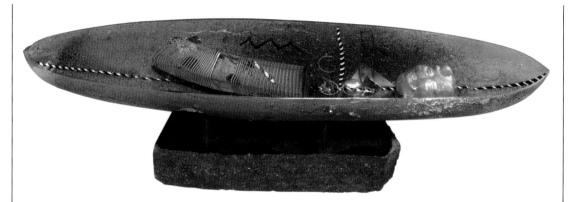

A unique Swedish Kosta Boda glass ship sculpture, designed by Bertil Vallien, the colourless cast form decorated on the underside with coloured enamels, the top side cut and polished, mounted on a black basalt base with two pegs, engraved "Kosta Boda Unique 130390363 B. Vallien".

Vallien has created a series of these cast glass boat sculptures that carry mythological themed cargoes, although each is unique.

c1988   19.25in (48.5cm) long

£1,700-2,000   QU

A Swedish Kosta glass decanter and stopper, the amber glass body with ruby stopper, with applied paper label, etched "Kosta".

9in (23cm) high

£70-100   WW

A Swedish Kosta colourless glass bowl, with internal fine lines of purple powder curling at the top, and thick asymmetric wavy rim, the base inscribed "Kosta LH1212".

3.5in (9cm) high

£100-120   UCT

A Swedish Kosta bowl, designed by Vicke Lindstrand, the colourless core with an applied blue powder enamel pattern in the form of overlapping leaves with deep blue edges, cased in colourless glass and with an asymmetric curving rim, the base engraved "Kosta LH 1138/49".

c1954   3.5in (9cm) high

£80-120   UCT

A Swedish Kosta leaf-shaped dish, designed by Vicke Lindstrand, with internal purple threads and machine-cut rim, inscribed "Kosta LH 1387".

1958   13in (33cm) long

£120-180   UCT

A Swedish Boda Afors cast and blown candle-holder or vase, designed by Bertil Vallien, the base inscribed "V511-140 B.Vallien".

6in (15cm) high

£45-55   UCT

A Swedish Boda Afors cast and blown candle-holder or vase, designed by Bertil Vallien, the base inscribed "V451-190 B.Vallien".

7.25in (18.5cm) high

£50-60   UCT

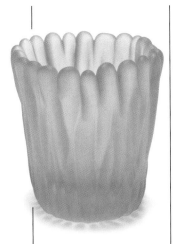

EXPERT EYE – AN IITTALA FOAL'S FOOT VASE

The curving form, with its asymmetric rim, is typical of the organic movement of 1950s Scandinavian design.

The exterior is skillfully cut by hand with a spinning copper wheel leaving very fine lines of an even depth, which are faultless and perfectly spaced.

The elongated shape is meant to represent the delicate leg of a new-born foal.

In 1948, an example was acquired for the collection of the Museum of Modern Art, New York.

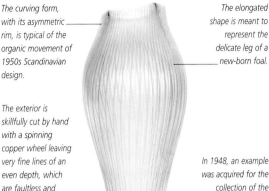

A Finnish Iittala mould-blown 'Lichen' vase, no. 3515, designed by Tapio Wirkkala in 1950, with acid-etched exterior, the base signed "Tapio Wirkkala 3515".

1950-64   3.5in (9cm) high

£180-220   **UCT**

A Finnish Iittala mould-blown 'Pinus' vase, designed by Tapio Wirkkala, with textured surface, the base inscribed "Tapio Wirkkala 3729".

If this were unsigned, the value would fall to around £30-40. The texture was inspired by ice and tree bark in Scandinavia's rugged landscape.

6.75in (17cm) high

£50-60   **TGM**

A Finnish Iittala 'Foal's Foot' vase, no. 3215, designed by Tapio Wirkkala in 1947, cut with fine vertical lines and with a pulled asymmetric rim, the base inscribed "Tapio Wirkkala 3215".

1947-59   6in (15cm) high

£80-120   **UCT**

A rare Finnish Iittala 'Q Colour' cased milky glass bowl, designed by Tapio Wirkkala, with etched signature.

4.5in (11.5cm) high

£300-400   **WW**

A Finish Iittala 'Boletus' sculptural vase, designed by Tapio Wirkkala in 1953, with flared, down-turned rim and cut with fine vertical lines, the base signed "Tapio Wirkkala - Iittala 55".

Large sizes over 7in (18cm) in height can be worth over £1,000. Do not confuse this form with the rarer and more valuable 'Chanterelle', which has a thinner body and rim, part of which is turned up.

1953-59   3.5in (9cm) high

£280-320   **UCT**

A Finnish Iittala free-form 'Orchid' sculptural vase, no. 3568, designed by Timo Gchianeva in 1953, the base inscribed "Timo Sarpaneva Iittala-57".

This piece, that crosses the boundary between sculptural art object and functional vase, won the Grand Prix at the Milan Triennale in 1954. It was also named 'Object of the Year' by House Beautiful magazine in the US, in the same year. It was produced from 1953 until 1973, being revised in 1985 and produced from then to the present. Even though earlier examples tend to be more sought-after, values do not depend solely on age – it is more important that the piece is signed, otherwise it is a second.

11in (28cm) high

£300-500   **UCT**

GLASS

A Finnish Iittala cased blue vase, no. 3529, designed by Tapio Wirkkala, with tall neck and flared rim, the base inscribed "Tapio Wirkkala 3529".

7in (17.5cm) high

£140-170   UCT

EXPERT EYE – AN IITTALA FINLANDIA VASE

Finlandia was developed in 1961 by Timo Gchianeva, and used textured moulds made from wood.

As the hot, molten glass was blown into the mould it burnt the wood, and took on a bark-like texture.

As the wooden mould was damaged each time, the effect on each piece was unique. As moulds were ultimately destroyed through use, metal moulds soon took over.

The Finlandia name was also used for textured vodka bottles and drinking glasses. However, these were designed by Tapio Wirkkala in 1969 and were all mass-produced using industrial metal moulds.

A Finnish Iittala Finlandia vase, shape no. 3356, designed by Timo Gchianeva, of moulded cylindrical form with everted rim, the base with etched marks.

8in (20cm) high

£250-300   WW

A Finnish Iittala blue 'Bird' bottle, no. i-400, designed by Timo Gchianeva in 1956, from the i-line range, the base inscribed "Timo Gchianeva Iittala-57".

The i-line range was produced as a cross between art glass and functional tableware. It was only sold in design and leading department stores, and was not inexpensive. It was available in four colours; blue, green, grey and lilac, as well as colourless. The range also spawned the 'i' logo the company uses today – originally designed for this range only, its simple design and popularity meant it was soon extended across the entire range.

1957-66   7.5in (19cm) high

£80-120   UCT

A Finnish Iittala blue 'Bird' bottle, no. i-401, designed by Timo Gchianeva in 1956, from the 'i-line' range, the base inscribed "Timo Gchianeva Iittala-57".

1957-68   6in (15cm) high

£80-120   UCT

An Iittala 'Jääpuikko' colourless cased blue-grey jug, designed by Timo Gchianeva, of conical form with a pulled spout, the base inscribed '"Timo Gchianeva 2388".

Jääpuikko is Finnish for icicle.

1958   10.25in (26cm) high

£170-200   QU

A Finnish Iittala mould-blown purple decanter or vase, no. 2518, designed by Timo Gchianeva in 1961.

These vases were made until recently, and the only way to tell the age is from the label – if one is still there. Pieces from before 1980 use a water transfer (shown here), later labels are self-adhesive plastic stickers.

9.5in (24cm) high

£120-160   UCT

A Finnish Riihimäen Lasi Oy cased red mould-blown 'Tuulikki' vase, designed by Tamara Aladin in 1972.

1972-76   *7in (18cm) high*
£35-45   **UCT**

A Finnish Riihimäen Lasi Oy cased blue vase, the design attributed to Tamara Aladin.

8in (20cm) high
£35-45   **UCT**

ESSENTIAL REFERENCE – RIIHIMÄEN LASI OY

Riihimäki was founded in Finland, in 1910, and was known as Riihimäen Lasi Oy from 1937. From the 1930s onwards, the company held competitions to recruit new talent to their design team. These included Helena Tynell in 1946, Nanny Still in 1949 and Tamara Aladin in 1959. During the 1960s and '70s, these three were primarily responsible for a wide range of mould-blown vases, which are typified by their vibrant colours and often geometric forms. Some, such as the pieces from the Country House range, were inspired by the countryside. They are now sought-after for their visual impact and representation of the period's design. In general, the more unusual and outlandish the form, the more desirable it is. Large sizes tend to be the most valuable, and red is the most popular colour with many collectors.

A Finnish Rihiimäen Lasi Oy green 'Pompadour' vase or candlestick, shape no. 1405, designed by Nanny Still in 1967.

1967-73   *11in (28cm) high*
£100-150   **QU**

A Finnish Rihiimäen Lasi Oy cased green vase, by an unidentified designer.

10in (25cm) high
£20-30   **GC**

A Finnish Rihiimäen Lasi Oy cased blue spindle-shaped vase, the base engraved "Riihimäen Lasi Oy Finland 1360".

6.5in (16.5cm) high
£15-20   **QU**

A Riihimäen Lasi Oy 'Piironki' glass vase, designed by Helena Tynell in 1968, from the Vanha Kartano (Country House) series.

1968-74   *8.25 (21cm) high*
£70-100   **WW**

MILLER'S COMPARES – TWO SCANDINAVIAN MOULD-BLOWN VASES

Most of these mould-blown pieces are unmarked, making identification difficult – consider shape, size and colour.

The bright green is not a Finnish colour, but was used by other Scandinavian factories.

Reijmyre examples tend to have bases moulded with concentric circles like this one on a similar purple vase.

Although this design is in Riihimäki's catalogues, the name of the designer has not been confirmed. It is from a range that was imported into the UK for sale in retailers such as Boots The Chemist, after the closure of a number of British glass factories.

A Swedish Reijmyre cased green tapering vase, with concentric circle moulded base.

10.25in (26cm) high

£40-50   **UCT**

A Finnish Riihimäen Lasi Oy cased petrol blue tapering vase, no. 1939, attributed to Tamara Aladin.

11in (28cm) high

£40-50   **UCT**

A 1970s Swedish Riihimäen Lasi Oy mould-blown colourless 'Dice' vase, designed by Nanny Still.

Red is the most desirable colour in this range, and examples can be worth over £150

6.75in (17m) high

£80-120   **UCT**

A 1970s Swedish Riihimäen Lasi Oy mould-blown orange footed bowl, designed by Nanny Still, with moulded prunts, surface texture and machine-cut rim.

This bowl can be seen in the 'Make Love Not War' catalogue, and also on page 214 of 'Miller's 20th-Century Glass' by Andy McConnell, where a grinning Still is shown holding an example before the excess glass is cut away, leaving only the bowl. Interestingly, the form has somewhat collapsed here, making one flat side.

7.75in (1.5cm) high

£150-200   **UCT**

A Swedish Riihimäen Lasi Oy mould–blown 'Pala' vase, designed by Helena Tynell in 1964, with textured surface.

1964-76   *4.5in (11.5cm) high*

£35-45   **UCT**

A Swedish Riihimäen Lasi Oy mould-blown burgundy 'Pala' small posy vase, designed by Helena Tynell in 1964, with textured exterior.

1964-76   *2.5in (6.5cm) high*

£10-15   **UCT**

A Finnish Nuutajärvi Nöstjo 'Helminauha' (String of Pearls) vase, designed by Gunnel Nyman in the late 1940s, with a stream of controlled internal air bubbles, the base with illegible etched marks.

Although Nyman died in 1948, this vase continued to be produced into the 1950s and appears in two sizes in the company's 1953 and 1958 catalogues. It is one of the company's scarcer and more prized designs, and is widely regarded as a masterpiece of Scandinavian glass design of the period.

9in (23cm) high

£400-600   UCT

A Finnish Nuutajärvi Nöstjo tapering vase, designed by Gunnel Nyman, the amber bowl with trails of controlled internal bubbles, and a heavy cased colourless foot, the base etched "G.Nyman Nuutajärvi Nöstjo".

7.75in (19.5cm) high

£250-300   UCT

A Finnish Nuutajärvi Nöstjo mould-blown cobalt blue 'Hourglass' vase, no. KF245, designed by Kaj Franck in 1956.

This design is multifunctional and can be used as a goblet, vase or even a candle-holder. Colours included yellow, violet, lilac, green, and light and dark blue.

1956-69   6.75in (17cm) high

£50-90   UCT

A Finnish Nuutajärvi Nöstjo bird, designed by Oiva Toikka, the green body with applied coloured chips, the applied head with colourless beak, the base with "Nuutajarvi O. Toikka" acid stamp.

9in (23cm) long

£80-120   UCT

A Finnish Nuutajärvi Nöstjo bird, designed by Oiva Toikka, the orange body with internal bubbles, and applied head with colourless beak, the base with "Nuutajärvi O. Toikka" acid stamp.

Toikka's wide range of bird figures was introduced in 1981, and at least one has been released each year since. In 1988, Iittala and Nuutajärvi merged, so birds can be found with both Nuutajärvi acid marks and Iittala labels. The range continues to be produced by Iittala today, although some shapes have been discontinued.

2002   8in (20cm) long

£70-90   UCT

A Finnish Nuutajärvi Nöstjo 'Northern Duck' bird, designed by Oiva Toikka, with iridescent swirled body. the applied head with colourless beak, the base with "Nuutajärvi O. Toikka" acid stamp.

1991   6.75in (17cm) long

£80-100   UCT

A Finnish Nuutajärvi Nöstjo 'Whip-Poor-Will' blown bird, designed by Oiva Toikka, with applied head and spiralling green stripes to body, the base with acid stamp "O.Toikka Nuutajärvi.

This model is currently still being sold by Iittala.

5.75in (14.5cm) long

£40-60   TGM

A Swedish Strömbergshyttan large glass vase, engraved with deer grazing in a glade, the base engraved "Strömbergshyttan 1664 = 1168" and with an artist's signature.

The deer are engraved on one side and the trees on the other, giving a sense of perspective. The technique used for the bark on the trees is interesting, as the glass has been chipped away to give the almost sparkling effect of early morning, dew-laden trunks.

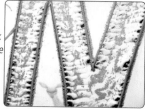

12in (30.5cm) high

£300-400   GC

A 1950s-60s Swedish Strömbergshyttan clear glass vase, unsigned, probably designed by Gerda Stromberg, with thick, cut rim.

6.75in (17cm) high

£20-30   AEM

A Swedish Strömbergshyttan colourless cased brown vase, possibly designed by Gunnar Nyland, with offset well and asymmetric curving pulled rim, the base inscribed "Strömberg B775".

4.25in (10.5cm) high

£80-100   UCT

A Swedish Strömbergshyttan brown torpedo vase, designed by Gunnar Nylund in 1955, the base signed "Strömbergshyttan".

10in (25.5cm) high

£55-75   TGM

A Swedish Strömbergshyttan brown-toned vase, designed by H.J. Dunne-Cooke, of flower-like form.

8.25in (21cm) high

£70-90   GC

A Swedish Strömbergshyttan hollow blown bird figurine, with applied eyes, beak, neck and wings, and with plastic label to base, the machine-cut base rim inscribed "AB 7405 Strömbergshyttan".

Strömberg was taken over by Orrefors in 1976 and closed in 1979, meaning this bird must have been made during the 1960s or '70s, or else Orrefors used the name later.

6.75in (17cm) high

£60-80   UCT

A Swedish Afors colourless cased purple glass vase, designed by Ernest Gordon, the base inscribed "5H 3130 E.Gordon Lila".

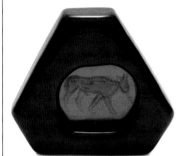

Ernest Gordon (b.1926) worked for Afors from 1954 to 1961, and his designs followed the organic Scandinavian Modern movement, but also conformed to more Modernist lines. Unless signed, his designs are difficult to attribute.

7in (17.5cm) high

£100-150   UCT

A Swedish Aseda colourless cased mottled deep blue vase, designed by Bo Borgstrom, with powder inclusions, heavy base and 'folded' rim.

Although they appear black, the powder inclusions are in fact a very dark blue. The rim, which has been tightly folded down over the neck, is one of the most interesting features of this vase – it is a challenging technique requiring skill and experience.

7in (17.5cm) high

£50-80   UCT

A Swedish Björkshult mould-blown figural decanter, by an unknown designer, with original paper label.

The original blown stopper typically fits loosely in the neck.

9.5in (24cm) high

£80-100   GC

A Swedish Boda cast orange paperweight, designed by Erik Höglund, with impressed deer.

The strong colour and chunky, comparatively unrefined, form and motif are typical of Höglund's designs. Among other themes, he was also inspired by cave paintings, an inspiration that can be clearly seen in the animal motif.

4.5in (11.5cm) high

£40-50   UCT

A Swedish Boda cast green paperweight, designed by Erik Höglund, with impressed stylized walking deer.

4in (11.5cm) diam

£35-45   UCT

A Swedish Boda cast colourless glass paperweight, designed by Erik Höglund, with impressed stylized boy's head and shoulders.

4in (11.5cm) high

£35-45   UCT

A Swedish Boda cast orange paperweight, designed by Erik Höglund, with impressed stylized face.

4.5in (11.5cm) wide

£35-45   UCT

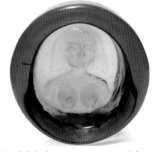

A Swedish Boda cast green paperweight, designed by Erik Höglund, with impressed stylized bust of a busty woman.

4in (11.5cm) diam

£35-45   UCT

GLASS

A Swedish Flygsfors ovoid cased vase, possibly designed by Paul Kedelv, with heavy colourless foot and angular cut and polished rim, the base engraved "Flygfors 65".

1965   12.5in (32cm) high

£70-100   P&I

A Swedish Flygsfors vase, designed by Paul Kedelv, the burgundy core cased in colourless glass, with opaque white pulled rim, the base signed "Flygsfors 55 Kedelv'.

1955   12in (30.5cm) high

£70-100   QU

A Swedish Flygsfors colourless cased green and opaque white 'Coquille' small dish, designed by Paul Kedelv, the base inscribed "Flygsfors-63 Coquille".

The Coquille range, with its opaque white layer, was launched in 1952 and sold into the 1960s. Kedelv worked at Flygsfors from 1949 until 1956.

4.75in (12cm) wide

£60-90   UCT

A late 1950s Swedish Gullaskruf red pressed glass 'Randi' bowl, designed by Arthur Percy in 1952, with moulded grid-like pattern of rectangles made up of lines.

This range typifies the Modernist aspect of the Scandinavian aesthetic of the 1950s, and comprised a number of bowls, dishes and vases of different sizes.

3in (7.5cm) high

£25-35   UCT

A Swedish Gullaskruf red mould-blown bottle vase, designed by Arthur Percy.

13in (33cm) high

£30-50   GC

A Swedish Gullaskruf 'Double Walled Coiled Bowl', designed by Hugo Gehlin, the polished base engraved "Gehlin, Gullaskruf".

As well as being one of Gehlin's most popular designs, it is the most commonly found signed. Most other Gullaskruf glass is very rarely signed.

7.25in (18.5cm) wide

£30-40   PC

A late 1960s-70s Swedish Johansfors spherical vase, probably designed by Bengt Orup, with internal bubbles of varying sizes and powder inclusions, the base engraved "Johansfors Orlys".

Orup worked for Johansfors from 1951 until 1973, first as a staff designer, then as art director.

6in (15cm) high

£40-60   BH

A Norwegian Randsfjord translucent white and mottled blue spherical vase, designed by Torbjörn Torgersen, with flared rim, the base with embossed paper and gilt label.

4.25in (10.5cm) high

£32-38   **TGM**

A 1960s Swedish Skruf cut glass vase, designed by Bengt Edenfalk, with stylized sunburst design, the base etched "Edenfalk Skruf".

8.25in (21cm) high

£100-150   **GC**

EXPERT EYE – A SCANDINAVIAN GLASS VASE

It is hard to be sure which factory made this vase, but the form suggests Johansfors or, more probably, Lindshammar.

Swards decorated pieces from Gullaskruf, hence the name on the label, but also bought pieces from other factories such as Johansfors and Lindshammar.

The decoration is extremely unusual and contrasts with the organic form. Gilt bands are more commonly associated with Czechoslovakian glass design of the same period.

The label bears the names 'Swards' and 'Gullaskruf'. Edvin and Freda Sward were originally glass decorators at Gullaskruf, before leaving to found their own glass decorating company.

A very rare 1960s Swedish Lindshammar or Johansfors shouldered vase, possibly designed by Sixten Wennerstrand, the applied gilt and white enamelled banding by Swards, with asymmetric, pulled rim, and gold and silver foil Swards label.

With thanks to members of the Glass Message Board for the above information (see www.glassmessages.com).

10.75in (27cm) high

£80-120   **PC**

A 1970s Swedish Skruf Glasbruk mould-blown full lead crystal vase, designed by Lars Hellsten in c1970, with scrolling design, the base engraved "Hellsten Skruf H 18 2".

Lars Hellsten (b1933) worked as a designer at Skruf Glasbruk from 1964 to 1972, before moving to Orrefors.

6.5in (16.5cm) high

£100-150   **GC**

A 1960s Swedish Skruf Glasbruk bottle vase, designed by Bengt Edenfalk, the red body cased in colourless glass, the base marked "Edenfalk Skruf Inka 6".

10.5in (26.5cm) high

£80-120   **QU**

FIND OUT MORE...

'Miller's 20th-Century Glass', *by Andy McConnell, published by Miller's, 2006.*

'Scandinavian Ceramics & Glass In The Twentieth Century', *by Jennifer Opie, published by V&A Publications, 1989.*

'20th Century Factory Glass', *by Leslie Jackson, published by Mitchell Beazley, 2000.*

GLASS

ESSENTIAL REFERENCE

- Stuart (founded 1787) produced a wide range of brightly coloured enamelled table and decorative wares from 1928 until 1939. Over 600 patterns were designed, including geometric, figural, floral and foliate motifs. The majority were designed by the company's leading cutter and designer, Ludwig Kny. Geoffrey Stuart also produced designs after 1933.
- Outlines were applied by transfer, with teams of women and girls filling them in with colour. As these paintresses were less costly to pay than glass cutters, the enamelled wares could be sold for less than cut glass.
- Geometric designs typically followed the prevalent Art Deco style of the day, and reached the peak of their popularity in the mid-1930s.
- Look out for complex decoration. Decorative ware is usually worth more than tableware. Cocktail shakers are the exception as they attract interest from cocktail shaker collectors and those buying for use. Scarce and desirable designs include 'Red Devil', introduced in 1933, and the spider web pattern produced from c1935. Similar pieces were produced by other companies and in other countries, so always look on the base for Stuart's acid stamp.

A 1930s Stuart enamelled decanter and pair of matching glasses, decorated with a blue and black geometric pattern in alternating acid-etched and plain columns, the decanter with facet-cut stopper.

Decanter 10.5in (26.5cm) high

£450-550   **FLD**

A 1930s Art Deco Stuart enamelled conical decanter and two matching goblets, decorated with a yellow and black wavy line pattern and alternating frosted and plain columns, the decanter with slice-cut neck and stopper, the base with acid stamp.

Decanter 12in (30.5cm) high

£420-480   **FLD**

A 1930s Stuart decanter and set of six matching glasses, enamelled with a mounted huntsman, the decanter with slice-cut neck and spire form stopper, the bases with acid marks.

Decanter 12.25in (31cm) high

£300-400   **FLD**

A 1930s Art Deco Stuart enamelled footed posy vase, decorated with a stylized floral garland and green curl border, the base with acid stamp.

5.5in (14cm) high

£120-180   **FLD**

A pair of Art Deco Stuart enamelled candle-holders, decorated with an abstract geometric pattern of cogs and flashes, the base with acid stamp.

3.25in (8cm) high

£150-200   **FLD**

A 1930s Art Deco Stuart enamelled preserve pot, decorated with clover flowers and bees, the base with acid stamp.

4in (10cm) high

£60-80   **FLD**

ESSENTIAL REFERENCE

- Studio glass is the name given to glass produced by individual artists working outside of the confines of a factory environment. The movement as it is known today began in the US, in the early 1960s, when Harvey Littleton and Dominick Labino developed a process that allowed individuals to melt, form and blow glass themselves. Glassmakers in other countries had also made similar developments, and soon the movement spread.
- Although there are no new techniques in glass, which has been made since Roman times, skills have developed enormously over the past 20 years. Pieces are now generally more finely made, using increasingly complex techniques. Glass has also been seen increasingly as an art form, rather than a craft, and since the 1980s leading museums and galleries have been adding studio glass to their collections.
- The work of major names, such as Dale Chihuly and Marvin Lipofsky, already make high sums on the secondary market. However, works by those they taught, or lesser known makers, can be more affordable. The market for second and third generation artists is lively. Some have attracted, or are attracting, large groups of fans and collectors – a factor that has caused demand, and thus prices, to rise.
- Learn about an artist's background to see who they studied with, and build up an eye for their style and work. Many pieces are signed, but signatures can be hard to read, and some are not signed at all. Also learn a little about how glass is made as this will help you spot complex pieces, which were time-consuming to make, and so were probably expensive at the time, and may be rare today.
- Also learn about the key movements and styles of any given period. Date is not always an indicator of value, and some early examples are crudely formed, although they do represent this important development in glass-making history. Large pieces, and those by makers who already have a large following could be good investments as interest in this vibrant area is developing every year.

An Adam Aaronson ball vase, covered with a layer of fragmented silver foil, the base signed "The Handmade Glass Co 1998 Adam Aaronson Design".

1998   *5in (12cm) high*

£30-50   **TGM**

A Sarah Cable large vase, the matte green body with iridescent, low relief mottles, and pink petal rim, the base signed "Sarah Cable".

New studio glass artist Sarah Cable first blows a coloured body. This is then overlaid with another layer of dark glass that is iridised to make it opaque. The petal-like pink lobes are added by hand. She then applies protective decals in the forms of the mottles and sandblasts any unprotected areas away. These vases are produced in a number of sizes, colours and patterns.

c2007   *15in (38cm) high*

£80-120   **TGM**

A Sarah Cable large vase, the matte beige-yellow body with iridescent, low relief stripes, and blue petal rim, the base signed "Sarah Cable".

c2007   *8.75in (22cm) high*

£60-70   **TGM**

A Sarah Cable large vase, the matte blue body with iridescent, low relief mottles, and lime green petal rim, the base signed "Sarah Cable".

c2007   *8.75in (22cm) high*

£60-70   **TGM**

A Jane Charles ribbed footed ball vase, the blue and green mottled body with short neck and flat rim, the base signed "Jane Charles".

3.75in (9.5cm) high

£32-38   **TGM**

GLASS

A Norman Stuart-Clarke vase, with mottled beige effect, applied cane and chips to form a tree motif, and iridescent surface, the base with broken pontil mark and signed "Norman Stuart Clarke 86".

Norman Stuart-Clarke's hot-worked designs, inspired by the Cornish landscape around him, have become increasingly sought-after over the past few years.

1986	8in (20cm) high
£140-160	**TGM**

A Carin von Drehle ovoid vase, the exterior with randomly applied trails and heavy iridescence, the base signed "Carin von Drehle 1990".

US glass artist Carin von Drehle trained under Peter Layton at the London Glassblowing Studios, which were then in Rotherhithe, during the mid-late 1980s. Designs with iridescence and applied trails were typical of production at the time. Unlike her colleagues Siddy Langley and Norman Stuart-Clarke, von Drehle gave up glassmaking in the early 1990s.

	4.75in (12cm) high
£80-120	**TGM**

A Norman Stuart-Clarke bowl, the lower half covered with coloured chips to represent the ground and with applied iridescent moon, the base signed "Norman Stuart Clarke 88".

1988	6.5in 16.5cm (high)
£120-160	**TGM**

A Julia Donnelly flattened oval vase, the mottled surface with coloured chips, signed "Julia Donnelly 1995".

1995	4.25in (10.5cm) high
£32-38	**TGM**

A Carin von Drehle bottle vase, the light blue body decorated with a random pattern of coloured trails, canes and chips, with an iridescent surface effect, the base signed "Carin von Drehle"

	8in (20cm) high
£70-100	**TGM**

A Julia Donnelly cylinder vase, with flared rim, with applied shards of glass, and mottled and veiled decoration, the base signed "Julia Donnelly 1998".

Donnelly studied under Peter Layton and worked with Siddy Langley, but no longer makes glass.

1998	6.25in (15.5cm) high
£35-45	**TGM**

A Carin von Drehle disc vase, the tapered translucent white body with applied mottled brown-black bands, the base signed "Carin von Drehle 1986".

This is similar to designs produced by Layton at the time, such as the piece shown on page 275, however, it has an outer layer of colourless glass.

	3in (7.5cm) high
£70-100	**TGM**

A Sam Herman bottle vase, with applied mottling and iridescent trailing, the base inscribed "Samuel J Herman 1972".

1972   8.75in (22cm) high
£700-900   **WW**

A Sam Herman vase, signed "Samuel J Herman HW5".

The torso-like form is a favoured shape for Herman, who studied anthropology and sculpture.

8in (20cm) high
£350-450   **AMAC**

EXPERT EYE – A SAM HERMAN VASE

Sam Herman (b.1936), studied the new studio glassmaking techniques, developed in 1962 by Dominick Labino and Harvey Littleton in the US. From late 1966, he worked and taught at the Royal College of Art, London. His students became the first wave of British studio glass artists.

This was made in Southern Australia where Herman taught and made glass from 1974 to 1979.

This is a large piece and is typical of his hand-formed shapes. Herman often adapts his preconceived ideas to suit the piece as it is being made.

The expressive and free pattern is typical of his work, with Herman trailing, speckling and swirling molten glass over the surface, much like a painter.

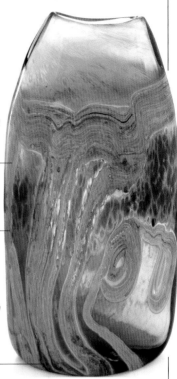

A Sam Herman vase, with mottled inclusions and applied iridescent trails, the base inscribed "Samuel J Herman 1977 SA".
1977   13.75in (35cm) high
£850-950   **WW**

A Sam Herman large free-form charger, with marbled, streaked and mottled brown, yellow, green and blue coloured enamel inclusions, the base inscribed "Sam Herman 1976".

Dish forms, which are spun out, are rare compared to vases and sculptural forms.
1976   20.5in (52cm) wide
£700-1,000   **FLD**

A Jonathan Harris Studio Glass 'Monsoon' bowl, with multicoloured applied fragmented gold foil, trails, straps and chips, and applied colourless footed base signed "Jonathan Harris Ironbridge England 2000".
2000   6.75in (17cm) high
£250-300   **TGM**

A Robert Eickholdt studio glass 'Chip' vase, the body overlaid with spirals of fused and melted blue and green chips, with an iridescent finish and a wide flared rim, the base signed "Eickholdt 1995.5"
1995   7.5in (19cm) high
£80-120   **TGM**

GLASS

A Toan Klein 'Catfish' triple-cased vase, the opaque white core overlaid with a colourless glass layer, a silk-screened enamel image of a cat's head with fish as eyes, and an outer layer of colourless glass.

An example of this complex and witty vase can be seen in the Corning Museum of Glass. Toan Klein (b.1949) is a Canadian studio glass artist, and his work can also be seen in The Royal Ontario Museum and the Smithsonian Institute.

c1981   7in (18cm) high

£900-1,100   **SHAND**

EXPERT EYE – A SIDDY LANGLEY VASE

Langley (b.1955) still produces glass today, and it is becoming increasingly sought-after on the secondary market.

She trained under Peter Layton at the London Glassblowing Workshops between 1979 and 1987. This series was made during the 1980s.

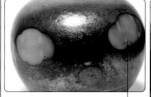

The techniques used to 'paint' the cloud and sun motifs into the glass are complex, and cleverly use iridisation to indicate the sky.

The ground is indicated by heavy trailing and a darker iridised effect.

A Siddy Langley 'Clouds' ovoid vase, with small neck rim, with applied opaque white 'clouds', orange 'sun', heavily iridised sky and trailed ground, the base signed "Siddy Langley 1983".

1983   5in (12.5cm) high

£120-160   **TGM**

A Siddy Langley bowl, made at the London Glassblowing workshop, with a spiralling green and brown pattern, the base signed "Siddy Langley 6.12.86".

1986   4.25in (10.5cm) high

£80-100   **TGM**

A Siddy Langley perfume bottle, the green body with applied coloured powdered enamel and glass chips, overlaid with green and white applied trails, the base signed "Siddy Langley 2003".

2003   6.25in (15.5cm) high

£40-60   **TGM**

An early 1970s Peter Layton part mould-blown vase, with pulled neck and applied rim, the base signed "Peter Layton".

6.25in (15.5cm) high

£70-100   **TGM**

A Ludlow Cameo Company double gourd shaped cameo vase, decorated with a wheel-cut pattern of hydrangeas and fuchsias, the base with cut signature.

14.5in (37cm) high

£300-400   **FLD**

A Peter Layton cylinder vase, with flared rim, the opaque white body overlaid with black powdered enamels in a random geometric pattern. signed "Peter Layton 1983" in one of the black areas.

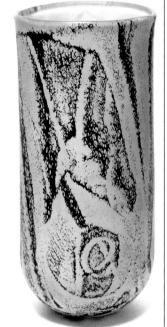

1983   *8.75in (22cm) high*

£140-160   **TGM**

A Dominick Labino deep ruby red vase, with applied swirling prunts, the base inscribed "Labino 1973".

Dominick Labino (1910-87) is one of the founding fathers of the studio glass movement. Along with Harvey Littleton, he developed the glass formula and small furnace that allowed glassmaking to move out of the factory and become economical and viable for individual artists. His students went on to become the first studio glass artists. As such, his work is highly sought-after, particularly in the US. This is typical of his free-formed works, which appear in many museums around the world.

1973   *6.25in (16cm) high*

£900-1,100   **ANT**

An Isgard Moje-Wohlgemuth bowl, with melted coloured enamels in triangular and dripped patterning giving the effect of ink staining, engraved "MOJE 1972".

1972   *6.25in (15.5cm) diam*

£200-300   **QU**

A William Walker mould-blown bowl, the spiralling optic opaque white body with a brown randomly applied streak, and with a coiled rim cased in colourless glass, the base signed 'William Walker".

The applied and tightly folded down rim requires great skill to achieve successfully.

3.25in (8.5cm) high

£35-40   **TGM**

An early 1980s David Wallace vase, the heavy colourless body overlaid with randomly applied pink striped canes and cased in an outer layer of colourless glass, the base signed "David Wallace".

3.75in (9.5cm) high

£50-60   **TGM**

A David Wallace perfume bottle, with applied black arms, central disc and matching black stopper, the base signed "David Wallace".

4in (10cm) high

£35-45   **TGM**

A David Wallace perfume bottle, the colourless body with applied canes twisted into a spiral, the base signed "David Wallace 1988".

1988   *5.25in (13cm) high*

£28-32   **TGM**

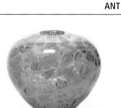

GLASS

ESSENTIAL REFERENCE

- Powell & Sons was founded in 1680, in London. The original site was once a monastery, and the company became more commonly known as Whitefriars. In 1923, the company moved to Wealdstone, Middlesex and in 1962 the name Whitefriars was officially adopted. The company grew to prominence during the late 19thC producing art glass, some inspired by Venetian and European styles.
- In 1954, Royal College of Art graduate Geoffrey Baxter (1922-95) was employed as designer, and produced the most important Whitefriars designs of the late 20thC. His designs are also the most collectable and in many instances the most valuable, and some have become icons of 20thC glass design. His designs were strongly modern, and were inspired by Scandinavian glass of the same period. Other important designers include Peter Wheeler and William Wilson.
- Baxter's most characteristic output was the Textured range, designed in 1966 and introduced the following year. All pieces were handmade, being blown into textured moulds, and were produced in bright colours with inventive, abstract shapes drawing inspiration from many sources including the natural world and geometry.
- Consider the form, colour and size of pieces, as these factors affect value considerably. New colours were introduced in 1969, and dates shown represent a combination of the colours and shapes. Prices for iconic designs such as the 'Banjo' and 'Drunken Bricklayer' have reached a plateau over the past few years, but are still very strong. Look for examples with good levels of sharp detail, as moulds tended to wear down over time, leaving lower levels of texture.
- Look out for organically knobbly and lobed cased pieces from the 1950s, designed in association with William Wilson, and pieces from the Late Textured range of the 1970s, as these are possibly under-priced. Most were free-formed, so exact sizes and colours will differ, making each piece unique. Similarly unique are the pieces from the Studio ranges, which continue to rise in price and popularity.

A 1960s Whitefriars Ruby red 'Molar' lobed vase, no. 9410, designed by William Wilson.

c1955   *7.25in (18cm) high*

£60-70   **TGM**

A Whitefriars Sea green 'Twisted Molar' vase, no. 9386, designed by William Wilson.

c1953   *8in (20cm) high*

£40-60   **GC**

A Whitefriars cased Emerald green 'Knobbly' vase, no. 9611 designed by Harry Dyer in 1963.

1964-72   *7in (17cm) high*

£50-60   **TGM**

A Whitefriars cased Kingfisher blue five-lobed bowl, no. 9407, designed by Geoffrey Baxter in 1957.

1957-70   *5.5in (14cm) high*

£50-70   **TGM**

A Whitefriars cased Meadow green 'Knobbly' thin vase, no. 9612, designed by Harry Dyer in 1963.

Meadow green is a desirable colour.

1964-72   *9.5in (24cm) high*

£50-60   **TGM**

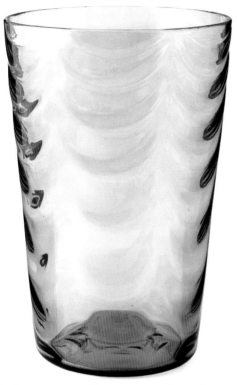

A Whitefriars Aqua full-lead crystal lobed vase, no. 9858, designed by Geoffrey Baxter in 1980.

The full lead crystal range was designed between 1978 and 1980, to replace the 'tired' Textured range. Colours comprised of Gold, Aqua and Sky blue, and shapes were new. Examples can be hard to find today as the factory closed in 1980.

1980   9in (23cm) high

£45-55   TGM

A Whitefriars Sea green tumbler vase, no. 8473, designed by Marriott Powell in 1938, with wavy optic ribbing.

This was also produced in Amethyst purple until 1949.

1938-70   10in (25.5cm) high

£80-120   GC

A Whitefriars Ruby red footed bowl, no. 7170, designed by William Butler in the 1920s, with wavy optic moulding.

This colour was used from c1940.

4.75in (12cm) high

£70-90   GC

A Whitefriars Kingfisher blue cased flared vase, no. 9562, designed by Geoffrey Baxter in 1959, with internal optic moulding.

1960-67   6.75in (17cm) high

£35-45   GC

A Whitefriars Kingfisher blue cased small vase, no. 9094, designed by Geoffrey Baxter in 1959, with internal optic moulding.

1960-67   5.75in (14.5cm) high

£20-30   GC

A Whitefriars Kingfisher blue 'Pear' vase, no. 9578, designed before 1964 by Geoffrey Baxter, with internal optic moulding.

1964-67   4in (10cm) high

£20-30   GC

A Whitefriars Ruby red 'Pear' vase, no. 9578, designed by Geoffrey Baxter before 1964.

1964-67   4.25in (10.5cm) high

£18-22   TGM

GLASS

A Whitefriars Amethyst purple goblet vase, no. 9593, attributed to Geoffrey Baxter, from the Blown Soda range.

1963   6in (15cm) high
£50-70   GC

A Whitefriars Amethyst purple vase, no. 9598, designed by Geoffrey Baxter in 1963, from the Blown Soda range.

The mould-blown, Blown Soda range was introduced in 1962 and was typified by undecorated and simple, almost geometric, forms in strong colours. Shapes were designed into the late 1960s and were popular, meaning they can be easy to find today, although certain shapes and sizes are rare.

7in (17.5cm) high
£50-80   GC

EXPERT EYE – A WHITEFRIARS VASE

The applied white enamel streaks were trailed over the blue body, but did not adhere successfully and consistently, causing production delays and technical problems.

This range was also made in Ruby red, with the same problems, meaning that the range was only made for a short period during 1961 and as a result, very few pieces were produced. This is a desirable shape.

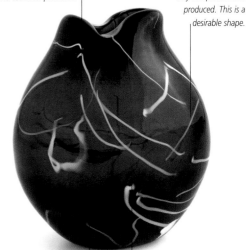

Designed in 1961, this range was due for release at the 1962 Blackpool trade fair – its failure led to the development of the Blown Soda range shown on this page.

The colour and free form organic shape was inspired by Scandinavian glass of the time, but given an English twist by Baxter.

A Whitefriars Cobalt blue experimental vase, no. 9577, designed by Geoffrey Baxter in 1961, with internal white trails.

5.75in (14.5cm) high
£550-650   WW

A Whitefriars Ruby red bulbous vase, no. 9599, designed by Geoffrey Baxter in 1963, from the Blown Soda range.

7in (17.5cm) high
£30-40   GC

A Whitefriars Midnight blue disc-bodied vase, no. 9597, designed by Geoffrey Baxter in 1963, from the Blown Soda range, with long flared neck.

5in (14.5cm) high
£40-50   GC

A Whitefriars Pewter grey tapered vase, no. 9553, designed by Geoffrey Baxter, from the Blown Soda range.

c1965   4.5in (11.5cm) high
£15-20   GC

A Whitefriars Kingfisher blue 'Ribbon Trailed' vase, no. 9706, designed by Geoffrey Baxter in 1969, with green ribbons.

1969-c1971   *10.25in (26cm) high*

£70-100   **TGM**

A Whitefriars orange baluster vase, no. 9803, designed by Geoffrey Baxter in 1972, from the New Studio range, with flared rim, the body overlaid with randomly trailed orange streaks highlighted with silver chloride.

All items in the Studio ranges were relatively highly priced and made in comparatively small quantities. As Whitefriars was also going through a decline in sales, at this time, examples are rare today.

1972-80   *7in (18cm) high*

£200-300   **GC**

EXPERT EYE – A WHITEFRIARS STUDIO VASE

The Studio range was introduced in 1969 in answer to the growing interest in, and the influence of, the Studio glass movement that had sprung up at that time.

There were three designs within it – an opaque white core cased in orange streaks, created in silver chloride. The final casing makes it appear as if the design is floating above the core. This was produced in 1969 only.

Some designs were produced by Geoffrey Baxter, but the specific 'Studio Range' was designed by art school graduate Peter Wheeler, who worked with Baxter during 1969.

Shapes are simple and solid, providing a monumental feel, and the design was also available in 'Old Gold' with a silvery cream ground and gold-brown stripes.

A Whitefriars Studio vase, no. S6, designed by Peter Wheeler, with opaque white glass cased in brown lined orange.

c1969   *10.25in (26cm) high*

£220-280   **WW**

A Whitefriars Sapphire blue jug, no. M104, designed by William Wilson.

Geoffrey Baxter produced cut designs for this jug the following year. Cut examples are scarce. The jug was also sold as part of a water set with tapering drinking glasses.

c1958   *9.25in (23cm) high*

£30-40   **GC**

A Whitefriars cut and polished glass vase, of tapering cylindrical form with an asymmetric rim and cut with a shoal of small fish and a larger fish.

Whitefriars' cut glass is relatively hard to find. A production date for this unique piece is unknown as it was never catalogued.

9in (22.5cm) high

£250-300   **WW**

A Whitefriars Sky blue bubbled paperweight, no. 9303, designed by Geoffrey Baxter.

1980   *3in (7.5cm) diam*

£20-25   **TGM**

GLASS

MILLER'S COMPARES – FAKE & AUTHENTIC DRUNKEN BRICKLAYERS

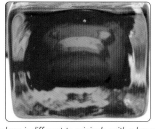

The base is different to originals, with a less well executed polished concave pontil mark. There is also no sign of wear through use, such as small criss-crossing scratches.

The green vase is a recent fake – the colour is intended to mimic Meadow Green, but is the wrong tone. A dark cobalt blue and a strong amber can also be found and again, were never used by Whitefriars.

The texture on the original is slightly sharper and better defined. Although textures differ depending on the age of the mould, they are usually crisper and in higher relief than on reproductions.

The authentic vase is cased all over the body, whereas the green vase is not, and the casing on the base is different.

A fake Whitefriars green 'Drunken Bricklayer' vase.

c2007   8.5in (21.5cm) high

£20-30   **PC**

A Whitefriars aubergine 'Drunken Bricklayer' small vase, no. 9673, designed by Geoffrey Baxter in 1966.

1972   *8in (20cm) high*

£250-300   **GC**

A Whitefriars Kingfisher blue small 'Drunken Bricklayer' vase, no. 9673, designed by Geoffrey Baxter in 1966.

This popular form was produced in two sizes, and this is the smallest. This colour was available from 1969 to 1974, even though the shape was introduced in 1966.

1969-74   8.25in (21cm) high

£220-260   **TGM**

A Whitefriars Kingfisher blue 'Banjo' vase, no.9861 designed by Geoffrey Baxter in 1966.

The iconic 'Banjo' was available in Kingfisher blue from 1969.

1969-c1973   12.5in (32cm) high

£600-800   **MAX**

A Whitefriars Tangerine 'Banjo' vase, no. 9681, designed by Geoffrey Baxter in 1966.

1966-c1973   13in (33cm) high

£600-800   **GC**

A Whitefriars Tangerine 'Bark' vase, no. 9691, designed by Geoffrey Baxter in 1966.
1967-80   *7.75in (18.5cm) high*
£50-60   **TGM**

A Whitefriars Pewter grey 'Bark' vase, no. 9690, designed by Geoffrey Baxter in 1966.
1969-72   *6in (15cm) high*
£35-45   **TGM**

A Whitefriars Aubergine 'Nailhead' vase, no. 9683, designed by Geoffrey Baxter in 1966.
1967-80   *6.75in (17cm) high*
£35-45   **TGM**

A Whitefriars Kingfisher blue 'Hoop' vase, no. 9680, designed by Geoffrey Baxter in 1966.

This was not released in Kingfisher blue or Tangerine until 1968, with Aubergine following in 1972.
1969-73   *7.25in (18.5cm) high*
£80-120   **WW**

A Whitefriars Kingfisher blue 'Coffin' vase, no. 9686, designed by Geoffrey Baxter in 1967.

1969-80   *5.25in (13cm) high*
£50-60   **TGM**

A Whitefriars Willow 'Nuts and Bolts' or 'Hobnail' vase, no. 9668, designed by Geoffrey Baxter in 1966.

Do not confuse this with the similar 'Mobile Phone' vase, no. 9670, which has round instead of square moulded prunts, and is smaller at 6.5in (16.5cm) high.
1967-70   *10.5in (27cm) high*
£250-300   **WW**

A Whitefriars Indigo 'TV' vase, no. 9667, designed by Geoffrey Baxter in 1966.
1967-c1973   *7.25in (18.5cm) high*
£150-200   **WW**

GLASS

A Whitefriars Kingfisher blue 'Dimple' vase, no. 9809, designed by Geoffrey Baxter in 1971, from the Late Textured range.

1971-74   *4.45in (11cm) high*

£35-45   **TGM**

A Whitefriars Pewter grey 'Traffic Light' vase, no. 9760, designed by Geoffrey Baxter in 1971, from the Late Textured range.

1971-74   *4.75in (12cm) high*

£40-60   **TGM**

A Whitefriars Tangerine 'Double Diamond' vase, no. 9759, designed by Geoffrey Baxter in 1971, from the Late Textured range, with original label.

Many designs from the Late Textured range of the 1970s are currently more affordable. Although many collectors think that the range is not as fresh or inventive as the first Textured range of the late 1960s, some innovative and characteristic shapes such as this can be found.

1971-74   *6in (15cm) high*

£80-120   **TGM**

A Whitefriars Tangerine 'Aztec' textured vase, pattern no. 9816, designed by Geoffrey Baxter in 1972, from the Late Textured range.

1972-74   *7in (18cm) high*

£60-80   **GC**

A Whitefriars Ruby red 'Chess' textured vase, no. 9817, designed by Geoffrey Baxter in 1972, from the Late Textured range.

1972-74   *6in (15cm) high*

£60-80   **GC**

A Whitefriars Glacier range decanter, pattern no. 9725, designed by Geoffrey Baxter.

The Glacier range of tableware was designed between 1967 and 1974, and was produced until 1980.

11.25in (28cm) high

£60-70   **GC**

A pair of late 1930s Bagley orange pressed glass owl bookends, with moulded registered design no. 798842 for 18th December 1934.

A 1930s Bagley 'Sunburst' amber pressed glass jug.

A smaller version is known and is usually worth around £20-30. Both sizes can also be found in frosted, and frosted and clear finishes.

8.75in (22.5cm) high

The ears on these charming owls are often damaged, so it is unusual to find a set in perfect condition, as here. Damaged examples are usually worth over 30 per cent less.

5.75in (14.5cm) high

£100-150   AAB

£30-50   AAB

A rare Chance Glass intaglio-cut white 'Pearl' rectangular dish.

Introduced in 1957 and in production for two to three years, the Intaglio range was comprised of colourless pieces flashed (thinly coated) in opal white, blue or red glass. A pattern was then cut through the upper coloured layer, revealing the colourless layer beneath.

A Caithness Glass sand-cast display piece, designed by Sarah Peterson, with coloured enamel decoration in an abstract design.

c2001   7.75in (19.5cm) high

A Caithness Glass sand-cast display piece, designed by Sarah Peterson, with coloured enamel decoration in an abstract design.

c2001   5in (13cm) high

1957-c1960   11.25in (28.5cm) high

£80-100   GC

£80-100   GC

£50-70   GC

A rare Chance Glass 'Green Leaves' small rectangular dish, designed by Margaret Casson in 1958.

Despite being approved by the Design Centre, this design seems not to have been popular with the public and is rare today.

5.5in (14cm) long

£30-40   GC

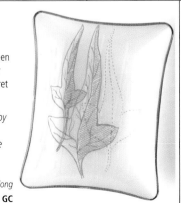

A very rare Dartington Glass Kingfisher blue one-pint tankard, no. FT5, designed by Frank Thrower in 1967.

As its low FT number indicates, this tankard was one of the earliest designs produced by Thrower for Dartington, when it opened in 1967. It was available in (colourless) Clear, Kingfisher blue and Midnight grey, and in one-pint, three-quarters of a pint and half-pint sizes. The handles are particularly prone to damage.

5.25in (13.5cm) high

£60-80   PC

GLASS

A 1930s Daum amber large stepped vase, with flared rim and acid-cut low relief tessellated block pattern, with wheel-cut signature and cross of Lorraine mark.

14.5in (36.5cm) high

£350-400   FLD

A 1960s Higgins large slump glass ashtray, with moulded cigarette rests, internal gold applied star transfers and signature, together with original foil label.

13.75in (35cm) wide

£150-250   TCF

EXPERT EYE – A PRESSED GLASS LION

John Derbyshire founded his short-lived company in Manchester, in August 1873, after leaving the family company James Derbyshire & Bros. Known in 1877 as The Regent Flint Glass Co., it seems to have merged with the family company a few years later.

The figure was available in uranium yellow, green, turquoise, colourless and acid-etched. This matte black colour, similar to Wedgwood's black basalt, is the most desirable.

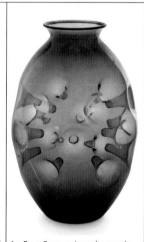

Modelled after Sir Edward Landseer's lions at the base of Nelson's Column, it was registered on 3rd July 1874 and can have crossed or straight paws.

It was one of the company's most popular items, but look out for their similarly posed Sphinx, which can be worth around £2,000 in this colour.

A late 19thC John Derbyshire matte black pressed glass figurine of a recumbent lion, after Sir Edward Landseer, with gilt highlights and moulded marks to base.

5in (12.5cm) high

£280-320   FLD

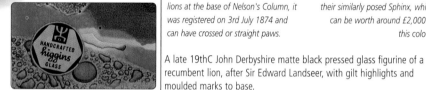

A 1930s Jobling 'Opalique' opalescent pressed glass elephant, with moulded registration diamond.

Jobling's Opalique is known for its strong blue tone. This elephant is scarce.

1934-39   *6in (15cm) long*

£600-800   FLD

A Lauscha or Bimini snake shaped solifleur vase, with orange stripes and applied eyes.

Thin and delicate lampworked pieces such as this are often attributed to Austrian company Bimini, founded by Fritz Lampl during the 1930s. However, a number of factories continued to produce these designs after WWII, many around Lauscha in Germany.

8.5in (21.5cm) high

£5-8   PAS

An East German Lauscha purple free-blown vase, with spikey internal indentations.

5in (13cm) high

£10-15   PC

A Leerdam attenuated bottle, designed by Floris Meydam in 1970, the body of orangey-brown opaque glass and the neck of transparent cobalt blue.

17in (43cm) high

£120-180   QU

A 1930s Dutch Leerdam 'Ariel' sea-green glass ovoid vase, designed by Andreas Dirk Copier, with internal seaweed and fish decoration, the base inscribed "W 1618".

This vase uses the complex Ariel technique developed at Orrefors in Scandinavia, in 1937, for more information, see page 257.

13.75in (35cm) high

£1,200-1,800   FLD

EXPERT EYE – A MONART VASE

Influenced by Monart's owner's wife Isobel Montcrieff, and inspired by the Cloisonné enamels coming from the Far East, the range was surprisingly unpopular and is rare today.

To gain the colour, a colourless body would be rolled over red powdered enamels, followed by crushed opaque white enamel chips – all would be melted onto the surface in the furnace.

To gain the effect, the still hot and partially formed body would be dipped into cold water causing the surface to fracture. The body would then be blown to shape, pulling the separate white parts apart, revealing the red beneath.

Finally the piece was fumed in metallic salts to give the white areas an iridescent appearance. This pattern was also available without an iridescent finish.

A Monart Cloisonné vase, shape D, size IX, colour code 64, coral red cased in clear with iridescent crackle white enamel, unsigned.

A similar vase featured on the cover of the landmark 1987 book 'British Glass Between The Wars', edited by Roger Dodsworth.

6.5in (16.5cm) high

£350-450   WW

A 1950s Dutch Leerdam 'Unica' vase, designed by Floris Meydam, the compressed ovoid body with crescent rim decorated with internal cased bands of blue and green, the base with inscribed signature and numbered "1-133".

7.5in 19cm) high

£300-400   FLD

A Loetz corseted vase, designed by Michael Powolny, with flared rim in semi-opaque white glass with cobalt trailing, the base engraved "Prof Powolny Loetz".

5in (12.5cm) high

£800-1,000   SDR

A Monart 'Stoneware' range baluster vase, ref. FA, decorated with a mottled green and blue powdered enamel over a sea green ground, the base with polished pontil mark.

8.5in (22cm) high

£500-600   FLD

GLASS

A Muller Frères spherical vase, with everted rim, of mottled blue to yellow glass with matte acid-etched surface, the base with acid etched "Muller Frères Luneville" mark.

6.25in (16cm) high

£180-220   **WW**

An Italian Opalina Fiorentina mould-blown opaque blue vase, with stylized flower design.

These vases are often mistakenly attributed to Dartington due to the flower motif. Opalina Fiorentina was based in Empoli, Italy. This vase is one of their most common, and can be found in beige, green, yellow, orange and blue. Many are lined with an opaque white, making the colours vibrant, although transparent examples are also known.

12in (30.5cm) high

£30-40   **GC**

A rare Stevens & Williams grey-green glass vase, with applied foot, the base with acid-etched mark and facsimile signature to base.

12in (30.5cm) high

£700-900   **WW**

EXPERT EYE – A CUT GLASS VASE

Glass designed by architect and ceramics designer Keith Murray is high quality and is also rare, as it was only produced for a few years before WWII.

Although this shape was designed by Keith Murray, the strongly Art Deco cut design does not appear to be his, as it is not in the company's pattern book of Murray's designs.

However, the pattern book starts at 100, possibly indicating that the first 99 designs are missing.

If further research, or the discovery of any missing designs by Murray, show that this design is indeed by him, the value of this large vase could rise to over £2,500.

A 1930s (Stevens & Williams) Royal Brierley cut glass vase, shape no. 716A or 725A, designed by Keith Murray, and cut with Art Deco chevron design bands and lenses.

The dark green colour is typical of Royal Brierley at this time.

12in (30.5cm) high

£400-600   **PC**

A Belgian Val St Lambert green cased cut vase, inscribed with factory name on base.

11in (28cm) high

£100-150   **BH**

A 1960s Belgian Val St Lambert bowl, of dynamic form, the pink core cased in colourless glass, with factory gilt label.

13.5in (34cm) long

£150-200   **QU**

GLASS

A Vedar enamelled glass vase, decorated with brightly coloured buildings, on square foot, painted "Vedar VII", chip to foot rim.

Perhaps surprisingly, this enamelled vase was made in Milan, Italy, by Vetri D'Arte Fontana. The name Vedar was taken from the first two letters of the first two words of the company's name. The range was introduced by Dr Carlo Vezzoli in 1925 and produced until 1930. Like most, this is signed and dated with Roman numerals 'VII' for 1927.

1927   8.75in (22.5cm) high

£80-120   **WW**

A John Walsh Walsh 'Albany' pattern cut glass vase, designed by Clyne Farquharson, decorated with elliptical lozenge cuts and wavy lines, with engraved signature to base.

9.75in (24.5cm) high

£400-500   **FLD**

A Belgian Val St Lambert dish, the champagne coloured glass pulled into four lobes.

Always examine the forms, colours and bases of these dishes carefully, as many of this type were also made in France and Murano. These tend to be worth less than this example.

c1960   16.5in (42cm) long

£100-200   **QU**

A 1960s East German 'Vereinigte Lausitzer Glas' light blue pressed glass 'Lyon' vase, with shallow well base.

VLG were based in Saxony, east of Dresden. This is also found in smokey grey and light green.

8in (20cm) high

£20-30   **GC**

A 1960s East German 'Vereinigte Lausitzer Glas' smokey grey pressed glass 'Gent' vase, with shallow well base.

8in (20cm) high

£25-35   **GC**

A Thomas Webb vase, with internal bubbles and green bands.

c1935   8in (20cm) high

£70-100   **GC**

A 1930s Thomas Webb purple lidded jar, the base with "Thos Webb England" acid-etched mark.

6in (15cm) high

£25-30   **GC**

An American graduated pink satin glass rose bowl, with purple and red colour tones.

3.25in (8cm) high

£30-45 BH

A Mother of Pearl pink satin glass herringbone pattern rose bowl.

4.75in (12cm) high

£50-70 BH

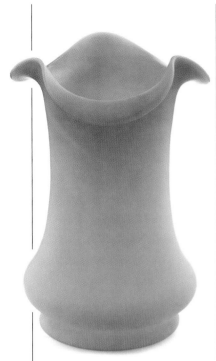

An American Peach Blow ruffled vase, possibly by Mt Washington.

Peach Blow, fading from creamy white to pink, was made in different ways by a number of companies including Mt Washington, Gunderson-Pairpoint, and New England Glass Co., who introduced their range in 1885. As this is not cased and is lighter in weight than Pairpoint examples, it is likely to have been made by Mt Washington.

5in (12.5cm) high

£30-45 BH

A W.M.F. Ikora 'Dexel-Ei' glass vase, designed by Walter Dexel, graduated brown to mustard, cased in clear glass with air bubble inclusions, unsigned.

6in (15cm) high

£100-150 WW

A Romanian blue mould-blown hooped vase, with applied gilt bands, the base with a small circular gold and silver foil reading "Made in Romania" around a wine glass motif.

Previously thought to be Czechoslovakian due to the use of gilt banding, these vases are also found in colourless, amber and smoked glass. Probably dating from the late 1960s to 1970s, the blue is the most desirable and valuable.

10.75in (27cm) high

£20-30 PAS

A 1970s Polish Zabkowicze Glassworks pressed glass vase, designed by Jan Sylvester Drost in 1972.

Although this vase has the characteristic 'bird bath' recession on the base, surrounded by a machine-cut rim, it was not produced by one of the Sklo Union factories in Czechoslovakia. Unusually for such vases, the interior is moulded with a design, as well as the exterior. The interior has moulded vertical ribs, while the exterior has moulded horizontal ribs, the combination giving an appealing optical effect.

6.75in (17cm) high

£30-40 PAS

A large mould-blown sculptural display object or light fitting, moulded with a lion's face to each side, with ground base.

Although the maker is currently unknown, it may have originated in Czechoslovakia or France during the 1970s.

18.25in (46cm) high

£300-400 WW

ESSENTIAL REFERENCE

- Hair is collected as it offers a unique and direct link to a historic personality or celebrity. Hair has been kept for centuries in memory of a person, with special forms of jewellery, such as lockets or rings, being made to house it. Today, many parents keep a lock of their baby's first growth of hair as a memento. Some companies have even extracted DNA from the hair of famous people and included it in jewellery, or other personal items such as pens.
- Provenance is key to value. Locks or strands should be accompanied by a verifiable document detailing how the lock was obtained. If it is from an historic figure, being able to firmly trace it over the years is important. The amount of

hair is also important to value, with locks commanding higher sums. They are often then broken down into strands for resale.

- The fame of the celebrity, and how commonly their hair appears on the market, also affects value. Celebrity hairdressers often kept locks when they cut their patrons' hair – in 2002, a jar of Elvis Presley's hair collected by his barber sold for over £57,000. Interesting stories can add value. Also consider how the hair is housed – when framed and glazed with a photograph or other visual items, such as a letter or signature, it offers an appealing display.

Three strands of Charles Dickens' hair, with a note of certification written by Georgina Hogarth, Dickens' sister-in-law, mounted and framed.

£400-500   MAS

Several strands of King Edward VII's hair, certified by a handwriting expert, framed.

£100-150   MAS

Three strands of Andrew Jackson's hair, certified by an autograph expert, framed.

£150-250   MAS

Three strands of Abraham Lincoln's hair, certificated by University Archives, framed.

£400-500   MAS

Four strands of John F. Kennedy's hair, with a note of certification from Harry Gelbart, barber to John Kennedy.

£100-150   MAS

Several strands of George Washington's hair, certified by a handwriting expert, framed.

£280-320   MAS

ESSENTIAL REFERENCE

- Over the past five years, handbags have become one of the hottest and most desirable fashion accessories the world-over. Shows such as 'Sex and The City' and celebrities like Victoria Beckham have inspired thousands to buy, and collect, vintage and contemporary designs. Values depend on a number of factors, including the quality of materials used, quality of construction, the maker, the condition, and the style and date of the bag.
- Always look for high quality materials and construction. Leather is one of the most desirable and varied materials, with crocodile, lizard and snake skin being scarcer and adding value. Details, including straps and metal clasps, should also be made from good quality materials and be able to withstand use. Good quality stitching and construction usually indicate a good maker, or at least an expensive price tag in its day.

- Maker's names are important, with the most notable designers and names adding instant value and cachet. Hermès, Chanel, Judith Lieber, Fendi and Gucci lead the field, but many fine quality names of the past have faded from wider knowledge. In these instances look at the location of the maker, as those in prestigious locations, such as Fifth Avenue in New York, are likely to have been important.
- Look out for handbags that sum up the styles of the day in terms of colour, style and material. In the 1920s and '30s, beaded bags were popular, as were leather bags with Art Deco geometric patterns. These are likely to appeal to collectors and those wishing to have an individual, period look. Bags in truly mint condition will command a premium, so always look at corners, clasps and the bag's interior for signs of wear and damage.

A 1950s American pearlised Lucite handbag, attributed to Jilly Originals, the transparent violet lid and front panel cut with diamond shapes.

Lucite bags are typical of the 1950s. Those in bright colours, with pearlised patterns or carved details tend to be the most sought-after, as are those by well-known makers such as Wilardy or Rialto. Avoid examples with a chemical smell, or with a fine network of lines on the surface, as these indicate the plastic is degrading irreversibly.

9in (23cm) high

£220-280 QU

A 1950s American Jilly Originals pearlised grey Lucite handbag, with silver foil strip inclusions and transparent curved facet-cut Lucite handle.

9in (23cm) high

£200-300 QU

A 1940s-50s French pearlised ivory Lucite handbag, with moulded gold-look plastic catch and rigid handles.

10.25in (26cm) long

£100-120 TSIS

A 1960s transparent amber and brown Lucite handbag, the lid etched with roses.

8.25in (21cm) long

£50-70 TSIS

A Jerri's Original box handbag, the wooden body with woven cord decoration, the Lucite lid decorated with hand-painted flying carpet scene.

11.5in (29.5cm) wide

£150-200 GCHI

A 1920s-30s French beaded and embroidered handbag, the gold-tone frame set with white glass cabochons, and with gold tone chain handle.

Always examine beaded bags carefully. Tears and missing beads are almost impossible to repair satisfactorily thereby reducing values by over 75 per cent.

5in (12.75cm) high

£30-50   **PC**

A 1930s Art Deco beaded handbag, with a metal internal frame, and white and clear glass beads in a floral design.

6in (15cm) wide

£10-15   **PC**

A 1930s French handmade beaded evening handbag, with gilt metal frame.

9.25in (23.5cm) wide

£70-100   **GCHI**

A 1950s black velvet handbag, with applied fabric flowers and beaded designs, the bag with a rigid frame.

11.75in (30cm) high

£80-120   **GCHI**

A black 1950s woven straw handbag, with applied fabric and beaded decoration, and "Made in Japan" label.

15.5in (39cm) high

£70-100   **GCHI**

A 1950s navy blue fabric handbag, with all-over beaded decoration in the form of a sleeping Mexican.

As well as a funky pattern, the beads glow in the dark.

12in (30.5cm) wide

£25-35   **GCHI**

A black fabric and tapestry handbag, with ridged frame and beaded details, and black plastic handle.

13in (33cm) high

£100-140   **GCHI**

A 1960s Art Deco-style leather clutch handbag, printed and stamped with a geometric design in light brown over a burgundy-brown background.

10in (25cm) long

£10-20   PC

A 1950s Koret alligator handbag, rich golden brown leather with hinged top frame opening, single top loop handle, brass hardware and sable leather interior with multiple pockets and coin purse.

£180-220   FRE

A 1960s Roger Vivier umber patent leather handbag, with an oversized faux-tortoiseshell link handle, snap-top closure, lined in kid leather, embossed "Roger Vivier Paris".

£100-150   FRE

A Chanel chevron-quilted red leather handbag, rectangular bright red top-zip bag with double-chain handle shoulder straps, exterior pockets on each side.

£180-220   FRE

A 1980s Judith Leiber suede leather gold charm evening handbag, with removable chain handle and applied gold Asian-themed designs.

Judith Leiber is particularly notable for her rhinestone encrusted metal-bodied bags, often in the form of animals, known as minaudières. She shot to fame after a number of celebrities and notable personalities, including many of America's First Ladies, were seen with her bags.

£200-300   FRE

EXPERT EYE – A HERMÈS HANDBAG

This design has enormous classic appeal. With its double handles and flap it recalls the more valuable and iconic Birkin.

The attention to detail is also high. Note the H-shaped clasps and the way the leather has been cut to give a symmetrical pattern.

All Hermès bags are handmade using quality materials including leather linings and fully stamped metalware.

This leather is farmed in Australia and is considered by many to be the premier Hermès leather. Its fine sheen is gained by repeated buffing with a smooth stone.

A Hermès chocolate brown 'Drage' handbag, covered with 'Crocodylus porosus' crocodile skin and lined in soft brown leather, the gilt brass 'H' closures with maker's name and also stamped in gold to the front panel under the closure flap.

12in (30cm) long

£2,000-3,000   KT

A Whiting & Davis Co. gilt mesh 'miser's purse', with pink satin interior, the expandable neck closing with a lid.

Whiting & Davis, founded in 1876, are renowned for their metal mesh handbags. During the 1930s, they collaborated with designers such as Paul Poiret and Elsa Schiaparelli. Although their bags went out of fashion in the 1950s, their sparkle ensured a comeback during the Disco era of the 1970s and '80s, and they are highly collectable.

5in (13cm) high

£32-38 　　　　BB

An American Lin Bren aqua suede slouch handbag, with Lucite circular handle and gold-coloured compact clasp.

11in (28cm) high

£150-200 　　　　GCHI

A 1950s woven bent-wood box handbag, with red plastic banding, and cherry and leaf decoration to lid.

8in (20cm) wide

£80-120 　　　　GCHI

An Edwardian brown crocodile leather suitcase, with canvas 'storm' cover monogrammed "BJ", and gilt brass locks.

c1910 　　　18in (46cm) wide

£120-180 　　　　ROS

EXPERT EYE – AN EMILIO PUCCI HANDBAG

Italian nobleman and flying ace Emilio Pucci (1914-92) rose to prominence during the 1960s with his printed fabrics and easy-to-wear dresses that typified the decade.

Vintage Pucci is always in vogue. It has seen a further surge in popularity since Bernard Arnault's LVMH group relaunched the brand in 2000.

This is typical of his printed designs, with its bright, psychedelic colours, and asymmetric geometric and abstract pattern.

Due to Pucci's success and the high cost of vintage and new pieces, imitations are known. Always look closely, as authentic examples bear the 'Emilio' name repeated within the design.

An Emilio Pucci printed silk handbag, bright canary yellow printed with grey and earth tone geometric designs, with black leather single strap and brass loops at the side, hidden snap at the front flap closure, lined in black leather and embossed "Emilio Pucci".

£200-300 　　　　FRE

An early 20thC leather-bound travelling case, the interior with fitted compartments, and with oval plaque to lid above lock.

£100-150 　　　　BRI

ESSENTIAL REFERENCE

- Hallowe'en memorabilia is the second most popular area of holiday collecting after Christmas memorabilia, particularly in the US. Much reflects the holiday's rural origins in 18thC Scotland, as the custom was brought to the US by Scottish settlers during the 1880s. Despite this, most of the earliest pieces from the 1900s to '30s were made in Germany and exported.

- Pumpkin-shaped jack-o-lanterns or sweet containers are the most commonly found form, but figurines, skulls and other related items can also be found. The majority are made from card, which was pressed into moulds when wet, before being painted. Papier–mâché, pressed pulp, crêpe paper, lithographed tinplate and plaster-of-Paris were also used. Most pieces were decorated in typical oranges and blacks.

- The fragile materials used means that much did not survive as it was worn through play or use over the years. Always look for the original paper inserts on jack-o-lanterns as these add value. Damage such as tears or wear to the paint can reduce values by 50 per cent or more. Large pieces tend to be rare, partly as they were expensive to begin with. They were also more easily damaged through use.

- Look out for novelty or amusing forms and unusual colourways, as they can add value. During the 1950s and '60s, plastic was increasingly used as it was more robust, cheaper and easier to produce in quantity. Although values are still not as high as for earlier pieces, rare forms, such as those with moving parts or unusual poses, can fetch hundreds of pounds. As earlier pieces also become harder to find and more expensive, these are rising in desirability.

A 1950s American pressed pulp Hallowe'en witch, with black cape and hat.

9in (23cm) high

£150-200   SOTT

A 1950s American pressed pulp Hallowe'en witch, with orange cape and large hat.

This is the rarer and more visually appealing version of this form. The black and white colourway on the left is easier to find, and less valuable.

9in (23cm) high

£220-280   SOTT

A 1950s American printed card Hallowe'en 'Fanny Farmer' witch double-sided sweets box, with paper labels.

8in (20cm) high

£50-80   SOTT

A 1940s-50s American pressed pulp witch and cauldron sweets container.

This is a very rare shape. This example is in very good condition, but has repairs to the cauldron and hat. Examples in better condition can be worth around £150-200.

4.75in (12cm) high

£80-120   SOTT

An American 1950s-60s plastic Hallowe'en witch-on-motorcycle lolly holder.

This is an extremely rare shape.

7.25in (18cm) long

£200-250   SOTT

A rare pair of 1950s-60s American plastic Hallowe'en pastry cooks-on-wheels lolly holders.

5in (13cm) high

£220-280   SOTT

A 1920s-30s German painted plaster miniature Hallowe'en veggie man sweets box, with removable card base printed "Made in Germany".

This more commonly found shape is not a nodder, which explains why the value is lower.

3.25in (8cm) high

£150-200   SOTT

A 1920s-30s German painted plaster Hallowe'en boy-eaten-by-pumpkin nodder sweets container, with removable card disc base.

This is a valuable container, despite its diminutive size. Nodders are easily damaged, making complete examples rarer and more desirable.

2.75in (7cm) high

£180-220   SOTT

A 1920s-30s German painted plaster and card Hallowe'en child-riding-pumpkin nodder sweets container.

3.75in (9.5cm) high

£250-300   SOTT

A 1920s-30s German painted plaster and card Hallowe'en child-riding-pumpkin nodder sweets container.

3.75in (9.5cm) high

£200-300   SOTT

A very rare and early pair of German painted plaster Hallowe'en old woman and old man nodders.

c1910-15

£800-1,200

7in (17.5cm) high

SOTT

A 1920s-30s German painted plaster Hallowe'en red devil nodder.

6in (15cm) high

£200-250   SOTT

A rare German Hallowe'en clicker, with composition head and felt clothes, the back of one trouser leg printed "D.R.G.M. 18284".

The clicker works by holding the handle and shaking the body, causing the figure to bend at the waist and make a clicking sound.

c1910-20   *10in (25.5cm) high*

£250-350   SOTT

A 1930s-40s American pressed pulp large Hallowe'en roly-poly pumpkin man lantern.

Always look at the top of the head, as this area is usually damaged by being pushed in and broken. Although this example shows some signs of pressing, it is not broken.

9.25in (23cm) high

£250-300   **SOTT**

EXPERT EYE – A HALLOWE'EN DEVIL

The head was also produced separately and is rare. On its own, it can be worth over £500.

Figures are hard to find, but examples of this size and level of detail are almost once-in-a-lifetime finds, particularly when complete.

This probably unique piece was most likely to have been a special commission from a wealthy client, or made as a shop display.

It is incredible to think that the delicate crêpe paper clothes have survived in this condition for over 80 years – this accounts for a large part of the value.

A 1920s-30s German large Hallowe'en devil, constructed from card, papier-mâché, crêpe paper and wire, complete with original paint, paper insert, clothes, base and fork.

20.75in (52.5cm) high

£1,500-2,000   **SOTT**

A 1920s-30s German double-sided printed card and crêpe paper Hallowe'en squeeky toy, the crêpe tube printed "Germany".

The crêpe paper tube and printed card surfaces in particular are easily damaged. This example is in excellent condition.

4.5in (11cm) high

£120-180   **SOTT**

A 1950s American pressed pulp Hallowe'en black cat sweet container.

7.25in (18cm) high

£180-220   **SOTT**

A 1950s American painted pressed pulp Hallowe'en cat sweet container, with rare heavy gloss finish.

6.75in (17cm) high

£200-250   **SOTT**

A 1930s-40s American pressed pulp Hallowe'en owl lantern.

10in (25cm) high

£80-120   **SOTT**

EXPERT EYE – A HALLOWE'EN JACK-O-LANTERN

The pulped paper, eggbox-like material used here is typical of American production of the 1950s.

This double-faced form is very rare, and the singing 'choir boy' expression is both scarce and desirable.

During the 1930s-40s, the colour was added to the pulp mix as a dye, but during the 1950s, the surface was painted with colour, as here.

German factories pressed wet card into moulds, which was then covered in a layer of strengthening plaster, before being painted. US factories did not use these materials.

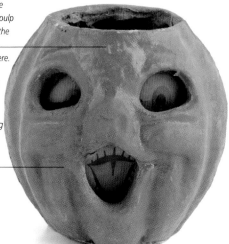

A 1950s American pressed pulp Hallowe'en double-faced jack-o-lantern, with 'choir boy' expression and original printed paper inserts.

4.5in (11.5cm) high

£70-100   SOTT

A large 1920s-30s German Hallowe'en jack-o-lantern, with original printed paper insert and card base.

7.5in (19cm) high

£250-300   SOTT

A German card oversized Hallowe'en jack-o-lantern, with original printed paper insert.

1910-20   10.75in (27cm) wide

£900-1,000   SOTT

A 1930s-40s American sprayed pressed pulp Hallowe'en jack-o-lantern, with original insert and black 'wrinkle' lines.

5.25in (13cm) high

£100-150   SOTT

A 1950s American pressed pulp Hallowe'en jack-o-lantern, with spray painted decoration and black outlined features.

3.5in (9cm) high

£35-45   SOTT

A 1920s-30s German spray painted pressed card Hallowe'en skull jack-o-lantern.

This was produced using the more common pumpkin mould, but was sprayed white to be a skull.

5in (13cm) high

£180-200   SOTT

A 1910s-20s German large pressed card Hallowe'en watermelon jack-o-lantern, hand-painted in blue and green, with original paint, card base and printed tissue insert.

Melon jack-o-lanterns are the hardest to find, probably as they were considered less suitable and appealing as Hallowe'en decorations at the time. They are also usually very early in date. This form is also known in a smaller size at around 4in (10cm) wide, which could be worth up to £500 in similar condition.

6.25in (16cm) wide

£800-1,200   SOTT

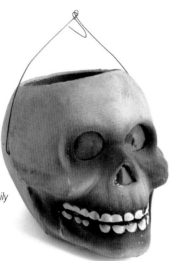

A German sprayed and painted composition Hallowe'en skull jack-o-lantern.

This is a rare size and is in surprisingly good condition for such an easily damaged material.

1910-15   4.25in (11cm) high
£450-550   SOTT

An early German heavy plaster-over-card Hallowe'en simian skull jack-o-lantern, with original printed paper insert.
1910-20   3.25in (8cm) high
£250-300   SOTT

An early German heavy plaster Hallowe'en small skull jack-o-lantern, with original red paper insert.
1910-20   3.25in (8cm) high
£200-250   SOTT

A German painted pressed card and plaster coated Hallowe'en skull jack-o-lantern, with original rosette crêpe paper base.

Note how detailed and well painted the expression is executed.

1910-20   5.5in (14cm) high
£350-450   SOTT

An extremely rare and large 1920s-30s German hand-painted papier-mâché Hallowe'en devil's head jack-o-lantern, with original paint and printed paper insert for eyes and mouth.

This would have been made for display, possibly in a shop, or as a table centrepiece. Its size and high original cost meant that few would have been sold and even fewer would have survived in this condition.

11.25in (28.5cm) high
£1,000-1,200   SOTT

A German plaster coated papier-mâché Hallowe'en devil's head jack-o-lantern, with replaced printed paper insert.
1910-20   2.75in (7.5cm) high
£200-250   SOTT

A 1930s-40s American pressed pulp Hallowe'en devil's head jack-o-lantern, with original paper insert.

This form, with its strongly moulded and deep features, is very rare.

6.5in (16.5cm) high
£180-220   SOTT

A rare and early German composition Hallowe'en old lady jack-o-lantern, with original paper inserts.

3.5in (9cm) high

£250-350   **SOTT**

A very rare 1950s Rosen Co. printed card box for moulded plastic Hallowe'en 'Sweets Pops' lolly holders, containing five witches and five cats.

Although the lolly holders themselves are not rare, the box is extremely rare as most were thrown away by shops once the contents had been sold.

Box 13.5in (34cm) long

£120-150   **SOTT**

A 1920s American Marks Bros. Co. printed card and crêpe paper Hallowe'en horn, printed "US Patent Sept,13,1921 Marks Bros. Co. Boston Mass".

The fact this retains its original crêpe paper makes it more valuable, although not all horns were fitted with crêpe.

10.75in (27cm) long

£60-90   **SOTT**

A late 1940s American Hallowe'en printed card 'Screech Owl' siren horn.

6.75in (17cm) high

£25-35   **SOTT**

A card and die-cut crêpe paper Hallowe'en sweets container favour, with die-cut black cat card.

4.5in (11cm) high

£35-50   **SOTT**

A 1950s-60s American orange and black plastic sweets basket, with witch on a broomstick handle.

5.5in (14cm) long

£10-15   **SOTT**

An American colour printed 'Happy Hallowe'en' postcard, with dated copyright wording for the International Art Pub. Co.

1908   *5.5in (14cm) wide*

£12-18   **SOTT**

A 1930s American colour printed and embossed 'Hallowe'en' postcard, with two pumpkins beneath a smiling moon, printed by the International Art Pub. Co. of New York.

5.5in (14cm) high

£12-18   **SOTT**

ESSENTIAL REFERENCE

- The most desirable and valuable pieces of Christmas memorabilia were made in Germany during the early 20thC. Most were made from composition or papier-mâché / pressed pulp, which was then hand-painted. The larger or more complex a piece is, the more valuable it is likely to be. Clothes and accessories are similarly handmade. Makers' names do not generally appear, with most being simply marked 'Germany'.

- Also look out for rare variations in terms of colour, or the accessories the figure may be holding, as these can add value. The same goes for later moulded plastic memorabilia made from the 1950s and '60s onwards, which is rising in value. Nevertheless, a great many examples can still be found for under £25, with prices rarely rising above £150.
- Condition is important for both areas, with examples in truly mint condition being worth a premium.

A 1920s-30s German painted plaster Santa Claus sweets container, with rare moss green felt coat and fur beard, holding a brass basket and feather tree.

11in (28cm) high

£1,000-1,200   SOTT

EXPERT EYE – A 1920S GERMAN SANTA FIGURINE

At nearly 15in high, this is a very rare large example of a figurine.

He is in near mint condition and is complete with a fur beard and all of his accessories.

The mottled green, brown and tan woven mohair coat is both unusual and extremely rare.

His wicker backpack still contains its rare original gifts, which are individually wrapped.

A very rare 1920s-30s large Santa Claus figurine, with painted plaster face, fur beard and multicoloured mohair coat, holding a stocking and a wire-and-feather tree, with a wicker pack on his back containing separately made gifts.

14.75in (37cm) high

£1,600-2,000   SOTT

An early German painted plaster stooped Santa Claus figurine, with red mohair coat, holding a feather tree and a gift-filled bag, and a gift-filled wicker basket on his back.

c1910   10in (25.5cm) high

£700-1,000   SOTT

A 1920s-30s German Santa Claus figurine, with long coat, feather Christmas tree, in a woven wicker car with wooden wheels.

7.25in (18cm) long

£400-500   SOTT

A 1920s-30s German painted plaster Santa Claus sweets container, opening at the waist.

4.25in (10.5cm) high

£70-100   SOTT

A 1920s-30s German painted plaster Belsnickle figure, with wire-and-feather tree, red chenille trim and applied clear Venetian glass or Coralene beads.

Coralene are tiny glass beads that are glued onto the surface of an object. Wear and loss of the beads is common, and reduces value.

An early German blue painted plaster Belsnickle figurine, decorated with glass chips, red chenille trim and a feather tree.

8.5in (21.5cm) high

£500-700   SOTT

10.5in (26.5cm) high

£400-600   SOTT

A 1920s-30s German composition 'Santa on a log' figure, with a pack of toys on his back, the base painted "Germany".

2.75in (7cm) high

£50-70   SOTT

A large Annalee Christmas poseable reindeer soft toy.

4in (10cm) high

£6-9   AEM

An American Schoenhut hand-painted composition smiling Santa Claus 'Roly Poly' toy, with weighted bottom, repair to top of head.

9in (23cm) high

£300-400   BER

A set of 12 Santa Claus picture blocks, the wooden cubes with colour lithographed images of Santa Claus in different scenes.

2.25in (5.5cm) wide

£250-350   BER

A 'Santa Claus In Africa Picture Puzzle' box, published by McLoughlin Bros., New York, with colour lithographed label showing children riding ostriches followed by Santa on his sleigh, lacks contents.

10.25in (26cm) high

£200-250   BER

ESSENTIAL REFERENCE

- Most of what is termed and collected as Inuit art today was created from the 1950s onwards, although the heritage goes back many centuries to the Athabascan and Thule cultures of Alaska and Northern Canada. The work of these peoples came to light in 1949, when a young Canadian artist called James Houston visited the Canadian Arctic to find out if the native art was appealing and could be sold. He found that it was and during the 1950s and '60s, the creation of and trade in these works became increasingly organised.

- Most works are sculptural, and use the soft yet durable soapstone found across the area that ranges in colour from a deep grey through to green. It can also be polished to a high sheen, which has led to its reputation as 'Canadian jade''. Drawings, textiles and prints are also created. Subject matter ranges from Inuit daily life and experiences, such as hunting, to their myths, and more abstracted ideas.

- The primary consideration as regards value is the artist, with works by influential sculptors and artists such as John Pangnark, Osuitok Ipeelee, Pauta Saila, Jessie Oonark and Judas Ullulaq being highly collectable and valuable. Many of the most valuable pieces were made during the 1950s to

'70s by artists who are now dead. The subject matter and appearance also count greatly – look for well-executed, stylized and even abstracted designs, often with an inherent wit or humour. Mythical creatures and 'transformation' sculptures are also often highly desirable.

- Due to the growing popularity of Inuit art and increased trade over the past two decades, there are also a great many average, and even poor, artworks available. These have little chance of becoming desirable or collectable in future, so learn about forms, artists and market trends from books and by visiting dealers and auctions to view examples. Of the many contemporary artists in the market, only a few look set to become considered as masters of the art.

- Many pieces are signed on the bottom with syllabics, the Inuit form of verbal lettering, or with a disc number beginning with an 'E' or 'W', that identifies the artist. An example is shown on this page. Numbers given after the artist's name in the caption indicate the disc number, if known. The market in Inuit art has seen rapid development over the last 25 years, with interest growing across the world, and this looks sets to continue.

A carved and polished seated Inuk soapstone sculpture, with washing pulled over a pole, unsigned.

6.5in (17cm) long

£80-120   THG

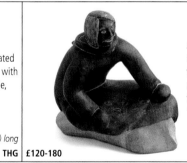

A carved grey soapstone sculpture of a seated Inuk, with polished and unpolished areas of stone, the base inscribed "C 87 11-53-'8".

5in (13cm) high

£120-180   THG

A carved soapstone sculpture of a Inuk holding a seal, by Simon Kasudluak (b.1925), E9-1716, with syllabics and disc number.

7in (18cm) high

£120-180   THG

An carved and polished soapstone sculpture of bear and Inuk fighting, by Aibilie Echalook, E9-1647, signed in syllabics and with disc number.

Born in 1940, Echalook's work has been exhibited at the Winnipeg Art Gallery and by UNESCO. His work was sold at Sotheby's as early as 1982.

16.5in (42cm) wide

£1,000-1,200   THG

A dark soapstone Inuit woman, by an unidentified artist, signed in syllabics, dated "'72".

1972   *10in (25cm) high*

£1,500-2,000   **WAD**

A soapstone 'Man Playing Accordian' figure, by an unidentified artist.

8in (20.5cm) high

£500-700   **WAD**

A soapstone figure, by Mathew Aqigaaq, E2-350, signed in syllabics.

Born in 1940 into the Qamani'tuaq community, Aqigaaq's work has been included in many publications and exhibitions, including 'Sculpture/Inuit: Masterworks of the Canadian Arctic', organised by the Canadian Eskimo Arts Council. He was also mentioned in an article by James Houston.

c1972   *12in (33cm) high*

£3,200-3,800   **WAD**

A stone figure of a seated woman, by Leonie Qunnut (b.1941), E5-417, from Igloolik, signed in Roman, with disc number.

15in (6cm) wide

£500-600   **WAD**

A soapstone 'Woman With Kudlik' figure, by Timothy Naralik (b.1942), signed in Roman.

5in (12.5cm) high

£500-600   **WAD**

A stone figure of a mother and child, by Mathew Aqigaaq, E2-350, from Baker Lake, signed in syllabics.

9in (23cm) high

£800-1,200   **WAD**

A soapstone, ivory and wood 'Hunter' figure, by an unidentified artist.

c1967   *13in (33cm) high*

£600-800   **WAD**

An antler, skin and stone figure of a hunter, by Judas Ullulaq, E4-342, from Gjoa Haven.

13in (33cm) high

£3,000-4,000   **WAD**

EXPERT EYE – JUDAS ULLULAQ

Judas Ullulaq (1937-98) began by carving ivory miniatures, later moving to larger soapstone sculptures – most include details made from other materials, such as inset bone, ivory, or antler eyes.

He was heavily influenced by his nephew, Karoo Ashevak, who is one of the most desirable artists in today's market. Both focused on spirits and the supernatural in their abstracted figural works.

His forms are typically bulging and exaggerated with bizarre distorted or grotesque faces, often with open mouths with teeth, which give a highly expressive appearance to his work.

Ullulaq was a founder of the important Netsilik school, known for its asymmetrical styles inspired by mysticism, His work is more humourous and whimsically amusing.

A soapstone and antler 'Mother and Child' figure, by Judas Ullulaq, E4-342, from Gjoa Haven, signed in syllabics.

17in (43cm) high

WAD

£4,000-5,000

A dark soapstone shaman, by Judas Ullulaq, E4-342, from Gjoa Haven, with inset eyes and teeth, being attacked by a bone creature and holding an antler axe, signed in syllabics.

12in (30cm) high

£3,500-4,000   **WAD**

A soapstone and antler 'Hunter' figure, by Judas Ullulaq, E4-342, from Gjoa Haven.

16in (40.5cm) high

£3,000-5,000   **WAD**

A soapstone and antler 'Shaman' figure, by Judas Ullulaq, E4-342, from Gjoa Haven, signed in syllabics.

16in (40.5cm) high

£3,500-4,500   **WAD**

A stone, figure of a demon collecting eggs, by Abraham Kingmiatuq (b.1933), E4-329, from Spence Bay, signed in syllabics.

14in (35.5cm) high

£2,500-3,000   **WAD**

INUIT ART

A stone figure of a dancing polar bear, by Paulassie Pootoogook (b.1927), E7-1176, from Cape Dorset.

13in (33cm) high

£1,200-1,800   **WAD**

ESSENTIAL REFERENCE – THE POLAR BEAR

Sharing the Arctic circle with the Inuit people, polar bears are both admired and feared. Known as 'Nanuk', they are considered to be wise, dangerous and powerful, being able to outrun, outswim and outfight a man. They are also considered 'man-like' as they could walk on two legs. When hunted and killed, great respect is paid to their skins and bodies, nearly all parts of which are used for survival in harsh conditions. The bear's power and mystical nature has led it to be depicted in Inuit and pre-Inuit sculpture and art for many centuries. During the 20thC, one of the most notable artists of polar bear sculptures was Pauta Saila (b.1916). He became known for his monumental, heavily stylized dancing bears that poked gentle fun at the animal, yet drew attention to its great strength and power. Born in Cape Dorset in 1977, Pootoogook works in a similar style to Saila, and manages here to convey a superb sense of movement. Dancing polar bears have become one of the most desirable types of Inuit sculpture in recent years.

A carved soapstone figure of an acrobatic polar bear, by Mosesie Pootoogook from Cape Dorset, signed in Roman.

2in (5cm) high

£1,800-2,200   **WAD**

A stone figure of a dancing polar bear, by George Arluk (b.1949), E3-1049, from Arviat, signed in Roman.

1995   *12.5in (32cm) high*

£300-500   **WAD**

A stone figure of a polar bear, by David Ruben Piqtoukun (b.1950), W3-1119, signed in Roman and dated "1986".

1986   *9in (23cm) wide*

£550-750   **WAD**

A soapstone 'Polar Bear' figure, by Mannumi Shaqu (b.1917), signed in syllabics.

11in (28cm) long

£1,200-1,800   **WAD**

A carved and polished black soapstone polar bear, by Joe Kovik (b.1950), E9-188, signed with syllabics and disc number.

8in (20.5cm) high

£400-600   **THG**

A soapstone 'Exhausted Polar Bear' figure, by Kananginak Pootoogook (b.1935), signed in Roman.

5in (12.5cm) long

£320-380   **WAD**

A stone and antler musk ox figure, by Lucassie Ikkidluak (b.1947), E7-765, from Lake Harbor, signed in syllabics, dated "1992".

1992   *16in (40.5cm) wide*

£4,000-5,000   **WAD**

A stone and antler musk ox figure, by Seepee Ipellie (b.1940), E7-511, from Iqaluit, signed in syllabics.

13in (33cm) wide

£1,200-1,800   **WAD**

A stone and ivory floating walrus figure, by Markoosie, E7-647, signed in Roman and with disc number.

c1970   *4in (10cm) high*

£280-320   **WAD**

A carved light grey soapstone perching bird, probably by Mary Sanguvia Qumala (b.1946) from Povungnituk, the base inscribed "1346".

7.25in (19cm) high

£120-180   **THG**

A soapstone 'Musk Ox' figure, by Nuveeya Ipellie, with antler horns.

6.5in (16.5cm) long

£500-700   **WAD**

A stone figure of a bird, by Abraham Etungat (1911-99), E7-809, from Cape Dorset.

9in (23cm) long

£850-950   **WAD**

A stone bird figure, by Abraham Etungat, E7-809, from Cape Dorset, signed in syllabics.

3in (7.5cm) high

£800-1,000   **WAD**

A dark soapstone otter, by an unidentified artist.

c1960   *20cm (8in) wide*

£500-700   **WAD**

A stone Sedna, by Gideon Qauqjuaq, E4-392, Spence Bay.

6in (15cm) high

£180-220   **WAD**

A stone bird woman figure, by Tivi Anasuga, signed in syllabics.

6.5in (16.5cm) high

£150-200   **WAD**

A grey soapstone animal figure, by Andy Miki, E1-436, from Arviat.

Like Pangnark, Miki (1918-83) is known for his simplification of form and strong stylisation that recalls ancient and primitive sculpture. His work is similarly sought-after.

7in (18cm) high

£5,000-7,000   **WAD**

EXPERT EYE – JOHN PANGNARK

Pangnark (1920-80) is known for his highly abstracted forms that are reminiscent of hills, mountains, rocky outcrops or even Inuit huddled together.

The simplest of facial features, consisting of mere lines, are lightly carved or inscribed on a small part of the sculptures.

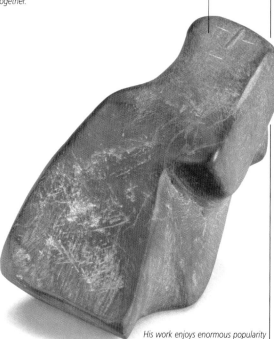

Although typically tiny in size, the simple forms make them appear massive and monumental, and recall the other tribal statues like the Moai statues on Easter Island.

His work enjoys enormous popularity with values varying, depending on the size, sense of weight and form, and visual appeal of the piece..

A stone figure, by John Pangnark, E1-104, from Arviat.

9in (23cm) long

£5,000-7,000   **WAD**

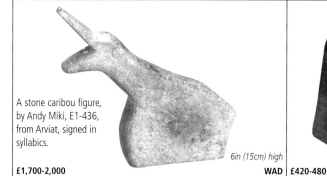

A stone caribou figure, by Andy Miki, E1-436, from Arviat, signed in syllabics.

6in (15cm) high

£1,700-2,000   **WAD**

A stone figure, by John Pangnark, E1-104, from Arviat, signed in syllabics.

2.75in (7cm) high

£420-480   **WAD**

A carved weathered bone drummer figure, with ivory baton and skin drum.

6.75in (17cm) high

£280-320   THG

A carved weathered bone standing hunter figure, with ivory knife, unsigned.

6in (15cm) high

£200-300   THG

A carved weathered dark grey bone hunter figure, with carved bone spear, unsigned.

7.25in (18cm) high

£320-380   THG

A carved weathered bone standing polar bear figure, unsigned.

The artist has cleverly used the weathered side to give the impression of a spine.

12.25in (31cm) high

£100-150   THG

A weathered whale vertebrae bone, carved as a polar bear's head.

Whalebone has been used for centuries by Inuit and pre-Inuit communities such as the Thule. It was usually found in distressed, weathered condition, resulting in interesting textures and colours. Dating a piece of bone can be extremely difficult, if not impossible. Most are also not signed by the sculptor. Collectors should make themselves fully aware of the guidelines for the sale and export of these works of art.

19.25in (49cm) long

£600-900   THG

A carved weathered bone polar bear figure, unsigned.

8in (20cm) long

£180-220   THG

INUIT ART

A limited edition engraving of a bird, untitled, by Pauta Saila (b.1916), from an edition of 50.

1962   11.75in (30cm) wide

£450-550   **WAD**

A limited edition 'Geese With Hawk' engraving, by Kenojuak Ashevak (b.1927), from an edition of 50.

1963   11.75in (30cm) wide

£280-320   **WAD**

EXPERT EYE – A LUKE ANGUHADLUQ INUIT PRINT

Anguhadluq was in his late sixties when he was inspired to become an artist by his cousin Jessie Oonark, who was becoming increasingly successful.

His first drawings were made between 1960 and 1961, and by 1970 his work had become part of the Baker Lake Annual Print Collection, to which he contributed until 1982.

His style of small figures in a large area of blank white paper reflects the focus and experience of the hunter in the vast expanse of the frozen, white Arctic.

His work has appeared in over 70 exhibitions in Canada and around the world. His strictly limited edition prints are highly sought-after.

A limited edition 'Muskox' stonecut and stencil print, by Luke Anguhadluq (1895-1982), from an edition of 50.

1977   37in (94cm) wide

£1,000-1,500   **WAD**

A limited edition 'Young Owls' stonecut print, by Lucy Qinnuayuak (1915-82), E7-1068, from Cape Dorset, from an edition of 50, unframed.

24.5in (62.5cm) wide

£850-950   **WAD**

A limited edition 'Caribou Hunters' engraving, by Kiakshuk (1886-1966), from an edition of 50, signed in syllabics.

1963   12in (31cm) wide

£250-350   **WAD**

A limited edition 'Geese With Hawk' engraving, by Kenojuak Ashevak (1927-), from an edition of 50.

1963   11.75in (30cm) wide

£280-320   **WAD**

FIND OUT MORE...

The Inuit Art Center: www.ainc-inac.gc.ca/art/index_e.html

'Inuit Art: An Introduction', by Ingo Hessel, Dieter Hessel and George Swinton, published by Douglas & McIntyre, 2003.

'Sculpture of the Inuit', by George Swinton, published by McLelland & Stewart, 1999.

ESSENTIAL REFERENCE

- Much like 19th and early 20thC kitchenalia, post-WWII domestic and kitchen accessories and equipment is primarily collected for its decorative appeal. The 1950s in particular saw an explosion in design, and the production of labour-saving devices to make looking after a home easier. Look out for pieces that represent the dominant styles of the period. Major manufacturers often employed important designers, and these will usually fetch a premium.
- Solid teak kitchen and tablewares have seen a rise in interest and values recently. Forms are usually very simple, with the style leaders being Scandinavian, primarily Danish. The most notable name is Dansk, founded in 1954 by US entrepreneur Ted Nierenberg. The company's main designer until the 1980s was Jens Quistgaard, who produced innovative designs in teak, iron and steel. These have become hotly sought-after today.
- Not all of Dansk's designs were by Quistgaard – look at the base for stamped marks including an 'IHQ' monogram. His most famous design was an ice bucket inspired by the prow of a Viking longboat. Other countries also producing teak wares included Italy and South America. As teak is now an endangered wood, it cannot be used to make solid items, and only limited supplies exist. Always consider style and condition, looking for typically modern forms.

A pair of 1950s-60s Danish solid teak candlesticks, unmarked.

11.5in (29cm) high

£45-55   UCT

A pair of Danish solid teak candlesticks, with curving asymmetric rims, unmarked.

These are said to be by Jens Quistgaard (b.1919), but this cannot be confirmed as they they are typically unmarked.

9in (23cm) high

£45-50   UCT

A pair of Danish solid teak salt and pepper shakers, with inset metal 'S' and 'P', unmarked.

4.75in (12cm) high

£25-35   UCT

A 1960s Dansk solid teak pepper grinder, designed by Jens Quistgaard, with stamped marks to base.

3.5in (9cm) high

£45-65   UCT

A Danish Woodline solid teak cylindrical ice bucket, with double-ringed handles, hinged lid and metal liner, the base impressed "Woodline Denmark".

6.5in (16.5cm) high

£80-100   UCT

A Danish Anri Form solid teak ice bucket, with two shaped handles and a metal liner, the base with inset factory metal medallion.

9in (23cm) high

£40-60   UCT

KITCHENALIA

A 1950s-60s Danish solid teak bowl, with asymmetric curved rim, unmarked.

4in (10cm) high

£30-40   **UCT**

A Danish solid teak three-legged candle-holder, with brass insert, unmarked.

4.5in (12cm) high

£25-35   **UCT**

A Danish Digsmed carved solid teak meat cutting tray, with impressed mark to base.

As well as having a decorative central boss that grips the joint of meat, the surface is sloped so the meat juices drain away.

c1964   *17in (43cm) diam*

£35-45   **UCT**

A 1950s Gotthilf Singer 'Type T.V.E. 20' desk fan, with turquoise rubber blades, and maker's mark to base.

10.75in (28cm) high

£50-80   **QU**

EXPERT EYE – A TEAK ICE BUCKET

The form is similar to a Shaker 'dipper', used for getting water from a barrel or stream, or a cylindrical folk art candle box.

The simple, almost geometric form is typical of its day and is similar to those produced in Denmark at the time.

The design and placement of the handle also allows it to be hung on the wall.

It is built from slats of wood like a barrel, with the vertical lines and different colour tones and grains adding interest.

An Italian Anri Form solid teak ice bucket, with single handle and metal liner, the base with inset factory metal medallion.

15in (38cm) high

£50-80   **UCT**

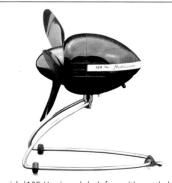

A 1950s Spanish '125 Hurricane' desk fan, with mottled green bakelite body, three red blades and chromed metal stand.

The mottled green body and red blades make this an unusually colourful piece. The form and stand also suggest a rocket or a aeroplane's propeller engine, which is another attractive feature.

6.75in (17cm) high

£200-300   **QU**

A 1950s-60s hand-painted 'Granny' utensil holder.

10.25in (26cm) high

£4-6   AEM

A 1950s-60s hand-painted 'Grated Cheese' chef cheese sprinkler.

8in (20cm) high

£4-6   AEM

A seated teddy bear chocolate mould, numbered "40" but otherwise unmarked.

The teddy bear is a desirable subject, and the seated bear is much harder to find. Additionally, as he is seated, the resulting chocolate is more three-dimensional.

4.75in (12cm) high

£100-150   SOTT

An American 'Man With Flowers' cast iron doorstop, painted in colours.

Depicted in 18thC clothing, this is a very well detailed stop.

9in (23cm) high

£300-400   BER

A 1950s-60s Wilton Prod. painted cast iron bottle opener.

Intended for opening beer bottles, the double-eye effect gives the impression of being drunk.

3.75in (9.5cm) high

£30-40   BH

A Japanese Holt Howard hand-painted cat's head string dispenser, dated "1958".

1958   *5.25in (13cm) wide*

£10-15   AEM

A 1950s American Ice-o-Mat ice crusher, by Rival Manufacturing Co. Kansas City 289, Missouri, in Wood Tone with Sandalwood, mint condition together with original box.

Boxed 10.75in (27cm) high

£15-25   MA

A late 1950s German AEG KMEG offee bean grinder, designed by Hans Krebs in 1954, in white and brown plastic, with maker's plaque to base.

6.25in (15.5cm) high

£80-120   QU

A German Rommler AG poseable office desk lamp, designed by Christian Dell, in dark brown bakelite.

Dell's lamp designs continued to be very popular during the 1950s.

c1930   15.75in (40cm) high

£120-180   **QU**

A 1950s German Osram 'Vitalux' aluminium folding desk lamp, with maker's mark to base.

11.5in (29cm) high

£120-180   **QU**

A 1950s floor lamp, with spherical plasticized paper shade hanging from a curving support on a black finished metal wire tripod with brass ball and rubber feet.

The planet-like shade hints at the 1950s fascination with outer space, and the tripod legs and ball support are also typical of 1950s design, and recall molecular or atomic structures.

55.25in (140cm) high

£220-280   **QU**

A 1950s American brown lacquered metal organic-form table lamp, with rectangular metal base and original printed paper shade, some chips to the lacquer.

This biomorphic form is typical of 1950s lamp designs, and similar forms can also be found in ceramic. Always look for original shades as not only do they look better, but they also add considerably to the value.

29.5in (75cm) high

£220-280   **QU**

A late 1950s Philips table lamp, the design attributed to Louis Kalff, with a brass angled stand and black lacquered metal shade.

As with the floor lamp above, the influence of the 1950s obsession with UFOs and outer space is clear.

15.75in (40cm) high

£100-150   **QU**

A 1950s German floor lamp, with rhombic rocket-form woven shade on a black finished metal wire tripod.

52in (132cm) high

£150-200   **QU**

A 1950s-60s desk lamp, probably French, with red acrylic shade and brass curving stand with lacquered metal angled support.

10.5in (26cm) high

£150-200   **QU**

A 1950s German Schleiss & Co. Gmundner Keramik table lamp, the black ceramic figure holding a raffia parasol and shield and wearing a raffia skirt.

21.25in (54cm) high

£800-1,200   **QU**

A pair of 1950s Italian frosted glass wall lamps.

As well as harking back to the Art Deco feel for modern shapes, the rocket-like lamps echo the public interest in outer space.

c1957   *14in (37cm) high*

£30-50   **MA**

A 1950s green glazed ceramic fireplace television lamp, unmarked.

The small pots at the front were meant to contain plants, despite the fact that these were intended to be placed on top of a television.

10in (25.5cm) long

£30-50   **TSIS**

A 1950s hand-painted ceramic horse television lamp.

12.75in (32cm) high

£30-50   **TSIS**

A 1970s 'Sirrah' table lamp, distributed by the Design Gallery, Milan, comprised of an opaque white glass tubular shade and a base made of a pleated green silk sack filled with beads.

14in (35.5cm) high

£150-250   **GM**

A 1970s Italian Artemide 'Telegono' table lamp, designed by Vico Magistretti in 1969, with white and orange plastic body.

16in (41cm) high

£100-150   **QU**

A late 1960s-70s Italian Artemide orange moulded plastic 'Nesso' table lamp, designed by Gruppo Architetti Urbanista Citta Nuova in 1965.

13.5in (34cm) high

£200-300   **QU**

ESSENTIAL REFERENCE

- Vintage collectable marbles fall into one of two distinct categories: handmade marbles and machine-made marbles. Handmade marbles were produced primarily in Germany from the 1860s to the 1920s. Machine-made marbles were produced in the US after 1905 when M.F. Christensen developed a marble-making machine. Production reached a peak in the 1920s and '30s. In the 1950s and '60s machine-made marbles began to be produced in large numbers in the Far East and South America, but these are generally of little interest to collectors.

- Handmade marbles can be distinguished by the presence of rough pontil marks, where they were broken away from the glass rod to be formed into a sphere. Although traditionally the most sought after, the scarcity of fine hand-made examples has meant that collectors' interest in the best machine-made marbles is now almost as fervent.

- Machine-made marbles have no pontil mark. Notable manufacturers include the short-lived Christensen Agate Company, which operated between 1905 and 1917, and Akro Agate, that produced marbles from 1910 until the factory's closure in 1951.

- The type of marble can affect value considerably. Patterns, colours and sizes are all important. Symmetry in design and unusual or very bright colours have proved consistently popular. Chips, scuffs, marks and play wear will reduce value, particularly of machine-made marbles, or if the marble's pattern is affected. Marbles in truly mint condition can be worth up to double the value of a worn example.

A German handmade Joseph's Coat marble.

This type of marble has many tightly packed thin multicoloured strands under a very thin surface layer of clear glass.

c1880-1920   0.75in (2cm) diam

£50-70   **AB**

A German handmade pink Onionskin marble.

c1880-1920   0.75in (2cm) diam

£20-30   **AB**

A German handmade Custard Swirl marble.

c1880-1920   0.75in (2cm) diam

£40-50   **AB**

A German handmade Latticinio Core Swirl marble, with an alternating colour core.

c1880-1920   1in (2.5cm) diam

£40-60   **AB**

A German handmade Divided Core marble.

c1880-1920   1.75in (4.5cm) diam

£100-150   **AB**

A German handmade Latticinio Core Swirl marble.

c1880-1920   1.25in (3cm) diam

£50-70   **AB**

A German handmade Solid Core Swirl marble.

c1880-1920   1in (2.5cm) diam

£25-30   **AB**

A German handmade Coreless Swirl marble.
c1880-1920   *0.75in (2cm) diam*
£8-12   **AB**

A German handmade Banded Swirl marble.
c1880-1920   *0.5in (1.5cm) diam*
£5-10   **AB**

A German handmade Indian Swirl marble, with white, green, blue and purple bands.

Indian marbles have black bases. The greater the variety of colours in the swirls, the more valuable it is likely to be.
c1880-1920   *0.75in (2cm) diam*
£20-30   **AB**

Three German handmade 'End of Day' Onionskin marbles.

Rather than indicating they were made at the end of a glassmaker's day, as the term usually implies, 'End of Day' here indicates that the marble was made with stretched flecks of left-over glass rather than rods.
c1880-1920   *0.75in (2cm) diam*
£50-70 (each)   **AB**

A German or American handmade Transitional Oxblood marble.
c1880-1910   *0.75in (2cm) diam*
£250-350   **AB**

EXPERT EYE – A MICA MARBLE

The glass rod used to make the marbles was rolled in mica chips, which give a glittering effect, before being coated in another layer of glass.

The mica chips usually run through the marble, with distinct sections, known as 'panels', being very rare.

Red is a very rare colour, most are colourless.

The spread of the mica chips within the panels, and the panels themselves, are even and symmetrical, which makes this example appealing.

A German floating panelled Mica Onionskin marble.
c1880-c1920   *1.25in (3cm) diam*
£2,000-2,300   **AB**

An American Christensen Agate Company 'Cobra' marble.

With its tornado-like interior swirl, this is a very rare marble.
1927-29   *0.5in (1.5cm) diam*
£1,000-1,500   **AB**

MARBLES

A German or American handmade Clearie marble.

c1880-1920   *0.5in (1.5cm) diam*

£8-12   **AB**

An American handmade Melted Pontil Transition marble.

c1880-1910   *0.75in (2cm) diam*

£40-60   **AB**

EXPERT EYE - A GUINEA MARBLE

Guineas are among the most desirable and rarest machine-made marbles.

Bases are usually transparent, with colourless being very common, amber and blue being less so, and green and red being the rarest.

They are characterised by their random stretched flecks and blotches of multicoloured glass that cover the surface. The manufacturers named them for the colours on the Guinea cocks roaming around the factory yard.

Reproductions are known, so always compare to an original or seek professional advice.

An American Christensen Agate Company machine-made Guinea marble.

c1927-29   *0.75in (2cm) diam*

£150-220   **AB**

An American Peltier Glass Company machine-made Clear Rainbow marble.

c1930-1935   *0.75in (2cm) diam*

£8-12   **AB**

An American Peltier Glass Company machine-made National Line Rainbow 'Flaming Dragon' marble.

National Line Rainbow marbles are renowned for their vibrant colours and are among the most popular produced by Peltier. Their often unusual names have been given by collectors.

c1925-32   *0.75in (2cm) diam*

£30-50   **AB**

An American Akro Agate Company machine-made Limeade marble.

Marble names with 'ade' suffixes contain uranium, which makes them glow under ultra-violet light.

0.75in (2cm) diam

£30-50   **AB**

An American Christensen Agate Company machine-made swirl marble.

c1928-29   *0.5in (1.5cm) diam*

£12-20   **AB**

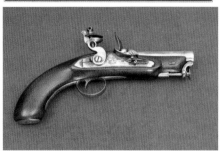

A 73rd Highlanders regimental engraved silver medal, the obverse with crowned "GR", "73" above and "Second Battn. Highlanders" below, the reverse inscribed "A Reward for Military Merit given by the Officers to John Williams 1816, Mangalore", with fixed ring suspension, in excellent condition.

£500-600 DNW

An 1821 Coronation silver medal, naming Jno. Tripp, First Regiment, Buckinghamshire Yeomanry Cavalry Hussars, pierced, with ring suspension, minor edge bruising, in good condition.

£200-300 DNW

An Indian General Service medal, with one clasp "Burma 1889-92", naming 2831 Private J. Edmons Second Battalion Oxfordshire Light Infantry, in very good condition, with damaged card box of issue.
1854-95

£250-350 DNW

A Board of Trade silver medal for Gallantry in Saving Life at Sea, naming Paul Holland Millar, unmounted, minor edge bruise, in excellent condition.

£700-800 DNW

A Llandudno Commemorative bronzed metal plaque, moulded in raised letters "The Urban District of Llandudno" and engraved "Robert Jones, Private, R.W.F.", set on a wooden base, in very good condition.
1914-19   Base 12in (30cm) wide

£180-220 DNW

A silver presentation cigarette case, with regimental badge to lid, engraved inside "Presented to Colonel RND Frier MC by the officers The Assam Regimental Centre", hallmarked "S&BM", Birmingham.
1946   6.25in (16cm) high

£100-150 W&W

A late 19thC Shepard Hardware Co. cast iron 'Uncle Sam' mechanical money bank, designed by Charles Shepard and Peter Adams and patented on 8th June 1886.

Pushing the button makes a coin in Sam's hand drop into his bag. His jaw also moves throughout.

£600-800   BER

An American J. & E. Stevens Tammany cast iron money bank, with sliding coin trap, marked 'put a coin in his hand and see how promptly he pockets it and how politely he bows his thanks', some chips to paint and wear to edges, otherwise in good condition.

c1870   6.5in (17cm) high
£35-45   VEC

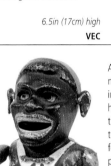

A Starkie's Jolly N aluminium money bank, marked 'place coin in the mans hand and push lever, he raises his arm and swallows the coin as his eyes roll down, tongue flips in and ears rotate forward', some paint loss, particularly to edges, otherwise in good condition.
c1920   7in (18cm) high
£50-80   VEC

A Sydenham & McOustra cast iron 'Save And Smile' money bank, with black finish, painted eyes and lips.
4in (10cm) high
£100-150   BER

A National Products burgundy painted diecast metal 1947 Chevrolet Fleetline promotional automobile money bank, with silver details and impressed wording reading "Chevrolet Grand Rapids, MICH".
6.5in (16.5cm) long
£100-150   BER

A 1950s cast metal rocket and moon 'Strato Bank', with transfer for the 'Midstates Federal Savings & Loan Association'.
8.25in (21cm) long
£60-90   AEM

An 1850s-60s St Louis double clematis paperweight, with amber ground and pink flower.

2.25in (5.5cm) diam

£550-650   BGL

A 1970s Perthshire paperweight, with blue ground and millefiori rods arranged in a chain-link star, with factory paper label to base.

2.25in (6cm) diam

£100-150   BGL

A unique William Manson footed 'Strawberry Patch' paperweight, signed to the base "William Manson SNR 1/1 1999 Joyce Manson", with paper label to base.

2.75in (7cm) diam

£80-120   BGL

A Joe St Clair 'Kewpie' sulphide marble or sphere, the colourless glass containing a moulded three-dimensional hand-painted figure, signed.

Great skill is needed to produce sulphide marbles containing porcelain-like forms. The form must be at the same temperature as the glass, otherwise the paperweight or sphere will crack, and the form must be carefully cased to avoid trapping air bubbles.

2in (5cm) diam

£100-150   BGL

A David P. Salazar 'paperweight style' sphere, with hot-worked forms of a butterfly over a pink hibiscus flower and cut faceted sides, signed.

Salazar is the most noted exponent of the Californian 'painting with glass' technique. The facet cuts, known as 'six and one' due to their arrangement, are a rare feature.

2in (5cm) diam

£120-180   BGL

ESSENTIAL REFERENCE

- Waterman, Parker, Montblanc and Dunhill Namiki remain the most sought-after brands, with large pens and early precious metal-covered examples being particularly valuable. Fine examples of Dunhill's 1930s maki-e lacquer models occupy the pinnacle of the market. Pens from lesser known companies that are now closed, such as Conklin, De La Rue and Mabie Todd are also collectable, although these generally attract lower prices.
- Collectors have traditionally been most interested in pens produced in their own countries, yet with a maturing market and increasing prices, this has recently changed. Those interested in pens are now looking further afield and, with the help of internet trading, are adding formerly less appreciated brands to their collections. England's Conway Stewart, for example, is now proving popular on both sides of the Atlantic. More modern pens, such as the Parker 75,

are also receiving greater attention.

- Modern limited editions are often produced in large numbers and are only of value if kept in pristine condition with their boxes and paperwork. Used examples are less desirable and collectors should look for early editions, such as Parker's 'Spanish Treasure' and 'Hall of Independence', or editions produced in smaller numbers, ideally under 1,000.
- Condition and completeness are paramount. As many collectors use their pens, they should be in working order. Avoid cracked or chipped examples and try to ensure that replaceable parts, such as nibs and clips, are correct.
- Fountain pens were mass-produced before the ballpoint became universal and many standard pens are worth under £20, even with original gold nibs. However, those at the lower end of the market can still make useful and interesting writing instruments.

An exceptionally rare American Parker 51 Blue Diamond 'Red Band' button-filling pen, with red housing and medium nib, in mint condition with a used gold-filled Custom cap.

The 'Red Band' 51 is extremely rare as it was only made between July 1946 and late 1947. It used a new, supposedly quick, button-filling mechanism attached to the barrel by a red collar – hence its nickname. However, this collar tended to split with use and any other problems with the pen (such as a nib replacement) required its removal, as the nib hood was fixed to the barrel.
1946-47

£500-600   BLO

An American Parker 51 Blue Diamond Vacumatic-filling pen, Buckskin body with gold-filled Custom cap, 'jewel' clip screw and barrel tassie and medium nib, in very good condition.

1945

£180-220   BLO

A mid-1940s American Parker 51 Blue Diamond Classic De Luxe Vacumatic-filling pen, burgundy body with brushed stainless steel 'wedding ring' cap and fine nib.

£60-90   BLO

A 1950s English Parker 51 Custom pen, burgundy body with rolled gold Insignia design cap and fine nib, in 'inked mint' condition, with remains of chalk marks.

In used condition, particularly with any signs of wear, this pen is usually worth around £20-30.

£100-150   BLO

An American Parker Demi-51 Custom pen, Plum Lucite body with gold-filled Custom cap and medium nib, in very good condition.

Plum is by far the rarest of the standard 51 colours and was only produced in the USA for a couple of years.
1949

£120-180   BLO

A new-old-stock 1970s American Parker 51 Custom MkIII pen and ballpoint duo set, black body with gold-filled Insignia design cap, metal clip screw and fine nib, in mint condition, with tag on the pen.

£100-150   BLO

PENS & PENCILS

An English Parker 61 Custom pen, black body with gold-filled Insignia design cap and medium nib, in excellent condition with remains of chalk marks on barrel.
1962-67

£60-80   BLO

An English Parker 61 'Heirloom' capillary action-filling pen, Vista Blue body with pink and green rolled-gold 'Rainbow' cap and medium nib, in near mint condition with chalk marks.
c1964-67

£100-150   BLO

An American Parker 61 'Legacy' capillary action-filling pen, grey body with nickel and silver 'Rainbow' cap and medium nib, assembled from mint new-old-stock parts, but later Classic barrel with chalk marks.

Parker's three Rainbow caps are hard to find, particularly in good condition, as they were easily scratched and worn. The Legacy is by far the rarest of the three, as it was only produced for two years.
1957-59

£70-90   BLO

An English Parker 61 Custom Insignia duo pen set, rolled gold barrel and cap with Insignia design, and medium nib, together with matching push-cap ballpoint, in mint condition, with swing tag on pen.

Examine these pens all over for engraved names, serious scratches or dents, as these will reduce this value.
1966-68

£70-100   BLO

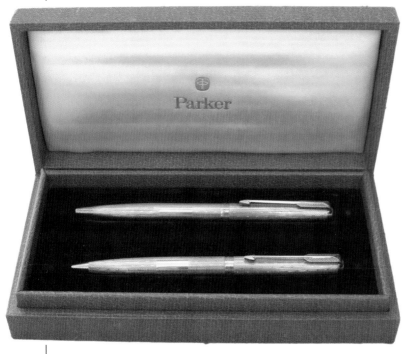

An English Parker 61 Presidential 9ct gold 'Waterdrop' pattern ballpoint pen and propelling pencil, in Parker duo Presidential presentation box, in near mint condition, London hallmarks for 1965.

£400-500   BLO

A 1960s English Parker 61 Custom Heirloom capillary action-filling pen, dark grey body with yellow and brown rolled gold Rainbow cap, fine nib, in excellent condition.

While only being worth around £20-30 on its own, this style of Parker 61 presentation box is very rare.

£80-120   BLO

A rare English Parker 61 Consort cartridge/convertor-filling pen trio set, black body with rolled gold Consort pattern (horizontal and vertical line) cap, fine nib, and with matching push-cap ballpoint and rotary pencil, in Parker trio hard box, in near mint condition, box excellent.
1967-69

£180-220   BLO

A French Parker 75 Laqué duo pen set, Jasper Red Quartz barrel and cap with Parker .585 France fine nib, together with matching push-cap ballpoint, in mint condition, with tag on pen.
1979

£120-180   BLO

A rare French Parker 75 Laqué duo pen set, Malachite green cap and barrel, with fine nib unit and matching push-cap ballpoint, very good but has replaced American nib unit.
1980

£80-120   BLO

A new-old-stock French Parker 75 'Godron' pattern pen, gold-plated cap and barrel, with flat clip screw and barrel tassie, "20¬µ" mark, broad gold-plated section ring with '0' reference and Parker .750 France medium nib, inked mint.

A rare example of an early Parker 75 made at Meru, in France, retaining the flat tassies found on the first series of pens, and using the ¬µ symbol to indicate the thickness of gold electroplate. These features were phased out during the early to mid-1970s.
c1968-71

£300-400   BLO

A slightly rare mid-1970s French Parker 75 Place Vendôme 'Flammé' pen, gold-plated cap and barrel, with (slightly later) Parker .585 France fine nib, in mint condition.

£80-120   BLO

A late 1970s French Parker 75 Place Vendôme 'Perlé' pattern pen, gold-plated cap and barrel with line-and-dot design, with plain cartouche on the cap, and Parker .585 France broad nib, in mint condition.

£120-180   BLO

A 1970s French Parker 75 Flighter pen, satin-finish brushed steel barrel and cap with chrome clip, blue cap decal and titanium nib, a rare variation, in excellent/near mint condition.

£80-120   BLO

A late 1960s American Parker 75 Vermeil 'Ciselé' pattern duo pen set, marked "Sterling & 14k gf" with flat clip screws and barrel tassies, section ring with '0' reference, and Parker 14k USA code 66 [medium] nib, with matching propelling pencil in hard box, with booklet and card outer, in near mint/mint condition, a rare finish.

This vermeil version of the Ciselé finish is rarer than the plain sterling silver version also on this page. The pens have a satin matte finish when new and become shinier through use.

£200-300   BLO

A new-old-stock late 1960s American Parker 75 'Ciselé' pattern duo pen set, marked "Sterling silver Made in U.S.A.", with flat clip screws and barrel tassies, '0' reference on the section ring and Parker 14K USA code 65 [fine] nib, with matching rotary pencil, in Parker 75 box with leaflet 'From a Thrifty Scot', and card outer box, in mint condition.

£180-220   BLO

A limited edition English Parker 75 'R.M.S. Queen Elizabeth', from an edition of 5,000, green patinated brass, salvaged from the sunken luxury liner, with Parker 14K point medium nib, in velvet-lined wooden presentation case with brass plaque, card sleeve, key, certificate of authenticity, 75 leaflet, facsimile invitation, and rare Business Reply card in place of the usual envelope, pen inked mint.
1977

£600-700   BLO

A rare American Parker model 45 eyedropper-filling pen, with faceted mother-of-pearl barrel overlay, two chased gold-filled bands and matching cap crown, with Parker Lucky Curve Pen 3 broad nib, in very good condition.

Check the mother-of-pearl overlay carefully as replaced panels, identifiable by their different colour and signs of adhesive, will reduce the value.
1905-18

£700-900

BLO

A very rare American Parker baby Jack-Knife Safety eyedropper-filling pen, with Bakelite barrel and hard rubber cap, Parker 'lazy S' Lucky Curve Pen 2 nib, in very good condition.

Originally designed as in-store demonstrators, these transparent barrelled pens were popular with the buying public as it was easy to tell how much ink was left. They were put into general production in a number of sizes.
1914-25

£800-1,200

BLO

An American Parker model 16 eyedropper-filling pen, gold-filled three-leaf filigree overlay signed on the barrel overlay, with Parker Lucky Curve Pen 2 nib, crack in hard rubber of cap lip, with scarce three-leaf filigree used on late production of this model.
c1917-25

£180-220

BLO

A very rare American Parker sub-Junior Vacuum-filling pen, the burgundy pearl laminated celluloid lockdown-filler with "Parker Vacuum-filler" imprint, pearl section, and two-colour Arrow medium-firm nib, barrel broken at a hoop and repaired, black blind cap.

During development and early test-marketing this range was known as the Vacuum-Filler, but was renamed the more succinct Vacumatic not long after it went into general production. These early examples are popular with collectors today.
1932-33

£80-120

BLO

An American Parker oversize Vacumatic filling pen and similar Canadian pencil, the pen with silver pearl laminated celluloid, with pearl section, aluminium lockdown-filler and two-colour arrow nib, in Parker duo box, in very good condition, pencil engraved.
1935

£180-220

BLO

An American Parker oversize Vacumatic filling pen, burgundy pearl laminated celluloid lockdown-filler, with pearl section, cap crown and tassie, and later small two-colour medium oblique Arrow nib, professionally restored.

These 'oversize' Vacumatics are the most valuable of the standard range. The nib has been replaced with a smaller and later example, which reduces the value.
1936

£180-220

BLO

A rare American Parker sub-Junior Vacumatic filling pen, solid Jet black celluloid lock-down plunger-filler with short section and Parker USA Arrow broad nib, cap lip slightly shortened, minor brassing.

Parker made a small number of 'opaque' or solid colour Vacumatics, thought to have been discontinued by 1936 because the public preferred the laminated Vacumatics, which catered for the 1930s craze for visible ink supply. The lock-down plunger was discontinued in 1937, however, it would seem that Parker retained it for this model at least, as the short size of a lock-down filler was in keeping with the reduced proportions of the rare 'sub-Junior' model.
1939

£60-80

BLO

An American Parker Slender-Maxima Blue Diamond Vacumatic filling pen, golden pearl laminated celluloid aluminium speedline-filler, 'wedding band' cap band, Parker U.S.A. arrow fine nib, in very good condition, with three initials on cap band.
1940

£70-100

BLO

An American Waterman's 414 silver 'Filigree' pattern eyedropper-filling pen, three-leaf filigree overlay signed "Sterling" on the barrel, with Clip-Cap and Waterman's 4 nib, in Waterman's hard eyedropper box, in very good condition.
1908-15
£200-250   **BLO**

An American Waterman's 452 1/2 silver 'Hand-Engraved Vine' pattern lever-filling pen, marked "Sterling" on cap, barrel, clip and lever, with matching 'hand engraved' clip and lever, and Waterman's 2 medium-fine nib, three initials, tiny bruise in crown, otherwise in very good condition.
1924-27
£150-200   **BLO**

An American Waterman's 552 1/2 LEC gold 'Basketweave' pattern lever-filling pen, marked "14kt" on clip, cap, barrel and lever, with Waterman's Reg US 2 nib, in excellent condition, three initials.

LEC stands for 'Lower End Covered' and indicates that the metal barrel overlay extends to cover the end of the barrel. Some patterns can be found in either version, others, such as Hand Engraved Vine have only been found with 'LEC'.
1928-30
£220-280   **BLO**

A very rare American Waterman's 58 'Cardinal' lever-filling pen, cardinal red hard rubber, with Clip-Cap and Waterman's 8 medium nib, in Waterman's blue and cream hard box, but imprints faint, and hairline crack in cap through clip rivets.
1924-27
£450-550   **BLO**

An exceptionally rare English Waterman's 58 'Barleycorn' pattern lever-filling pen, silver overlaid black hard rubber with hallmarked cap and barrel, 'Ideal' clip, and hallmarked 14ct gold Waterman's Canada 8 broad nib, London hallmark, in Waterman's box, in excellent condition.

An outstanding example of Waterman's largest lever-filler with a precious metal overlay. This pen is so rare it does not appear in Waterman's catalogues of the time and, therefore, must have been made as a custom order or special production.
1927
£4,000-5,000   **BLO**

A Canadian Waterman's 94 'Steel Quartz' (red-flecked grey marble) lever-filling pen, with chrome trim and Waterman's 4 medium nib, engraved name and light surface marks, generally in good to very good condition.

1934-39
£40-60   **BLO**

A Canadian Waterman's 92 'Silver Lizard' lever-filling pen, silver pearl 'lizardskin' celluloid with Waterman's Canada 2 oblique medium nib, in excellent condition.
1931-34
£220-280   **BLO**

An American Waterman's Hundred Year lever-filling pen, smooth red transparent body with triple cap band, with medium Hundred Year Pen nib, cap lip shortened.

A popular model with collectors, always check the cap lip as they are often cracked, or have been shortened. Also check the transparent barrel end, which is prone to cracking or 'crystallisation'. Examples with replaced barrel ends can also be found. The oversized version is particularly desirable.
c1941
£70-100   **BLO**

An American Mabie, Todd & Bard half-overlaid Swan eyedropper-filling pen, marked "Sterling" on the 'Scroll Chased' pattern overlay, with hard rubber over/underfed Swan nib, in Mabie, Todd & Bard hard presentation case, in very good/excellent condition.

An unusual variation of this attractive pattern, with 'C' scrolls rather than 'snail' whorls.
1890s-1906
£700-1,000   **BLO**

A rare English Mabie, Todd & Co. Swan 9ct rose-gold 'Rosette' pattern [265/19] Self-Filler, with gold section and Swan 2 broad nib, three initials and seam split in cap, London hallmark, in leather case.

A rare example of a precious metal Self-Filler made in England; most lever-fillers were made in the USA, with metal overlay production in the UK concentrating on the top-line Leverless filling system introduced in 1934.
1933

A rare 1920s English Mabie, Todd & Co Swan Eternal 444B/61 lever-filling pen, mottled red and black hard rubber with Swan Eternal 4 medium nib, in very good condition.

£150-200   **BLO**   **£150-200**   **BLO**

A Mabie Todd & Co Swan Leverless L112/49 pen, with 'Mother O' Pearl' celluloid barrel and cap, and Swan No.1 broad nib.

This is a rare pen, however the usual darkening to the plastic and two engraved initials, reduces the value.
1937-40

A English Mabie, Todd & Co. Blackbird Self-Filler BB2/46 lever-filling pen, 'Oriental Blue' light blue and dark blue with bronze-gold marble celluloid, with Blackbird 14ct medium nib, in excellent condition.
1934-37

£200-250   **BLO**   **£30-40**   **BLO**

An English Mabie Todd & Co Blackbird BB2/45 lever-filling pen, with greenish silver and black marbled celluloid, and Blackbird medium-oblique nib, in near mint condition.

A Mabie Todd & Co Swan Leverless L312/88 twist-filling pen, with green lizardskin celluloid with later Swan 3G medium nib, excellent, restored.

This attractive celluloid is prone to opening up along the seams, particularly on the cap, so always inspect examples carefully.
c1937

c1937

£70-100   **BLO**   **£120-180**   **BLO**

An English Mabie Todd & Co. un-numbered pearl grey snakeskin and green veined celluloid Self-Filler, with chrome trim and narrow cap band, with Swan No.1 fine nib, mint new-old stock.

A Mabie Todd & Co 'Le Merle Blanc' pen, with silver and black marbled celluloid with chrome trim, and Warranted 14ct broad nib, in mint condition.

This pen was produced for export to the French market, as indicated by the partially French barrel imprint. This is the same form as Mabie Todd's 'Big Blackbird' series, which is very hard to find, particularly in multicoloured celluloid.
c1937

c1937

£30-40   **BLO**   **£150-200**   **BLO**

A 1920s American Le Boeuf Unbreakable 40 ringtop lever-filling pen, black and ivory striped celluloid, in excellent condition but lacks nib and feed.
£40-60 BLO

A late 1920s American Le Boeuf 80 lever-filling pen, bronze and black marble celluloid with Le Boeuf Springfield Mass 6 nib, in very good to excellent condition.
£280-320 BLO

A rare late 1920s American Le Boeuf Unbreakable 75 lever-filling pen, 'tiger's eye' celluloid with Le Boeuf Springfield, Mass. 8 fine nib, brassing on band, otherwise in excellent condition.
£220-280 BLO

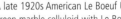

A late 1920s American Le Boeuf Unbreakable 75 lever-filling pen, jade green marble celluloid with Le Boeuf Springfield, Mass. 8 fine nib, slight discolouration.
£150-200 BLO

A very rare late 1920s American Le Boeuf Unbreakable 75 lever-filling pen, 'cocobolo' celluloid with Le Boeuf Springfield, Mass. 8 medium nib, barrel threads replaced with similar celluloid.
£180-220 BLO

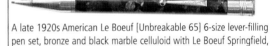

A late 1920s American Le Boeuf [Unbreakable 65] 6-size lever-filling pen set, bronze and black marble celluloid with Le Boeuf Springfield, Mass. 6 fine nib, and similar rotary pencil, pen in excellent condition, pencil in very good condition.
£220-280 BLO

A late 1920s American Le Boeuf Unbreakable 40 ringtop lever-filling pen, grey-white swirl celluloid with black trim and Le Boeuf 4 nib, in near mint condition.
£100-150 BLO

A rare American Le Boeuf 'Asperges' holy water sprinker, black celluloid with cruciform clip, in excellent condition.
c1930
£200-300 BLO

ESSENTIAL REFERENCE – LE BOEUF

An American Le Boeuf 8-size sleeve-filling pen, pearl and black marble celluloid with one-piece sleeve and Le Boeuf-pattern medium stub nib with 'p' imprint only, in very good to excellent condition, a rare large size.

The Le Boeuf Fountain Pen Company was founded by Frank Le Boeuf in 1918, in Springfield, Massachusettes. Due to a patented manufacturing process, Le Boeuf were able to produced pens in plastics not used by other companies and it is these unusual, jewel-like plastics that the company is prized for today. As the company was forced to close due to bankruptcy in 1933, examples are scarce today. As with all vintage celluloid, the material can become brittle over time, so always check examples carefully for cracks and chips.
c1930-32
£400-500 BLO

PENS & PENCILS

An American Aiken Lambert 2-size 'Golpheresque' eyedropper-filling pen, gold-filled overlay on a black hard rubber barrel and cap with black cap crown, Aiken Lambert Co. No. 2 nib, in very good condition, light wear to plating.
c1910
£120-180   **BLO**

An American Carters Superwear 9223 lever-filling pen, green celluloid with Carter's Superwear Pen medium nib, in near mint or mint condition.
1928-30
£120-180   **BLO**

An American Conklin Endura Senior lever-filling pen, Sapphire Pyroxlin with red bands and Conklin Toledo medium crescent nib, in excellent condition, with a bright, clean colour.
1926-30
£300-350   **BLO**

An English Conway Stewart 60, blue and black herringbone with Duro medium-fine nib, in very good condition, with remains of price sticker.
1958-63
£80-120   **BLO**

ESSENTIAL REFERENCE – MAKI-E LACQUER PENS

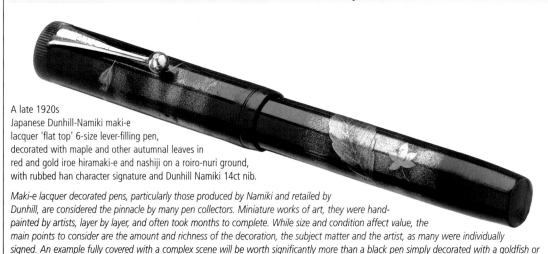

A late 1920s
Japanese Dunhill-Namiki maki-e
lacquer 'flat top' 6-size lever-filling pen,
decorated with maple and other autumnal leaves in
red and gold iroe hiramaki-e and nashiji on a roiro-nuri ground,
with rubbed han character signature and Dunhill Namiki 14ct nib.

Maki-e lacquer decorated pens, particularly those produced by Namiki and retailed by Dunhill, are considered the pinnacle by many pen collectors. Miniature works of art, they were hand-painted by artists, layer by layer, and often took months to complete. While size and condition affect value, the main points to consider are the amount and richness of the decoration, the subject matter and the artist, as many were individually signed. An example fully covered with a complex scene will be worth significantly more than a black pen simply decorated with a goldfish or bird. The use of other materials, such as mother-of-pearl (aogai) and silver plaques, also adds to the value.

5in (13cm) long

£1,800-2,200   **L&T**

A 1920s Canadian Eclipse gold-filled filigree lever-filling pen, with three-leaf design and warranted medium nib, in very good condition.

£50-80   **BLO**

An American Moore gold-filled filigree safety filling pen, signed "Moore's" around the post and with Heath mark on cap and barrel, with The Moore Pen fine nib, minor wear on post.

Filigree overlaid Moore safety fillers are very rare.
c1919
£350-400   **BLO**

A rare 1920s English National Security 'Rosemary' Dinkie-style Casein ringtop, with National Security 14ct gold nib, in near mint condition.

For a long time collectors have speculated that these attractive pens were by Conway Stewart. The discovery of a British Carbon Fibres Ltd instruction leaflet with instructions for both National Security and Rosemary pens confirms that they were manufactured by the same source for the same supplier.

£70-90   BLO

A 1920s American Salz Bros. Peter Pan red mottled hard rubber ring-top eyedropper-filling pen, with Peter Pan nib.

2.25in (6cm) long

£15-25   BB

ESSENTIAL REFERENCE – SHEAFFER PFM PENS

A new-old-stock American Sheaffer's PFM V 'Snorkel' filling pen, black with gold-plated cap and Sheaffer's 14K fine nib, in mint condition.

PFM stands for Pen For Men and was produced in one, man-sized, version. Of the five colours produced, grey is the rarest, having been added to the range late. There were nine variations with differing trim and cap finishes. PFM I came with stainless steel clip, cap band and a Palladium silver nib. PFM II had a solid stainless steel cap with a Palladium nib, and so on, up to the solid gold PFM VIII, which was probably never produced. The Snorkel filling system can be difficult to repair, so only buy from an experienced repairer.

1959-63

£150-200   BLO

An American Sheaffer's PFM III 'Snorkel' filling pen, black plastic with gold-plated trim and Sheaffer 14K fine nib, in excellent/near mint condition.

1959-63

£80-120   BLO

An American Sheaffer Imperial Touchdown trio set, marked "Sterling Silver" with lattice design, and fine nib, with matching rotary pencil and push-clip ballpoint in Sheaffer box with card outer, mint new-old-stock with three stickers.

c1970

£180-220   BLO

An early 1930s American Wahl-Eversharp oversize Gold Seal Equipoised lever-filling pen, jade green Pyrolin, Gold Seal Signature medium nib, a rare pen with light discolouration.

£220-280   BLO

An American Wahl-Eversharp Gold Seal 'Deco Band' lever-filling pen set, pearl and black Pyralin with Gold Seal flexible nib and matching propelling pencil, rare but cap lip crack to band, otherwise in very good condition.

These large, handsome pens were Wahl's answer to Parker's Duofold.

1929-31

£150-250   BLO

A 1940s American Eversharp 'Solid' Skyline lever-filling pen set, brown, with gold-filled Derby and broad band, unusual blue section and Eversharp Skyline medium nib, with matching push-button pencil in Eversharp mock-cloth double box with leaflet, in very good condition.

£70-100 (set)   BLO

An Eversharp 'Coronet', the gold-filled body with Dubonnet Pyralin inlay and Eversharp flexible fine nib, replaced feed and wear to end of barrel, otherwise very good.

£200-300   BLO

A limited edition German Montblanc 'Marcel Proust', from an edition of 21,000, octagonal piston-filling pen, the barrel with engraved silver overlay, dated two-colour 'hourglass' 4810 M nib, boxed with service certificate, in 'inked mint' condition.
1999
£600-900   BLO

A limited edition German Montblanc 'Imperial Dragon' pencil, from an edition of 1,500, with silver dragon clip, in near mint condition.

A fountain pen and ballpoint were also produced but the pencil is the rarest as is was only available as part of a trio set limited to 1,500.
1993
£500-700   BLO

A limited edition German Montblanc 'Oscar Wilde' pencil, from an edition of 12,000, pearl and black resin 0.9mm propelling pencil with vermeil clip marked 925, with box and papers, in near mint condition.
1994
£150-200   BLO

ESSENTIAL REFERENCE – MONTBLANC LIMITED EDITIONS

A limited edition German Montblanc 'Lorenzo de Medici', from an edition of 4,810, faceted piston-filling pen with hand-engraved silver overlay, two-colour 4810 18k M nib, in box with paperwork, pen sealed mint; some wear to box card outers.

This was the first issue from Montblanc's Patron of Arts series and is one of the most sought-after models today. The pens were sold sealed in small plastic bags and examples should still be sealed to be of interest to most collectors. It is also important that the pen retains all of the packaging and paperwork. The edition of 4,810 (the height of Mont Blanc in meters) is relatively small, which helps keep the value buoyant.
1992
£4,000-5,000   BLO

A limited edition Italian OMAS 'Colombo II', 12-sided briar wood finish on black resin, with 1992 section date and two-colour Omas 750 medium nib, in mint condition and boxed.

Made to commemorate the Italian Navy's new sailing vessel 'Colombo II'. Each pen required four months to produce and production was limited to 1992 to 1994, with the year of production being engraved on the section.
1992
£450-550   BLO

A limited edition German Pelikan '1931', from an edition of 5,000, black resin with 18k barrel sleeve marked ag 750, Pelikan 750 18 Karat M nib, in box with paperwork, in mint condition.
1997
£350-450   BLO

A limited edition American Pelikan M800 green 'demonstrator' and K800 ballpoint, from an edition of 3,000, with two-colour 18C-750 medium nib, in mint condition with two Pelikan Collector's Edition boxes and leaflets, with M800 registration card.
1992
£400-500   BLO

A scarce limited production French Waterman Man 100 'Bicentenaire de la Revolution Française' duo set, black, with '1789-1989' clip and cap decal, and two-colour Waterman Ideal medium nib, with matching ballpoint, each mint with papers and boxes with string and wax seal.

This pen was only produced for one year and is sought-after today.
1989
£200-300   BLO

FIND OUT MORE...

'The Fountain Pen: A Collector's Companion', *by Alexander H.I. Crum Ewing, published by Running Press, April 1997.*
'Fountain Pens of the World', *by Andreas Lambrou, published by Philip Wilson Publishers Ltd, 31 Mar 2006.*
'Pens and Writing Equipment: A Collector's Guide', *by Jim Marshall, published by Millers, February 1999.*

ESSENTIAL REFERENCE

- Although the first plastics were developed in the 19thC, it wasn't until the early 20thC that they really came into their own. In 1907, Belgian chemist Dr Leo Baekeland developed Bakelite, which was the first entirely synthetic plastic and came to be known as 'the material of 1,000 uses'.
- Economical to produce, and adaptable, it went on to be used for all manner of decorative and functional domestic wares, and was also used in industry. Today, domestic Bakelite items are the most commonly found items.
- Black, brown, and mottled brown and cream are the most common colours, with red, green and blue being scarcer. Bakelite saw the start of a golden age of plastic that lasted until the 1950s, when cheaper injection moulded plastics took over. Catalin is one of the most desirable forms of early plastic, and is noted for its vibrant colours. It was used to house radio sets and for stylish jewellery, among other uses.
- Always consider style and colour when looking to buy or sell. Items that follow the dominant Art Deco style of the day will always be more popular. Bright, cheerful colours such as cherry red, green and orange are more desirable than dull browns. Decorative items and radios also tend to be more sought-after than kitchenware. Although shallow chips can be polished out, cracks and deeper chips will reduce value dramatically.

Three 1930s Beetlware pink and white mottled jelly moulds.

2.75in (7cm) diam

£2-3 (each)   **MHC**

A 1930s-40s multicoloured urea formaldehyde eggcup and bowl.

4in (10cm) diam

£2-4 (each)   **MHC**

A 1930s 'Bandalasta' ware orange and black marbled trio set, by Streetly Manufacturing for Brookes & Adams, comprising teacup, saucer and side plate.

These were often included in picnic sets. Red and black marbling is the most desirable.

Side plate 6.5in (16.5cm) diam

£10-15   **MHC**

Three 1930s marbled octagonal bakelite napkin rings.

1.75in (4.5cm) diam

£3-5 (each)   **MHC**

A set of six cherry red bakelite napkin rings, four engraved in gilt 'Mummy', 'Andrew', 'Linda' and 'John'.

2in (5cm) diam

£20-25   **P&I**

A 1930s Art Deco mottled brown Bakelite and chrome sprung toast rack, unmarked.

5.5in (14cm) long

£10-15   **MHC**

A 1930s set of silver-plated knives, with orange marbled galalith handles, in original faux leather paper-covered fitted case.

Knives 7.25in (18.5cm) long

£8-12   **MHC**

A Rolls Razor mottled red and black bakelite lidded shaving dish, the base marked "RR102", the lid titled 'The Whetter'.

4in (10cm) diam

£28-32   P&I

A 1930s Stadium mottled plastic pen tray, the base moulded "A Stadium Product British".

9.75in (24.5cm) long

£10-15   MHC

A 1930s yellow and black Catalin lidded box, with ribbed body and stepped lid.

2.5in (6.5cm) diam

£30-40   P&I

A very rare hand-carved black marbled orange Catalin scarab desk accessory or paperweight.

Egyptian themes and motifs became popular after the discovery of Tutankhamun's tomb by Howard Carter in 1922.

c1925   *3.25in (8.5cm) long*

£80-120   PC

EXPERT EYE – A PAIR OF BAKELITE CANDLESTICKS

These large candlesticks were made in a number of different colours and types of mottled Bakelite. The colours on these differ showing they are a matched pair, which reduces the value slightly.

Each candlestick is comprised of four separate pieces that screw together, rather than being made from a single moulded piece. This is indicative of higher quality.

Despite being made in the late 1920s or early 1930s, the style owes more to the Arts & Crafts movement, and even Charles Rennie Mackintosh, than the Art Deco style of the period.

They are rare and deemed classics of Bakelite design.

A pair of Linsden Ware mottled brown bakelite candlesticks, the bases, candle-holders, drip trays and stems screwing together, the bases moulded "Linsden Ware Made in England".

c1930   *14.25in (36cm) high*

£120-180   MHC

A British green and cream marbled plastic 'bowling ball' spirits decanter, with metal foot and moulded brass sculpture of a bowler, opening to reveal six shot glasses with chromed metal dispenser with red bakelite lid.

12.75in (32cm) high

£250-350   QU

A pair of 1950s British Bristol moulded marbled acrylic toilet brushes, in duck-shaped holders.

11in (28cm) high

£180-220   QU

A postcard showing 'Pearks Stores, Leamington Spa', post-dated "9.SP.14".

'Location' postcards that show smaller events, local scenes or buildings that are no longer in existence tend to be more desirable and valuable than examples showing historic buildings that are still standing, or were very well-known, such as churches. Certain towns can also be more popular than others.

5.5in (14cm) wide

£20-25   CANT

A postcard showing '12 O'Clock Street, Sheffield'.

5.5in (14cm) wide

£15-20   CANT

A postcard showing 'Royal Agricultural Show, Doncaster. 191', published by Regina Co.

5.5in (14cm) wide

£8-12   CANT

A 1930s postcard showing 'Royal Edward Dock, Avonmouth', published by J. & C. McKenna.

5.5in (14cm) wide

£6-8   CANT

A WWI postcard showing 'S.S. Iris on War Service later renamed Royal Iris'.

5.5in (14cm) wide

£7-10   CANT

A 'King Orry ashore at New Brighton' postcard.

The King Orry was part of the Isle of Man Steam Packet Co.'s fleet during peacetime, and ran aground at New Brighton due to fog, on 19th August 1921. Amazingly, no damage was done and she floated off on the next tide.

1921   *5.25in (13.5cm) wide*

£12-16   CANT

A postcard showing 'Beta The Army Airship', by F. Scovell & Co.

c1914   *5.5in (14cm) high*

£20-25   CANT

A WWI 'Big Lizzie off to the Boys' postcard, published by T.H. Co., Coventry.

5.5in (14cm) wide

£8-12   CANT

A railway postcard showing 'Salford Priors. 3.', post-dated 12.6.08.

c1908   *5.5in (14cm) wide*

£12-18   CANT

A location postcard of local Brighton celebrity 'Blind Harry'.

Henry Vowles (1861-1919) went blind at the age of three and spent his life entertaining visitors to Brighton by playing musical instruments on the seafront.

5.5in (13.5cm) high

£5-8   LG

A German 'To my Darling' textured and embossed Silka series postcard, published by E.A. Schwerdeleger & Co.

5.5in (14cm) high

20-50p   CANT

A coloured postcard of a young courting couple.

5.5in (14cm) high

50p-£1   CANT

A 1920s-30s German colour lithographed 'Happy Hallowe'en' postcard, showing a boy and pumpkin jack 'o lantern.

1911   *5.5in (14cm) high*

£10-15   SOTT

ESSENTIAL REFERENCE

- Travel posters evoke a sense of the romance, glamour or relaxation of travelling and holidays, with their striking or picturesque images aimed at tempting people away from their working lives. As modes of travel expanded and became more affordable during the mid-20thC, more people were able to afford holidays away from home. Posters were produced to advertise railways, cruise liners, motoring and airlines, as well as general tourism. Most collectors focus on one area, or a single style, such as Art Deco posters.
- The 1910s to '50s was arguably the golden age, before television and other forms of advertising took over from the 1960s onwards. Railways and cruise liners were the first to be widely advertised, with the former being a particularly large market. Cruise liner posters continued into the 1930s, with their heyday being during the Art Deco period, but declined with the introduction of air travel in the 1950s.

- Look out for major names in travel, such as the White Star Line, GWR, LNER, Canadian Pacific, Air France and Pan American. Values are also dependent on leading and influential designers and artists, with names such as (Adolphe Mouron) Cassandre, Jean Carlu and Paul Colin pulling in the highest prices. Many of these worked in a modern or Art Deco style, and posters in these styles tend to be the most sought-after regardless of the designer.
- The image itself is also of vital importance to value. Those that show the excitement or luxury of the mode of travel, and are executed in bright, appealing colours with eye-catching images are likely to be popular.
- Always consider condition. Most posters before the 1970s were folded, and these folds can often be removed by a professional restorer. Tears may also be restored, although any damage to the image itself will reduce the value considerably.

'S.S. France', Richard Rummell French Line, chromolithograph, loss to bottom left corner, tears and creases.

42.5in (108cm) wide

£350-450   ON

'Shaw Savill Line, Cape Town & Table Mountain', by E.J. Waters, printed by Gibbs & Gibbs Ltd, tear to top margin.

39.75in (101cm) high

£300-350   ON

'Union-Castle, South & East Africa', signed illegibly, printed on japan paper by Thomas Forman & Sons Ltd.

1949   *101in (256.5cm) high*

£350-450   VSA

'Aberdeen & Commonwealth Line, England to Australia', by A. Eger, printed by Gibbs & Gibbs, with loss to bottom margin.

40.5in (103cm) high

£500-700   ON

'Holland-Amerika Linie Nieuw Amsterdam', designed by Alphons Dullaart, printed by Johann Enschedé en Zonen.

1949   *37in (94cm) high*

£350-450   VSA

POSTERS

'Holland-Amerika Lijn, S.S.
Statendam', designed by Reyn
Dirksen, printed by Kunstdruk Luii
& Co., Amsterdam.

c1956   37.5in (95.5cm) high

£700-800   **VSA**

'Holland-America
Line', designed by
Frans Mettes.

c1955

95.5in (242.5cm) high

£500-600   **VSA**

'American President Lines,
Bombay', lithographed in the US.

1960   101.5in (258cm) high

£120-180   **VSA**

'American President Lines
Bangkok', designed by J. Clift,
lithographed in the US.

1958   86in (218.5cm) high

£200-300   **VSA**

'American President Lines
Singapore', designed by J. Clift,
lithographed in the US.

1958   86in (218.5cm) high

£250-350   **VSA**

'Europe-Canada Linie M.S. Seven
Seas', designed by Reyn Dirksen.

c1955   96in (244cm) high

£350-450   **VSA**

'SAL – Svenska Amerika Linien', designed by Rittmark, printed on
japan paper by Isacsons, Göteborg, Sweden.

c1935   100in (254cm) high

£3,800-4,200   **VSA**

'Royal Interocean Lines', designed by Teyn Dirksen, printed in Holland.
c1955 92in (233.5cm) high
£550-650 VSA

'United States Lines', designed by Charles Shepherd, printed in England.
c1930 101.5in (258cm) high
£1,200-1,800 VSA

EXPERT EYE – A QUEEN MARY II POSTER

Despite having only been produced four years ago, this poster is already making healthy prices on the secondary market, partly due to the fame of the liner and the recently renewed interest in cruising.

Razzia is the pseudonym for Gerard Courbouleix, who is lauded as one of the finest living poster artists. He does not use a computer for designing, instead painting the original image traditionally.

He has produced work for a number of clients including Louis Vuitton, L'Oreal, Harrod's and Macy's, and may be a hot collecting tip for the future.

His designs are inspired by Surrealism and Cubism, but also the best poster designs from the pre-war golden age. The large ship, angular design, and colours are reminiscent of designs by Adolphe Mouron (Cassandre).

'Cherbourg, Le 14 April 2004, Queen Mary II', designed by Razzia.
2004 176in (447cm) high
£100-150 VSA

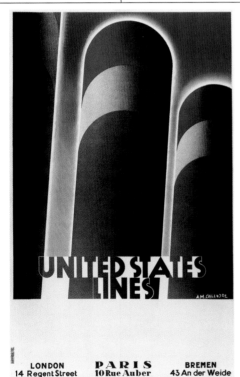

'United States Lines', designed by Adolphe Mouron 'Cassandre' (1901-68), and printed by Hachard, Paris, restoration to folds and edges.

Cassandre's designs draw the attention of collectors, as well as high prices. For more information about this notable poster designer, see the railway poster on P.342.
1928 39.5in (100.5cm) high
£7,000-10,000 SWA

'Fascinating South America', designed by Mark von Arenburg.
c1955 89in (226cm) high
£150-200 VSA

'Ireland Overnight, Dublin via Holyhead – Belfast via Heysham', by Claude Buckle, printed for BR(LMR) by Haycock Press Ltd.
50in (127cm) wide
£280-320 ON

'County Durham', by J.C. Moody, printed for LNER by Jordison & Co. Ltd.

50in (127cm) high

£450-550   ON

'Moulsham Mill, Chelmsford Essex', designed by Wesson, printed for BR(ER) by Jordison & Co. Ltd, folds.

50in (127cm) high

£100-150   ON

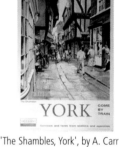

'Norwich', by Rowland Hilder, printed for LNER by Vincent Brooks Day & Son Ltd, mounted on linen.

39.75in (101cm) high

£350-450   ON

'Portrush, Northern Ireland', by Ronald Lampitt, printed for BR(LMR) by Jordison, some folds.

40.25in (102cm) high

£350-450   ON

'The Shambles, York', by A. Carr Linford, printed for BR(NER) by Chorley & Pickersgill Ltd, some folds.

40.25in (102cm) high

£120-180   ON

LOUGH DERG

IRELAND *for* **HOLIDAYS**

BRITISH RAILWAYS

'Lough Derg Ireland for Holidays', by Paul Henry, printed for LMS by Jordison & Co. Ltd.

1949   *40.25in (102cm) high*

£650-750   ON

'Come and Explore Quiet Towns', by S.R. Badmin, printed for 'BT and HA' by Chromoworks Ltd.

1953   *30in (76cm) high*

£220-280   ON

'The Dales of Derbyshire, Monsal Dale and the River Wye', by S.R. Badmin, printed for BR(LMR) by McCorquodale.

40.25in (102cm) high

£400-500   ON

'Skegness is SO Bracing', after John Hassall, printed for the Skegness town council by R. B. Macmillan Ltd.

Hassall's 1908 design was so successful that it was used later by the town council to promote tourism. At this point, the format was made portrait.

'Woodhall Spa', by Frank Newbould, printed for LNER by Vincent Brooks Day Ltd, mounted on linen.

40.25in (102cm) high

£450-550   ON

30in (76cm) high

£60-80   ON

'Skegness is SO Bracing', designed by John Hassall, printed for LNER by Waterlow & Sons Ltd.

This original poster, featuring the 'Jolly Fisherman' is probably the most famous railway holiday poster produced. A number of versions are known, with later examples having the town's pier in the background. Hassall was paid 12 guineas for this design.

c1910   *40.25in (102cm) wide*

£1,000-1,500   ON

'Yorkshire Coast', by Tom Purvis (1888-1959), printed for the LNER by The Dangerfield Printing Co., London, lithograph in colour, linen-backed.

c1930   *50in (127cm) wide*

£800-1,200   BLNY

'Ireland for Holidays', original colour photographic poster, printed for BR(LMR) by The Haycock Press Ltd, with folds.

50in (127cm) wide

£80-120   ON

'InterCity APT, The Shape of Travel to Come', colour photographic poster.

40.25in (102cm) high

£5-8   ON

'Inter-City 125. It's the Changing Shape of Rail', colour photographic poster printed for BR by Impress.

40.25in (102cm)

£7-10   ON

POSTERS

'Vers Le Mont-Blanc', by George Dorival, printed by Lucien Serre & Cie., Paris, lithograph in colours, in near mint condition, linen-backed.

1928   *41in (104cm) high*

£1,500-2,000   **BLNY**

'1962 Emprunt SNCF', designed by Bernard Villemot.

1962   *99.5in (252.5cm) high*

£200-250   **VSA**

EXPERT EYE – A CASSANDRE RAILWAY POSTER

Using the pseudonym 'Cassandre', Adolphe Mouron (1901-68) was a highly influential poster and graphic designer who was influenced by Surrealism and Cubism and became known for his innovative designs.

The railway tracks are used to give a strong sense of perspective, which is a typical feature of Cassandre's designs, they also cleverly suggest distance and travel.

Cassandre frequently used a muted palette of colours. Here he uses black, silver and blue, which summon up steam engines and railways track.

Typography was an important part of his designs, and he developed his own modern font styles, including Bifur and Acier Noir.

'Étoile du Nord', designed by Cassandre (Adolphe Mouron), printed on japan paper by Hachard & Cie, Paris.

£4,500-5,500   **VSA**

'Wank Bahn', designed by Ludwig Hohlwein, printed by Herman Sonntag & Co., Munich.

c1935   *59in (150cm) high*

£280-320   **VSA**

'German Railroads, Safety, Speed, Comfort', designed by Hermann Schneider, printed in Germany, mounted on linen.

c1936   *100.5in (255cm) high*

£150-200   **VSA**

'Far Better Travel By BOAC', by Abram Games, printed in Great Britain, mounted on linen.

1952   30in (76cm) high
£350-450   ON

'L'Europe voyagez par BOAC', by an unknown designer, printed in Great Britain, mounted on linen.

1957   30in (76cm) high
£50-80   ON

'Jet Your Way by B.O.A.C. Around the World', designed by Adelman.

1958   101in (256.5cm) high
£300-350   VSA

'British European Airways – The Key to Europe', by Lee-Elliott, printed by Curwen, dry mounted.

1946   40in (102cm) high
£60-80   ON

'Air France', designed by Edmond Maurus, printed by Goossens Publicité, France, losses and repaired tears to margins.

Air France is a popular airline with a global reputation, and released a large number of well-designed posters that are sought-after today. Maurus was one of their best designers, and is known for his images of planes flying over buildings or locations symbolic of the destination. Africa, shown here was, and continues to be, an important destination for the airline. The bold colours that recall the African desert, and a dizzying feel of perspective and speed also make this a desirable poster.

1947   39.5in (100.5cm) high
£1,500-2,000   SWA

'Swissair', designed by Carlo L. Vivarelli, printed by Fretz Bros. Ltd Zürich.

c1950   102in (259cm) high
£350-400   VSA

'Swissair Coca-Cola OK', printed in Switzerland.

1987   102in (259cm) high
£80-120   VSA

POSTERS

'American Airlines to Boston', by Edward McKnight Kauffer, lithograph in colours, in near mint condition, linen-backed.

1953   40in (102cm) high

£350-450   **BLNY**

'New York – Capital Airlines', by an unknown designer, lithograph in colours, in near mint condition, not linen-backed.

c1960   35in (89cm) high

£550-650   **BLNY**

'New Orleans – Delta Air Lines'.

c1960   71.5in (181.5cm) high

£150-250   **VSA**

'Pan American – The Philippines', designed by A. Amspoker, screen-processed in the US.

1960   89in (226cm) high

£200-300   **VSA**

'Fly TWA – New York', designed by David Klein.

c1955   63.5in (161cm) high

£350-450   **VSA**

'Western Airlines – New York', printed on linen.

c1985   93.5in (237.5cm) high

£100-150   **VSA**

EXPERT EYE – A PAN AMERICAN AIRLINE POSTER

Jean Carlu (1900-97) was a leading French poster designer during the 1920s and '30s, along with Adolphe Mouron Cassandre and Paul Colin.

He trained as an architect, turning to poster design in 1919. He was heavily influenced by Surrealism and Cubist art – inspirations that can be clearly seen in this poster.

He went to the US in 1939 and remained there until 1953, producing a series of posters for Pan Am. He also worked for Air France, Larousse and Firestone.

Posters for the now defunct Pan Am are popular for their typically stylish corporate branding. Combined with the designer and appeal of the design, this is a valuable poster.

'To Paris via Pan American', by Jean Carlu, lithographed in colours, linen-backed.

1954   42.5in (106cm) high

£1,000-1,500   **BLNY**

ESSENTIAL REFERENCE – SKIING POSTERS

'Sports D'Hiver dans les Vosges', designed by Theo Doro, printed on japan paper by C. Courtois Imp., Paris.

Skiing posters have shot up in desirability and value in recent years. Their bold and striking imagery combines the romance of foreign destinations with the excitement of the sport, and appeals to a wealthy international clientele. Certain resorts have more appeal, particularly if well-known as more people will have visited them, leading to greater demand. However, the primary indicator to value is the quality of the image itself. Those suggesting drama, speed, bright sunshine and strong stylization, like this example, tend to be worth more. Rare examples that fulfil these criteria can be worth many thousands of pounds. As most buyers are private individuals looking for a statement piece that displays their fondness for the sport, condition is paramount.

1929   96in (244cm) high

£2,000-3,000   **VSA**

'Österreiche Verkehrswerbung', designed by Paul Kirnig, printed by Christoph Reisser's Söhne, Wien.

1935   95in (241cm) high

£600-700   **VSA**

SWITZERLAND

'Switzerland', photographed by A. Perren-Barberini, printed on linen by Poster Prints, Norristown.

                        90in (228.5cm) high

£450-550   **VSA**

'Switzerland', by Alois Cariget, printed by Eidenbenz- Seitz Co., St. Gall, lithograph in colours, in near mint condition, not linen-backed.

c1950   40in (102cm) high

£400-600   **BLNY**

'Norge', printed by Grøndhal & Søn.

1954   100in (254cm) high

£180-220   **VSA**

'Berner Oberland', designed by Franco Barberis, printed by J.C. Müller, Zürich.

                        102in (259cm) high

£700-800   **VSA**

'Sapada, Dolomite', by an unknown designer, offset lithograph in colours, backed on linen.

c1940   37in (94cm) high

£800-1,000   **BLNY**

'Villars Chesières Switzerland', by
an unknown designer, printed by
Brygger.

40.25in (102cm) high

£150-250   **ON**

'Adelboden Bernese Oberland
4500 Feet Switzerland', by Gyger,
printed by Brugger Ltd.

40.25in (102cm) high

£150-250   **ON**

'Berne, Switzerland', by Reber,
printed by Steiger Ltd.

40.25in (102cm) high

£150-250   **ON**

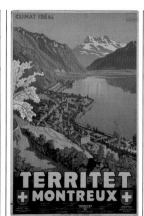

'Territet Montreux, Climat Ideal',
by JEM, printed by Roth & Sauter.

40.25in (102cm) high

£300-350   **ON**

'Schwimmbad Dianabad',
designed by Hans Marek, printed
on japan paper by F. Ademetz,
Wien.

1941   *86in (218.5cm) high*

£650-750   **VSA**

'See America, Welcome to Montana', designed by Richard Halls
(1906-1976), and printed by Works Progress Administration Federal Art
Project, NYC, silkscreened paper, loss to upper right corner.

c1935   *28in (71cm) high*

£3,200-3,800   **SWA**

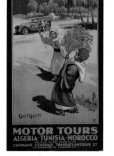

'Pamplona', designed by Fr. de
Sotes, printed by Ortega, Valencia,
minor losses along folds, possibly
trimmed.

1954   *39.25in (99.5cm) high*

£1,000-1,500   **SWA**

'The Magic of Islam, Motor Tours
Algeria Tunisia Morocco', by
E.J. Kealey, printed for Compagnie
Generale Transatlantique Ltd by
Hill Siffken.

39.75in (101cm) high

£700-900   **ON**

ESSENTIAL REFERENCE

- The most popular poster sizes with collectors are the US one-sheet measuring 27in (68.5cm) by 41in (104cm) and the similar UK quad measuring 30in (76cm) by 40in (84cm).
- Posters for films that captured the public's imagination or are considered classics or cult films are among the most popular. Posters for little known or unpopular films are generally less desirable, unless featuring artwork by a particular artist.
- A particularly appealing image or style may add to desirability. Look for designs that sum up the emotion or drama of the film, or portray key characters or scenes.
- Some collectors pursue posters by individual artists, such as Robert Peal or Giuliano Nistri. Saul Bass, who worked with Martin Scorsese, Alfred Hitchcock and Stanley Kubrick on many well-known films, is another popular poster artist.
- Film posters are not subject to any generally recognised grading system, but any form of folding, tear, stain or other damage will have a detrimental effect on value, particularly if the image is affected. However, it can be hard to find a poster in absolutely mint condition, and some damage can be restored. Posters can be professionally backed onto linen or other materials to make them more robust.

- Posters are quite often re-issued if the film is re-released, if it has won an award or following the release of the film on video or DVD. Buyers should be careful that they are not buying a poster for a re-release, instead of an original, as these tend not to be as valuable.
- 'Teasers' are posters produced prior to a film's release and offer another area of interest to collectors. These can be rare and are often of a different design to the main release poster, usually featuring a key image from the film accompanied by a minimal amount of text.
- Posters are produced for each country a film is released in and can have different artwork. Look for posters from the film's country of origin as these generally prove the most popular.
- Fakes and forgeries are increasing in number, and can be hard to spot. Reproductions are much more common. These are often photographic images of the original which have been printed on to shiny poster paper. Gaining familiarity with originals from reputable dealers or auction houses will enable you to recognise a reproduction. The actual image in a forged or reproduced poster may be slightly pixelated or in different tones of colour, which can be a tell-tale sign.

'The African Queen', US one-sheet poster.
1951   *41in (104cm) high*
£300-400   **AAC**

'Dorucak Tifanija' [Breakfast at Tiffany's], Yugoslavian poster, in near mint condition.

This poster, with its iconic image of Audrey Hepburn, has become a classic of film poster design. Desirable in any language, English language examples are the most sought-after and can be worth in excess of £15,000 in large sizes.
1961   *27.5in (70cm) high*
£500-600   **RTC**

'Annie Get Your Gun', US insert card, in very good condition.

1950
36in (91.5cm) high
£220-280   **RTC**

'Boulevard du Crepuscule' [Sunset Boulevard], Belgian poster, linen-backed and in very good condition.
1950   *22in (56cm) high*
£350-450   **RTC**

'British Intelligence', US insert card, in good condition.

1940
36in (91.5cm) high
£150-200   **RTC**

'Buck Rogers', US one sheet poster, artwork by Victor Gadino.

1979   *41in (104cm) high*

£20-30   **AAC**

'Cat on a Hot Tin Roof', US one-sheet poster, linen-backed and in near mint condition.

1958   *41in (104cm) high*

£400-500   **RTC**

EXPERT EYE – A CASABLANCA POSTER

Casablanca is considered one of the greatest films of all time, spawning a number of now legendary phrases, including 'We'll always have Paris" and "Of all the gin joints in town, she walks into mine".

The poster features the two leads, Ingrid Bergmann and Humphrey Bogart in a bold and classic pose.

'Charley's Aunt', US one-sheet poster, linen-backed and in near mint condition.

1941   *41in (104cm) high*

£120-180   **RTC**

This design is the same as the highly desirable US poster, and is one of the more colourful posters produced for the film.

It is backed on linen and is in near mint condition with bright colours and no wear or damage.

'Casablanca', Belgian poster, linen-backed and in near mint condition.

1942   *16in (40.5cm) high*

£1,700-2,000   **RTC**

'City for Conquest', US insert card, in near mint condition.

1940   *36in (91.5cm) high*

£500-700   **RTC**

'Dial M for Murder', US one-sheet poster, linen-backed and in very good condition.

The blood red background and telephone motif with its 'spoken' line add a sense of drama to this poster. The extended hand hints at the fact this film was filmed in 3-D, after the technique had taken hold in 1953. However, the fad had tailed off by the film's release in 1954, and it wasn't until c1980 that the film could be seen in its 3-D glory.

1954   *41in (104cm) high*

£700-900   **RTC**

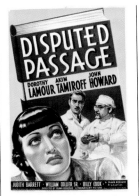

'Disputed Passage', US one-sheet poster, linen-backed and in very good condition.

1939   *41in (104cm) high*

£60-80   RTC

'Doctor Blood's Coffin', US insert poster.

1961   *36in (91.5cm) high*

£25-40   AAC

EXPERT EYE – A DR STRANGELOVE POSTER

The design hints at Pablo Ferro's influential and innovative opening titles to the film, where B-52 bombers are seen refuelling in formation. The wording is hand-drawn in strongly contrasting letters.

The design was by Tomi Ungerer (b.1931), a notable French political, erotic and children's illustrator known for his work with the New York Times and for the anti-Vietnam war campaign.

'Dr. Jekyll and Mr. Hyde', US one-sheet poster, linen-backed and in very good condition.

1941   *41in (104cm) high*

£120-180   RTC

The design is symmetrical, cleverly making the hands around the politician on the right not immediately noticeable.

A recent exhibition of his work included another, more dynamic design for the poster, showing a general pushing a button on his coat as his head explodes.

'Dr. Strangelove', by Tomi Ungerer, US three-sheet poster, in near mint condition.

1964   *81in (205.5cm) high*

£450-550   RTC

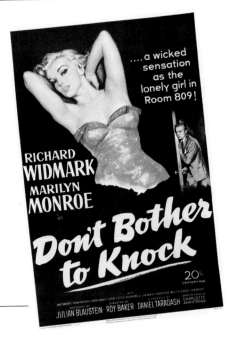

'Don't Bother to Knock', US one-sheet poster, linen-backed and in very good condition.

Ravaged dames were the favoured subject matter of paperback cover artists such as Reginald Heade and F.W. Perle. This particular dame and the positioning of the title echo the covers of these popular books.

'Easter Parade', US insert card, in near mint condition.

1952   *41in (104cm) high*

£300-400   RTC

1948   *36in (91.5cm) high*

£200-300   RTC

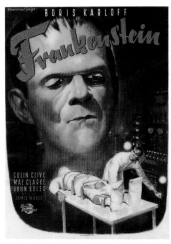

'Frankenstein', German A1 one-sheet poster, linen-backed and in near mint condition.

This is a postwar release of the enduringly popular poster showing Boris Karloff. Posters for horror and science fiction films are among the most sought-after genres, with some originals being worth vast sums. In 1993, an original 1931 Frankenstein film poster, one of only five known, sold for a then record price of £99,000. In 2007, an original Universal lobby card from 1931 fetched over £16,500.

1947   33in (84cm) high

£1,800-2,200   **RTC**

'Far from The Madding Crowd', US half sheet.

1967   28in (71cm) wide

£70-100   **AAC**

'The Gay Falcon', US insert card, in very good condition.

1941   36in (91.5cm) high

£120-180   **RTC**

'Heaven Can Wait', US insert card, in very good condition.

1942   36in (91.5cm) high

£120-180   **RTC**

'How Green Was My Valley', US one-sheet poster, linen-backed and in near mint condition.

1941   41in (104cm) high

£250-350   **RTC**

'Ringaren I Notredame' [The Hunchback of Notre Dame], Swedish one-sheet, in near mint condition.

1939   41in (104cm) high

£1,500-2,000   **RTC**

'The Karate Killers', US insert poster for a Man from U.N.C.L.E. film.

1967   36in (91.5cm) high

£150-250   **AAC**

'Délicieuse' [Mad About Music], Belgian one-sheet poster, linen-backed and in near mint condition.

1938   33in (84cm) high

£70-90   **RTC**

'Ocho Sentencias de Muerte' [Kind Hearts and Coronets], Spanish one-sheet, linen-backed and in near mint condition.

1949   *39in (99cm) high*

£120-180   **RTC**

'King Solomon's Mines', US insert card, in near mint condition.

1935   *36in (91.5cm) high*

£400-500   **RTC**

'Kon-Tiki', US insert poster for the Norwegian film.

So far, this is the only Norwegian film to win an Oscar.

1950   *36in (91.5cm) high*

£20-30   **AAC**

'Lady in the Dark', US one-sheet poster, linen-backed and in near mint condition.

1944   *41in (104cm) high*

£120-180   **RTC**

'Laughing Sinners', US one-sheet poster, linen-backed and in near mint condition.

As well as featuring a stern looking Joan Crawford, the film also starred Clark Gable, further adding to the attraction of this early poster with its bold and striking artwork.

1931   *41in (104cm) high*

£500-600   **RTC**

'The Littlest Rebel', US one-sheet poster, linen-backed and in very good condition.

As well as the strongly patriotic design, this poster shows Shirley Temple, a highly collectable name, who is noted for her dancing in this film. However, the film has since been criticised for its overt racism.

1935   *41in (104cm) high*

£850-950   **RTC**

'Licence To Kill', US insert poster.

1989   *36in (91.5cm) high*

£30-40   **AAC**

'The Lost Weekend', US one-sheet poster, linen-backed and in near mint condition.

1945   *41in (104cm) high*

£400-500   **RTC**

'A Man for All Seasons',
US three-sheet poster,
linen-backed and in near
mint condition.

*This is a rare pre-Oscar
version. The film won six
Oscars including Best
Actor for Paul Schofield,
Best Director and Best
Film and was nominated
for a further two.*

1966   81in (205.5cm) high
£350-500   RTC

'Marie Antoinette', Belgian poster,
in near mint condition.

1938   33in (83.5cm) high
£200-300   RTC

'The Misfits', US one-sheet poster,
linen-backed and in near mint
condition.

1961   41in (104cm) high
£180-220   RTC

'My Gal Sal', US one-sheet poster,
linen-backed and in near mint
condition.

1942   41in (104cm) high
£350-400   RTC

'Monster On The Campus', US
insert poster.

*Also known as 'Stranger on The
Campus', this low-budget film
was the last of Universal's science
fiction/monster films released
before 'Island of Terror' in 1966.*

1958   30in (76cm) high
£25-35   AAC

'Night has a Thousand Eyes', US
insert card, in near mint condition.

1948   36in (91.5cm) high
£200-300   RTC

'The Night of the Hunter', US one-
sheet poster, linen-backed and in
near mint condition.

1955   41in (104cm) high
£250-350   RTC

'Personal Property', US one-sheet poster, linen-backed and in near mint
condition.

1937   41in (104cm) high
£500-600   RTC

'Pillow of Death', US one-sheet poster, linen-backed and in near mint condition.

1945 *41in (104cm) high*

£150-200 **RTC**

'A Place in the Sun', US insert card, in near mint condition.

1951 *36in (91.5cm) high*

£320-380 **RTC**

EXPERT EYE – A US INSERT CARD

This film featured Lana Turner in one of her most memorable roles as a femme fatale Cora Smith, who lures drifter Frank Chambers into a plot to kill her older husband.

The "Their love was a Flame that Destroyed!" wording at the top was used on all the posters and represents the characters' murderous and illicit love.

Turner and Garfield are shown in characteristic poses, with Turner's expression, in particular, hinting at Cora's character.

It is widely considered to be one of the best film noirs ever made, and was a prototype of the erotic thriller genre, so has a large following.

'The Postman Always Rings Twice', US insert card, in near mint condition.

1946 *36in (91.5cm) high*

£1,000-1,500 **RTC**

'Pride and Prejudice', US insert card, in very good condition.

1939 *36in (91.5cm) high*

£250-350 **RTC**

'Raintree County', US insert card, in very good condition.

1957 *36in (91.5cm) high*

£120-180 **RTC**

'The Shining', UK quad poster.

1980 *40in (84cm) wide*

£18-22 **GAZE**

POSTERS

'Smash-Up', US three-sheet poster, linen-backed and in near mint condition.

1925   81in (205.5cm) high

£1,500-2,000   RTC

'Some Like it Hot', Australian day bill poster, linen-backed and in near mint condition.

1959   30in (76cm) high

£350-450   RTC

'A Star is Born', US one-sheet poster, linen-backed and in near mint condition.

1954   41in (104cm) high

£180-220   RTC

'Suddenly Last Summer', UK quad poster, linen-backed and in very good condition.

Despite it being a relatively monochrome poster, this film starred three of the biggest names in Hollywood at the time; Elizabeth Taylor, Katharine Hepburn and Montgomery Clift.

1959   40in (101.5cm) wide

£300-400   RTC

'Too Many Girls', US one-sheet poster, linen-backed and in very good condition.

1940   41in (104cm) high

£250-350   RTC

'White Heat', US insert card, in near mint condition.

1949   36in (91.5cm) high

£500-600   RTC

'Who's Afraid of Virginia Woolf?', US insert card, signed by Elizabeth Taylor, in very good condition.

1966   36in (91.5cm) high

£200-300   RTC

'Ziegfeld Follies', US insert card, in near mint condition.

1946   36in (91.5cm) high

£220-280   RTC

'Beau Geste', US jumbo window card, in near mint condition.

1939   28in (71cm) high
£350-450   RTC

'Double Indemnity', US window card, in very good condition.

The graphics are very similar to those used on mass-produced 'pulp fiction' paperbacks of the period, the stories of which focused on passion and crime.

1944   22in (56cm) high
£500-600   RTC

ESSENTIAL REFERENCE – FILM POSTER SIZES

The most common size of vintage US movie poster is the 'one-sheet', which measures approximately 27x41in (68.5x104cm). After 1983, the size dropped to 27x40in (68.5x101.5cm). Inserts were issued in the US until the 1980s and were 14x36in (35.5x91.5cm) high. Window cards typically feature the same artwork as the movie poster, but were printed on card rather than paper, and measure 14x22in (35.5x56cm). They were used to advertise the film in locations other than movie theatres, such as shops. They typically have a blank area at the top which would bear the details of the cinema the film could be seen at. However, this has been cut off on some. Both inserts and window cards are popular with collectors due to their smaller size. Some inserts are rarer than one sheets.

'Crime School', US window card, paper-backed and in near mint condition.

1938   22in (56cm) high
£750-1,000   RTC

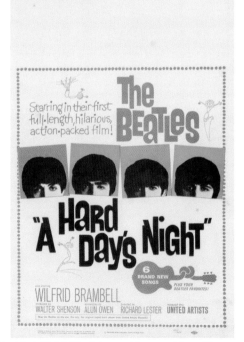

'A Hard Day's Night', US window card, in near mint condition.

1964   22in (56cm) high
£700-800   RTC

'House of Wax', US window card, in excellent condition.

1953   22in (56cm) high
£80-120   RTC

POSTERS

'Niagara', US window card, in excellent condition.

1953   22in (56cm) high
£150-200   RTC

'Once Upon a Time in the West', US window card, in near mint condition.

1968   22in (56cm) high
£250-350   RTC

'Walt Disney's Peter Pan', US window card, in near mint condition.

1953   22in (56cm) high
£80-120   RTC

'Phantom of the Rue Morgue', US window card, in excellent condition.

1954   22in (56cm) high
£80-120   RTC

'The Producers', US window card for the Broadway production, signed by five members of the cast including Matthew Broderick and Nathan Lane, in near mint condition.

2005   22in (56cm) high
£170-200   RTC

'Walt Disney's Saludos Amigos' [Hello Friends], US window card, in excellent condition.

1942   22in (56cm) high
£150-200   RTC

'The Treasure of the Sierra Madre', US window card, in excellent condition.

22in x 14in is the typical size for window cards, but all 'Sierra Madre' window cards are 22in x 13in.

1948   22in (56cm) high
£450-600   RTC

'It's Here!', US promotional poster for the Beatles 'White Album', in near mint condition.

1968   37in (94cm) high

£280-320   **CO**

EXPERT EYE – A RICHARD AVEDON BEATLES POSTER

The posters were commissioned by NEMS, the Beatles' management company and licensed to US magazine 'Look', UK newspaper 'The Daily Express' and German magazine 'Stern'.

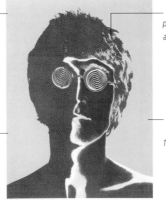

These four posters are from the later US edition of 1967 and are larger in size.

Heavily 'solarised', they reflect the psychedelic styles of the day, as well as Andy Warhol's influential pop art portraits.

They are considered the first major rock star posters. A year later in 1968, Avedon was commissioned to produce portraits for the Beatles' legendary White Album.

'John, Paul, George & Ringo', by Richard Avedon, printed by Cowles Education Corporation, New York, set of four posters (one shown), offset lithographs in colours, in near mint condition, linen-backed.

1967   31in (79cm) high

£2,200-2,800 (set of four)   **BLNY**

'Don't Look Back', by Alan Aldridge & Harry Willock, original UK version, offset lithograph in colours, in near mint condition, linen-backed.

This was produced for the Don Pennebaker documentary that followed Dylan on his 1965 'Don't Look Back' tour of the UK. Released in 1967, it is considered by many to be the best rock documentary ever made. Aldridge is a notable graphic designer and artist within the psychedelic style.

1967   30in (76cm) high

£280-320   **BLNY**

'Ball 67', German concert poster, designed by Gunther Kieser.

1967   36.5in (69.5cm) high

£170-220   **QU**

'Oz', designed by Martin Sharp.

1967   75in (190.5cm) high

£250-300   **VSA**

'Don Pullen Quartet', by Niklaus Troxler, German concert poster, lithographed in colours, printed by Siebdruck Bosch, Luzern.

1978   50in (127cm) high

£300-400   **BLNY**

POSTERS

'Funk Night Willis', by Niklaus Troxler, German colour-lithographed concert poster, printed by Siebdruck Bosch, Luzern.

1987 5in (127cm) high

£250-350 BLNY

'Thelonius Monk', by Niklaus Troxler, German concert poster, lithographed in colours, printed by Siebdruck Bosch, Luzern.

1986 5in (127cm) high

£250-350 BLNY

EXPERT EYE – AN OSIRIS VISIONS POSTER

Psychedelic poster designers of the late 1960s were partly inspired by Art Nouveau styles, hence the curving organic forms and the presence of the lady, although made over in acid colours of the day.

The use of silver and gold metallic inks was common, adding an extra dimension to the visual impact of the design.

Michael English (b.1941) was a notable psychedelic poster designer. In 1967 he joined with Nigel Waymouth to form the legendary 'Hapsash & The Coloured Coat' design team, who worked with Osiris Vision.

Designed in June 1967, this poster was used to advertise a performance at the UFO club, which launched a number of famous bands.

'UFO Coming', designed by Michael English, printed by Osiris Visions Ltd.

1967

£200-300 VSA

ESSENTIAL REFERENCE

- Posters produced in Britain during the two world wars primarily focus on a number of important themes including recruitment, rationing, health, savings and the importance of the Home Front.
- Unlike other countries, officially produced posters generally did not enter the realm of political propaganda by denigrating other nations, but instead promoted the strength of Britain.

- Different themes appeal to different collectors, although savings posters tend to be less desirable. The main indicators to value lie in the artist or designer, and the visual impact and appeal of the image. A striking image will often lead a poster to be as desirable and valuable as one by a notable artist. Rarity also counts. So many variations were produced, and posters were not intended to last, meaning that certain examples can be scarce.

'Troops Who Fly by Night, Buy War Savings', by an unknown designer, printed for HMSO by W.R. Royle & Son Ltd WFP 354.

20in (51cm) high

£120-180   ON

'Salute the Soldier – Save More – Lend More', by Forster, printed for HMSO by Chromoworks Ltd, WFP 345, with small loss to corner.

30in (76cm) high

£12-18   ON

'Soldiers at Sea, Set your Course for War Savings', by an unknown designer, printed for HMSO by W.R. Royle & Son Ltd WFP 356.

It's the mint condition of this poster that helps to make it so valuable.

20in (51cm) high

£220-280   ON

'Keep on Saving, Salute the Soldier', by Elgar, printed for HMSO by Chromoworks, in poor condition with losses.

30in (76cm) high

£5-8   ON

'Roslagens Forsvarsforenings Lotteri', Swedish National Lottery poster, depicting a crouching soldier.

c1925   28in (71cm) high

£70-100   CLG

'Salute the Soldier – Save More – Lend More', by J.A. May, printed for HMSO by Stafford & Co.

39.5in (100cm) high

£20-30   ON

POSTERS

'Well Saved Forces, National Savings', by an unknown designer, issued by National Savings, with creases and loss to one corner.

1945   *30in (76cm) high*

£10-20   **ON**

'He Did His Duty. Will You Do Yours?', by an unknown designer, PRC no. 20, printed by Johnson, Riddle & Co. Ltd, London, S.E., with creases and losses.

30in (76cm) high

£18-22   **ON**

'Men of London, Each Recruit Means Quicker Peace', published by the Central Recruiting Office.

17in (43cm) high

£25-35   **ON**

'Why Drop Out?', designed by Abram Games, in very good condition, with folds.

30in (76cm) high

£350-450   **ON**

'Fly with the RAF – Men Under 33 Can Volunteer', by an unknown designer, photo montage printed for HMSO by J Weiner Ltd.

59.5in (151cm) wide

£30-50   **ON**

'Civil Aeronautics Division', designed by Edward McKnight Kauffer, printed on linen by the US Government Printing Office.

This is typical of the slightly Surreal, Modernist designs produced by McKnight Kauffer (1891-1954). It also recalls designs by Abram Games (1914-96), another notable mid-century and wartime graphic designer, examples of which are also shown on this page.

1943

£800-1,200   **VSA**

'Commando Medical Services' for the Red Cross, designed by Abram Games, with folds.

30in (76cm) high

£700-800   **ON**

'Blood Donors', designed by Abram Games, printed by Field Sons & Co., in excellent condition.

25.5in (65cm) high

£150-200   **ON**

'Get First Aid At Once', by Tom Eckersley, printed by Loxley Bros. Ltd, lithograph in colours, linen-backed.

1943   *29in (74cm) high*

£300-400   **BLNY**

'Air Raid Precautions', by Edward McKnight Kauffer, printed by Fosh & Cross Ltd, London, lithograph in colours, linen-backed.

1938   *29.75in (76cm) high*

£300-400   **BLNY**

EXPERT EYE – A JEAN CARLU WARTIME POSTER

The fact that the efforts of workers on the home front were as important to the war effort as soldiers fighting is clearly shown in this clever design.

The flat planes of bright colours and highly Modern stylization are typical of the designs of Jean Carlu, who was one of the designers responsible for revolutionising poster design between the wars.

The inclusion of the worker is also relevant to Carlu's life as he was staunchly left-wing.

Carlu was inspired by the Cubist art of Albert Gleize and Juan Gris in the early decades of the 20thC.

'Give 'Em Both Barrels', by Jean Carlu, lithograph in colours, linen-backed.

c1916   *20in (51cm) wide*

£400-600   **BLNY**

'Hendon War Display, Only Mass Action Of Workers Can Stop War', by an anonymous designer, in excellent condition.

The grim image and striking choice of colours of this rare poster were intended to shock. It was probably published in the mid-1930s by British Communist Party members in response to the pre-war Air Shows held at Hendon.

                    30in (76cm) high

£850-950   **ON**

'A 2oz Chop Bone will make…', designed by an unknown designer, printed for HMSO by Chromoworks Ltd, with folds, small losses and tears.

60in (152cm) high

£200-300   **ON**

'Freedom is in Peril…' and 'Your Courage…', each red background with white lettering, published by HMSO, in excellent condition with folds.

19.75in (50cm) high

£70-100 (pair)   **ON**

ESSENTIAL REFERENCE

- 20thC Chinese posters show the fascinating social, political and economic history of Communist China, and how it developed with the 'Great Leap Forward' between 1958 and 1960. Earlier posters tend to be traditional in design and imagery, focusing on ancient Chinese stories or characters, or beautiful women and characteristic Chinese landscapes.

- Communism swept away this traditionalism, and introduced internal propaganda posters that were executed in a new modern style using contemporary imagery. Many were based on similar posters from Communist Russia, hence the Western appearance of some faces. One overriding aim was to inspire the people to unite, build themselves up and work not only for their own good, but for the good of the Republic.

- Mao Tse-tung (1893-1976), chairman of the Communist party of China from 1945 to 1976, was commonly depicted, being shown over the decades as a hard political or military leader, a benevolent leader loved by the people, or an almost god-like figure, as time went on. Chinese military power was also a popular topic, particularly in relation to the perceived threat from the West.

- The market for these items is still new, meaning values may change as the market develops. Often many thousands of these posters were printed, although sizes of print-runs varied. The quality of paper used was poor, and many are damaged. Iconic or visually powerful imagery is likely to be more desirable, as are key messages. Beware of reproductions, which can often be identified from the printing methods and the type of paper used.

'Sleepless', by Tang Xiu, printed by Cheng Zheng Tai Printing Factory, The French Territory, offset coloured lithograph.

c1925   20.75in (52.5cm) high

£300-450   BLNY

'The New Moon' by Tung Xau, printed by Zhen Xing Printing Factory, offset coloured lithograph.

c1930   30.5in (77.5cm) high

£200-300   BLNY

'The Beauty By The Huang Pu River', by Ying Shi, offset coloured lithograph.

c1930   30.75in (78cm) high

£200-300   BLNY

'Stop the Use of Bio-Chemical Weapons by War Criminals', by An Lin, published by The People's Arts Publishing Company, Beijing.

The text reads that, in December 1949, the Soviet Union Supreme Court tried Japanese war-criminals for the use of bio-chemical weapons.

1952   30.75in (78cm) wide

£750-850   BLO

'Our Motherland is Leaping Forward', by an unknown artist, published by Beijing People's Art Publishing House, printed by Tianjin People's Printing Factory.

1958   30in (76cm) high

£200-300   BLO

'Advance Bravely Holding The Red Flag Of Chairman Mao's Thought Aloft', unknown artist, published by The Pictorial Of The People's Liberation Army Of China, Beijing.

1960   30in (76cm) high

£280-320   BLO

'Obey All the Orders of Chairman Mao', unknown artist, losses to bottom edge and creased edges.

1960s   29.5in (75cm) wide
£80-120   **BLO**

'Policy and Tactics are the Life of the Party, the Leading Comrades of Different Levels Must Pay Attention and Must not be Negligent', by an unknown artist, minor tears and handling creases to the edges.

1960s   30in (76cm) wide
£200-250   **BLO**

'Firmly Support the Justice Struggle of American Black People', by an unknown artist, published by The People's Art Publishing House, Beijing.

The quote is from Mao Tse-tung and reads, "The vicious colonialism and imperialism thrived on the slavery and selling of black people, and will end with the complete liberation of black people".

1963   42.25in (107cm) high
£1,800-2,200   **BLO**

[Female Artillery Soldiers], by an unknown artist, purple staining to centre and creases, loss and repair to the left side and bottom corner.

c1967   30in (76cm) high
£150-200   **BLO**

'The Revolutionary 'Three Combinations' Are the Guarantee to Take Over Power and Win the Success', by an unknown artist, published by Tianjin People's Art Publishing House, Tianjin, several short tears and creases.

1967   30in (76cm) wide
£100-150   **BLO**

'Grasp Revolution and Great Criticism Movement', unknown artist, published by The Shanghai People's Art Publishing House, some damage.

The slogans on the poster reads 'Grasp Revolution, Promote Production' and 'Deeply and Continuously Develop the Great Revolution, Promote Production'.

1969   41in (104cm) wide
£250-300   **BLO**

'People of the World Unite and Defeat the American Invaders and All their Running Dogs', published by The Shanghai People's Publishing House, several tears.

The caption reads: 'All The Reactionaries Are Paper Tigers'.

1970   41.25in (105cm) wide
£600-700   **BLO**

'Chinese Communist Party Members Should be the Advanced Element of the Proletarian Class, unknown artist, folds and creases.

1971   29.5in (75cm) high
£200-250   **BLO**

FIND OUT MORE...

The International Institute of Social History, http://www.iisg.nl/~landsberger/

[The February Revolution of 1917], by Aleksandr Rodchenko, lithograph in colours, backed on paper.

Aleksandr Rodchenko (1891-1956) was an important Russian artist, photographer and graphic designer, and was one of the founders of Constructivism. Many of his powerful images are typified by photomontages and bold planes of colour, as here, and photographs are often taken from striking angles. In 2005, rock group Franz Ferdinand based the cover artwork for their 'You Could Have It So Much Better' album on one of his most famous images.

1925-26   27.5in (70.5cm) high
£1,000-1,500   **BLNY**

[Death to Fascism! Freedom to the People!], by Aleksej Alekseevich Kokorekin (1906-59), lithograph in colours, backed on japan paper.

1944   34.5in (87.5cm) high
£350-450   **BLNY**

Communist Party Politics, issued by the Central Committee of the Communist Party of the Soviet Union to all voters, folds.

1974   39.75in (101cm) wide
£70-100   **ON**

[Alliance for the Struggle for Liberation of the Working Classes], by Aleksandr Rodchenko, lithograph in colours, linen-backed.

1925-26   27in (68cm) high
£1,000-1,500   **BLNY**

[The Cooperative], attributed to Aleksandr Alekseev, lithograph in colours, linen-backed.

1930   40.5in (103cm) high
£500-700   **BLNY**

EXPERT EYE – A RUSSIAN PROPAGANDA POSTER

Valentina Kulagina (1902-87) is considered an important Soviet avant-garde artist and designer, although her husband Gustav Klutsis' work is better known.

This is typical of her style, in terms of its Modern stylization, use of a striking angular line, different spatial areas, and bold colours.

The imagery shows modern workers uniting together like soldiers to defend the USSR - note the factory in the bottom left corner, from which a stream of planes is leaving.

Only a very few posters and designs under her own name are known, making this rare, although she regularly contributed much to her husband's work.

[Defending the USSR], by Valentina Kulagina (1902-87), lithograph in colours, linen-backed.

1930   35.5in (91cm) high
£2,800-3,200   **BLNY**

ESSENTIAL REFERENCE

- Advertising posters promoting products had their golden age from the late 19thC until the late 20thC. The 1920s and '30s were particularly innovative, with a number of prolific designers pushing boundaries and producing innovative and influential designs. Many of these are sought today due to their visual and decorative appeal, as well as for their importance to 20thC poster and graphic design.
- As well as looking for notable artists such as Jean Carlu, Paul Colin or Bernard Villemot, always consider the brand. Posters advertising smoking are becoming more

sought-after as the habit becomes less popular. Those that have large and strong followings will generally be worth more. Images with cross-market interest, such as for cars or cycling, may also prove to be more desirable and valuable.

- Always look for strong images with bold, bright colours, as well as designs that are typical of the period, as these tend to be more popular. Stylized, modern images tend to be more popular, as do those with a sense of humour or witticism.

'Lucky Strike Cigarettes', designed by Baz.

48.5in (123cm) high

£120-180   VSA

'Lucky Strike Cigarettes', designed by Baz.

Ben-Hur Baz (1906–2003) was born in Mexico and became widely know for his designs produced for Esquire magazine during the 1940s and '50s. Extremely prolific, he designed for calendars, centrefolds, story illustrations and paperback cover artwork. This glamour girl's similarity to Marilyn Monroe is obvious, making it an appealing image.

48.5in (123cm) high

£120-180   VSA

'Sud', by P. Bellenger, printed by De La Vasselais, Paris, lithographed in colours, linen-backed.

c1950   *61in (155cm) high*

£200-300   BLNY

'Perrier', by Jean Carlu, printed by Hertig Imp. La Chaux-De Fonds, offset lithograph in colours, in near mint condtion, linen-backed.

51in (130cm) high

£1,000-1,200   BLNY

'Black & Decker', by Francis Bernard (1900-79), printed by Editions Paul Martial, Paris, lithographed in colours, linen-backed.

1930   *62in (158cm) high*

£800-1,200   BLNY

'Les Progrès', by Paul Colin, printed by S.A. Courbet, Paris, lithograph in colours, linen-backed.

1954   *31in (79cm) high*

£400-600   BLNY

'Cinzano', by Paul Colin, printed by Publicitas-Paris, lithograph in colours, in near mint condition, linen-backed.

1951   45in (114cm) high
£500-600   BLNY

'La Tendre Ennemie', by Paul Colin, printed by Doc Publicite, Paris, lithograph in colours, in near mint condition, linen-backed.

1930   59in (150cm) high
£2,000-2,200   BLNY

'La Maison du Porte-Plume', by Jean Dylen, printed by E.V. Ferdi, Bruxelles, lithograph in colours, in near mint condition, linen-backed.

Although this poster advertising a stationery and pen shop shows a number of famous models by Waterman and Parker, none are named, presumably as no permission had been sought to include their designs. Even the ink bottle labels are blank.

c1930   63in (160cm) high
£1,500-2,000   BLNY

'Jaffa Grapefruit', designed by Frans Mettes, Dutch-language poster.

1958   116in (295cm) high
£180-220   VSA

'Bonnet', by Herve Morvan (1914-80), printed by De La Vasselais, Paris, lithograph in colours, linen-backed.

c1950   44.5in (113cm) high
£400-600   BLNY

EXPERT EYE – A SHELL POSTER

Shell petrol and oil advertising posters, produced from the 1930s to '50s, are highly sought-after by collectors.

The bold colours, feeling of perspective, modern fonts and simple, abstract forms are typical of McKnight Kauffer's best work.

Shell posters were produced in a number of styles, but the highly stylized or Modernist images by designers such as Richard Guyatt, Hans Schleger and McKnight Kauffer tend to be more desirable than those with natural motifs or animals.

This appealing and scarce example is also in excellent condition and is backed on linen.

'For Pull, Use Summer Shell', by Edward McKnight Kauffer, printed by Waterlow, lithograph in colours, in near mint condition, linen-backed.

1930   45in (114cm) wide
£850-950   BLNY

'Essolube', designed by Jean Walther, printed on japan paper.

1935   96.5in (245cm) high
£1,000-1,500   VSA

ESSENTIAL REFERENCE – LEONETTO CAPPIELLO

'Cachou LaJaunie', by Leonetto Cappiello, printed by Devambez, Paris, lithograph in colours, in near mint condition, linen-backed.

Italian born self-taught artist, caricaturist and graphic designer Leonetto Cappiello (1875-1942) is credited with being one of the leading poster artists of his day, moving poster design away from Art Nouveau styles into the modern age. His first poster was designed in 1899, and between 1901 and 1914, he released several hundred influential designs in addition to caricatures. Many featured his hallmark style of brightly coloured figures on a black background with bold branding above, which differed so much from the work of those who surrounded him. Many of his designs are witty or humourous, and executed in a lively manner. This poster for breath fresheners is a good example, with the smoking lady breathing out noxious fumes before popping a sweet into her mouth. After WWI, he devoted himself to poster design, working with the publisher Devambrez from 1919 until 1936.

1920   59in (150cm) high
£1,200-1,800   **BLNY**

'Cachou LaJaunie', by Leonetto Cappiello, printed by P. Vercasson, Paris, lithograph in colours, in near mint condition, linen-backed.
1900   *55in (140cm) high*
£2,000-2,500   **BLNY**

'Le Thermogène', by Leonetto Cappiello, printed by Marci Bruxelles.
1907   *39.45in (100cm) high*
£80-120   **ON**

'Aurore', by Leonetto Cappiello (1875-1942), printed by Devambez, Paris, lithograph in colours, in near mint condition, linen-backed.

1928   *62in (158cm) high*
£1,000-2,000   **BLNY**

'Nitrolian', by Leonetto Cappiello, printed by Devanbez, Paris, lithograph in colours.

'Cognac Pellisson', by Leonetto Cappiello, printed by Vercasson, Paris, lithograph in colours, in near mint condition, linen-backed.
c1920   *47in (119cm) high*
£400-600   **BLNY**

'Contratto', by Leonetto Cappiello, printed by Affiches Cappiello, Paris, lithograph in colours, in near mint condition, linen-backed.
1922   *54.5in (138cm) high*
£1,200-1,500   **BLNY**

1929   *63in (160cm) high*
£1,500-2,000   **BLNY**

'Paris Exposition Internationale', designed by Paul Colin, printed by Jules Simon, mounted on linen.

1937 23.5in (59.5cm) high

£250-350 ON

'6eme Festival International du Film Cannes', by Leon and Jean Luc, Nice, printed by Robaudy, Cannes, original French issue, offset lithograph in colours, in near mint condition, linen-backed.

1953 39in (99cm) high

£400-600 BLNY

'Weersport Kampen' [Army Sports Camp], by an unknown designer, produced in the Occupied Netherlands.

As well as being typical of the Nazi ideal of youth, the young man's healthy and strong appearance conforms to Modernist principles of the day, which promoted exercise to help create prosperity and modernity.

1943 79.5in (202cm) high

£60-80 VSA

'New York World's Fair 1939', by Albert Staehle (1899-1974), printed by Grinnell Litho. Co; NYC, lithograph in colours, in near mint condition, linen-backed.

With the fireworks and the Trylon and Perisphere in the background, the modernity and positivity about the future celebrated by the fair is accentuated by the smart dressed lady in the foreground, with her arm outstretched as if reaching for the future. World's Fair memorabilia is also a highly collectable market.

1939 30.5in (76cm) high

£1,200-1,800 BLNY

'The Great Sorcar', single sheet magic show poster.

Protul Chandra Sorcar (1913-71), known as 'The Great Sorcar', is often called 'the father of Indian magic'.

£70-100 MAS

'De Architekt Mart Stam', architecture exhibition poster, designed by Paul Schuitema.

Modernist architect Stam had himself used similarly modern typography for an exhibition poster in 1928, with avant-garde graphic designer Schuitema playing on this fact.

1972

£120-180 SWA

'Der Humor in der Reklame' (Humour in Advertising), designed by Julius Klinger (1876-1942), printed by Hollerbaum & Schmidt, Berlin.

1909 37.75in (94cm) wide

£500-600 SWA

ESSENTIAL REFERENCE

- Pot lids are decorative, usually coloured, ceramic lids used on pots of products such as food, hair preparations and toothpaste.
- Blue and white pot lids were produced during the 1820s and in bulk from the 1830s. The first coloured lids appeared in the early 1840s and often featured bears, as bear's grease was used as a popular hair preparation for men at the time. Manufacturers were based in Staffordshire and include F. & R. Pratt, who were granted a related patent in 1848, T.J. & J. Mayer and J. Ridgway.
- It is not possible to date the majority of pot lids with any accuracy as they are usually undated and were often produced for long periods of time. Examples that commemorate a specific event, such as 'The Interior of the Grand International Building 1851' (below), can be dated to c1851, as production was unlikely to have taken place much after that date. Otherwise, registration dates, changes in design and some maker's marks can date lids to a period.

- Before 1860, lids were flat and lightweight and often had a screw thread. As the quality at this time was so high, these are usually the most desirable. Between 1860 and 1875 lids became heavier and more convex and, after 1875, became even heavier but with flat tops once again.
- Collectors have sought pot lids almost since they were first introduced, and they first appeared at auction in 1924. Today collectors look for examples in excellent condition and those with unusual variations in the main design or borders.
- The numbers given in the description are those used in K.V. Mortimer's "Pot-Lids Reference & Price Guide", the standard reference for pot lids.

A Staffordshire 'The Interior of the Grand International Building 1851' pot lid, no. 143, produced by the Mayer factory, with title and other wording around the rim.

The version without the wording around the rim can be worth twice as much.

5.25in (13cm) diam

£280-320   **SAS**

EXPERT EYE – A STAFFORDSHIRE POT LID

This pot lid was produced to mark the opening of the Exhibition of the Industry of All Nations that opened in New York City in 1853. It was inspired by the success of the Great Exhibition of 1851, held in London. The fair even had its own Crystal Palace, but this was destroyed by fire in 1858.

This is the first version issued for this pot lid. A version with a gold band around the rim is much rarer and can be worth twice as much.

Due to the subject matter, this pot lid would also be of interest to collectors of exhibition memorabilia.

A number of later re-issues were made into the 20thC, but these are of significantly less interest to collectors.

A Staffordshire 'New York Exhibition 1853' pot lid, no. 154, produced by the Mayer factory, with oak leaf border, minor hairline crack to rim.

c1853   *5.25in (13cm) diam*

£600-700   **SAS**

A Staffordshire 'L'Exhibition Universelle de 1867' pot lid, no. 152, produced by the Pratt factory.

c1867   *4.75in (12.5cm) diam*

£70-100   **SAS**

A Staffordshire 'Albert Memorial' pot lid, no. 240, probably produced by Bates, Brown-Westhead, Moore & Co., without carriage in the foreground.

4in (10cm) diam

£80-120   **SAS**

A Staffordshire 'The New Blackfriars Bridge' pot lid, no. 244, produced by the Pratt factory.

4.5in (11cm) diam

£22-28   **SAS**

A Staffordshire 'Thames Embankment' pot lid, no. 245, produced by the Pratt factory.

4.25in (10.5cm) diam

£45-55   **SAS**

POT LIDS

ESSENTIAL REFERENCE – PEGWELL BAY POT LIDS

A Staffordshire 'Pegwell Bay, Established 1760' pot lid, no. 32, with sandy road and pathway.

Pegwell Bay in Kent was a tourist resort from the 1760s, peaking in popularity between 1847 and 1875, and competing with its larger and more popular neighbour, Ramsgate. It was noted for the fresh shrimp teas served at the Belle Vue tavern and pots of shrimp paste sold to tourists as souvenirs. The pot lids were decorated with scenes of the village and surrounding countryside as well as shrimping and fishing scenes. Today, collectors group these seemingly disparate lids together to form a small collecting area of their own. They would also appeal to historians of the local area.

4in (10cm) diam

£45-55   SAS

A Staffordshire 'Belle Vue Tavern, Pegwell Bay' pot lid, no. 37, with flat lid, dark cliffs, no name on tavern.

3.5in (9cm) diam

£1,000-1,500   SAS

A Staffordshire 'Pegwell Bay, Ramsgate, Still Life Game' pot lid, no. 43, produced by the Mayer factory, hairline crack.

4.25in (10.5cm) diam

£45-55   SAS

A Staffordshire 'Pegwell Bay, Ramsgate (Farmyard Scene)' pot lid, no. 45, produced by the Mayer factory.

4in (10cm) diam

£150-200   SAS

A Staffordshire 'Royal Harbour, Ramsgate' pot lid, no. 50, probably produced by the Cauldon factory.

4in (10cm) diam

£70-100   SAS

A Staffordshire 'Walmer Castle' pot lid, no. 53, version with two horsemen.

Pot lid no. 54 also titled 'Walmer Castle', with pedestrians replacing the horsemen, is very rare and can be worth over four times as much.

4.25in (10.5cm) diam

£50-70   SAS

A Staffordshire 'Lobster Sauce' pot lid, no. 57, produced by the Pratt factory, second issue with no title or window.

4.25in (10.5cm) diam

£80-120   SAS

A Staffordshire 'Hauling in the Trawl' pot lid, no. 60, produced by the Pratt factory for Crosse & Blackwell.

4.25in (11cm) diam

£70-100   SAS

A Staffordshire 'Alas Poor Bruin' pot lid, no. 1, produced by the Pratt factory, with lantern on pub sign, and double line-and-dot border.

3.5in (8.5cm) diam

£120-180 SAS

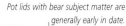 A very early Staffordshire 'Bear's Grease Manufacturer' advertising pot lid, no. 3, attributed to the Mayer factory, no lettering, restored.

Some versions of this rare pot lid carry advertising for Clayton & Co., Bears Grease, 58 Watling Street, London and these can be worth about 20 per cent more.

3.25in (8cm) diam

£3,000-4,000 SAS

A Staffordshire 'Bear Hunting' pot lid, no. 4, produced by Pratt factory, with "119 & 120 Bishopsgate" wording, blue chequered border, hairline crack.

There are a number of variations of this pot lid. While the picture stays the same, the border changes. The most desirable version features the "119 & 120 Bishopsgate" address and additional gold line border.

3.5in (9cm) diam

£550-650 SAS

A Staffordshire 'Shooting Bears' pot lid, no. 13, produced by the Pratt factory, no lettering.

3.25in (8cm) diam

£100-150 SAS

A very early Staffordshire 'Bear in Ravine' advertising pot lid, no. 14, probably produced by the Ridgway factory, flange restored.

2.5in (6.5cm) diam

£1,500-2,000 SAS

EXPERT EYE – BEAR POT LID

This is probably the first coloured pot lid produced, as it is recorded, as early as 1846.

Pot lids with bear subject matter are generally early in date.

There is another version with a moon in the sky and a more overall blue tone, which can be worth about double this version.

While black or brown bears are a much more common subject matter, polar bears also appear on 'Arctic Expedition in search of Sir John Franklin', which refers to an incident in 1848, dating it with some certainty.

A Staffordshire 'Polar Bears' pot lid, no. 18, without moon, gold border.

3.25in (8cm) diam

£320-380 SAS

A Staffordshire 'The Ins' pot lid, no. 15, with fancy lettering, flange restored.

'The Ins' and 'The Outs' (below) were produced as a pair. The producer is unknown but it has been suggested that it could be Pratt or possibly Ridgway. Examples of either pot lid with a fancy ribbon border will be worth slightly more.

3.5in (8.5cm) diam

£350-450 SAS

A Staffordshire 'The Outs' pot lid, no. 16, with fancy border, restored.

3.5in (9cm) diam

£700-800 SAS

POT LIDS

A Staffordshire 'The Queen God Bless Her' pot lid, no. 269, produced by the Pratt factory, with fancy border.

5in (12.5cm) diam

£45-55   **SAS**

A Staffordshire 'Deerhound Guarding Cradle' or 'Fidelity' pot lid, no. 270, with marbled border.

3.25in (8cm) diam

£70-100   **SAS**

A Staffordshire 'Deer Drinking' pot lid, no. 277, produced by the Pratt factory, hairline crack.

A larger version with a seaweed surround can be worth about double this version.

4.25in (10.5cm) diam

£45-55   **SAS**

A Staffordshire 'The Boar Hunt' pot lid, no. 288, produced by the Mayer factory, without border.

This pot lid was reissued by Kirkhams up to 1960. The version with a decorative border can be worth half as much again.

A Staffordshire 'The Shepherdess' pot lid, no. 279, produced at the Cauldon factory by Bates, Brown-Westhead Moore & Co.

4in (10cm) diam

£35-45   **SAS**

4.25in (10.5cm) diam

£450-550   **SAS**

A Staffordshire 'The Master of the Hounds' pot lid, no. 295, produced by the Pratt factory.

Later examples have a line and dot border and a title, they are usually worth much less.

4.25in (10.5cm) diam

£100-150   **SAS**

A Staffordshire 'The Fair Sportswoman' pot lid, no. 297, produced at the Cauldon factory by Bates, Brown-Westhead Moore & Co.

4.25in (10.5cm) diam

£40-50   **SAS**

A Staffordshire 'Summer' pot lid, no. 335, produced by Bates, Elliot & Co.

Look for early examples with a registration mark on the underside, as these can be worth twice as much. 'Autumn' also exists as a pot lid and 'Spring' can be found on a plaque, however 'Winter' has yet to be seen.

4.5in (11cm) diam

£35-45   **SAS**

A Staffordshire 'The Packman' pot lid, no. 103, probably produced by J. Ridgway & Bates, restored.

The most desirable version of this pot lid is the one with 'Bandoline Pomade' advertising around the rim. It can be worth ten times as much as this.

3.25in (8cm) diam

£50-70   SAS

A Staffordshire 'Letter from the Diggings', no. 131, produced by the Pratt factory, with fancy border.

The Australian gold rush of the early 1850s was the inspiration for this pot lid. The version with the seaweed surround can be worth about twice the value.

5in (13cm) diam

£50-70   SAS

A Staffordshire 'Queen Victoria and Prince Consort' pot lid, no. 167, probably produced by the Pratt factory, with oak leaves and acorn border.

This pot lid would also appeal to collectors of Royal memorabilia.

5in (13cm) diam

£200-300   SAS

A Staffordshire 'Windsor Castle' or 'Prince Albert (Hare Coursing)' pot lid, no. 176, produced by the Mayer factory, minor hairline crack.

4.25in (10.5cm) diam

£120-180   SAS

A Staffordshire 'Wellington with Cocked Hat' pot lid, no. 183, with lettering, restored.

5.25in (13.5cm) diam

£500-600   SAS

A Staffordshire 'Wellington with Clasped Hands' pot lid, no. 184, produced by the Mayer factory.

One of four variations of this design. The values do not differ greatly, but the version with a blue bow below the title is slightly more desirable.

4.75in (12cm) diam

£700-800   SAS

A Staffordshire 'The Blue Boy' pot lid, no. 196, produced by the Pratt factory.

Based on Thomas Gainsborough's famous painting of Master Jonathan Butall, this pot lid was produced for many years by Pratt and very early examples are scarce. Look for examples with a seaweed border and flange, and a gold border as these can be worth much more.

4.75in (12cm) diam

£60-80   SAS

A Staffordshire 'Little Red-Riding Hood' pot lid, no. 200, produced by the Pratt factory.

Unsurprisingly, this design is also found on nursery plates.

3in (7.5cm) diam

£100-150   SAS

A Staffordshire 'A Fix' pot lid, no. 302, produced by the Mayer factory, no border.

4.25in (11cm) diam

£150-200   SAS

POT LIDS

A Staffordshire 'The Times' pot lid, no. 307, produced by the Pratt factory.

4.25in (10.5cm) diam

£50-70   SAS

A Staffordshire 'A False Move' pot lid, no. 308, produced by the Mayer factory, restored.

The version lacking a title and border can be worth twice as much.

5.25in (13cm) diam

£55-65   SAS

A Staffordshire 'The Village Wakes' pot lid, no. 321, produced by the Pratt factory, with fancy border and bullnose rim.

4in (10m) diam

£280-320   SAS

A Staffordshire 'Xmas Eve' pot lid, no. 323, produced by the Pratt factory, with double-lined border in black.

3.75in (9.5cm) diam

£380-420   SAS

A Staffordshire 'May Day Dancers at the Swan Inn' pot lid, no. 324, probably produced by the Bates, Brown-Westhead & Moore Co. factory.

4.25in (10.5cm) diam

£60-80   SAS

A Staffordshire 'Children of Flora' pot lid, no. 326, probably produced at the Cauldon factory.

4.75in (12cm) diam

£80-120   SAS

A Staffordshire 'The Dentist' pot lid, no. 331, produced by the Pratt factory.

4.25in (10.5cm) diam

£120-180   SAS

A Staffordshire 'The Poultry Woman', no. 349, produced by the Pratt factory, with small leaf border.

The version with the wide gold border can be worth ten times as much.

4.25in (10.5cm) diam

£120-180   SAS

A 1930s American Bendix 0526C black and, green and yellow marbled Catalin radio.

This was the only Catalin-cased radio that Bendix made.

11in (28cm) long

£600-800   QU

A late 1940s French Sonora mottled brown bakelite radio, with chrome detailing.

Note the design echoes the dashboard, bonnet and grille of cars of the same period.

18.25in (46cm) wide

£180-220   QU

A 1950s American Clarion red bakelite radio.

(12.75in) 32.5cm wide

£280-320   QU

An American Zenith Radio Corp. burgundy bakelite radio, with circular dial and side speakers.

13.5in (34cm) wide

£150-200   QU

An Ultra Electric Ltd 'Twin-De-Luxe' radio, with sliding doors concealing the dial and knobs, and snakeskin-effect case.

This is the scarcer 'luxury' version, examples with less ostentatious coverings are worth less.

14.5in (37cm) wide

£150-250   QU

A 1950s Russian Oceanic radio, with laminated wood veneer case, cream plastic surround and knobs with sprayed brown detailing.

24.5in (62cm) wide

£120-180   QU

An Italian Brionvega 'Stereo RR 126' combined radio, turntable and speakers, designed by Achille Castiglioni in 1965, with detachable cube speakers.

Important architect and product designer Castiglioni intended this to be a 'musical pet', as well as being highly modern in form and design. The dials and knobs form a face, with the detachable side speakers acting as 'ears'. It was mounted on casters so it could be moved around the house.

36.25in (92cm) wide

£800-1,200   QU

RAILWAYANA

ESSENTIAL REFERENCE

- Railwayana is a hugely popular collecting area. Items that hark back to the early 20thC 'golden age' of steam and the glamour of train travel, as well as some later pieces, being highly sought-after.

- Memorabilia and ephemera from the 'big four' railway companies: London, Midland & Scotland (LMS), London & North-Eastern Railway (LNER), Great Western Railway (GWR) and the Southern Railway (SR), all of which operated from 1924 to 1948, are very popular with collectors. Items from some of the smaller companies that also existed in this period can be rarer and hold as much interest with collectors. Railwayana prior to 1924 is very rare and, as a result, does not have a wide collecting base.

- The period of the big four ended with nationalisation in 1948 and the creation of British Railways. The rationalisation, which followed the Beeching Report from 1963, saw the beginning of the end of steam-powered trains in Britain and the closing down of a number of lines and stations. Railwayana from the 1950s is enthusiastically collected, although it is perhaps not quite as valuable or sought-after as earlier items.

- Station signs and locomotive nameplates traditionally occupy the top end of the market. Those that are worth the highest values are generally in original condition and fresh to the market. Nameplates of well-known locomotives also demand a significant premium. Shedplates and smokebox plates are popular, and are often more affordable. Be aware that signs in particular are being reproduced, so only buy from reputable sources.

- More common items, such as carriage prints, tickets, timetables and handbills offer an accessible form of railwayana collecting. Later items from the period of diesel and electric traction may also be of interest to the budding collector with an eye for the future.

A London Underground enamel locomotive destination board, with 'Via Charing X' to one side and 'Via Bank' on the other side, finished in black lettering on a yellow background, in good condition.

£30-50   VEC

A High Barnet-Morden double-sided destination plate for an 'N7' smokebox door, with two holes for clipping on the smokebox door, in good condition.

£35-45   VEC

An Eastern Region 'Ladies Room' station sign, finished in dark blue with white lettering, in excellent condition.

18in (45.75in) wide

£80-120   VEC

A 'Bend' road sign, with original reflective studs, of pressed alloy construction, retaining the original post clamps.

21in (53.5cm) high

£45-55   GWRA

A Lancashire & Yorkshire Railway 'Notice The Company's Road Not Public' cast iron sign, with raised border, top and bottom fixing lugs, in ex-lineside condition.

23.5in (59.5cm) wide

£280-320   GWRA

A Vulcan Foundry workplate, from Newton-le-Willows Lancashire, no. 4423, dated.

From an ex-Nigerian Railways Class 806 4-8-2 locomotive number 806, rebuilt in 1950-51.

1930

£400-500   GWRA

An '8E' shedplate, without paint or surface rust.

Used at Brunswick from May 1950 until April 1958 and then Northwich until 1968.

£60-100 GWRA

A '9G' painted cast iron shedplate, in ex-locomotive condition.

Used at Northwich from May 1950 until April 1958, and then at Gorton from April 1958 until June 1965.

£180-220 GWRA

EXPERT EYE – A '17D' SHEDPLATE

Shedplates were fixed to locomotives and indicated their home depot.

This plate was used at Rowsley from 1948 for ten years only, when the shed's designation was changed to 17C. '17D' was never used again.

The number indicated the railway area, and the letter the size of the shed, with 'A' being the largest and 'D' being much smaller and housing fewer locomotives, meaning fewer plates existed.

Although it has been restored, it does contain its original paint underneath. Plates in original 'locomotive' condition are the most desirable.

A '16F' painted cast iron shedplate, face restored over original paint, otherwise in ex-locomotive condition.

Used at Burton-on-Trent from September 1963 until May 1973.

£100-150 GWRA

An extremely rare '17D' painted cast iron shedplate, face restored over original paint, in ex-locomotive condition.

£280-320 GWRA

A rare '20D' painted cast iron shedplate, LMS pattern, in ex-locomotive condition.

Used at Normanton until February 1957.

£500-600 GWRA

A '21B' painted cast iron shedplate.

Used at Bourneville from 1948 until February 1960, then at Bescot until September 1963.

£180-220 GWRA

A rare '25F' painted cast iron shedplate, LMS pattern, in ex-locomotive condition, recovered from Derby Works, "47355" painted on the reverse.

Used at Low Moor until September 1956.

£220-280 GWRA

An LNER Great Northern Triple piecrust pattern three-aspect handlamp, with embossed brass plate titled 'C.Vicar', reservoir, burner and red and blue aspect glasses.

This was painted in silver to indicate the authority of C. Vicar, who was the Head Shunter at Kings Cross Goods Depot.

£45-55   GWRA

A Great Northern Railway lorry or cart lamp, with handled chimney, brass rimmed front cowl and bevelled glass side aperture, stamped "GNR" on chimney, missing bullseye lens.

£350-450   GWRA

A Crown Staffordshire North Eastern Railway Hotels Department china cup, with colour transfer-printed crest and blue and gold trimmed rim.

2in (5cm) diam

£35-45   GWRA

A Bridgwood Great Western Railway Hotels plate, with blue and gold rim around a Moorish inspired brown transfer-printed design.

7in (17.5cm) diam

£35-45   GWRA

A Southern Railway brass ashtray, with embossed wording around the rim and embossed 'SR Shipping House Flag' beneath.

4in (10cm) diam

£45-55   GWRA

A Beatles printed ring binder, by Nems Enterprises Limited, with photographic print and printed signatures to the cover.

11.5in (29.5cm) high

£180-220   NOR

A 'Beatles for Sale' album cover, signed by Paul McCartney.

£200-300   MAS

A mid-1960s 'Beatles Dress', black print of the Fab Four with facsimile signatures on white cotton labelled "Authorized design, copyright NV Stoonweverij, Nijverheid, Enschede, Holland".

Bust 34in (86cm)

£350-450   KT

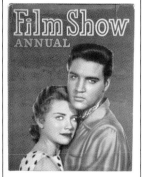

A Film Show Annual, with Elvis Presley 'Loving You' cover.

1956   *11in (28cm) high*

£10-15   MA

A 'Discland' hardback book, published by The Daily Mirror.

1956   *11in (28cm) high*

£6-8   MA

ROCK & POP

A Mattel 'Marie Osmond' poseable figure, mint and boxed.

The high value is due to the immense, devoted following the Osmonds have attracted. The box also has great artwork typical of the period. You'll also note that the sticky price label is still on the box. Be very careful about removing labels as they can tear the surface of the package, or leave an unsightly stain, which will reduce desirability. If you must remove a price tag, it is best to gently steam it off.

1976   Box 13in (33cm) high
£55-65   MTB

An Aladdin Industries Donny & Marie Osmond vinyl lunchbox and Thermos flask.

1977   Thermos 6.5in (16.5cm) high
£35-45   BH

A late 1960s Rolling Stones transfer sheet, with black line portraits and facsimile signatures.

£20-30   GAZE

A Knebworth Fair official programme for 1976, the line-up including Rolling Stones, Lynyrd Skynyrd, 10CC and others, printed by Frederick Bannister Ltd.

1976   11.75in (30cm) high
£15-25   GAZE

A Sid Vicious Sex Pistols punk commemorative mug, with applied chain and safety pin, hand-painted with punk messages and 'Sid Vicious 1957-1979...', the base with additional (rude) message.

5.25in (13cm) high
£80-120   WW

A Play Along 'Britney Spears' doll, from the Video Performance Collection, in airline stewardess costume.

13in (33cm) high
£5-8   BH

ROYAL MEMORABILIA

ESSENTIAL REFERENCE

- Although earlier examples are well known, the production of royal memorabilia boomed during the reign of Queen Victoria. Ceramics were the first and most common item to be produced, and with the advent of transfer-printing and the railways, they could be produced and distributed economically. Their popularity grew from the late 19thC into the early 20thC, and examples are still produced today.

- Collectors tend to focus on one monarch, or even one event, as the variety produced is so wide. Queen Victoria and the current Queen tend to be the most popular subjects, partly due to the enormous amount and variety of pieces that can be collected. However, interest in pieces produced to celebrate events in the lives of the younger members of the current Royal family is growing.

- Always consider the quality and maker of the piece. Well-known makers such as Royal Worcester, Royal Crown Derby, Minton and Copeland typically produced high quality, finely decorated pieces. However, even if a piece is not by a major maker, but is well-decorated, it is likely to be of interest to collectors. Connected to this is 'eye appeal', which is another important factor. If a piece is brightly coloured and detailed, it is likely to appeal to more collectors. The desirability of portraits and armorials is largely down to taste.

- Always examine a piece carefully for damage, as condition is important. Many 19thC items were not made to last, so some wear or restoration is understandable, but cracks and chips will reduce desirability and value. Damage on more recent pieces will reduce value considerably.

- The event is also important. For example, many more pieces were produced for Queen Victoria's Golden Jubilee than for her marriage. This can make certain pieces rare. Look out for limited editions, particularly in editions of 250 pieces or less. If demand rises to exceed supply, values will rise. Keep all paperwork and boxes, as these are important to value.

- Above all, bear in mind that rarity is by far the most important factor when assessing value.

A Queen Victoria Coronation earthenware plate, the moulded central portrait within a border of moulded coronation trophies and flowers of the Union, lined in underglaze blue, chipped.

1838   *7.75in (19.5cm) diam*

£180-220   **SAS**

A rare Queen Victoria Coronation earthenware plate, printed in underglaze blue with a named portrait, the reverse printed "Manufactured for D. Brandon, Kingston, Jamaica".

1838   *9in (23cm) diam*

£450-550   **SAS**

A Queen Victoria commemorative earthenware mug, printed in blue and flanked by flowers of the Union, hairline crack to base and rim chip.

1837-38   *2.5in (6.5cm) high*

£400-500   **SAS**

A Queen Victoria commemorative pearlware jug, printed in blue with named portraits, restored chips.

1837-38

£300-400   **SAS**

A Queen Victoria & Prince Albert Royal Wedding nursery plate, the border moulded with flowers of the Union, the centre printed in brown with named portraits.

1840   *7in (18cm) diam*

£100-150   **SAS**

A Queen Victoria Golden Jubilee pottery plate, with scalloped edge, printed with a portrait encircled by views of four palaces, with gilt rim.

1887

£20-30   SAS

A Wallis Gimson Queen Victoria Golden Jubilee pottery plate, with gilt rim.

This plate is from a series, each of which shows a portrait of a late 19thC personality.

1886

£25-35   SAS

A Doulton Lambeth Queen Victoria Diamond Jubilee glazed stoneware mug, moulded with a young and old profile portrait of the Queen in green.

1897

£50-70   SAS

A Doulton Lambeth stoneware jug, the mottled green glazed body moulded with a portrait of Queen Victoria, the words 'Hoisting the Flag', flags and national emblems of the United Kingdom.

1900   *8.25in (21cm) high*

£250-350   SAS

A Queen Victoria white biscuit figure, seated upon a throne moulded with the Royal Arms, left hand missing.

c1840   *7in (18cm) high*

£100-150   SAS

A rare Copeland for Thomas Goode Queen Victoria pottery goblet, moulded with a portrait of the Queen on a gilt reserve and well-decorated in gilt and colours, hairline crack.

Thomas Goode is a well-known and long established ceramics and glass retailer in Mayfair, London. As expected from Copeland, this is a fine quality piece, with detailed decoration.

6in (15.5cm) high

£350-450   SAS

A pair of Queen Victoria and Royal Family commemorative nursery plates, the borders moulded with flowerheads, decorated in enamels and printed with a named portrait of Victoria and the Prince of Wales with attendant Princesses, the borders lined in pink lustre.

c1847   *6in (15cm) diam*

£250-350   SAS

A Queen Victoria 'The Royal Children' commemorative nursery plate, the border moulded with flowers and foliage, the centre printed with the Prince of Wales on a pony, with two of his sisters.

c1846   *7in (17.5cm) diam*

£200-300   SAS

An Edward, Prince of Wales commemorative nursery plate, the border moulded with flowerheads, the centre printed with the Prince on a pony.

c1845   7.25in (18.5cm) diam

£70-100   **SAS**

A Queen Victoria 'Royal Nursery Polka' commemorative nursery plate, the border moulded with flowers of the Union, the centre printed with the Prince of Wales and two of his sisters playing.

c1844   6.25in (16cm) diam

£120-180   **SAS**

A Princess Victoria, Princess Royal & Prince Friedrich of Prussia Royal Wedding cup and saucer, printed in black with portraits and views of the palace.

1858

£70-100   **SAS**

A Queen Victoria 'Holyrood House' commemorative pottery plaque, printed with a view of the Royal residence.

c1860   6.5in (16.5cm) diam

£10-15   **SAS**

A Royal Doulton Edward VII Coronation stoneware mug, glazed in blue with moulded designs of Edward and Alexandra within medallions, surrounded by Art Nouveau style flowers.

1902

£100-150   **SAS**

A Fieldings King Edward VII In Memoriam transfer-printed pottery beaker, with silver rim.

1910

£60-80   **SAS**

A Royal Doulton King George V Coronation plate, with underglaze blue transfer-printed design.

1911   10.5in (26.5cm) diam

£80-100   **RCC**

A Royal Doulton King George V 'A Royal Exemplar' in memoriam loving cup.

1936   4.75in (12cm) high

£50-80   SAS

A Royal Doulton George VI & Elizabeth Coronation porcelain beaker, printed with superimposed profiles in grey on a blue ground, with gilt highlights.

1937

£180-220   SAS

EXPERT EYE – A GEORGE V TOBY JUG

This is from a set of 11 toby jugs that included other military and political leaders during WWI, such as Lord Kitchener.

They were designed by Sir Francis Carruthers Gould (1888-1925), a famous and important political cartoonist of the time.

Produced from 1915-20, only limited numbers of each were made meaning some characters, and full sets in particular, are very rare today.

The colours are rich and strong, and the facial modelling is true to the character of the individual.

A Wilkinson Ltd 'George V' naval character jug, designed by Sir Francis Carruthers Gould, the base with printed marks.

12.5in (31cm) high

£450-550   FLD

A limited edition Minton King George VI & Queen Elizabeth Coronation beaker, from a limited edition of 2,000, enamelled with super-imposed profiles within a gilt starburst.

1937

£120-180   SAS

A John Maddock & Sons 'Royal Ivory' commemorative transfer-printed plate, commemorating the visit of George VI & Queen Elizabeth to the Dominion of Canada in 1939, and showing the coats-of-arms for the nine different dominions of Canada.

c1939   8.75in (22cm) wide

£18-22   TCF

A Grimwade's Royal Winton commemorative transfer-printed ashtray, commemorating the visit of George VI & Queen Elizabeth to Canada and the US in 1939.

c1939   4in (10cm) wide

£35-50   TCF

A Paragon London Pride Princess Elizabeth & the Duke of Edinburgh commemorative ashtray, with sepia transfer-printed image of the Houses of Parliament, London, with border reading 'HRH Princess Elizabeth Canada HRH Duke of Edinburgh Oct 1951'.

This commemorates the first visit Queen Elizabeth II (then Princess Elizabeth) made to Canada with her husband, in October 1951.

c1951   4.75in (12cm) diam

£18-22   **TCF**

A Wedgwood Queen Elizabeth II Golden Jubilee mug, with hand-painted gilt pattern, based on a design by Eric Ravilious.

2002   4in (10.5cm) high

£50-100   **WW**

A Doulton for Whiteley Prince George, Duke of York & Mary of Teck Royal Wedding commemorative pottery mug, printed in brown and decorated in colours, with gilt rim.

1893

£60-80   **SAS**

EXPERT EYE – A POOLE POTTERY CHARGER

The bright colours and swirling linear pattern are typical of Poole's 'Contemporary' range that was being produced at this time.

It was produced in a very limited edition of 25. Demand from both Poole Pottery collectors and royal memorabilia collectors means examples are scarce and valuable.

It is a large piece, and chargers are popular as they make a superb display.

It is fully signed on the back.

The design was produced by Alfred Read, the pottery's designer at the time, and is part of a number of designs he produced to commemorate the Coronation, all including either the Royal coat of arms, EIIR monogram or celebratory phrases.

A limited edition Poole Pottery Queen Elizabeth II Coronation charger, designed by Alfred Read and decorated by Ruth Pavely, from an edition of 25, the reverse with impressed and painted marks.

1953   15in (38cm) diam

£600-700   **WW**

A Doulton for Mortlocks Prince George, Duke of York & Mary of Teck Royal Wedding stoneware jug, with applied moulded foliate decoration, date and monogrammed oval.

John Mortlock & Co. was a distillery, which explains the grape and hop motifs in the decoration.

1893

£25-35   **SAS**

A Royal Worcester kidney-shaped plate from the Royal Household, with ER monogram surmounted by a crown printed in blue, the reverse with printed Royal coat-of-arms, ribboned inscription and dated 1905.

This plate was sold with a copy of a letter from Reverend Cannon F.A.J. Hervey, formerly the chaplain to King Edward VII at Sandringham.

c1905   8.25in (21cm) wide

£150-200   **SAS**

A 1930s Dutch earthenware commemorative charger, titled 'Prinses Juliana 30 April 1909-1934' and bearing heraldic crest, inscribed verso "Juliana bord no. 270 Schoonhoven Holland".

12.25in (31cm) diam

£80-120   **BIG**

ESSENTIAL REFERENCE

- Although they have been produced for centuries, it is instruments from the 19thC, and possibly from the late 18thC, that are most likely to be found today. Many are made from lacquered brass, although other materials were also used, including mahogany, and occasionally precious metals. Collectors tend to focus on one category, such as navigational or optical instruments, or one type such as microscopes.
- The period and maker are two of the most important factors that count towards value. Although a piece may look similar, the presence of a notable maker's name such as Cuff, Powell & Lealand or Dollond indicates quality and accounts for the value. Similarly, complex, finely made examples will be worth more. The presence of a complete set of original accessories, including a box, will add value. Values have fallen somewhat as the area has become largely unfashionable, so now may be a good time to buy.

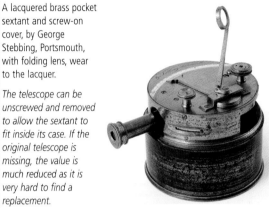

A lacquered brass pocket sextant and screw-on cover, by George Stebbing, Portsmouth, with folding lens, wear to the lacquer.

The telescope can be unscrewed and removed to allow the sextant to fit inside its case. If the original telescope is missing, the value is much reduced as it is very hard to find a replacement.

A late 19thC Troughton & Simms lacquered brass and mahogany-bound telescope, mounted on a copper tripod stand.

£250-300   **SWO**

A late 19thC unmarked brass pocket microscope, with tube cover and sliding objective.
2.25in (5.5cm) high

£40-60   **BA**

£280-320
2.25in (5.5cm) diam
     BA

A French 18thC Butterfield-type silver sundial compass, the gnomon in the form of a bird, the back engraved with 20 French, Spanish, and English cities and their latitudes, the compass base engraved with a river landscape, in a fitted velvet-lined shagreen case.

These silver or brass dials were named after the late 17thC Parisian instrument maker Michael Butterfield. The gnomon can be moved to match the latitude of a city, enabling the owner to tell the correct time in that city – making this an early form of travelling clock. The presence of the original case adds markedly to the value.
2.25in (6cm) wide

£1,000-1,500   **SWO**

A double-sided pocket barometer, the silvered dial inscribed "D. Norris, Rio de Janeiro" and "C.F. Casella & Co. Ltd., London S.W.", no. 9916 with a rotating outer altitude scale and thermometer verso, all within a double-hinged leather case.

£300-400   **SWO**

A 19thC gold pocket shipmaster's compass, by Gilbert & Co., London, dial inscribed "Gilbert & Co, London".

Gold cased compasses are scarce. This would have been an expensive version of the instrument in its day.
2in (5cm) diam

£600-700   **L&T**

A Stanley brass surveyor's scale, with two folding sight arms on a spoked circular frame with central glazed aperture, within engraved silvered dial, with fitted mahogany case.
7in (18cm) wide

£150-200   **ROS**

SCIENTIFIC INSTRUMENTS

A late 19thC folding mahogany graphoscope viewer, with inlaid ebony stringing and large magnifying lens.

Graphoscopes were used for magnifying and viewing prints and photographs in detail.

15.5in (39cm) high

£120-180   ATK

A late 19thC mahogany cased and glazed barograph, with five bellows, detachable cover, lacquered brass clockwork action, and drum and ink bottle, all on a stepped plinth.

14.5in (37cm) wide

£450-550   BIG

A rare mahogany and brass magic lantern, by J.T. Chapman, Manchester, with slide carrier and gas light burner.

Magic lanterns are effectively early slide projectors. With its mahogany and brass construction, this is a fine quality example, with Chapman being a notable maker.

21in (53.5cm) high

£600-800   ATK

A French Lantern Riche painted tinplate magic lantern, some parts repainted, but retaining original burner.

Despite their inexpensive appearance, these delicate painted tinplate magic lanterns are very rare. The rarest version is shaped like the Eiffel Tower.

c1880   *16in (40.5cm) high*

£200-300   ATK

A German Gebruder Bing 'Faust' child's magic lantern, with 12 3in slides, contained in a fitted card and wood box, converted to electrical power.

c1904   *14.5in (37cm) high*

£150-200   ATK

ESSENTIAL REFERENCE

- Very early pieces of golf memorabilia from the early to mid-19thC are rare and can be extremely valuable. Examples from the late 19thC and early 20thC are more readily available and generally more affordable. Golf clubs and balls form the basis of many collections and these items are consistently highly sought-after. Early, rare or high-quality examples made by renowned manufacturers tend to occupy the upper echelons of the market. As most equipment was used in play, items in good condition will generally fetch the largest sums.
- The on-going popularity of the sport across the world has ensured that a huge amount of golfing-themed items are available to collectors, including metalware, glass, artwork and books, some of which are easily affordable. Ceramics celebrating the game were also produced by a number of factories, including Doulton, Shelley and Spode, these are of interest to collectors of both sporting and ceramic items. Ephemera related to games and tournaments, such as programmes and tickets, are also popular and often more affordable. Those related to important games or players, and in good condition, will tend to attract the most interest.
- Although golf is one of the oldest sports still played today, it was not until the early 20thC that women began to participate. Memorabilia associated with female players is therefore rare and can command a premium, particularly as interest in the women's game is still increasing. Specialist auctions are quite common, with a number taking place in July, around the time of the Open Championship.

A 'Gyro' bramble pattern gutty ball, retaining much of its original paint, several hack marks.

£200-300   L&T

A Haskell bramble gutty ball, retaining much of the original finish, some light hack marks.

£250-350   L&T

A Goodrich 'Haskell Bramble 10' bramble pattern gutty ball.

£280-320   L&T

A 'Henley B Marking' mesh pattern gutty ball, in mint condition.

£700-1,000   L&T

A Hyde Imperial 'Woodley Flier 27 1/2' mesh pattern gutty ball.

£200-300   L&T

A Musselburgh mesh pattern gutty ball, retaining much of the original paint.

£500-600   L&T

SPORTING MEMORABILIA

A Silvertown mesh pattern gutty ball, with large letters, retaining most of its original paint.

£250-350   **L&T**

A Wilsden's Rocket mesh pattern gutty ball, retaining much of the original paint.

£240-350   **L&T**

EXPERT EYE – A HAND-HAMMERED GUTTY BALL

Gutta percha balls were introduced in 1848. Gutta percha is a hard latex-like natural plastic made from the resin of a tree.

Balls were hand-hammered until moulds were introduced in the 1860s.

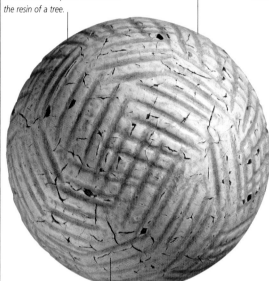

Initially smooth, it was soon discovered that cuts and marks, created by use, improved the aerodynamics of the ball and were then added intentionally by manufacturers.

The rarest type of gutty balls are those painted red for use in snow, smooth examples are particularly desirable.

A hand-hammered gutty ball, in virtual mint condition, with only slight paint loss.

£1,400-1,800   **L&T**

A steel ball mould, no. 365, with a shield and cross clubs pattern to both poles with numerous circles.

£300-500   **L&T**

A mesh pattern gutty ball, marked with a single star at both poles.

£250-350   **L&T**

A US Rubber Company 'Electronic US True Blue 3' rubber core ball, in mint condition.

£90-120   **L&T**

A MacSmith aluminium-headed putter, the hickory shaft with channelled huntly grip, hosel cracked.

£200-300   L&T

A Robert Black Wilson 'OK Special A1' putter, lacks hosel, with hickory shaft.

£550-650   L&T

A longnose putter, with horn insert to sole, lead counterweight, hickory shaft, the scared beech head stamped "H. Philip".

£750-850   L&T

A Grosse Ile Putter Co. patent brass-headed putter, with alignment flange, hickory shaft.

£800-900   L&T

A Jack Randall of Sundridge Park patent mallet head putter, the face of the aluminium head fitted with 13 plugs of lead weight, the sole stamped with patent no. 186522, with unusual oval section hosel, hickory shaft and leather-covered grip.

£80-120   GBA

A 'Bennie no. 2 Putter', the aluminium head with unusual circular projection for striking the ball, hickory shaft.

£550-650   L&T

A Carston Mfg. Corp. Ping Anser putter, steel shaft, the head stamped "Phoenix Ariz." and numbered "85029".

£250-350   L&T

An Otto G.A. Hackbarth aluminium-headed putter, with forked hosel, hickory shaft.

£450-550   L&T

A Tom Morris lofting iron, with hickory shaft, the head stamped "F.G. Curtis", with Stewart cleek mark.

£550-650   L&T

A Gibson of Kinghorn 'The Skoogee' niblick, with smooth dished face and hickory shaft.

£250-350   L&T

A R. Forgan & Son of St. Andrews transitional scared neck wood, with Prince of Wales's Feathers stamp, the replacement hickory shaft stamped "John Wisden & Co.", with sheepskin grip.
c1902

A Tom Morris St Andrews long-nosed driver, with beech head and hickory shaft, good condition.
c1870

£1,500-2,000   GBA

An Anderson Anstruther 'Hold-Em' mashie niblick, with deep-grooved face and hickory shaft.

£300-500   L&T

£180-220   GBA

A Bussey-Type caddie, by Jacques, London, with wooden and brass mounted frame, leather handles, and canvas cylindrical club holder and ball pouch.

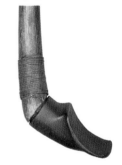

An Andrew Herd Scott of Elie and Earlsferry spliced neck wood, with hickory head and hickory shaft, Prince of Wales's Feathers stamp.
c1900

A dual-faced chole clubhead, with dished upper portion and upright front blade positioned at the heel end, attached to a sawn-off ash shaft, with an area of binding.

£180-220   GBA | **£450-550**   L&T | **£200-300**   GBA

A National Open Championship gilt metal and enamel contestant's badge, by the Whitehead & Hoag Company, Newark, NJ, dated "June 23 to 25, 1932", centrally with the initials of the "USGA", lacking pin to the reverse.

1.25in (3cm) wide

£450-550   L&T

A Club Professional Championship Contestant money clip, from The Professional Golfers Association of America.

1968

£200-300   L&T

A 33rd National Open Golf Championship Marshal's medal, made by The Whitehead & Hoag Company, Newark, NJ, the yellow ribbon inscribed 'Winged-Foot Golf Club, June 27-28-29, 1929', the medal of ball pattern with superimposed club crest, the pin inscribed 'Marshal' within a chased-gilt metal border.

3.5in (9cm) high

£850-950   L&T

A Professional Golfer's Association of America member white metal badge.

1916

£180-220   MAS

A Blackheath Royal Golf Club 'The Calcutta Cup' white metal medal, the obverse relief decorated with a trophy and inscribed 'The Calcutta Cup', the reverse with the crest and motto of the Blackheath Royal Golf Club, with blue suspension silk ribbon and white metal clasp, in a Baddeley Bros. case.

c1900

£700-800   L&T

A silver golfing medal, of Maltese Cross form, Birmingham, centrally engraved with a golfer at the top of his swing, ring suspension, cased, the lid inscribed "Ruthwell Golf Club 1895".

1894   *1.25in (3cm) wide*

£350-450   L&T

An English Searle & Co. silver golfing trophy, the front engraved 'Presented to the Ottawa Golf Club by Cleveson-Gower 1910', the sides engraved with winners' names and years, with maker's marks and London hallmarks for 1907.

1907   *9.25in (23.5cm) high*

£1,000-1,500   TCF

A Ladies' Amateur Championship silver-plated golfing trophy, from Manitou Beach, Saskatoon, mounted on a wooden base with applied plaques.

15.5in (39cm) high

£450-650   TCF

FIND OUT MORE...

'Golf Memorabilia', by Sarah Fabian-Baddiel, published by Miller's, 1994.

An official daily programme for the Open Championship 1957, The Old Course St. Andrews, Wednesday 3rd July.

£350-450   L&T

A Royal & Ancient Golf Club of St. Andrews Open Champions dinner menu, 17th July 1990, the cover with numerous signatures of former champions including Arnold Palmer, Fred Daly, Nick Faldo, Gary Player and Greg Norman.

An official daily programme for the Open Golf Championship at Muirfield, Thursday 9th May 1929.

£650-750   L&T

£500-600   L&T

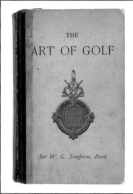

Sir Walter G. Simpson, "The Art of Golf", published by David Douglas, first edition, engraved vignette on the title page, photographic plates, original printed paper boards.

1887

£550-650   L&T

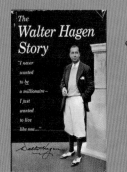

RHOD McEWAN GOLF

Francis Bowler Keene, "Lyrics of the Links: Poetry, Sentiment and Humour of Golf", published by Cecil Palmer, first edition, original decorative cloth, dust jacket, verse inscription from the author on the front free endpaper, dated "Rome, Oct. 28, 1924".

1923

£250-350   L&T

ESSENTIAL REFERENCE

- The popularity of football has ensured that memorabilia connected with the sport has long been in great demand. Items connected to famous teams, popular players or important matches, tend to gain the most interest and the highest values.
- Past stars, including Pelé, George Best, Bobby Charlton and Bobby Moore, remain popular today and items associated with these men are in high demand. Nevertheless, the enormous popularity of today's football stars and teams ensures that memorabilia associated with them can also attract equally significant sums. Shirts, boots and other equipment used or worn by well-known players are highly sought-after and some can demand very large sums, particularly if worn during an important match or signed by the player and their team mates.
- Programmes are another popular area of collecting. There is a large variety available, and values vary widely.

- Modern programmes are printed in large numbers, and many fans store them in good condition, meaning that these can be an affordable entry into collecting. Programmes from FA and European Cup finals, international and early, pre-WWI games generally fetch larger sums. Nevertheless, the enormous significance of some matches ensured that programmes were kept in large enough numbers to keep values relatively modest. A large amount of programmes from the 1966 World Cup final, for example, were kept as souvenirs. Programmes should be in clean condition. Annotated examples will fetch lower sums than those in mint condition.
- Caps are also popular. Those that date from before WWII were traditionally made from a velvet-like material and have the date of the match on the narrow peak, and often the location, tour or organisation. Those from after the war have both teams' names and the date embroidered onto them.

David Beckham's match-worn L.A. Galaxy no. 23 long-sleeved jersey, with MLS flash, the reverse lettered 'Beckham', unwashed.

This jersey was released from within the club as match-worn. The particular match was not stipulated but the August 2007 release date, points towards the Superliga match against DC United .

2007

£1,800-2,200　　　　GBA

Wayne Rooney's match-worn Manchester United no. 8 short-sleeved jersey, for the 2005-06 season, with F.A. Premier League flashes, the reverse lettered 'Rooney'.

This jersey was worn by Rooney in the Premier League match at Tottenham Hotspur in season 2005-06. The jersey was gained in a swap by a Spurs player.

2005-06

£300-400　　　　GBA

Alan Shearer's match-worn Newcastle United short-sleeved jersey and captain's armband, from the F.A. Cup semi-final against Tottenham Hotspur played at Old Trafford 11th April 1999, the reverse lettered 'Shearer'; together with a signed handwritten note of authenticity from Shearer.

Newcastle United won this game 2-0 with Alan Shearer scoring both goals during extra-time.

£1,200-1,800　　　　GBA

Patrick Vieira's match-worn France no. 4 short-sleeved jersey, worn in the international match against England at the Stade de France on 2nd September 2000, inscribed 'France, Angleterre, 02-09-2000', the reverse lettered 'Vieira', together with a note of authenticity.

£550-650　　　　GBA

An F.A. Cup final programme for Aston Villa v Huddersfield Town, played at Stamford Bridge Chelsea on 24th April 1920.

1920

£2,000-2,500   GBA

An F.A. Cup final programme for Aston Villa v Newcastle United, played on 26th April 1924, with original colour pictorial covers preserved, areas of professional restoration.

This is considered one of the rarest Wembley Cup final programmes, for two reasons. Firstly, it rained on the day of the match, ruining many examples, which had thin paper covers. The Football Association had also doubled the price of the programme that year making it too expensive for many fans during the economically depressed 1920s.

1924

£7,000-8,000   GBA

An F.A. Cup final programme Bolton Wanderers v Manchester City, played on 24th April 1926.

1926

£1,200-1,800   GBA

An F.A. Cup final programme for Arsenal v Cardiff City, played on 23rd April 1927.

£2,000-3,000   GBA

An F.A. Cup final programme Blackburn Rovers v Huddersfield Town, played on 21st April 1928.

£800-1,000   GBA

An F.A. Cup final programme for Bolton Wanderers v Portsmouth 27th April 1929.

1929

£1,000-1,500   GBA

An F.A. Cup final programme for Birmingham v West Bromwich Albion, played on 25th April 1931.

1931

£700-900   GBA

A Charlton Athletic official home programme, vol. III, from the 1934-35 season.

£120-180   GBA

An England v Spain international match programme, played at Highbury on 9th December 1931.

1931

£400-500 GBA

An England v Ireland international programme, played at Bloomfield Road, Blackpool on 17th October 1932.

1932

£1,200-1,800 GBA

An England v Wales international programme, played at Ayresome Park on 17th November 1937.

1937

£300-400 GBA

A Germany v England international programme, played at the Olympic Stadium, Berlin on 14th May 1938.

£500-600 GBA

An England v Norway international programme, played at St James' Park on 9th November 1938.

1938

£700-900 GBA

An England v Ireland international programme, played at Old Trafford on 16th November 1938, tied with a green ribbon.

1938

£300-400 GBA

A very rare England v Wales wartime international programme, played at the City Ground, Nottingham 26th April 1941.

1941

£700-800 GBA

A Belgium v England international programme, played at the Heysel Stadium, Brussels on 21st September 1947.

1947

£350-450 GBA

A Football Association steward's badge for the F.A. Cup final between Bury and Derby County, at Crystal Palace 18th April 1903.

1903

£550-650   GBA

A Football Association steward's enamelled badge for the 1929 F.A. Cup final at Wembley Stadium.

1929

£200-300   GBA

A Football Association steward's enamelled badge for the 1932 F.A. Cup final at Wembley Stadium.

1932

£200-300   GBA

A Football League 9ct gold medal for the 1935-36 season, inscribed 'The Football League, Champions, Division 3, Northern Section, Chesterfield F.C., Season 1935-36, M.Dando'.

This medal was awarded to the Spireites' Maurice 'Mick' Dando (1905-49) who scored 29 goals in just 27 games. Dando played for Bath City and Bristol Rovers before moving north in the summer of 1933 to join York City where he scored 46 goals in two seasons. He joined Chesterfield in June 1935 and finished his career at Crewe. Dando suffered from ill-health and died prematurely, aged 44, in 1949.

£850-950   GBA

A silver medallion presented to Sir Stanley Matthews by the French Football Federation on the occasion of their 75th anniversary, sold with a certificate of authenticity signed by Sir Stanley Matthews' daughter.

£350-450   GBA

Mal Donaghy's Manchester United 1991 European Super Cup winner's gold metal medal, inscribed "UEFA, Super Competition 1991", in original fitted case.

Manchester United beat Red Star Belgrade 1-0 at Old Trafford. The away leg was never played due to political unrest in the former Yugoslavia. Malachy Donaghy was signed by Alex Ferguson from Luton Town for £650,000 in October 1988. The Northern Ireland international repaid the manager's faith with consistent performances at centre-back and at full-back in his four year spell at United.

£1,200-1,800   GBA

A miniature gold-plated replica of the FIFA World Cup trophy, by Bertoni of Milan, set on a square marble base with a plaque inscribed 'FIFA World Cup, Germany 2006'.

6.25in (16cm) high

£500-800   GBA

ESSENTIAL REFERENCE

- Cricket equipment has changed very little since the game's inception in the 17thC. The most notable change being the move to straight, from curved, bats from the mid-18thC onwards. Interest and value of memorabilia is therefore largely based on association with a famous player or an important match or event.
- Notable past players include Dr. W.G. Grace (1848-1915), Gary Sobers (b.1936), Geoffrey Boycott (b.1940) and Don Bradman (1908-2001). Memorabilia connected to these players, or signed by them, will tend to demand a high level of interest, although firm provenance is required. Items connected to modern players with a significant following, or to more recent events, can also attract interest. The recent

popularity of Andrew Flintoff may ensure that items associated with him become collectable, particularly if he continues to succeed.
- A large amount of memorabilia dates from the mid-19thC onwards and a wide variety of items are available from this period. Ceramics, programmes, tickets, photographs and accessories are all popular with collectors. Note that these should be kept in as good a condition as possible.
- Wisden Cricketers' Almanack, a fact-filled review of the sport, has been published annually since 1864 and continues to be produced. This book is held in high regard by cricketing fans and early copies in good condition are rare and can fetch significant values.

A Doulton Lambeth Art Nouveau-style stoneware beaker, moulded in relief with figures of Bobby Abel, Sammy Woods and Gregor MacGregor, with later silver rim, hallmarked Birmingham 1938 and engraved "G.J.T. Hawke batting av B.C.C. 1938, from J.T.", Doulton Lambeth impressed mark and initials "E.B." and "8236".

4.75in (12cm) high

£900-1,000   **DN**

A Westerwald beaker, moulded in relief with three cameo panels of a cricketer after W.G. Grace, the body decorated with vines on a cobalt blue ground.

c1890   6in (15cm) high

£500-600   DN

A Doulton Lambeth beaker, by John Broad, moulded in relief with figures of a batsman in different poses, Doulton Lambeth impressed mark to base, chips, rim restored.

c1891   5.25in (13cm) high

£800-1,000   DN

A Victorian brown slipware mug, inscribed "Fred Lee Champion 1885", decorated with a bat.

A Doulton Lambeth stoneware tobacco jar, decorated in relief with figures of cricketers, the lid decorated with a figure of a crouching wicket-keeper, Doulton Lambeth impressed mark to base.

This is one of less than five examples known to exist.

4.5in (11.5cm) high

£350-450   DN

1884   4in (10cm) high

£4,500-5,500   DN

A Minton M.C.C. commemorative mug, the rim decorated in the club's colours, with monogram of 1787-1937 to both sides, stamped to base and impressed mark "H328".

5.25in (13cm) high

£200-300   **DN**

A Victorian Staffordshire mug, by Ford & Riley, printed in brown with a cricket match and a football match of four players, with Bee Sports F. & R. mark to base.

c1887   *4in (10cm) high*

£180-220   **DN**

A Doulton Lambeth stoneware tyg, decorated in relief with three figures of a batsman, a fielder and a wicket-keeper, the handles as cricket bats and boaters, with a silver rim, hallmarks for Birmingham, 1880, Doulton impressed mark to base.

5in (12.5cm) high

£850-950   **DN**

A terracotta circular plaque, entitled 'Australian Test Match Players England v Australia 1926', with the Australian crest and facsimile signatures of players and management, stating to reverse 'Clay plaque signed at the Hotel Cecil London 12th May 1926' and signed by the artist Maud O'Reilly.

13.5in (33.5cm) diam

£1,800-2,200   **DN**

A MacIntyre of Burslem heart-shaped pin tray, with gilded and scalloped rim and printed with Tom Richardson in bowling pose, with MacIntyre stamp to base and Rg. 319664.

1898

£600-700   **DN**

A porcelain plaque, with moulded scroll and floral decoration, printed with a photographic image of a batsman at the crease, coloured, some staining to border.

6.5in (16.5cm) high

£250-300   **DN**

A Victorian ivory novelty propelling pencil, in the form of a cricket bat, scuffed.

This would appeal to collectors of novelty pencils as well as those of cricket memorabilia.

3.5in (9cm) long

£150-200   **DN**

An official programme commemorating the visit of the Australian cricketers to the US in September and October 1912, scheduling the matches to be played in Philadelphia, New York, Bermuda, Winnipeg and Victoria B.C., printed with blank scoring pages, which have been completed in pencil by the original owner at the matches played at Merion CC, Philadelphia.

£500-700   **GBA**

A Surrey County Cricket Club banquet menu, in honour of the 11th Australian cricket team at the Oval Pavilion 12th May 1902, complete with an invitation numbered 43 for W.W. Read Esq.

The banquet took place on the first day of the Surrey v Australia match. The game marked the first of Victor Trumper's 11 centuries in England in 1902.

£450-550   **GBA**

D. G. Bradman, Captain (South Australia)—Born 27th August, 1908. Brilliant right hand batsman. Played his first Test in 1928. Has captained Australia on many occasions, also New South Wales and South Australia in Sheffield Shield Games. Has compiled over 100 centuries and 37 double centuries in first class matches, and has broken almost all Australian and many world records.

A P. & O. R.M.S. 'Strathaird' souvenir booklet for the 1948 Australian cricket tour to England, fully-signed in ink by the Australian tour party besides their photographic portraits, signatures comprising Bradman, Hassett, Barnes, Brown, Hamence, Harvey, Johnson, Johnston, Lindwall, Loxton, McCool, Miller, Morris, Ring, Saggers, Tallon, Toshack and the team manager, Keith Johnson.

£650-750   **GBA**

A signed dinner menu in honour of the West Indies cricket team and Mr A.P. Freeman's XI in 1933, held at the Town Hall, Gravesend, 22nd April, the interior signed in pencil and ink by both teams; sold together with a postcard of the 1933 West Indies Team.

£300-400   **GBA**

A portrait print of W.G. Grace, published by J.W. Arrowsmith, Bristol, bearing a signature in pencil but not believed to be in the hand of W.G. Grace, mounted, framed and glazed.

1890   Image 27in (69cm) high

£60-80   **GBA**

After Philip Hermogenes Calderon (1861-1926) 'Captain of the Eleven', a chromolithograph presented with Pear's Soap Christmas Annual 1898, repaired, mounted, framed and glazed.

Image 28in (71cm) high

£100-150   **GBA**

SPORTING MEMORABILIA

A Converse 'Fundamentals for Better Basketball' booklet.

1975   8.5in (21.5cm) high
£1-2   BH

A Fleer 'Cliff Hagan' basketball card, no. 18, sealed in box with PSA rating of 'Mint 9'.

1961-62
£600-700   MAS

EXPERT EYE – A FLEER BASKETBALL CARD

PSA is a third-party trading card authentification service, which will authenticate and grade the condition of trading cards or other memorabilia for a fee. Cards such as this are sealed in a 'slab' so that they maintain the condition at which they were graded.

The Fleer 1961 card set is considered one of the top three basketball card sets produced. The others being the Bowman 1948 set and the Topps 1957 set.

Wilt Chamberlain's rookie card is one the most valuable from the Fleer set. Also desirable is Oscar Robertson's rookie card, no. 36 and Jerry West's rookie card, no. 43.

Wilt Chamberlain is widely considered the NBA greatest offensive player.

A Fleer 'Wilt Chamberlain Rookie Card' basketball card, no. 8, sealed in box with PSA rating of 'NM-MT 8'.
1961-62
£1,000-1,500   MAS

A T9 Turkey Red Cabinets 'James Jeffries' boxing card, no. 55, sealed in box with PSA rating of 'VG-EX 4'.
£180-220   MAS

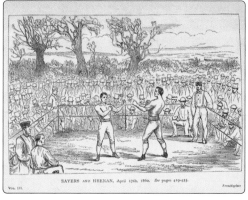

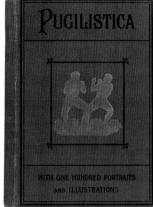

"Pugilistica: The History of British Boxing", by Henry Downes Miles, Edinburgh, three volumes.
1906
£120-180   MAS

An Art Deco style Royal Winter Fair Horse Show silver-plated trophy, mounted on a black finished wooden base, engraved 'Royal Winter Fair Horse Show, 1937, Class 39 Pony Four In Hands 1st Prize Won By'.

c1936   *6in (15cm) high*

£250-350   **TCF**

An piece of original artwork depicting ice hockey centre Bobby Clarke, in his Philadelphia Flyers uniform.

£60-80   **MAS**

A salesman's sample of Wayne Gretzky's Edmonton Oilers 1984 Stanley Cup Champions ring.

c1984

£650-750   **MAS**

An Adidas sports shoe, signed by Heide Rosendahl and other athletes at the 1972 Olympic Games.

Rosendahl competed in and won the 4 x 100m women's relay race for West Germany.
c1972

£120-180   **QU**

A pair of Carl Lewis Seoul Summer Olympics signed race-used track spikes.

Canada's Ben Johnson came first in the 100m final but later tested positive for steroid abuse. Second place Lewis was awarded gold and his time of 9.92 seconds was recognised as an Olympic and world record time.
1988

£400-500   **MAS**

A Muhammad Ali signed 1986 Olympics commemorative gold basketball.

This would appeal to collectors of Ali memorabilia as well as those of Olympics memorabilia.

£200-300   **MAS**

A 1950s German transfer-printed tinplate Dunlop Tennis Balls tin.

8in (20cm) high

£60-80   **QU**

ESSENTIAL REFERENCE

- Teddy bears were named after US president Theodore (Teddy) Roosevelt, who refused to shoot a bear on a hunting trip in 1902. The media picked up on his act of kindness and a cartoon was published. Entrepreneur Morris Michtom produced a soft toy teddy bear to commemorate the event, starting a craze that is still with us today.
- Despite the teddy's origins in the US, German company Steiff (founded 1886) are considered the best maker, with their bears being the most desirable and valuable. Gebruder Hermann, Bing, and Schreyer & Co. (Schuco), are other notable German names to look out for. British companies include Farnell (1908-60s) who are often called the 'English Steiff', Merrythought (1920-2006) and Chad Valley (1915-78). In the US, bears were produced by a large number of factories including Ideal, Gund and Knickerbocker.
- Bears from before WWII tend to have long limbs with large, upturned paw pads, pronounced snouts and humped backs. They are usually made from mohair and solidly stuffed with wood shavings or wool known as kapok. After the war,

limbs became shorter, bodies became plumper and snouts less pronounced, on more rounded heads. Other, largely synthetic, materials were used from the 1960s onwards.
- Bears can be identified and dated from labels, if they are still present, or from the materials, colour and overall form. Consult reference books and handle as many as possible so you can build up an eye for the different styles. Always consider condition as tears, stains, replaced pads and particularly worn fur, reduces value considerably. However, apart from fur, bears can be restored professionally, giving new life to old friends.
- Modern limited edition bears by major names, such as Steiff, are beginning to make good prices on the secondary market, as are bears made by contemporary bear artists. Many are replicas of older bears, so do not confuse these with original versions, which can be worth many times more. When buying a modern replica or limited edition, always retain the box and paperwork with the bear, keeping everything in mint condition.

A limited edition Steiff 'Black Bear' replica 1907 black mohair bear, from an edition of 4,000, with white ear tag numbered "0173/40", chest tag and certificate, in excellent condition, with box in good condition.
1988
£250-300   VEC

A Steiff original honey mohair teddy bear, with yellow ear tag numbered "0201/36" and chest tag, in excellent condition.
c1990   *14in (36cm) high*
£35-45   VEC

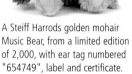

A Steiff Harrods golden mohair Music Bear, from a limited edition of 2,000, with ear tag numbered "654749", label and certificate.
1996   *17in (44cm) high*
£80-120   VEC

A limited edition Steiff 'Teddy Peace' replica 1925 teddy bear, from an edition of 1,500, with tags certificate, in mint condition.
1999   *25.5in (65cm) high*
£80-120   VEC

A Steiff 'George' teddy bear, from an exclusive edition for Teddy Bears of Witney, with ear tag, in mint condition, with felt bag.
2000   *12in (30cm) high*
£100-150   VEC

A limited edition Steiff British Collectors honey golden mohair teddy bear, from an edition of 4,000, with white ear tag numbered "660728", card tag and certificate.

2000   *13.75in (35cm) high*

£80-120   **VEC**

A limited edition Steiff British Collectors honey golden mohair teddy bear, from an edition of 4,000, with tags and certificate, in mint condition and with near mint condition box.

2002   *13.75in (35cm) high*

£80-120   **VEC**

A limited edition Steiff replica 1909 'Rolly Polly' beige mohair bear, from an edition of 3,000, with white ear tag numbered "406652", chest tag, certificate and box, in mint condition.

2003   *6.25in (16cm) high*

£70-100   **VEC**

A 1950s German Steiff pull-along bear on wheels, with metal frame and tinplate wheels.

23.75in (60cm) long

£180-220   **QU**

EXPERT EYE – A STEIFF CENTRE SEAM TEDDY BEAR

The term 'centre seam' applies to the sewn seam that runs down the centre of his head.

To enable the factory to use the mohair economically, every seventh bear was made by joining two pieces of fabric. This meant the bear had a seam down his nose and makes them rarer than standard bears.

The centre seam also gives bears a typically appealing and charming facial expression, which makes them popular with collectors.

This early example is large in size and in superb condition, also retaining his early button and original pads.

A Steiff blond mohair 'centre seam' teddy bear, with original boot button eyes, stitched nose, paw pads, and early blank ear button.

c1905   *16in (40.5cm) high*

£2,200-2,800   **SOTT**

A rare limited edition Steiff Club Members 'Haute Couture' teddy bear, from an edition of 500, made with pastel woven fabric embellished with silver metallic sequins, with stainless steel 'edition' button to ear, black embroidered tag to side seam, book and boxes, in mint condition.

As well as being from a very small edition, recipients were chosen by a prize draw at Steiff. The unusual sparkling, tweedy fabric was designed at the Jakob Schlaepfer studio in St. Gall and was woven in Northern Italy, the eyes are made from Murano glass, and the pads are covered with Indian silk.

2004-05   *12.25in (31cm) high*

£400-500   **VEC**

A 1950s-60s Farnell 'Alpha' blond mohair teddy bear, with amber and black plastic eyes, black vertically stitched nose, fully jointed rexine pads, label to torso, paw pad covering worn.

10in (25cm) high

£60-80   **VEC**

A 1960s Farnell 'Alpha' blond mohair teddy bear, amber and black plastic eyes, black plastic nose, fully jointed, rexine pads, remains of label to side seam, paw pads with cracked surface.

20in (51cm) high

£50-70   **VEC**

A 1960s Merrythought 'Cheeky' golden mohair teddy bear, with amber and black plastic eye, velvet inset muzzle, black vertically stitched nose, bells within ears, fully jointed, with worn areas and losses and damage to stitching, and with one eye missing.

Had it been in better condition, it may have been worth twice as much. However, despite the wear, its fur is in good condition, so it is likely that it could be restored professionally.

13in (33cm) high

£50-80   **VEC**

An American Ideal blond mohair teddy bear, with original eyes, stitched nose and paw pads.

This bear shows a number of features typical of Ideal bears, including a triangular head with widely spaced apart ears set on the sides of the head. Arms set low on the body are another typical feature.

c1910   *13in (33cm) high*

£280-320   **SOTT**

A 1930s German golden mohair musical bear, by an unknown maker.

Squeezing his body activates the musical mechanism which, was obviously a popular amusement for the original owner, judging by the wear on his back.

15in (38cm) high

£200-300   **SOTT**

A 1970s Gabrielle Design beige plush Paddington Bear, unjointed, wearing an orange hat, red duffle coat, blue Dunlop Wellington boots, label to rear seam, in very good condition.

18in (46cm) high

£70-90   **VEC**

A 1990s Channel Island Toys Miller's Books promotional teddy bear, with woven navy blue jumper with embroidered logo.

These bears were produced for bookstore displays in the early 2000s.

8.25in (21cm) high

£7-10   **PC**

A 1950s Twyford wool plush monkey soft toy, with amber and black glass eyes, jointed neck and wire limbs, felt face, hands, ears and feet, red felt waistcoat and fez, label to side seam, in good condition.

12in (31cm) high

£30-40   **VEC**

EXPERT EYE – A STEIFF 'CHRISTMAS' FOX

This red fox was made especially for a Christmas campaign at New York department store FAO Schwartz during the 1950s.

They were usually made in brown, for which the value is around £50-100.

It is in excellent, unplayed with condition with a bright, fresh colour.

A late 19thC American Arnold Print Works 'Tabby's Kitten' printed fabric cat soft toy, the paws printed "Pat.July 5.92 and Oct 4.92'.

These were purchased on fabric panels, which were cut out, sewn together and stuffed at home.

6.5in (16.5cm) high

£8-12   **HGS**

This example retains its ribbon bow, Steiff card tag and the FAO Schwartz card tag, which are extremely rare.

An extremely rare 1950s Steiff red mohair 'Christmas' fox, made exclusively for FAO Schwartz, complete with two card tags.

6.75in (17cm) high

£700-900   **SOTT**

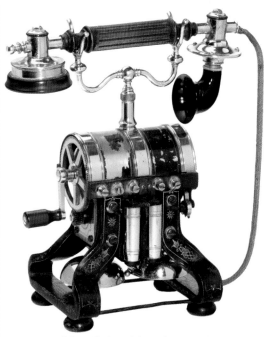

A French Grammont wood-cased telephone, with marbled base and brass plaque to front, in excellent condition.

£750-850   ATK

A rare Swedish L.M. Ericsson table telephone, for 10 lines, with wooden case and nickel-plated cast metal fittings.

1905

£1,000-1,500   TK

A very rare Swedish Stockholms Telefon AB 'TUNNAN' (tunnel) telephone, the cast iron base painted black and decorated with floral transfers.

This rare model was made for nationwide operation under the state-owned 'Rikstelefon' network, which was taken over by the Bell Company in 1901. It is one of the earliest and rarest non-Ericsson telephones in the world.

c1892

£1,500-2,000   ATK

A Danish black bakelite telephone, on metal base with lettered dial and cradle-type handset holder.

7.5in (19cm) long

£100-150   GORL

A 1930s Bakelite and metal telephone, the rotary dial with alphabet and numerical band, black geometric Bakelite case, signed on dial.

c1929   *9.75in (25cm) wide*

£800-1,200   SK

A 1930s G.P.O. black Bakelite 'Series 200' pyramid telephone, fully refurbished and operational.

Designed in 1929, this became the standard GPO telephone during the 1930s. Examples with bells in the base are scarce.

£350-400   TDG

A very rare 1950s G.P.O. red Bakelite 'Series 300' telephone, in excellent condition, restored and fully operational.

Designed by Ericsson in 1932, and produced during the 1940s-50s, the green version is slightly rarer.

£800-1,200   TDG

A 20thC Ericsson rotary dial 'Ericofon' telephone, designed by Ralph Lysell and Hugo Blomberg in 1955, with a pale blue finish and rotary dial in the base, in the original box.

This classic mid-century Modern telephone is still being produced in a variety of colours. This pale blue is typical of the 1950s.

8.25in (21cm) high

£80-120   FRE

A Kirk Plus wall-mounted purple plastic telephone, with paper labels.

9in (23cm) long

£25-35   WW

A Trimphone turquoise push button telephone.

This design classic was the first to have the handset over the keypad or earlier dial.

8in (20cm) long

£80-120   MHT

A 1980s Swatch Twin-Phone, florescent green plastic construction, in original packaging and box.

9.75in (24.5cm) long

£60-100   WW

A Creil & Montreau ceramic plate, titled 'Telegraph' depicting a news agency with telegraph station and French text.

8.25in (21cm) diam

£80-120   ATK

ESSENTIAL REFERENCE

- Dinky toys began life as 'Model Miniatures' in 1931. Produced by the makers of Hornby train sets and Meccano toys, they were intended as accessories to model railways. They proved so popular that in 1934 they were given their own brand, taking on the name Dinky. By 1935 over 200 models were available. Although the range mainly consisted of road vehicles, Dinky aeroplane and ship models were also produced. The models were made at factories at Binns Road, Liverpool until 1979 and also in Bobigny, France from 1937 to 1972.

- The 1930s are widely recognised as the golden age of Dinky, ensuring that examples from this period are extremely highly sought-after. These pre-war models can be rare, partly as they were made from an alloy which tended to crumble over time, and few have survived in good condition.

- Dinky toys from the 1950s and '60s are more readily available. Some models from the '60s featured opening doors and fingertip steering. Boxed gift sets from these decades are particularly popular and can fetch high values.

- The Supertoys range was launched in 1947 and became instantly popular. The Speedwheels range was introduced in 1969 to compete with the Hot Wheels models from US company Mattel.

- Condition is of crucial importance. Models must be in as near to shop-sold condition as possible to make the highest prices. Variations are also vital; models with different colours or markings, or versions released only in certain countries, such as Canada, America or South Africa, can command high values. Examples accompanied by their original boxes will be worth around 40 per cent more. Boxes, and any packaging, must be in good, or better, condition.

- Following the closure of the Binns Road factory, the Dinky name was taken over by Matchbox in 1987, and subsequently by Mattel, who have not used it since 2001.

A Dinky 167 A.C. Aceca Coupé, cream body, brown roof, pale tan ridged hubs, in excellent condition, with good condition correct colour spot card picture box.

1958-63

£100-150   **VEC**

A Dinky 161 Austin Somerset Saloon, black lower body, cream upper body and ridged hubs, in near mint condition, with excellent condition correct colour spot card picture box.

Two-tone paintwork is rarer and more valuable. Another variation has a yellow upper and red lower body.

1956-59

£350-450   **VEC**

A Dinky 147 Cadillac 62, metallic blue, red interior, shaped spun hubs, white tyres, in near mint condition, with excellent condition card picture box.

1962-69

£70-100   **VEC**

A French Dinky 530 Citroën DS19, red body, cream roof, ivory interior, concave spun hubs, silver base, very minor paint touch-ins, otherwise in near mint condition, with near mint condition full-colour card picture box.

This was made by Meccano in Paris and sold in the UK.

1965-66

£120-180   **VEC**

A Dinky 558 Citroën 2CV Modele 61, yellow body, brown roof, red interior, grey concave hubs, in near mint condition, with excellent condition card picture box.

£150-200   **VEC**

A Dinky 545 De Soto Diplomat, metallic green body, off-white roof, silver side stripe, concave spun hubs, white tyres, in excellent condition, with excellent condition card picture box, pen mark to one end flap.

£150-200   **VEC**

A Dinky 545 De Soto Diplomat, salmon pink, black roof, silver-coloured side stripe, concave spun hubs, in near mint condition, with near mint condition yellow card picture box.

£150-200   **VEC**

A Dinky 148 Ford Fairlane, pale green body, cream interior, shaped spun hubs, black tyres, in excellent condition, with excellent condition card picture box.

Metallic green paintwork can double the value of this model, depending on the colour tone. The rarest versions are in blue and were produced for the South African market in 1966 only; they can be worth over four times as much.
1962-65

£70-100   **VEC**

EXPERT EYE – A DINKY OXFORD MORRIS SALOON

This Oxford Morris Saloon was produced for one year only, in 1954, making it rarer than many other models.

It is in near mint condition and retains its correct 'colour spot' box, which is also in excellent condition.

There are two other variations with two-tone paintwork; one has a green upper and cream lower body, and the other has a rarer turquoise upper and cream lower body, and can be worth around twice as much.

The rarest variation has a beige body and hubs, and was produced for export, it can be worth more than three times as much as this one.

A Dinky 159 Morris Oxford Saloon, cream upper body, cerise lower, beige ridged hubs, in near mint condition, with excellent condition picture box.
1954

£350-450   **VEC**

A Dinky 165 Humber Hawk, cream, maroon roof and side panels, in excellent condition, with good condition later card box.

This is slightly more valuable than the black and green version with a black roof.
1959-60

£100-150   **VEC**

A Dinky 102 MG Midget, pale green body, dark cream interior, light cream ridged hubs, grey driver, in near mint condition, with good condition yellow colour spot card picture box.

1957-60

£380-420   **VEC**

A Dinky 197 Morris Mini Traveller, fluorescent green, red interior, chrome spun hubs, in near mint condition, with good condition carded box.

1961-71

£180-220   **VEC**

A Dinky 173 Nash Rambler, turquoise, red side flashes, shaped spun hubs, white tyres, in excellent condition, with excellent condition plain card box.
1958-62

£180-220   VEC

A French Dinky 24D Plymouth Belvedere, grey body, red roof and side flash, plated convex hubs, in excellent condition, with near mint condition yellow card picture box.

£120-180   VEC

A Dinky 518 Renault 4L, dark blue, second type grille, white interior, shaped spun hubs, in mint condition, with near mint condition card picture box.

£80-120   VEC

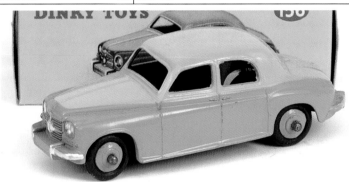

A Dinky 156 Rover 75 Saloon, light green upper, mid green lower and ridged hubs, in near mint condition, with excellent condition correct colour spot card picture box.

Look out for the rare version with the green upper body and the turquoise lower body as this can be worth up to four times the value of this model.
1956-59

£250-350   VEC

A Dinky 105 Triumph TR2 Sports Car, grey body, red interior and ridged hubs, grey driver, in near mint condition, with yellow colour spot card picture box.
1957-60

£180-220   VEC

A Dinky 114 Triumph Spitfire, metallic silver grey body, red interior, plastic lady driver, shaped spun hubs, in near mint condition, with excellent condition card picture box.

Look out for the rarer metallic purple paintwork, which can be around 25 per cent more valuable.
1963-66

£100-150   VEC

A French Dinky 24L Vespa 400 2CV, blue body, grey roof, plated convex hubs, in near mint condition, needs cleaning, with excellent condition card picture box.

£60-80   VEC

A Dinky 181 VW Saloon, grey body, mid-blue ridged hubs, in near mint condition, with excellent condition correct colour spot card picture box.
1956-70

£100-150   VEC

A rare Dinky 232 Alfa Romeo, red, with plastic hubs, racing number 8, in excellent condition.
1954-60
£150-200 VEC

A Dinky 109
Austin Healey 100 sports car,
yellow body, mid-blue interior and ridged hubs, white driver, racing number 21 to bonnet and doors, in near mint condition, with excellent condition correct colour spot card picture box.
1955-59
£250-350 VEC

A Dinky 233 Cooper Bristol, green, mid-green ridged hubs, in excellent condition, with excellent condition card picture box.
1954-60
£100-150 VEC

A Dinky 111 Triumph TR2 Sports Car, turquoise body, red interior and ridged hubs, racing number 25, in near mint condition, with excellent condition correct colour spot card picture box.
1956-59
£220-280 VEC

MILLER'S COMPARES – TWO DINKY 239 VANWALL RACING CARS

The combination of a yellow driver and yellow hubs is appealing, desirable and rare.

This version was made later, between 1962 and 1965. Fewer examples were likely to have sold as the model had already been available for a number of years. It is therefore rarer.

Green or aluminium hubs are more common – yellow plastic hubs are rare.

Even though this example retains its box, it is still not as valuable.

A rare Dinky 239 Vanwall racing car, in green, with yellow driver and yellow plastic hubs, racing number 35, in excellent condition.

1962-65
£120-180 VEC

A Dinky 239 Vanwall racing car, green body, mid-green ridged hubs, white driver, decals, in excellent condition, with excellent condition card picture box.
1958-60
£70-100 VEC

A Dinky 481 'Ovaltine' Bedford van, blue body, ridged hubs, printing to both sides, in near mint condition, with good condition card picture box.

1955-60
£180-220   VEC

A Dinky 923 Heinz Bedford Van, red cab and chassis, yellow back and hubs, in good condition, with fair condition plain blue striped lift-off lid box, with split to one seam.

Look out for the rare variation with Heinz 'Tomato Ketchup' advertising, as this can be worth over five times as much as this model.

1955-58
£120-180   VEC

A Dinky 472 'Raleigh Cycles' Austin van, dark green body, yellow ridged hubs, printing to both sides, in near mint condition, with good condition card picture box.

£220-280   VEC

A Dinky 930 Bedford Pallet Jekta, orange lower, yellow upper body and Supertoy hubs, two plastic pallets, light wear and small paint touch-ins, otherwise in good condition, with good condition blue and white striped box.

1960-64
£180-220   VEC

A Dinky 414 Dodge Rear Tipping Wagon, blue cab, chassis, ridged hubs, grey tipping back, in near mint condition, with good condition correct colour spot card box.

1954-64
£80-120   VEC

A Dinky 901 Foden 8-wheel Diesel Wagon, red cab, chassis, Supertoy hubs, fawn back, in good condition, with blue and white striped lift-off lid picture box.

Along with smaller advertising vans, Foden lorries and trucks are extremely popular among collectors, with rare paintwork variations, and those in the best condition, being worth the most.

1954-57
£220-280   VEC

A Dinky 503 Foden Flat Truck, with tailboard, red cab and body, ridged hubs, black chassis, wheel arches and flash, paint chipping mainly to front of cab, overall in good condition, the good condition plain brown card box with red and white label to lid.

As with many Foden trucks, there are a number of colour variations. The rarest and most valuable has a dark orange cab and chassis with a yellow flatbed and hubs, and was produced from 1952 to 1953.

1947-48
£180-220   VEC

A Dinky 502 Foden Flat Truck, orange cab, chassis, mid-green back and hubs, in excellent condition.

1948-52
£180-220   VEC

A Dinky 514 'Lyons' Guy van, dark blue cab and body, mid-blue ridged hubs, printing to both sides and doors, rear axle in cast mounts, in good condition, with fair condition blue card lift-off lid box, hole to picture face and writing to sides.

The yellow variation with the 'Weetabix' advertising decals is the rarest version, and can be worth over double the value of this example.
1952
£350-450   **VEC**

A Dinky 934 Leyland Octopus Wagon, yellow cab and chassis, green back, highband and bumper, red metal hubs, back rivetted on, paint touch-in to cab, otherwise excellent condition, with excellent condition striped lift-off lid box.

The rarest and most valuable variations have blue cabs with yellow backs, and can be worth around twice the value of this example.
1958-63
£350-450   **VEC**

A Dinky 948 Tractor-Trailer McLean, red cab, plastic hubs, grey back, all decals present, poor moulding quality to one rear hubs otherwise near mint condition, with near mint condition striped lift-off lid picture box.
1961-67
£130-200   **VEC**

A Dinky 260 'Royal Mail' Morris J van, red body, ridged hubs, black roof, printing to both sides, very slightly sunfaded, otherwise near mint condition, with excellent condition card picture box.
1955-61
£120-180   **VEC**

A Dinky 451 Dunlop Trojan van, red body, ridged hubs, printing to both sides, in near mint condition, with excellent condition picture box, shop sticker to one picture face.
1954-57
£180-220   **VEC**

A rare Dinky 453 'Oxo' Trojan van, dark blue, with mid-blue ridged hubs, in excellent condition.

This is a rare model and was made for just one year, unlike the other Trojan advertising vans made by Dinky. Along with the 'Dunlop', 'Esso' and 'Chivers' models, it was also one of the first to be released.
1954
£550-650   **VEC**

A Dinky 450 'Esso' Trojan Van, red body and ridged hubs, decals to both sides, in near mint condition, with good condition card picture box.
1954-57
£200-300   **VEC**

A Dinky 454 'Cydrax' Trojan van, mid-green body, ridged hubs, decals to both sides, in near mint condition, with good condition card picture box.
1957-59
£200-250   **VEC**

A Dinky 967 BBC TV Mobile Control Room, dark green, grey middle stripe, Supertoy hubs, very minor loss to decals, otherwise near mint condition, with excellent condition striped lift-off lid picture box.

£180-220 VEC

A Dinky 968 BBC TV Roving Eye Vehicle, green body, grey centre stripe, roof and Supertoy hubs, camera man, grey plastic aerial, in excellent condition box which has two packing pieces.

£180-220 VEC

A Dinky 969 BBC TV Extending Mast Vehicle, dark green, grey side stripes, hubs, working metal mast with metal/plastic aerial, in near mint condition, with excellent condition striped lift-off lid style box with packing piece and instructions.

£220-280 VEC

A French Dinky 80F Renault Military Ambulance, matte finish, red crosses, spun hubs, in excellent condition, with all-yellow earlier box.

£60-100 VEC

A Dinky 622 10-ton Army Truck, matte olive green, ridged hubs, driver, ridged roof, in excellent condition, with excellent condition striped lid box.

1954-64

£80-120 VEC

A French Dinky 816 Berliet Rocket Launcher, light military green, black launcher, white and red rocket, in near mint condition, with plain card inner packing and good condition detailed picture box.

1969-71

£150-250 VEC

A French Dinky 823 GMC Military Tanker, military green, black cab canopy, spun hubs, in mint condition, complete with excellent condition, inner card stand and no. 595B Traffic Sign in original unopened polythene bag, with good condition detailed picture box.

£350-450 VEC

A French Dinky 890 Berliet T6 Tank Transporter, military green body and ridged hubs, in near mint condition, with excellent condition Supertoy striped box with inner stand.

£180-220 VEC

A Dinky 100 'Thunderbirds' Lady Penelope's FAB1, pink with roof slides, Parker and Lady Penelope figures, Penelope detached and some missiles and rockets loose, in otherwise excellent condition, with good condition inner pictorial stand, in excellent condition outer carded picture box.

1967-75

£220-280   VEC

A Dinky 102 'Joe 90' Joe's Car, finished in green, with chrome and red engine thrusters, in near mint condition, with mint condition inner pictorial stand and polystyrene tray, and excellent condition outer carded picture box, complete with instruction sheet.

1969-75

£250-350   VEC

A Dinky 352 Ed Straker's Car, gold-plated body, blue interior, in excellent condition, with good condition card picture box and instructions.

1971-75

£100-150   VEC

A Dinky 103 Spectrum Patrol Car, metallic red, white base, yellow interior, white aerial, in near mint condition, with excellent condition card picture pack, internal packing pieces and instructions.

1968-75

£150-200   VEC

EXPERT EYE – A DINKY THUNDERBIRD 2

A variation can be found in metallic dark green. Although it was made for one year only, it is worth roughly the same as this version.

Thunderbird 2 is one of the best loved of the Thunderbirds vehicles, making it popular with a large number of Dinky, and film and TV memorabilia collectors.

The rarest and most valuable variation has a turquoise body, and can be worth over £1,000.

It must be complete with the Thunderbird 4 vehicle inside its detachable pod, otherwise the value is dramatically reduced.

A Dinky 101 'Thunderbirds' Thunderbird 2, green, red chrome rear thrusters, yellow legs, complete with Thunderbird 4 pod, in excellent condition, with inner pictorial stand, in good condition outer carded picture box.

1967-73

£350-450   VEC

A Dinky 353 'UFO' Shado 2 Mobile, in blue with black base, rollers and tracks, with white plastic interior, in near mint condition, contained in a mint condition inner polystyrene packing and card window box in good condition.

This can also be found with a green finish, although it is generally worth less, unless it has a smooth flat roof, in which case it can be of a similar value as this version.

1971-79

£300-400   VEC

TOYS & GAMES

ESSENTIAL REFERENCE

- Corgi toys were first introduced in 1956 by the Welsh toy company, Mettoy. The company has produced model cars, aircraft, farm vehicles, commercial vehicles and boats, and continues to produce limited editions today.
- Corgi toys were released to compete with Dinky's Supertoys series. They were the first toys to have plastic windows, a feature which was copied by competitors. Doors and boots that opened were also included, as was sprung suspension, which was marketed as Glidamatic and introduced in 1959.
- As with other die-cast models, condition is paramount when determining value. Collectors look for examples in very good, or excellent condition, with top prices going to examples in mint condition. Never attempt to paint over any scuffs or chips, as this will reduce value. Models should ideally be accompanied by their original boxes, which should also be in good condition.
- Variations are similarly important to value. Look for models

with rare colours or interiors as these are generally worth more. Superdetailing kits were sold in the 1960s and included stickers with which to decorate a Corgi. The addition of these stickers to a model will usually decrease value. For a complete guide to colours, variations and models, consult a dedicated reference book, such as Ramsay's British Die-cast Model Toys Catalogue.
- A number of models were produced during the 1960s and 1970s to tie-in with popular TV programmes and films. These included James Bond vehicles, Batman's Batmobile and Batboat and the Chitty Chitty Bang Bang car. These were very popular when released, and have remained so with collectors. Other popular special models include the range of Chipperfield Circus vehicles. Boxed gift sets are also of great interest to collectors. These should still have their original internal packaging to be considered complete and make the highest prices.

A Corgi 236 'Motor School' Austin A60, in pale blue with red interior and roof turning disc, and spun hubs, in near mint condition, with correct issue folded instruction sheet, and good condition outer blue and yellow carded box.

1964-68

£80-120   **VEC**

A Corgi 229 Chevrolet Corvair, in mid-blue with lemon interior and spun hubs, in mint condition, with mint condition blue and yellow carded box complete with Collectors Club folded leaflet.

1961-66

£120-180   **VEC**

A Corgi 240 Fiat Ghia 600 Jolly, in blue with red and silver plastic canopy, two figures, and spun hubs, in near mint condition, with good condition blue and yellow carded box.

1963-64

£80-120   **VEC**

A Corgi 233 Heinkel Trojan Economy car, the orange body with lemon interior and cast hubs, in near mint condition, with near mint condition blue and yellow carded box with Collectors Club folded leaflet.

Metallic blue, turquoise or fawn bodies are rarer and can be worth at least 50 per cent more in this condition.

1962-72

£70-100   **VEC**

A Corgi 213 'Fire Service' Jaguar 2.4, in orangey-red with flat spun hubs, grey plastic aerial and roofbox, in near mint condition, with excellent condition blue and yellow carded box.

Look out for the rarer, and slightly more valuable, version produced from 1961 until 1962 with suspension and shaped spun wheels.

1959-61

£150-250   **VEC**

A Corgi 247 Mercedes Benz 600 Pullman, in maroon with cream interior, spun hubs and chrome trim, in mint condition, with mint condition correct instruction sheet and folded collectors leaflet, with outer blue and yellow carded box in excellent condition.

1964-69

£70-100   **VEC**

A Corgi 327 MGB GT, the red body with pale blue interior with gold steering wheel, black luggage case and wire wheels, complete with Collectors Club folded leaflet and unapplied racing number 6 decal sheet, in near mint condition, with mint condition blue and yellow carded box.
1967-69
£100-150   **VEC**

A Corgi 349 Morris Mini-Minor 'Pop-Art Mostest', in orangey-red with psychedelic roof, side and bonnet decals, lemon interior and cast hubs, in mint condition.

This is one of the rarest versions of the popular Mini. It was only made for one year in 1967, and few examples were produced. It is also in mint condition.
1967
£800-1,200   **VEC**

A Corgi 237 'County Sheriff' Oldsmobile Super 88, in black and white with red interior and roof-light, in near mint condition, with near mint condition, inner packing card and Collectors Club folded leaflet, and excellent condition outer blue and yellow carded box.
1962-67
£100-150   **VEC**

A Corgi 219 Plymouth Sports Suburban Station Wagon, the cream body with beige roof, red interior and flat spun hubs, in near mint condition, with Collectors Club folded leaflet excellent condition blue and yellow carded box.
1959-63
£100-150   **VEC**

A Corgi 445 Plymouth Sports Suburban Station Wagon, the pale lilac body with red roof, lemon interior and spun hubs, in mint condition, with near mint condition blue and yellow carded box complete with Collectors Club folded leaflet.
1963-66
£150-200   **VEC**

A Corgi 205 Riley Pathfinder Saloon, in red with flat spun hubs and silver trim, in good condition, with near mint condition all-carded blue box with correct issue folded colour leaflet.

1956-62
£140-200   **VEC**

A Corgi 506 'Police' Sunbeam Imp, in blue and white with brown interior with figure driver, cast hubs and blue roof-light, in mint condition, with excellent condition blue and yellow carded picture box with Collectors Club folded leaflet.
1968-69
£120-180   **VEC**

A Corgi 154 Ferrari Formula 1 Racing Car, in red with cast hubs and racing number 36, in near mint condition, with mint condition correct issue blue and yellow window box, still has original price ticket to front.
1963-72

£40-60   VEC

A Corgi 314 Ferrari Berlinetta 250 Le Mans, the red body with blue tinted windows, wire wheels, racing number 4, in excellent condition, with near mint condition blue and yellow carded box complete with Collectors Club leaflet.
1965-72

£50-80   VEC

A Corgi 158 Lotus Climax Formula 1 Racing Car, in orange and white with cast hubs and racing number 8, in mint condition, with mint condition, inner carded packing and instruction sheet, outer blue and yellow carded box.
1969-73

£30-40   VEC

A Corgi 505 Maserati Sport 2000, the red body with concave spun hubs, white driver, racing number 9 decals and Italian flag added, otherwise in excellent condition, with excellent condition card picture box.

£70-100   VEC

A Corgi 345 MGB GT, the yellow body with black interior, bonnet and hatch, luggage case, wire wheels, Collectors Club folded leaflet and unapplied racing number 6 decal sheet, in mint condition, with near mint blue and yellow carded box.

The fact that the racing number decals have not been applied makes this more desirable.
1969

£120-180   VEC

A Corgi 339 'Rallye Monte Carlo' BMC Mini Cooper S, in red, the white roof with chrome roof-rack and two spun hubs, racing number 177, in mint condition, the blue and yellow carded box without picture.
1967-71

£180-220   VEC

A Corgi 317 'Rallye Monte Carlo' Morris Mini Cooper, in red with white roof and chrome spotlight, lemon interior, spun hubs, racing number 37, in good condition, with near mint condition blue and yellow carded plain box.

Look out for the rarer variation with a pink roof, which can be worth around 50 per cent more in similar condition.
1964-65

£120-180   VEC

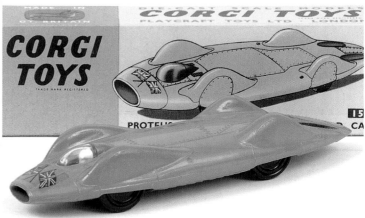

A Corgi 153 Proteus Campbell Bluebird Record Car, the blue body with black plastic wheels, two Union Jack decals, in near mint condition, with excellent condition blue and yellow box.

This is a variant of the standard model, which has one US and one UK flag on the bonnet.
1961-65

£180-220   VEC

A Corgi 405 'Fire Dept' Bedford, in red with black roof ladders, flat spun hubs and mechanical motor, with near mint condition all-carded blue box, with colour folded leaflet.

With its mechanical motor, this red version is a more valuable variation of the standard model produced from 1956 to 1960 in green. That version is generally worth around two thirds of the value of this model.
1956-59

£250-350   **VEC**

A Corgi 1140 'Mobilgas' Bedford TK Articulated Petrol Tanker, the red body with silver gantry, spun hubs and lemon interior, in near mint condition, with excellent condition blue and yellow carded box with inner carded packing and Collectors Club folded leaflet.

Ensure the inner packaging is retained, otherwise it will generally not be worth as high a price.
1965-67

£280-320   **VEC**

A Corgi 408 'AA Road Service' Bedford, in yellow with black roof and flat spun hubs, in mint condition, with excellent condition all-carded blue box, with colour folded leaflet.

Variations with undivided windscreens are more common and usually worth slightly less.
1957-59

£100-150   **VEC**

A Corgi 403M 'K.L.G. Plugs' Bedford, with mechanical motor, in red with flat spun hubs, in excellent condition, with good condition all-carded blue box with pink Collectors Club leaflet.

This is a motorised variation of the more common and slightly less valuable 'Daily Express' van, which has a blue body and is also shown on this page.
1956-60

£120-180   **VEC**

A Corgi 403 'Daily Express' Bedford, the dark blue body with flat spun hubs, in near mint condition, with good condition all-carded box.
1956-60

£80-120   **VEC**

A Corgi 462 'Hammonds' Commer Van, in green, white and blue with red interior and cast hubs, in excellent condition, with correct issue blue and yellow carded box.

The Hammonds version is about 25 per cent more valuable than the other Commer van in blue and white, and with a 'CO-OP' transfer.
1971

£100-150   **VEC**

A Corgi Major 1143 American La France Aerial Rescue Truck, red including cast hubs, yellow ladders, six plastic fireman figures, in near mint condition, with excellent condition inner polystyrene tray, and good condition outer blue and yellow window box with Mr Retailer pop-up card.

£120-180   **VEC**

A Corgi 471 'Patates Frites' Smiths Karrier Mobile Snack Bar Canteen, the blue body with spun hubs, in mint condition, with good condition blue and yellow carded box with correct issue instruction sheet.

The 'Patates Frites' wording indicates this is the rare Belgian version, the wording usually says 'Joe's Diner'. The presence of the correct instruction sheet is also rare.
1965-66

£250-350   **VEC**

A Corgi 926 'James Bond' Stromberg Helicopter, in black and yellow, lacks missiles, otherwise mint condition, with excellent condition striped window box.

This is the Stromberg helicopter taken from the 1977 Bond film "The Spy Who Loved Me".
1978-80

£70-100   **VEC**

EXPERT EYE – A CORGI JAMES BOND LOTUS ESPRIT

This was based on the Lotus in the 1977 James Bond film 'The Spy Who Loved Me'. The scene where it emerges from the sea onto the beach is a much-loved classic.

In 1977, 10 gold plated models were produced with special mountings and boxes, these can be worth over £2,000.

The earlier versions had instruction manuals inside, which must be present, rather than having instructions printed on the base of the box.

Collectors prefer the missiles to be still attached to the sprue and all components to be in mint condition, as with this model.

A Corgi 929 Superman 'Daily Planet' Jetcopter, in red and white, the missile still attached to sprue, in mint condition, with mint condition striped window box, ex-shop stock.
1979-80

£60-80   **VEC**

A Corgi 269 'James Bond' Lotus Esprit, in white and black, the missiles still attached to sprue, in mint condition, with mint condition inner carded display, and excellent condition outer film strip window box with 'Hammer & Sickle' logo.
1977-83

£120-180   **VEC**

A Corgi 342 'The Professionals' Ford Capri, in metallic silver, complete with three figures, in mint condition, with mint condition inner carded tray, and excellent condition outer striped window box.
1980-82

£100-150   **VEC**

A Corgi 292 'Starsky & Hutch' Ford Torino, in red and white with two figures, in excellent condition, with excellent condition inner plastic tray and carded display, and good condition outer striped window box.
1977-82

£80-120   **VEC**

A Corgi 805 'The Hardy Boys' 1912 Rolls Royce Silver Ghost, in yellow, red, blue with gold trim, in excellent condition, with mint condition figures in dome, with good condition outer window box.
1970-71

£80-120   **VEC**

A Corgi 804 Noddy's Car, in yellow and red with chrome trim, complete with Noddy figure, in near mint condition, with excellent condition later issue window box.
1975-78

£100-150   **VEC**

ESSENTIAL REFERENCE

- Matchbox toys were originally produced by the Lesney Products company, which was founded in London, in 1947. The company produced their first toys in 1949. From the early 1950s the company devoted itself to toy production and went on to manufacture a large variety of die-cast model road vehicles, aircraft, ships, boats and trains.
- During the 1950s, the company developed the very popular 1-75 (launched in 1953) and Models of Yesteryear ranges. Toys from these ranges are in high demand from collectors. Early Matchbox toys were distributed by the Moko company (bought by Lesney Products in 1959) and may bear the name Moko or Moko-Lesney. After 1965, the name Matchbox or Matchbox Series was marked on the base or chassis of models. The Superfast range was introduced from 1969, with these models featuring suspension.

- Later ranges included Super-Kings and Speed Kings, both produced after c1971. These are not currently as popular with collectors as earlier models, and will generally not be worth the higher prices.
- Collectors will only be seriously interested in toys in very good to mint condition, and with their original boxes. Variations are the second major key to value, with versions in rare colours sometimes being worth as much as ten times more than those in standard colours.
- Lesney Products went into receivership in 1982. In 1992, the Matchbox brand was acquired by Tyco Toys, who continued to produce toys under the name. Tyco Toys merged with Mattel Inc. in 1996 and Matchbox branded toys, aimed at children and collectors, are still produced.

A Matchbox 36a Regular Wheels Austin A50 Cambridge, the turquoise body with silver-coloured trim, grey plastic wheels, in mint condition, with near mint condition type B Moko box.

This version is usually around 25 per cent more valuable than variations with a blue-green body.

£50-80   VEC

A Matchbox 65b Regular Wheels Jaguar 3.8 Saloon, in deep metallic red with green tinted windows, silver-coloured base and plastic wheels, in mint condition, with near mint condition type B Moko box.

£40-60   VEC

A Matchbox 32a Regular Wheels Jaguar XK140, in orange-red with black base and grey plastic wheels, in near mint condition, with mint condition type B Moko box.

£100-150   VEC

A Matchbox 19a Regular Wheels MG TD, the cream body with red seats, beige figure driver and metal wheels, in near mint condition, with excellent condition type B Moko box.

£100-150   VEC

A Matchbox 34a Regular Wheels 'Matchbox International Express' VW Transporter Van, the greyish blue body with black base and knobbly grey plastic wheels, in mint condition, with near mint condition type B Moko Lesney box, small original pen price mark to two sides.

£150-200   VEC

A Matchbox 47a Regular Wheels 'Brooke Bond Tea' Trojan Van, the red body with black base and knobbly grey plastic wheels, in mint condition, with type B Moko box with model numbers in white circles to end flaps.

£50-80   VEC

A Matchbox 20a Regular Wheels ERF truck, the light maroon body with silver trim and grille, and metal wheels, in mint condition, with type B Moko box.

£100-150   VEC

A Matchbox 38a Regular Wheels Karrier Bantam 'Cleansing Dept' refuse truck, the silver-coloured body with grey plastic wheels, in mint condition, with type B Moko box.

£120-180 VEC

A Matchbox 5b Regular Wheels 'Buy Matchbox Series' London Bus, in red with gold radiator and metal wheels, in mint condition, with near mint condition type B Moko box.

£70-100 VEC

A Matchbox 58a Regular Wheels 'British European Airways' Airport Coach, the blue body with grey plastic wheels and white lettering, in mint condition, with near mint condition type B Moko box.

£60-80 VEC

A Matchbox Superfast 'Nigel Mansell' F1 Renault Racing Car, finished in white, blue, yellow and red, with racing number 5, in mint condition, with mint condition blue and yellow carded box.

This is from a very limited number produced for the Variety Club Children's Charity Nigel Mansell Tribute Dinner 18th June 1993.

£50-60 VEC

A Matchbox Thunderbirds die-cast 'Rescue Pack', containing five models, mint and boxed.

The box on this example is a little crushed and water damaged. If it were mint like the models it contains, the value could rise to around £35.
1992 *12.5in (31.5cm) high*

£20-25 MTB

A limited edition Matchbox silver- and gold-plated die-cast Thunderbirds set, from an edition of 7,500, with information card, certificate and original display box.

The models in this set are the same as those in the other Thunderbirds gift set shown on this page, but are silver- and gold-plated. Produced to celebrate the 30th anniversary of Thunderbirds, it is from a limited edition that would appeal to both Matchbox collectors and fans of the TV series. In order to be worth this amount, the models and box must be in mint condition and complete with all paperwork, as here.
1995 *Box 12.25in (31cm) wide*

£100-150 MTB

A Matchbox James Bond 'Licence to Kill' die-cast gift set, licensed by Eon Productions.
1989 *12.25in (31cm) wide*

£30-50 MTB

ESSENTIAL REFERENCE

- The US toy manufacturer Mattel released its Hot Wheels range of model vehicles in 1968. The eye-catching models were designed to appeal to boys looking for more exciting toys than those offered by competing UK manufacturers Corgi, Dinky and Matchbox.

- Hot Wheels specialised in producing models of 'muscle cars' and hot rods, some of which were decorated with a special metallic finish called Spectraflame, developed to make their cars look different from the competition. Cars finished in Spectraflame were produced in a number of different colours with pink and purple generally the rarest, as these were considered too 'girly' by many boys and bought in fewer numbers.

- Redline models, which feature red stripes around the wheels, were produced between 1968 and 1977 and tend to be popular with collectors. Hot Wheels models are still produced by Mattel and the company currently produces a range of toys aimed at both children and older collectors.

- As with all die-cast models, condition has a great affect on value. But, unlike the toys from most other manufacturers, Hot Wheels were packaged in blister packs, rather than boxes, which were usually badly damaged and then discarded when opened. As a result, it is much more difficult to find Hot Wheels models still with their packaging. Those that have their complete and intact packaging will generally command a significant premium.

A Mattel Hot Wheels 'red line' purple Custom Fleetside, no. 6213.

1967   *3.25in (8cm) long*

£15-20   **SOTT**

A Mattel Hot Wheels 'red line' metallic lime Deora with surfboards, no. 6210.

1968   *2.75in (7cm) long*

£40-50   **SOTT**

A Mattel Hot Wheels gold 'red line' Custom Mustang, no. 6206, with brown interior, open bonnet scoops, in excellent condition, with excellent condition tin badge.

1968

£280-320   **VEC**

A Mattel Hot Wheels 'red line' bronze Twinmill, with stickers.

1968   *3in (7.5cm) long*

£22-32   **SOTT**

A Mattel Hot Wheels 'red line' green Silhouette, no. 6209.

1968   *2.75in (7cm) long*

£15-20   **SOTT**

A Mattel Hot Wheels 'red line' orange Splittin' Image, no.6261.

1969   *3in (7.5cm) long*

£22-28   **SOTT**

A Mattel Hot Wheels 'red line' purple Sand Crab, no. 6403, with chipped windscreen and Crane Arms decal.

1970   *2.5in (6cm) long*

£12-18   SOTT

A Mattel Hot Wheels 'red line' turquoise Stripteaser, no. 6188, with 'Firestone' transfer.

1971   *3.25in (8cm) long*

£40-60   SOTT

A Mattel Hot Wheels 'red line' blue Cement Mixer, no. 6452, from The Heavyweights range.

1970   *3.5in (9cm) long*

£20-30   SOTT

A Mattel Hot Wheels 'red line' burgundy Snorkel, no. 6020, from the The Heavyweights range, with broken platform rail.

1971   *3.5in (8.5cm) long*

£35-50   SOTT

A Mattel Hot Wheels green Ranger Rig, with replaced wheels.

1975   *3in (7.5cm) long*

£22-28   SOTT

A Mattel Hot Wheels white All American Firebird, no. 9518.

This is a colour and transfer variation of the no. 2014 Hotbird.

1977   *3in (7.5cm) long*

£20-30   SOTT

A Mattel Hot Wheels T-Bird, no. 2013, with pink and green side streaks and plastic base.

1978   *3in (7.5cm) long*

£3-5   SOTT

A Mattel Hot Wheels purple Turboa, no. 2061, made in Malaysia, from the 'Speed Demons' series.

1986   *3in (7.5cm) long*

£5-8   SOTT

An ATC (Model Pet) Honda S800 Coupé, yellow with black interior and base and chrome trim, in near mint condition, unboxed.

£150-200   VEC

A Mercury no. 19 Fiat 600 Multipla, blue and turquoise with red interior, in near mint condition, with near mint condition carded box.

£100-150   VEC

A Tekno no. 419 'N.L. Dehn' Ford Taunus Van, type one, blue with red chassis and chrome hubs, in excellent condition, with good condition correct issue carded colour picture box.

£220-280   VEC

An early 1970s Topper metallic bronzy-red Johnny Lightning Custom Mako Shark, with chipped paintwork.

Introduced in 1969, in light of Mattel's success with Hot Wheels, 'Johnny Lightning' cars came with 'friction free' wheels that were said to leave both Hot Wheels and Superfast Matchbox on the 'starting grid'. Although they were successful, they did not catch the imagination as much as Hot Wheels and were withdrawn in the mid-1970s.

3in (7.5cm) long

£10-15   SOTT

A scarce Tri-ang Spot-On AEC Mammoth Major 8, with float and sides and oil drum load (110/3D), in yellow with light grey chassis, complete with nine oil drums, boxed with packaging, minor wear, vehicle in very good condition with one or two minor chips.

£1,200-1,800   W&W

A Tri-ang Spot-On 217 Jaguar E-type, yellow with a cream interior, in excellent condition, with excellent condition colour collectors card and folded leaflet and excellent condition carded box.

£550-650   VEC

A Tri-ang Spot-On 161 'RAC Radio Rescue' Land Rover, blue with red interior, plastic figure driver, spun hubs and plastic roof box, in excellent condition, with good condition carded box complete with colour collectors card and folded leaflet.

£150-250   VEC

TOYS & GAMES

ESSENTIAL REFERENCE

- Model trains were first produced in the 1850s, but they were stylized, bulky and rather unrealistic. By the 1890s, German makers such as Märklin (est. 1859) and Gebruder Bing (1863-1933) had introduced more realistic tinplate models, with clockwork or steam mechanisms. Many of these were exported to the US and other European countries. Production and exports ceased during the two world wars.

- Märklin introduced gauge sizes in 1891, with the larger gauges of I, II and III being eclipsed in 1910 by the smaller I and 0, as demand for smaller trains and sets grew. Gauge I was discontinued by 1938, and gauge 0 itself was replaced in 1935 with the even smaller 00-gauge. The H0-gauge appeared in 1948.

- Hornby began making trains in 1920 and the name has since become synonymous around the world with model trains. Their pre-WWII gauge 0 trains are widely collected. Postwar examples tend to be of poorer quality, which led to the range being discontinued in 1969.

- Their Dublo range, introduced in 1938, was designed to compete with small gauge sets by Märklin and Trix, and is highly collectable. Nationalised livery trains from 1953-1957 tend to be less desirable, but after this date, the range was refreshed. The company was taken over by Tri-ang in 1964.

- Condition is paramount for value, as trains were made to be played with, and usually were. The precise model, date and livery are also important factors with regard to price, and a premium is paid for rarer models. Sets from the 1950s to '60s, such as those by Tri-ang, are now worth looking out for, particularly if in mint and complete condition with their boxes. These are still reasonably priced, but may rise in the future.

A Hornby 0-gauge LNER EM120 0-4-0 tank locomotive, no. 2900, 20v electric, in very good condition.

£280-320   VEC

A Hornby 0-gauge LNER E320 'Flying Scotsman' 4-4-2 locomotive and tender, no. 4472, 20v electric, in good condition.

£250-350   VEC

A Hornby 0-gauge Southern Railways no. 2 special 4-4-2 tank locomotive, no. 2091, 20v electric, with original bulb, locomotive lamps, spanner and a guarantee slip date coded "22/11/36", with the base of a repaired box, locomotive in very good condition.

£400-500   VEC

A Hornby 0-gauge LMS clockwork no. 2C special 4-4-0 locomotive and tender, 'Compound' no. 1185, in excellent condition, with original boxes, locomotive box has some reconstruction and in fair condition, tender box in good condition.

1929-41

£1,500-2,200   VEC

A Hornby 101 LNER 0-4-0 tank locomotive 460, in original box and in good condition.

£50-60   SAS

EXPERT EYE – A HORNBY DUBLO TRAIN

This was made in 1947 only, with a pre-war body but an electric motor and automatic couplings.

As with all early models, it has the the usual gold block on the bunker back – later models have a silver block.

With its green Southern livery, it is the most valuable variation of the EDL7 models, which were made at various times from 1947 to 1954.

It is in excellent condition, retaining its dated instruction booklet and its box, which are both in very good condition.

A Hornby Dublo three-rail EDL7 Southern olive green 0-6-2 tank locomotive, no. 2594, with gold decal to bunker rear and fitted with a horseshoe-type motor, with instruction booklet dated "9/47", minor paint loss to smokebox door, in otherwise excellent condition, with a pale blue box in good condition dated "6/48".
1947

£850-950   VEC

A Hornby Dublo three-rail GWR green EDG7 tank locomotive, no. 6699, with gold decal to bunker rear and fitted with horseshoe-type motor and complete with instruction booklet dated "8/49", in excellent condition and with good condition pale blue box with GW sticker to one end and dated "6/48".
c1949

£700-800   VEC

A Hornby Dublo three-rail LNER green EDG7 N2 class 0-6-2 tank locomotive, no. 9596, with silver decal to bunker rear and fitted with horseshoe-type motor, in excellent condition, with repair box with repair label "14955" to both ends and complete with blue end packing pieces and printed cover strip.

£100-150   VEC

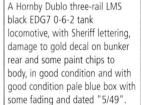

A Hornby Dublo three-rail LMS black EDG7 0-6-2 tank locomotive, with Sheriff lettering, damage to gold decal on bunker rear and some paint chips to body, in good condition and with good condition pale blue box with some fading and dated "5/49".

£120-180   VEC

A Hornby Dublo three-rail LNER black EDL7 N2 class 0-6-2 tank locomotive, no. 9596, with gold decal to bunker rear and fitted with horseshoe-type motor, some minor damage to gold decal and paint loss to smokebox door, unboxed, in good condition.

£180-220   VEC

A Hornby Dublo three-rail GWR EDL7 0-6-2 tank locomotive, no. 6699, with BR-type totem applied to both tank sides, unboxed, in good condition.

£150-200   VEC

A Hornby Dublo three-rail LNER blue 'Sir Nigel Gresley' EDL/D1 A4 class 4-6-2 locomotive and tender, no. 7, fitted with a horseshoe-style motor, locomotive in near mint condition, tender in excellent condition but plastic coal section has minor distortion, both contained in pale blue boxes in excellent condition, locomotive box dated "6/48" and complete with all inner packing sections, printed cover strips and complete with spanner, tender box dated "1/49".

Early models in the earlier light blue boxes are more desirable and are therefore valuable.
c1949

£600-700 VEC

A Hornby Dublo three-rail LNER blue 'Sir Nigel Gresley' EDL1 A4 class 4-6-2 locomotive, no. 7, marked "EDL1" to inside of cab roof, slight distortion to plastic tender top, in good condition, unboxed.

£80-120 VEC

A rare Canadian issue Hornby Dublo three-rail BR green class 20 L30/3230 Bo-Bo diesel locomotive, no. D8000, some marks to roof, in otherwise good condition, with picture box in good condition with instruction booklet dated "11/58", guarantee slip dated "1/59", Meccano Magazine order form and yellow test tag.

The Canadian models are identical to the standard models, with moulded plastic bodies, but have no buffers.

£180-220 VEC

A Hornby Dublo two-rail BR green 'Cardiff Castle' 2221 4-6-0 locomotive, no. 4075, with instruction booklet dated "8/60", in excellent condition and with excellent condition box.

£100-150 VEC

A Hornby Dublo two-rail BR green 'Golden Fleece' A4 class 2211 4-6-2 locomotive, no. 60030, with instruction booklet dated "9/60", also including metal talisman head board, in excellent condition and with excellent condition box with two surface tears where sticky tape has been removed.

£180-220 VEC

A Hornby Dublo two-rail BR green 'Barnstaple' West Country class 2235 4-6-2 locomotive, no. 34005, with instruction booklet dated "3/61", amended instruction flyer dated "June/1961" and purple guarantee slip, two small paint chips to tender front left side and minor lining loss to left side cylinder, otherwise in excellent condition and with excellent condition box, base torn to one side.

£120-180 VEC

A Hornby Dublo two-rail BR maroon 'City of London' Princess Coronation class 2226 4-6-2 locomotive, no. 46245, with instruction booklet dated "10/59", in excellent condition and with excellent condition box but some minor scuffing to lid.

£100-150 VEC

A Hornby Dublo BR black 8F class two-rail 2224 2-8-0 locomotive, no. 48073, with instruction booklet dated "8/60", in very good condition and with excellent condition box.

£120-180 VEC

EXPERT EYE – A HORNBY DUBLO 'GREEN ARROW' TRAIN

This is from a limited edition of only 210 models, and is numbered '11'. Its ticket is glued to the inside of the box lid.

It was produced to celebrate the Golden Jubilee of Hornby's Dublo trains in 1988.

It retains its certificate and special reproduction picture box, which is also in mint condition.

This item is in truly mint condition, a common feature of many limited edition toys. The edition was very small, hence the high value.

A limited edition Hornby Dublo two-rail BR green 'Green Arrow' V2 class 2240 2-6-2 locomotive, no. 60800, from an edition of 210, with numbered certificate, in mint condition with mint condition box.

£800-1,000   VEC

A Hornby Dublo two-rail BR green class 20 2231 0-6-0 diesel shunter, no. D3302, split-rod type, complete with instruction booklet dated "7/60" and purple guarantee slip, in excellent condition and with excellent condition box with Tri-ang/Hornby sticker to left side of lid and with unused tube of oil.

£100-150   VEC

A Hornby Dublo three-rail Southern malachite green EDL7 0-6-2 tank locomotive, no. 2594, fitted with horseshoe-type motor and having gold decal to bunker rear, in excellent condition, with pale blue box in good condition dated "6/48" and with Southern Railways sticker to one end.

£400-500   VEC

A Hornby Dublo two-rail BR green 2232 Co-Co diesel locomotive, with instruction booklet dated "7/60" and purple guarantee slip, in excellent condition and with excellent condition box.

£60-80   VEC

A Hornby Dublo two-rail 2006 tank goods train set, consisting of 0-6-0 BR green R1 class tank locomotive, no.31340, three Superdetail goods wagons, brown steel open, United Glass & Bottle Co. open and BR (WR) grey brake van, track, instruction booklet dated "11/59" and guarantee slip, rolling stock appears unrun, small paint loss to rear buffer beam on tank loco, in excellent condition and with very good condition box but with some minor graffiti to lid.

£70-100   VEC

A Hornby Dublo two-rail 2019 tank goods set, consisting of 2-6-4 BR black standard class 4 tank loco, no. 80033, four goods vehicles, low-sided with meat container, low-sided with tractor, double bolster with timber load and SD6 BR (ER) brown brake van, track and instruction booklet dated "10/59", in very good condition and with good condition box with excellent condition inserts for goods wagons, locomotive insert missing.

£100-150   VEC

A rare Hornby 0-gauge 'Coleman's Mustard' private owner van, finished in yellow with "Colemans Mustard", "Royal Appointment" and bulls head figure transfers to both sides, sides in good condition, roof in fair condition.

This is a very rare van, and was only produced for one year. Coleman's advertising memorabilia is also popular with collectors. There is a Coleman's museum in Norwich.

£600-700   VEC

A Hornby 0-gauge 'Fyffes' private owner van, with black base and red roof, sides in excellent condition, roof in good condition, with a box dated "3/40" in excellent condition.

£150-200   VEC

A Hornby 0-gauge 'Cadburys' private owner van, with a green base and a white roof, sides in excellent condition, with box in excellent condition.

£400-500   VEC

A Hornby 0-gauge 'Fyffes' private owner van, with red base and roof, sides in excellent condition, roof in near mint condition, with box in excellent condition.

It is the excellent to near mint condition of this model, which also has an undamaged roof, that makes it more valuable than the other example shown above.

£350-450   VEC

A Hornby 0-gauge 'Power Ethyl' petrol tank wagon, in excellent condition, with a good condition box date coded "6/38".

£300-400   VEC

A Hornby 0-gauge 'Redline–Glico' petrol tank wagon, in excellent condition, with a fair condition box date coded "12/39".

£200-300   VEC

A Hornby 0-gauge Southern Railways breakdown van and crane, with small gold SR lettering to van sides, finished in green and blue with black chassis, in excellent condition with a box in excellent condition.

£180-220   VEC

A Hornby Series LMS gunpowder van, in original box, with 'LMS' roundel, over-painted roof, and some white letter embellishment, lacks two tabs, one end flap detached, some damage.

£100-150   SAS

A Wrenn LNER blue 'Mallard' A4 class W2110 4-6-2 locomotive, no. 4468, in excellent condition with very good condition box.

£80-120   VEC

A Wrenn LNER blue 'Sir Nigel Gresley' A4 class W2212 4-6-0 locomotive, no. 7, fitted with plastic bogie, pony truck and tender wheels, with instruction booklet, in excellent condition with excellent condition Tri-ang Wrenn box.

£70-100   VEC

A Wrenn BR maroon 'City of London' Princess Coronation class 2226 4-6-2 locomotive, no. 46245, fitted with plastic bogie, pony truck and tender wheels, in excellent condition with good condition Tri-ang Wrenn box without 'W' prefix to end number.

£60-80   VEC

A Wrenn BR green 'Dorchester' West Country class W2236 4-6-2 locomotive, no. 34042, fitted with plastic bogie, pony truck and tender wheels, in excellent condition with very good condition Tri-ang Wrenn box.

£60-100   VEC

A Wrenn BR green 'City of Birmingham' Princess Coronation class W2228 4-6-2 locomotive, no. 46235, with instruction booklet, in excellent condition with very good condition box.

£150-200   VEC

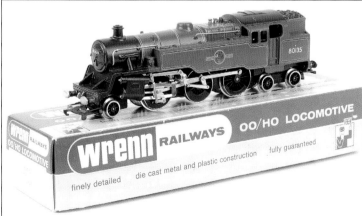

A Wrenn BR green standard class 4 W2270 2-6-4 tank locomotive, no. 80135, in excellent condition with mint reproduction box.

The value would have been greater if the box was an original.

A Wrenn BR green standard class 4 W2270 2-6-4 tank locomotive, no. 80135, in mint condition with excellent condition box.

£250-350   VEC

£150-200   VEC

A Basset-Lowke Midland maroon 'Compound' gauge 1 4-4-0 live steam locomotive and tender, no. 1000, locomotive has some repairs with most of the paint removed from the boiler and fire box, and requires some restoration, otherwise sound locomotive, tender finished in maroon with 'Lowke' transfer to rear and running number '1000' to tender sides, in fair condition.

£850-950   VEC

A Bing LB & SCR brown 12 Class clockwork 0-gauge 4-4-2 tank locomotive, no. 11, expertly repainted, lined and transferred in brown and black with 'LB & SCR' lettering to tank sides, running number to bunker sides, body originally electric, with keyhole added.

£220-280   VEC

A 3.5in gauge 'Juliet' 0-4-0 coal-fired black tank locomotive, with copper boiler, tubes, firebox, and fitted with lubricator, finished in black overall and lined in white and red, complete with original hydraulic/steam test certificate and with home-made wooden case.

Live steam, coal-fired locomotives are valuable and desirable examples of engineering. The finer and more realistic the construction, and the larger the model, the more valuable it is likely to be.
c1995

£1,500-2,000   VEC

A Marklin 0-gauge four-wheeled passenger coach, finished in brown, black and blue, lined in orange and yellow with '1st' in gold to coach sides, the coach has two opening doors on both sides, couplings are broken, the interior overpainted, in good condition.
c1905   *5in (13cm) long*

£150-200   VEC

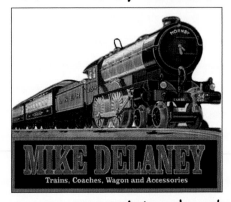

A kit-built BR black Z class 00-gauge 0-8-0 tank locomotive, no. 30954, professionally built and painted, in excellent condition.

£180-220   VEC

A kit-built Royal Scot class 'The Royal Artilleryman' 00-gauge 4-6-0 BR green parallel boiler locomotive, no. 46157, constructed from brass, missing footstep to tender right side front, well-built and painted, in excellent condition.

£70-100   VEC

A kit-built BR Clan class 'Clan Stewart' 00-gauge DJH 4-6-2 locomotive, no. 72009, professionally built and detailed with paintwork by Larry Goddard, signed under right side running plate, in excellent condition.

2000

£500-600   VEC

A kit-built LMS crimson 'Queen Victoria's Rifleman' Royal Scot class 00-gauge F131 parallel boiler 4-6-0, no. 6160, mounted on proprietary chassis with scale driving wheels, in very good condition.

£50-80   VEC

A kit or scratch-built LMS parcels coach, running no. 31059, in mint condition.

£180-220   VEC

Two kit-built LNER green 00-gauge steam locomotives, comprising 4-4-0 class D49 Shire no. 246 'Morayshire' and 2-6-2 class L1 no. 9000, both of brass construction, well-painted and in excellent condition.

£250-350 (pair)   VEC

Two kit-built 00-gauge steam locomotives, comprising 4-6-0 Great Central lined black livery Class 1A no. 4 'Glenalmond', and 0-6-0 GWR green Dean opencab saddle tank no. 1853.

£80-120   VEC

Two kit-built LNER black 00-gauge steam locos, comprising 0-8-0 class Q1 ex-Great Central hump shunter, no. 9929 mounted on Hornby Dublo chassis, and 0-6-0 J15 no. 5393, in very good condition.

£120-180   VEC

TOYS & GAMES

ESSENTIAL REFERENCE

- Tinplate toys were made from the mid-19thC as toymakers started to appreciate the material's advantages over wood. Manufacturers produced toys with finer details as tinplate can be fashioned and decorated more intricately and economically. By the late 19thC tinplate toys were being produced in large quantities.
- Germany became the epicentre of 19thC and early 20thC tinplate toy manufacture. A number of famous German tinplate manufacturers were founded and flourished during this period, including Märklin (founded 1856), Gebrüder Bing (1863-1933) and Schreyer & Co. (1912-78), known as Schuco. Toys bearing these names are keenly collected. Note that toys from German manufacturers were not exported during wartime.
- Tinplate toy manufacturing also took place in the US from the 1880s onwards. Toys by makers such as Marx (1896-c1982) and Ferdinand Strauss (c1914-42), particularly cars and aeroplanes, are avidly collected.
- Early tinplate toys were generally hand-painted. To identify these, look closely at the surface of the decoration for signs of brush marks. Later examples were transfer-printed; the decoration on these toys tends to be shinier, more detailed and more uniformly smooth.
- After WWII the centre of production moved to Japan and tinplate toys became more novelty in theme. Developments during this period included the addition of battery-operated features, which saw tinplate toys adorned with lights and able to produce electronic sounds. Robots from the 1960s are popular and notable Japanese manufacturers include Yoshiya, and Horikawa who produced toys under the SH Toys brand. Extra detailing and features usually add value.
- Value is dependent upon the type of toy, the maker, size, date and condition. Toys by major manufacturers such as Märklin are very desirable. Large ships, aircraft and early cars tend to fetch high prices, as do smaller penny toys, if rare and in excellent condition.
- Be aware that modern reproductions of a number of original toys have been produced. Check colours with reference books to ensure you are buying an original. Reproduction boxes, aimed at collectors, are also currently available. Beware of rust and scratched lithography, as this is almost impossible to restore.

A German Tipp & Co. clockwork two-door saloon, with permanent key, red, cream with tinplate wheels, chauffeur to interior, some wear to edges of roof, otherwise in good condition.

8.75in (22cm) long

£200-250　　　　　　　　　　　　　　　　　　**VEC**

A Wells or similar tinplate Citröen four-door sedan, in red, with cream upper, opening rear boot, clockwork operation with permanent key, tin-printed wheels, some wear to edges of roof and bonnet, otherwise in good condition.

11.5in (29cm) long

£150-200　　　　　　　　**VEC**

A Mettoy tinplate clockwork two-door car, red, with cream tin-printing, tinplate wheels, clockwork operation with permanent key, some wear to rear boot and slight fading to plated parts, otherwise in good condition.

9in (23cm) long

£150-200　　　　　　　　**VEC**

A Chad Valley tinplate clockwork two-door coupé, in red, with black trim and running boards, tin-printed wheels, nut and bolt assembly from the Ubilda Series, in good condition.

10.25in (26cm) long

£80-120　　　　　　　　**VEC**

A pre-war French tinplate fire car, with hinged roof, possibly used as a biscuit tin, red, black, with detailed tin-printing including fireman, with 'SP9' numberplate to rear and "Fabrication Francaise" to base, in good condition,

6.75in (17cm) long

£50-80　　　　　　　　**VEC**

A rare German Arnold Lizzie tinplate novelty car, yellow with opening dickey seat, steerable front wheels, lacks front head-lights and windscreen but includes four composition passengers, with novelty graffiti to car bodywork, otherwise in fair condition.

10in (25cm) long

£180-220　　　　　　　　　　　　　　　　　　　　**VEC**

A German Tipp & Co. tinplate four-door car, dark green, plated parts including plastic hubs, black plastic wheels, in near mint condition.

7.5in (19cm) long

£70-100 VEC

A rare German Distler tinplate Jaguar XK120, blue, with detailed tin-printing, rubber tyres with steerable front wheels, plated parts, battery operation, very light scratches to roof and bonnet, otherwise in excellent condition.

8.75in (22cm) long

£120-180 VEC

A German Arnold tinplate Mercedes four-door saloon, cream, clockwork operation, detailed interior, plated parts, includes motif to radiator grille, in excellent condition.

9.5in (24cm) long

£120-180 VEC

A Japanese ATC Subaru tinplate car, friction-drive model in brick red, with detailed tin-printed interior and hub caps, plated parts, friction drive, in near mint condition.

Made by the Asahi Toy Company (ATC), this is a rare model and is in near mint condition.

6.25in (16cm) long

£350-450 VEC

A 1950s Japanese Asahi Toy transfer-printed tinplate battery operated 'Musical Car', with original card box and maker's mark.

9in (23cm) long

£180-220 QU

A rare Japanese Yonezawa tinplate Opel Olympic, large scale battery operated car in light blue, with cream roof, detailed tin-printed interior, with operating switch to driver's door, wired for illuminated head-lights, rubber tyres with steerable front wheels, plated parts, in excellent condition.

c1954   *11.75in (30cm) long*

£250-350 VEC

A Japanese tinplate Ford Thunderbird, by an unknown maker, large scale battery operated tinplate model in orange, with detailed interior and hub caps, plated parts, opening driver's door, clear plastic windscreen, in excellent condition.

11in (28cm) long

£80-120 VEC

A Japanese tinplate 'James Bond' no. M101 Aston Martin DB5, with remote control, finished in silver with black base, some slight loss of chrome around bumpers, otherwise in excellent condition, in fair condition lift-off lid box.

£180-220 VEC

EXPERT EYE – A GERMAN TINPLATE MOTORCYCLE

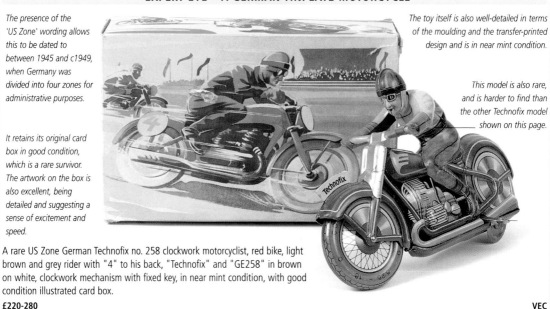

The presence of the 'US Zone' wording allows this to be dated to between 1945 and c1949, when Germany was divided into four zones for administrative purposes.

It retains its original card box in good condition, which is a rare survivor. The artwork on the box is also excellent, being detailed and suggesting a sense of excitement and speed.

The toy itself is also well-detailed in terms of the moulding and the transfer-printed design and is in near mint condition.

This model is also rare, and is harder to find than the other Technofix model shown on this page.

A rare US Zone German Technofix no. 258 clockwork motorcyclist, red bike, light brown and grey rider with "4" to his back, "Technofix" and "GE258" in brown on white, clockwork mechanism with fixed key, in near mint condition, with good condition illustrated card box.

£220-280   VEC

A 1930s Spanish Rico clockwork touring rider-on-motorcycle, mechanism with fixed key, red bike, brown and blue rider, plain brown tinplate wheels, stabilisers, "RSA" to tank sides, clockwork mechanism requires some attention, in good condition.

6.5in (16.5cm) long

£220-280   VEC

A Russian Touring clockwork motorcyclist, with red and yellow bike, green and blue rider with brown helmet, tinplate tyres with small outriders, in working order and in near mint condition, unboxed.

£40-60   VEC

A French SFA motorcyclist and sidecar, red bike and sidecar, blue rider, "SFA-Paris" to tank sides and sidecar, registration no. "2139-RP9", in near mint condition.

£70-100   VEC

A 1950s German Technofix no. 255 clockwork trick motorcycle, light brown bike, red and blue Rider with "2" to his back and rear wheels and "Technofix" and "GE255" to front in white on red, in good condition, unboxed.

£80-120   VEC

A Japanese MT clockwork police rider, mechanism driven with fixed key, on green bike with eagle logo to tank sides, rider in silver suit with green helmet and "PD" to helmet and on arm, meant for variable cable action, in near mint condition, unboxed.

£60-100   VEC

A 1950s West German MF2 'Hurricane' transfer-printed tinplate clockwork boat, in mint condition with original box with pictorial lid, marked "Made in Western Germany".

Box 9.75in (24.5cm) long

£8-12   MTB

A Sutcliffe 'Meteor' clockwork drive speedboat, white plastic body with wood-effect deck, "Meteor" and "Sutcliffe" transfers, in original box with instructions and key, in excellent condition.

£60-100   VEC

A German CKO Kellerman clockwork Atlantic liner, black/red hull, detailed tin-printing to superstructure, two red funnels, includes rudder, propeller and key, in excellent condition, with good condition colourfully illustrated box.

13.75in (35cm) long

£80-120   VEC

A pre-war German tinplate clockwork submarine, unknown maker, with grey hull and superstructure, upper part of hull has three colour camouflage effect, lacks propeller but includes swivelling rudder, otherwise in good condition.

11.5in (29cm) long

£50-80   VEC

A 1950s Czechoslovakian transfer-printed tinplate clockwork car scene, unmarked, in mint condition with original card box.

In similar condition but without the box, this is worth around £10-15.

9.5in (24cm) long

£18-22   MTB

A 1950s-60s Czechoslovakian lithographed tinplate clockwork train toy, the sides printed with scenes of buses, people in a city and trains speeding towards tunnels, the top with trains moving through buildings.

The streamlined style of the trains is typical of the styling of the period.

9.5in (25cm) long

£8-12   PC

TOYS & GAMES

A 1950s-60s Japanese TM Modern Toys transfer-printed tinplate and plastic battery powered 'Space Explorer Ship', marked "Made in Japan TM", with original card box.

10in (25.5cm) diam

£350-450   **QU**

EXPERT EYE – A LI'L ABNER MECHANICAL TOY

Unique Art Manufacturing Co. of Newark, New Jersey, were known for their mechanical tinplate character toys, which also included 'Gertie The Goose'.

This toy was produced for Christmas 1945, and was based on a popular comic strip of the time.

The movement is superb. When wound and set off, every character moves with Abner dancing, Daisy Mae playing the piano, Mammy Yokum keeping time, and Pappy Yokum playing the drums.

The form is complex, involving many separate components, and the transfer-printed decoration is detailed and colourful, covering all parts of the toy.

A 1950s American Unique Art Manufacturing Co. 'Li'l Abner and his Dogpatch Band' tinplate mechanical lithographed toy, with attached figures of Daisy Mae, Abner, Mammy and Pappy Yokum, in good condition.

12in (30cm) wide

£220-280   **VEC**

A 1950s-60s Japanese Nogura transfer-printed tinplate and plastic robot, marked "Made in Japan".

This robot is modelled after the iconic robot Robby, first seen in the 1956 film 'Forbidden Planet'.

12in (31cm) high

£500-600   **QU**

A US Zone German Schuco Turn Miki 881 mouse toy, grey felt body, green trousers, yellow neck ribbon, grey wire arms with brown felt hands, black tail, in near mint condition, with good condition box and instruction leaflet.

5.5in (14cm) high

£180-220   **VEC**

A US Zone German Schuco Solisto 985/1 clockwork monkey drummer, green jacket, blue trousers, red beret, brown hair, tin drum, yellow bow tie, slight discolouration to felt, tiny marks to face of drum, otherwise in good condition, with fair condition box.

4.5in (11cm) high

£100-150   **VEC**

A 1950s Japanese Haji transfer-printed tinplate and wood clockwork mother and child in pram, the pram sides printed with a detailed childhood scene, with maker's mark.

6.25in (16cm) long

£300-400   **QU**

ESSENTIAL REFERENCE

- Cast and painted lead figures saw their golden age from the late 19thC until the late 1950s, when cheaper plastic took over. Soldiers are the most popular category, although domestic and pastoral themes such as farming and zoos were produced, particularly after WWI. There are a number of makers, with Britains (founded 1845) being the largest and most popular. Other names include Charbens, Taylor & Barrett, and John Hill Co.

- Look for fine detailing and original paint. Paint which is completely opaque, overly bright or has unusual colour tones may indicate a repainted figure. These, or figures that have had parts replaced, re-attached or customised, should be avoided. If buying a set, ensure that it is complete and does not contain incorrectly duplicated figures. Original boxes will add value, particularly in excellent condition, as they were often thrown away or became damaged.

A Britains Royal Scots Greys set 32, comprising five mounted troopers, in scarlet dress uniform, in original box tied to stringing card.

c1953   *3.25in (8.5cm) high*

£70-100   **W&W**

A scarce Britains Danish Guard Hussar regiment set 2018, comprising of six men with swords and an officer, all on brown horses, and a trumpeter on a grey horse, in original box.

3.25in (8.5cm) high

£350-450   **W&W**

A Britains Greek Army Evzones set 196, containing seven marching soldiers with shouldered rifles, some wear and paint chips.

3in (7.5cm) high

£100-150   **W&W**

A rare Britains 1937 Coronation state coach set 1470, with seated figures of George VI & Elizabeth pulled by Windsor grey horses, in original box.

Box 22in (56cm) wide

£120-180   **W&W**

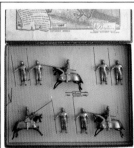

A rare Britains metal knights in armour set 1307, in original box.

£80-120   **W&W**

A Britains US Airmen set 334, comprising six Marching Airmen in service dress with peak caps, brown belts and boots, all very good, rare figures to find in this condition.

£220-280   **VEC**

A Britains Farmers Gig, no. 20F, one shaft damaged, boxed.

4.75in (12cm) wide

£60-80   **GAZE**

TOYS & GAMES

A Barclay Manoil soldier throwing a grenade, with rifle.

3.25in (8cm) high

£5-7   PWE

A Barclay soldier carrying two ammunition boxes, moulded on the base "Barclay U.S.A. Made 3734".

3.25in (8cm) high

£10-15   PWE

A Manoil M44 25 'Sniper' figure, with folding rifle.

This figure is rare as the folding rifle was easily broken. Manoil was founded in 1935 in New York and closed in 1959. As well as soldiers, they produced the 'Happy Farm', and 'My Ranch' series of cowboys and Indians. Although they did not copy each other, figures by Manoil and Barclay are very similar and could be mixed with each other.

2.25in (6cm) high

£100-150   PWE

A Manoil Kneeling Sniper figure, with long rifle.

With the non-folding rifle, this is generally worth around a tenth of the example with the folding rifle. However, examples with tinplate hats can be worth around £20-25.

2.25in (6cm) high

£10-15   PWE

A Barclay Manoil armoured car with cannon.

4.25in (10.5cm)

£8-12   PWE

A rare Taylor & Barrett fire escape engine, red painted die-cast lead, with detachable two-piece ladder on wheels and three original firemen.

Fire engines are popular models. Taylor & Barrett was only in existence from 1920 to 1939, and is best known for its zoo series.

4in (10cm) long

£180-220   W&W

ESSENTIAL REFERENCE

- While Star Wars memorabilia covers such diverse areas as film props, posters, clothing, breakfast cereal boxes and Christmas ornaments, it is the toys, and especially the 3.75in action figures, that most fans associate with the subject and therefore tend to make the highest prices.
- The merchandising license was initially offered to Mego Corp., but they declined and it was eventually taken up by Kenner in the US and Palitoy in the UK.
- Before Star Wars, the standard size for action figures was 8 to 12in. Kenner chose to produce the figures at around 3.75in so spaceships like the Millennium Falcon could be in scale with the figures, something that would have been prohibitively expensive with the large figures. This also meant they could be sold more cheaply than the larger versions, making them a popular choice with parents as well as children.
- The first 12 figures were released in 1978 and were sold mounted on cards illustrating the 12 figures in the range.

These cards are known as '12-backs' and are generally the most sought-after today. As more figures were released, the card backs were updated. More toys were issued to coincide with each new film in the original trilogy but following the release of Return of the Jedi in 1983, the toy franchise was beginning to tire. The line was retired in 1985 but then resurrected in 1990. The recent prequel trilogy has resulted in a huge number of new toys being released.

- Today, the market for vintage toys has now levelled off as older collectors have mature collections, younger fans have little interest in the older characters, and a number of large collections have come to the market. Toys produced for the new trilogy are unlikely to reach the high prices of vintage examples today. While the films are aimed at the juvenile market, the toys are geared towards the collectors market where mint and boxed pieces are the norm, rather than the exception.

"Star Wars", issue 1, published by Marvel Comics, 1 July 1978, with 30¢ cover price.

Look for the edition of the first issue with the 35¢ cover price. It is possible as few as 1,500 copies where printed and it can be worth over 10 times as much as the regular 30¢ edition.

1978   10.25in (26cm) high

£12-18   KNK

A "Star Wars Punch Out and Make It" activity book, published by Random House.

1977   12in (30cm) high

£4-6   KNK

A "Star Wars Intergalactic Passport", first edition, by Ballantine Books, designed by Charles R. Bjorklund.

450 Intergalactic Passports were originally produced for visitors to the Empire Strikes Back set and can be worth over £300. This example was on release to the general public in far greater numbers.

1983   6in (15cm) high

£7-10   KNK

A Star Wars themed first day cover commemorating the Viking Mission to Mars, post dated 20th July 1978.

This card is dated five days before the Viking 2 orbitor failed due to a fuel leak. The lander continued to operate on the surface of Mars until 11th April, 1980.

1978   7in (17.5cm) wide

£8-12   KNK

A Star Wars: The Empire Strikes Back printed card party centrepiece, produced by Designware, unopened and unused.

c1980   14in (35.5cm) high

£12-18   KNK

A Star Wars: The Empire Strikes Back themed Puffs facial tissue box, illustrated with a scene from Bespin Cloud City, with 'cut-out and colour' Luke Skywalker on the back.

Boxes with scenes from Hoth and Dagobah were also produced and each had one of two 'cut-out and colour' scenes on the back.

1980   13.5in (34cm) high

£8-12   KNK

A Canadian Star Wars: Droids – The Adventures of R2-D2 and C-3PO 'R2-D2' action figure, by Kenner, mounted on dual language card with collectors coin.

The figures in this range are the same as those produced for the original movies, but are painted in 'cartoon' colours.

c1985   *Card 9in (23cm) high*

£50-70   **KNK**

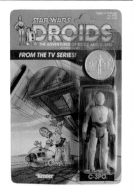

A Star Wars: Droids 'C-3PO' action figure, by Kenner, mounted with collectors coin.

Droids was a short-lived cartoon series, which aired with its companion series 'Ewoks'. A series of figures was released for the first series, of which Boba Fett (always a fan favourite) and Vlik, produced only in Brazil, are the most desirable.

c1985   *Card 9in (23cm) high*

£50-70   **KNK**

EXPERT EYE – AN UNLICENSED STAR WARS FIGURE

As official Star Wars figures were not licensed to Communist Europe, local toy manufacturers made moulds from licensed figures.

Moving parts such as limbs were removed during the moulding process and were often reassembled incorrectly. For example, this figure has the correct torso for an AT-AT Commander, but the limbs are from another figure.

Figures were also produced with differing details and colourings and this can make them sought-after by collectors. The Polish 'Stormtrooper' figure is bright blue and can be worth up to £400.

The card would appear to have been used for a number of different figures. While the 'AT-AT Commander' is an Imperial character, the card is illustrated with an Alliance Y-Wing starfighter.

An unlicensed Polish Star Wars: Return of the Jedi 'AT-AT Commander' action figure, unopened and mounted on a Polish language card with an illustration of an Y-Wing starfighter.

c1985   *Card 8.25in (21cm) high*

£150-200   **KNK**

A Star Wars 'Holographic Princess Leia' carded transparent action figure, by Hasbro, sold exclusively at the San Diego Comic-Con 2005, in mint condition.

The figure is taken from the 1998 Power of the Force II action figure.

2005   *9in (22.5cm) high*

£3-5   **MTB**

A Star Wars: Episode I 'Darth Sidious' carded action figure, by Hasbro, with 'Com Talk' chip, in mint condition.

9in (22.5cm) high

£2-4   **MTB**

A Star Wars: Episode I 'Watto' carded action figure, by Hasbro, with 'Com Talk' chip, mint and carded.

9in (22.5cm) high

£2-4   **MTB**

A Star Wars 'Imperial Cruiser' diecast ship, by Kenner, with sliding cargo bay doors to base, containing removable 'Rebel Blockade Runner' ship.

If the Rebel Blockade Runner is not present, the value falls to well below £5. The condition of the paintwork also affects the value considerably.

c1979   7in (18cm) long

£12-18   **KNK**

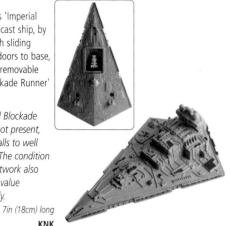

EXPERT EYE – A STAR WARS DIECAST SHIP

The TIE Bomber was originally intended to feature in the original Star Wars film, but instead made its first, brief, appearance in The Empire Strikes Back.

An example with the original box could be worth nearly three times as much.

The white plastic wings have yellowed with age, while the diecast body has stayed white.

Planned for the second series of diecast ships by Kenner, a limited number of TIE Bombers were produced to test the market. Little interest was shown and the ship was never put into general production, making it scarce today.

A rare Star Wars: The Empire Strikes Back diecast 'TIE Bomber' ship, by Kenner.

c1979   5.25in (13cm) wide

£100-120   **KNK**

A Star Wars: Return of the Jedi '"Battle Damaged" Imperial TIE Fighter' vehicle, by Kenner, with decals and TIE fighter pilot.

These mid-sized models are hard to find, especially complete with the 'damage' decals and pilot. A button on the back of the cockpit collapses the 'wings'.

c1983   4.75in (12cm) high

£12-15   **KNK**

A scarce Star Wars: The Empire Strikes Back '"Battle Damaged" X-Wing Fighter' vehicle, by Kenner, with decals and pilot.

A button on the back of the cockpit collapses the nose.

c1982   7.75in (20.5cm) long

£12-15   **KNK**

A Star Wars: Return of The Jedi 'Laser Rifle Carry Case' action figure carrying case, by Kenner, with original card packaging.

This case was the last one produced by Kenner from their first range of cases. Compared to others in the range, such as 'C-3PO' and 'Darth Vader', this case held fewer figures and was also rather large for a child to carry, making it less popular. Its shape also meant it was often played with as a gun and suffered damage as a result. While this example is discoloured, it does retain its cardboard base adding to the value.

c1984   25.5in (64.5cm) long

£40-50   **KNK**

A Star Wars: The Empire Strikes Back 'Switcheroo' Darth Vader shaped lightswitch cover, by Kenner.

The eyes show red for 'on' and white for 'off'.

1980   6.25in (15.5cm) high

£8-12   **KNK**

A Star Wars: Return of the Jedi 'Wicket W. Warrick the Ewok' soft toy, by Kenner, with original head-dress, fabric tag and card tag, in near mint condition.

Kenner made five Ewok plush soft toys and Wicket is the most easily found as he was the most popular character. The value drops to £6-8 without the head-dress and tags.

1983   14.75in (37.5cm) high

£10-12   **KNK**

A scarce Star Wars: Return of the Jedi 'Latara' Ewok plush soft toy, with head-dress and fabric tag, in excellent condition.

£10-12   **KNK**

A scarce Star Wars: Return of the Jedi 'Wiley' Wokling plush soft toy, by Kenner, with fabric tag, in excellent condition.

Wiley is Latara's little brother. Both characters featured in the ABC animated TV series 'Ewoks'.
1983

£4-6   **KNK**

A rare Star Wars: Return of the Jedi Ewoks plush soft toy shop display box, by Kenner.

As these boxes were usually thrown away by shops after use, they are rare today.
c1984   21in (53.5cm) wide

£70-100   **KNK**

A Star Wars: Return of the Jedi yellow vinyl child's raincoat, by Adam Joseph, with Yoda transfer to back.

A version with Darth Vader and the Imperial Guard on the back was also made.
1983   22.5in (57cm) long

£12-18   **KNK**

A Star Wars blue and white satin jacket, by Bright Red Group, with Greg and Tim Hildebrandt iron-on artwork to the back, and with woven badge to front, size 2.
c1977

£40-60   **NOR**

A pair of Star Wars: Return of the Jedi 'Darth Vader' roller skates, by Brookfield Athletic, with original box.

c1983

£20-30   **W&W**

A Star Wars: Return of the Jedi bag, by Frankel & Roth, with Jabba the Hutt and Bib Fortuna on one side and a hanger bay scene on the other.

c1983   12in (30.5cm) wide

£3-5   **W&W**

ESSENTIAL REFERENCE

- As nostalgia for vintage children's shows from the 1960s onwards grows, so does demand for vintage toys and merchandise connected to them.
- While shows like the Six Million Dollar Man and Charlie's Angels were broadcast internationally and will have collectors world-wide, others such as the Partridge Family in the US and the Magic Roundabout in the UK will attract the majority of attention in their country of origin.
- Much like Star Wars merchandise, the action figure is often the most popular toy produced and US manufacturer Mego Corp. is perhaps the best known producer.
- Mego was started by a husband-and-wife team in 1954 and initially made bargain-basement toys. The founders' son joined in 1971 and was responsible for transforming the company. The first action hero figure 'Action Jackson' was released in 1971. The line was not popular but did lead to the concept of producing a standard body for a range of characters and this economy played a major role in Mego's success. The first successful range was 'World's Greatest Super-Heroes' featuring Captain America, Superman and Batman among others. This was followed up by the Planet of the Apes line – Mego's most successful film and TV franchise. These figures showed Mego's attention to detail, and high quality sculpting and clothing. Merchandising licenses were soon snapped up and the company became the first port of call for film and TV studios, hitting a peak in 1976-77.
- In 1977, Mego famously failed to obtain the license for the Star Wars, either through some miscommunication or perhaps through choice. While the success of Kenner's line was not the direct reason for Mego's demise, it certainly was a factor, and the company closed in 1982.
- Today, collectors prize Mego figures for their realistic head sculpts with excellent likeness to the characters, and quality costumes and accessories. Action figures from short-lived series such as Space: 1999 are often more valuable as production runs were shorter. Female characters are often harder to find as young boys would have preferred the male heroes, meaning fewer were made and sold.
- See the Character Collectables section (pages 147-151) for non-toy Film & TV related merchandise.

A Doctor Who 'Third Doctor' action figure, by Dapol, modelled on Jon Pertwee, mint and carded.

c1996   7.75in (19.5cm) high

£7-9   **MTB**

An Italian Doctor Who 'Fourth Doctor' action figure, by Harbert, SpA, modelled on Tom Baker, complete with scarf and rare sonic screwdriver, mint and boxed.

The Denys Price Doctor Who range was produced by Mego in the US. Unsurprisingly the figure of the Doctor was the most popular, which perhaps explains why Harbert chose to issue only this figure. The sonic screwdriver is frequently lost. The version issued by Denys Price is worth a similar amount.

c1979   Box 10.25in (26cm) high

£75-85   **MTB**

A Doctor Who 'Melanie Bush' action figure, by Dapol, with blue shirt, mint and carded.

The artwork on the card makes this version more desirable than the other version on this page. The back of the card also shows the range of figures available. Mel has proven to be one of the Doctor's least popular companion with fans, hence prices for her are comparatively low.

c1987   7.75in (19.5cm) high

£8-10   **MTB**

A Doctor Who 'Melanie Bush' action figure, by Dapol, with pink shirt, mint and carded.

This figure and its packaging are an excellent example of 'plastic melt'. The different injection moulded plastics used in the figurine have begun to break down, giving off a gas. This can cause the packaging to warp (note the bubble by her head), and even crack, due to the pressure of the gas in the sealed bubble. Loose, she is usually worth around £3-4 in excellent condition.

7.75in (19.5cm) high

£7-8   **MTB**

TOYS & GAMES

A Doctor Who 'Ace' action figure, by Dapol, mint and carded.

This was the last form of packaging produced by Dapol before the BBC withdrew the license in 2002.

c1996   7.75in (19.5cm) high

£5-7   **MTB**

A Doctor Who 'Silurian' action figure, by Dapol, mint and carded.

c1996   7.75in (19.5cm) high

£7-8   **MTB**

A Doctor Who 'Talking K-9' battery operated toy, by Palitoy, mint and boxed.

The audio is supplied by a crude miniature record player inside. The drive band that runs the player to prone to breaking but can be replaced. Examples should be in working order to be worth the full amount.

c1978   Figure 6in (15cm) high

£75-85   **MTB**

A Doctor Who 'Robot Action Dalek' battery operated toy, by Marx Toys, licensed by the BBC, mint and boxed.

This is a re-issue of the first Doctor Who toy produced, in 1964 by Marx. It was produced in other colours including yellow and silver.

c1974   6.5in (16.5cm) high

£200-250   **MTB**

A Doctor Who 'Talking Dalek' battery operated toy, by Palitoy, licensed by the BBC, mint and boxed.

The delicate eyepiece and weapons are often damaged or lost through play. Replacements are being made and can be recognised by their shiny, vinyl appearance.

1975   6.25in (16cm) high

£220-280   **MTB**

An A-Team 'Off Road Attack Cycle' moulded plastic toy, by Galoob, mint and boxed.

Only the early pieces from this range are desirable to collectors.
c1983   5.5in (14cm) high
£45-55   **MTB**

A 1970s Alice in Wonderland 'Alice' doll, by Pedigree, based on the 1951 Walt Disney film, mint and boxed.

The doll is based on Pedigree's Sindy doll but with a slightly altered head. This makes it popular with collectors of Sindy dolls and Alice in Wonderland.
                                        Box 12in (30.5cm) high
£20-30   **MTB**

A World of Annie 'Annie' poseable figure, by Knickerbocker, modelled on the characters from the 1982 'Annie' musical film, mint and boxed.

The most popular figure from the full range of characters, Annie originally cost $2 (£1).
c1982   Box 8.25in (21cm) high
£8-12   **MTB**

A World of Annie 'Daddy Warbucks' poseable figure, by Knickerbocker, modelled on the characters from the 1982 'Annie' musical film.

c1982   Box 8.25in (21cm) high
£8-12   **MTB**

A World of Annie 'Punjab' poseable figure, by Knickerbocker, modelled on the characters from the 1982 'Annie' musical film.

This figure originally retailed for $2.97 (£1.50).
c1982   Box 8in (20.5cm) high
£8-12   **MTB**

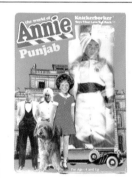

A Battlestar Galactica 'Imperious Leader' action figure, by Mattel, mint and carded.

A range of 3.5in action figures were made, based on the Battlestar Galactica series, and the 'bad guys' were a popular subject. While Starbuck and Adama were recreated in miniature form, other popular characters such as Apollo and Boomer were curiously overlooked.
c1978   9in (23cm) high
£18-22   **MTB**

A Battlestar Galactica 'Ovion' action figure, by Mattel, mint and carded.
c1978   9in (23cm) high
£18-22   **MTB**

A Battlestar Galactica 'Cylon Raider' plastic toy, by Mattel, mint and boxed.

Initially the toy spaceships were produced with firing missiles but safety concerns lead to these missiles being removed.
c1978   Box 9.75in (25cm) high
£50-60   **MTB**

TOYS & GAMES

TOYS & GAMES

A 'Battlestar Galactica' spiral-bound notebook, by The Mead Corporation, with photographic cover showing Starbuck, Apollo, Boomer and a Colonial Viper firing.

c1978   *10.75in (27cm) high*

£3-5   **BH**

A Bionic Woman 'Jamie Sommers' action figure, by Denys Fisher and licensed by Universal Studio Inc., complete with clothes, in mint condition in factory sealed box.

c1975   *Box 14in (15.5cm) high*

£80-120   **MTB**

EXPERT EYE – A BUCK ROGERS ACTION FIGURE

Despite being well-made, figures from the Buck Rogers range did not prove popular. This may be partly due to the figures being based solely on the pilot movie, aired several months before the series began, and many of the characters did not become series regulars or were re-cast for the series.

Mego figures are prone to 'plastic melt', as can be seen by Buck's grey face. As the plastic degrades, a gas is released that discolours the plastic and, in bad cases, can freeze joints when the gas cannot escape from the packaging. If this example was not discoloured it could be worth around £90.

Perhaps due to their poor sales, boxed examples are not hard to find. A loose figure with all its clothing and accessories would be worth about £20. As Buck is one of the most popular characters from the series, his figure is one of the easiest to find.

A Buck Rogers in the 25th Century 'Buck Rogers' action figure, by Mego Corp., mint and boxed.

1979   *Box 13.5in (34cm) high*

£40-60   **MTB**

A Buck Rogers in the 25th Century 'Dr. Huer' action figure, by Mego Corp., mint and boxed with no discolouration.

Dr. Huer was less popular at the time, making him harder to find today.

13.5in (34cm) high

£70-90   **MTB**

A Buck Rogers in the 25th Century 'Draco' action figure, by Mego Corp., mint and boxed with no discolouration.

13.5in (34cm) high

£70-90   **MTB**

A Buck Rogers in the 25th Century 'Killer Kane' action figure, by Mego Corp., mint and boxed with no discolouration.

13.5in (34cm) high

£70-90   **MTB**

A Buck Roger in the 25th Century 'Walking Twiki' battery operated plastic figure, by Mego Corp., mint and boxed.

Box 8.25in (21cm) high

£30-50   **MTB**

A Charlie's Angels 'Jill' action figure, UK-issue by Hasbro, licensed by Spelling Goldberg Productions, mint and carded.

c1977   *12in (30.5cm) high*

£55-65   **MTB**

A Charlie's Angels 'Sabrina' action figure, by Hasbro, licensed by Spelling Goldberg Productions, mint and carded.

c1977   *12in (30.5cm) high*

£45-55   **MTB**

A Charlie's Angels boxed gift set, US-issue by Hasbro, comprising 'Sabrina', 'Kris' and 'Kelly', mint and boxed.

Loose but complete, these figures can be worth around £5-7.

c1977   *Box 12.25in (31cm) wide*

£80-120   **MTB**

A Charlie's Angels 'The Slalom Caper' outfit set, by Hasbro, comprising of two complete outfits.

c1977   *Box 12in (30.48cm) high*

£40-50   **MTB**

A Chitty Chitty Bang Bang 'Truly Scrumptious' soft vinyl doll, by Mattel, mint and boxed.

Box 14.75in (37.5cm) high

A Charlie's Angels 'Black Magic' outfit set, by Hasbro.

c1977   *11in (27.94cm)*

£35-45   **MTB**

A C.H.i.P.S. 'Ponch' action figure and motorbike, by Mego Corp., mint and carded.

Despite the popularity of the series, these figures were deemed unexciting by children at the time and were only available for a short period, making them rare today.

c1981   *Card 8.5in (21.5cm) high*

£30-40   **MTB**

£300-400   **MTB**

TOYS & GAMES

A Chitty Chitty Bang Bang 'Truly Scrumptious' soft vinyl talking doll, by Mattel, mint and boxed.

This talking version is more valuable than the non-talking version on the previous page. The boxes must be in mint condition to be worth this amount of money.

Box 14.75in (37.5cm) high

£400-500   MTB

A Chitty Chitty Bang Bang plastic car, by Mattel and Gildrose Productions Ltd, complete with inflatable raft, characters and parts, in unopened packaging, mint and boxed.

This model inspired Corgi to release their diecast version of Chitty Chitty Bang Bang, however they chose not to include the inflatable raft. Examples in this condition with the box are extremely rare. The small parts were often lost or broken, particularly the windscreen.

1968   Box 7in (18cm) wide

£100-150   MTB

A Dempsey and Makepeace action figure set, by Rainbow Toys, licensed by LWT, comprising Lt. James Dempsey, Chief Supt. Gordon Spikings and a uniformed policeman, complete with accessories and in mint, carded condition.

c1984   Card 11in (28cm) high

£18-22   MTB

A Dukes of Hazzard 'Luke' action figure, by Mego Corp., mint and carded.

c1980   11in (28cm) high

£40-60   MTB

A Dune 'Fremen Tarpel Gun', by LJN, battery operated, mint and boxed.

Produced to coincide with the release of David Lynch's 1984 film version, the 'Tarpel Gun' does not appear in the original Frank Herbert novel.

c1984   Box 11in (28cm) wide

£30-40   MTB

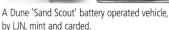

A Dune 'Sand Scout' battery operated vehicle, by LJN, mint and carded.

The rarest toy from this scarce range is the 'Sandworm', and is hidden under the 'Top Secret' banner above. It seems few were ever sold and today they can be worth over £150.

c1984   10in (25cm) wide

£20-30   MTB

A Happy Days boardgame, by Parker Bros., complete and boxed.

c1976   Box 18.25in (46.5cm) wide

£6-9   BH

An International Velvet 'Sarah Velvet Brown' action figure, by Kenner, complete with clothing, mint and boxed.

1978   13.25in (33.5cm) high
£35-45   **MTB**

A M.A.S.H. 'Hot Lips Houlihan' action figure, by Aspen Productions, complete, mint and carded.

c1969   Card 13in (33cm) high
£35-45   **MTB**

A Mork & Mindy 'Mindy' doll, by Mattel, mint and boxed.

c1979   9.75in (25cm) high
£40-50   **MTB**

A Mork & Mindy 'Mork' talking doll, by Mattel, mint and boxed.

As with most Mattel talking dolls, Mork is made to speak by pulling a cord in his back, which operates a small spinning record. This mechanism was notorious for breaking easily. Examples with broken mechanisms are worth about a third less than this example.

1979   Box 14.25in (36cm) high
£55-65   **MTB**

A Muppet Show 'Rowlf' figure, by Bendy Toy, mint and boxed.
1980   Box 8.75in (22cm) high
£15-25   **MTB**

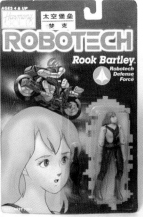

A Police Woman 'Sgt. Leanne "Pepper" Anderson' action figure, by Horseman Dolls, USA, in original box.

Box 12in (30.48cm) high
£25-35   **MTB**

A Robotech 'Miriya' action figure, by Harmony Gold, mint and carded.

Robotech was adapted from three Japanese mecha anime series, which were re-written and dubbed into English. This combination resulted in three 'generations', with story arcs taken from each of the original series. A number of follow-up films and series were planned but only some were released. This character is based on 'Milia Fallyna Jenius' from The Super Dimension Fortress Macross, which formed the first generation of Robotech.

c1992   9in (22.5cm) high
£7-10   **MTB**

A Robotech 'Rook Bartley' action figure, by Harmony Gold, mint and carded.

Rook is based on the character Houquet et Rose from 'Genesis Climber MOSPEADA', which formed the third generation of the Robotech storyline.

c1992   9in (22.5cm) high
£7-10   **MTB**

A Robotech 'Micronized Zentraedi Warrior' action figure, by Harmony Gold, mint and carded.

The evil Zentraedi appeared as giants in the animated show and the original Zentraedi figures made by Matchbox were much larger than the Robotech figures, although not to scale. This is a 'Micronized' figure, so it the same size as the human characters.

c1992   9in (22.5cm) high

£7-10   MTB

A Six Million Dollar Man 'Steve Austin' action figure, by Denys Fisher, in mint condition, complete with carrying case.

Mint and boxed, the value can rise to £80-120. The case on its own can be worth £7.

12.75in (32.5cm) high

£12-18   MTB

A Space 1999 'Commander Koenig' action figure, by Mattel, mint and carded.

These figures are rare, particularly in unopened, mint condition.

1975   12in (30.5cm) high

£55-75   MTB

A Space 1999 'Doctor Russell' action figure, no. 9544, by Mattel, mint and carded.

The rarest 9in figure is the alien 'Zython'. Planned for release in 1976, the figure was dropped from production and only a few examples, possibly samples or prototypes, were released. The second, and final, season of the series was not as successful as the first and this may account for further toys not being released.

1975   12in (30.5cm) high

£50-80   MTB

A Star Trek – The Motion Picture 'Klingon' action figure, by Mego Corp., with signs of discolouration to his face, mint and boxed.

The modelling of the Klingon's head differs greatly from the action figure produced for the original Star Trek series. In the original series the Klingons generally appear human. For the first motion picture, an increased budget for make-up and better techniques meant the race was redesigned with the now typical ridged forehead, and the new figure reflects this. This change was given an official explanation in the Star Trek: Enterprise episodes "Affliction" and "Divergence".

1979   Box 12.5in (32cm) high

£50-70   MTB

A Starsky & Hutch 'Starsky' action figure, by Mego Corp., mint and carded.

1975   9.25in (23cm) high

£30-50   MTB

A Japanese Terrahawks 'Action Zeroid' toy, by Bandai, mint and boxed.

It is hard to find mint and boxed examples of this now popular toy. Always check the collar where the ball fits onto the column as this is frequently broken. Loose but in mint condition, it can be worth up to £20.

1983   Box 7.25in 18.5cm) high

£75-85   **MTB**

A Tom & Jerry plastic friction-powered toy, by Louis Marx, mint with printed card original box.

1972   4.35in (10.5cm) high

£75-85   **MTB**

A Toy Story 'Buzz Lightyear' speaking poseable action figure, by Chinese Thinkway Toys, in full working order.

1995-99   11.75in (30cm) high

£8-12   **PC**

A pair of Waltons 'Grandma and Grandpa' figures, by Mego Corp., licensed by Lorimar Productions, mint and boxed.

Note Grandpa's hair, which is a darker shade than the actor's own hair. The rarest Waltons toy is the truck, which is made from diecast parts and can be worth up to £40.

Box 15in (38cm) high

£35-45   **MTB**

A pair of Waltons 'Mom and Pop' figures, by Mego Corp., licensed by Lorimar Productions, mint and boxed.

Box 15in (38cm) high

£35-45   **MTB**

A pair of Waltons 'John Boy and Ellen' figures, by Mego Corp., licensed by Lorimar Productions, mint and boxed.

Box 15in (38cm) high

£35-45   **MTB**

A Wizard of Oz 'The Cowardly Lion' large plush soft toy, by Chinese Presents, licensed by Loews Inc. ©1939, Metro Goldwyn Mater Inc. and Turner Entertainment, in mint condition with original tag and medal.

Turner Entertainment went bankrupt some time after these toys were made, making them hard to find today.

13.75in (35cm) high

£20-25   **MTB**

A Wizard of Oz 'Scarecrow' plush large soft toy, by Chinese Presents, licensed by Loews Inc ©1939, Metro Goldwyn Mater Inc. and Turner Entertainment, in mint condition complete with original paper scroll and tag.

Without the scroll in his right hand, the value is reduced by around 50 per cent.

16in (40.5cm) high

£20-25   **MTB**

FIND OUT MORE...

www.megocentral.com
www.megomuseum.com
'Miller's Sci-Fi & Fantasy Collectibles', *by Phil Ellis, published by Miller's 2003.*

TOYS & GAMES

A 1960s Airfix Volkswagen 1200 32-scale model kit, in mint condition with original packaging.

7.25in (18cm) high

£20-30   MTB

A 1960s Airfix Aston Martin DB5 32-scale model kit, in mint condition with original packaging.

These transparent bags were used before card boxes.

7.25in (18cm) high

£20-30   MTB

A 1960s Airfix Triumph Herald 32-scale model kit, in mint condition with original box.

7.25in (18cm) high

£20-30   MTB

A 1960s Airfix Mirage & MiG 15 72-scale airplane model kit, in mint condition with original box.

During the late 1970s, artwork on the boxes of children's toys was not allowed to depict images of firing guns or rockets, or explosions. As well as helping to date a model or toy, there are collectors that seek out these great graphics.

7.25in (18cm) high

£20-30   MTB

EXPERT EYE – A LINES BROS. BUCCANEER MODEL

To achieve this price, it must be complete and in this condition. The box is particularly crucial as it contains the winding mechanism which allows the plane to fly.

Model planes such as this were once every boy's dream. They are now collected by those nostalgic for their youth.

Lines Bros., who owned the Tri-ang brand, were an important maker of toys including this range of planes.

Without its box it could still be worth up to £50 due to the popularity of this model.

A 1950s Lines Bros. moulded plastic Buccaneer 'ready to fly' model plane, with wind-up motor, in mint condition with instructions and box with fitted winding mechanism.

Box 16.25in (412cm) long

£80-120   MTB

A Meccano No.00 model aircraft, built as a low-wing monoplane, the wings and tail fins finished with a red sunburst pattern, in good condition.

£100-150   VEC

A Meccano no. 01 Constructor Car, expertly repainted in cream and red with a number of spare components including seat, bonnet and others.

£200-300   VEC

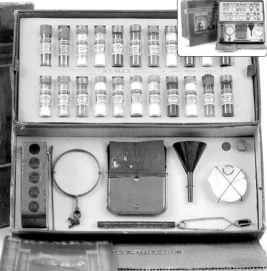

A Hornby Meccano Racer 3 speedboat, finished in two-tone blue and white, contained in original box with key and instruction booklet dated "12/37", in very good condition.

£250-350   VEC

A rare Meccano 'Kemmex 2B' outfit, including glassware, chemical bottles, stand, funnel and other items, together with the instruction booklet for outfits no. 2 and no. 3, contents in good to excellent condition, box in fair condition.

c1933-34

£350-450   VEC

An American Hubley cast iron Racing Car, in light brown with black driver, plated wheels, operating engine cylinders, some wear to edges, otherwise in good condition.

31.75in (27cm) long

£40-60   VEC

An American Kingsbury pressed steel clockwork two-door coupé, yellow with black chassis, opening rear Dickey seat, wired for electric lights, some cracking to the rubber tyres and light wear, with key.

12.5in (32cm) long

£180-220   VEC

An American Wyandotte pressed steel WWII Navy Airplane model, with blue wings, silver fuselage, 'US Navy' stencil, four engines and some scratching to paintwork.

c1944   *14.5in (37cm) wide*

£300-400   BER

An early 1960s Louis Marx plastic friction-powered 'Vanwall Racing Car', made in Hong Kong, in mint condition with original box.

Box 6.25in (16cm) long

£15-25   MTB

A rare French Marx Toys plastic La France Pumper Fire Truck, with silver-coloured upper, yellow removable plastic ladder, friction drive with siren, in excellent condition, with good condition illustrated card box with French printing.

9.5in (24cm) long

£70-100   VEC

A Commedia dell'Arte Mezzetino wood and papier-mâché marionette, painted features, woollen hair, removable mask, wearing a multicoloured costume and carrying a lute, with Fritz Boss type hand controls.

23in (58cm) high

£80-120   **VEC**

A Luntoy 'Mr Turnip' die-cast puppet, missing his 'top knot' root, top of head missing paint and indented, otherwise in good condition, with box in good condition.

7in (18cm) high

£30-50   **VEC**

A 1950s Louis Marx Fairykin TV Scene set, with 'Mary had a Little Lamb', mint and boxed.

For more information about Marx's similar range of Disneykins, please see the Disneyana section, p173-175.

3in (7.5cm) high

£20-25   **MTB**

A 1950s Louis Marx Fairykins 'Little Red Riding Hood' miniature figurine, made in Hong Kong, mint and boxed.

2.25in (5.5cm) high

£6-12   **MTB**

A Marx Toys Playpeople 'U.S. Cavalry Super Set', complete and in mint condition.

Growing in popularity in Germany as well as the US, sets tend to be worth around the same value, while mint and carded single figures are valued at around £10.

17.5in (44.5cm) long

£25-30   **MTB**

A Playskool Richard Scarry's Puzzletown People 'Nurse Nellie' figurine, mint and carded.

Richard Scarry (1913-94) is best known for his 'Busytown' children's books, as well as his human-like animal characters. Mint and carded figurines are growing in popularity among a new generation of collectors who loved his books as children.

1967   *Card 5.75in (14.5cm) high*

£8-12   **MTB**

ESSENTIAL REFERENCE

- Chess, in its closest format to the game known today, is thought to have originated in 6thC India, where it was known as 'Chaturanga'. However, a similar game was also developed in China during the 2ndCBC. The rules used today were set down in Italy during the 15thC, but it wasn't until the 18thC and 19thC that the game mushroomed in popularity.

- Although older sets are known, collectors are most likely to come across sets that date no earlier than the late 18thC, but most will date from the 19thC and 20thC. Chess crosses language barriers and is played internationally, so sets were produced in many countries, with the Eastern export markets of China and India being particularly strong. Sets were also made in the UK and the rest of Europe.

- The form and style of figures differs from country to country, as does the material. Ivory was commonly used in India and China, with hardwoods the favoured material in Europe, although bone and ceramic were also used. Styles also changed over time, particularly during the late 18thC and early 19thC. The styles were often named after famous chess players or locations.

- The quality of the carving also affects value. Eastern sets are usually intricately carved. Although well-carved, most central European sets, and those by the best London makers, are simpler. Sets should be complete and undamaged to be of interest to most collectors, unless very early or very well-carved. Boxes can add value, particularly if they were made for the set, or are similarly well-made.

- The market continues to be strong, with interest from across the globe. Although the internet sees a lively trade, the traditional auction world offers some of the highest quality sets available. Older, good quality sets are becoming harder to find and more valuable, meaning previously less expensive sets are rising in value. Before buying or selling, learn about any national limitations on the trade and transport of ivory.

An English ivory chess set, by John Calvert, one side stained red, the other natural, kings with double 'fountains', queens with single 'fountains', bishops with mitres, knights as horses' heads, rooks as turrets, white king signed "Calvert Maker 189 Fleet Strt London".

c1810   *King 3.5in (9cm) high*

£1,200-1,800   **BLO**

An English ivory chess set, by John Calvert, with one side stained red, the other natural, kings with Maltese crosses and punched decoration, queens with fleur-de-lys , bishops with open mitres, knights as horses' heads, rooks as turrets, white king signed, "Calvert Maker 189 Fleet Strt London".

John Calvert, a member of the Worshipful Company of Turners, was located at Fleet Street from c1790 to 1840. He specialised in finely detailed chess sets for the aristocracy and London coffee shops, where chess was a popular pastime. The type, typified by the other examples on this page, was reproduced later in the mid-19thC by John Jaques and Lund. Many 'Old English' pieces are 'monobloc', ie; made from a single piece of wood. *c1810*

£1,500-2,000

BLO

An English ivory chess set, by John Calvert, one side stained red, the other natural, kings with double pierced 'fountains', queens with single 'fountains', bishops with mitres, knights as horses' heads, rooks as turrets, the white king signed "Calvert Maker 189 Fleet Strt London".

c1810   *King 3.5in (9cm) high*

£1,200-1,800   **BLO**

A 19thC English small-size 'Lund' pattern ivory chess set, one side stained red, other natural, kings with Maltese crosses, queens with reeded ball finials, bishops with mitres, knights as horses' heads, rooks as turrets, pawns with reeded ball finials, in mahogany box.

King 2.75in (7cm) high

£250-350   **BLO**

A weighted machined-brass chess set, by Carlton of England, one side with black patination, the other in unfinished brass, knights with horses' heads, lead heads on brass side, stamped "Carlton England", in wooden box with sliding lid.

c1930   *King 3.25in (8cm) high*

£170-200   **BLO**

TOYS & GAMES

A 19thC English 'Old English' pattern chess set, one side in rosewood, the other in boxwood, kings surmounted with Maltese crosses, queens with ball finials topped with spikes, bishops as mitres, knights as horses' heads, rooks as turrets, pawns with ball finials.

King 4.75in (12cm) high

£200-300 **BLO**

A 19thC 'Old English' pattern boxwood and ebonised chess set, the king and queens with ball finials, knights as horse's heads and bishops as mitres.

King 4.75in (12cm) high

£100-150 **BLO**

EXPERT EYE – AN 'OLD ENGLISH' CHESS SET

The turned single-piece forms identity this as being in the 'Old English' style, particularly the handling of the rook and the rounded discs on the other pieces.

This set may be by Jaques considering the precise design. It is also a large, weighted set.

Always examine knights carefully, as they had to be carved rather than turned – the better and more finely detailed the carving, the more the set is likely to be worth.

The bases have been re-covered with felt over the original pads, and the set has possibly been revarnished at some point, but the 'toffee' patination is attractive and desirable.

A 19thC English 'Old English' pattern boxwood and ebony large-size weighted chess set, probably re-varnished and with new felt bases.

King 4.75in (12cm) high

£500-600 **BLO**

An English silver and silver-gilt chess set, the kings surmounted with crosses, queens with petal-shaped tops, and bishops with mitres and chased crucifix decoration, with hallmarks for Birmingham, 1974, in a leather covered and gilt-tooled casket.

1974

King 4in (10cm) high

£2,200-2,600 **BLO**

An unusual 19thC Scottish boxwood and ebony chess set, in a late 19thC brass-mounted oak box with steel carrying handle.

This unusual set is similar in style to both the 'Staunton' and 'Edinburgh Upright' forms and, partly due to the latter, is most probably Scottish in origin.

King 4in (10cm) high

£450-550 **BLO**

A 'Silette' Catalin chess set, by Grays of Cambridge, with one side black, other side yellow, in mahogany box with sliding lid.

c1925

King 2.75in (7cm) high

£90-120 **BLO**

An English 'Rose Chess' set, one side black, the other side red, in original card box.

King 2.25in (6cm) high

£150-200 **BLO**

A 19thC Jaques 'In Status Quo' travelling chess set, with bone pieces stained red and natural, in mahogany board, signed, "J. Jaques & Son, Makers, London".

Board 9in (23cm) wide

£380-420 **BLO**

ESSENTIAL REFERENCE – STAUNTON SETS

As chess became ever more popular during the late 18thC and early 19thC, demand grew for a standardised set. The vast array of styles available were typically tall and cumbersome in play. Also, a different style may put certain players off their game as it was unfamiliar. In 1849, legendary sports and games equipment maker John Jaques of London devised a set that would become the standard across the world. The design is attributed to his brother-in-law, Nathaniel Cook, who registered the design in March 1849. The set is characterised by simple curving necks on a standard base, each topped with a different 'head' representing the piece. As well as being elegant and well-proportioned, it was also easy and economical to carve and produce. It was given the name 'Staunton' in honour of the then chess world champion, Howard Staunton (1810-74), who endorsed and promoted it heavily. Weighted sets, like this one, and those carved from ivory are highly desirable. Green is a rare colour. 'Staunton pattern' sets were not made by Jaques and tend to be less desirable.

A 19thC Jaques Staunton weighted boxwood and ebony chess set, the white king stamped,"Jaques London", in mahogany box.

£1,500-2,000   BLO

A 19thC Jaques Staunton weighted boxwood and ebony chess set, both kings stamped, "Jaques London", in mahogany box.

King 4in (10cm) high

£1,000-1,500   BLO

A 19thC Jaques Staunton boxwood and ebony chess set, the white king stamped "Jaques London", in mahogany box with sliding lid.

King 3.5in (9cm) high

£550-650   BLO

A mid-19thC Jaques Staunton boxwood and ebony chess set, the white king stamped "Jaques London", including a number of pieces with chipped collars and other areas, and loss to varnish.

King 3.25in (8.5cm) high

£100-150   BLO

A Jaques Staunton ivory chess set, one side stained red, the other natural, in red leather mounted casket of sarcophagus shape with "The Staunton Chessmen" on lid.

Ivory Staunton sets are scarcer than wood, particularly when well-carved as with this set. This box is both appealing and rare, and adds to the desirability and value.

Casket 7in (18cm) wide

£4,000-5,000   BLO

A 20thC Staunton style boxwood and ebony weighted chess set, one side in boxwood, other side black.

King 4.25in (11cm) high

£180-220   BLO

TOYS & GAMES

A Chinese export Cantonese ivory figural 'King George' chess set, one side stained red, the other side left natural, the Chinese versus the Europeans, white king and queen as George III and Queen Charlotte.

c1810　　　　　　　　　*King 5.5in (14cm) high*

£1,800-2,200　　　　　　　　**BLO**

An early 19thC Chinese export ivory 'Bust' chess set, one side stained red, the other side natural, the king and queen as monarchs' heads, bishops as mandarins or counsellors, knights as horses' heads, rooks as turrets with flags, pawns as foot soldiers.

King 3.5in (9cm) high

£1,200-1,800　　　　　　　　**BLO**

EXPERT EYE – A CHINESE EXPORT CHESS SET

The style of carving on both sides is identical, so we can be sure that this is a complete set from one workshop.

Chinese export sets are usually stained in red, with green being a very unusual and rare colour.

As with other Cantonese sets, the carving is typically complex, with many fine details.

Each side has an identical European monarch king and consort queen, which is another rare feature. European monarchs are usually limited to one side, or do not appear at all.

A Chinese export Cantonese ivory 'King George' chess set, one side stained green, the other side left natural, kings as King George III, queens as Charlotte, bishops as clergy, knights as rearing horse, rooks as elephants bearing towers, pawns as foot soldiers with shields and raised spears.

c1800　　　　　　　　　*King 5in (12.5cm) high*

£2,500-3,000　　　　　　　　**BLO**

An early 19thC Cantonese 'Burmese' pattern ivory chess set, one side stained red, the other side natural, the chessmen with intricate carved foliate decoration, knights as horses' heads, rooks as turrets with flags, the white rook with Union flag.

King 3.25in (8cm) high

£450-550　　　　　　　　**BLO**

A 20thC Chinese hardwood 'puzzleball' chess set, made in Hong Kong, one side in boxwood, the other side in coromandel, kings surmounted with crosses, queens with crowns, bishops with split mitres, knights as horses, rooks as turrets, pawns with spire finials, contained in a wooden box.

King 6in (15.5cm) high

£70-90　　　　　　　　**BLO**

An early 19thC Chinese export Cantonese ivory king chess piece, the figure depicting an Emperor or Chinese Worthy, holding a fan in his right hand, with pearls around his neck and a pigtail under his cap, seated on a Chinese-style chair or throne.

Early or finely carved single pieces can hold a value of their own. This sculptural and realistic piece is such an example.

3.5in (9cm) high

£280-320　　　　　　　　**BLO**

A 19thC Indian export ivory chess set, one side stained green, the other side left natural, kings with pierced tops and spray finials, over nautical crown collars, queens with bud finials, bishops with feathered mitres, knights as horses' heads, rooks as rusticated turrets with spire finials, pawns with baluster knops, in a mahogany and boxwood inlaid box/board.

King 3in (7.5cm) high

£300-400   BLO

An early 19thC Indian ivory chess set, probably Vizagapatam, one side stained red, other side natural, kings with large reeded ball finials over castellated galleries, queens similar in smaller size, bishops with unusually shaped mitres, knights as horses' heads, rooks with spiked or petal-shaped finials, pawns with baluster knops.

King 3.25in (8cm) high

£1,000-1,500   BLO

A 19thC Anglo-Indian 'Staunton' pattern ivory chess set, one side stained red, the other side left natural, in a mahogany box with a sliding lid.

King 2.75in (7cm) high

£400-600   BLO

A 20thC Indian carved stone chess set, one side black, the other side a light green colour, kings with pierced crowns, queens similar, bishops with further pierced decoration and elongated finials, knights as horses' heads, rooks as turrets, pawns with domes, all raised on circular bases, together with a wooden box carved with intricate floral patterns.

King 2.75in (7cm) high

£50-70   BLO

An East India (John Company) ivory sepoy (Indian soldier) pawn, wearing a shako, pearls around neck, holding a musket.

c1850   *3.125in (8cm) high*

£180-220   BLO

An 18thC collection of Indian ivory chessmen, from Rajasthan, including two elephant kings, two elephant queens, four temple bishops or rooks, three horsemen knights and 12 foot soldier pawns, with polychrome decoration, some restoration.

King 3.25in (8cm) high

£3,200-3,800   BLO

A 19thC French 'Régence' pattern boxwood and ebony chess set, with rosewood, boxwood and mahogany edged chess board.

This set is so-named due to its association with the Café de la Régence in Paris, during the mid-19thC. A haunt of Voltaire, Diderot and Benjamin Franklin, it was a popular place for thinkers and 'celebrities' to play chess.

King 3.5in (9cm) high

£220-280   BLO

An Islamic wooden chess set, one side painted light red with yellow highlights, other side olive green with yellow highlights, all of abstract form.

King 3.25in (8cm) high

£700-900   **BLO**

A Japanese ivory figural chess set, one side tea stained, the other side natural, king and queen as a Japanese Emperor and Empress, bishops as counsellors, knights as Samurai, rooks as pagodas, pawns as peasants with staffs, in wooden presentation box.

c1950   *King 2.25in (6cm) high*

£200-300   **BLO**

A 20thC Nigerian wooden figural tribal chess set, with one side predominately dark brown, other side lighter, kings as chieftains, queens as consorts, bishops carrying bags or sacks on backs, knights as horsemen, rooks as tribal huts, pawns as pot-bellied tribesmen, with wooden board.

King 4in (10cm) high

£150-200   **BLO**

A 20thC Algerian ivory chess set, with an interesting tribal variation on the French 'Régence' pattern, one side stained blue, other side natural, kings and queens as tribal elders.

King 4in (10cm) high

£200-300   **BLO**

A 20thC 'American Civil War' resin figural chess set, the brown side as the Union, the white side as the Confederates, Union king as Lincoln, Union queen as Mary Todd Lincoln, Union bishop as Ulysses S. Grant, Union knight as cavalry, Union rook as Capitol, Union pawn as infantry, Confederate king as Jefferson Davis, Confederate queen as Varina Davis, Confederate bishop as Robert E.

Lee, Confederate knight as cavalry, Confederate rook as Confederate Capitol, Confederate pawns as infantry.

King 6.25in (16cm) high

£100-150   **BLO**

A rare Wedgwood Jasperware chess pawn, after a design by Joseph Flaxman, depicting a knight in armour holding a shield and sword, stamped "Wedgwood" on underside of base.

The designs were produced by notable 18thC sculptor Joseph Flaxman, and were modelled on Shakespeare's 'Macbeth'. This set was reproduced in limited numbers in the 1960s, and only a very few sets have been made since. Each pawn had a different pose.

2.75in (7cm) high

£500-600   **BLO**

A rare 18thC Indian Mysore double-sided chess board, with alternate squares in hardwood and ivory with polychrome painted decoration, board decoration on borders with leaves and foliage ivory inlay.

Although most chess collectors and players only require one or two boards, this example is both an extremely old survivor and very rare, partly as it would have cost so much in its day. The condition is also excellent.

18in (46cm) wide

£9,500-10,500   **BLO**

ESSENTIAL REFERENCE

- Dexterity games became popular during the late 19thC. Produced in France, Germany, the UK and the US, early examples were handmade and were typically finely printed, often with complex images. Many were made from printed paper over wood, some coming with their own box-like covers. From the early 20thC onwards, they were produced in larger numbers in Germany, often from printed tinplate, but quality fell. These smaller, typically circular, games were exported around the world and were sold inexpensively.
- The presence of a makers' name generally increases value, particularly if a game is early and finely made. More challenging games with extra details may also be worth more. Look for scenes that may have cross-market appeal, including magic, sporting, advertising and travel themes. Amusing novelty themes or scenes will also be popular.
- Always examine a game thoroughly, considering the condition. Many had mirror backs, and these are often broken. While not impossible to replace, values will be reduced. Similarly, many of the printed card inserts have faded or been stained.

A 1920s-30s 'Chicken Shed' printed tinplate and card dexterity game, with mirror back.

This is a detailed and well-printed scene.

2.25in (6cm) diam

£30-50   BH

A German 'Chicken Feeding' tinplate and printed card dexterity game, marked "D.R.G.M."

2.25in (5.5cm) diam

£15-18   BH

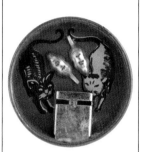

A 'Cat and Mouse' printed card and tinplate dexterity game, probably German.

2.25in (5.5cm) diam

£12-18   BH

A Japanese 'Three Blind Mice' printed paper-over-card and glass dexterity game, marked "Japan".

4in (10cm) diam

£12-18   BH

A 1920s-30s French 'Kleber Colombes Au Coq Boîtes et Chaussures' printed card and tinplate shoes advertising dexterity game.

Given away as promotional items, games advertising major brands are highly collectable as they also attract interest from advertising collectors.

2.25in (5cm) diam

£18-22   BH

A late 1940s-50s German 'Juggling Clown' card-backed dexterity game, printed "Made in US Zone Germany".

2.25in (5.5cm) diam

£22-28   BH

TOYS & GAMES

An early German tennis-themed printed card and tinplate dexterity game, marked "Germany".

1.5in (3.5cm) diam

£35-45   BH

A 1920s-30s German 'Wer Gewinnt – Rot Oder Blau' printed card and tinplate hockey dexterity game, with mirror back and star-printed paper insert inside.

The text translates as 'Who will win? Red or blue?'.

2.25in (5.5cm) diam

£18-22   BH

A colour-printed tinplate dexterity game, probably German.

Here the old man has come down from his bedroom, having been disturbed by a burglar. The aim of the game is to get both of the hinged, reflective cupboard doors closed.

2.5in (6cm) diam

£25-35   BH

An early German printed card and metal dexterity game.

The aim of the game is to place the balls on the girl's earlobes, to give her earrings.

1.75in (4.5cm) diam

£30-35   BH

A 1920s-30s English 'Performing Seal' printed tinplate, card and glass dexterity game, printed "Made in England".

Note how different makers in different countries copied each other when a scene proved popular.

2.25in (5.5cm) diam

£20-30   BH

A 1920s-30s German 'Performing Seals' dexterity game, with mirror back, printed "Made in Germany".

2.25in (5.5cm) diam

£15-25   BH

A 1920s 'Drivers' printed card and tinplate dexterity game, with mirror back.

Sporting or automotive themes are very popular and are usually more valuable. This is due to added demand from sporting or automobilia collectors. Examples such as the three on this page are also interesting as they show early forms of dress. This example also shows an early car.

2.25in (3.5cm) diam

£35-45   BH

A printed tinplate and card dexterity game, possibly French, showing a lady in a hat.

1.5in (4cm) diam

£15-20   BH

A 1920s-30s German double-sided red and green star dexterity game, marked '"D.R.G.M."

2in (5cm) diam

£22-28   BH

An early R. Journet 'The Dovecote Puzzle' paper-covered wood and glass dexterity game.

5.5in (14cm) high

£15-25 BH

An R. Journet 'The Stork Puzzle' paper-covered wood and glass dexterity game.

Typical of Journet, the game is more complex than just trying to get the plastic pods into the 'bed' slots. Boys are black pods and girls are pink pods – each has to be matched against the respective male or female names.

5in (12.5cm) wide

£55-65 BH

An R. Journet 'Pootles The Pup' paper-covered wood and glass dexterity game.

4.5in (12cm) high

£40-60 BH

An R. Journet 'The Salmon Tin Puzzle' dexterity game, with red tinplate salmon.

Even the tin has an unseen printed paper 'label' around it.

3.5in (8.5cm) high

£50-80 BH

ESSENTIAL REFERENCE – ROBERT JOURNET

Robert Journet started a toy shop in 1878, in Paddington, London. Puzzles were initially made by his father during the 1890s, but this expanded to an increasingly large team when sales mushroomed after the company attended trade fairs. Quality remained high, with paper-covered wood frames, vibrantly coloured and detailed images and innovative themes. Exports grew rapidly, and the US became a major market. From the 1920s onwards, the company grew to become the most popular producers of 'Popular Perplexing Puzzles' in the world. In 1965, it was sold to Abbey Corinthian Games who continued to produce the puzzles into the 1970s. The growing popularity of board games and the arrival of the home computer and electronic games led to a decline in sales, and the range was discontinued. The back of each puzzle advertised the other games available (starting at no. 50) and acts as a handy checklist for collectors, although variations of popular games do exist, widening the variety available.

An R. Journet 'The Brooch Puzzle' printed card and paper-covered wood dexterity game.

Note the nicely decorated embossed paper frame. Like many Journet games, the reverse bears a label showing the many games the company produced.

4.5in (11cm) high

£40-50 BH

An R. Journet 'The Whirlpool Puzzle' paper-covered card and glass dexterity game.

5.25in (13cm) high

£8-12 BH

An R. Journet 'Motorist Puzzle' paper-covered wood and glass dexterity game, signed "R.J. London".

5.25in (13cm) wide

£12-18 BH

An R. Journet 'Four Leaf Clover' printed tinplate and glass dexterity game.

4.25in (10.5cm) high

£14-16 BH

TOYS & GAMES

An R. Journet 'The Television Puzzle' paper-covered wood and glass dexterity game.

This can be dated to the early 1950s from the style of the TV set, which was just beginning to proliferate in homes across the Western world. At the time of the coronation of Queen Elizabeth II in 1953, 2.5million TV sets were in use across the UK.

5in (12.5cm) high

£15-25   BH

An R. Journet 'The Hand-Some Puzzle' paper-covered wood and glass dexterity game, made for Woolworths.

3.25in (8.5cm) high

£20-30   BH

An R.Journet 'The Green Eyed Kitty Puzzle' paper-covered wood and glass dexterity game, and made for Woolworths, printed "Made in England".

The use of the yellow card and red box is typical of R. Journet. Journet made a series of 12 dexterity games for Woolworths.

2.5in (9cm) high

£40-60   BH

An early 1940's 'V For Victory' printed card, metal and glass dexterity game, printed "Made in U.S.A."

The aim of the game is to fill up the 'V' with the coloured rods and fill the holes with silver balls.

5.25in (13cm) high

£12-18   BH

EXPERT EYE – A DEXTERITY GAME

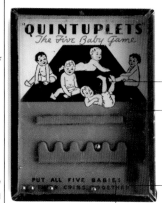

This game is by a named US maker, which makes it desirable. It is also a more difficult version of the 'put the ball in the hole' game and this also makes it sought-after.

Games with individual themes are often more desirable and valuable. As quins are an unusual subject, it is also rare.

Although not dated, this is likely to have been made in late 1934. In May that year the Dionne Quintuplets were born, becoming the first identical quins to survive birth.

This is borne out by the style of the wording, and the general style and choice of colours, which are all strongly Art Deco.

A James R. Irvin & Co. Inc. of Chicago printed card and tinplate 'Quintuplets The Five Baby Game' dexterity game.

4.5in (11cm) high

£18-22   BH

A 1930s Japanese printed paper-over-card and glass dexterity game, showing an owl perched on a branch with a town in the background, marked "Made in Japan".

2.5in (6cm) high

£15-20   BH

A 1940s American 'Flight Formation' painted tin, card and glass dexterity game.

5.25in (13cm) wide

£18-22   BH

A 1940s 'Wot! No Eyes?' printed card, paper-over-card and glass dexterity game.

Known as Chad or Kilroy, this popular form of graffito was first seen during WWI, primarily in response to rationing, where any particular item could be added after "Wot no...".

2.5in (6.5cm) high

£20-30   BH

A 19thC English bone and ebony domino set, in a spruce wooden box with sliding lid.

11.75in (30cm) long

£12-18 **BLO**

A 'prisoner of war' bone cribbage and domino box, with red and black decoration, sliding lid, interior with dominoes, die and counters.

'Prisoner of war' objects were made and sold, or used by French soldiers taken prisoner during the Napoleonic wars. They used materials that were found in the prisons they were housed in, such as wood, bone, paper, straw and, occasionally, ivory. Other objects included ship models.

c1800 *6in (15cm) long*

£200-300 **BLO**

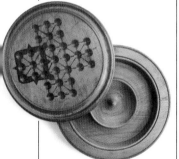

A late 19thC or early 20thC English tulipwood solitaire board, opening to reveal storage for marbles.

1880-1930 *8in (20.5cm) diam*

£40-60 **AB**

A wooden and metal mounted roulette wheel, with case, stamped cipher to underside.

8.75in (22cm) wide

£12-18 **BLO**

An American 'Brownie Stamps and Coloring Outfit No. 1401', the card box containing an inkpad and 12 stamps.

10.75in (27cm) wide

£70-100 **SOTT**

A set of 1950s 'Lenny The Lion's Snap!' playing cards, with original box.

3.75in (9.5cm) high

£10-15 **MTB**

A Schaper Manufacturing Company 'Casper The Friendly Ghost' board game, licensed by Harvey Friendly Comics Inc.

1974 *11.5in (29cm) wide*

£12-18 **SOTT**

A J. Jaques & Son and Hamley Bros. 'Ping Pong or Gossima' set, including two vellum covered bats, with original box, in very good condition.

c1900 *Box 18.5in (47cm) long*

£50-80 **VEC**

ESSENTIAL REFERENCE

- Interest in vintage wristwatches, and wristwatches in general, has grown over the past few years. This has been led by attention from men's fashion magazines, and a generally smarter and more luxurious look returning to fashion. Wristwatches are now more widely sought-after not only by collectors, but by those wishing to own an elegant watch different from high street examples. Many also buy as an investment, particularly high quality, complex watches, or those produced in limited editions.
- There are a number of indicators to value, including the maker, the complexity of the movement, the style and the materials used. High-end brands such as Patek Philippe and Rolex will always be sought-after due to their high quality. Within their ranges, iconic models will be the most

desirable. The more complex a watch is, the more it is likely to be worth; chronographs and watches with extra features such as moon phases, alarms or perpetual calendars will usually be valuable.
- The style of a watch can also help you to date it, as well as adding value. Small, round pocket watch-like examples generally date from the early 20thC. Rectangular watches are typically 1930s, although examples were produced in the 1950s too. From the late 1940s onwards, watch cases became more stylized and innovative in form, often taking on period jewellery styles. During the 1950s, simple circular styles with pared down faces were also popular. During the late 1960s and '70s, watches became strongly influenced by fashion and often had large, sculptural cases and futuristic styles.

A 1930s Hamilton 'Perry' wristwatch, with white gold-filled oval dial, luminous hands and markers, and Hamilton 987 17-jewel movement.

White gold-filled versions of this watch are always a little more valuable than yellow gold-filled, as they are rarer.

£150-190   ML

A 1930s Hamilton 'Sidney' wristwatch, the gold-filled case with 18ct solid gold applied numbers, and 17-jewel movement.

A 1930s Hamilton 'Perry' wristwatch, with yellow gold-filled oval dial, luminous hands and markers, and Hamilton 987 17-jewel movement.

£140-160   ML

Interestingly, all applied numbers on Hamilton watches from the 1930s are solid gold, regardless of whether the case is solid gold or not.

£90-120   ML

A 1930s Hamilton 'Cushion' wristwatch, with 10ct yellow gold-filled shaped case, silvered dial with luminous 'exploding' Arabic numbers and subsidiary seconds dial at six o'clock, and 17-jewel movement.

£120-140   ML

A 1930s Hamilton 'Greenwich' wristwatch, the yellow gold-filled case with stepped bezel, white dial with luminous hands and numbers, subsidiary seconds dial at six o'clock, and 17-jewel movement.
c1931

£140-160   ML

A 1930s Hamilton wristwatch, with white gold-filled 'cut corner' case, white dial with black Arabic numerals, and Hamilton 17-jewel movement.

£120-150   ML

A 1930s Hamilton 'Square B' wristwatch, with white gold-filled case, white dial with luminous numbers, subsidiary seconds dial at six o'clock, and Hamilton 987 17-jewel movement.

This case is typical of the 1930s and can also be found with engraved decoration.

£140-160   ML

A 1940s Hamilton 'Myron' wristwatch, with curving rectangular 10ct gold-filled case, silvered dial with Arabic numerals, subsidiary seconds dial at six o'clock, and Hamilton 980 17-jewel movement.

This is a very popular watch due to the shaped lugs.

£90-120   ML

A 1930s Hamilton 'Stanley' wristwatch, with yellow gold-filled case, solid gold applied numbers and subsidiary seconds dial at six o'clock, and Hamilton 401 17-jewel movement.

The 401 is the rarest of Hamilton's movements. Only a few of the desirable Stanley models were fitted with this movement, making this example doubly desirable. c1931

£350-400   ML

EXPERT EYE – A HAMILTON WRISTWATCH

This is an early driver's watch, and was introduced in c1938.

The curved case was made to fit on the side of the wrist so that it could be more easily seen when driving.

The overall elongated rectangular shape is typical of 1930s watches.

The streamlined tapered and curved form is reminiscent of automobile design, such as a radiator grille, and is an appealing feature.

A late 1930s Hamilton 'Brooke' wristwatch, with shaped gold-filled case, subsidiary seconds dial at six o'clock, and 17-jewel movement.

£220-250   ML

A 1930s Hamilton 'Sienna' wristwatch, with 14ct solid gold elongated case, and Hamilton 982 19-jewel movement.

Although similar to the Linwood, the case is not as long, nor as curved, as that watch. Fewer of this model were made in solid 14ct gold, so rarity accounts for much of its value.

£300-350   ML

A 1930s Hamilton Art Deco wristwatch, the platinum rectangular case with hooded 'barrel' lugs, diamond markers, and Hamilton 980 17-jewel movement.

The hooded 'barrel' lugs are a typical feature of 1930s watches.

£1,800-2,200   ML

A 1930s Hamilton wristwatch, the 14ct solid white gold case with ribbed bezel at the top and bottom, diamond-set dial, subsidiary seconds dial at six o'clock, and Longines 17-jewel movement.

Many diamond dial watches have curved or cut crystals to accommodate the diamonds which protrude from the dial.

£420-520   ML

A 1940s Hamilton 'Gilbert' wristwatch, with 14ct solid gold rectangular case, dial with applied solid gold numbers, subsidiary seconds dial at six o'clock, and Hamilton 982 19-jewel movement.

c1941

£200-240   ML

A 1940s Hamilton 'Essex' driver's wristwatch, with pink gold-filled case, 'Coral' face, and Hamilton 980 17-jewel movement.

The moving lugs, also known as 'Tuxedo' lugs, allowed this to be worn on the side of the wrist, making it easier to read while driving.

£140-160   ML

A 1940s Hamilton 'Endicott' wristwatch, with 10ct gold-filled case, the two-tone silvered dial with Roman numerals.

A version with a subsidiary seconds dial at six o'clock was also produced, as was one with gold-filled Arabic numerals, both variations are shown on the watch to the right.

c1941

£70-100   ML

A 1940s Hamilton 'Endicott' wristwatch, with 10ct gold-filled case and the two-tone silvered dial with Arabic numerals.

c1941

£70-100   ML

A 1950s Hamilton 'Electric Titan' wristwatch, with 10ct gold-filled stepped bezel and flared lugs, and Hamilton 505 battery powered movement, signed four times on the dial, case, movement and crown.

This was Hamilton's first attempt at a battery powered watch. It was a commercial failure as the movement was so hard to repair. Surprisingly, replacement batteries are still available today.

£60-90   ML

A late 1950s Hamilton 'Masterpiece' wristwatch, with 10ct solid gold case, silvered dial with solid gold applied numbers, subsidiary seconds dial at six o'clock, and Hamilton 17-jewel manual wind movement.

£100-120   ML

ESSENTIAL REFERENCE – A HAMILTON 'THE PIPING ROCK' WRISTWATCH

Along with the 'Spur' and the 'Coronado', the 'Piping Rock' is one of the most sought-after and desirable Hamilton watches. It was originally designed and released in 1929, and was named after the exclusive Piping Rock Country Club on Long Island, NY, which opened in 1912. It was re-designed and re-released in 1948, with many collectors preferring the shape of the later case design (shown right). It came with either a 17- or 19-jewel movement, and either a 14ct yellow or white solid gold case, meaning it was very expensive in its day. Only 3,815 examples with yellow gold cases were made, making it scarce, but the white gold case is even rarer as even fewer were made. Always check the enamelled bezel, as it can become chipped, and look out for a rare variation with an engraved case-back commemorating the New York Yankees baseball team winning the World Series in 1928, as this is extremely rare.

A very rare Hamilton 'Piping Rock' wristwatch, the 14ct solid white gold case with black enamelled bezel, and early Hamilton 17-jewel movement.
c1928

£1,000-1,300   ML

A rare Hamilton 'Piping Rock' gentleman's wristwatch, the 14ct solid yellow gold case with black enamelled bezel, and early Hamilton 17-jewel movement.
c1948

£800-1,200   ML

A 1950s Hamilton 'Tyrone' wristwatch, the 10ct gold-filled bezel with stainless steel back, seconds subsidiary dial at six o'clock, and Hamilton 17-jewel movement, signed "Tyrone" on inside of case back.

£70-100   ML

A 1950s Hamilton 'Sinclair' wristwatch, with yellow gold-filled angled case, black dial with subsidiary seconds dial at six o'clock, and 22-jewel movement.

c1957

£120-140   ML

A 1950s Hamilton wristwatch, possibly a 'Milton', with yellow gold-filled shaped rectangular case, champagne dial with solid gold applied markers, subsidiary seconds dial at six o'clock, and Hamilton 22-jewel movement.

£70-100   ML

A 1950s Hamilton 'Brockton' gentleman's wristwatch, with 10ct solid gold rectangular case, the dial with solid gold applied numbers, and Hamilton 982 19-jewel movement

£150-180   ML

A late 1960s Hamilton 'Selfwinding' automatic wristwatch, no. 941572, with 10ct gold-filled case, date aperture, the Swiss-made movement with full rotor.

The back of the case is solid, meaning the movement is removed through the dial.

£50-70   ML

A 1930s Longines 'Tank' wristwatch, with 14ct solid gold rectangular case, applied gold numbers, full 60-second subsidiary dial, and Longines 17-jewel movement.

£180-220   ML

A 1930s Art Deco Longines wristwatch, with platinum case, diamond-set dial, seconds sub-dial at 6 o'clock, and Longines 17-jewel movement.

Made in Switzerland, this would have been a top of the range wristwatch offered by Longines, and would have been affordable only to the wealthy.

£1,000-1,200   ML

A 1930s Longines wristwatch, the rectangular stainless steel case with wire lugs, silvered dial with subsidiary second dial at six o'clock, and early 17-jewel movement, triple signed.

Stainless steel is desirable, as is the early movement that dates from before the LT movement. The movement is covered inside the case, to protect it from shocks and dust.

£160-190   ML

WATCHES

A 1950s Longines wristwatch, with solid platinum rectangular case, the black dial set with diamonds, subsidiary seconds dial at six o'clock, and Longines 17-jewel movement.

£650-800   ML

A 1950s Longines wristwatch, the 14ct solid gold case with applied fancy stepped bell lugs, diamond-set dial, and Longines 17-jewel movement.

£450-550   ML

A 1950s Longines wristwatch, with 14ct solid yellow gold rectangular case, diamond-set dial, and Longines 17-jewel movement.

£550-650   ML

A 1950s Longines 'Admiral' automatic wristwatch, with 10ct gold-filled waterproof case, and Longines Swiss-made 17-jewel automatic movement.

As the case is sealed, the movement is removed through the dial aperture. This clean and classic style of watch has become popular once again.

£100-120   ML

EXPERT EYE – A LONGINES WRISTWATCH

The minutes are indicated by the dot, and the hours by the arrow. Both are on revolving discs, making them appear to move without being connected to the dial, hence the term mystery dial.

Red is a rare colour, followed by yellow and then blue. It is also found in two-tone black and white, and brown and green variations.

This example is in excellent condition - the dot and the arrow usually discolour to a yellow over time.

This watch was rare as the space age design was deemed too avant-garde for period tastes, so comparatively few were sold.

A late 1960s Longines 'Comet' wristwatch, with stainless steel cushion-shaped case, the red and black direct-read mystery dial with rare two disc arrow pointing minute hand, and 17-jewel manual wind movement.

£500-600   ML

A 1950s Longines wristwatch, with 10ct white gold-filled case, the silvered airbrushed dial with subsidiary dial at six o'clock, and Longines 17-jewel movement.

£70-100   ML

A 1970s Longines automatic wristwatch, with pillow-shaped stainless steel case, blue dial and date window, signed four times on the movement, dial, case and crown.

£70-120   ML

A 1930s Bulova wristwatch, the white gold-filled case with Art Deco enamelled bezel, two-tone dial with luminous hands and numbers, and Bulova 17-jewel movement.

£140-180   ML

A 1930s Bulova wristwatch, with elongated gold-filled case, the champagne dial with blue steel hands, and 17-jewel movement.

This watch is hard to find in this case, as it was deemed too long in its day and few were sold. The movement is from a ladies watch – as this case is so slim, the thinnest and smallest movement was needed.

£120-140   ML

A 1940s Bulova wristwatch, with 14ct solid pink gold rectangular case, silvered dial, and Bulova 21-jewel movement.

Bulova produced a large number of watches in pink gold during the 1940s.

£170-200   ML

A 1950s Bulova wristwatch, the 14ct white solid gold rectangular case with bell lugs, the black dial with subsidiary seconds dial and magnifying curved crystal, and Bulova 21-jewel movement.

£180-220   ML

A 1950s Bulova wristwatch, with 10ct rolled gold high arched Shell design case, silvered dial with gold markers and hands, subsidiary second dial at six o'clock, and 17-jewel movement.

The desirable case design is the result of an Art Deco style revival in wristwatch design during 1950s. Stamped 'L1', this watch can be dated to 1951.

£140-160   ML

A 1950s Bulova wristwatch, with 10ct gold-filled rectangular ribbed case, the 'hour glass' two-tone dial with second dial at six o'clock, marked "L".
1951

£120-140   ML

A Bulova 'Photo' or 'Flip Up' wristwatch, the 10ct gold-filled case with catch to base releasing the sprung flap, and 21-jewel Swiss-made Bulova movement, signed four times on the case, dial, movement and crown.

The 'L0' marking on the back mean this was made in 1950. 'L' indicates the 1950s, with the following number indicating the year of manufacture. Despite the watch itself being very ordinary, this case style is sought-after, with many buyers placing photographs of loved ones under the flip cover.

£180-220   ML

WATCHES

An Elgin wristwatch, the white gold-filled case with fancy engraved bezel, original dial and ball lugs, and Elgin 15-jewel movement.
c1925-26

£120-150   ML

A 1930s Elgin wristwatch, the white gold-filled case with stepped bezel, and manual-wind Elgin 15-jewel movement.

This early watch is currently highly desirable, but condition is everything. Examples in poorer condition can be worth under half as much.

£120-160   ML

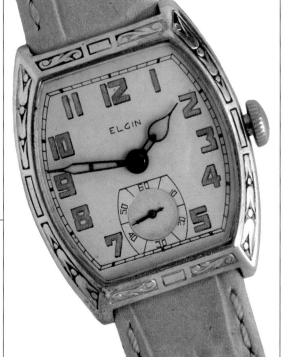

A 1930s Elgin wristwatch, the solid 14ct white gold case with engraved and enamelled bezel with stylized floral pattern, the white face with luminous hands and numbers and subsidiary seconds dial at six o'clock, and 17-jewel movement.

£220-280   ML

A 1930s Elgin wristwatch, with 'cut corner' 14ct white gold case, seconds dial at 6 o'clock, luminous dial and hands, and 15-jewel movement.

£240-280   ML

A 1950s Lord Elgin Shockmaster 'Stingray' wristwatch, with yellow gold-filled shaped case, dial with horizontal lines, subsidiary seconds dial, and 21-jewel movement.

Lord Elgin is the company's high-end brand. The Elgin version has a 19-jewel movement.

£150-180   ML

A 1950s Lord Elgin 'mystery' wristwatch, with gold-filled case, the hour hand on a revolving inner disc, the minute hand on an outer disc, the arrow heads marking the time, and Lord Elgin 21-jewel movement.

£100-120   ML

A 1950s Lord Elgin wristwatch, the gold-filled stepped case with matching articulated strap, dial with fancy numbers, and Lord Elgin 21-jewel movement.

£80-120   ML

ESSENTIAL REFERENCE – JAEGER LECOULTRE

LeCoultre was founded in Le Sentier, Switzerland, in 1833. After expansion in the 1860s, it quickly became known for its extremely fine quality precision movements and, in fact, supplied Patek Philippe with its movements for around 30 years from 1902. In 1903, the founder's son, Jacques-David LeCoultre, met Parisian watchmaker Edouard Jaeger and the two formed an alliance, although the combined name only appeared on watches from 1937 onwards. However, due to a licensing problem, only the LeCoultre name could be used in the US until the early 1970s. 1931 saw the design and release of the famous 'Reverso' polo watch, although it did not become popular until its revival later in the century. LeCoultre produced its first automatic watch in 1946 and continued to improve on the mechanism in subsequent years. The striking 'Memovox' range was introduced in 1950, with the automatic alarm feature being released in 1956. The company continues to produce fine quality, complex precision mechanisms today.

A 1940s LeCoultre wristwatch, with stainless steel case, the two-tone military style 24-hour dial with luminous hands and numbers, and LeCoultre 17-jewel movement, triple signed on the case, dial and movement.

£200-250   ML

A 1940s LeCoultre chronograph wristwatch, with stainless steel case, original dial with overlapping pulsations, and LeCoultre 17-jewel movement, triple signed on the case, dial and movement.

£700-1,000   ML

A 1950s LeCoultre 'Memovox' alarm wristwatch, with yellow gold-filled case, revolving inner dial with arrow head to mark the alarm time, and signed LeCoultre 487 17-jewel Vacheron movement, signed "VXN".

£350-400   ML

A 1950s LeCoultre automatic wristwatch, with 18ct solid gold case with rare 'hobnail' bezel, and Swiss full-rotor 17-jewel automatic movement.

£600-650   ML

EXPERT EYE – A JAEGER LECOULTRE WRISTWATCH

The movement is very desirable as it bears markings for the high quality maker Vacheron, as indicated by the VXN marking.

LeCoultre is a highly collectable name currently, and the Memovox range, and alarm wristwatches in general, are particularly popular.

The simple, classic style is desirable. The central dial is moved to set the time for the alarm, indicated by the arrow head.

In this instance steel is rarer than gold-filled, as it was more expensive at the time of manufacture.

A 1950s Jaeger LeCoultre 'Memovox' alarm wristwatch, with stainless steel case, and 17-jewel movement with VXN markings.

£600-750   ML

An early 1950s LeCoultre 'Wrist Alarm' wristwatch, with a signed Memovox gold-filled case, and 17-jewel alarm movement, the back stamped "Memovox".

Earlier models used a lower quality movement, this was the first upgrade to a higher quality movement.

£400-500   ML

A rare LeCoultre gentleman's automatic 'Memovox' alarm wristwatch, with egg-shaped stainless steel case, three-tone blue dial, and LeCoultre 916 17-jewel movement, signed four times.

The unusual shape is typical for this short period of time, and was deemed avant-garde, as well as being expensive. 'HPG' stands for 'High Precision Guaranteed', further denoting its expense at the time.
1969-72

£600-700   ML

WATCHES

A Swiss Gruen 'Curvex Precision' gentleman's wristwatch, 10ct white gold-filled case, original metallic grey dial and original 'pyramid' faceted glass crystal.

This example is in superb condition. Not only is it hard to find the original dial, but it is even harder to find the original faceted crystal. This watch is also rare as it was unpopular at the time due to the elongated size of the case at 2in (5cm).

£320-420 **ML**

A 1940s Gruen Curvex Precision wristwatch, with pink gold-filled case, two-tone pink gold dial, and 17-jewel movement, signed four times on the case, dial, crown and movement.

The rectangular stepped design still shows strong influences of the Art Deco period of the preceding decade.

£150-180 **ML**

A 1940s Gruen Curvex Precision wristwatch, with 10ct gold-filled rectangular, shaped case, and 17-jewel movement, signed on the case, movement, dial and crown.

The inset lines on the case were once enamelled, as indicated by the remains of the enamel on the bottom of the case.

£150-180 **ML**

A 1950s Gruen gentleman's wristwatch, with 14ct solid gold case, pink dial, and 17-jewel movement, signed four times on the case, movement, dial and crown.

Even though the pink face is more desirable, much of the value of this watch is in the gold case.

£150-200 **ML**

A 1950s Gruen 'Continental' gentleman's wristwatch, the 14ct solid white gold case with saucer bezel, black face, and Gruen signed 17-jewel manual movement.

£160-220 **ML**

A 1970s Swiss Gruen gentleman's wristwatch, the 16ct gold-plated case with stainless steel back, silvered dial, date, and 17-jewel movement.

£50-70 **ML**

A 1950s Benrus 'Wristalarm' gentleman's wristwatch, with gold-filled case with brushed silvered dial, and 17-jewel movement.

£100-120 **ML**

A 1950s Benrus 'Jump Hour' gentleman's wristwatch, with gold-filled waterproof case, hour and minutes apertures, and Benrus 17-jewel movement.

This model was top of the range at the time, and was also Benrus' 'dressiest' design.

£170-200 **ML**

A 1950s Benrus 10ct gold-filled 'bottle cap' gentleman's watch, numbered 545697, with 21-jewel movement.

The leaf logo under the name indicates the company's best 21-jewel movement is inside. Standard movements have 15- or 17- jewels. This case takes its name from the inspiration behind it: a bottle cap.

£80-120 **ML**

A Benrus wristwatch, the 'Hunting' or 'Polo' gold-filled case with flip-up protective cover and lug button release at bottom of case, stainless steel back, subsidiary seconds dial at six o'clock, and 17-jewel movement.

£120-140   ML

A Breitling Colt Military automatic watch, with revolving bezel, black face and stainless steel case.
c1992

£400-500   RSS

A Swiss Corum wristwatch, with 18ct solid gold case, bezel enamelled with Roman numerals, and 17-jewel ultra-thin manual movement.

A 1930s Illinois 'Mate' wristwatch, the white gold-filled case with engraved bezel, two-tone dial with luminous hands and numbers, seconds dial unusually at nine o'clock, and 17-jewel movement.

A 1990s Swiss International Watch Co. oversized wristwatch, with chrome-plated steel case, the white face with black Arabic numerals, and subsidiary seconds dial at nine o'clock.

£620-780   ML

£150-180   ML

£750-900   RSS

A 1950s Junghans wristwatch, with asymmetrical gold-filled case, and 17-jewel movement.

Typical of 1950s style, asymmetric cases are very popular today.

£70-90   ML

A late 1950s or early 1960s Swiss Jules Jurgensen wristwatch, with square solid 14ct gold case, and signed Jules Jurgensen 17-jewel manual wind movement.

Swiss maker Jules Jurgensen's pocket watches and watches from before the 1970s are of good quality, but despite this their popularity is surprisingly low, particularly in the US.

£140-150   ML

A 1960s Swiss Jules Jurgensen automatic wristwatch, with large brushed stainless steel case, azure blue dial, and Jules Jurgensen 21-jewel movement.

The superb colour of the dial really makes this watch, as does the high quality movement.

£70-100   ML

WATCHES

A 1950s Swiss Movado wristwatch, with gold-filled case, and a Zenith 17-jewel manual wind movement.

£80-120   ML

A 1940s Movado chronograph, with 18ct solid gold case, and 17-jewel movement, signed on the case, dial and movement.

The presence of pulsations at the end of a time period and the additional registers may indicate that this was an aviator's watch.

£1,100-1,300   ML

A 1950s Movado 'Kingmatic' wristwatch, with stainless steel case, the silvered face with day and date apertures, and 28-jewel movement.

This was a high quality and expensive watch during the 1950s. The back is stamped "Sub-Sea" indicating it is waterproof.

£120-150   ML

A limited edition Swiss Franck Muller 'Endurance 24' manual-wind chronograph wristwatch, from an edition of 500, with stainless steel case, true 24-hour orange dial, and original signed Franck Muller strap.

Surprisingly, manuals are worth more than automatics, as fewer were made. Born in 1958, Franck Muller is known as the 'master of complications' due to his highly complex watches. He studied at the famous Geneva School of Watchmaking and launched his first watches in 1983. The car racing theme is also desirable.
1995

£2,000-2,500   ML

EXPERT EYE – A ROLEX 'BUBBLE BACK'

The 'bubble back' was launched in 1934 and was produced until the 1950s – the reference number allows this watch to be dated to around 1942-45.

Look out for the 'hooded' version, filled in between the lugs, which was introduced in 1941. It was not as popular making it rarer today.

The term 'bubble back' refers to the bulging back containing a rotor that moved 360 degrees – its size required a thicker case.

The case is made from solid gold, and is in excellent condition with the original face and intact back milling, hence the high value.

A Rolex 'Bubble Back' wristwatch, with 14ct solid yellow gold case, and 18-jewel automatic movement, reference no. 3131.

£1,300-1,700   ML

A 1960s Omega 'Constellation' wristwatch, the stainless steel case with 'Observatory' back, and Omega Caliber 561 24-jewel movement with five adjustments.

As this contains a 561 movement, it is deemed a true Constellation. In 2007, an Omega Constellation Grand Luxe in platinum from 1958 sold for £175,500 setting the world record price for an Omega watch.

£300-400   ML

A late 1950s Rolex 'Air King' Oyster Perpetual automatic wristwatch, with brushed stainless steel case and band, and signed Rolex 26-jewel full-rotor movement.

Introduced in the late 1950s, the Air King is one of the less valuable Rolex watches, but is still of excellent quality.

A 1930s Swiss Art Deco Semca wristwatch, the yellow and white gold case with engraved bezel, and 15-jewel movement.

This was intended for the Swiss or Canadian market, rather than the US or European market.

A 1970s Tressa Lux 'Spaceman' automatic wristwatch, designed by André Le Marquand the brushed stainless steel oval case with black face, and original 'Corfam' plastic strap.

Values drop by more than a third if the strap has been replaced or is in poor condition.

£550-650   ML   **£180-220**   ML   **£80-120**   RSS

A Tudor military-style 'Ranger' wristwatch, with stainless steel Oyster case, matching articulated strap, black dial, and ETA 25-jewel movement.

Tudor is a sub-brand of Rolex, and was launched in 1945. Other sub-brands include Unicorn and Rolco.

A 1990s Swiss Universal 'Compax' manual-wind chronograph wristwatch, the white dial with three registers, sapphire crystal, and signed Universal Geneve 31-jewel movement, signed seven times.

A desirable watch, the manual version is rarer than the automatic. In solid gold this watch could be worth £3,000-3,500.

A 1930s Waltham Ford Merit Club presentation watch, with elongated white gold-filled case, silvered dial with gold Arabic Art Deco style markers, and 17-jewel movement.

Presentation engravings usually devalue a watch, however this example was presented by the Ford Merit Club in 1935, which makes it more interesting and valuable. The length of the case, at 42mm, is rare as it was very large for the time.

£320-380   ML   **£600-750**   ML   **£120-140**   ML

A 1930s Waltham 'Cushion' wristwatch, with white gold-filled case, the white dial with luminous hands and numbers, subsidiary seconds dial at six o'clock, and with 17-jewel movement.

A 1930s Waltham wristwatch, the 14ct white gold 'Solidarity' case with highly engraved bezel, silvered dial with subsidiary seconds dial at six o'clock, and matching Solidarity engraved solid 14ct white gold buckle.

It is hard to find the buckle and watch together. It is also hard to find a watch with this much decoration on the case.

A 1970s Zenith 'Respirator' automatic wristwatch, with stainless steel case and matching articulated bracelet, and blue face.

£70-100   ML   **£200-220**   ML   **£250-300**   RSS

A 1970s Zenith 'Respirator' automatic watch, with rectangular metal case and matching bracelet, the silvered face with date aperture.

£300-350   RSS

A 1960s Swiss Zodiac 'Seawolf' automatic diver's wristwatch, in sealed case, with date and two-tone high fluorescent bezel and dial chapter ring.

£120-140   ML

A 1940s Bailey Banks & Biddle wristwatch, with solid platinum case, hooded lugs, diamond-set dial, and Swiss-made 27-jewel movement, the back stamped "Platinum".

High-end jewellery retailer Bailey Banks & Biddle was founded in Philadelphia in 1832 and now has over 70 stores in 24 US states. This watch would have been made and assembled in Switzerland under contract, and the dial marked with their name. A number of retailers sold watches marked and produced in this way.

£1,100-1,350   ML

A 1940s May's wristwatch, with 14ct solid pink gold square case and Swiss made 17-jewel movement.

Made for May's, the parent company of Macey's, this is another example of a 'contract' watch.

£150-180   ML

A Tiffany & Co. 18ct gold demi-hunter wristwatch, with presentation engraving inside back "1871 Sept 7th 1896", signed on the dial and movement, and the case signed "Tiffany & Co. 18K".

c1895

£500-600   ML

A 1960s Pierre Cardin wristwatch, with brushed stainless steel case, silvered dial, and Jaeger 17-jewel movement.

Early Pierre Cardin branded watches like this example were fitted with high quality Jaeger movements. The stainless steel case is unusual.

£120-140   ML

A Schochet 'Coin' wristwatch, the solid 18ct gold case made from a $20 coin, and with an unsigned movement, marked "Schochet" on the gold-tone face.

This was probably made by a jeweller, as it is not quite as well-made as the Piaget coin watch on the next page. For example, compare the two catches – the catch on this example is not as well concealed.

£750-900   ML

A late 1920s-30s Art Deco Roxy lady's pendant watch, the sterling silver case with enamelled design, and Swiss 17-jewel movement, with restored enamel.

£200-250   **ML**

A 1920s-30s Swiss lady's pendant watch, with hand-engraved Sterling silver hexagonal case, and Swiss 17-jewel movement.

The 12 o'clock is at the bottom of the pendant, allowing it to be 'turned up' and easily read.

£150-180   **ML**

EXPERT EYE – A LADY'S PENDANT WATCH

Founded in 1883 in Switzerland, Turler are a high quality watchmaker and jeweller. They moved to their current location in Zurich, in 1907.

Probably dating to the late 1920s, the Art Deco styling is desirable. It is also rare to find an original box.

The black enamelled exterior with enamelled gold dots is in excellent condition with no damage, and it retains its original leather strap and bow.

Twisting the bottom hemisphere makes the top hemisphere open like an iris to reveal the watch face - this is a complex mechanism.

This example has superb iridescence, making it more desirable.

A Swiss Turler lady's pendant watch, within a spherical case decorated with black enamel and gold enamel dots, stamped "Swiss Watch Co.", with an ETA movement, together with leather strap and bow and original box.

£150-180   **ML**

A Swiss Gallet & Co. lady's pendant watch, the conical sterling silver case decorated with alternate bands of black and green enamel and stamped ".935" and "Gallet & Co Geneva Switzerland", with sterling silver rose bud and leaf finial, unsigned face and Gallet 15-jewel movement with two adjustments.

£150-200   **ML**

A Swiss Movado 'Ermeto' travelling watch, solid 9ct gold case sliding open and closed to wind the watch, decorated with Japanese maki-e lacquer scenes of the Nihon Bashi in Kyoto, import marks for Glasgow 1929, and signed Movado 17-jewel movement.

c1929

£1,400-1,800   **DN**

A Piaget 'Coin Watch', the solid 18ct gold case made from a $20 coin, the spring-loaded flap activated by a hidden side release, with Piaget signed 17-jewel movement.

This is a superbly and finely engineered example, with the opening catch being skillfully concealed inside the milled edge of the coin. A number of companies made these, including Corum and Piaget, as well as a number of jewellers, and qualities vary. They were usually carried around in a bag or used on a night stand.

£1,200-1,500   **ML**

GLOSSARY

A

Acid etching A technique using acid to decorate glass to produce a matt or frosted appearance.

Albumen print Photographic paper is treated with egg white (albumen) to enable it to hold more light-sensitive chemicals. After being exposed to a negative, the resulting image is richer with more tonal variation.

Applied Refers to a separate part that has been attached to an object, such as a handle.

Automatic Used to describe a wristwatch movement that is wound using a revolving weighted disc or half-disc. As the wearer's wrist moves, the disc revolves and winds the watch. Automatic movements became commercially widespread from the 1930s onwards.

B

Baluster A curved form with a bulbous base and a slender neck.

Base metal A term describing common metals such as copper, tin and lead, or metal alloys, that were usually plated in gold or silver to imitate more expensive and luxurious metals. In the US, the term 'pot metal' is more commonly used.

Bisque A type of unglazed porcelain used for making dolls from c1860 to c1925.

Boards The hard covers of a book.

Brassing On plated items, where the plating has worn off to reveal the underlying base metal.

C

Cabochon A large, protruding, polished, but not faceted, stone.

Cameo Hardstone, coral or shell that has been carved in relief to show a design in a contrasting colour.

Cameo glass Decorative glass made from two or more layers of differently coloured glass, which are then carved or etched to reveal the colour beneath.

Cartouche A framed panel, often in the shape of a shield or paper scroll, which can be inscribed.

Cased Where a piece of glass is covered with a further layer of glass, sometimes of a contrasting colour, or clear and colourless. In some cases the casing will be further worked with cutting or etching to reveal the layer beneath.

Charger A large plate or platter, often for display, but also for serving.

Chromolithography A later development of 'lithography', where a number of printing stones are used in succession, each with a different colour, to build up a multi-coloured image.

Composition A mixture including wood pulp, plaster and glue used as a cheap alternative to bisque in the production of dolls' heads and bodies.

Compote A dish, usually on a stem or foot, to hold fruit for the dessert course.

Craze/Crazed/Crazing A network of fine cracks in the glaze caused by uneven shrinking during firing. It also describes plastic that is slowly degrading and has the same surface patterning.

Cuenca A technique used for decorating tiles where moulded ridges separate the coloured glazes, like the 'cloisonne' enamelling technique.

Cultured pearl A pearl formed when an irritant is artificially introduced to the mollusc.

D

Damascened Metal ornamented with inlaid gold or silver, often in wavy lines. Commonly found on weapons or armour.

Dichroic Glass treated with chemicals or metals that cause it to appear differently coloured depending on how it is viewed in the light.

Diecast Objects made by pouring molten metal into a closed metal die or mould.

Ding A very small dent in metal.

E

Earthenware A type of porous pottery that requires a glaze to make it waterproof.

Ebonized Wood that has been blackened with dye to resemble ebony.

E.P.N.S. Found on metal objects and standing for 'electroplated nickel silver', meaning the object is made from nickel which is then electroplated with silver.

F

Faience Earthenware that is treated with an impervious tin glaze. Popular in France from the 16th century and reaching its peak during the 18th century.

Faceted A form of decoration where a number of flat surfaces are cut into the surface of an object such as a gem or glass.

Faux A French word for 'false'. The intention is not to deceive fraudulently but to imitate a more costly material.

Finial A decorative knob at the end of a terminal, or on a lid.

Foliate Leaf and vine motifs.

G

Gather The term used to describe the mass of molten glass that the glassmaker forms into an object.

Guilloché An engraved pattern of interlaced lines or other decorative motifs, sometimes enamelled over with translucent enamels.

H

Hallmark The series of small stamps found on gold or silver that can identify the maker, the standard of the metal and the city and year of manufacture. Hallmarks differ for each country and can consist only of a maker's or a city mark. Nearly all English silver made after 1544 was required to be fully marked.

Hotworked Descriptive of a technique in glassmaking, where the shape and decoration are created and finished by the glassmaker at the furnace, when the glass is still hot and molten. The mass of glass is often re-inserted into the furnace to keep it molten and at a high enough temperature to ensure it can be 'worked'.

IJKL

Incised Applied to surface decoration or a maker's mark that has been scratched into the surface of an object with a sharp instrument.

Inclusions Used to describe all types of small particles of decorative materials embedded in glass.

Inscribed Usually related to a signature on the base of a piece, or else a design, which has been scratched into the surface using a sharp tool.

Iridescent A lustrous finish that subtly changes colour depending on how light hits it. Often used to describe the finish on ceramics and glass.

Lithography A printing technique developed in 1798 and employing the use of a stone upon which a pattern or picture has been drawn with a grease crayon. The ink adheres to the grease and is transferred to the paper when pressed against it.

MNO

Manual Used to describe a wristwatch movement that needs to be wound using a winder on the side of the case.

Millefiori An Italian term meaning 'thousand flowers' and used to describe cut, multi-coloured glass canes which are arranged and cased in clear glass. When arranged with the cut side facing the exterior, each circular disc (or short cane) resembles a small flower.

Mint A term used to describe an object in unused condition with no signs of wear and derived from coinage. Truly 'mint' objects will command a premium.

Mould Blown Descriptive of glass which has been blown into a mould to give it form. The inside of the mould is usually decorated with a three dimensional design, giving he surface of the piece a raised pattern.

Mount A metal part applied to an object made of ceramic, glass or another material, with a decorative or functional use. Murrine Slices of coloured transparent, translucent or opaque glass canes, typically with an internal pattern ranging from stylised flowers to abstract patterns. They are usually applied to the exterior of a vase and melted into and bonded to it in the furnace.

Nappy A shallow dish or bowl with a handle used for drinking.

Opalescent An opal-like, milky glass with subtle gradations of colour between thinner more translucent areas and thicker, more opaque areas.

P

Paisley A stylized design based on pinecones and foliage, often with added intricate decoration. It originated in India and is most often found on fabrics, such as shawls.

Paste (jewellery) A hard, bright glass cut the same way as a diamond and made and set to resemble them.

Patera An oval or circular decorative motif often with a fluted or floral centre. The plural is 'paterae'.

Piqué A decorative technique where small strips or studs of gold are inlaid onto ivory or tortoiseshell on a pattern and secured in place by heating.

Pontil A metal rod to which a glass vessel is attached when it is being worked. When it is removed it leaves a raised disc-shaped 'pontil mark'.

Pot metal Please see 'Base metal'.

Pounce pot A small pot made of wood (treen), silver or ceramic. Found on inkwells or designed to stand alone, it held a gum dust that was sprinkled over parchment to prevent ink from spreading. Used until the late 18th century.

Pressed (Press moulded) Ceramics formed by pressing clay into a mould. Pressed glass is made by pouring molten glass into a mould and pressing it with a plunger.

R

Reeded A type of decoration with thin raised, convex vertical lines. Derived from the decoration of classical columns.

Relief A form of moulded, pressed or carved decoration that protrudes above the surface of an object. Usually in the form of figures of foliate and foliage designs, it ranges in height from 'low' to 'high'.

Rhinestone Faceted, highly reflective crystal or glass 'stones' cut to resemble gemstones. The original rhinestones were quartz stones (rock crystal) dug out from the Rhine river in Germany. Usually of great clarity, they may be colourless or coloured, and may be treated with chemicals to give an iridescent surface effect.

Repoussé A French term for the raised, 'embossed' decoration on metals such as silver. The metal is forced into a form from one side causing it to bulge.

S

Sgraffito An Italian word for 'little scratch' and used to describe a decorative technique where the outer surface of an object, usually in glazed or coloured ceramic, is scratched away in a pattern to reveal the contrasting coloured underlying surface.

Sommerso Technique developed in Murano in the 1930s. Translates as 'submerged' and involves casing one or more layers of transparent coloured glass within a layer of thick, clear, colourless glass.

Stoneware A type of ceramic similar to earthenware and made of high-fired clay mixed with stone, such as feldspar, which makes it non-porous.

T

Tazza A shallow cup with a wide bowl, which is raised up on a single pedestal foot.

Tinplate A thin sheet of steel which has been plated with tin to prevent rusting. It is usually die-cut and bent into shapes and may also be decorated with painted or transfer printed designs.

Tooled Collective description for a number of decorative techniques applied to a surface. Includes engraving, stamping, punching and incising.

V

Vermeil Gold-plated silver. Vesta case A small case or box, usually made from silver, for carrying matches.

W

White metal Precious metal that is possibly silver, but not officially marked as such.

Y

Yellow metal Precious metal that is possibly gold, but not officially marked as such.

INDEX TO ADVERTISERS

Every item illustrated in the Miller's Collectables Price Guide by Judith Miller and Mark Hill has a letter code that identifies the dealer, auction house or private collector that owns or sold it. In this way the source of the item can be identified. The list below is a key to these codes. In the list, auction houses are shown by the letter A, dealers by the letter D, and private collectors by the letter P. Inclusion in this book in no way constitutes or implies a contract or a binding offer on the part of any of our contributors to supply or sell the goods illustrated, or similar items, at the prices stated.

AAB Ⓓ
ASHMORE & BURGESS
Mob: 07702 355122
info@ashmoreandburgess.com
www.ashmoreandburgess.com

AAC Ⓐ
ALDERFER AUCTION COMPANY
501 Fairground Road,
Hatfield, PA 19440 USA
Tel: 001 215 393 3000
info@alderferauction.com
www.alderferauction.com

AB Ⓟ
AUCTION BLOCKS
P.O. Box 241 Shelton
CT 06484, USA
blockschip@yahoo.com

AEM Ⓓ
ANTIQUES EMPORIUM
29 Division Street, Somerville
NJ 08876, USA
Tel: 001 908 218 1234
bkr63@patmedia.net

AMAC Ⓓ
ANDREW MCAULAY
The Quad, Alfie's Antiques Market,
13 Church Street,
Marylebone, London NW8 8DT
www.alfiesantiques.com

ANT Ⓓ
THE ANTIQUE GALLERY
8523 Germantown Avenue,
Philadelphia PA 19118, USA
Tel: (001) 215 248 1700
info@antiquegal.com
www.antiquegal.com

ART Ⓓ
ARTIUS GLASS
Street, Somerset BA16 0AN
Tel: 01458 443694
Mob: 07860 822666
wheeler.ron@talktalk.net
www.artiusglass.co.uk

ATK Ⓐ
AUCTION TEAM KÖLN
Otto-Hahn-Str. 10
50997 Köln (Godorf),
Germany
Tel: (0049) 2236 38 4340
auction@breker.com
www.breker.com

BA Ⓓ
BRANKSOME ANTIQUES
370 Poole Road, Branksome,
Poole, Dorset BH1 1AW
Tel: 01020 763 324/679 932

BAD Ⓓ
BETH ADAMS
Unit GO23-25 Alfie's Antique
Market, 13 Church Street,
Marylebone, London NW8 8DT
Mob: 07776 136 003
www.alfiesantiques.com

BB Ⓓ
BARBARA BLAU
South Street Antiques Market
615 South 6th Street, Philadelphia,
PA 19147-2128 USA
Tel: (001) 215 592 0256
bbjools@msn.com

BEL Ⓐ
BELHORN AUCTION SERVICES
PO Box 20211, Columbus,
OH 43220 USA
Tel: 001 614 921 9441
auctions@belhorn.com
www.belhorn.com

BER Ⓐ
BERTOIA AUCTIONS
2141 De Marco Drive
Vineland, NJ 08360 USA
Tel: 001 856 692 1881
toys@bertoiaauctions.com
www.bertoiaauctions.com

BEV Ⓓ
BEVERLEY ADAMS
Ground Floor, Alfie's Antiques
Market, 13 Church Street,
Marylebone, London NW8 8DT
Mob: 07776 136 003
www.alfiesantiques.com

BGL Ⓓ
BLOCK GLASS LTD
blockglss@aol.com
www.blockglass.com

BIG Ⓐ
BIGWOOD AUCTIONEERS
The Old School, Tiddington
Stratford-upon-Avon,
Warwickshire CV37 7AW
Tel: 01789 269 415
www.bigwoodauctioneers.co.uk

BH Ⓓ
**BLACK HORSE ANTIQUES
SHOWCASE**
2180 North Reading Road
Denver, PA 17517, USA
Tel: 001 717 335 3300
www.blackhorselodge.com/Antiques
.asp

BLNY Ⓐ
**BLOOMSBURY AUCTIONS
NEW YORK**
6 West 48th Street, New York
NY 10036-1902, USA
Tel: (001) 212 719 1000
newyork@bloomsburyauctions.com
www.bloomsburyauctions.com

BLO Ⓐ
BLOOMSBURY AUCTIONS
Bloomsbury House,
24 Maddox St, London W1S 1PP
Tel: 020 7495 9494
info@bloomsburyauctions.com
www.bloomsburyauctions.com

BRI Ⓐ
BRIGHTWELLS
Easters Court, Leominster
Herefordshire, HR6 0DE
Tel: 01568 611 166
www.brightwells.com

C Ⓐ
COTTEES
The Market, East Street, Wareham,
Dorset BH20 4NR
Tel: 01929 552 826
auctions@cottees.fsnet.co.uk
www.auctionsatcottees.co.uk

CANT Ⓐ
CARLTON ANTIQUES
43 Worcester Road, Malvern
Worcestershire WR14 4RB
Tel: 01684 573 092
dave@carlton-antiques.com
www.carlton-antiques.com

CHEF Ⓐ
CHEFFINS
Clifton House, 1 & 2 Clifton Road,
Cambridge CB1 7EA
Tel: 01223 213 343
fine.art@cheffins.co.uk
www.cheffins.co.uk

CHT Ⓐ
CHARTERHOUSE
The Long Street Salerooms,
Sherborne, Dorset DT9 3BS
Tel: 01935 812 277
enquiry@charterhouse-
auctions.co.uk
www.charterhouse-auctions.co.uk

CLV Ⓐ
CLEVEDON SALEROOMS
The Auction Centre,
Kenn Road, Kenn, Clevedon,
Bristol BS21 6TT
Tel: 01934 830 111
Fax: 01934 832 538
info@clevedonsalerooms.co.uk
www.clevedon-salerooms.com

CN Ⓓ
COLIN NARBETH
Colin Narbeth & Sons Ltd, 20 Cecil
Court, Leicester Square, London
WC2N 4HE
Tel: 0207 379 6975
colin.narbeth@btinternet.com
www.colin-narbeth.com

CO ⒹⒶ
COOPER OWEN
Tel: 01753 855 858
enquiry@cooperowen.com
www.cooperowen.com

CW Ⓟ
CHRISTINE WILDMAN
wild123@allstream.net

DN Ⓐ
DREWEATTS
Donnington Priory Salerooms,
Donnington, Newbury,
Berkshire RG14 2JE
Tel: 01635 553 553
donnington@dnfa.com
www.dnfa.com/donnington

DNW Ⓐ
DIX NOONAN WEBB
16 Bolton Street, Piccadilly, London
W1J 8BQ
Tel: 0207 016 1700
coins @dnw.co.uk
www.dnw.co.uk

DRA Ⓐ
DAVID RAGO AUCTIONS
333 North Main Street, Lambertville,
NJ 08530 USA
Tel: 001 609 397 9374
info@ragoarts.com
www.ragoarts.com

FFM Ⓐ
FESTIVAL FOR MIDWINTER
No longer trading

FLD Ⓐ
FIELDING'S AUCTIONEERS
Mill Race Lane, Stourbridge,
West Midlands DY8 1JN
Tel: 01384 444140
info@fieldingsauctioneers.co.uk
www.fieldingsauctioneers.co.uk

FRE Ⓐ
FREEMAN'S
1808 Chestnut Street, Philadelphia,
PA 19103 USA
Tel: 001 215 563 9275
info@freemansauction.com
www.freemansauction.com

GAZE Ⓐ
THOS. WM. GAZE & SON
Diss Auction Rooms, Roydon Rd,
Diss, Norfolk IP22 4LN
Tel: 01379 650 306
sales@dissauctionrooms.co.uk
www.twgaze.com

GBA Ⓐ
GRAHAM BUDD AUCTIONS
P.O. Box 47519,
London N14 6XD
Tel: 020 8366 2525
gb@grahambuddauctions.co.uk
www.grahambuddauctions.co.uk

GC Ⓟ
GRAHAM COOLEY COLLECTION
Mob: 07968 722 269
graham.cooley@universalsensors.co.
uk

GCA Ⓓ
GRIFFIN COOPER ANTIQUES
South Street Antiques Market
615 South 6th Street, Philadelphia,
PA 19147-2128 USA
Tel: 001 215 592 0256

GCHI Ⓓ
THE GIRL CAN'T HELP IT!
Grand Central Window, Ground
Floor, Alfie's Antiques Market, 13-25
Church Street, London NW8 8DT
Tel: 0207 724 8984
Mob: 07958 515 614
info@thegirlcanthelpit.com
www.thegirlcanthelpit.com

GGRT Ⓓ
GARY GRANT CHOICE PIECES
18 Arlington Way,
London EC1R 1UY
Tel: 020 7713 1122
garyjamesgrant@btinternet.com

GHOU Ⓐ
GARDINER HOULGATE
Bath Auction Rooms,
9 Leafield Way, Corsham,
Nr Bath SN13 9SW
Tel: 01225 812 912
auctions@gardinerhoulgate.co.uk
www.gardinerhoulgate.co.uk

GM Ⓐ
GALERIE MAURER
Kurfürstenstrasse 17
D-80799 Munich, Germany
Tel: 0049 89 271 13 45
info@galeriemaurer.de
www.galerie-objekte-maurer.de

GORL Ⓐ
GORRINGES
15 North Street, Lewes,
East Sussex BN7 2PD
Tel: 01273 472 503
www.gorringes.co.uk

GROB Ⓓ
GEOFFREY ROBINSON
Stand GO77-78 & GO91-92, Alfies
Antiques Market,
13-25 Church Street,
London NW8 8DT
Tel: 020 7723 0449
www.alfiesantiques.com

GWRA Ⓐ
**GLOUCESTERSHIRE
WORCESTERSHIRE RAILWAY
AUCTIONS**
Tel: 01684 773 487 /
01386 760 109
www.gwra.co.uk

H&G Ⓓ
HOPE AND GLORY
131A Kensington Church Street,
London W8 7LP
Tel: 020 7727 8424

HAMG Ⓐ
DREWEATTS
Valuation Office
Baverstock House
93 High Street, Godalming
Surrey GU7 1AL
Tel: 01483 423 567
godalming@dnfa.com
www.dnfa.com

HGS Ⓓ
HARPER GENERAL STORE
lauver5@comcast.com

HLM Ⓓ
HI & LO MODERN
161 Montclair Avenue
Montclair NJ 07042 USA
sales@hiandlomodern.com
www.hiandlomodern.com

JN Ⓐ
JOHN NICHOLSON AUCTIONEERS
The Auction Rooms, 'Longfield',
Midhurst Road, Fernhurst,
Haslemere, Surrey GU27 3HA
Tel: 01428 653 727
sales@johnnicholsons.com
www.johnnicholsons.com

KCS Ⓓ
KCS CERAMICS
Tel: 020 8384 8981
karen@kcsceramics.co.uk
www.kcsceramics.co.uk

KNK Ⓓ
KITSCH-N-KABOODLE
South Street Antiques Market,
615 South 6th Street, Philadelphia,
PA 19147-2128 USA
Tel: 001 215 382 1354
kitschnkaboodle@yahoo.com

KT Ⓐ
KERRY TAYLOR AUCTIONS
Unit C25,
Parkhall Road Trading Estate
40 Martell Road, London SE21 8EN
Tel: 0208 676 4600
info@kerrytaylorauctions.com
www.kerrytaylorauctions.com

L&T Ⓐ
LYON AND TURNBULL LTD.
33 Broughton Place,
Edinburgh EH1 3RR
Tel: 0131 557 8844
info@lyonandturnbull.com
www.lyonandturnbull.com

LG Ⓓ
LEGACY
No longer trading

LH Ⓓ
LUCY'S HAT
Pine Street, Philadelphia, PA, USA

MA Ⓓ
MANIC ATTIC
Alfies Antiques Market, Stand
S48/49, 13-25 Church Street,
London NW8 8DT
Tel: 020 7723 6105
ianbroughton@hotmail.com

MAS Ⓐ
MASTRO AUCTIONS
7900 South Madison Street, Burr
Ridge, Illinois 60527, USA
Tel: 001 630 472 1200
customerservice@mastroauctions.com
www.mastroauctions.com

MAX Ⓐ
MAXWELLS AUCTIONEERS
133a Woodford Road
Woodford Cheshire SK7 1QD
Tel: 0161 439 5182
info@maxwells-auctioneers.co.uk
www.maxwells-auctioneers.co.uk

MEM Ⓓ
MEMORY LANE
45-40 Bell Blvd, Suite 109
Bayside, NY 11361, USA
Tel: (001) 718 428 8181
memlnny@aol.com

MHC Ⓟ
MARK HILL COLLECTION
Mob: 07798 915 474
books@markhillpublishing.com
www.markhillpublishing.com

MHT Ⓓ
MUM HAD THAT
info@mumhadthat.com
www.mumhadthat.com

ML Ⓓ
MARK LAINO
Mark of Time, 132 South 8th Street,
Philadelphia, PA 19107 USA
Tel: 001 215 922 1551
lecoultre@verizon.net
eBay ID: lecoultre

MTB Ⓓ
THE MAGIC TOYBOX
210 Havant Road, Drayton,
Portsmouth, Hampshire PO6 2EH
Tel: 02392 221 307
magictoybox@btinternet.com
www.magictoybox.co.uk

MTS Ⓓ
THE MULTICOLOURED TIMESLIP
dave_a_cameron@hotmail.com
eBay ID: dave65330

NEA Ⓐ
NEALES OF NOTTINGHAM
192 Mansfield Road,
Nottingham NG1 3HU
Tel: 0115 962 4141
nottingham@dnfa.com
www.dnfa.com/nottingham

NOR Ⓓ
NEET-O-RAMA
14 Division Street, Somerville,
NJ 08876 USA
Tel: 001 908 722 4600
www.neetstuff.com

ON Ⓐ
ONSLOWS
The Coach House, Manor Road,
Stourpaine, Dorset DT11 8TQ
Tel: 01258 488 838
enquiries@onslows.co.uk
www.onslows.co.uk

OUT Ⓓ
OUTERNATIONAL
14 Lübeckerstrasse, Cologne
D50670, Germany
info@outernational.eu
www.outernational.eu

P&I Ⓓ
PAOLA & IAIA
Unit S057-058, Alfie's Antiques
Market, 13-25 Church Street,
London NW8 8DT
Tel: 07751 084 135
paolaeiaialondon@hotmail.com

PAS Ⓓ
PAST CARING
54 Essex Road, London N1 8LR

PC Ⓟ
PRIVATE COLLECTION

PGO Ⓓ
PAMELA GOODWIN
Goodwin Antiques, 11 The Pantiles,
Royal Tunbridge Wells, Kent TN2 5TD
Tel: 01435 882200
mail@goodwinantiques.co.uk
www.goodwinantiques.co.uk

PSA Ⓐ
**POTTERIES SPECIALIST
AUCTIONS**
271 Waterloo Road, Cobridge,
Stoke-on-Trent ST6 3HR
Tel: 01782 286 622
enquiries@potteriesauctions.com
www.potteriesauctions.com

PWE Ⓐ
**PHILIP WEISS AUCTION
GALLERIES**
1 Neil Court, Oceanside,
NY 11572 USA
Tel: 001 516 594 073
info@philipweissauctions.com
www.philipweissauctions.com

QU Ⓐ
**QUITTENBAUM
KUNSTAUKTIONEN**
Hohenstaufenstrasse 1,
D-80801 Munich, Germany
Tel: 0049 89 33 00 756
info@quittenbaum.de
www.quittenbaum.de

RCC Ⓐ
ROYAL COMMEMORATIVE CHINA
Paul Wynton & Joe Spiteri
Tel: 020 8863 0625
Mob: 07930 303 358
royalcommemoratives
@hotmail.com

ROS Ⓐ
ROSEBERY'S
74-76 Knight's Hill, West Norwood,
London SE27 0JD
Tel: 020 8761 2522
auctions@roseberys.co.uk
www.roseberys.co.uk

ROW Ⓐ
ROWLEY FINE ART AUCTIONEERS
8 Downham Road, Ely,
Cambridgeshire, CB6 1AH
Tel: 01353 653 020
silas@rowleyfineart.com
www.rowleyfineart.com

RSS Ⓐ
ROSSINI SVV
7 Rue Drouot, Paris 75009, France
0033 1 53 34 55 00
contact@rossini.fr
www.rossini.fr

RTC Ⓐ
RITCHIES
380 King Street East, Toronto
Ontario, M5A 1K9, Canada
Tel: (001) 416 364 1864
auction@ritchies.com
www.ritchies.com

SAE Ⓐ
ANTIQUES EMPORIUM
29 Division Street, Somerville
NJ 08876, USA
Tel: (001) 908 218 1234
bkr63@patmedia.net

SAS Ⓐ
SPECIAL AUCTION SERVICES
Kennetholme, Midgham,
Nr. Reading, Berkshire RG7 5UX
Tel: 0118 971 2949
mail@specialauctionservices.com
www.specialauctionservices.com

SDR Ⓐ
SOLLO:RAGO MODERN AUCTIONS
333 North Main Street, Lambertville, NJ 08530 USA
Tel: 001 609 397 9374
info@ragoarts.com
www.ragoarts.com

SHAND Ⓓ
THE SHAND GALLERY
Toronto Antiques on King
276 King Street West, Toronto, Ontario M5V 1J2 Canada
Tel: 001 416 260 9056
kenshand@allstream.net
www.torontoantiquesonking.com

SK Ⓐ
SLOANS & KENYON
7034 Wisconsin Avenue, Chevy Chase, Maryland 20815 USA
Tel: (001) 301 634 2330
info@sloansandkenyon.com
www.sloansandkenyon.com

SMP Ⓟ
ANTIQUEXPLORER PUBLISHERS
The Old Glove Factory, Bristol Road, Sherborne, Dorset DT9 4HP
Tel: 01935 814995
info@antiquexplorer.com
www.antiquexplorer.com

SOTT Ⓓ
SIGN OF THE TYMES
Mill Antiques Center, 12 Morris Farm Road, Lafayette, NJ 07848 USA
Tel: 001 973 383 6028
jhap@nac.net
www.millantiques.com

SWA Ⓐ
SWANN GALLERIES IMAGE LIBRARY
104 East 25th Street, New York, NY 10010 USA
Tel: 001 212 254 4710
swann@swanngalleries.com
www.swanngalleries.com

SWO Ⓐ
SWORDERS
14 Cambridge Road, Stansted Mountfitchet, Essex CM24 8BZ
Tel: 01279 817 778
auctions@sworder.co.uk
www.sworder.co.uk

TCF Ⓓ
CYNTHIA FINDLAY
Toronto Antiques on King
276 King Street West, Toronto, Ontario Canada M5V 1J2
Tel: 001 416 260 9057
www.torontoantiquesonking.com

TDG Ⓓ
THE DESIGN GALLERY
5 The Green, Westerham, Kent TN16 1AS
Tel: 01959 561 234
sales@designgallery.co.uk
www.designgallery.co.uk

TGM Ⓓ
THE STUDIO GLASS MERCHANT
Tel: 07775 683 961
Tel: 0208 668 2701
info@thestudioglassmerchant.co.uk
www.thestudioglassmerchant.co.uk

THG Ⓓ
HERITAGE
Toronto Antiques on King
276 King Street West, Toronto, Ontario M5V 1J2 Canada
Tel: 001 416 260 9057
www.torontoantiquesonking.com

TOA Ⓓ
THE OCCUPIED ATTIC
Tel: 001 518 899 5030
occattic@aol.com
seguin12@aol.com

TOJ Ⓓ
THESE OLD JUGS
Tel: 001 410 626 0770
susan@theseoldjugs.com
www.theseoldjugs.com

TSIS Ⓓ
THREE SISTERS
South Street Antiques Market, 615 South 6th Street, Philadelphia, PA 19147-2128 USA
Tel: 001 215 592 0256

TWF Ⓓ
TWICE FOUND
608 Markham Street, Mirvish Village, Toronto, Ontario M6G 2L8, Canada
Tel: 001 416 534 3904
twicefound@bellnet.ca

UCT Ⓓ
UNDERCURRENTS
28 Cowper Street, London, EC2A 4AS
Tel: 0207 251 1537
shop@undercurrents.biz
www.undercurrents.biz

VC Ⓓ
VICTOR CAPLIN
Stand G075-76, Alfie's Antiques Market, 13-25 Church Street, London NW8 8DT
Mob: 07947 511 592
victorcaplin@aol.com
www.alfiesantiques.com

VE Ⓓ
VINTAGE EYEWEAR OF NEW YORK CITY INC.
1A The Fantastic Umbrella Factory 4820 Old Post Road, Charlestown Rhode Island, USA
Tel: 001 917 721 6546
vintageyes60@yahoo.com

VEC Ⓐ
VECTIS AUCTIONS LTD
Fleck Way, Thornaby, Stockton on Tees TS17 9JZ
Tel: 01642 750 616
admin@vectis.co.uk
www.vectis.co.uk

VSA Ⓐ
VAN SABBEN AUCTIONS
Appelsteeg 1-B, NL-1621 BD, Hoorn, Netherlands
0031 229 268 203
uboersma@vansabbenauctions.nl
www.vansabbenauctions.nl

VZ Ⓐ
VON ZEZSCHWITZ
Friedrichstrasse 1a, 80801 Munich, Germany
Tel: 00 49 89 38 98 930
www.von-zezschwitz.de

W&L Ⓐ
W&L ANTIQUES
Stand G060, Alfie's Antiques Market, 13-25 Church Street, London NW8 8DT
Tel: 0207 723 6066
Mob: 07788 486 297
teddylove@blueyonder.co.uk

WAD Ⓐ
WADDINGTON'S AUCTIONEERS
111 Bathurst Street, Toronto, Ontario, Canada M5V 2R1
Tel: 001 416 504 9100
www.waddingtons.ca

W&W Ⓐ
WALLIS & WALLIS
West Steet Auction Galleries, Lewes, East Sussex BN7 2NJ
Tel: 01273 480 208
auctions@wallisandwallis.co.uk
www.wallisandwallis.co.uk

WDL Ⓐ
KUNST-AUKTIONSHAUS MARTIN WENDL
August-Bebel-Straße 4, 07407 Rudolstadt, Germany
Tel: 0049 3672 424 350
www.auktionshaus-wendl.de

WW Ⓐ
WOOLLEY & WALLIS
51-61 Castle Street, Salisbury, Wiltshire SP1 3SU
Tel: 01722 424 500
enquiries@woolleyandwallis.co.uk
www.woolleyandwallis.co.uk

If you wish to have any item valued, it is advisable to contact the dealer or specialist in advance to check that they will carry out this service and whether there is a charge. While most dealers will be happy to help you with an enquiry, do remember that they are busy people with businesses to run. Telephone valuations are not possible. Please mention the Miller's Collectables Price Guide 2009 by Judith Miller and Mark Hill when making an enquiry.

ADVERTISING

Dan Tinman
Lipka Arcade (Portobello Road),
Unit 13-14 Lower Ground,
282 Westbourne Grove,
London W11
Tel: 01761 462 477 or
07768 166 808
www.dantinman.com

Huxtins
Saturdays at: Portobello Road,
Basement Stall 11/12,
288 Westbourne Grove,
London W11
Tel: 07710 132 200
david@huxtins.com
www.huxtins.com

Junktion
The Old Railway Station,
New Bolingbroke,
Boston, Lincolnshire
Tel: 01205 480068 or
07836 345 491
junktionantiques@hotmail.com

The Tin Shop
Market Vaults, Scarborough,
North Yorkshire YO11 1EU
Tel: 01723 351 089
www.tinshop.co.uk

ANIMATION ART

Animation Art Gallery
13-14 Great Castle Street,
London W1W 8LS
Tel: 020 7255 1456
Fax: 0207 436 1256
gallery@animaart.com
www.animaart.com

ART DECO

Art Deco Etc
73 Gloucester Road, Brighton,
Sussex, BN1 3LQ
Tel: 01273 329 268
johnclark@artdecoetc.co.uk

AUTOGRAPHS

Lights, Camera Action
6 Western Gardens, Western
Boulevard, Aspley,
Nottingham, HG8 5GP
Tel: 0115 913 1116
Mob: 07970 342 363
nick.straw@lca-
autographs.co.uk
www.lca-autographs.co.uk

Special Signings
Tel: 01438 714 728
sales@specialsignings.com
www.specialsignings.com

The Autograph Collectors Gallery
7 Jessops Lane,
Gedling, Nottingham
Tel: 0115 961 2956
www.autograph-gallery.co.uk

AUTOMOBILIA

Automobilia Planet
P.O. Box 624, Yarm TS15 9WT
info@automobiliaplanet.com
www.automobiliaplanet.com

C.A.R.S. of Brighton
The White Lion Garage
Clarendon Place,
Kemp Town, Brighton Sussex
Tel: 01273 622 722
Fax: 01273 622 722
whiteliongarage@fsmail.net
www.carsofbrighton.co.uk

Finesse Fine Art
Tel: 07973 886 937
tony@finesse-fine-art.com
www.finesse-fine-art.com

Junktion
The Old Railway Station,
New Bolingbroke,
Boston, Lincolnshire
Tel: 01205 480068 or
07836 345 491
junktionantiques@hotmail.com

BOOKS

Biblion
1-7 Davies Mews,
London W1K 5AB
Tel: 020 7629 1374
info@biblion.com
www.biblion.com

Zardoz Books
20 Whitecroft, Dilton Marsh,
Westbury, Somerset BA13 4DJ
Tel: 01373 865 371
www.zardozbooks.co.uk

Banknotes, Bonds & Shares
Colin Narbeth & Sons Ltd
20 Cecil Court, Leicester
Square, London WC2N 4HE
Tel: 0207 379 6975
colin.narbeth@btinternet.com
www.colin-narbeth.com

Intercol
43 Templar's Crescent, Finchley,
London N3 3QR
Tel: 020 8349 2207
sales@intercol.co.uk
www.intercol.co.uk

BREWERIANA

Junktion
The Old Railway Station,
New Bolingbroke,
Boston, Lincolnshire
Tel: 01205 480068 or
07836 345 491
junktionantiques@hotmail.com

Gordon Litherland
25 Stapenhill Road,
Burton on Trent, Staffordshire
Tel: 01283 567 213 or
07952 118 987
gordon@jmp2000.com

CERAMICS

A1 Collectables
Hampton Wick Antiques
Market, 97B High Street,
Hampton Wick, Surrey
Tel: 0208 977 7230
www.a1-collectables.co.uk

Beth Adams
Unit GO43/4, Alfies Antique
Market, 13 Church Street,
Marylebone, London NW8 8DT
Mob: 07776 136 003
www.alfiesantiques.com

The Ceramic Studio
2 Potters Hill Farm Cottages,
Langley, Witney, Oxfordshire
wwww.theceramicstudio.co.uk

China Search
P.O. Box 1202, Kenilworth,
Warwickshire CV8 2WW
Tel: 01926 512 402
Fax: 01926 859 311
helen@chinasearch.uk.com
www.chinasearch.uk.com

Collectables
134B High Street, Honiton,
Devon EX14 1JP
Tel: 01404 470 024
chris@collectableshoniton.co.uk
www.collectableshoniton.co.uk

Cornishware.biz
Vintage-Kitsch, 1 Crown &
Anchor Cottages, Horsley,
Newcastle, Tyne & Wear
Tel: 07979 857 599
info@cornishware.biz
www.cornishware.biz

Adrian Grater
25-26 Admiral Vernon Antiques
Centre, 141-149 Portobello
Road, London W11 2DY
Tel: 0208 579 0357
adriangrater@tiscali.co.uk

Gallery 1930
18 Church St, London NW8 8EP
Tel: 020 7723 1555
Fax: 020 7735 8309
gallery1930@aol.com
www.susiecooperceramics.com

Gary Grant Choice Pieces
18 Arlington Way,
London EC1R 1UY
Tel: 020 7713 1122

Gillian Neale Antiques
P.O. Box 247,
Aylesbury HP20 1JZ
Tel: 01296 423754
Fax: 01296-334601
gillianneale@aol.com
www.gilliannealeantiques.co.uk

Tony Horsley
P.O. Box 3127,
Brighton, East Sussex
Tel: 01273 550 770

KCS Ceramics
Tel: 0208 384 8981
www.kcsceramics.co.uk

Louis O'Brien
Tel: 01276 32907

Nick Ainge
Tel: 01832 731 063
Mob: 07745 902 343
nick@ainge1930.fastnet.co.uk
decoseek.decoware.co.uk

ReMemories Antiques
74 High Street, Tenterden, Kent
Tel: 01580 763 416

Retroselect
info@retroselect.com
www.retroselect.com

Rick Hubbard Art Deco
Tel: 01794 513133
www.rickhubbard-artdeco.co.uk

Geoffrey Robinson
Stand GO77-78 & GO91-92,
Alfies Antiques Market,
13-25 Church Street,
London, NW8 8DT
Tel: 020 7723 0449
unknown@unknown.com
www.alfiesantiques.com

Rogers de Rin
76 Royal Hospital Rd, Paradise
Walk, London SW3 4HN
Tel: 020 7352 9007
Fax: 020 7351 9407
rogersderin@rogersderin.co.uk
www.rogersderin.co.uk

Sue Norman
Antiquarius, Stand L4, 135
King's Rd, London SW3 4PW
Tel: 020 7352 7217
sue@sue-norman.demon.co.uk
www.sue-norman.demon.co.uk

Undercurrents
28 Cowper Street,
London, EC2A 4AS
Tel: 0207 251 1537
shop@undercurrents.biz
www.undercurrents.biz

Richard Wallis Antiks
Tel: 0208 529 1749
sales@richardwallisantiks.com
www.richardwallisantiks.com

CIGARETTE CARDS

Carlton Antiques
43 Worcester Road, Malvern,
Worcestershire WR14 4RB
Tel: 01684 573 092
dave@carlton-antiques.com
www.carlton-antiques.com

COINS & MONEY

British Notes
P.O. Box 257, Sutton,
Surrey SM3 9WW
Tel: 0208 641 3224
pamwestbritnotes@aol.com
www.britishnotes.co.uk

Coincraft
44-45 Great Russell Street,
London WC1B 3LU
Tel: 0207 636 1188
www.coincraft.com

Colin Narbeth
20 Cecil Court, Leicester
Square, London WC2N 4HE
Tel: 0207 379 6975
colin.narbeth@btinternet.com
www.colin-narbeth.com

Intercol
43 Templar's Crescent, Finchley,
London N3 3QR
Tel: 020 8349 2207
sales@intercol.co.uk
www.intercol.co.uk

COMICS

Phil's Comics
P.O. Box 3433, Brighton
Sussex BN50 9JA
Tel: 01273 673 462
phil@phil-comics.com
www.phil-comics.com

The Book Palace
Bedwardine Road, Crystal
Palace, London SE19 3AP
Tel: 020 8768 0022
Fax: 020 8768 0563
www.bookpalace.com

COMMEMORATIVE WARE

Hope & Glory
131a Kensington Church Street,
London W8 7LP
Tel: 020 7727 8424

Commemorabilia
15 Haroldsleigh Avenue,
Crownhill, Plymouth
Tel: 01752 700 795
www.commemorabilia.co.uk

Recollections
5 Royal Arcade, Boscombe,
Bournemouth, Dorset BH1 4BT
Tel: 01202 304 441

Royal Commemorative China
Paul Wynton & Joe Spiteri
Tel: 020 8863 0625
Mob: 07930 303 358
royalcommemoratives@
hotmail.com

COSTUME & ACCESSORIES

Beyond Retro
110-112 Cheshire Street,
London E2 6EJ
Tel: 020 7613 3636
sales@beyondretro.com
www.beyondretro.com

Cad van Swankster at The Girl Can't Help It
Alfies Antiques Market, Grand
Centre Window, Ground Floor,
13-25 Church Street,
London NW8 8DT
Tel: 020 7724 8984
Mob: 07958 515 614
sparkle@sparklemoore.com
www.thegirlcanthelpit.com

Decades
20 Lord Street West,
Blackburn BB2 1JX
Tel: 01254 693320

Echoes
650a Halifax Road, Eastwood,
Todmorden
Tel: 01706 817 505

Fantiques
Tel: 020 8840 4761
paula.raven@ntlworld.com

Linda Bee
Grays Antiques Market, 1-7
Davies Street, London W1Y 2LP
Tel/Fax: 020 7629 5921
www.graysantiques.com

Old Hat
66 Fulham High Street,
London SW6 3LQ
Tel: 020 7610 6558

RetroBizarre
25 St Mary's Row, Moseley,
Birmingham, B13 8HW
Tel: 0121 442 6389
info@retrobizarre.biz
www.retrobizarre.biz

Rokit
101 Brick Lane, London E1 6SE
(and other London locations)
Tel: 0207 375 3864
www.rokit.co.uk

Sparkle Moore at The Girl Can't Help It
Alfies Antiques Market, Grand
Centre Window, Ground Floor,
13-25 Church Street,
Marylebone, London NW8 8DT
Tel: 020 7724 8984 or
07958 515 614
sparkle@sparklemoore.com
www.thegirlcanthelpit.com

Steptoe's Dog Antique & Vintage Online Store
Tel: 07731475164
www.steptoesantiques.co.uk

Vintage Modes
Grays Antiques Market, 1-7
Davies Mews, London W1Y 5AB
Tel: 020 7409 0400
info@vintagemodes.co.uk
www.vintagemodes.co.uk

Vintage to Vogue
28 Milsom Street, Bath,
Avon BA1 1DG
Tel: 01225 337 323

Wardrobe
51 Upper North Street,
Brighton, East Sussex
Tel: 01273 202 201

COSTUME JEWELLERY

Cristobal
26 Church St, London NW8 8EP
Tel: 020 7724 7230
steven@cristobal.co.uk
www.cristobal.co.uk

Eclectica
Tel/Fax: 020 7226 5625
liz@eclectica.biz
www.eclectica.biz

Richard Gibbon
neljeweluk@aol.com

Ritzy
7 The Mall Antiques Arcade,
359 Upper Street,
London N1 0PD
Tel: 020 7704 0127

William Wain at Antiquarius
Stand J6, Antiquarius, 135
King's Road, London SW3 4PW
Tel: 020 7351 4905
w.wain@btopenworld.com

Crested China
The Crested China Company
Highfield, Windmill Hill,
Driffield, East Riding of
Yorkshire YO25 5YP
Tel: 01377 257042
dt@thecrestedchinacompany
.com
www.thecrestedchinacompany
.com

DOLLS

Bébés & Jouets
c/o Lochend Post Office, 165
Restalrig Road,
Edinburgh EH7 6HW
Tel: 0131 332 5650
bebesjouets@tiscali.co.uk

British Doll Showcase
squibbit@ukonline.co.uk
www.britishdollshowcase.co.uk

Lolli Dollies Online
8 Athol Terrace, Dover, Kent
www.lolli-dollies-online.co.uk

Pollyanna
34 High Street, Arundel,
West Sussex
Tel: 01902 885 198 or
07499 903 457

Sandra Fellner
A18-A19 and MB026,
Grays Antique Market
Tel: 020 8946 5613
sandrafellner@blueyonder.co.uk
www.graysantiques.com

Victoriana Dolls
101 Portobello Road,
London W11 2BQ
Tel: 01737 249 525
Fax: 01737 226 254
heather.bond@totalserve.co.uk

FIFTIES, SIXTIES & SEVENTIES

Twentieth Century Marks
Whitegates, Rectory Road,
Little Burstead, Near Billericay,
Essex CM12 9TR
Tel: 01268 411 000
info@20thcenturymarks.co.uk
www.20thcenturymarks.co.uk

Design20c
Tel: 01276 512329 /
0794 609 2138
sales@design20c.co.uk
www.design20c.co.uk

Fragile Design
14-15 The Custard Factory,
Digbeth, Birmingham B9 4AA
Tel: 0121 224 7378
info@fragiledesign.com
www.fragiledesign.com

High Street Retro
39 High Street, Old Town,
Hastings, East Sussex TN34 3ER
Tel: 01424 460 068
www.highstreetretro.co.uk

InRetrospect
37 Upper St James Street,
Kemptown, Brighton,
East Sussex BN2 1JN
Tel: 01273 609 374

Luna
139 Lower Parliament Street,
Nottingham NG1 1EE
Tel: 0115 924 3267
info@luna-online.co.uk
www.luna-online.co.uk

Manic Attic
Alfie's Antiques Market,
Stand S48/49,
13-25 Church St,
London NW8 8DT
Tel: 020 7723 6105
ianbroughton@hotmail.com

Modern Warehouse
243b Victoria Park Road,
London E9 7HD
Tel: 0208 986 0740 or
07747 758 852
info@themodernwarehouse
.com
www.themodernwarehouse
.com

Multicoloured Timeslip
eBay Store: multicoloured
timeslip
eBay ID: dave65330
Mob: 07971 410 563
dave_a_cameron@hotmail.com

Planet Bazaar
397 St John Street,
London EC1V 4LD
Tel; 0207 278 7793 or
07956 326 301
www.planetbazaar.co.uk

Retrocentre
Tel: 01189 507 224
al@retro-centre.co.uk
www.retro-centre.co.uk

Retropolitan
24 Wells House,
London NW10 6EE
Tel: 07870 422 182
lesley@retropolitan.co.uk
www.retropolitan.co.uk

FILM & TV

The Prop Store of London
Great House Farm, Chenies,
Rickmansworth, Herts WD3 6EP
Tel: 01494 766 485
steve.lane@propstore.co.uk
www.propstore.co.uk

GLASS

**Andrew Lineham
Fine Glass**
Tel/Fax: 01243 576 241
Mob: 07767 702 722
andrew@antiquecoloured
glass.com
www.antiquecolouredglass.com

**Antique Glass at
Frank Dux Antiques**
33 Belvedere, Lansdown Road,
Bath, Avon BA1 5HR
Tel/Fax: 01225 312 367
www.antique-glass.co.uk

Artius Glass
Tel: 07860 822 666
wheeler.ron@talktalk.net
www.artiusglass.co.uk

Cloud Glass
info@cloudglass.com
www.cloudglass.com

Francesca Martire
Stand F131-137, First Floor, 13-
25 Alfies Antiques Market, 13
Church St, London NW8 0RH
Tel: 020 7724 4802
www.francescamartire.com

Glass etc
18-22 Rope Walk, Rye,
East Sussex TN31 7NA
Tel: 01797 226 600
andy@decanterman.com
www.decanterman.com

Grimes House Antiques
High Street, Moreton in Marsh,
Gloucestershire GL56 0AT
Tel: 01608 651 029
grimes_house@cix.co.uk
www.cranberryglass.co.uk

**Jeanette Hayhurst
Fine Glass**
32A Kensington Church Street,
London W8 4HA
Tel: 020 7938 1539

Mum Had That
info@mumhadthat.com
www.mumhadthat.com

**Nigel Benson
20th Century Glass**
Mob: 07971 859 848
nigel@20thcentury-glass.com
www.20thcentury-glass.com

No Pink Carpet
Tel: 01785 249 802
www.nopinkcarpet.com

Pip's Trip
Tel: 08451 650 274
www.pips-trip.co.uk

**The Studio Glass
Merchant**
Tel: 07775 683 961
Tel: 0208 668 2701
info@thestudioglassmerchant
.co.uk
www.thestudioglassmerchant
.co.uk

KITCHENALIA

Appleby Antiques
Geoffrey Vans' Arcade,
Stand 18, 105-107 Portobello
Road, London W11
Tel/Fax: 01453 753 126
mike@applebyantiques.net
www.applebyantiques.net

**Below Stairs of
Hungerford**
103 High Street, Hungerford,
Berkshire RG17 0NB
Tel: 01488 682 317
Fax: 01488 684294
hofgartner@belowstairs.co.uk
www.belowstairs.co.uk

Ken Grant
F109-111 Alfies Antiques
Market, 13-25 Church Street,
Marylebone, London NW8 8DT
Tel: 020 7723 1370
k-grant@alfies.clara.net

Jane Wicks Kitchenalia
Country Ways,
Strand Quay, Rye,
East Sussex TN31 7AY
Tel: 01424 713 635
janes_kitchen@hotmail.com

Mechanical Music
Terry & Daphne France
Tel: 01243 265 946
Fax: 01243 779 582

The Talking Machine
30 Watford Way,
London NW4 3AL
Tel: 020 8202 3473
Mob: 07774 103 139
talkingmachine@gramophones.
ndirect.co.uk
www.gramophones.ndirect
.co.uk

MILITARIA & MEDALS

Jim Bullock Militaria
P.O. Box 217, Romsey,
Hampshire SO51 5XL
Tel: 01794 516 455
jim@jimbullockmilitaria.com
www.jimbullockmilitaria.com

The Old Brigade
10a Harborough Road,
Kingsthorpe,
Northampton NN2 7AZ
Tel: 01604 719 389
stewart@theoldbrigade.co.uk
www.theoldbrigade.co.uk

West Street Antiques
63 West Street,
Dorking, Surrey RH4 1BS
Tel: 01306 883 487
www.antiquearmsandarmour
.com

MODERN TECHNOLOGY

Junktion
The Old Railway Station,
New Bolingbroke,
Boston, Lincolnshire
Tel: 01205 480068 or
07836 345 491
junktionantiques@hotmail.com

Pepe Tozzo
pepe@tozzo.co.uk
www.tozzo.co.uk

PAPERWEIGHTS

Sweetbriar Gallery Ltd
56 Watergate Street
Chester, Cheshire, CH1 2LA
Tel: 01244 329249
sales@sweetbriar.co.uk
www.sweetbriar.co.uk

PENS & WRITING

Battersea Pen Home
PO Box 6128,
Epping CM16 4CG
Tel: 01992 578 885
Fax: 01992 578 485
orders@penhome.com
www.penhome.com

Hans' Vintage Pens
Tel: 01323 765 398 or
07850 771 183
hseiringer@aol.com
www.hanspens.com

Henry The Pen Man
Admiral Vernon Antiques
Market, 141-149 Portobello Rd,
London W11
Tel: 020 8530 3277
Saturdays only

PLASTICS & BAKELITE

Paola & Iaia
Unit S057-58, Alfies Antiques
Market, 13-25 Church Street,
London NW8 8DT
Tel: 07751 084 135
paolaeiaialondon@hotmail.com

POSTERS

At The Movies
info@atthemovies.co.uk
www.atthemovies.co.uk

Barclay Samson
By appointment only
Tel: 020 7731 8012
richard@barclaysamson.com
www.barclaysamson.com

DODO
Stand F073/83/84,13-25
Church Street, Marylebone,
London NW8 8DT
Tel: 020 7706 1545
www.dodoposters.com

Limelight Movie Art
135 King's Road, London
Tel: 0207 751 5584
www.limelightmovieart.com

The Reelposter Gallery
72 Westbourne Grove,
London W2 5SH
Tel: 020 7727 4488
info@reelposter.com
www.reelposter.com

Rennies
47 The Old High Street,
Folkestone, Kent CT20 2RN
Tel: 01303 242427
info@rennart.co.uk
www.rennart.co.uk

POWDER COMPACTS

Sara Hughes Vintage Compacts, Antiques & Collectables
Mob: 0775 9697 108
sara@sneak.freeserve.co.uk
http://mysite.wanadoo-members.co.uk/sara_compacts/

Mary & Geoff Turvil
Vintage Compacts, Small
Antiques & Collectables
Tel: 01730 260 730
mary.turvil@virgin.net

Wildewear
Tel: 01395 577 966
www.wildewear.co.uk

RADIOS

On the Air Ltd
The Vintage Technology Centre,
Hawarden, Deeside CH5 3DN
Tel/Fax: 01244 530 300
info@vintageradio.co.uk
www.vintageradio.co.uk

Junktion
The Old Railway Station,
New Bolingbroke,
Boston, Lincolnshire
Tel: 01205 480068 or
07836 345 491
junktionantiques@hotmail.com

Philip Knighton
1c South Street, Wellington,
Somerset TA21 8NS
Tel: 01823 661 618
philip.knighton@btconnect.com

ROCK & POP

Beanos
Middle Street, Croydon,
Surrey CR0 1RE
Tel: 0208 680 1202
www.beanos.co.uk

Briggs Rock & Pop Memorabilia
Loudwater House, London
Road, Loudwater, High
Wycombe, Buckinghamshire
Tel: 01494 436 644
music@usebriggs.com
www.usebriggs.com

Collectors Corner
P.O. Box 8, Congleton,
Cheshire, CW12 4GD
Tel: 01260 270 429
dave.popcorner@ukonline.co.uk

More Than Music
PO Box 2809, Eastbourne,
East Sussex BN21 2EA
Tel: 01323 649 778
morethnmus@aol.com
www.mtmglobal.com

Spinna Disc Records
2b Union Street, Aldershot,
Hampshire GU11 1EG
Tel: 01252 327 261
www.spinnadiscrecords.com

Sweet Memories Vinyl Records
www.vinylrecords.co.uk

Tracks
PO Box 117, Chorley,
Lancashire PR6 0UU
Tel: 01257 269726
sales@tracks.co.uk
www.tracks.co.uk

SCIENTIFIC, TECHNICAL, OPTICAL & PRECISION INSTRUMENTS

Arthur Middleton Antiques
Tel: 020 7281 8445
Mob: 07887 481 102
www.antique-globes.com

Branksome Antiques
370 Poole Rd, Branksome,
Dorset BH12 1AW
Tel: 01202 763 324

Charles Tomlinson
Tel: 01244 318 395
charlestomlinson@tiscali.co.uk

Early Technology
Monkton House, Old
Craighall,Musselburgh,
Midlothian EH21 8SF
Tel: 0131 665 5753
michael.bennett-levy@virgin.net
www.earlytech.com

SMOKING MEMORABILIA

Richard Ball
richard@lighter.co.uk
www.lighter.co.uk

Tom Clarke
Admiral Vernon Antiques
Centre, Unit 36, Portobello Rd,
London W11
Tel: 020 8802 8936

SPORTING MEMORABILIA

Manfred Schotten
109 High Street, Burford,
Oxfordshire OX18 4RH
Tel: 01993 822 302
enquiries@schotten.com
www.schotten.com

Old Troon Sporting Antiques
49 Ayr St, Troon KA106EB
Tel: 01292 311 822

Rhod McEwan
Glengarden, Ballater,
Aberdeenshire AB35 5UB
Tel: 01339 755 429
www.rhodmcewan.com

Simon Brett
Creswyke House,
Moreton-in-Marsh GL56 0LH
Tel: 01608 650 751

Warboys Antiques
St. Ives, Cambridgeshire
Tel: 01480 463891
Mob: 07831 274774
johnlambden@
sportingantiques.co.uk
www.sportingantiques.co.uk

Graham Budd
P.O. Box 47519,
London N14 6XD
Tel: 020 8366 2525
gb@grahambuddauctions.co.uk
www.grahambuddauctions.co.uk

TELEPHONES

Candlestick & Bakelite
P.O. Box 308, Orpington,
Kent BR5 1TB
Tel: 0208 467 3743
candlestick.bakelite@mac.com
www.candlestickandbakelite.com

Retrobrick (Mobile Phones)
www.retrobrick.co.uk

Telephone Lines
304 High Street, Cheltenham,
Gloucestershire GL50 3JF
Tel: 01242 583 699
info@telephonelines.net
www.telephonelines.net

TOYS & GAMES

Automatomania
Logie Steading, Forres, Moray
IV36 2QN, Scotland
Tel: 01309 694 828
Mob: 07790 71 90 97
www.automatomania.com

Collectors Old Toy Shop & Antiques
89 Northgate, Halifax,
West Yorkshire HX11XF
Tel: 01422 360 434
collectorsoldtoy@aol.com

Colin Baddiel
B24-B25, Grays Antique
Market, 1-7 Davies Mews,
London W1K 5AB
Tel: 020 7408 1239
Fax: 020 7493 9344
toychemcol@hotmail.com
www.colinsantiquetoys.com

Andrew Clark Models
Unit 113, Baildon Mills,
Northgate, Baildon,
Shipley BD17 6JX
Tel: 01274 594 552
andrew@andrewclarkmodels
.com
www.andrewclarkmodels.com

Dave's Classic Toys
Antiques Centre Gloucester,
1 Severn Road,
The Historic Docks,
Gloucester
Tel: 01452 529 716

Donay Games
Tel: 01444 416 412
info@donaygames.co.uk
www.donaygames.com

Garrick Coleman
75 Portobello Rd,
London W11 2QB
Tel: 020 7937 5524
www.antiquechess.co.uk

Gerard Haley
Hippins Farm, Black Shawhead,
nr Hebden Bridge, Yorkshire
Tel: 01422 842 484
gedhaley@yahoo.co.uk

Hugo Lee-Jones
Tel: 01227 375 375
Mob: 07941 187 2027
electroniccollectables@hotmail.
com

Intercol (Playing Cards)
43 Templars Crescent,
Finchley, London N3 3QR
Tel: 020 8349 2207
Mob: 077 68 292 066
sales@intercol.co.uk
www.intercol.co.uk

John & Simon Haley
89 Northgate, North Bridge,
Halifax, Yorkshire
Tel: 01422 360 434
collectorsoldtoys@aol.com
www.collectorsoldtoyshop.com

Karl Flaherty Collectables
Tel: 02476 445 627
kfcollectables@aol.com
www.kfcollectables.com

The Magic Toybox
210 Havant Road, Drayton,
Portsmouth
Tel: 02392 221 307
www.magictoybox.co.uk

Metropolis Toys
31 Derby Street,
Burton on Trent, Staffordshire
Tel: 01283 740 400
www.metropolistoys.co.uk

Mike Delaney
Tel: 01993 840 064 or
07979 910 760
mike@vintagehornby.co.uk
www.vintagehornby.co.uk

Mimififi
27 Pembridge Road,
Notting Hill Gate,
London W11
Tel: 0207 243 3154
www.mimififi.com

Sue Pearson Dolls & Teddy Bears
18 Brighton Square,
'The Lanes', Brighton,
East Sussex BN1 1HD
Tel: 01273 774851
info@suepearson.co.uk
www.suepearson.co.uk

Teddy Bears of Witney
99 High Street, Witney,
Oxfordshire OX28 6HY
Tel: 01993 706 613
bears@witneybears.co.uk
www.teddybears.co.uk

Toydreams
sales@toydreams.co.uk
www.toydreams.co.uk

The Vintage Toy & Train Shop
Sidmouth Antiques &
Collectors' Centre,
All Saints' Road,
Sidmouth EX10 8ES
Tel: 01395 512 588

Vintage Toy Box
contact@vintagetoybox.co.uk
www.vintagetoybox.co.uk

Wheels of Steel (Trains)
Gray's Mews Antiques Market,
B10-B11, 58 Davies Street,
London W1K 5LP
Tel: 020 7629 2813
wheelsofsteel@grays.clara.net
www.graysantiques.com

WATCHES

Kleanthous Antiques
144 Portobello Road,
London W11 2DZ
Tel: 020 7727 3649
antiques@kleanthous.com
www.kleanthous.com

70s Watches
graham@gettya.freeserve.co.uk
www.70s-watches.com

The Watch Gallery
1129 Fulham Road,
London SW3 6RT
Tel: 020 7581 3239

The following list of general antiques and collectables centres and markets is organised by region. Any owner who would like to be listed in the our next edition, space permitting, or to update their contact information, should email info@millersguides.com by 1st February 2009.

LONDON

Alfie's Antiques Market
13-25 Church St, NW8 8DT
Tel: 020 7723 6066
info@alfiesantiques.com
www.alfiesantiques.com
(Closed Monday)

Antiquarius
131-141 King's Road, SW3 5EB
Tel: 020 7823 3900
info@antiquarius.co.uk
www.antiquarius.co.uk

Bermondsey Market
Crossing of Long Lane &
Bermondsey St, London SE1
Tel: 020 7351 5353
Every Friday morning from 5am

Camden Passage Antiques Market
Camden Passage, Angel,
Islington N1
(Wednesday & Saturday mornings)

Covent Garden Antiques Market
Jubilee Hall, Southampton
Street, Covent Garden WC2
Tel: 0207 240 7405
(Mondays from 6am)

Gray's Antiques Market
South Molton Lane, W1K 5AB
Tel: 0207 629 7034
www.graysantiques.com

Kensington Antiques Centre
58-60 Kensington Church
Street W8 4DB
Tel: 0207 376 0425

Northcote Road Antiques Market
155a Northcote Road,
Battersea SW11 6QB
Tel: 0207 228 6850
www.spectrumsoft.net/nam
.htm

Palmers Green Antiques Centre
472 Green Lanes, Palmers
Green N13 5PA
Tel: 0208 350 0878

Past Caring
76 Essex Road, N1 8LT
(Opens 12pm)

Portobello Rd Market
Portobello Rd, W11
Every Saturday from 6am

Spitalfields Antiques Market
Lamb Street,
Commercial Street, E1
Tel: 0207 240 7405
(Thursdays from 7am)

The Mall Antiques Arcade
Camden Passage, 359 Upper
Street, Islington N1 8DU
Tel: 0207 351 5353

BEDFORDSHIRE

Ampthill Antiques Emporium
6 Bedford Street,
Ampthill, Bedford
Tel: 01525 402131

Woburn Abbey Antiques Centre
Woburn Abbey,
Woburn, WK17 9WA
Tel: 01525 290 333
www.woburnantiques.co.uk

BERKSHIRE

Great Grooms at Hungerford
Riverside House, Charnham St,
Hungerford, RG17 0EP
Tel: 01488 682 314
Fax: 01488 686677
antiques@great-grooms.co.uk
www.great-grooms.co.uk

Stables Antiques Centre
1a Merchant Place (off Friar
Street), Reading, RG1 1DT
Tel: 01189 590 290

BUCKINGHAMSHIRE

Jackdaw Antiques Centre
25 West Street,
Marlow SL7 2LS
Tel: 01628 898 285

Marlow Antiques Centre
35 Station Road,
Marlow SL7 1NW
Tel: 01628 473 223

CAMBRIDGESHIRE

Cambridge Antiques Centre
206 Mill Road,
Cambridge CB1 3NF
Tel: 01223 247 324

Waterside Antiques Centre
The Wharf, Ely CB7 4AU
Tel: 01353 667 066
waterside@ely.org.uk
www.ely.org.uk/waterside.html

DERBYSHIRE

Alfreton Antique Centre
11 King Street,
Alfreton DE55 7AF
Tel: 01773 520 781

Chappells Antiques Centre
King Street, Bakewell DE45 1DZ
Tel: 01629 812 496
www.chappellsantiquescentre
.com

Heanor Antiques Centre
11-3 Ilkeston Rd, Heanor,
Derbyshire
Tel: 01773 531 181
sales@heanorantiquescentre
.co.uk
www.heanorantiquescentre
.co.uk

Matlock Antiques & Collectables
7 Dale Road, Matlock DE4 3LT
Tel: 01629 760 808
www.matlock-antiques-
collectables.cwc.net

DEVON

Quay Centre
Topsham, Nr Exeter EX3 0JA
www.quayantiques.com

ESSEX

Debden Antiques
Elder Street, Debden, Saffron
Walden CB11 3JY
Tel: 01799 543 007
www.debden-antiques.co.uk

GLOUCESTERSHIRE

Gloucester Antiques Centre
1 Severn Road, The Historic
Docks, Gloucester GL1 2LE
Tel: 01452 529 716
www.gacl.co.uk

Church Street Antiques Centre
3-4 Church Street,
Stow-on-the-Wold, GL54 1BB
Tel: 01451 870 186

Durham House Antiques
Sheep Street,
Stow-on-the-Wold GL54 1AA
Tel: 01451 870 404
www.durhamhousegb.com

Top Banana Antiques Mall
1 New Church Street,
Tetbury GL8 8DS
Tel: 0871 288 1102
www.topbananaantiques.com

HAMPSHIRE

Dolphin Quay Antique Centre
Queen Street,
Emsworth PO10 7BU
Tel: 01243 379 994

Lymington Antiques Centre
76 High Street,
Lymngton SO41 9AL
Tel: 01590 670 934

Squirrel Collectors Centre
9 New Street,
Basingstoke RG21 1DE
Tel: 01256 464 885

HEREFORDSHIRE

Hereford Antique Centre
128 Widemarsh Street,
Hereford HR4 9HN
Tel: 01432 266242

HERTFORDSHIRE

By George Antique Centre
23 George Street,
St Albans AL3 4ES
Tel: 01727 853 032

Riverside Antiques Centre
The Maltings, Station Road,
Sawbridgeworth CM21 9JX
Tel: 01279 600 985 or 07956
844 792

IRELAND

Archives Antiques Centre
88 Donegall Pass, Belfast,
County Antrim BT7 1BX
Tel: 02890 232383

Powerscourt Centre
59 South William Street
Dublin 2
Tel: (+353) (0)1 6717000

KENT

Burgate Antiques Centre
23A Palace Street,
Canterbury CT1 2DZ
Tel: 01227 456 600

Castle Antiques
1 London Road,
Westerham TN16 1BB
Tel: 01959 562 492

Copperfields Antiques & Crafts Centre
3c-4 Copperfields, Spital Street,
Dartford DA9 2DE
Tel: 01322 281 445

Nightingales
89-91 High Street, West
Wickham BR4 0LS
Tel: 0208 777 0335

Otford Antiques and Collectors Centre
26-28 High St,
Otford TN15 9DF
Tel: 01959 522 025
Fax: 01959 525858
info@otfordantiques.co.uk
www.otfordantiques.co.uk

Tenterden Antiques Centre
66-66A High Street,
Tenterden TN30 6AU
Tel: 01580 765 655

LANCASHIRE

The Antiques & Decorative Design Centre
56 Garstang Road,
Preston PR1 1NA
Tel: 01772 882 078
www.paulallisonantiques.co.uk

GB Antiques Centre
Lancaster Leisure Park,
Wyresdale Road,
Lancaster LA1 3LA
Tel: 01524 844 734

Heskin Hall Antiques
Heskin Hall, Wood Lane,
Heskin, Chorley PR7 5PA
Tel: 01257 452 044

Kingsmill Antiques Centre
Queen Street, Harle Syke,
Burnley BB10 2HX
Tel: 01282 431 953
www.kingsmill.demon.co.uk

LINCOLNSHIRE

Hemswell Antiques Centre
Caenby Corner Estate,
Hemswell Cliff,
Gainsborough DN21 5TJ
Tel: 01427 668 389
enquiries@hemswell-antiques.com
www.hemswell-antiques.com

St Martins Antiques Centre
23a High Street, St Martins,
Stamford PE9 2LF
Tel: 01780 481 158
www.st-martins-antiques.co.uk

NORFOLK

Tombland Antiques Centre
AugustineSteward House, 14
Tombland, Norwich NR3 1HF
Tel: 01603 761 906
www.tomblandantiques.co.uk

Old Granary Antiques Centre
King Staithe Lane,
King's Lynn PE30 1LZ
Tel: 01553 775509

NORTHAMPTONSHIRE

Brackley Antique Cellar
Drayman's Walk,
Brackley NN13 6BE
Tel: 01280 841 841

Magpies Antiques & Collectables Centre
1 East Grove,
Rushden NN10 0AP
Tel: 01933 411 404

NOTTINGHAMSHIRE

Castlegate Antiques Centre
55 Castlegate,
Newark NG24 1BE
Tel: 01933 411 404

Newark Antiques Centre
Regent House, Lombard Street,
Newark NG24 1XP
Tel: 01636 605 504

Occleshaw Antiques Centre
The Old Major Cinema,
11 Mansfield Road,
Edwinstowe NG21 9NL
Tel: 01623 825 370

Top Hat Antiques Centre
70-72 Derby Road,
Nottingham NG1 5FD
Tel: 0115 941 9143

OXFORDSHIRE

Deddington Antiques Centre
Laurel House, Market Place,
Bull Ring, Deddington,
Nr Banbury OX15 0TT
Tel: 01869 338 968

Lamb Arcade Antique Centre
High Street,
Wallingford OX10 0BX
Tel: 01491 835 166

The Quiet Woman Antiques Centre
Southcombe,
Chipping Norton OX7 5QH
Tel: 01608 646 262

The Swan Antiques Centre
High Street Tetsworth, Nr
Thame OX9 7AB
Tel: 01844 281777
Fax: 01844 281770
antiques@theswan.co.uk
www.theswan.co.uk

SCOTLAND

Now and Then
9 West Crosscauseway,
Edinburgh EH8 9JW
Tel: 0131 668 2927
www.oldtoysandantiques.co.uk

Rait Village Antiques Centre
Rait, Perthshire PH2 7RT

Scottish Antiques & Arts Centre
Abernyte, Perthshire PH14 9SJ
Tel: 01828 686 401
www.scottish-antiques.com

The Peebles Antiques Centre
Innerleithen Road,
Peebles EH45 8BA
01721 724666

SHROPSHIRE

Shrewsbury Antiques Market
Frankwell Quay Warehouse,
Shrewsbury SY3 8LG
Tel: 01743 350 916

Stretton Antiques Market
Sandford Avenue, Church
Stretton SY6 6BH
Tel: 01694 723 718

SOMERSET

Assembly Antiques
6 Saville Row, Bath BA1 2QP
Tel: 01225 448 488

Bath Antiques Market
Guinea Lane (off Landsdown
Road), Bath BA1 5NB
Tel: 07787 527 527

Bartlett St Antiques Centre
5-10 Bartlett St, Bath BA1 2QZ
Tel: 01225 466689
Monday to Saturday (excluding
Wednesday)

Old Bank Antiques Centre
14-17 & 20 Walcot Buildings,
London Rd, Bath BA1 6AD.
Tel: 01225 469282 or 01225
338818
www.oldbankantiquescentre
.co.uk

STAFFORDSHIRE

Compton Mill Antique Emporium
Compton Mill, Compton, Leek
Tel: 01538 373396

Curborough Hall Antiques
Watery Lane, Lichfield
Tel: 01543 417100

Lion Antiques Centre
8 Market Place, Uttoxeter (opp.
War Memorial)
Tel: 01889 567717

Potteries Antique Centre
271 Waterloo Rd, Cobridge,
Stoke-on-Trent ST6 3HR
Tel: 01782 201 455
Fax: 01782 201518
www.potteriesantiquecentre
.com

Rugeley Antique Centre
161 Main Road, Brereton,
Nr Rugeley WS15 1DX
Tel: 01889 577 166
www.rugeleyantiquecentre
.co.uk

CENTRES, MARKETS & SHOPS

SUFFOLK

Badgers Den Antique & Collectables Centre
6 Sun Lane, off High Street, Newmarket
Tel: 01638 666 676

Meltord Antiques Warehouse
Hall Street, Long Melford
Tel: 01787 379 638

Snape Maltings Antiques & Collectors Centre
Saxmundham IP17 1SR
Tel: 01728 688038

SURREY

Great Grooms Antiques Centre
51-52 West Street, Dorking RH4 1BU
Tel: 01306 887 076
www.greatgrooms.co.uk

Kingston Antiques Centre
29-31 London Road, Kingston-upon-Thames KT2 6ND
Tel: 0208 549 2004
www.kingstonantiquescentre.co.uk

Pilgrims Antiques Centre
7 West Street, Dorking, RH4 1BL
Tel: 01306 875028

Serendipity Antiques Centre
7 Petworth Road, Haslemere GU27 2JB
Tel: 01428 642 682

SUSSEX (EAST)

The Brighton Lanes Antiques Centre
12 Meeting House Lane, Brighton BN1 1HB
Tel: 01273 823 121

Brighton Flea Market
31a Upper St. James's Street, Brighton BN2 1JN
Tel: 01273 624 006

Church Hill Antiques Centre
6 Station Street, Lewes BN7 2DA
Tel: 01273 474 842

The Emporium Antiques Centre Too
24 High Street, Lewes BN7 2LU
Tel: 01273 477 979

Lewes Antiques Centre
20 Cliffe High Street, Lewes BN7 2AH
Tel: 01273 476 148

Snooper's Paradise
7-8 Kensington Gardens, Brighton BN1 4AL
Tel: 01273 602558
www.northlaine.co.uk/snoopers paradise/snoopers.html

SUSSEX (WEST)

Antique & Collectors Market
Old Orchard Building, Old House, Adversane, Nr Billingshurst RH14 9JJ
Tel: 01403 782 186

Arundel Antiques Centre
51 High Street, Arundel BN18 9AJ
Tel: 01903 882 749

WALES

Afonwen Antiques
Afonwen, nr Caerwys, nr Mold, Flintshire CH7 5UB
Tel: 01352 720 965

Offa's Dyke Antiques Centre
4 High Street, Knighton, Powys LD7 1AT
Tel: 01547 528 635

Second Chance Antiques & Collectables Centre
Ala Road, Pwlheli, Gwynedd LL53 5BL
Tel: 01758 612 210

WARWICKSHIRE

Stratford-upon-Avon Antique Centre
59-60 Ely St, Stratford-upon-Avon CV37 6LN
Tel: 01789 204180

WEST MIDLANDS

Birmingham Antiques Centre
1407 Pershore Road, Stirchley, Birmingham B30 2JR
Tel: 0121 459 4587

WORCESTERSHIRE

Worcester Antiques Centre
Reindeer Court, Mealcheapen Street, Worcester WR1 4DF
Tel: 01905 610 680
www.worcesterantiquecentre.com

YORKSHIRE

The Antiques Centre York
Allenby House, 41 Stonegate, York YO1 8AW
Tel: 01904 635 888
www.theantiquescentreyork.com

Cavendish Antique & Collectors Centre
44 Stonegate, York YO1 8AS
Tel: 01904 621 666
www.cavendishantiques.com

The Collectors' Centre
35 St Nicholas Cliff, Scarborough YO11 2ES
Tel: 01723 365 221
www.collectors.demon.co.uk

The Ginnel Antiques Centre
Off Parliament St, Harrogate, North Yorkshire HG1 2RB
Tel: 01423 508·857
info@theginnel.com
www.redhouseyork.co.uk

Stonegate Antiques Centre
41 Stonegate, York YO1 8AW
Tel: 01904 613 888

MAJOR FAIR & SHOW ORGANISERS

DMG Antiques Fairs
Newark (Nottinghamshire), Ardingly (Sussex), Detling (Kent) and Shepton Mallet (Somerset)
www.dmgantiquefairs.co.uk

Clarion Events
Antiques for Everyone, Birmingham
www.antiquesforeveryone.co.uk
Olympia Antiques Fairs, London
www.olympiaartsinternational.com

Nelson Fairs
Alexandra Palace, London
www.nelsonfairs.com

Arthur Swallow Fairs
Swinderby Airfield, Lincolnshire
www.arthurswallowfairs.co.uk

The following list of auctioneers who conduct regular sales by auction is organised by region. Any auctioneer who would like to be listed in the our next edition, space permitting, or to update their contact information, should email info@millersguides.com by 1st February 2009.

LONDON

Bloomsbury Auctions
Bloomsbury House,
24 Maddox Street W1 S1PP
Tel: 020 7495 9494
Fax: 020 7495 9499
info@bloomsburyauctions.com
www.bloomsburyauctions.com

Bonhams
101 New Bond Street,
W1S 1SR
Tel: 020 7629 6602
Fax: 020 7629 8876
info@bonhams.com
www.bonhams.com

Christies (South Kensington)
85 Old Brompton Road,
SW7 3LD
Tel: 020 7581 7611
Fax: 020 7321 3311
info@christies.com
www.christies.com

Chiswick Auctions
1 Colville Road,
Chiswick W3 8BL
Tel: 0208 992 4442
info@chiswickauctions.co.uk
www.chiswickauctions.co.uk

Criterion Auctioneers
53 Essex Road,
Islington N1 2SF
Tel: 0207 359 5707
41-47 Chatfield Road,
Wandsworth, SW11 3SE
Tel: 0207 228 5563
info@criterion-auctioneers.co.uk
www.criterionauctions.co.uk

Graham Budd Auctions
P.O. Box 47519, N14 6XD
Tel: 020 8366 2525
gb@grahambuddauctions.co.uk
www.grahambuddauctions.co.uk

Lots Road Auctions
71 Lots Road,
Chelsea SW10 0RN
info@lotsroad.com
www.lotsroad.com

Rosebery's
74-76 Knights Hill,
West Norwood, SE27 0JD
Tel: 020 8761 2522
Fax: 020 8761 2524
auctions@roseberys.co.uk
www.roseberys.co.uk

Sotheby's
34-35 New Bond Street,
W1A 2AA
Tel: 0207 293 5000
Fax: 0207 293 5989
info@sothebys.com
www.sothebys.com

BEDFORDSHIRE

W. & H. Peacock
The Auction Centre,
26 Newnham St,
Bedford MK40 3JR
Tel: 01234 266366
Fax: 01234 269082
info@peacockauction.co.uk
www.peacockauction.co.uk

BERKSHIRE

Dreweatts
Donnington Priory, Donnington,
Nr. Newbury RG142JE
Tel: 01635 553553
Fax: 01635 553599
donnington@dnfa.com
www.dnfa.com

Special Auction Services
First Floor, Kennetholme, Bath Road, Midgham,
Nr Reading RG7 5UX
Tel: 0118 971 2949
Fax: 08717 146 905
info@specialauctionservices.com
www.specialauctionservices.com

BUCKINGHAMSHIRE

Amersham Auction Rooms
125 Station Road,
Amersham HP7 0AH
Tel: 08700 460606
Fax: 08700 460607
info@amershamauctionrooms.co.uk
www.amershamauctionrooms.co.uk

CAMBRIDGESHIRE

Cheffins
Clifton House, 1&2 Clifton Road, Cambridge CB1 7EA
Tel: 01223 213 343
Fax: 01223 271 949
fine.art@cheffins.co.uk
www.cheffins.co.uk

CHANNEL ISLANDS

Martel Maides Ltd.
The Old Bank,
29 High Street GY1 2JX
Tel: 01481 713463
Fax: 01481 700337
sales@martelmaides.co.uk
www.martelmaides.co.uk

CHESHIRE

Bonhams (Chester)
New House, 150 Christleton Road, Chester CH3 5TD
Tel: 01244 313 936
Fax: 01244 340 028
info@bonhams.com
www.bonhams.com

Bob Gowland International Golf Auctions
The Stables, Claim Farm,
Manley Rd Frodsham, WA6 6HT
Tel/Fax: 01928 740668
bob@internationalgolfauctions.com
www.internationalgolfauctions.com

CLEVELAND

Vectis Auctioneers (Toys & Dolls)
Fleck Way Thornaby,
Stockton-on-Tees TS17 9JZ
Tel: 01642 750616
Fax: 01642 769478
www.vectis.co.uk

CORNWALL

W. H. Lane & Son
Jubilee House, Queen Street,
Penzance TR18 4DF
Tel: 01736 361447
Fax: 01736 350097
info@whlane.co.uk
www.whlaneauctioneersandvaluers.co.uk

David Lay FRICS
The Penzance Auction House,
Alverton, Penzance TR18 4RE
Tel: 01736 361414
Fax: 01736 360035
david.lays@btopenworld.com
www.davidlay.co.uk

CUMBRIA

Mitchells Fine Art Auctioneers
Station Road, Cockermouth CA13 9PZ
Tel: 01900 827800
Fax: 01900 828073
info@mitchellsfineart.com
www.mitchellsfineart.com

Penrith Farmers' & Kidds
Skirsgill Saleroom, Skirsgill,
Penrith CA11 0DN
Tel: 01768 890781
Fax: 01768 895058
info@pfkauctions.co.uk
www.pfandk.co.uk

DERBYSHIRE

Bamfords Ltd
The Old Picture Palace,
133 Dale Road,
Matlock DE4 3LT
Tel: 01629 574460
www.bamfords-auctions.co.uk

DEVON

Bearne's
St Edmund's Court,
Okehampton Street,
Exeter EX41LX
Tel: 01392 207000
Fax: 01392 207007
enquiries@bearnes.co.uk
www.bearnes.co.uk

Bonhams
Dowell St, Honiton,
Devon EX14 1LX
Tel: 01404 41872
Fax: 01404 43137
honiton@bonhams.com
www.bonhams.com

DORSET

Charterhouse
The Long Street Salerooms,
Sherborne, Dorset DT9 3BS
Tel: 01935 812277
Fax: 01935 389387
enquiry@charterhouse-auctions.co.uk
www.charterhouse-auctions.co.uk

HY Duke & Sons
Weymouth Avenue, Dorchester,
Dorset DT1 1QS
Tel: 01305 265080
Fax: 01305 260101
enquiries@dukes-auctions.com
www.dukes-auctions.com

Onslows
The Coach House, Manor Road,
Stourpaine DT11 8TQ
Tel/Fax: 01258 488 838
info@onslows.co.uk
www.onslows.co.uk

Semley Auctioneers
Station Rd, Semley,
Nr Shaftesbury SP7 9AN
Tel: 01747 855122
Fax: 01747 855222
semley.auctioneers@
btinternet.com
www.semleyauctioneers.com

ESSEX

Sworder & Sons
14 Cambridge Road,
Stansted Mountfitchet
CM24 8DE
Tel: 01279 817778
Fax: 01279 817779
auctions@sworder.co.uk
www.sworder.co.uk

GLOUCESTERSHIRE

Simon Chorley
Prinknash Abbey Park GL4 8EX
Tel: 01452 344499
Fax: 01452 814533
info@simonchorley.com
www.simonchorley.com

Dreweatt's
St. John's Place,
Apsley Road, Clifton,
Bristol BS8 2ST
Tel: 0117 973 7201
Fax: 0117 973 5671
bristol@dnfa.com
www.dnfa.com/bristol

Cotswold Auction Co.
Chapel Walk, Cheltenham,
Gloucestershire GL50 3DS
Tel: 01242 256363
Fax: 01242 571734
info@cotswoldauction.co.uk
www.cotswoldauction.co.uk

**Mallams Fine Art
Auctioneers & Valuers**
26 Grosvenor Street,
Cheltenham GL52 2SG
Tel: 01242 235712
Fax: 01242 241943
cheltenham@mallams.co.uk
www.mallams.co.uk/fineart

Moore, Allen & Innocent
The Norcote Salerooms,
Burford Road, Norcote,
Nr Cirencester, GL7 5RH
Tel: 01285 646 050
fineart@mooreallen.co.uk
www.mooreallen.co.uk

HAMPSHIRE

Andrew Smith & Son
The Auction Rooms,
Manor Farm, Itchen Stoke,
Nr Winchester SO24 0QT
Tel: 01962 735988
Fax: 01962 738879
auctions@andrewsmithandson
.com
www.andrewsmithandson.com

**Jacobs & Hunt Fine Art
Auctioneers**
Lavant Street,
Petersfield GU32 3EF
Tel: 01730 233 933
Fax: 01730 262 323
auctions@jacobsandhunt.com
www.jacobsandhunt.com

HEREFORDSHIRE

Brightwells
The Fine Art Saleroom,
Ryelands Road,
Leominster HR6 8NZ
Tel: 01568 611122
Fax: 01568 610519
fineart@brightwells.com
www.brightwells.com

HERTFORDSHIRE

Tring Market Auctions
Brook Street,
Tring HP23 5EF
Tel: 01442 826 446
Fax: 01442 890 927
sales@tringmarketauctions
.co.uk
www.tringmarketauctions.co.uk

ISLE OF WIGHT

Shanklin Auction Rooms
79 Regent Street,
Shanklin, PO37 7AP
Tel: 01983 863441
enquiries@shanklinauctiorooms
.co.uk
www.shanklinauctionrooms
.co.uk

KENT

Dreweatts (Office)
The Pantiles,
Tunbridge Wells TN2 5QL
Tel: 01892 544500
Fax: 01892 515191
tunbridgewells@dnfa.com
www.dnfa.com/tunbridgewells

Gorringes (Office)
15 The Pantiles,
Tunbridge Wells TN2 5TD
Tel: 01892 619 670
Fax: 01892 619 671
auctions@gorringes.co.uk
www.gorringes.co.uk

Humberts Fine Art
The Estate Office,
Stone Street,
Cranbrook TN17 3HD
Tel: 01580 713828
www.humberts.co.uk

Lambert & Foster
102 High Street,
Tenterden TN30 6HT
Tel: 01580 762083
saleroom@lambertandfoster
.co.uk
www.lambertandfoster.co.uk

LANCASHIRE

Capes Dunn & Co.
38 Charles St,
Manchester M17DB
Tel: 0161 273 1911
Fax: 0161 273 3474
capesdunn@googlemail.com
www.capesdunn.com

LEICESTERSHIRE

Gilding's
64 Roman Way, Market
Harborough, LE16 7PQ
Tel: 01858 410414
Fax: 01858 432956
sales@gildings.co.uk
www.gildings.co.uk

Tennants Co.
Millhouse, South Street,
Oakham,
Rutland LE15 6BG
Tel: 01572 724666
Fax: 01572 724422
oakham@tennants-ltd.co.uk
www.tennants.co.uk

LINCOLNSHIRE

Golding Young & Co.
Old Wharf Rd, Grantham,
Lincolnshire NG31 7AA
Tel: 01476 565118
Fax: 01476 561475
enquiries@goldingyoung.com
www.goldingyoung.com

MERSEYSIDE

Cato, Crane & Co
6 Stanhope St, Liverpool L8 5RE
Tel: 0151 709 5559
Fax: 0151 707 2454
www.cato-crane.co.uk

NORFOLK

T. W. Gaze & Son
Diss Auction Rooms, Roydon
Road, Diss IP22 4LN
Tel: 01379 650306
Fax: 01379 644313
sales@dissauctionrooms.co.uk
www.twgaze.com

**Keys Auctioneers &
Valuers**
Aylsham Salerooms,
Palmers Lane,
Aylsham, NR11 6JA
Tel: 01263 733195
Fax: 01263 732140
www.keysauctions.co.uk

**Knights Sporting
Auctions**
Cuckoo Cottage, Town Green,
Alby, Norwich NR11 7PR
Tel: 01263 768488
Fax: 01263 768788
www.knights.co.uk

NOTTINGHAMSHIRE

Mellors & Kirk
Gregory Street,
Nottingham NG7 2NL
Tel: 0115 9790 000
Fax: 0115 9781 111
enquiries@mellors-kirk.com
www.mellors-kirk.co.uk

Neales of Nottingham
192 Mansfield Road,
Nottingham NG1 3HU
Tel: 0115 962 4141
Fax: 0115 969 3450
nottingham@dnfa.com
www.dnfa.com/neales

**Vennett-Smith
Auctioneers and Valuers**
11 Nottingham Road, Gotham,
Nottingham NG11 0HE
Tel: 0115 9830541
Fax: 0115 9830114
info@vennett-smith.com
www.vennett-smith.com

OXFORDSHIRE

Mallams
Dunmore Court, Wootton Road,
Abingdon, OX13 6BH
Tel: 01235 462840
Fax: 01235 534788
abongdon@mallams.co.uk
www.mallams.co.uk

Mallams
Bocardo House,
24a St. Michaels Street,
Oxford OX1 2EB
Tel: 01865 241358
Fax: 01865 725483
oxford@mallams.co.uk
www.mallams.co.uk

Soames Country Auctions
Pinnocks Farm Estate,
Northmoor, Witney OX8 1AY
Tel: 01865 300626
soame@email.msn.com
www.soamesauctioneers.co.uk

SHROPSHIRE

Halls Fine Art
Welsh Bridge,
Shrewsbury SY3 8LA
Tel: 01743 231 212
Fax: 01743 271 014
fineart@halls.to
www.hallsgb.com

Walker Barnett & Hill
Cosford Auction Rooms,
Long Lane, Cosford, TF11 8PJ
Tel: 01902 375555
Fax: 01902 375566
wbhauctions@lineone.net
www.walker-barnett-hill.co.uk

Mullock Madeley
The Old Shippon,
Wall-under-Heywood,
Nr Church Stretton SY6 7DS
Tel: 01694 771771
Fax: 01694 771772
info@mullocksauctions.co.uk
www.mullocksauctions.co.uk

SOMERSET

Clevedon Salerooms
The Auction Centre,
Kenn Road, Kenn, Clevedon,
North Somerset BS21 6TT
Tel: 01934 830111
Fax: 01934 832538
info@clevedon-salerooms.com
www.clevedon-salerooms.com

Gardiner Houlgate
9 Leafield Way, Corsham,
Bath SN13 9SW
Tel: 01225 812912
Fax: 01225 811777
auctions@gardiner-
houlgate.co.uk
www.invaluable.com/gardiner-
houlgate

**Lawrence's Fine Art
Auctioneers Ltd**
South Street,
Crewkerne, TA18 8AB
Tel: 01460 73041
Fax: 01460 74627
enquiries@lawrences.co.uk
www.lawrences.co.uk

STAFFORDSHIRE

**Potteries Specialist
Auctions**
271 Waterloo Road,
Cobridge,
Stoke-on-Trent, ST6 3HR
Tel: 01782 286622
Fax: 01782 213777
www.potteriesauctions.com

Richard Winterton
School House Auction Rooms,
Hawkins Lane,
Burton-on-Trent DE14 1PT
Tel: 01283 511224

Wintertons
Lichfield Auction Centre
Fradley, Lichfield, WS13 8NF
Tel: 01543 263256
Fax: 01543 415348
enquiries@wintertons.co.uk
www.wintertons.co.uk

SUFFOLK

Diamond Mills
Orwell Hall, Orwell Rd,
Felixstowe IP11 7BL
Tel:01473 218 600
diamondmills@btconnect.com
www.diamondmills.co.uk

Neal Sons & Fletcher
26 Church St,
Woodbridge IP12 1DP
Tel: 01394 382263
Fax: 01394 383030
enquiries@nsf.co.uk
www.nsf.co.uk

SURREY

Barbers
The Mayford Centre,
Smarts Heath Road,
Woking GU22 0PP
Tel: 01483 728939
Fax: 01483 762552
www.thesaurus.co.uk/barbers

Clark Gammon
Bedford Road,
Guildford GU1 4SJ
Tel: 01483 880915
Fax: 01483 880918
fine.art@clarkegammon.co.uk
www.clarkegammon.co.uk

Ewbank Auctioneers
The Burnt Common Auction
Rooms,
London Rd, Send,
Woking GU23 7LN
Tel: 01483 223101
Fax: 01483 222171
www.ewbankauctions.co.uk

**Dreweatt Neate
(Formerly Hamptons)**
Baverstock House,
93 High Street,
Godalming GU7 1AL
Tel: 01483 423 567
Fax: 01483 426 392
godalming@dnfa.com
www.dnfa.com/godalming

SUSSEX (EAST)

Burstow & Hewett
Lower Lake, Battle TN33 0AT
Tel: 01424 772 374
www.burstowandhewett.co.uk

**Dreweatt Neate
(Eastbourne)**
46-50 South St,
Eastbourn BN21 4XB,
Tel: 01323 410419
Fax: 01323 416540
eastbourne@dnfa.com
www.dnfa.com

Gorringes
Terminus Road,
Bexhill-on-Sea TN39 3LR
Tel: 01424 212994
Fax: 01424 224035
www.gorringes.co.uk

Gorringes
15 North Street,
Lewes BN7 2PD
Tel: 01273 472503
Fax: 01273 479559
www.gorringes.co.uk

Raymond P. Inman
The Auction Galleries,
98A Coleridge Street,
Hove BN3 5AA
Tel: 01273 774777
Fax: 01273 735660
r.p.inman@talk21.com
www.invaluable.com/
raymondinman

Wallis & Wallis
West St Auction Galleries,
Lewes BN7 2NJ
Tel: 01273 480208
Fax: 01273 476562
auctions@wallisandwallis.co.uk
www.wallisandwallis.co.uk

TYNE & WEAR

Anderson and Garland
Anderson House, Crispin Court,
Newbiggin Lane, Westerhope,
Newcastle upon Tyne NE5 1BF
Tel: 0191 430 3000
andersongarland@aol.com
www.andersonandgarland.com

Corbitts
5 Mosley St,
Newcastle-upon-Tyne NE1 1YE
Tel: 0191 232 7268
Fax: 0191 261 4130
collectors@corbitts.com
www.corbitts.com

WARWICKSHIRE

Locke & England
18 Guy Street,
Leamington Spa CV32 4RT
Tel: 01926 889100
Fax: 01926 470608
valuers@leauction.co.uk
www.leauction.co.uk

WEST MIDLANDS

Bonhams
Knowle, The Old House,
Station Road, Knowle,
Solihull B93 0HT
Tel: 01564 776151
Fax: 01564 778069
knowle@bonhams.com
www.bonhams.com

Fellows & Sons
Augusta House,
19 Augusta St, Hockley,
Birmingham B18 6JA
Tel: 0121 212 2131
Fax: 0121 212 1249
info@fellows.co.uk
www.fellows.co.uk

WEST SUSSEX

John Bellman
New Pound Wisborough Green,
Billingshurst RH14 0AZ
Tel: 01403 700858
Fax: 01403 700059
enquiries@bellmans.comuk
www.bellmans.co.uk

Denhams
The Auction Galleries,
Dorking Road,
Warnham,
Nr Horsham RH12 3RZ
Tel: 01403 255699
Fax: 01403 253837
enquiries@denhams.com
www.denhams.com

Rupert Toovey
Spring Gardens,
Washington RH20 3BS,
Tel: 01903 891955
auctions@rupert-toovey.com
www.rupert-toovey.com

WILTSHIRE

Finan & Co
The Square, Mere,
Wiltshire BA126DJ
Tel: 01747 861411
Fax: 01747 861944
post@finanandco.co.uk
www.finanandco.co.uk

Henry Aldridge & Sons
The Devizes Auctioneers,
Unit 1,
Bath Rd Business Centre,
Devizes SN10 1XA
Tel: 01380 729199
Fax: 01380 730073
www.henry-aldridge.co.uk

Woolley & Wallis
51-61 Castle St,
Salisbury SP1 3SU
Tel: 01722 424500
Fax: 01722 424508
enquiries@woolleyandwallis
.co.uk
www.woolleyandwallis.co.uk

WORCESTERSHIRE

Andrew Grant
St Mark's House,
St Mark's Close,
Cherry Orchard,
Worcester WR5 3DJ
Tel: 01905 357547
Fax: 01905 763942
fine.art@andrew-grant.co.uk
www.andrew-grant.co.uk

**Gloucestershire
Worcestershire
Railwayana Auctions**
'The Willows',
Badsey Road,
Evesham WR117PA
Tel: 01386 760109
www.gwra.co.uk

Phillip Serrell
The Malvern Saleroom,
Barnards Green Road,
Malvern WR143LW
Tel: 01684 892314
Fax: 01684 569832
www.serrell.com

EAST YORKSHIRE

Dee, Atkinson & Harrison
The Exchange Saleroom,
Driffield YO25 6LD
Tel: 01377 253151
Fax: 01377 241041
exchange@dee-atkinson-
harrison.co.uk
www.dahauctions.com

NORTH YORKSHIRE

David Duggleby
The Vine St Salerooms,
Scarborough YO11 1XN
Tel: 01723 507111
Fax: 01723 507222
www.davidduggleby.com

Tennants
The Auction Centre,
Leyburn DL8 5SG
Tel: 01969 623780
Fax: 01969 624281
enquiry@tennants-ltd.co.uk
www.tennants.co.uk

SOUTH YORKSHIRE

A. E. Dowse & Sons
Cornwall Galleries,
Scotland Street,
Sheffield S3 7DE
Tel: 0114 2725858
Fax: 0114 2490550
aedowes@aol.com
www.aedowseandson.com

BBR Auctions
Elsecar Heritage Centre,
5 Ironworks Row,
Wath Rd, Elsecar,
Barnsley S74 8HJ
Tel: 01226 745156
Fax: 01226 361561
www.onlinebbr.com

Sheffield Railwayana
43 Little Norton Lane,
Sheffield S8 8GA
Tel: 0114 274 5085
ian@sheffrail.freeserve.co.uk
www.sheffieldrailwayana.co.uk

WEST YORKSHIRE

Andrew Hartley Fine Arts
Victoria Hall Salerooms,
Little Lane, Ilkle LS29 8EA
Tel: 01943 816363
info@andrewhartleyfinearts.co.uk
www.andrewhartleyfinearts.co.uk

SCOTLAND

Bonhams Edinburgh
65 George St,
Edinburgh EH22JL
Tel: 0131 225 2266
Fax: 0131 220 2547
edinburgh@bonhams.com
www.bonhams.com

Loves Auction Rooms
52-54 Canal St, Perth,
Perthshire PH2 8LF
Tel: 01738 633337
Fax: 01738 629830

Lyon & Turnbull
33 Broughton Place,
Edinburgh EH1 3RR
Tel: 0131 557 8844
Fax: 0131 557 8668
info@lyonandturnbull.com
www.lyonandturnbull.com

Lyon & Turnbull
4 Woodside Place,
Glasgow G3 7QF
Tel: 0141 353 5070
Fax: 0141 332 2928
info@lyonandturnbull.com
www.lyonandturnbull.com

**Thomson, Roddick &
Medcalf Ltd.**
44/3 Hardengreen Business Park,
Eskbank, Edinburgh,
Midlothian EH22 3NX
Tel: 0131 454 9090
Fax: 0131 454 9191
www.thomsonroddick.com

WALES

Bonhams Cardiff
7-8 Park Place, Cardiff,
Glamorgan CF10 3DP
Tel: 02920 727 980
Fax: 02920 727 989
cardiff@bonhams.com
www.bonhams.com

Peter Francis
Curiosity Salerooms,
19 King St, Carmarthen,
South Wales
Tel: 01267 233456
Fax: 01267 233458
www.peterfrancis.co.uk

Welsh Country Auctions
2 Carmarthen Road,
Cross Hands, Llanelli,
Carmarthenshire SA14 6SP
Tel: 01269 844428
Fax: 01269 844428
enquiries@welshcountryautions
.com
www.welshcountryauctions.com

IRELAND

HOK Fine Art
4 Main St, Blackrock,
Co Dublin, Ireland
Tel: 00 353 1 2881000
fineart@hok.ie
www.hokfineart.com

Mealy's
The Square, Castlecomer,
County Kilkenny, Ireland
Tel: 00 353 56 41229
/41413
Fax: 00 353 56 41627
info@mealys.com
www.mealys.com

The following list is organised by the type of collectable. If you would like your club, society or organisation to appear in our next edition, or would like to update details, please contact us at info@millersguides.com before 1st February 2009.

ADVERTISING

Antique Advertising Signs
The Street Jewellery Society, 11 Bowsden Ter, South Gosford, Newcastle-Upon-Tyne NE3 1RX

AUTOGRAPHS

A.C.O.G.B. (Autograph Club of Great Britain)
info@autographcouncil.co.uk
www.acogb.co.uk

AUTOMOBILIA

Brooklands Automobilia & Regalia Collectors' Club,
P.O. Box No 4,
Chapel Terrace Mews,
Kemp Town, Brighton,
East Sussex BN2 1HU
www.barcc.co.uk

BAXTER PRINTS

The New Baxter Society
c/o Reading Museum & Art Gallery, Blagrave Street, Reading, Berkshire RG1 1QH
baxter@rpsfamily.demon.co.uk
www.rpsfamily.demon.co.uk

BANK NOTES

International Bank Note Society
43 Templars Crescent,
London N3 3QR

BOOKS

The Enid Blyton Society
93 Milford Hill, Salisbury,
Wiltshire SP1 2QL
Tel: 01722 331937
www.enidblytonsociety.co.uk

The Followers of Rupert
www.see.ed.ac.uk/~afm/followers

BOTTLES

Old Bottle Club of Great Britain
2 Strafford Avenue,
Elsecar, Nr Barnsley,
South Yorkshire S74 18AA
Tel: 01226 745 156

BREWERIANA

The British Beermats Collectors' Society
69 Dunnington Avenue,
Kidderminster DY10 2YT
enquires@britishbeermats.org.uk
www.britishbeermats.org.uk

CERAMICS

Beswick Collectors Club,
PO Box 310, Richmond,
Surrey TW10 7FU
barryjhill@hotmail.com
www.collectingdoulton.com

Carlton Ware Collectors' International
The Carlton Factory Shop,
Copeland St, Stoke-upon-Trent,
Staffordshire ST4 1PU
Tel: 01782 410 504
cwciclub@aol.com
www.lattimore.co.uk/deco/carlton.htm

Clarice Cliff Collectors Club
PO Box 2706,Eccleshall,
Stafford ST21 6WY
www.claricecliff.com

Fieldings Crown Devon Collectors Club
P.O. Box 462
Manvers,
Rotherham S63 7WT
www.fieldingscrowndevclub.com

Friends of Blue Ceramics Society
PO Box 122, Didcot D.O.,
Oxford OX11 0YN
terrysheppard45@@aol.com
www.fob.org.uk

Goss Collectors' Club
Tel: 01159 300 441
www.gosschina.com

Hornsea Pottery Collectors' & Research Society
128 Devonshire St, Keighley,
West Yorkshire BD21 2QJ
hornsea@pdtennant.fsnet.co.uk
www.easyontheeye.net/hornsea/society.htm

M.I. Hummel Club (Goebel)
Porzellanfabrik, GmbH & Co. KG, Coburger Str.7, D-96472 Rodental, Germany
Tel: +49 (0) 95 63 72 18 03
Fax: +49 (0) 95 63 9 25 92

Keith Murray Collectors' Club
Fantasque House, Tennis Drive, The Park, Nottingham NG7 1AE
www.keithmurray.com

Lorna Bailey Collectors' Club
Newcastle Street,
Dalehall, Burslem,
Stoke-on-Trent ST6 3QF
Tel: 01782 837 341

Mabel Lucie Attwell
Abbey Antiques,
63 Great Whyte, Ramsey,
Huntingdon PE26 1HL
Tel: 01487 814753

Moorcroft Collectors' Club
Sandbach Rd, Burslem,
Stoke-on-Trent,
Staffordshire ST6 2DQ
Tel: 01782 820500
cclub@moorcroft.com
www.moorcroft.com

Myott Collectors Club
P.O. Box 110,
Sutton SM3 9YQ
www.myottcollectorsclub.com

Pendelfin Family Circle
Cameron Mill,
Howsin St, Burnley,
Lancashire BB10 1PP
Tel: 01282 432 301
www.pendelfin.co.uk

Poole Pottery Collectors' Club
The Quay, Poole,
Dorset BH15 1RF
Tel: 01202 666200
Fax: 01202 682894
www.poolepottery.co.uk

Potteries of Rye Collectors' Society
22 Redyear Cottages,
Kennington Rd, Ashford,
Kent TN24 0TF
barry.buckton@tesco.net
www.potteries-of-rye-society.co.uk

Royal Doulton International Collectors' Club
Minton House, London Road,
Stoke-on-Trent,
Staffordshire ST4 7QD
Tel: 01782 292292
Fax: 01782 292099
enquiries@royal-doulton.com
www.royal-doulton.com/collectables

Royal Winton International Collectors' Club
Dancers End, Northall,
Bedfordshire LU6 2EU
Tel: 01525 220 272
Fax: 01525 222 442

The Shelley Group
7 Raglan Close, Frimley,
Surrey GU16 8YL
Tel: 01483 764097
www.shelley.co.uk

Susie Cooper Collectors' Group
Panorama House,
18 Oaklea Mews,
Aycliffe Village,
County Durham DL5 6JP
www.susiecooper.co.uk

The Sylvac Collectors' Circle
174 Portsmouth Rd, Horndean,
Waterlooville, Hampshire
admin@sylvacclub.com
www.sylvacclub.com

Novelty Teapot Collectors' Club
Tel: 01257 450 366
vince@totallyteapots.com
www.totallyteapots.com

Official International Wade Collectors' Club
Royal Works, Westport Rd,
Stoke-on-Trent, Staffs ST6 4AP
Tel: 01782 255255
Fax: 01782 575195
club@wade.co.uk
www.wade.co.uk

Wade Collectors Club
PO Box 3012
Stoke-on-Trent ST3 9DD
Tel: 0845 246 2525
www.wadecollectorsclub.co.uk

Royal Worcester Collectors' Society
Severn Street,
Worcester, WR1 2NE
Tel: 01905 746 000
sinden@royal-worcester.co.uk
www.royal-worcester.co.uk

CLUBS & SOCIETIES

CIGARETTE CARDS

Cartopulic Society of GB
7 Alderham Avenue, Radlett,
Herts WD7 8HL

COINS, BANKNOTES & PAPER MONEY

British Numismatic Society
c/o The Warburg Institute,
Woburn Square,
London WC1H 0AB
www.britnumsoc.org

Royal Numismatic Society
c/o The British Museum,
Great Russell Street,
London WC1B 3DG
Tel: 020 7636 1555
rns@dircon.co.uk
www.users.dircon.co.uk/~rns

International Bank Note Society
www.theibns.org

International Bond and Share Society
www.scripophily.org

COMMEMORATIVE WARE

Commemorative Collectors Society & Commemoratives Museum
Lumless House, 77
Gainsborough Road,
Winthorpe, Newark,
Nottinghamshire NG24 2NR
http://commemoratives
collecting.co.uk

COMICS

Association of Comic Enthusiasts
L'Hopiteau, St Martin du
Fouilloux 79420, France
Tel: 00 33 549 702 114

Comic Enthusiasts Society
80 Silverdale, Sydenham,
London SE26 4SJ

The Beano & Dandy Collectors' Club,
PO Box 3433,
Brighton BN50 9JA
www.phil-comics.com/
collectors_club

COSTUME & ACCESSORIES

The British Compact Collectors' Society
P.O. BOX 64, Langford,
Biggleswade SG18 9BF
www.compactcollectors.co.uk

The Costume Society
28 Eburne Road,
London N7 6AU
www.costumesociety.org.uk

Hat Pin Society of GB
PO Box 74, Bozeat,
Northamptonshire NN29 7UD

DISNEYANA

Walt Disney Collectors' Society
c/o Enesco, Brunthill Road,
Kingstown Industrial Estate,
Carlisle CA3 0EN
Tel: 01228 404 062
www.wdccduckman.com

DOLLS

Barbie Collectors' Club of GB
117 Rosemount Avenue,
Acton, London W3 9LU
wdl@nipcus.co.uk'

British Doll Collectors Club
'The Anchorage', Wrotham Rd,
Culverstone Green,
Meopham,
Kent DA13 0QW
www.britishdollcollectors.com

Doll Club of Great Britain
PO Box 154, Cobham,
Surrey KT11 2YE

The Fashion Doll Collectors' Club of GB
PO Box 133, Lowestoft,
Suffolk NR32 1WA
Tel: 07940 248127
voden@supanet.com

EPHEMERA

The Ephemera Society
PO Box 112, Northwood,
Middlesex HA6 2WT
Tel: 01923 829079
www.ephemera-society.org.uk

FILM & TV

James Bond 007 Fan Club
PO Box 007,
Surrey KT15 1DY
Tel: 01483 756007

Fanderson – The Official Gerry Anderson Appreciation Society
2 Romney Road,
Willesborough,
Ashford,
Kent TN24 0RW

GLASS

The Carnival Glass Society
P.O. Box 14, Hayes,
Middlesex UB3 5NU
www.carnivalglasssociety.co.uk

The Glass Association
150 Braemar Road,
Sutton Coldfield B73 6LZ
www.glassassociation.org.uk

Isle of Wight Studio Glass
Collectors' Club
Old Park, St Lawrence,
Isle of Wight, PO38 1XR
www.isleofwightstudioglass
.co.uk

Jonathan Harris Studio Glass Collectors Club
Woodland House,
24 Peregrine Way,
Apley Castle,
Telford TF1 6TH
www.jhstudioglass.com

Pressed Glass Collectors' Club
4 Bowshot Close,
Castle Bromwich B36 9UH
Tel: 0121 681 4872
www.webspawner.com/users/
pressedglass

KITCHENALIA

National Horse Brass Society
2 Blue Barn Cottage,
Blue Barn Lane,
Weybridge,
Surrey KT13 0NH
Tel: 01932 354 193

The Old Hall Stainless Steel Tableware Collectors Club,
Sandford House, Levedale,
Stafford ST18 9AH
www.oldhallclub.co.uk

The British Novelty Salt & Pepper Collectors Club
Coleshill,
Clayton Road,
Mold,
Flintshire CH7 15X

MARBLES

Marble Collectors Unlimited
P.O. Box 206
Northborough,
MA 01532-0206 USA
marblesbev@aol.com

MECHANICAL MUSIC

Musical Box Society of Great Britain
PO Box 299,
Waterbeach,
Cambridge CB4 4PJ

The City of London Phonograph & Gramophone Society
2 Kirklands Park,
Fyfe KY15 4EP
Tel: 01334 654 390

METALWARE

Antique Metalware Society
PO Box 63, Honiton,
Devon EX14 1HP
amsmemsec@yahoo.co.uk

MILITARIA

Military – Crown Imperial
37 Wolsey Close, Southall,
Middlesex UB2 4NQ

Military Historical Society
National Army Museum,
Royal Hospital Rd,
London SW3 4HT

Orders & Medals Research Society
123 Turnpike Link,
Croydon CR0 5NU

PAPERWEIGHTS

Paperweight Collectors Circle
P.O. Box 941, Comberton,
Cambridgeshire CB3 7GQ
Tel: 02476 386 172

Caithness Glass Paperweight Collectors' Society
Caithness Glass
Perth PH1 3TZ Scotland
www.caithnessglass.co.uk/
collectors

PENS & WRITING

The Writing Equipment Society
wes.membershipsec@virgin.net
www.wesoc.co.uk

PERFUME BOTTLES

International Perfume Bottle Association
396 Croton Road,
Wayne,
PA 19087 USA
www.ipba-uk.co.uk

PLASTICS

Plastics Historical Society
31a Maylands Drive,
Sidcup,
Kent DA14 4SB
mail@plastiquarian.com
www.plastiquarian.com

POSTCARDS

Postcard Club of Great Britain
Drene Brennan,
34 Harper House,
St.James Crescent,
London SW9 7LW
Tel: 0207 771 9404

POTLIDS

The Pot Lid Circle
Collins House,
32/38 Station Road,
Gerrards Cross,
Buckinghamshire SL9 8EL
Tel: 01753 279 001
ian.johnson@bpcollins.co.uk
www.thepotlidcircle.co.uk

QUILTS

The Quilters' Guild of the British Isles
Room 190,
Dean Clough, Halifax,
West Yorks 3HX 5AX
Tel: 01422 347 669
Fax: 01422 345 017
info@quiltersguild.org.uk
www.quiltersguild.org.uk

RADIOS

The British Vintage Wireless Society
59 Dunsford Close,
Swindon,
Wiltshire SN1 4PW
Tel: 01793 541 634
www.bvws.org.uk

RAILWAYANA

Railwayana Collectors Journal
7 Ascot Rd,
Moseley,
Birmingham B13 9EN

SCIENTIFIC & OPTICAL INSTRUMENTS

Scientific Instrument Society
90 The Fairway,
South Ruislip,
Middlesex HA4 0SQ
sis@sis.org.uk
www.sis.org.uk

SEWING

International Sewing Machine Collectors' Society
www.ismacs.net

The Thimble Society
1107 Portobello Road,
London W11 2QB
antiques@thimblesociety.co.uk
www.thimblesociety.co.uk

SMOKING

Lighter Club of Great Britain
Richard Ball
richard@lighter.co.uk

SPORTING

International Football Hall of Fame
info@ifhof.com,
www.ifhof.com

UK Football Programme Collectors Club,
PO Box 3236,
Norwich NR7 7BE

British Golf Collectors Society
anthonythorpe@ntlworld.com
www.britgolfcollectors.wyenet
.co.uk

Rugby Memorabilia Society
PO Box 57,
Hereford HR1 9DR
www.rugby-memorabilia.co.uk

STAMPS

Postal History Society
60 Tachbrook Street,
London SW1V 2NA
Tel: 020 7545 7773
john.scott@db.com

Royal Mail Collectors' Club
Freepost, NEA1431,
Sunderland SR9 9XN

STANHOPES

The Stanhope Collectors' Club
jean@stanhopes.info
www.stanhopes.info

STAINLESS STEEEL

The Old Hall Club
Sandford House,
Levedale,
Stafford ST18 9AH
Tel: 01785 780 376
oht@gnwiggin.freeserve.co.uk
www.oldhallclub.co.uk

TEDDY BEARS & SOFT TOYS

British Teddy Bear Association
PO Box 290
Brighton, Sussex
Tel: 01273 697 974

The Dean's Collectors Club
PO Box 217,
Hereford HR1 9AB
www.deansbears.com

Merrythought International Collectors' Club
Ironbridge, Telford,
Shropshire TF8 7NJ
Tel: 01952 433 116

Steiff Club Office
Margaret Steiff GmbH,
Alleen Strasse 2,
D-89537 Giengen/Brenz,
Germany

TOYS

Action Man Club
PO Box 142,
Horsham, RH13 5FJ

The British Model Soldier Society
www.btinternet.com/~model.so
ldiers

Corgi Collectors' Club
PO Box 323, Swansea,
Wales SA1 1BJ

Hornby Collectors Club
PO Box 35, Royston,
Hertfordshire SG8 5XR
Tel/Fax: 01223 208 308
hsclubs.demon.co.uk
www.hornby.co.uk

The Matchbox Toys International Collectors' Association
P.O. Box 120, Deeside,
Flintshire CH5 3HE
kevin@matchboxclub.com
www.matchboxclub.com

International Society of Meccanomen
72a Old High Street,
Headington, Oxford OX3 9HW
www.internationalmeccanomen
.org.uk

The Historical Model Railway Society
Tel: 01773 745 959
www.hmrs.org.uk

The English Playing Card Society
11 Pierrepont St, Bath,
Somerset BA1 1LA
Tel: 01225 465 218

The Hornby Railway Collectors Association
PO Box 3443, Yeovil,
Somerset, BA21 4XR
chairman@hrca.net
www.hrca.net

Train Collectors' Society
P.O. Box 20340,
London NW11 6ZE
Tel: 020 8209 1589
tcsinformation@btinternet.com
www.traincollectors.org.uk

William Britain Collectors Club
P.O. Box 32,
Wokingham RG40 4XZ
Tel: 01189 737080
Fax: 01189 733947
ales@wbritaincollectorsclub
.com
www.britaincollectorsclub.com

The British Smurf Collectors Club
PO Box 96, Deeping St James
Peterborough PE6 8YN
www.kittyscavern.com

WATCHES

British Watch & Clock Collectors' Association
5 Cathedral Lane, Truro,
Cornwall TR1 2QS
Tel: 01872 264010
Fax: 01872 241953
tonybwcca@cs.com
www.timecap.com

COLLECTING ON THE INTERNET

Collectables are particularly suited to online trading. When compared with many antiques, most collectables are easily defined, described and photographed, whilst shipping is relatively easy, due to average sizes and weights. Collectables are also generally more affordable and accessible, and the internet has provided a cost effective way of buying and selling without the overheads of shops and auction rooms. A huge number of collectables are offered for sale and traded daily over the internet, with websites varying from global online marketplaces, such as eBay, to specialist dealers' sites.

• There are a number of things to be aware of when searching for collectables online. Some items being sold may not be described accurately, meaning that general category searches, and even purposefully misspelling a name, can yield results. If something looks, or sounds, too good to be true, it probably is. Using this book should give you a head start in getting to know your market, and also enable you to tell the difference between a real bargain, and something that sounds like one. Good colour photography is absolutely vital

– try to find online listings that include as many images as possible, including detail shots, and check them carefully. Be aware that colours can appear differently between websites, and even between computer screens.

• Always ask the vendor questions about the object, particularly regarding condition. If no image is supplied, or you want to see another aspect of the object, ask for more information. A good seller should be happy to cooperate if approached politely and sensibly.

• As well as the 'e-hammer' price, you will very likely have to pay additional transactional fees such as packing, shipping and possibly regional or national taxes. Ask the seller for an estimate of these additional costs before leaving a bid, as this will give you a better idea of the overall amount you will end-up paying.

• In addition to large online auction sites, such as eBay, there are a host of other online resources for buying and selling. The internet can also be an invaluable research tool for collectors, with many sites devoted to providing detailed information on a number of different collectables.

INTERNET RESOURCES

Live Auctioneers
www.liveauctioneers.com
info@liveauctioneers.com
A free online service which allows users to search catalogues from selected auction houses in Europe, the USA and the United Kingdom. Visitors to the site can bid live via the Internet into salerooms as auctions happen. Registered users can also search through an archive of past catalogues and receive a free e-mail newsletter.

The Saleroom.com
www.the-saleroom.com
A free online service that allows users to search catalogues from selected auction houses in Europe, the USA and the United Kingdom. Visitors to the site can bid live via the internet into salerooms as auctions happen. Registered users can also search through an archive of past catalogues and receive a free e-mail newsletter.

ArtFact
info@artfact.com
www.artfact.com
Provides a comprehensive database of worldwide auction listings from over 2,000 art, antiques and collectables auction houses. User can search details of both upcoming and past sales and also find information on a number of collectors' fields. Basic information is available for free, access to more in depth information requires a subscription. Online bidding live into auctions as they happen is also offered.

Invaluable.com
www.invaluable.com
sales@invaluable.com
A subscription service allowing users to search selected auction house catalogues from the United Kingdom and Europe. Also offers an extensive archive for appraisal uses.

The Antiques Trade Gazette
www.atg-online.com
The online edition of the UK trade newspaper, including British auction and fair listings, news and events.

Maine Antique Digest
www.maineantiquedigest.com
Online version of America's trade newspaper including news, articles, fair and auction listings and more.

La Gazette du Drouot
www.drouot.com
The online home of the magazine listing all auctions to be held in France at the Hotel de Drouot in Paris. An online subscription enables you to download the magazine online.

AuctionBytes
www.auctionbytes.com
Auction resource with community forum, news, events, tips and a weekly newsletter.

Auction.fr
www.auction.fr
An online database of auctions at French auction houses. A subscription allows users to search past catalogues and prices realised.

Auctiontalk
www.internetauctionlist.com
Auction news, online and offline auction search engines and chat forums.

Go Antiques/Antiqnet
www.goantiques.com
www.antiqnet.com
An online global aggregator for art, antiques and collectables dealers. Dealers' stock is showcased online, with users able to browse and buy.

eBay
www.ebay.com
Undoubtedly the largest and most diverse of the online auction sites, allowing users to buy and sell in an online marketplace with over 52 million registered users from across the world.

INDEX

INDEX